Opera

Opera
A Research and Information Guide
Second Edition

Guy A. Marco

Foreword by
Edward O. D. Downes

Garland Publishing, Inc.
New York and London
2001

Published in 2001 by
Garland Publishing, Inc.
29 West 35th Street
New York, NY 10001

Garland is an imprint of the Taylor & Francis Group

10 9 8 7 6 5 4 3 2 1

Library of Congress Cataloging-in-Publication Data

Marco, Guy A.
    Opera : a research and information guide / Guy A. Marco — 2nd ed.
       p. cm. — (Music research and information guides ; 21) (Garland reference library of the humanities ; v. 2180)
    Includes indexes.
    ISBN: 0-8153-3516-4 (alk. paper)
      I. Opera—Bibliography.   I. Title.   II. Music research and information guides ; vol. 21.   III. Garland reference library of the humanities ; vol. 2180.

ML128.O4 M28 2000
016.7821—dc21
                                      00-050302

Between the time Website information is gathered and the date of publication, individual sites may have moved or may no longer be active. Therefore, the publisher cannot guarantee that the Websites listed herein are still accessible at the URL provided.

Printed on acid-free, 250-year-life paper
Manufactured in the United States of America

Va pensiero, a Capri, nido di memorie, dove bella calma proverà.

Das Alles ist geheim, so viel geheim,
Und man ist dazu da, dass man's ertragt,
Und in dem "Wie"
Da liegt der ganze Untershied.
       —Der Rosenkavalier

Contents

Foreword

What a superb undertaking! When one considers the endless ramifications of the art of opera, it becomes clear that a critical bibliography of opera must be a frightening prospect to anyone rash enough to venture upon it. Yet there is a crying need for such a work. Despite the growing body of serious musicological work on opera, there is probably no other field of music so rife with amateurish popularizers and pseudoscholarship. And there is none so full of booby traps for the humble music lover in search of hard facts. When such a standard guide as Kobbé can pass through edition after edition with egregious errors left uncorrected and at least one of its descriptive analyses translated word for word from a familiar French dictionary of opera, it is clear that the layperson needs guidance. And all of us, including professionals, are necessarily laypersons in some of the many aspects of operatic history or performance.

Guy Marco, like all good scholars, invites additions, corrections, and comments from his readers. They will be forthcoming. For perfection is even more of a dream in this field than in many others. Donald Grout's bibliography for his *Short History of Opera* lists some 3,900 items. Marco does more than list. He evaluates, comments, and joins the fray, so to speak, with 2,833 titles. As one edition follows another, the field grows not only larger, but richer. May it continue to expand and refine and put us all into Marco's debt.

Edward O. D. Downes

Introduction

Bibliography is the art of the impossible. It was ever so, although the impossibility was not always recognized. The early compilers of lists of books—practitioners of what we came to call enumerative bibliography—hardly sensed the intractability of their projects. They worked alone. They wanted to find and report everything. Indeed, there used to be an ideal of "universal bibliography," a master list of all that had been written—an exotic mirage, not mentioned after around 1800.

We who work in music bibliography have shared in the grand illusion that we could make complete lists of scores or writings and do it single-handedly. Valiant efforts, lifetime toils, of Robert Eitner, Carl Becker, and Emil Vogel—mileposts of bibliographic history—are superseded by more inclusive (still incomplete) inventories created by teams and projects. The last warrior to face the challenge of totality in music bibliography was Franz Pazdirek, whose 14-volume *Universal-Handbuch der Musikliteratur aller Zeiten und Volker* (1904–1910) resonates, in title and scope, with the bluster of romanticism. Pazdirek identified a half million musical compositions, but they were not really from "all times" (it was an in-print list heavy with recent publications) or "all peoples" (it was primarily about Europe and the United States).

During the 20th century, we music bibliographers have picked smaller targets. Going from more to less requires selectivity, which demands criteria for choosing and rejecting. Nobody will compile a list of all the music written in the century, or all the books about music, and certainly not all the periodical articles. Instead, there are selective inventories of restricted patches, such as a list of critical writings about the Vienna performances of *Die Frau ohne Schatten*, or—a bigger patch—writings about Zoltán Kodály. Along with selectivity has come the useful practice of content description, at times offering critiques and comparisons. This mode seems more manageable than the earlier all-inclusive one, but it also remains impossible. There is far too much music and too much written about it, for anyone to discover. We tend to select from a selection made by others (librarians, other list-compilers), to skip troublesome languages, to step away from dissertations, and to omit journalistic work, and we have little idea how many conference papers we never find.

In this context I have approached the formidable patch called opera literature, which may in fact be too large for a valid bibliography. With the millions of writings in the field, I cannot claim more than a slight, often secondary, acquaintance. Since World War II opera has become musicology's busiest field. Seeing all I could see and finding out as much as possible about what I could not see, and hoping that the rest was not vital to the task, I have tried to identify a core literature and say some useful things about it. I hope the (impossible) result is not a complete mirage. To quote from *The Fairy Queen,*

> We hope to please, but if some critic here
> Fond of his wit, designs to be severe,
> Let not his patience be worn out too soon,
> In a few years we shall be all in tune.

* * *

In revising the first edition, I have felt like someone racing to catch a train as it leaves the station. At first it seems that the platform dash should succeed, but as the train gathers speed human acceleration is sorely tested. Keeping pace with the rush of operatic literature is an exhilarating run. I hope I have been able to make a movie finish (clinging to the last car), so that the result is a useful list of the core writings. There were 714 numbered entries in the first edition, extended to 2,822 in this one. Hundreds of other items are included without separate numbers as citations within composite books, and there are references, *passim,* to related materials listed in other bibliographies.

Among those other bibliographies are numerous titles in the Garland Composer Resource Manuals series. The expert guidance in those volumes has saved me countless hours and given me confidence that I have not overlooked significant material. The search for that material has taken me through the back files of the principal scholarly journals, dissertation lists, websites, and the online catalogues of the Library of Congress and other great libraries of Europe and America. I have also followed the "citation trail," noting what writings are referred to by the important authors. Most of the research was done in the University of Chicago Library.

The scope of the compilation is limited to writings on the opera of the Western world, covering Europe, North America, and South America; there is also attention to Australia and New Zealand. All kinds of opera are included, but musicals are not. Materials in English, German, French, Italian, and Spanish are emphasized, but contributions in other languages are entered when needed for certain topics. Access to the scholarship in Slavic languages is usually through references to other books that cover it.

I have included writings that give reliable summaries of their topics, those that are significant contributions to the development of scholarship, those that form clusters of views on a subject, those that have valuable bibliographies, those that are of current interest in the field, those that offer useful gatherings of facts, and those that offer stimulating perspectives of any kind. In the annotation for an item I try to bring out the features that justify its inclusion. Biographical material on individual singers and other artists is excluded from this compilation. It is a subject in itself, well attended to by Robert Cowden (#160, #161) and Andrew Farkas (#162). Collected and complete works of composers are listed selectively; I was looking for recent publications and those that include modern editions of operas with commentaries.

To be practical, I have not annotated dissertations or the contents of individual volumes in certain series (*Avant-scène opéra,* Cambridge Opera Handbooks, English National Opera Guides, and Rororo Opernbücher). Annotations are also lacking for the few works I was unable to examine, unless I was able to find something about them elsewhere; I think I have explicated the situation in each instance.

Each entry gives the names of principal authors, joint authors, editors, and translators. Titles of earlier editions and of original language publications (in the case of translations) are given, with dates and publishers. An ISBN (International Standard Book Number) is included for the edition examined, if the book has one (most American, British, and German books published from around 1968 have these numbers, but the situation is variable regarding the issues of other countries). An ISSN (International Standard Serial Number) is given for lesser-known periodicals. Entries for monographs have Library of Congress (LC) call numbers. Most American research libraries use the LC classification, so these numbers will assist someone in finding materials in their collections; however, libraries frequently modify the LC number, so this technique requires caution. In general I have accepted the authority of the LC for transliterations, forms of names, and bibliographic data. The imprint omits the name of the country of publication, unless the location of the publisher's city might be in doubt. Typically, a book in Italian is published in Italy, one in German is published in Germany or in a familiar Austrian city, and so on. The only crossover language is English, and for imprints published in a city that may not be well known, I specify the country.

To keep the annotations short, I use certain terms frequently. A "life and works" treatment of a composer is a basic biography with some discussion of the compositions. A "genesis" study of an opera is the account of its creation, which could include its literary or mythological sources, influences by other composers, details of the collaboration between composer and librettist, sketches and early revisions, and anything pertinent to the preparation of the work for the first performance. A "performance history" is the tale of the opera's stagings, from premiere onward, and "reception" deals with critical and public response to it. A "program note" describes an opera in layman's language, while an "analysis" offers a more technical discussion in terms familiar only to the musically trained reader.

My descriptions are for the most part noncritical—the presence of a writing in the list implies that it is of value—but I have thought it helpful to introduce some opinions to alert the reader to certain aspects of the content. It should be clear from the presentation when my views are added to the basic descriptions. Where there might be doubts over whose thought is expressed, I have put my glosses in square brackets. I frequently allude to the author's inclusion of footnotes and bibliography (estimating the number of entries), both to give a sense of the research level of the piece and to indicate whether it is useful to someone seeking additional references on its topic. My comments on the indexing in a monograph are intended to suggest how accessible the contents are. An "expansive" index is the preferred model, one in which index entries are expanded with subdivisions to avoid long lists of undifferentiated page citations. Within chapter subdivisions I have endeavored to group entries according to affinity, instead of arranging them alphabetically by authors' names. The reader will therefore often find several works that take up the same topic near one another.

Titles of operas are in their original languages, for works in English, German, French, Italian, and Spanish. Titles from other languages are in English translation, with the original titles given. I have left out of this revision the checklist of composers and their major works, which required about 50 pages of the first edition. Such a list is no longer necessary, since there is now a strong title list in *The Viking Opera Guide* (#57), available in most libraries, and a composer/works list in the *Mellen Opera Reference Index* (#24), to be seen in larger libraries. Kurt Pahlen's books (#48, #49) give composer and title approaches to thousands of operas. Nevertheless, operas specifically cited in the writings included in the present edition are in a separate index, which may also serve as a title guide to most of the historical repertoire.

I gathered material for the book during 1998 and 1999, with a cutoff date for inclusion in December 1999. I respectfully invite users of the volume to advise me of omissions, errors, or other infelicities they may notice. If there is a further revision, it will benefit—as this one has—from comments received.

I wish to thank librarians Janice Deal, Judith K. Meyers, and Diane Petit, who located elusive materials or data for me; M. R. Roberts and Paul Opel of Broude Brothers, who provided current data on their important series; and several scholars who sent me facts about their works: Elliott Antokoletz, Susan Borwick, Maureen Carr, and Patricia Lewy Gidwitz. I am grateful to Siegmund Levarie for guidance and encouragement, and to MaryFrances Watson for her technical support and critical reading. Ed and Ernie Maier helped solve computer problems and gave assistance in many ways. I also wish to express my appreciation to Carol Hartland, the ideal copyeditor.

Abbreviations

For items with entries in this guide, the entry number follows the title.

19CAMT	*Nineteenth-Century American Musical Theater* (#2730)
19thCM	*19th Century Music*
AfM	*Archiv für Musikwissenschaft*
AM	*Acta musicologica*
ASO	*Avant-scène opéra* (#146)
Baron	*Baroque Music: A Research and Information Guide* (#6)
Chefs	*Chefs d'oeuvre classiques de l'opéra français* (#2225)
COH	*Cambridge Opera Handbooks* (#147)
COJ	*Cambridge Opera Journal* (#148)
DSJ	*Donizetti Society Journal*
Duckles	*Music Reference and Research Materials* (#2)
ENOG	*English National Opera Guides* (#150)
ERO	*Early Romantic Opera* (#113)
FO	*French Opera in the 17th and 18th Centuries* (#2224)
GL	*Garland Library of the History of Music* (#63)
GO	*German Opera 1770–1800* (#2343)
GRB	*Guide to Reference Books* (#1)
HS	*Handel Sources* (#947)
IO–1640	*Italian Opera, 1640–1770* (#2422)
IO–1810	*Italian Opera, 1810–1840* (#2423)
IOM	*Information on Music* (#3)
JAMS	*Journal of the American Musicological Society*
JM	*Journal of Musicology*
JRMA	*Journal of the Royal Musical Association*
Kaufman	*"A Bibliography of House Annals"* (#126)
LOAM–3	*Literature of American Music III* (#2732)
M&L	*Music and Letters*

MGG	*Die Musik in Geschichte und Gegenwart* (#18)
MORI	*Mellen Opera Reference Index* (#24)
MQ	*Musical Quarterly*
MR	*Music Review*
NG	*New Grove Dictionary of Music and Musicians* (#19)
NGDO	*New Grove Dictionary of Opera* (#22)
NOHM	*New Oxford History of Music* (#58)
NRMI	*Nuova rivista musicale italiana*
OAS	*Operas of Alessandro Scarlatti*
OQ	*Opera Quarterly* (#156)
PRMA	*Proceedings of the Royal Musical Association*
RAM	*Recent Researches in American Music*
RdM	*Revue de musicologie*
RILM	*Répertoire international de la littérature musicale* (RILM Abstracts)
RIM	*Rivista italiana de musicologia*
RISM	*Répertoire international des sources musicales* (#11)
RMBE	*Recent Researches in Music of the Baroque Era*
RMCE	*Recent Researches in Music of the Classic Era*
RMI	*Rivista musicale italiana*
Rororo	Rororo Opernbücher (#159)
RRAM	*Recent Researches in American Music*
SIMG	*Sammelbände der Internationalen Musikgesellschaft*
Strunk	*Source Readings in Music History* (#96)
Viking	*Viking Opera Guide* (#57)
ZfM	*Zeitschrift für Musikwissenschaft*

Opera

I. Bibliographies

All Topics

1. *Guide to Reference Books*. 11th ed. Ed. Robert Balay. Chicago: American Library Association, 1996. xxvii, 2,020p. ISBN 0-8389-0669-9. Z1035.1 .G89. (Cited in this guide as *GRB*.)

   The primary bibliography of reference materials in all topics and languages. Some 16,000 annotated entries, with full bibliographic detail. Works on opera and theaters are well represented. Model index of authors, titles, and subjects.

Music in General

2. Duckles, Vincent H., and Ida Reed. *Music Reference and Research Materials: An Annotated Bibliography*. 5th ed. New York: Schirmer, 1997. xvii, 812p. ISBN 0-02-870821-0. ML113 .D83. (Cited in this guide as *Duckles*.)

   Vincent Duckles prepared the first edition of this standard tool in 1964 and completed a third edition (1974) before his death. This new edition is an outstanding continuation of his efforts to list and describe the essential reference works in music. There are 3,801 entries, most of them annotated, all of them giving bibliographic essentials. Although only a dozen titles are specifically about opera, many others give useful perspectives; for example, there are composer worklists, thematic catalogues, and bibliographies of writings on more general topics in which materials on opera may be found. The index (p.638–812), credited to Linda Solow Blotner, is an ideal specimen of its kind, presenting authors, titles, and subjects.

3. Marco, Guy A., Sharon Paugh Ferris, and Ann G[arfield] Olszewski. *Information on Music: A Handbook of Reference Sources in European Languages*. Littleton, Colo.: Libraries Unlimited, 1975–1984. 3v. Contents: v.1, *Basic and Universal Sources,* 1975 (164p. ISBN 0-87287-096-0); v.2, *The Americas,* 1977 (296p. ISBN 0-87287-141-X); v.3, *Europe,* 1984 (519p. ISBN 0-87287-401-X). ML113 .M33. (Cited in this guide as *IOM*.)

   An annotated list of 3,676 books, parts of books, articles, and dissertations, covering all aspects of music. V.1 is arranged by type of material and the other

1

volumes by country. Entries for opera and about theaters are found in country sections. Indexes by authors, titles, and subjects; updates and revisions appear in v.2 and v.3. See also Wehrle (#2182).

4. Tyrrell, John, and Rosemary Wise. *A Guide to International Congress Reports in Musicology, 1900–1975*. New York: Garland, 1979. 353p. ISBN 0-8240-9839-0. ML113 .T95.

   A list of about 10,000 papers included in published proceedings for international conferences in music and related subjects. Indexed by place, title, series, sponsor, author, editor, and subject. "Opera" has about one and a half columns of entries in the subject index; Wagner, a half column; other composers are also well represented.

5. Gerboth, Walter. *An Index to Musical Festschriften and Similar Publications*. New York: Norton, 1969. ix, 188p. ML128 .M8 G4.

   A list of dedicatory volumes with subject and author indexes of the essays they contain. Some 3,000 essays in more than 500 volumes are included, up to a 1967 cutoff date. The subject "Opera" in the index runs to two columns of entries.

6. Baron, John H. *Baroque Music: A Research and Information Guide*. Music Research and Information Guides, 16. New York: Garland, 1993. xviii, 588p. ISBN 0-8240-4436-3. ML116 .B37. (Cited in this guide as *Baron*.)

   An important guide to 1,423 books, parts of books, articles, and dissertations about music of the 17th and 18th centuries, with extensive, perceptive annotations. The opera chapter, p.469–500, includes sections on individual countries. Name, subject, and author indexes.

7. Brockman, William S. *Music: A Guide to the Reference Literature*. Littleton, Co.: Libraries Unlimited, 1987.

   558 reference works, mostly in English, are classified and evaluated, along with 109 periodicals and 172 music organizations. Name, subject, and author indexes.

8. *Garland Composer Resource Manuals* [series]. Guy A. Marco, series ed. New York: Garland, 1981–.

   With 49 volumes issued through 1999, each devoted to one composer (in a few cases, two composers), this set provides a useful base for research in many musical fields. Each manual has a selective, annotated bibliography of writings about the composer, along with worklists, information on resources, and indexes. Those volumes dealing with composers of opera are entered separately in the present guide.

9. *Bio-Bibliographies in Music* [series]. Westport, Conn.: Greenwood, 1984–.

   A useful series that has featured volumes about lesser-known composers; 72 published through 1999. Many of those volumes about opera composers are cited separately in the present guide.

10. Brook, Barry S., and Richard J. Viano. *Thematic Catalogues in Music: An Anno- tated Bibliography*. 2nd ed. Annotated Reference Tools in Music, 5. Stuy- vesant, N.Y.: Pendragon, 1997. l, 602p. ISBN 0-918728-86-X. ML113 .B86.

First edition, 1972. An important descriptive list of 1,444 catalogues, in com- poser order (or source, for multiple composers) with full bibliographic detail. Also background material on the history and bibliography of thematic cata- logues. The period covered is 1645–1996.

11. *Répertoire international des sources musicales = International Inventory of Musical Sources = Internationales Quellenlexikon der Musik*. Munich: Henle; London: Novello; Kassel: Bärenreiter, 1960–. ML113 .I6.

This massive project—generally known as *RISM* and cited thus in the present guide—of the International Musicological Society and the International Asso- ciation of Music Libraries began in 1952 under the chairmanship of Friedrich Blume. Its purpose was to present a complete bibliography of musical works, published or not, which appeared in all countries up to the year 1800; in fact, later materials are included in various series. Contents of the series are given in *IOM* 1, p.107–108; and *Duckles,* diverse entries, see index. *RISM Online* includes electronic (July 1999) versions of Series A/II: *Music Manuscripts after 1600; RISM-U.S. Libretto Database*; *RISM Libraries Directory*; and *RISM Bibliographic Citations Database*. The libretto database has records for more than 11,000 printed and manuscript libretti from the 16th to the 20th century.

12. *Répertoire international de la presse musicale: A Retrospective Index Series (RIPM)*. Ann Arbor, Mich.: UMI Center for Studies in Nineteenth-Century Music, University of Maryland, 1988–.

An endeavor to index individual music periodicals issued in the 19th century. A list of 34 periodicals covered through 1994 is in *Duckles* 4.123.

13. *A Basic Music Library: Essential Scores and Sound Recordings*. 3rd ed. Com- piled by the Music Library Association. Elizabeth Davis, coordinating ed. Chicago: American Library Association, 1997. 650p. ISBN 0-8389-3461-7. ML113 .B3.

A recommended core collection for libraries but also useful for anyone who needs to find a good edition or CD of a repertoire opera. Of the 3,000 scores listed, 140 are operas and 100 are operettas/musicals. Full bibliographic infor- mation is provided. Composer indexes to the score and recording sections.

Among the other indexes and bibliographies that serve the field of music, with coverage of opera, a number must be mentioned. Descriptions of them appear in *Duckles* at the entry numbers cited: *Music Index* (4.89), *RILM Abstracts of Music Literature* (4.90), *British Catalogue of Music* (5.14, 5.67), and *Doctoral Dissertations in Musicology* (4.136).

Opera

The next titles are bibliographies of material about opera, without national limi- tations. Bibliographies of opera for specific countries are listed in the country sections of this guide, and bibliographies of individual composers appear in their own sections.

14. Abert, Anna Amalie. "Die Oper zwischen Barock und Romantik. Ein Bericht über die Forschung seit dem zweitem Weltkrieg." *AM* 49 (1977): 137–193.

A thorough listing of post-1945 publications dealing with 18th- and 19th-century opera, arranged by country, then by genre. Brief annotations and unifying commentaries make this a useful guide to a large body of literature.

15. Turner, J. Rigbie. *Four Centuries of Opera: Manuscripts and Printed Editions in the Pierpont Morgan Library.* New York: The Library, and Dover, 1983. xii, 132p. ISBN 0-486-246602-7. ML141 .N4 P57.

Photos and commentaries on about 50 items in the library, dating from the first edition of the *Dafne* (1598) libretto to the autograph of John Eaton's *Danton and Robespierre* (1978). Most major composers are represented by sketches, first editions, or other material. With a selective checklist of operatic manuscripts in the library and printed opera libretti. Bibliography of references for the commentaries; no index.

16. Trowell, Brian. "Libretto." In *NGDO* 2, 1227–1252.

The bibliography consists of about 1,000 entries, in classified arrangement, without annotations. Its utility is considerable but diminished by the incomplete publication data given. See also *MORI* and Grout (#78).

II. Dictionaries and Encyclopedias

Music in General

The following titles have significant operatic coverage.

17. Randel, Don Michael. *The New Harvard Dictionary of Music*. Cambridge, Mass.: Harvard U.P., 1986. xxi, 942p. ISBN 0-6745-6152-5. ML100 .R3.

    Replaces *The Harvard Dictionary of Music* (1954; 2nd ed. 1969). The standard source of definitions and concise topical articles for English readers. No biographical entries (see #166). Some operas have individual entries (*Falstaff*), and some do not (*Carmen*). Charlotte Greenspan prepared the survey article on opera and a number of related entries, all of which are convenient overviews. Bibliographies accompany most articles in the dictionary. Lack of an index greatly inhibits use.

18. *Die Musik in Geschichte und Gegenwart*. 2nd ed. Ed. Ludwig Finscher. Kassel: Bärenreiter, 1994–. In progress. (Cited in this guide as *MGG*.)

    Status of this project as of August 1999: v.1–9, *Sachteil*, 1994–1998—complete. *Personenteil*, 12v., and *Register*—not published. Completion of the set is proposed for the year 2004. "Oper," v.7, columns 635–641, is mostly a list of cross-references to more specialized articles, plus a good basic bibliography (with incomplete data) by topic. A strong treatment of "Libretto" appears in v.5, columns 1116–1259, written by many authorities; it is a historical survey, with sections for countries and periods, and a six-page bibliography.

19. *The New Grove Dictionary of Music and Musicians*. Ed. Stanley Sadie. London: Macmillan; distributed in the U.S. by Grove's Dictionaries of Music, Washington, D.C., 1980. 20v. ISBN 0-333-23111-2. ML100 N48. (Cited in this guide as *NG*.)

    An indispensable but uneven work, said to contain 22,500 articles, with a total of 18,000,000 words, by 2,500 contributors. Weaknesses include the article bibliographies (important omissions; incomplete publication data) and the lack of an index to the set. Described in *IOM* 1333 and *Duckles* 1.48. Many spin-offs; those dealing with opera composers are cited separately in this guide. A new edition is scheduled for publication in the year 2000. See also #2739.

20. *Dizionario enciclopedico universale della musica e dei musicisti.* Ed. Alberto Basso. Turin: UTET, 1983–1990. 13v. ISBN 88-02-03820-1. ML100 .C61.

   The Italian counterpart to *NG*, divided into two parts: I has four volumes of subject entries, and II has eight volumes of biographical entries. V.13, *Appendice,* is a biographical supplement. Approximately 37,000 signed articles. Bibliographies are weak and have incomplete data. No general index.

Opera

21. Dent, Edward Joseph. "The Nomenclature of Opera." *M&L* 25 (1944): 132–140; 213–226.

   A fascinating review of opera's contorted identifications. Gives the names, with explanations and examples, by which operatic works have been labeled in Italy, France, Germany, and Britain. Among the tags described are *favola, dramma per musica, dramma musicale, commedia in musica, dramma giocoso, melodramma, opera semiseria, tragedia, commedia lirica, tragédie lyrique, opéra-ballet, parodie, drame lyrique, Singspiel, Lustspiel, Komische Oper, Bühnenfestspiel, mask,* and musical comedy. *Opera* is still a rare designator in Italy.

   Among other lists of operatic terms: Boldrey (#28), *Viking* (#57), Sadie (#79), and Reid (#355).

The next four items are the major multivolume references:

22. *New Grove Dictionary of Opera.* Ed. Stanley Sadie and Christine Bashford. New York: Grove's Dictionaries of Music, 1992. 4v. ISBN 0-935859-92-6. ML102 .O6 N5. (Cited in this guide as *NGDO.*)

   The premier reference source for opera, prepared by some 1,300 specialists. Entries for composers, singers, librettists, and everyone associated with production. Individual operas have entries, which include plot summaries and commentaries. Terms, opera houses, and a wide selection of opera topics are given strong presentations. A number of the articles are noted separately in this guide. List of role names in about 850 operas and first-line index of more than 5,000 arias and ensembles; no general index.

23. *International Dictionary of Opera.* Ed. C. Steven LaRue. Detroit: St. James, 1993. 2v. ISBN 1-55862-081-8. ML102 .O616.

   A gathering of about 1,000 articles by some 200 specialists, covering persons and individual operas. Despite contributions by a number of major scholars, this is a problematic work. Too much space goes to plots and to oversize portraits. Factual errors, misspelled names, and missing diacritics are ubiquitous. Bibliographies are a serious debility, where standard items are often missing, and all entries have incomplete imprint or pagination information. No general index.

24. *Mellen Opera Reference Index.* Ed. Charles H. Parsons. Lewiston, N.Y.: Edwin Mellen, 1986–1988. 21 [i.e., 23] v. ISBN 0-88946-400-6. ML102 .O6 P25. (Cited in this guide as *MORI*).

The 21st volume is actually three books, identified as 21a, 21b, and 21c. An impressive achievement by Parsons, providing much information in a form not otherwise available. V.1–4, opera composers and their works; v.5–6, librettists; v.7–8, theaters where operatic premieres occurred (by country, then city); v.9, operas in topical arrangement, identifying those about Aztecs, Joan of Arc, Dido, and so on, and those based on writings of literary figures; v.10–12, discography; v.13–14, premiere casts for operas of each composer; v.15–16, index of the cast members; v.17–18, bibliography of books about opera, in classified order, with full publication data (about 9,000 titles; no author index); v.19, index to contemporary reviews of the premiere performances; v.20, videography, listing 895 videos of 298 operas, with casts; v.21a-b-c, printed scores in American libraries (without library locations). It is easy to find errors, omissions, and oddities in this vast compilation, but its utility is considerable.

25. *Pipers Enzyklopädie des Musiktheaters: Oper, Operette, Musical, Ballett.* Ed. Carl Dahlhaus. Munich: Piper, 1986–. 6v. through 1997. ISBN (v.1) 3-492-02411-4. ML102 .O6 P563.

A major work, comprising six volumes (published) of composer entries and a projected two volumes of subject entries. For each composer, principal operas are described (premiere data, plot, commentary). Each volume has its title index. Although v.6 is entitled *Register,* it is simply the concluding (S–Z) book in the composer set. No index to the whole encyclopedia has been announced.

The next group, in alphabetical sequence, consists of diverse dictionaries and lists.

26. Barlow, Harold, and Sam Morgenstern. *A Dictionary of Opera and Song Themes, Including Cantatas, Oratorios, Lieder, and Art Songs.* New York: Crown, 1966. vi, 547p. ML128 .V7 B3.

A reprint of *A Dictionary of Vocal Themes* (Crown, 1950), unchanged except for the title. About 8,000 short musical themes are given, under their composers, including thousands of opera arias. Index of titles.

27. Boldrey, Richard. *Guide to Operatic Duets.* Dallas: Pst . . . Inc., 1994. 131p. ISBN 1-877761-65-6. ML102 .O2 B6.

A handy list of about 600 duets, arranged by first line. Each entry names the opera and role and identifies the voice types involved. Indexing by composer, title, role, and voice type.

28. Boldrey, Richard. *Guide to Operatic Roles & Arias.* Dallas: Pst . . . Inc., 1994. 554p. ISBN 1-877761-64-8. ML102 .O2 B62.

A valuable inventory of about 3,000 arias, arranged by first line. Each entry names the opera and role and identifies the voice type involved. There are many such types: a useful table lists 27 names for them, in four languages.

Another table gives their range, register, and timbre. Indexed by role, voice type, opera, and composer.

29. Bourne, Joyce. *Who's Who in Opera: A Guide to Opera Characters*. New York: Oxford U.P., 1998. xviii, 457p. ISBN 0-19-210023-8. ML102 .O6 B68.

    An alphabetical list of some 2,000 characters, with detailed accounts of their parts in the stories and titles of their arias. The first singer of each role is identified. List of composers represented and their operas, but no index.

30. Brockway, Wallace, and Herbert Weinstock. *The World of Opera: The Story of Its Origins and the Lore of Its Performance*. New York: Pantheon, 1962. 731p. ML1700 .B86 O7.

    An excellent handbook of data on 253 operas, generally representing the mid-century repertoire. Gives premiere date and theater, with cast, and a summary performance history, emphasizing the U.S. and offering negative as well as affirmative appraisals. Information is accurate; historical highlights are aptly selected.

31. Clément, Félix, and Pierre Larousse. *Dictionnaire des opéras* . . . Rev. ed. Ed. Arthur Pougin. Paris: Larousse, 1905. 1,203p. Reprint, New York: Da Capo, 1969; 2v. ML102 .O6 C42.

    First edition, 1869, as *Dictionnaire lyrique*. A list of about 20,000 operas and operettas that were actually performed, with dates of premieres, language, number of acts, and names of composers and librettists. Some non-French titles are given only in French translation. Composer index.

32. Dassori, Carlo. *Opere e operisti (dizionario lirico 1541–1902)* . . . Genoa: Istituto Sordomuti, 1903. 977p. Reprint, Bologna: Forni, 1979. ML102 .O6 D2.

    A list of 15,406 operas, with premiere dates, and birth and death dates for the composers.

33. Ewen, David. *The New Encyclopedia of the Opera*. 3rd ed. New York: Hill & Wang, 1971. vii, 759p. ISBN 0-8090-7262-9. ML102 .O6 E9.

    Ewen's 75th book, this is a well-revised version of the 1955 original. It presents a vast array of information: operatic terms, stories, characters, singers, houses, festivals, literary sources, and topical articles. Marred by frequent errors of historical fact and lack of an index.

34. Griffel, Margaret Ross. *Operas in German: A Dictionary*. New York: Greenwood, 1990. xxviii, 735p. ISBN 0-313-25244-0. ML102 O6 G75.

    A title list of 380 operas with German libretti, covering 1627–1989, with premiere data, plot, and program notes. Also an appendix of 1,250 other titles without details. All the composers were born before 1919, so most recent works are excluded. An earnest effort, but in sum it is useful only to someone who has to see a list of German operas. Good bibliography; index of characters and performers.

35. Gruber, Clemens M. *Opern-Uraufführungen. Ein internationales Verzeichnis von der Renaissance bis zur Gegenwart.* Vienna: Gesellschaft für Musiktheater, 1978. 3v. ISBN 3-85202-049-2. ML128 .O4 G88.

   A list of opera premieres by about 1,700 composers, with basic facts about those events. Indexed by opera title and by city.

36. *Herders Musiklexikon: Oper, Operette, Musical.* Ed. Gerhard Hellwig. 4th ed. Vienna: Herder, 1976. 370p. ISBN 3-451-16357-8. ML102 .O6 H5.

   Based on the 1962 *Das grosse Buch der Musik.* Essentially a collection of plots but includes for each of about 500 works considerable background data and names of arias or songs (in German translation, leading to quaint titles like "Good night mein Jemand" from *Music Man*). A first-line index gives approximately 800 songs and arias in original tongues. Also biographical and term entries and an index of composers and titles.

37. Kloiber, Rudolf. *Handbuch der Oper.* 9th ed. Kassel: Bärenreiter, 1978. 2v. ISBN 3-761-904229; 3-761-804237. MT95 .K66.

   Detailed consideration of 180 operas in the current repertoire (with a German slant). Facts for each work: plot, instrumentation, duration (not in every case, and occasionally dubious), premiere date, publication, historical background, and voice types used. Table of roles by voice type—including such impressionistic categories as soubrette, dramatic coloratura, lyric mezzo-soprano, and dramatic alto. Also a list of arias by those voice types. Indexed by composer and title.

38. Krause, Ernst. *Oper A–Z: Ein Opernführer.* 3rd ed. Leipzig: VEB Deutscher Verlag für Musik, 1978. 704p. MT95 .K91.

   Along with plots, presents useful information about each work: instrumentation, duration of each act, genesis, and performance history. Many of the operas are outside the usual repertoire, by such composers as Jan Cikker, Fritz Geissler, Jakov Gotovac, and Udo Zimmermann. Title and composer index.

39. *La Scala Encyclopedia of the Opera.* Ed. Giorgio Bagnoli. Trans. Graham Fawcett. New York: Simon & Schuster, 1993. 398p. ISBN 0-671-87042-4. ML102 .O6 L14.

   Originally published as *Opera* (Milan: Mondadori, 1993). Despite its name, this routine handbook has nothing to do with the Teatro alla Scala in Milan. It gives program notes on 468 operas, plus entries for performers, composers, and librettists. Good color illustrations; no index.

40. Leopold, Silke, and Robert Maschka. *Who's Who in der Oper.* Kassel: Bärenreiter, 1997. 380p. ISBN 3-7618-1268-X. ML102 .O6 L46.

   A convenient index to 800 operatic characters, with considerable detail on their roles and arias. Index of other characters named in those entries.

41. Lessing, Gotthold E. *Handbuch des Opern-Repertoires.* Rev. ed. London: Boosey & Hawkes, 1952. xv, 393p. ML102 .O6 L65.

   A useful compilation of facts about 392 operas, giving for each the cast, duration of each act, instrumentation, premiere data, and editions.

42. Manferrari, Umberto. *Dizionario universale delle opere melodrammatiche.* Florence: Sansoni, 1954–1955. 3v. ML102 .O6 M3.

   A list of about 30,000 operatic works, in composer order, with names of librettists and premiere data.

43. Martin, George Whitney. *The Opera Companion to Twentieth-Century Opera.* New York: Dodd, Mead, 1979. 653p. ISBN 0-396-07594-0. MT95 .M253.

   Information on 78 operas, which are offered as the standard recent repertoire: plots, premiere data, and commentary. Also a valuable statistics section, giving extensive lists of the works performed in leading opera houses of the U.S., Europe, and South America. Good bibliography of about 120 items; expansive index of titles, names, and topics.

44. *Metropolitan Opera Encyclopedia*: *A Comprehensive Guide to the World of Opera*. Ed. David Hamilton. New York: Simon & Schuster, 1987. 415p. ISBN 0-6716-1732-X. ML102 .O6 M47.

   Essays on the most popular operas by "guests" (singers and conductors) are interfiled with short entries in alphabetical order, covering operas and performers. A routine work, with no special connection to the Met. Good color plates; no index.

45. Moore, Frank L. *Crowell's Handbook of World Opera.* New York: Crowell, 1961. 683p. Reprint, Westport, Conn.: Greenwood, 1974. ISBN 0-8371-6822-8. ML102 .O6 M6.

   A fine variety of information, in dictionary format: entries for operas (plots and principal musical themes), characters, and topics; opera chronology and discography. Useful index of roles by voice type or by type of ensemble. No general index.

46. Orrey, Leslie. *The Encyclopedia of Opera.* London: Pitman, 1976. 376p. ISBN 0-684-13630-9. ML102 .O6 E56.

   A useful compilation of about 3,000 entries, written by 13 scholars, covering individuals, opera houses, festivals, terms, filmed opera, radio and television opera, and other topics. About 700 operas have separate articles. Many of the 371 illustrations are in color. Names of operas in less common languages are alphabetized only in English translations. Lack of an index is troubling, especially since cross-reference practice is inconsistent. Otherwise this is an accurate and attractive volume.

47. *Oxford Dictionary of Opera*. Ed. John Warrack and Ewen West. New York: Oxford U.P., 1992. xviii, 782p. ISBN 0-19-869164-5. ML102 .O6 W37.

   First edition, 1964, as *Concise Oxford Dictionary of Opera;* it was issued under that name up to 1986, but now it seems the *Concise* has had its day. The work has some 4,500 entries for countries, types of opera, opera companies, and topics, but the greatest space goes to persons and plots. Reliability is uneven. Weak bibliographies; no index.

48. Pahlen, Kurt. *Oper der Welt.* 4th ed. Zurich: SV International, 1987. 802p. ISBN 3-7263-6516-8. ML1700 .P26.

    A strong assemblage of data on about 2,500 operas, including premiere information, brief plots, musical examples, and commentaries. Arranged by composer, with title index. A very useful appendix (p.686–705) presents opera composers with their operas—titles in original languages and dates. Concludes with 200 illustrations of singers and scenes. No bibliography or general index. The next title is similar:

49. Pahlen, Kurt. *Pahlen Opern Lexikon.* 2nd ed. Munich: Heyne, 1995. 1,023p. ISBN 3-453-09088-8. ML102 .O6 P242.

    First edition, 1974, as *Das grosse Heyne Opernlexikon.* A composer list of about 1,600 operas, giving background, premiere information, and plots for major works. With two title indexes: one of original language titles, the other of German translations. Also a handy chronology of performances, 1986–1995, with details.

50. Pallay, Steven G. *Cross Index Title Guide to Opera and Operetta.* Music Reference Collection, 19. New York: Greenwood, 1989. viii, 214p. ISBN 0-313-2562-25. ML128 .O4 P3.

    Described as a list of "more than 5,500 vocal and instrumental excerpts from over 1,400 operas and operettas by 535 composers." All principal arias and numbers are identified under each opera title, and they are entered individually as well, with reference to each opera. It should be noted that only the names of the arias are given, not any musical "excerpts."

51. *Reclams Lexikon der Opernwelt in sechs Bänden.* Ed. Rolf Fath. Stuttgart: Reclam, 1998. 6v. ISBN 3-15-030018-5. ML102 .O6 F36.

    Articles for composers, singers, and others connected with operatic matters; extensive treatment of about 200 operas (plot, premiere data; titles in original language and German), cities—a strong feature—and terms. No attribution to authors of the articles, so it seems Fath wrote them all. Some bibliographies with the articles; index of opera titles but no general index.

52. Riemann, Hugo. *Opern-Handbuch.* 2nd ed. Leipzig: H. Seemann Nachfolger, [189?]. 862p. ML102 .O6 R5.

    There is no date in this revised edition; the first edition appeared in 1887 and a supplement in 1893 (included in the revision). Operas, operettas, ballets, and other stage works are listed by title. Information given is variable: plot synopses, premiere data, and historical notes may appear. Not all the works were performed. No index.

53. Seeger, Horst. *Opern Lexikon.* 3rd ed. Rev. Eberhard Schmidt. Wilhelmshaven: F. Noetzel, 1987. 702p. ISBN 3-795-90271-1. ML102 O6 S4.

    Cover title: *Opernlexikon.* A convenient resource, with more than 10,000 brief entries, covering persons, individual operas (without plots), terms, arias, characters, and companies by city. Strong on Eastern Europe and Russia, less valuable for U.S. No bibliographies, no index.

54. *Simon & Schuster Book of the Opera: A Complete Reference Guide.* Trans. Catherine Atthill et al. Ed. Riccardo Mezzanotte. New York: Simon & Schuster, 1977. 512p. ISBN 0-671-24886. ML102 .O6 O63.

Translation of *L'opera: Repertorio della lirica dal 1597* (Milan: Mondadori, 1977). Synopses and program notes for about 800 operas of historic as well as contemporary importance. Premiere data, critical reception, good photographs. Chronological arrangement requires constant reference to the indexes (title and composer) to find a given work.

55. Stieger, Franz. *Opernlexikon = Opera Catalogue = Lexique des opéras = Dizionario operistico.* Tutzing: Schneider, 1975–1983. 10v. Teil 1: *Titelkatalog,* 3v. Teil 2: *Komponisten,* 2v. Teil 3: *Librettisten,* 3v. Teil 4: *Nachträge,* 2v. ML102 .O6 S8.

A delayed publication of Stieger's compilation, presented by him to the Austrian National Library in 1934. The basic title list covers about 50,000 operas, operettas, *Singspiele,* and plays with music; plus about 6,000 oratorios. Information for each work: composer, librettist, and premiere facts. Includes corrections to Clément (#31), Riemann (#52), and Dassori (#32), but Stieger's list also has many errors. More than 15,000 persons are in the volumes devoted to librettists. The supplement has some interesting arrangements of historical material: a chronology of operatic performances to 1700; names of *Singspiele* performed, 1701–1900, and of all German stage works, 1901–1935; Italian operas, 1701–1800; list of premieres in Italy, 1701–1900; Italian operas premiered outside Italy; and Italian libretti set by non-Italian composers. There is a list of composers by city of birth, by year of birth, and by year of death, with a summary list of those who lived longest and who died youngest. (The oldest was neither Auber nor Verdi but Giacomo Tritto, 1733–1824, who wrote 51 operas before dying at age 91.)

56. Towers, John. *Dictionary Catalog of Operas and Operettas Which Have Been Performed on the Public Stage.* Morgantown, W.Va.: Acme, 1910. 2v. Reprint, New York: Da Capo, 1967. ML102 .O6 T8.

A list of 28,015 operas, thick with inaccuracies and confusingly alphabetized. Gives the name, nationality, and dates of the composers and alternative or translated titles of each work. Composer index.

57. *The Viking Opera Guide.* Ed. Amanda Holden, Nicholas Kenyon, and Stephen Walsh. New York: Viking, 1993. xxii, 1,305p. ISBN 0-670-81292-7. ML102 .06 V55. (Cited in the guide as *Viking.*)

An excellent handbook, covering 1,587 works, arranged by composer. Operetta, *Singspiele,* and musicals are included. Written by 104 specialists, the entries offer premiere data, editions, duration, source of libretto, plot, recordings, cast, instrumentation, and (a usually weak) bibliography. Although only the leading operas are given this full treatment, all the operas by the composer are listed. Seven-page glossary of terms, index of titles in original language and translation but no general index.

III. Histories

Music in General

Principal Reference Histories

58. *The New Oxford History of Music*. Ed. Jack A. Westrup et al. London: Oxford U.P., 1954–1990. ML160 .N44. (Cited in this guide as *NOHM*.)

For full contents see *Duckles* 2.26. Opera is well covered in these chapters:
V.4, *The Age of Humanism, 1540–1630*. "Music and Drama," by Edward J. Dent, rev. by F. W. Sternfeld; "Early Italian Opera," by Simon Towneley.
V.5, *Opera and Church Music, 1630–1750*. "Italian Opera from the Later Monteverdi to Scarlatti," by Hellmuth Christian Wolff; "Italian Opera 1700–1750," also by Wolff; "The Origins of French Opera," by Margaret M. McGowan; "French Opera from Lully to Rameau," by Paul-Marie Masson; "Opera in England and Germany," by Jack W. Westrup.
V.7, *The Age of Enlightenment, 1745–1790*. "Promotion and Patronage," "Italian Opera," "German Opera," and "The Operas of Mozart," by Anna Amalie Abert; "The Operas of Haydn," by H. C. Robbins Landon; "Opera in France," by Martin Cooper; "English Opera," by Roger Fiske; "The Rise of Russian Opera," by Gerald Seaman; and "Opera in Spain," by Gerald Abraham.
V.8, *The Age of Beethoven, 1790–1830*. "French Opera," "Italian Opera," and "German Opera," by Winton Dean; "Opera in Other Countries," by Gerald Abraham.
V.9, *Romanticism, 1830–1890*. On romantic opera (1830–1850): "Grand Opera" and "*Opéra-comique*," by David Charlton; "Italy," by David Kimbell; "Germany," by Siegfried Goslich; "Russia and Eastern Europe," by Gerald Abraham; and "Great Britain and the United States," by Nicholas Temperley. "Wagner's Later Stage Works," by Arnold Whittall, is in a separate section. On the period 1850–1890: "Germany," by Gerald Abraham; "France," by David Charlton; "Italy," by Julian Budden; "Russian and Eastern Europe," by Gerald Abraham; and "Great Britain and the United States," by Nicholas Temperley.

V.10, *The Modern Age, 1890–1960.* "Stage Works, 1890–1918," by Martin Cooper; "Music in the Soviet Union," by Gerald Abraham.

Typically a volume of this set offers clear and dependable introductions to its topics by recognized authorities. Essays are footnoted and provided with numerous musical examples. Each volume has a name index, with titles of compositions listed under composers (a general index to the 10 volumes is projected). Bibliographies are a weakness: awkwardly arranged, thick with trivia, and lacking basic facts of publication (such as the publishers of monographs and pagination of journal articles).

59. *Neues Handbuch der Musikwissenschaft.* Ed. Carl Dahlhuas. Wiesbaden: Akademische Verlagsgesellschaft Athenaion; Laaber: Laaber, 1980–1992. 14v. ISBN 3-89007-030-2. ML160 .N48.

   A strong presentation, each volume edited by a different scholar and consisting of topical chapters by experts. V.6, *Die Musik des 19. Jahrhunderts,* ed. Carl Dahlhaus (1980), was translated by J. Bradford Robinson as *Nineteenth-Century Music* (Berkeley: U. of California Press, 1989). Contents of the set in *Duckles* 2.11.

60. *Storia della musica.* Rev. ed. Turin: EDT, 1991–1993. 12v.

   First edition, 1976–1982. Volumes prepared by various authorities. Contents in *Duckles* 2.35.

61. Burney, Charles. *An Eighteenth-Century Musical Tour in Central Europe and the Netherlands; Being Dr. Charles Burney's Account of His Musical Experiences.* Ed. Percy A. Scholes. London: Oxford U.P., 1959. xiii, 268p. Reprint, Westport, Conn.: Greenwood, 1969. ISBN 0-313-21107-8 (Oxford). ML 195 .B962.

   Burney, pioneer English historian of music, made two trips to the continent to gather materials. In 1770 he visited France and Italy; in 1772 he went to the Low Countries and what are now Germany and Austria. The first tour resulted in *The Present State of Music in France and Italy . . .* (London: T. Becket, 1771); it is available in a modern edition: *Music, Men and Manners in France and Italy, 1770 . . .,* ed. H. Edmund Poole (London: Folio Society, 1969, see #2236). The second tour was described in Burney's *The Present State of Music in Germany, the Netherlands, and United Provinces* (London: T. Becket, 1773; 2nd ed. 1775). Burney's perceptive comments on all that he saw and heard form important contributions to our knowledge of musical life at the time.

62. *Companion to Baroque Music.* Ed. Julie Anne Sadie. London: Dent, 1990. xviii, 549p. ISBN 0-02-872275-2. ML193 .C56.

   A very useful compilation of material by Sadie and 12 other scholars, offering multiple viewpoints on the music of c. 1600–1750. Most of the book is organized around seven regions of Europe, giving histories and capsule biographies. Other sections deal with vocal and instrumental practice, forms, national styles, ornamentation, and authentic performance. With a 60-page chronology, a 150-item bibliography, and a general index.

Collections of Essays

63. *The Garland Library of the History of Music.* Ed. Ellen Rosand. New York: Garland, 1985. 14v. ISBN varies with each volume. ML1700 .O63. (Cited as *GL* in this guide.)

    Consists of reprints of 170 articles, most in English. A cross section of musicological endeavor is the result, with major operatic scholars well represented. As articles on opera are noted later in this guide, inclusion in the *Garland Library* will be noted.

64. *Festschrift Friedrich Blume zum 70. Geburtstag.* Ed. Anna Amalie Abert and Wilhelm Pfannkuch. Kassel: Bärenreiter, 1963. 426p. ML55 .B58.

    Many useful essays, including several on opera that have separate entries in this guide: #350 (Grout on early chorus), #1962 (Vetter on Wagenseil), and #2020 (Engel on *Das Liebesverbot*).

65. Cone, Edward T. *Music: A View from Delft; Selected Essays.* Ed. Robert P. Morgan. Chicago: U. of Chicago Press, 1989. ix, 334p. ISBN 0-276-11469-4. ML60 .C773 M9.

    A variety of writings by Cone, including two important pieces on opera; they are treated later in this guide: "The World of Opera and Its Inhabitants" (#405), and "The Old Man's Toys: Verdi's Last Operas" (#1880).

66. Cooper, Martin. *Judgements of Value: Selected Writings on Music.* Ed. Dominic Cooper. New York: Oxford U.P., 1988. xiv, 339p. ISBN 0-19-311929-3. ML60 .C822.

    Among the varied essays in this collection, there are several on operatic matters, including one on Gounod and another on Meyerbeer. Indexed.

67. *Essays on Music for Charles Warren Fox.* Ed. Jerald C. Grave. Rochester, N.Y.: Eastman School of Music, 1979. ix, 253p. ISBN 0-9603-1860-7. ML55 .F68 E844.

    Among the writings there are three of operatic interest, all dealt with later in this guide: Fritz Noske on *Otello* (#1907), Michael Collins on Alessandro Scarlatti's *Tigrane*" (#1622), and Robert M. Stevenson, "American Awareness of the Other Americas to 1900" (#2115).

68. *Music and Theatre: Essays in Honour of Winton Dean.* Ed. Nigel Fortune. New York: Cambridge U.P., 1987. xv, 389p. ISBN 0-521-3234-7. ML55 .D36.

    Four of the contributions are taken up later in this guide: Reinhard Strohm on *Giustino* (#986), Julian Budden on Wagnerian tendencies in Italian opera (#2472), Philip Brett on *Peter Grimes* and *The Rape of Lucretia* (#645), and John Warrack on Mendelssohn (#1181).

69. Dean, Winton. *Essays on Opera.* New York: Oxford U.P., 1991. x, 323p. ISBN 0-19-315265-7. ML1700 .D4.

    Previously published material, some of it revised for this anthology. Includes some brief and very general items and also some of Dean's major efforts, which have separate entries in this guide: on recitative (#358), on Beethoven (#495), and on *Sosarme* (#998).

70. *Essays Presented to Egon Wellesz.* Ed. Jack Westrup. Oxford: Clarendon Press, 1966. viii, 188p. ML55 .W38 W5.

   Sixteen essays; seven about opera, of which four are given separate treatment in this guide: F. W. Sternfeld on Gluck's *Orfeo* and *Alceste* (#899), Hans F. Redlich on Wagnerian elements in pre-Wagnerian opera (#2010), Jack Westrup on Bizet's *La jolie fille de Perth* (#587), and Gerald Abraham on Serov (#1659).

71. Lee, M. Owen. *First Intermissions: Twenty-One Great Operas Explored, Explained, and Brought to Life from the Met.* New York: Oxford U.P., 1995. xv, 248p. ISBN 0-19-509225-4. MT95 .L54.

   A gathering of Lee's entertaining and insightful intermission features from the Metropolitan radio broadcasts. Six are about Verdi, five about Wagner, three about Richard Strauss, and two about Puccini; there is one essay each about Mozart, Gounod, Berlioz, Offenbach, and Massenet. Index of names and titles.

72. *Essays on Opera and English Music: In Honour of Sir Jack Westrup.* Ed. F. W. Sternfeld, Nigel Fortune, and Edward Olleson. Oxford: Blackwell, 1975. x, 189p. ISBN 0-631-15890-1. ML55 .E78.

   Fourteen contributions; four are treated separately in this guide: Donald Jay Grout on *Griselda* (#1619), Winton Dean on *Sosarme* (#998), Gerald Abraham on opera in Poland (#2618), and Eric Walter White on opera at Oxford (#2728).

73. *Studies in Eighteenth-Century Music: A Tribute to Karl Geiringer on His 70th Birthday.* Ed. H. C. Robbins Landon. London: Allen & Unwin, 1970. 425p. ISBN 0-306-79519-1. ML55 .G24 S8.

   Consists of 38 essays, including the following on opera (those with entry numbers are treated later in this guide): George J. Buelow on Johann Mattheson's opera *Cleopatra* (#1171), Winton Dean, "Vocal Embellishment in a Handel Aria," Edith Vogel Garrett on Georg Benda (#522), Dolores Menstell Hsu on Weber (#2086), Emanuel Winternitz, "A Homage of Piccinni to Gluck," and Hellmuth Christian Wolff, "The Fairy Tale of the Neapolitan Opera" (#2530).

74. *Studies in Musical Sources and Analysis: In Honor of Jan La Rue.* Ed. Eugene K. Wolf and Edward H. Roesner. Madison, Wisc.: A-R Editions, 1990. xii, 555p. ISBN 0-89579-253-2. ML55 .L217.

   Of the 17 essays here, two on opera subjects have separate entries in this guide: Martin Chusid on *Don Carlos* (#1873), and Ellen Rosand on *L'incoronazione di Poppea* (#1233).

Opera

All Periods

75. Knapp, J. Merrill. *The Magic of Opera.* New York: Harper & Row, 1972. x, 371p. ML1700 .K67.

   Opera history is but one of the topics treated in this excellent presentation. The book is in fact a general text on the nature of opera, its terminology, conventions, and production. It is sensible and scholarly throughout. Expansive name and topic index.

76. Barblan, Guglielmo, and Alberto Basso. *Storia dell' opera.* Turin: UTET, 1977. 3v. in 6 parts. ML1700 .S884.

   Specialists from several countries contributed to this imposing work. The first two parts (v.1) are devoted to Italy; the next two parts (v.2) are about Europe and America; the final parts (v.3) consider aspects of the vocal art, give biographical data on hundreds of singers (many of them quite obscure), and discuss libretti. Name index to all volumes and a useful title index in original languages. The essays are outline presentations in encyclopedia style, with few footnotes and few musical examples. Countries that have complete chapters include the Scandinavian nations, Belgium and the Netherlands, Portugal, Switzerland, Czechoslovakia, USSR, Poland, Spain, Hungary, Yugoslavia, Romania, Bulgaria, Greece, Canada, and the U.S. Latin America also has a chapter.

77. *Oxford Illustrated History of Opera.* Ed. Roger Parker. New York: Oxford U.P., 1994. xv, 541p. ISBN 0-19-816282-0. ML1700 .O95.

   Also in paperback as *The Oxford History of Opera* (published in 1996). Operatic history approached through chapters by various scholars: 17th century, by Tim Carter; 18th century, by Thomas Bauman; 19th-century France, by David Charlton; 19th-century Italy, by William Ashbrook; 19th-century Germany, by Barry Millington, Russian-Czech-Polish-Hungarian opera to 1900, by John Tyrrell; and 20th century, by Paul Griffiths. Of special interest: "Staging of Opera," by Roger Savage, and essays by William Ashbrook on singers and John Rosselli on "Opera as a Social Occasion." With a valuable chronology by Mary Ann Smart and a bibliographic essay touching on some 300 titles. A strong index completes this handy reference.

78. Grout, Donald Jay, and Hermine Weigel Williams. *A Short History of Opera.* 3rd ed. New York: Columbia U.P., 1988. xix, 913p. ISBN 0-231-06192-7. ML1700 .G83.

   The standard history in English, marked by insights into style and movements. A good expansive index of names, titles, and topics renders the contents accessible. Here is a fine starting point for investigation into subjects like leitmotiv, patronage, and singing. Much acclaim has been accorded to the bibliography, and it is formidable in bulk, with some 2,700 entries for books, parts of books, dissertations, and journal articles, giving full publication data. However, it possesses no discernible criteria for inclusion; many items are too trivial to be of any interest, and several seem to belong in some other list (e.g., Pastor's *History of the Popes*). The arrangement, alphabetical by author, is fine for looking up a known book but unhelpful in discovering what has been written on a topic or composer.

79. Sadie, Stanley. *History of Opera*. The New Grove Handbooks in Music. New York: Norton, 1990. xii, 485p. ISBN 0-393-02810-0. ML1700 .H57.

   A useful gathering of material from *NG,* most of it revised and organized into a coherent presentation. Authors include Thomas Walker (Italy), Peter Branscombe (Germany and Austria), James R. Anthony (France), Curtis Price (England), Jack Sage (Spain), Manfred Boetzkes (design), and Roger Savage (production). Without footnotes but with a long, classified bibliography of more than 1,000 titles. A strong glossary gives extended information on about 250 terms. Expansive index.

80. Jellinek, George. *History through the Opera Glass: From the Rise of Caesar to the Fall of Napoleon*. London: Kahn & Averill, 1994. x, 405p. ISBN 1-8710-8247-1. ML2100 .J44.

   A fascinating narrative history of the world, which cites operas that pertain to each time and place. Then a chronology of events and operas dealing with them, from 14 B.C. to 1993. (What were three operas set in the 14th century?) Bibliography of about 100 entries; index of names, titles, and topics.

81. Lindenberger, Herbert Samuel. *Opera in History: From Monteverdi to Cage*. Stanford, Calif.: Stanford U.P., 1998. xi, 364p. ISBN 0-8047-3104-1. ML1700 .L54.

   An interesting ramble through numerous topics, although the endeavor to present opera as a sort of paradigmatic model of its times appears to dissolve en route. The author's knowledge and insights are pervasive. He suggests, for example, that acting in opera is nothing but a generalized expression of affect, having no connection to the character or situation: the aria is a musical pose. About the *Ring,* he observes that the topics concerned are not mythic themes but contemporary issues (incest, adultery, rebellion versus authority); the *Ring* actually "helped create a mid–19th century for us" by giving us a framework for rethinking the period. There is a good section on *Moses und Aron,* and on *Mahaggony,* works that Lindenberger takes as seriously as the *Ring,* and a fine account of John Cage's *Europeras,* which he takes even more seriously, wondering if they "put the aesthetic of opera in question." A 400-item bibliography, strong index.

82. Bokina, John. *Opera and Politics: From Monteverdi to Henze*. New Haven, Conn.: Yale U.P., 1997. xiv, 240p. ISBN 0-300-06935-9. ML1700 .B74.

   Opera seen as the medium "for the recording of the conscious and unconscious, explicit and implicit, historiography of society." It achieves this role through its libretti (music is not a concern here), which deal with issues and ideas of the day. *Fidelio,* for example, is about "republican virtue" and *Elektra* is about the new psychology. Other themes and libretti are matched as well.

Bokina notes that postmodern works (Cage, Adams, Corigliano) touch on contemporary issues "but take no clear and coherent position on them." Backnotes, 20-page bibliography, good index.

83. Wolff, Hellmuth Christian. *Geschichte der komischen Oper: Von den Anfängen bis zur Gegenwart.* Wilhelmshaven: Heinrichshofen, 1981. 264p. ISBN 3-7959-0304-1. ML1850 .W64.

    A scholarly account of the genre from the early Renaissance; emphasis on Europe, with some attention to American works. Illustrations, extended musical examples, unannotated bibliography of about 150 items. Name and topic index.

Precursors and 17th Century

84. Raguenet, François. *Parallel des Italiens et des François, en ce qui regarde la musique et las* [sic] *opéra.* Paris: J. Moreau, 1702. 140p.

    An important early discussion of Italian (which is favored) and French opera, foreshadowing the *querelle* that erupted a half century later. In *Strunk,* 671–678, the complete text is given, with source information and some notes. Fubini (#98) prints excerpts, with source information and more extensive notes (p.68–73). An English translation attributed to J. E. Gaillard appeared in 1709.

85. Le Cerf de La Viéville, Jean Laurent. *Comparaison de la musique italienne et de la musique françois.* Brussels: F. Foppeas, 1704–1706. 3v. in 1.

    A response to Raguenet (#84), partly translated into English in *Strunk.* The author was an ardent admirer of Lully and the French opera.

Other material on opera's first century is entered under the composers who created it: Giulio Caccini (#654ff.), Jacopo Peri (#377, #1398), Claudio Monteverdi (#1204), and their librettists: Gian Francesco Busenello (#236), and Ottavio Rinuccini (#268, #269).
See also #2438–#2446 for material on the Camerata.

18th Century

86. Jacquot, Jean, ed. *La fête théâtrale et les sources de l'opéra: Acts de la 4° session des Journées Internationales d'Étude du Baroque.* Mantaubon: Baroque Revue Internationale, 1972. 138p. ML1703 .J7.

    Fourteen papers on various arts of the musical theater (ballets, *intermèdes, fêtes,* etc.). Complete contents in *Baron,* 473.

87. Yorke-Long, Alan. *Music at Court: Four Eighteenth-Century Studies.* London: Weidenfeld & Nicolson, 1954. xviii, 158p. ML60 .Y6.

    Valuable background essays about music in Parma, Stuttgart, Dresden, and Berlin. They deal with the theaters, festivals, place of the musician, composers, singers, and the overarching role of the ruling personage. With footnotes and index.

88. Downes, Edward O. D. "*Secco* Recitative in Early Classical Opera Seria (1720–1780)." *JAMS* 14 (1961): 50–69.

    A valuable analysis of recitative that was not accompanied by the orchestra, stressing the emotional impact of its performance and the harmonic devices used by Pergolesi and others. Less *secco* was used in the reform operas. For performance practice issues, see Dean (#358).

89. Algarotti, Francesco. *Saggio sopra l'opera in musica*. Livorno: M. Coltellini, 1763. English translation, 1768. Reprinted in *Strunk*, 909–922.

    First edition, 1755. Algarotti, a Venetian who spent nine years in Berlin assisting Frederick the Great in the translation of opera libretti, expressed negative views about contemporary Italian opera. He found that composers were bent on flattering the ears of the audience, "but not at all either to affect the heart or kindle the imagination." He took the Gluckian (see #378) view on what needed reforming.

Material on the Quarrel of the Buffoons is at #2257ff.

90. *I vicini di Mozart: Il teatro musicale tra sette e ottocento. Atti del Convegno Internazionale di Studi . . . 7–9 settembre 1987*. Ed. Maria Teresa Muraro and David Bryant. Studi di musica veneta, 15. Florence: Olschki, 1989. 2v. ISBN 88-222-3685-8. ML170 .V5.

    A strong collection of papers from the conference, including three on opera in v.1 that are entered later in this guide: Rudolph Angermüller on Anfossi's *Il curioso indiscreto* (#459), Mercedes Viale Ferrero on operas given in Turin and Milan (#2525), and Gian Paolo Minardi on Paër (#1370). V.2 is on "La farsa musicale veneziana (1750–1810)." The lead article by David Bryant is at #2579.

91. *Opera and the Enlightenment*. Ed. Thomas Bauman and Marita Petzoldt McClymonds. New York: Cambridge U.P., 1995. xii, 317p. ISBN 0-521-46172-3. ML1720.3 O64.

    An important collection of essays by various scholars. These are covered later in this guide: Gary Tomlinson on pastoral (#2445), Mary Cyr on chorus in French opera (#351), Winton Dean on *Serse*" (#995), Julie E. Cumming on Gluck's Iphigenia operas (#903), and Richard Taruskin, "From Fairy Tale to Opera in Four Moves (Not So Simple)" (#1433). The volume has footnotes and a strong index but no bibliography.

92. Kelly, Michael. *Reminiscences*. Ed. Roger Fiske. New York: Oxford U.P., 1975. xx, 396p. ISBN 0-19255-4174. ML420 .K3 .A202.

    Originally published 1826. Kelly was a noted tenor (he sang in the premiere of *Le nozze di Figaro*) who performed extensively in London and on the continent. His memoir offers keen observations on music and singers, theater politics, and conditions of performance in various European cities. Useful comments by Fiske, chronology, bibliography, and index.

19th Century

93. Die *"opéra-comique"* und ihr Einfluss auf das europaische Musiktheater im 19. Jahrhundert: Bericht über den Internationalen Kongress Frankfurt 1994. Ed. Herbert Schneider and Nicole Wild. Musikwissenschaftliche Publikationen, 3. Hildesheim: Olms, 1997. 490p. ISBN 4871-0250-1. ML1720 .O63.

A valuable collection of 18 papers from the conference, with name and topic indexing. These are treated separately in this guide: David Charlton on the *romance* (#2261), Arnold Jacobshagen on the choral introduction (#2263), Odile Krakovitch on censorship (#2321), and Irmlind Capelle on Grétry and Lortzing (#931). The other papers: Philippe Blay, "Le fonds de l'Opéra-Comique: Préambule à un inventaire"; Philippe Vendrix, "L'opéra comique sans rire"; Patrick Taïeb, "Romance et mélomanie . . ."; Thomas Betzwiser, "Si tu veux faire un opéra comique . . ."; Albert Gier, "Volkslied und Bänkelsang: Einlagelieder von Grétry bis Jacques Offenbach"; Nicole Wild, "La mise en scène à l'Opéra-Comique sous la restauration"; Jean-Claude Yon, "Les débuts périlleux d'Offenbach à l'Opéra-Comique: *Barkouf* (1860)"; Marie-Claire Mussat, "Diffusion et réception de l'opéra comique dans les provinces françaises . . ."; Michael Fend, "Es versteht sich von selbst, dass ich von der Oper spreche, die der Deutsche und Französe will . . ."; Joachim Veit, "Das französische Repertoire der Schauspielgesellschaft August Pichlers zwischen 1825 und 1847"; Emilio Sala, "Réécritures italiennes de l'opéra comique française . . ."; Marco Marica, "Le traduzioni italiane in prosa di *opéras comiques* francesi (1763–1813)"; and Ramón Barce, "Das spanische Singspiel (*Sainete lirico*)."

94. De Van, Gilles. *"Fin de siècle* Exoticism and the Meaning of the Far Away." *OQ* 11-3 (1995): 78–94.

Trans. from Italian by William Ashbrook. Refers to exoticism at the end of the 19th century as "almost an obsession." It began with Cherubini and ended with *Turandot*. The effect was achieved in opera by an alien setting, either temporal or geographical. De Van interprets the movement as a "metaphor of desire" toward the "other which becomes a mirror of the self." The exotic closely relates to the erotic search for the mysterious woman, or femme fatale. Intriguing; also a well-documented guide to the other literature.

20th Century

95. *Oper heute: Formen der Wirklichkeit im zeitgenossischer Oper heute.* Ed. Otto Kolleritsch. Vienna: Universal, 1985. 274p. ISBN 3-7024-0170-9. ML55 .S9103, v.16.

Sixteen essays by various writers, dealing with recent operas. The studies are technical analyses, with footnotes and often inscrutable little music examples. These are of special interest: Wolf Konold, "Ligetis *Le grand macabre*: Absurdes Welttheater auf der Opernbühne"; Hans-Werner Heister, "Kinderoper als Volkstheater: Hans Werner Henzes *Pollicino*"; Jurgen Maehder, "Bussottis Operaballett: Zur Entwicklung der musikalischen Dramaturgie im Werk Sylvano Bussottis"; Ivanka Stofanova, "Prinzipien des Musiktheaters bei Luciano

Berio: *Passaggio, Laborintus II, Opera*"; and Georg Quander, "Von Minimal zum Maximal . . ." (about *Satyagraha* by Philip Glass).

Collections of Documents

96. Strunk, Oliver. *Source Readings in Music History.* 2nd ed. Ed. Leo Treitler. New York: Norton, 1998. xxii, 1,552p. ISBN 0-393-03752-5. ML160 .S89. (Cited in this guide as *Strunk.*)

    First edition, 1950. The new edition of this indispensable anthology considerably augments the number of readings in the first (from 87 items to 214) and provides new introductions by specialists for each period. Material from the 20th century is included (the first edition stopped with the 19th). Musicians and critics are represented, by English translations where necessary. Long treatises have extracts. Among the authors who wrote on opera: Padre de'Bardi, Ottavio Rinuccini, Giulio Caccini, Jacopo Peri, François Raguenet, Benedetto Marcello, Rousseau, Francesco Algarotti, Gluck, Weber, Berlioz, and Wagner. Expansive index of names and topics.

97. Weiss, Piero, and Richard Taruskin. *Music in the Western World: A History in Documents.* New York: Schirmer, 1984. 556p. ISBN 0-02-872900-5. ML160 .M865.

    A useful selection of 114 short documents or extracts, with commentaries. Among the writers on opera: Giulio Caccini, Monteverdi, Goldoni, Addison and Steele, Ferdinand Hiller, Gluck, Leigh Hunt, and Wagner. Index of names, works, and subjects.

98. *Music and Culture in Eighteenth-Century Europe: A Source Book.* Ed. Enrico Fubini. Chicago: U. of Chicago Press, 1994. x, 442p. ISBN 0-226-26731-8. ML240.3 .M8613.

    A fine collection of 50 writings, most of them on opera or relating to opera, translated into English. Extensive documentation and commentaries, with biographical information on the writers; bibliography and excellent subject index. Among the authors included are François Raguenet, Jean-Laurent Lecerf de la Viéville, Diderot, Friedrich Melchior Grimm, Francesco Algarotti, Metastasio, and Johann Mattheson.

99. Becker, Heinz. *Quellentexte zur Konzeption der europäischen Oper im 17. Jahrhundert.* Kassel: Bärenreiter, 1981. 200p. ML1703 .Q3.

    A gathering of 62 documents in their original languages, without translations, with extensive commentaries in German. Topics are Florentine, Venetian, French, and German opera of the 17th century, as discussed by such writers as Jacopo Peri, Giovanni Doni, Marc'Antonio Cesti, Pietro Ziani, Antonio Sartorio, and Lully. Name and title index.

100. Krause-Graumnitz, Heinz. *Von Wesen der Oper. Opernkomponisten über die Oper.* Berlin: Henschelverlag, 1969. 538p. ML90 .K73.

    Letters, prefaces, and other statements by about 100 composers of opera, from Peri to Shostakovich. Sources identified; commentaries; everything is in German. Name and title index.

101. Fisk, Josiah. *Composers on Music: Eight Centuries of Writings*. Boston: Northeastern U.P., 1997. xvi, 512p. ISBN 1-55553-278-0. ML90 .C77.

   An expanded version of a 1956 anthology by Samuel Morgenstern. A good selection of writings by about 80 composers, including all the major opera composers and a number of moderns (such as Poulenc, Cage, Copland, Bernstein, Ligeti, Berio, Henze, and Glass). Full source information is given for each extract, along with commentary. Well indexed.

102. *Composers on Modern Musical Culture: An Anthology of Source Readings on Twentieth- Century Music*. Ed. Bryan R. Simms. New York: Schirmer, 1999. xiii, 286p. ISBN 0-02-864751-3.

   All the leading opera composers are included in this useful gathering of original writings, many of them appearing in English for the first time. Commentaries, bibliography, and index.

103. Weisstein, Ulrich. *The Essence of Opera*. New York: Free Press of Glencoe, 1964. 372p. ML1700 .W35.

   An anthology of 68 selections on the topic of operatic poetics, all in English, with sources and commentaries. Authors include composers from the Florentines to Stravinsky and literary figures like Voltaire, Goethe, Schopenhauer, Shaw, Cocteau, Brecht, and Auden. Name and title index.

Chronologies

104. Zöchling, Dieter. *Die Chronik der Oper*. Dortmund: Chronik, 1990. 639p. ISBN 3-611-00128.7 ML102. O6 Z623.

   An excellent day-by-day review of operatic history, in newspaper style, from 1598 to 1990. Lavish color illustrations add to the value of the stories, which include accounts of premieres, openings of new buildings, deaths of artists, and other events related to opera. The composer index has titles (in German) under each name, with premiere date; there is also a name index.

Operatic highlights also appear in many general chronologies; of these the most useful have been described in *IOM* 0105–0112, 1410, and 1501, and *Duckles* 2.62–2.84. Surely the most fascinating of them is:

105. Slonimsky, Nicolas. *Music since 1900*. 5th ed. New York: Schirmer, 1994. 1,260p. ISBN 0-02872-4185. ML197 .S634.

   First edition, 1937. Major events in music from 1900 through 1991, including opera premieres, dates of composition, odd occurrences, and Slonimsky's peppery, perceptive observations on it all. Glossary of new terms, and name index, with compositions listed under their composers.

One of the pillars of opera reference is in chronological format:

106. Loewenberg, Alfred. *Annals of Opera, 1597–1940*. 2nd ed. Rev. and corrected Frank Walker. Geneva: Societas Bibliographica, 1955. 2v. ML102 .O6 L6.

   A reprint edition (Totowa, N.J.: Rowman & Littlefield, 1978) was described as "3rd edition, revised and corrected." The standard list of about 3,600 operas that have been performed, arranged by date of premiere. For each work the first and important performances outside the home country are given, with exact dates, language of each libretto and names of translators, plus miscellaneous observations. Opera titles appear in their original languages, with English translations for less common tongues. Indexes by title, composer, and librettist; also a general index with entries for individual countries and for topics. Performance histories are more complete for 17th- and 18th-century works. *Kaufman* gives an important critical commentary on this undertaking, noting various types of errors to watch for. A continuation of Loewenberg, by Harold Rosenthal, was announced for 1983 but has not appeared.

107. Kaufman, Thomas G. *Verdi and His Major Contemporaries: A Selected Chronology of Performances with Casts*. Garland Reference Library of the Humanities, 1,016. New York: Garland, 1990. xxiv, 590p. ISBN 0-8240-4106-2. ML128 .O4 K4.

The publisher has given two added titles: on the title page we find "Annals of Italian Opera," while the verso announces "Annals of Opera Vol.1." Since no further volume has appeared, the exact nature of the series remains undefined. This is an invaluable book in itself, with tabular performance histories for all of Verdi's operas through the 1980s and for the operas of 17 other composers. For works with relatively few performances, all productions are cited; for popular works there is a selection. (Kaufman estimates that "a repertory opera such as *Il trovatore* or *Aida* probably had 10,000 to 25,000 performances.") Arrangement is by country, then city. Cast information is given as available. A long bibliography of sources consulted, some 400 books and periodicals, presents many theatrical histories; it would have been more useful with complete bibliographic information. The only index is to opera titles. Linda Fairtile has enhanced the access to this book with composer and librettist indexes in *Verdi Newsletter* 20 (1992): 16–21.

See also the chronologies in *Oxford Illustrated History* (#77) and Jellinek (#80).

Iconographies

Opera lends itself admirably to pictorial treatment, or iconography. Many such treatments are cited in this guide under specific approaches that they represent (particular composers, designers, opera houses, and so forth). There is one general iconography of interest:

108. Wolff, Hellmuth Christian. *Oper, Szene und Darstellung von 1600 bis 1900*. Musikgeschichte in Bildern, 4/1. Leipzig, VEB Deutscher Verlag für Musik, 1968. 212p. ML89 .M9 v.4,1.

Part of a major series of iconographical works. Consists of more than 200 documented illustrations of productions, costumes, and all kinds of performers. Many sketches for stage design, including some published for the first time. Bibliography of about 150 entries; name and topic index.

See also the sections on iconography in *IOM* 0113–0136, and *Duckles* 2.40–2.61.

IV. Editions and Excerpts

Composer entries in this guide offer some information on modern editions of their operas. Citations to complete and collected works of all composers are given in *NOHM*. Several anthologies of music provide a variety of examples from the history of opera. These are especially useful:

109. *Anthology of Music.* Ed. Karl Gustav Fellerer. Cologne: Arno Volk, 1955–1976. 48v. M2 .M9872.

   Four volumes are devoted to opera: 5, 38, 39, and 40. The most popular arias are generally avoided, in favor of lesser-known but characteristic pieces. English libretto segments are given, along with commentaries and sources.

110. Brody, Elaine. *Music in Opera: A Historical Anthology.* Englewood Cliffs, N.J.: Prentice-Hall, 1970. 604p. M2 .B857 M9.

   About 100 long excerpts, covering all periods. Aria texts in original languages and English translations, stage directions, and commentaries. Popular arias are mingled with less familiar numbers. Name, title, and topic index.

111. *Historical Anthology of Music.* Rev. ed. Ed. Archibald T. Davison and Willi Apel. Cambridge, Mass.: Harvard U.P., 1949–1950. 2v. M2 .D25 H6.

   V.2 has numerous operatic excerpts, with commentaries. Texts are translated into English; sources are described.

Garland Publishing has issued some valuable series of scores, making available works not generally available before. The sets specific to countries are entered there; these are multinational:

112. *The Ballad Opera: A Collection of 171 Original Texts of Musical Plays Printed in Photo-Facsimile.* Selected and arranged by Walter H. Rubsamen. New York: Garland, 1974. 28v. ISBN 0-8240-0900-2. ML48 .B18.

   These works constitute the entire extant repertoire of English, Scottish, Irish, and American ballad opera—the 18th-century form that led to the comic opera. Among the better- known compositions are *The Beggar's Opera, Polly,*

The Devil to Pay, and *The Disappointment.* Scores and libretti are printed as they were first published, without notes, comments, or indexing.

113. *Early Romantic Opera.* Ed. with introductions by Philip Gossett and Charles Rosen. New York: Garland, 1978–1984. 44v. ISBNs and LC numbers vary per volume. (Cited in this guide as *ERO.*)

These are full orchestral scores, photocopied from manuscript or rare early printed sources. Major works by Bellini, Rossini, Meyerbeer, Donizetti, Auber, Cherubini, Halévy, Le Sueur, Méhul, and Spontini are included. All the operas in the set are noted individually under their composers in this guide.

The next work is a helpful guide to the musical anthologies:

114. Hill, George Robert, and Norris L. Stephens. *Collected Editions, Historical Series and Sets, and Monuments of Music: A Bibliography.* Fallen Leaf Reference Books in Music, 14. Berkeley, Calif.: Fallen Leaf, 1997. xliv, 1,349p. ISBN 0-914913-32-0. ML113 .H55.

Some 8,000 titles given, with every volume of a series listed. Inclusion is limited to works containing music (as opposed to writings about music). Full bibliographic data given, with reprint information. Effectively replaces the earlier guide to anthologies by Anna Harriet Heyer, *Historical Sets, Collected Editions, and Monuments of Music* (Chicago: American Library Association, 1980; *Duckles* 5.511), except that the planned index has not yet appeared.

V. Libraries

Catalogues

Several major libraries have issued lists of opera scores and/or libretti in their collections:

115. United States. Library of Congress. Music Division. *Catalogue of Opera Librettos Printed before 1800.* Prepared by O. G. T. Sonneck. Washington, D.C.: U.S. Government Printing Office, 1914. 2v. Reprints, New York: Burt Franklin, 1967; New York: Johnson Reprint, 1970. ML136 .U55 C45.

About 17,000 items in composer order with full bibliographic data and annotations usually that give information about the premiere. Useful for correct facts of publication on most operas before 1900, e.g., 21 by Auber and 36 by Grétry. V.1 is a title catalogue, and v.2 is an index of composers, librettists, and arias.

116. United States. Library of Congress. *Dramatic Music (Class M1500, 1510, 1520): Catalogue of Full Scores.* Comp. Oscar George Theodore Sonneck. Washington, D.C.: U.S. Government Printing Office, 1908. 170p. Reprint, New York: Da Capo, 1969. ML128 .O5 U5.

Some 1,700 entries with full bibliographic data and facts about premieres. In composer order with no index.

117. *Catalog of the Opera Collections in the Music Libraries: University of California, Berkeley; University of California, Los Angeles.* Boston: G. K. Hall, 1983. 697p. ISBN 0–8161-0392–5. ML136 .B47 U58.

A pair of composer lists, with about 4,000 entries from UCLA and 10,000 from Berkeley. Format is photoreproduction of catalogue cards, with full bibliographic data. No index.

118. Eckhoff, Annemarie. *Oper, Operette, Singspiel. Ein Katalog der Hamburger Musikbücherei.* Hamburg: Hamburger Öffentliche Bücherhallen, 1965. 206p. ML136 .H33 O4.

About 2,000 entries, in composer order with title index. Gives place and year of premiere, librettist, and publisher.

119. British Broadcasting Corporation. *Choral and Opera Catalogue.* London: British Broadcasting Corporation, 1967. 2v. ML128 .V7 B76.

> Composer and title lists, with the genres intermixed. Gives publisher and duration for about 60,000 works.

Numerous library inventories include operatic works along with other kinds of music. For major examples see *IOM* 0227–0240, 0370–0389, and *Duckles,* section 7. Special notice is due to the outstanding cooperative list for North American libraries:

120. *National Union Catalog: Pre–1956 Imprints.* London: Mansell, 1968–1981. 754v. Z1215 .U47.

> With about 13,000,000 entries, this is the largest bibliographic work ever published. It consists of photocopies from the card catalogues of 1,500 research libraries in the U.S., Canada, and Mexico, representing monographs published before 1956. Sequence of material is alphabetical by author. Musical works are listed under names of composers; they include all editions, transcriptions, arrangements, libretti in various languages, and so on. Library locations are given. To exemplify the scope of the set, there are 182 entries for versions of *Faust* and 289 for *Don Giovanni.*

121. United States. Library of Congress. *Library of Congress Catalog—Music, Books on Music, and Sound Recordings, 1953–.* Washington, D.C.: Library of Congress, 1953–. Semiannual; annual and quinquennial cumulations. ISSN 0092–2838. Z881 .U52 M8.

> From 1953 to 1972 the title was *Music and Phonorecords.* The title adopted in 1973, *National Union Catalog,* marked the inclusion of entries from a number of cooperating libraries. Materials processed in any of the libraries during the time period of each volume are included. Genres included are music scores, books about music, and sound recordings whether of music or speech. Since 1991 this title has been issued only in microfiche and as part of the CD-ROM and online versions of the *National Union Catalog* (described in *GRB*).

Other important library catalogues include those of the New York Public Library (*Duckles* 7.362) and the British Library (*Duckles* 7.258).

Guides to Resources

Guidance to library resources for musical scholarship is offered by a number of works. A good overview of resource guides appears in *Duckles,* section 7. *NGDO* 2, 1163–1185, has a strong entry for "Libraries and Archives" by John Wagstaff; it lists important collections by country and city and notes the writings about each one. Other useful titles:

122. *Directory of Music Research Libraries.* Ed. Rita Benton. Kassel: Bärenreiter, 1967–. ML12 .B45.

> A sweeping guide to the world's music libraries, with five volumes published to date. Issued originally in a "preliminary edition" by Rita Benton (U. of Iowa Press, 1967–1970; 2v.) and the International Association of Music Libraries; later assimilated into *RISM,* Series C. It is a country/city listing of libraries,

giving descriptions of the collections and administrative information. Coverage has thus far extended to North America, Europe, Australia, New Zealand, and Japan. Details in *Duckles* 7.1.

123. Seaton, Douglass. "Important Library Holdings at Forty-one North American Universities." *Current Musicology* 17 (April 1974): 7–68.

   A general survey, in which certain opera collections are identified. Some of them are in Boston University (Risë Stevens collection), Columbia (Berlioz), Cornell (18th- and 19th-century scores), Harvard (Rossini), Indiana (black music and Latin American music), Stanford (recorded sound; early singers), University of California, Berkeley (18th-century French libretti; 19th-century Italian and French scores), University of California at Los Angeles (18th-century libretti, including a 117-volume set of Venetian works), Texas (libretti), Washington (17th–19th century scores), and Western Ontario (editions and manuscripts, 1751–1800).

124. Bradley, Carol June. *Music Collections in American Libraries: A Chronology.* Detroit: Information Coordinators, 1981. 249p. ISBN 0-89990-002-X. ML111 .B79.

   An inventory of 374 institutions in the U.S., citing significant dates, special collections, published catalogues, and writings by and about the library. Index identifies major subject collections.

125. Penney, Barbara. *Music in British Libraries: A Directory of Resources.* 4th ed. London: Library Association, 1992. 112p. ISBN 0-85365-739-4. ML21 .L66.

   First edition, 1971. Describes holdings and facilities of some 700 libraries. Index of composers cited and of other special collections by subject.

VI. Opera Houses

Gathered in this chapter are works that describe the opera houses of more than one country. Books and articles that are entirely concerned with the theaters of a single country are listed under that country in Chapter XVIII. *NGDO* 4 has valuable entries by Edward A. Langhans: "Seating," 283–292, and "Theatre Architecture," 709–722. Plans are given for La Scala, King's Theatre Haymarket, Covent Garden, Deutsche Oper Berlin, Vienna Staatsoper, Palais Garnier (Paris), the new Metropolitan Opera, Bastille Opera, and Bayreuth Festspielhaus. There is also a useful glossary of terms in English, French, German, and Italian.

126. Kaufman, Thomas G. "A Bibliography of House Annals." *DSJ* 5 (1984): 317–381. (Cited in this guide as *Kaufman*.)

    A very useful list of about 400 works that include annals (chronologies of performances) in individual opera houses. Selects "the best available book on each city or house," omitting superseded materials. Books without annals are listed only if they have special importance or if there is no published chronology for the house in question. Valuable commentaries point out the strengths and weaknesses of the works. Diacritics are frequently missing in titles, and a fair number of misprints got into the foreign words, so the user will be wise to verify imprint data. Kaufman's "Corrections and Additions," in *Donizetti Society Journal* 6 (1988): 193–215, added about 100 entries.

127. Stoddard, Richard. *Theatre and Cinema Architecture: A Guide to Information Sources*. Detroit: Gale, 1978. 368p. ISBN 0-8103-1426-6. Z5784 .S8 S82.

    Consists of 1,586 annotated entries—books, pamphlets, and articles—on exterior and interior design, including acoustical questions. Arrangement by country. Reference value of the work is reduced by the absence of diacritical marks in languages that use them. Index of architects and designers; index of theaters by country.

128. Hughes, Patrick Cairns (Spike). *Great Opera Houses: A Traveller's Guide to Their History and Traditions*. London: Weidenfeld & Nicolson, 1956; New York: McBride, 1959. 362p. ML1720 .H8.

Descriptions of the major houses in Munich, Vienna, Venice, Milan, Parma, Florence, Rome, Naples, Palermo, Catania, Genoa, Turin, Paris, and London. The approach is historical but popular (no footnotes). It is a pleasant introduction to many of opera's greatest homes. With 13 illustrations, bibliography, and index.

129. Krause, Ernst. *Die grossen Opernbühnen Europas.* Kassel: Bärenreiter, 1966. 251p. ML1720 .K73.

A photo album of halls in Berlin, Vienna, Milan, Rome, Venice, Paris, London, Glyndebourne, Moscow, St. Petersburg, Prague, Budapest, Sofia, Warsaw, Stockholm, Zurich, Barcelona, Munich, Dresden, Stuttgart, Hamburg, Frankfurt, Cologne, Düsseldorf, Leipzig, Bayreuth, Salzburg, and Halle. Most of the views are exteriors, but some are scenes from productions. Index of persons and opera titles.

130. Beauvert, Thierry. *Opera Houses of the World.* Trans. Daniel Sheeler. New York: Vendome, 1996. 277p. ISBN 2-8766-0004.8. ML1700 .B27.

A splendidly illustrated coffee-table book, showing views of 50 theaters. Many floor plans, cross sections, and accounts of construction. Also miscellaneous facts (including quite a few errors) and chronologies. Much space goes to singers. With no documentation and a weak index. The author is director of exhibitions and publications, Bastille Opéra, Paris.

131. Burian, Karel Vladimir. *Svě tová operní divadla.* Prague: Supraphon, 1973. 222p. ML1700 .B935.

Although the Czech language may present a barrier, this is a useful gathering of facts and pictures (59 plates) on the world's opera houses. Dimensions, history, and persons associated with 149 theaters are given, in city sequence. Index of names and theaters.

132. Sachs, Edwin O., and Ernest A. Woodrow. *Modern Opera Houses and Theatres.* London: Batsford, 1896–1898. 3v. Reprint, New York: Benjamin Blom, 1968. NA6821 .S22.

Two volumes review the architectural history and dimensions of important 19th-century structures in Europe; the final volume is a treatise on theater planning and construction, with attention to stage machinery. Cities covered are Vienna, Budapest, Prague, Dresden, Halle, Berlin, Bayreuth, Worms, London, Wolverhampton, Manchester, Bristol, Amsterdam, Brussels, Oslo, Stockholm, Odesssa, Tiflis, Leningrad, Paris, Monte Carlo, Palermo, Milan, Turin, Bilbao, Salzburg, Laibach, Frankfurt, Rostock, Essen, Bromberg, Stratford-on-Avon, Leeds, Cambridge, Athens, Rotterdam, Bucharest, Geneva, and Zurich. Photographs and plans, index.

133. Zietz, Karyl Lynn. *Opera! The Guide to Western Europe's Great Houses.* Santa Fe, N. Mex.: J. Muir, distributed by Norton, 1991. vi, 287p. ISBN 0-945465-81-5. ML1720 .Z53.

Covers 92 theaters, giving historical background and current directory information. Seating plans are shown, with other material of interest to persons planning to attend a performance.

134. Filippi, Joseph de. *Parallèle des principaux théâtres modernes de l'Europe et des machines théâtrales françaises, allemandes, et anglaises.* Paris: A. Lévy, 1860. 163p. plus drawings. Reprint, New York: Benjamin Blom, 1968. NA6821 .F5.

A historical survey of theater architecture and planning, followed by a technical description of halls in France, England, Italy, Germany, Russia, Spain, Belgium, and Denmark. Most are 19th-century structures, but a few are older. With 133 plates, including plans.

135. Bauer-Heinhold, Margarete. *Baroque Theatre.* Trans. Mary Whittall. London: Thames & Hudson; New York: McGraw-Hill, 1968. 292p. PN2174 .B32.

Originally published as *Theater des Barock* (Munich: Callwey, 1966). A cultural approach to theaters in Italy, Germany, France, Spain, Russia, Switzerland, and Austria, considering patrons, composers, artists, and production matters as well as the houses themselves. With 16 color plates, 191 photos, and 146 figures. Bibliography of about 150 items; index of names, titles, and topics.

136. Izenour, George C. *Theater Design.* New York: McGraw-Hill, 1977. 631p. ISBN 0-07-032086-1. NA6821 .I94.

A history of theaters from ancient times, with technical descriptions and plans and sections that are usefully drawn to the same scale. Also essays on diverse aspects of design, acoustics, cost analysis, and so forth. About 900 illustrations; index to theaters by type and by location.

137. Aloi, Roberto. *Architetture per lo spettacolo.* Milan: Ulrico Hoepli, 1958. lxv, 504p. NA6821 .A4.

A useful handbook of about 100 theaters of the world, most of them dating from the 1950s. Vastly detailed with technical data ("reinforced concrete roofing 2.36 inches thick . . . cork panels 1.18 inches thick . . .") and profusely illustrated with 21 color plates, 345 black-and-white photos, and 454 designs. The descriptive matter is in Italian, French, English, and German. Index of architects and theaters.

VII. International Directories

Directories for individual countries are listed in Chapter XVIII. These are guides to the operatic world: people, companies, theaters, activities. They are current or at least recent. Some comments on retrospective directories are at the end of the section.

138. Cowden, Robert H. *Opera Companies of the World: Selected Profiles*. Westport, Conn.: Greenwood, 1992. xxvi, 336p. ISBN 0-313-26220-9. ML12. O63.

   A valuable compilation of facts about 139 companies: histories, directory data, and bibliographies. Indexed by personal names, institutions, and cities.

139. Turnbull, Robert. *The Opera Gazetteer*. New York: Rizzoli, 1988. 240p. ISBN 0-8478-0727-4. ML12 .T87.

   Describes about 100 world opera houses, including seating capacity of each, and gives practical information for obtaining tickets. Except for Eastern Europe, names are in original languages. With photos and a name index.

140. *International Who's Who in Music and Musicians' Directory. I. Classical*. 15th edition. Cambridge, England: International Who's Who in Music; Detroit: Gale, 1996–1997. ISBN 0-900332-51-4 (International); 0-8103-0427-9 (Gale). ML106 .G7 W4.

   This directory has had various titles and publishers since it started in 1935. Beginning with this edition it split into two publications: one for classical and light classical musicians and the other for popular musicians. The classical volume offers a universal directory of musical institutions, including opera companies, and of opera singers. Names of organizations are sometimes in their own languages, sometimes in English. Many omissions and a huge number of misprints detract from the usefulness of the work. No index.

141. *Music Industry Directory*. 7th ed. Chicago: Marquis Professional Publications, 1983. 678p. ISBN 0-8379-5602-1. ML13 .M505.

   With this edition, a change from the former title: *The Musician's Guide: The Directory of the World of Music*. Publisher has varied since the first edition of 1954. Lists of U.S. and Canadian agencies, organizations, libraries, periodicals (foreign included), music critics, schools, competitions, etc. About 600 opera companies are identified—amateur and college groups among them—with addresses and names of administrators. The "general index" is really an expanded table of contents.

142. Musical America. *International Directory of the Performing Arts*. Hights-town, N.J.: Primedia Information, 1999. 831p. ISBN 1-891131-01-X. ML13 .M497.

Title and publisher vary for this yearbook, which has been published since 1968. It presents useful data for the U.S. and Canada on performers, groups, agents, publishers, and business aspects of music. An index of names gives total access to the material. It is of interest that the list of opera companies (by state and city) runs to 27 pages for the U.S. and Canada and to only 6 pages for the rest of the world.

143. Couch, John Philip. *The Opera Lover's Guide to Europe*. 2nd ed. New York: Limelight, 1991. 300p. ISBN 0-87910-191-1. ML1700 .C68.

Ticket information, including seating, and local transportation facilities, for opera houses in major cities and also in smaller centers. Arranged by country and city.

144. Rabin, Carol Price. *Music Festivals in America: Classical, Opera, Jazz, Pops, Country, Old-Time Fiddlers, Folk, Bluegrass, Cajun*. 4th ed. Great Barrington, Mass.: Berkshire Traveller Press, 1990. 271p. ISBN 0-9301-4501-1. ML35 .R3.

Title varies; first edition, 1979. A handy inventory of 160 U.S. and Canadian festivals, arranged geographically under each category. Directors and typical participants are named, and ticket information is given. Regional maps pin-point the exact locations. With an index of the festival names.

Older directories will not be described here, but their value should be mentioned. On one level, they provide the researcher a slice of the past. On another, they often give facts that are still valid, in more detail than later publications offer; for example, we find floor plans of opera houses in Scandinavian cities in Eugène d'Harcourt's *La musique actuelle dans les états scandinaves* (1910; *IOM* 1861). *Pierre Key's Music Yearbook* (*IOM* 0153) provided directory information on opera companies with lists of singers and premieres during its period of issue, 1924–1938. A fine series of guides by Elaine Brody and Claire Brook, issued 1975–1978, covered eight European countries (*Duckles* 11.68; *IOM* 1438–1441). *The Opera Directory* by Anne Ross (1961; *Duckles* 1.468) covered about 7,000 singers and other personnel. Other retrospective directories are noted in *IOM* 0138–0140, 1442–1443, and 2499.

VIII. Periodicals, Yearbooks, and Series

A list of about 200 opera periodicals, compiled by Imogen Fellinger, is given in *NGDO* 3, 959–967; it includes full bibliographic data for each title. A useful list identifies periodicals about individuals:

145. Basart, Ann P. "Serials Devoted to Individual Composers and Musicians: A Checklist." *Cum notis variorum* 83 (1984): 14–22.

   A useful list of about 100 entries, by person, with issuing body, name changes, and Library of Congress call numbers.

These are the essential currently published periodical publications and publishers' series about opera, along with a few expired titles that are still of value for the years covered.

146. *Avant-scène opéra,* 1–, 1976–. Paris: Avant-Scène, 1976–. Irregular. MT90 .A92. (Cited in this guide as *ASO*.)

   Each issue is about an opera or several operas (usually by the same composer). The libretto is given in the original language and in French, together with extensive program notes, background material by various specialists, and photographs. The last one seen (October 1999) was number 191 (1999), on *Boris Godunov*. Recent issues have carried lists of the earlier numbers. In Chapter XVII of this guide, each number is noted at its respective opera.

147. Cambridge Opera Handbooks [series]. New York: Cambridge U.P., 1981–.

   A valuable series, each volume about one opera, consisting of essays by specialists, on the libretto, production history, and analysis of the work. Volumes do not have individual numbers in the series. The 33 volumes seen, issued through 1998, are individually noted in Chapter XVII of this guide.

148. *Cambridge Opera Journal,* 1–, 1989–. New York: Cambridge U.P., 1989–. 3 per year. ML5 .C255.

   The principal scholarly journal of the field.

149. *Central Opera Service Bulletin,* 1–30, 1959–1990. New York: Central Opera
     Service, 1959–. Quarterly. ML1 .C397.

     A useful 30-year record, including informative reports on current productions,
     especially for the U.S. and Canada, with full lists of repertoires for most com-
     panies. Also news items, appointments and resignations, book reviews, courses,
     and seminars.

150. English National Opera Guides [series]. London: Calder; New York: Riverrun,
     1980–.

     Each volume of this distinguished series concerns one opera or, in some cases,
     operas of one composer. Volumes are numbered; 48 have been seen, issued
     through 1994, none since. Contents include photos, essays by specialists,
     libretto in original language and English, musical themes, bibliography, and
     discography. All volumes are individually noted in Chapter XVII of this guide.

151. *Oper heute: Ein Almanach der Musikbühne,* 1–12, 1978–1990. Berlin: Hen-
     schelverlag, 1978–. ML1700.1 .O61.

     Continued two earlier titles: *Jahrbuch der Komischen Oper Berlin* (1–12,
     1960/1961–1971/1972; *IOM* 2081), and *Musikbühne: Probleme und Infor-
     mationen* (1–4, 1974–1977; *IOM* 1379a). An outstanding reference source,
     not only for worldwide activity of each year but for summary articles on indi-
     vidual opera houses and lists of premieres by country. Appropriate citations
     appear elsewhere in the present guide.

152. *Oper: Jahrbuch der Zeitschrift "Opernwelt,"* 1–, 1966–. Velber bei Hanover:
     Opernwelt, 1966–. ML5 .O615.

     See #157. Title and publisher vary. A world review of operatic activity, with
     details of casts, photographs, and critical comments. Also feature articles.

153. *Opera,* 1–, 1950–. London: Seymour, 1950–. Monthly. ML5 .O67.

     General articles, reviews of books and recordings, coming events, and com-
     ments on performances in the U.S., Britain, and some other cities.

154. *Opera Journal,* 1–, 1968–. University, Miss.: National Opera Association,
     1968–. Quarterly. ML1 .O486.

     The association was organized in 1955; the editorial home of the *Journal* has
     varied. Issues include articles, reviews of performances, and reviews of books.

155. *Opera News,* 1–, 1936/1937–. New York: Metropolitan Opera Guild, 1936–.
     Monthly; biweekly during radio-broadcast season. ML1 .O482.

     Frequency varies. General articles, city reports (mostly U.S.), coming events,
     recording reviews. Detailed program notes for the operas broadcast on Satur-
     day afternoon radio.

156. *Opera Quarterly,* 1–, 1983–. Chapel Hill: U. of North Carolina Press, 1983–.
     Quarterly. ISSN 0736–0053. ML5 .O63.

     Both scholarly articles and more popular material make this the most interest-
     ing of the opera periodicals. Important book review section, as well as enter-

taining crosswords and opera quizzes (the latter, by M. Owen Lee, could be much easier).

157. *Opernwelt*, 1–, 1960–. Velber bei Hanover: Opernwelt, 1960–. Monthly. ML5 .O672.

Publisher and location vary. Discussions of performances, worldwide; interviews, articles, recording reviews.

158. Ozer, Jerome S. *Opera Annual U.S., 1984–85*. Englewood, N.J.: Author, 1988. 642p. ISBN 0-89198-132-2; ISSN 0899–3645. ML1699 .O6.

A valuable yearbook, apparently to appear no more. It gave an inventory of operas staged by the four major American companies (in New York, Chicago, and San Francisco) and a selection of regional companies, arranged by opera. With onstage photos, photocopies of programs, and reprints of reviews. Name index. No further volumes had appeared as of July 1999.

159. Rororo Opernbücher [series]. Reinbek bei Hamburg: Rowohlt Taschenbuch, 1981–1989.

Each of the 28 volumes is about one opera (in one case, two operas). For each opera there are scholarly essays on genesis and productions, chronologies, letters, analyses, bibliographies, discographies, and the libretto in German. Library of Congress record shows no holdings after 1989.

IX. Biographies

Indexes and Bibliographies

General indexes to biographical writing, in which musicians will be found in abundance, include *Biography and Genealogy Master Index* (*GRB* AH9), its electronic version, *Biobase* (*GRB* AH8), and its spin-off, *Performing Arts Biography Master Index* (*GRB* BH28); and *Biography Index* (*GRB* AH10). *Biobase* gives the sources of biographical information on 8.5 million individuals. The items listed next are entirely about musicians.

160. Cowden, Robert. H. *Classical Singers of the Opera and Recital Stages: A Bibliography of Biographical Materials.* Music Reference Collection, 42. Westport, Conn.: Greenwood, 1994. 509p. ISBN 0-313-29332-5. ML128 .S295 C71.

Supersedes his *Classical and Opera Singers,* 1985. A valuable list of 1,532 artists, including all those with articles in *NGDO* and 323 who are not in *NGDO.* For each person there is a thorough bibliography of books, parts of books, and periodical articles; these sources are drawn from 30 languages. With an index of authors, compilers, and editors.

161. Cowden, Robert H. *Concert and Opera Conductors: A Bibliography of Biographical Materials.* Music Reference Collection, 14. New York: Greenwood, 1988. xvi, 285p. ISBN 0-313-25620-9. ML128 .B3 C68.

A fine inventory of material about 1,249 conductors, drawn from standard biographical references and periodicals, with full bibliographic data; no annotations. Also an index to the 1,615 conductors whose biographies appear in Baker (#165), 7th edition. With an author index.

162. Farkas, Andrew. *Opera and Concert Singers: An Annotated International Bibliography of Books and Pamphlets.* Garland Reference Library of the Humanities, 466. New York: Garland, 1985. xxiv, 363p. ISBN 0-8240-9001-2. ML128 .S295 F37.

An excellent list of books that cover 796 singers. There are 1,830 numbered entries, of which 1,536 are about individuals. The other titles, collective biographies, greatly extend the enumeration of such works in the present guide. Full bibliographic data are given, along with critical annotations. Author index.

163. Hixon, Donald, and Don A. Hennessee. *Women in Music: An Encyclopedic Biobibliography.* 2nd ed. Metuchen, N.J.: Scarecrow, 1994. 2v. ISBN 0-8108-2769-7. ML105 .H6.

First edition, 1975. An index to material about women musicians in 169 reference works. More than 28,000 names are included, about 700 of them opera singers. A useful index makes it possible to locate all the sopranos, contraltos, etc.

164. De Lerma, Dominique-René. *A Bibliography of Black Music.* Westport, Conn.: Greenwood,1981–1984. 4v. ISBN (v.1) 0-313-21340-2. ML128 .B45 D34.

A monumental inventory, consisting of 19,397 entries, of books, articles, and academic papers. Coverage is international, with emphasis on the U.S., and the most coverage before 1975. Citations give full data; annotations are thorough and perceptive. Author index.

Collective Biographies

This is a selection of the most useful works. Principal general gatherings of biographical information on musicians are listed first, followed by the specialized compilations on operatic musicians. A longer list of collective biographies of singers appears in Farkas (#162).

Musicians in General

165. *Baker's Biographical Dictionary of Musicians.* 8th ed. Ed. Nicholas Slonimsky. New York: Schirmer, 1991. xxxv, 2,115p. ISBN 0-02-872415-1. ML105 .B16.

First edition, 1900. The most useful and reliable handbook of musical biography and the most entertaining of all music reference tools. Perceptive, critical accounts of lives, with worklists and bibliographical notices. Slonimsky's witty entry for himself is a classic of its kind.

166. *Harvard Biographical Dictionary of Music.* Ed. Don Michael Randel. Cambridge, Mass.: Harvard U.P., 1996. xi, 1,013p. ISBN 0-614-37299-9. ML105 .H38.

A collection of about 6,000 entries, mostly for composers (musicologists are among the missing). Much overlap with #165. This volume serves as a partner to the *New Harvard Dictionary of Music* (#17), which has no biographies.

167. *International Dictionary of Black Composers.* Ed. Samuel A. Floyd Jr. Chicago: Fitzroy Dearborn, 1999. 2v. ISBN 1-884964-27-3. ML390 .I58.

An outstanding compilation, whose 1,273 pages are devoted to 185 composers, living or dead, concert or popular musicians. "Black" is used in the sense of persons in any country who are of African descent. Extensive bio-graphical accounts are enhanced with worklists, bibliographies, portraits, and long critical essays about principal works (including a number of operas). About 100 contributors did the writing, which is exemplary throughout. Alphabetical list of entries but no general index.

168. Mapp, Edward. *Directory of Blacks in the Performing Arts*. Metuchen, N.J.: Scarecrow, 1978. 444p. ISBN 0-8108-1126-X. PN1590 .B53 M3.

Opera singers are among the 850 artists whose biographies are given in this useful volume. A classified index identifies them.

169. Turner, Patricia. *Dictionary of Afro-American Performers: 78rpm and Cylin-der Recordings of Opera, Choral Music, and Song, c. 1900–1949*. Garland Reference Library of the Humanities, 590. New York: Garland, 1990. xxiii, 433p. ISBN 0-8240-8736-4. ML106 .U3 T87.

A bio-discography of 23 composers, 39 singers, three instrumentalists, and 14 vocal groups, all performers of classical or religious music. Six operas and musicals are also discussed. Books, articles, newspaper notices, and archival collections are cited. Much information difficult to find elsewhere, but it is not always reliable. Bibliography of about 250 items, no index.

Reprints from *NG* have appeared in separate volumes. The essays are in most cases updated or otherwise revised, and each volume has an index, which *NG* lacks. In this guide those books are listed in their national or subject areas, except for the following, which are multinational in scope:

170. *The New Grove North European Baroque Masters*. Ed. Joshua Rivkin. New York: Norton, 1985. 356p. ISBN 0-393-01695-1. ML390 .N4665.

Composers included are Schütz, Froberger, Buxtehude, Purcell, and Telemann.

171. *The New Grove Early Romantic Masters I*. Ed. Nicholas Temperley et al. New York: Norton, 1985. 392p. ISBN 0-333-38545-4. ML390 .T45.

Composers included are Chopin, Liszt, and Schumann.

172. *The New Grove Early Romantic Masters II*. Ed. John Warrack et al. New York: Norton, 1985. 314p. ISBN 0-333-39013-X. ML390 .T451.

Composers included are Weber, Berlioz, and Mendelssohn.

173. *The New Grove Late Romantic Masters*. Ed. Deryck Cooke et al. New York: Norton, 1985. 401p. ISBN 0-393-01697-8. ML390 .N474.

Composers included are Bruckner, Brahms, Dvořák, and Wolf.

174. *The New Grove Turn of the Century Masters: Janáček, Mahler, Strauss, Sibelius*. New York: Norton, 1985. 324p. ISBN 0-333-38541-1. ML390 .N48.

175. *The New Grove Modern Masters: Bartók, Stravinsky, Hindemith*. Ed. Vera Lampert et al. New York: Norton, 1984. 292p. ISBN 0-393-30097-8.

Singers and Performers of Opera

The largest compilation is the most valuable:

176. Kutsch, Karl Josef, and Leo Riemens. *Grosses Sänger-Lexikon.* 3rd ed. Bern: Saur, 1997. 6v. ISBN 3-598-11250-5. ML105 .K83.

     First edition, 1962, as *Kleiner Sängerlexikon* and reissued in a second edition under that title in 1966. In 1975 and 1982 there were revisions under the name *Unvergängliche Stimmen Sängerlexikon.* An English translation of the 1966 version appeared as *A Concise Biographical Dictionary of Singers* (Philadelphia: Chilton, 1969). In the current manifestation, there are entries for about 12,000 persons, many of them truly obscure (there are 5 named Albanese). Information given includes life and career and critical observations; some recordings are noted. No bibliographies. V.6 has an index of opera and operetta titles mentioned in the text.

The remaining books of collective opera biography are listed by author:

177. Barbier, Patrick. *La maison des italiens: Les castrats à Versailles.* Paris: Grasset, 1998. 302p. ISBN 2-246-52591-8. ML400 .B373.

     A narrative history of the castrati, with their social and economic life in Paris. Much biographical information about leading performers of the *ancien régime.* Backnotes, bibliography of about 100 entries, name index.

178. Blanchard, Roger, and Roland de Candé. *Dieux et divas de l'opéra.* Paris: Plon, 1986–1987. 2v. ISBN 22-5901-4291. ML400 .B59.

     A narrative account of opera with singer biographies interspersed as they appeared on the scene. Coverage is from 1600 to Maria Callas. Portraits, critical comments, footnotes, bibliography and name index in each volume.

179. Celletti, Rodolfo. *Le grandi voci.* Rome: Istituto per la Collaborazione Culturale, 1964. xiv, lp, 1,044 columns, lp. ML400 C44.

     Biographies of about 250 singers, with perceptive comments, portraits, and discographies.

180. Celletti, Rodolfo. *Voce di tenore.* Milan: IdeaLibri, 1989. 264p. ISBN 88-7082-1277. ML400 .C442.

     Biographical information is interwoven with a narrative account of tenor singing from the 16th to the 20th century. There are interesting sections on singers of certain styles, from various countries, and with composer associations. No notes or bibliography; with name and title index.

181. Christiansen, Rupert. *Prima Donna: A History.* New York: Viking, 1985. 366p. ISBN 0-670-80482-7. ML1700 .C56.

     A popular account of the leading stars, with quotations but no footnotes, and a weak bibliography. Of interest for comments in the affinity groups (singers of Mozart, of Wagner, etc.). Name and title index.

182. Heriot, Angus. *The Castrati in Opera*. London: Secker & Warburg, 1956. 243p. Reprints, London: Calder, 1960; New York: Da Capo, 1975. ISBN (Da Capo) 0-306-80003-9. ML400 .H47.

A basic study of the castrati, who constituted (Heriot says) 70 percent of all male opera singers, as late as the end of the 18th century. Filippo Balatri (1676–1756) gets special attention; about 50 others have bio-sketches. Footnotes, bibliography of 101 items, index of names and titles.

183. Rosselli, John. "The Castrati as a Professional Group and a Social Phenomenon, 1550–1850." *AM* 60 (1988): 143–179.

A review of earlier literature and a detailed history of the castrato era. The cultural, religious, and economic aspects of Italian life amalgamated to make possible a bizarre practice that is incomprehensible in our time.

184. Lahee, Henry C. *Famous Singers of Today and Yesterday*. Boston: Page, 1898. ix, 337p. ML400 .L183.

Brief, popular sketches of about 250 persons. Useful chronological table that arranges them in order of birthdates. Index of names.

185. Lahee, Henry C. *The Grand Opera Singers of Today*. Rev. ed. Boston: Page, 1922. x, 543p. ML400 .L185.

First edition, 1912. A running critical commentary, with biographical facts, about hundreds of singers who took the stage in New York, Chicago, or Philadelphia during the period after 1903. Name and title index.

186. Müller-Marein, Josef, and Hannes Reinhardt. *Das musikalische Selbstportrait, von Komponisten, Dirigenten, Instrumentalisten, Sängerinnen und Sänger unser Zeit*. Hamburg: Nannen, 1963. 508p. ML385 .M91.

Autobiographical: 50 artists discussing themselves and their work. Includes these singers: Berger, Streich, Seefried, M. Lorenz, Leider, Lemnitz, Mödl, Melchior, Varnay, Rosvaenge, Winters, Hotter, Kunz, Ludwig, and Windgassen; also director Rolf Liebermann. Name index.

187. Rasponi, Lanfranco. *The Last Prima Donnas*. New York: Knopf, 1982. 633p. ISBN 0-394-52153-6. ML400 .R37.

One of the better books about women singers (56 of them, from the 20th century) emphasizing their art over their personalities. Much of the material appeared first in *Opera News*. Expansive index of 70 pages.

188. Rosenthal, Harold D. *Great Singers of Today*. London: Calder & Boyars, 1966. 212p. ML400 .R79.

Facts, dates, and critical opinions concerning about 100 singers, male and female; in popular style but not chatty. Many photos, no bibliography or index.

189. Smith, Eric Ledell. *Blacks in Opera: An Encyclopedia of People and Companies, 1873–1993*. Jefferson, N.C.: McFarland, 1995. xi, 236p. ISBN 0-89950-8138. ML102 .O6 S6.

Life and career information on singers, directors, and producers; portraits, bibliographies, recordings. Indexed.

190. Steane, J. B. *The Grand Tradition: Seventy Years of Singing on Record*. London: Duckworth, 1974. xii, 628p. Reprint, Portland, Ore.: Amadeus, 1993. ISBN 0-931340-640. ML400 .S821.

     Although the Amadeus publication is labeled "2nd edition," it is (reading the small print) in fact "a reprint of the original book . . . [with] many corrections." An interesting narrative history of operatic and concert singing as displayed on recordings, with much discerning critical opinion. Useful chapters on singers of each country and on the interpreters of Mozart, Wagner, etc. This is not—despite the implication of the title—a discography; however, there is an appendix comparison of recorded performances of 12 arias. With 138 illustrations of singers, many in costume. Index of composers with their works, index of names.

191. Steane, J. B. *Singers of the Century*. London: Duckworth; Portland, Ore.: Amadeus, 1996–1998. 2v. ISBN 1-57467-009-3, 1-57467-040-9 (Amadeus). ML400 .S73 S5.

     About 50 brief, personalized biographies, originally published in *Opera News*. Among the artists covered are Emma Calvé, Geraldine Farrar, Régine Crespin, Arleen Auger, Jon Vickers, Lucia Popp, Jussi Björling, Maria Callas, Placido Domingo, Luciano Pavarotti, Lawrence Tibbett, and Kiri Te Kanawa. Perceptive critical comments on acting ability as well as the voice itself; with fascinating vignettes. Not strong in citations or bibliographic data, but indexed.

X. Opera Plots

Indexes

Summaries of the story lines are given in many of the sources already cited in Chapter II. The works that follow will widen the perspective. To sort out the great mass of opera plot books, three indexes are highly useful:

192. Studwell, William E., and David A. Hamilton. *Opera Plot Index: A Guide to Locating Plots and Descriptions of Operas, Operettas, and Other Works of the Musical Theater, and Associated Material*. Garland Reference Library of the Humanities, 1,099. New York: Garland, 1990. xxi, 466p. ISBN 0-8240-4621-8. ML128 .O4 S8.

A valuable guide to locations of plots and other information on 2,900 stage works from all Western nations of all periods. The locations are in about 200 books in several languages. Since there are so many repeats of popular operas, a useful coding system is applied to show which sources have certain features (musical examples, illustrations, historical information, analysis). Works are listed by their original language, with cross-references from translated titles. The composer/title index is useful in itself for a quick look at the works that have represented, for the plot writers, the standard repertoire.

193. Drone, Jeanette Marie. *Musical Theater Synopses: An Index*. Lanham, Md.: Scarecrow, 1998. 352p. ISBN 0-8198-3489-8. ML128 .O4 D76 Suppl.

First edition, as *Index to Opera, Operetta and Musical Comedy Synopses in Collections and Periodicals,* 1978. Works listed in the 1978 edition are included in the new edition, bringing the total number of titles covered to more than 11,000 by more than 4,000 composers; this is the most comprehensive of plot indexes. Sources indexed include 352 books, issues of 62 periodicals, and 14 websites; all of them are in English only. Title and composer indexes.

194. Rieck, Waldemar. *Opera Plots*. New York: New York Public Library, 1927. 102p. ML128 .O4 R4.

The oldest of the indexes, still useful for citations to non-English sources and early plot collections not included in Studwell or Drone. Covers about 200 books of synopses, in English, French, German, and Danish. Cites 2,775 operas by 998 composers.

Books of Plots

195. Czech, Stan. *Das Operettenbuch: Ein Führer durch die Operetten und Singspiele der deutschen Bühnen.* 4th ed. Stuttgart: Muth, 1960. 424p. MT95 .C93.

    Detailed synopses of about 125 light operas that have held the German stage. In addition to familiar composers like Kálman and Lehár, we find the works of such lesser-known persons as Bromme, Burkhard, Dellinger, Dostal, Jarno, Meisel, Nick, Raymond, and Vetterling. Only one American composition is included: *Küss mich Kätchen* (yes, all titles and arias are in German only). A useful feature is the citation of films made of each operetta, with dates and casts. There are also brief performance histories and comments. No indexes.

196. Davidson, Gladys. *The Barnes Book of the Opera.* New York: Barnes, 1962. 890p. MT95 .D2 B4.

    Long, chatty stories; useful for coverage of unusual works. There are 22 Russian operas, as well as representations by Bantock, Benedict, Benjamin, Bliss, Boughton, Bush, Holbrooke, Lloyd, Philpot, Rankl, and Smyth.

197. Fellner, Rudolph. *Opera Themes and Plots.* New York: Simon & Schuster, 1958. xii, 354p. MT95 .F319.

    A valuable guide to plots of the standard operas, because the stories are keyed to many brief musical examples (e.g., 34 extracts from *Un ballo in maschera*). Covers 32 operas in that manner, with a list of the arias and vocal numbers in the index.

198. Jacobs, Arthur, and Stanley Sadie. *Great Opera Classics.* New York: Gramercy, distributed by Crown, 1987. 563p. ISBN 0-517-64108-9. MT95 .J32.

    A book of many names, originally published as the *Pan Book of Opera* (London: Pan Books, 1964), then as *Limelight Book of Opera* (New York: Limelight, 1985), which was a revision of *Great Operas in Synopsis* (1964); also a manifestation as *Opera: A Modern Guide.* It offers plots and program notes for 87 operas by 41 composers. Commentary is extensive and valuable. With a bibliography but no index.

199. Kobbé, Gustave. *The New Kobbé's Complete Opera Book.* 9th ed. Ed. and rev. the Earl of Harewood. New York: Putnam, 1976. xvii, 1,694p. ISBN 399-11633-8. MT95 .K52.

    The title of this popular book has varied considerably over its publishing history, which began in 1919. It gives long summaries of about 220 standards, with historical notes and a name and title index. The 1989 version has pictures but fewer plots: *Kobbé's Illustrated Opera Book: Twenty-six of the World's Favorite Operas.* A new edition was announced in 1999.

200. Lubbock, Mark Hugh. *The Complete Book of Light Opera.* With an American section by David Ewen. London: Putnam; New York: Appleton-Century-Crofts, 1962. xviii, 952p. MT95 .L85.

About 300 plots, covering the European repertoire and American musicals. Premiere information is given along with the story. Another book by Ewen includes fewer plots but adds more background facts: *The Book of European Light Opera* (New York: Holt, Rinehart & Winston, 1962); it has a useful chronology and an aria index.

201. Martens, Frederick Herman. *A Thousand and One Nights of Opera.* New York and London: Appleton, 1926. ix, 487p. Reprint, New York: Da Capo, 1978.

Seems to be the largest collection of plots (1,550 works), but ballets are included as well as operas. Title and composer indexes.

202. Melitz, Leo. *Opera Goers' Complete Guide.* Rev. ed. New York: Garden City, 1921. xvii, 508p. MT95 .M31.

First edition, 1908. Plots and names of musical numbers (in English only), with casting, for 268 works. Useful for many nonstandard inclusions, by such composers as Adam, Auber (8 operas), Blech, Blockx, Breil, Breton, Cadman, Erlanger, Goldmark (5), Massenet (10), and Pfitzner (3).

203. *The Metropolitan Opera Stories of the Great Operas.* Ed. John W. Freeman. New York: Metropolitan Opera Guild, distributed by Norton, 1997. 2v. ISBN 0-393-01888-1, 0-393-04051-8. MT95 .M49.

Advertised as the only plot collection "authorized by the Metropolitan Opera," this set covers 275 works with biographical information on the composers.

204. Newman, Ernest. *Stories of Great Operas.* New York: Vintage, 1958. 2v. MT95 .N5.

Incorporates his *Stories of Famous Operas, More Stories of Famous Operas,* and *Seventeen Famous Operas.* (For another, *The Wagner Operas,* see #2004.) These are literate, detailed summaries of standard repertoire material, with musical examples and background information. A dependable first-choice reading for the works covered.

205. Payne, Alexis. *Grand opéras du répertoire.* Paris: Fayard, 1979. 574p. ISBN 2-213-00675-X. ML102 .O6 P346.

Detailed plots for about 120 operas, including the numerous works by French composers, with lists of arias and numbers and background data. Indexes of characters and titles and a chronological array. Also a list of theaters by country, with most names in original languages.

206. Renner, Hans. *Renner's Führer durch Oper, Operette, Musical: Das Bühnenrepertoire der Gegenwart.* 6th ed. Zurich: Atlantis, 1997. 728p. ISBN 3-254-08203-0. MT95 .R423.

First edition, 1969, as *Oper, Operette, Musical* (Munich: Südwest). About 350 plots, reflective of the current German stage. Premiere information, facts about the first German performance, synopsis, and commentary. Titles and arias are identified in German only. Composer and title indexes.

207. Sadie, Stanley. *The New Grove Book of Operas*. London: Macmillan, 1996. ix, 758p. ISBN 0-312-15443-7. ML102 .O6 N4.

Material, drawn from *NGDO,* on 264 operas: plot, with premiere data, commentary, and illustrations. Index of aria and ensemble first lines, index of role names, glossary, composer index.

208. Schumann. Otto. *Der grosse Opern- und Operettenführer*. 11th ed. Wilhelmshaven: Heinrichshofen's Verlag, 1983. 748p. ISBN 3-88-1991-085. MT95 .S393.

In addition to standard repertoire, presents a fine cross section of less familiar material by Germans like Weismann, Braunfels, Gerster, Sehlbach, and Lothar. Composer biographies, illustrations, index of titles and of characters (with their German names only: who remembers Mackie Messer?).

209. Sénéchaud, Marcel. *Le répertoire lyrique d'hier et d'aujourd'hui*. Paris: Billaudot, 1971. 301p. MT95 .S48.

Plots to 343 works, with special concern for operas popular in Paris or by French composers.

210. Wagner, Heinz. *Das grosse Operettenbuch: 120 Komponisten und 430 Werke*. Berlin: Parthas, 1997. 376p. ISBN 3-932529-0202. ML102 .O6 W3.

Plots and premiere data, with cast roles (not the performers); titles in German and original languages. By composer, with title index.

211. *The Victor Book of the Opera*. 13th ed. Ed. Henry W. Simon. New York: Simon & Schuster, 1968. 475p. MT150 .V4.

Title varies. First published in 1912, this familiar work has been frequently revised. It covers 120 operas with leisurely synopses, photos of famous singers in the various roles, and discographies of Victor recordings.

XI. Libretti and Librettists

Bibliographies

There are lists of librettists in Loewenberg (#106, v.2) and *MORI* (v.5–6). *RISM* includes a U.S. libretto database of more than 11,000 items. See also the Library of Congress *Catalogue* (#115) and other titles in Chapter V.

212. Alm, Irene. *Catalog of Venetian Librettos at the University of California, Los Angeles*. University of California Publications in Catalogs and Bibliographies, 9. Berkeley: U. of California Press, 1993. xxviii, 1,053p. ISBN 0-520-09762-9. ML136 .L842 .U682.

   A catalogue with bibliographic descriptions of 1,286 items, dated 1637–1769, covering "virtually every opera libretto printed in Venice." In date order, with 17 indexes, including titles, artists, dedicatees, and roles.

213. Columbro, Marta. *La raccolta di libretti d'opera del Teatro San Carlo di Napoli*. Ancilla musicae, 3. Lucca: Libreria Musicale Italiana, 1992. xiii, 107p. ISBN 8-8709-6062-5. ML136 .N21 T43.

   A title list of 262 entries, with full bibliographic descriptions, names of opera characters, and persons associated with productions related to the published libretti. They are all Italian or translated into Italian. Indexes of the characters, persons, and places, as well as a chronological list.

214. Conservatorio Benedetto Marcello, Venice. Biblioteca. *Catalogo dei libretti del Conservatorio Benedetto Marcello*. Florence: Olschki, 1994–1995. 4v. ISBN 88-222-4112-6; 88-222-4194-0; 88-222-4226-2; 88-222-4299-8. ML136 .V3 C64.

   A detailed inventory of a major libretto collection, consisting of 3,221 entries in title order. Full bibliographic descriptions, characters named in the texts, and extensive commentaries. Nearly all the libretti are by Italian composers, or translated into Italian, but there is a representation of French material as well. Indexes to be published (not seen as of October 1999).

215. Fabbri, Paolo. *Il secolo cantante: Per una storia del libretto d'opera nel seicento*. Bologna: Il Mulino, 1990. 350p. ISBN 88-15-02473-5. ML1733 .F22 S42.

A well-documented narrative account of libretto history, quoting many original sources. The Venetian model is emphasized: its early subjects and style and its exportation. By the late 17th century public demand for novelty had brought a focus on spectacular stage effects and a "*gusto erotico*" that included racy dialogue and nudity. But the heroic themes that had marked the early libretto began to return. Backnotes, bibliographic essay, indexes of names and titles.

216. Fuld, James J. *Book of World-Famous Libretti: The Musical Theater from 1598 to Today*. Rev. ed. New York: Pendragon, 1994. xxxviii, 363p. ISBN 0-9451-9348-3. ML128.04 .F8.

First edition, 1984. Introduction to the revised edition indicates that it has corrections and "new and variant editions." Facsimiles, bibliographic descriptions, commentaries, and *RISM* sigla for locations. Indexes of librettists and composers.

History and Criticism

Two useful articles in *NGDO*: "Libretto," by Richard Macnutt and Brian Trowell, 2, 1185–1191, with a bibliography of more than 1,000 entries; and "Versification," by Tim Carter et al., 4, 964–972.

217. Smith, Patrick J. *The Tenth Muse: A Historical Study of the Opera Libretto*. New York: Knopf, 1970. xii, 417, xvii p. Reprint, New York: Schirmer, 1975. ISBN 0-394-44822-7 (Schirmer). ML2110 .S62.

One of the earlier studies to regard the libretto and the music as equal partners (while admitting that the music carries the ultimate value, in the sense that inferior music cannot survive even with a superb libretto). The major librettists are studied, including Goldoni, Busenello, Quinault, Metastasio, W. S. Gilbert, Boito, and von Hofmannsthal, with attention to Brecht, Gertrude Stein, and many others. Smith has praise and glory for all of them. Footnotes, weak bibliography, good index.

218. *Reading Opera*. Ed. Arthur Groos and Roger Parker. Princeton, N.J.: Princeton U.P., 1988. vii, 352p. ISBN 0-691-09132-3. ML2110 .R4.

A collection of 13 essays, most of them first presented at a conference on the libretto at Cornell University, October 1986. Emphasis is on the later-19th-century libretto. In his introduction Groos notes the approaches of recent scholars to the libretto: as verbal artifact, as object of study through various critical "strategies," as text for music, and in terms of the relation between words and music. Primacy of the music is not questioned (Stendhal is quoted: "Who would dream of judging an opera by the words?"). Each essay has a separate entry in the present guide; see #219, #582, #601, #741, #1348, #1744, #1833, #1906, #1914, #2059, #2062, and #2067. Footnotes, strong index, no bibliography.

219. Robinson, Paul. "A Deconstructive Postscript: Reading Libretti and Misreading Opera." In *Reading Opera* (#218), 328–346.

"Intended as a polemical dissent to certain assumptions informing the essays in this collection, and indeed, informing most operatic criticism that I have read." Robinson holds that "any interpretation of opera derived exclusively, or even primarily, from the libretti is likely to result in a misreading." For one thing, the words in a performance are rarely intelligible to the audience, because they may be in a foreign language, or obscured by the singing itself, or lost in ensembles, or drowned out by the orchestra. (Robinson recognizes that these problems vanish if there is prior study of the libretto or if the presentation has supertitles.) The question is not what does the text say, but "how is the text realized, or at least addressed, in the music?" The words do count but simply as "emblems of human volition"; they "identify the singer as a human actor with specific feelings, giving voice to specific thoughts."

220. *Opera and Libretto I*. Florence: Olschki, 1990. viii, 460p. ISBN 88-222-3825-7. ML1699 .S88 v.1.

A collection of 18 papers presented at five conferences that did not have published proceedings. Name index. Three are noted separately later in this guide: #222 (Osthoff on Goethe translations), #1374 (Piperno on Paisiello), and #516 (Lippmann on *Norma*). See next entry.

221. *Opera and Libretto II*. Florence: Olschki, 1993. viii, 496p. ISBN 88-222-40642. ML1699 .S88 v.2.

A collection of 22 papers read at earlier conferences; continues the preceding entry. Name index. Two papers are treated separately later in this guide: #1315 (Osthoff on *Die Entführung*) and #2099 (Gallerati on *Oberon*).

Translations

222. Osthoff, Wolfgang. "*La maga Circe* di Pasquale Anfossi nella traduzione di Goethe per il teatro di Weimar." In *Opera and Libretto I* (#220), 51–76.

Examines Goethe's approach to translation, with examples of his handling of passages in the Anfossi libretto. His intent was always to write a text to the music, not to make a direct transfer of the original text into German.

Libretti Associated with Specific Authors and Texts

223. Tedeschi, Rubens. *D'Annunzio e la musica*. Florence: Discanto, 1988. 229p. ISBN 88-221-0357-2. ML80 .A6 T4.

A narrative account of the use made of D'Annunzio's works by opera librettists and composers. Among the composers are Franchetti, Malipiero, Montemezzi, and Zandonai. There is no actual list of the collaborations. The book also includes a selection of D'Annunzio's critical articles and reviews. Indexed.

224. Gooch, Bryan N. S., and David Thatcher. *A Shakespeare Music Catalogue*. New York: Oxford U.P., 1991. 5v. ISBN 0-19812-941-6. ML134.5 .S52 G6.

An impressive undertaking, which uncovered 21,362 musical works based in some way on Shakespearian writings. In v.1–3 these works are listed under the name of the play or poem that inspired them, with full bibliographic detail, performance information, and library locations as appropriate; v.4 has indexes of titles, composers, editors, arrangers, and actual Shakespeare lines that were set to music, and v.5 is a classified bibliography, with full data, of 3,232 entries.

225. *NGDO* 4, 318–347, "Shakespeare," by Christopher B. Wilson, offers a list of about 270 operas, entered under each play. *The Tempest* has 48, leading all the rest.

226. Hotaling, Edward. *Shakespeare and the Musical Stage: A Guide to Sources, Studies, and First Performances.* Boston: G. K. Hall, 1990. xxv, 517p. ISBN 0-8161-9070-4. ML128 .O4 H68.

Deals with "any composition which anyone had proposed as being based on Shakespeare and any work whose title suggested that it might be based on Shakespeare," excluding only what might be called generic tales, like those of Julius Caesar or Cleopatra. For each of the 600 or so works listed, in composer order, there are bibliographic descriptions, with premiere information, casts, and comments. Indexes by title, city, date of premiere (covering 1611–1981), text authors, and the Shakespeare plays.

227. Schmidgall, Gary. *Shakespeare and Opera.* New York: Oxford U.P., 1990. 394p. ISBN 0-19-506450-X. ML3858 .S373.

Consists of 12 essays: an introduction, and discussions of 11 plays in their operatic manifestations. Similarities between 19th-century Italian opera and Shakespearian drama include aria/soliloquy, each preceded by a duet or ensemble, and more generally that both are "aural experiences," made for listening, with sound and spectacle supreme over sense. Verdi gets the most emphasis among composers cited.

228. Giraud, Yves F.-A. *La fable de Daphné.* Histoire des idées et critique litteraire, 92. Geneva: Droz, 1968. 574p. NX652 .D21 G52.

An absorbing, scholarly exploration of the Dafne myth in literature and the arts through the 17th century. About 500 works are noted. Operas by Peri, Marco da Gagliano, Cavalli, Schütz, Bontempi, and Richard Strauss are discussed. With bibliography and index of names and titles.

229. Lühning, Helga. "Titus-Vertonungen im 18. Jahrhundert: Untersuchungen zur Tradition der Opera seria von Hasse bis Mozart," *Analecta musicologica* 20 (1983): 1–530.

Mozart's *La clemenza di Tito* (1791) is the most renowned opera based on Pietro Metastasio's text, which told of the benevolent Roman emperor Titus Vespasianus (reigned 78–81). But many other works stemmed from that source, which is described in detail to begin this volume. The Mozart libretto, by Caterino Tommaso Mazzolà, is analyzed, and other setting are discussed in depth. Among the composers included are Hasse, Gluck, Anfossi, Wagenseil, Galuppi, and Jommelli. Chronology of the settings, composer index, sources and bibliography (about 250 items) but without index.

On Tasso, see Balsano (#2450). Other works on libretto matters are in Chapter XIII.

Individual Librettists

230. Engelbert, Barbara. "Wystan Hugh Auden, 1907–1973: Seine Opern-aesthetis-che Anschaung in seine Tätigkeit als Librettist." Ph.D. diss., U. of Cologne, 1982.

231. Weisstein, Ulrich. "Reflections on a Golden Age: W. H. Auden's Theory of Opera." *Comparative Literature* 22 (1970): 108–124.

    Offers "guidelines for an understanding of Auden's poetic theory . . . and reasons for his choice of opera and the dance as the preferred artistic media of our age." Auden preferred universal subjects: "a secondary world" but one which has "something significant to say . . . about our present life." His views are compared to those of Kierkegaard (see #1312) and found similar. Auden was modest about the role of the libretto, considering it "a private letter to the composer," which the composer would use as it seemed fit. He definitely opposed the Gluckian view of music in the service of poetry, favoring instead the Mozartian idea of poetry being "the obedient daughter" of the music.

232. Tintori, Giampiero, ed. *Arrigo Boito: Musicista e letterato.* N.p.: Nuove Edizioni, 1986. 199p. ML410 .B694 A85.

    A collection of essays on Boito, with a chapter by Michele Girardi on "Verdi e Boito: Due artisti fra tradizione e rinnovamento." Includes a catalogue of his musical and literary works.

233. Borwick, Susan. "Weill's and Brecht's Theories on Music in Drama." *Journal of Musicological Research* 4 (1982): 39–67.

    "Both men were practitioners first and theoreticians only second." They did not define concepts and were not consistent in "thought or terminology." Borwick gives special attention to the term "gestus"—to which they each gave different meanings. List of 47 essays by Weill or Brecht, 43 backnotes.

234. Borwick, Susan [Susan Harden]. "The Music for the Stage Collaborations of Weill and Brecht." Ph.D. diss., U. of North Carolina, 1972, 252 p.

235. Wagner, Gottfried. *Weill und Brecht: Das musikalische Zeittheater.* Munich: Kindler, 1977. 338p. ISBN 3-4630-0706-1. ML410 .W518 W17.

    Working relationship between Weill and Brecht, their theories (including their use of "gestus"), analysis of the operas with musical examples, political background in the Weimar Republic. Backnotes, bibliography, name index.

236. Brizi, Bruno. "Teoria e prassi melodrammatica di G. F. Busenello e *L'incoronazione di Poppea*." In Muraro (#2575), 51–74.

    An examination of Busenello's prefaces and prologues, concluding that his basic principle was that the libretto should follow the requirements of the music. With a metric and lingustic analysis of portions of *L'incoronazione.*

See also #1236.

237. Marri, Federico, ed. *La figura e l'opera di Ranieri de Calzabigi. Atti del Convegno di Studi, Livorno, 1987.* Florence: Olschki, 1989. ix, 232p. ISBN 88-2223-6243. ML423 C.25 F5.

Consists of eight papers, dealing with Calzabigi's theories, his association with Gluck and with other composers, *Sémiramis, La festa di Pierre,* and *Ipermestra.* Footnoted but without bibliography; name and title index.

238. Lazzeri, Ghino. *La vita e l'opera letteraria di Ranieri Calzabigi: Saggio critico con appendice di documenti inediti or rari.* Città di Castello: Lapi, 1907. 220p. ML410 .C3 L3.

Life and works of Calzabigi, emphasizing his collaboration with Gluck in the reform operas. Letters, documents, bibliography.

239. Michel, Hertha. "Ranieri Calzabigi als Dichter von Musikdramen und als Kritiker." *Gluck-Jahrbuch* 4 (1918): 99–171.

Life and works in detail, with an assessment of Calzabigi's influence on Gluck. For more on Calzabigi, see Robinson in #2462.

240. Black, John. *The Italian Romantic Libretto: A Study of Salvadore Cammarano.* Edinburgh: Edinburgh U.P., 1984. ix, 325p. ISBN 0-85224-4630. ML429 .C16 B6.

A detailed biography, followed by an analysis of the writer's methods and principles and his part in preparing works for production. Chronology of his libretti, bibliography, and index.

241. Da Ponte, Lorenzo. *Memorie di Lorenzo Da Ponte da Ceneda scritte da se stesso.* 2nd ed. New York: 1823–1827. Trans. Elisabeth Abbott. Philadelphia: Lippincott, 1929. x, 512p. Reprint, New York: Dover, 1967. ML423 .D15 A22.

The colorful memoir of author/adventurer Da Ponte, who is best remembered as Mozart's librettist; his recollections embrace that connection, as well as his curious final years (1811–1818) in Pennsylvania.

242. Hodges, Sheila. *Lorenzo Da Ponte: The Life and Times of Mozart's Librettist.* New York: Universe, 1985. xiv, 274p. ISBN 0-87662-489-7. ML423 .D15 H6.

A plain account, with many extracts from the *Memorie.* Weak bibliography but strong index.

243. Goldin, Daniela. "Mozart, Da Ponte, e il linguaggio dell'opera buffa." In Muraro (#2576), 2, 213–277.

Assigns a high value to Da Ponte's role in the success of his three Mozart operas. In comparison to his sources and to other libretti based on them, he created dramatic texts that were ideal for Mozart's music. Goldin's analyses of these texts are absorbing.

244. Winton, Calhoun. *John Gay and the London Theatre.* Lexington: U.P. of Kentucky, 1993. xvi, 212p. ISBN 0-8131-1832-8. PR3473 .B6 W56.

Gay wrote the libretto for *The Beggar's Opera* (1728), which was popular for a century. From many books about him, this one is chosen for its scope, recency, and scholarly approach. Covers genesis of *The Beggar's Opera,* its reception, and its place in theater history; also deals with other works by Gay. Backnotes, expansive index, no bibliography.

245. Benini, Aroldo. *L'operosa dimensione scapigliata di Antonio Ghislanzoni. Atti del Convegno di Studi svoltosi a Milano, a Lucca, a Caprena Bergamasco nell'autunno 1993.* Milan: Istituto per la Storia del Risorgimento Italiano, 1995. 277p.

Papers dealing with the life and varied output of Ghislanzoni, who is mostly remembered for the libretto to *Aida.*

246. Gossett, Philip. "Verdi, Ghislanzoni, and *Aida*: The Uses of Convention." *Critical Inquiry* 1 (1974): 291–334.

A look at the genesis of the libretto, through the extensive correspondence (35 letters from Verdi to Ghislanzoni). Since the letters were published in the wrong order in the *Copialettere* (#1813), Gossett organizes them into chronological sequence.

247. Emery, Ted. *Goldoni as Librettist: Theatrical Reform and the "drammi giocosi per musica."* New York: Peter Lang, 1991. xxvii, 237p. ISBN 0-8204-1230-9. PQ4699 .E53.

A consideration of Goldoni's early intermezzi, his "reform and counter-reform libretti, 1748–1783," comic operas, and Arcadian themes. With long accounts of individual works, concentrating entirely on the texts. Backnotes, bibliography of about 150 items, no index.

248. Mangini, Nicola. *Bibliografia goldoniana, 1908–1957.* Venice: Istituto per la Collaborazione Culturale, 1961. 465p. PQ4697.5 .M3.

A continuation of Arnaldo della Torre, *Saggio di una bibliografia delle opere intorno a Carlo Goldoni, 1793–1907* (Florence, 1908), giving 276 Italian editions of individual works; some 300 translations (arranged by language); and literature about Goldoni (by year and author), covering 225 pages. No annotations and a strikingly poor index.

249. Tocchini, Gerardo. "Libretti napoletani, libretti tosco-romani: Nascita della commedia per musica goldoniana." *Studi musicali* 26 (1997): 377–416.

Goldoni wrote 55 comic libretti from 1735 to 1779; they are listed here. Only one dates from the period 1737–1748, the writer having fled Venice in 1743 to avoid debtors' prison. He practiced law in Pisa and Florence to 1748, then returned to Venice and back to his texts. Tocchini considers the influence of Gennarantonio Federico (librettist for Pergolesi and a leader in developing the Neapolitan *buffa* libretto) on Goldoni. While in Florence Goldoni heard his operas, and they formed an "apprenticeship" for his new mature style.

250. Heartz, Daniel. "*Vis comica*: Goldoni, Galuppi, and *L'Arcadia in Brenta.*" In Muraro (#2576), 2, 33–73.

Galuppi's comic opera *L'arcadia in Brenta* (Venice,1749) was the first of a series he wrote with Goldoni. Heartz gives background on Venetian opera of the period, genesis of this work, story and musical examples. Innovations were brought about through the composer/librettist collaboration: the complex finale, aria varied according to the character who sings, varying lengths for numbers, and through-composed pieces. Great inventiveness was displayed by both Galuppi and Goldoni, exemplifying what the latter called *vis comica*.

251. Heartz, Daniel. "Goldoni, *opera buffa*, and Mozart's Advent in Vienna." In *Opera buffa* (#2141), 25–49.

Mozart's first *opera buffa*, *La finta giardiniera*, was written for Vienna but not performed there because of his father's "clumsy manipulations"; meanwhile, it was Salieri and Paisiello who were the successful comic composers there. Not until *Le nozze di Figaro* (1786) was there a Mozart *buffa* premiere in Vienna.

252. Robinson, Michael F. "Three Versions of Goldoni's *Il filosofo di Campagna*." In Muraro (#2576), 2, 75–85.

The third act of the *opera buffa* gradually disappeared in the 1760s and 1770s; Robinson attributes the cause more to the librettists than to the composers. Goldoni, taken as the example here, dropped the third act as he reduced the number of serious roles in his comic texts. He settled on just two serious characters, a man and woman who represented an upper social stratum, opposed by five to seven comic characters. Comparing the three versions of the text, it seems the plot improved with the elimination of the third act.

253. Goldoni, Carlo. *Memoirs of Goldoni, Written by Himself: Forming a Complete History of His Life and Writings*. Trans. John Black. London: Henry Colburn, 1814. 2v. PQ4698 .A6 E5 B58.

Originally published in French, 1787. Frequently translated and reissued. Of interest for its panoramic view of contemporary life in Venice and Paris but of little use for information on Goldoni as librettist. Although his libretti accounted for 283 of the 2,000 comic operas (set by Galuppi, Piccinni, Duni, and others) produced in Italy alone during the 18th century, his journals—which cover his life to his 80th year—hardly mention music. His narrative is of daily life and his personal tribulations, with comments about his plays and comedies; the reader would hardly know they were musical enterprises. Goldoni came from the melodic Italian tradition and had to adjust to the spare French mode. His first visit to the Opéra, to hear Rameau's *Castor et Pollux*, brought this reaction: "Everything was beautiful, grand, and magnificent, except the music."

254. Weiss, Piero. "Carlo Goldoni, Librettist: The Early Years." Ph.D. diss., Columbia U., 1970. 180p.

255. Strauss, Richard. *The Correspondence between Richard Strauss and Hugo von Hofmannsthal*. Trans. Hanns Hammelmann and Ewald Osers. New York: Cambridge U.P., 1980. xx, 558p. ISBN 0-521-23476-X. ML410 .S93 A463.

The translation is taken from the 1955 edition by Atlantis Verlag in Zurich. Covering 1900–1929, the letters deal with each opera in great detail. A useful appendix identifies the items by opera. Index of persons mentioned.

256. Arshagouni, Michael Hrair. "Aria Forms in *opera seria* of the Classic Period: Settings of Metastasio's *Artaterse* from 1760–1790." Ph.D. diss., U. of California at Los Angeles, 1994. 438p.

257. Sprague, Cheryl Ruth. "A Comparison of Five Musical Settings of Metastasio's *Artaterse*." Ph.D. diss., U. of California at Los Angeles, 1979. xiv, 386 leaves.

258. Wilson, J. Kenneth. "*L'Olimpiade*: Selected Eighteenth-Century Settings of Metastasio's Libretto." Ph.D. diss., Harvard U., 1982. 640p.

259. *Metastasio e il mondo musicale*. Ed. Maria Teresa Muraro. Florence: Olschki, 1986. 350p. ISBN 88-222-3409-X. ML423 .M587 M5.

A collection of essays on various aspects of Metastasio's life and works.

260. Joly, Jacques. *Les fêtes théâtrales de Métastase à la cour de Vienne (1731–1767)*. Clermont-Ferrand: Université de Clermont-Ferrand, 1978. 525p. ISBN X-20-001762-3. ML1723 .J6.

An important consideration of Metastasio's role in refining the old Baroque libretto. He brought a simplicity and directness to the writing that worked well with the reform operas of his time. He and Calzabigi are credited with comparable achievements in this regard. With bibliography.

261. *NGDO* 3, 351–361, "Metastasio," by Don Neville, lists and discusses all settings of all his libretti.

262. Monelle, Raymond. "The Rehabilitation of Metastasio." *M&L* 57 (1976): 268–291.

Considers the history of opinion about Metastasio's libretti and finds his reputation growing.

263. *Studies in Music* (University of Western Ontario) 16 (1997).

A special issue on Metastasio, including seven papers from a symposium. Topics include Metastasio before and during his Vienna period, adaptations for the London stage, *Demofoonte,* and his texts in North America.

264. Jorgenson, James Lee. "Metastasio: Revaluation and Reformulation." Ph.D. diss., U. of Minnesota, 1980. 285p.

Further material on Metastasio is at #1007, #1962, and #2462.

265. Auld, Louis. *The Lyric Art of Pierre Perrin, Founder of the French Opera*. Henryville, Penn.: Institute of Mediaeval Music, 1986. 3v. ISBN 0-9319-0282-2. ML423 .P37 A95.

A biography of Perrin, first director of the Académie de Musique (1669), composer and librettist. V.1 presents a strong historical context, along with writings of Perrin; v.2 considers Perrin's lyrics; v.3 prints all his poetry.

266. Giovanella, Paola Daniela. "La storia e la favola dell'*Oberto*." *Studi verdiani* 2 (1983): 29–37.

The librettist of *Oberto*, Antonio Piazza, drew on two different stylistic traditions: neoclassic and romantic. His approach to versification is described, with a genesis study of the opera.

267. Howard, Patricia. "The Influences of the *précieuses* on Content and Structure in Quinault's and Lully's *tragédies-lyriques*." *AM* 3–1 (1991): 57–72.

The *précieuses* were women of a movement in mid–17th-century France who might be described as early feminists. They supported Quinault, whose libretti met their requirements concerning representation of love as romance, with "effete heroes." Women were shown as prudish or coquettish, in either case empowered to choose their men. Quinault's influence extended to Piccinni, Philidor, Gossec, and Paisiello. Lully's operas *Amadis* and *Thésée* are used as examples to illustrate Quinault's procedures.

See also Howard's essay, #1127.

268. Tomlinson, Gary. "*Ancora su* Ottavio Rinuccini." *JAMS* 28 (1975): 351–356.

A commentary on an earlier article by Barbara Hanning, "*Apologia pro* Ottavio Rinuccini," *JAMS* 26 (1973): 240–262. Disagrees with her view that Rinuccini "had a program—one that was deeply influenced by the Greek, and especially Aristotelian, concept of the power and function of music." Tomlinson does not find "a neat succession of signposts" but rather that "each seems to represent the author's response to the set of circumstances and exigencies peculiar to the work itself." Various versions of *Dafne* are described to demonstrate this position.

269. Tomlinson, Gary. "Music and the Claims of Text: Monteverdi, Rinuccini, and Marino." *Critical Inquiry* 8–3 (1982): 565–589.

In setting a text, a composer's approach is shaped by "his view of the nature and capabilities of musical discourse," which is developed from the aspirations of his culture and the tradition of his musical predecessors. Attitudes of the text-writer are also involved. Rinuccini's basic perspective was introspective, while Giambattista Marino's was more sensual. Monteverdi moved from close following of the text (*Affektenlehre*) to a looser interaction of music and word. He was the "last Renaissance composer" and then "spokesman for a new world view."

See also the author's #384.

270. *Felice Romani: Melodrammi, poesie, documenti*. Ed. Andrea Sommariva. Florence: Olschki, 1996. vi, 363p. ISBN 88-2224-4087. ML423 .R76 F3.

Papers given at a Romani conference, dealing with Romani's libretti for Simone Mayr, Donizetti, and Bellini. A valuable list of some 300 Romani libretti, by John N. Black (p.203–256), gives bibliographic details from the earliest versions and library locations. Indexed.

271. Mariano, Emilio. "Felice Romani e il melodramma." In *Opera and Libretto I* (#220), 165–209.

Biographical highlights on Romani; his implementation, with Bellini, of reform principles in *Il pirata* (1827). The aim was to simplify the dramatic structure and metrical elements. *Norma* was a model of reformed melodramaturgy.

272. Roccatagliati, Alessandro. "Felice Romani, Librettist by Trade." *COJ* 8-2 (July 1996): 113–146.

Describes Romani's collaborations with impresarios, composers, singers, administrators, stage designers, and journalists; success depended on smooth relationships in all these areas. His specific works are discussed in this sense, along with a useful account of the early-19th-century libretto. With 53 footnotes as guides to the earlier literature and relevant documents.

273. Rinaldi, Mario. *Felice Romani dal melodramma classico al melodramma romantico.* Rome: De Santis, 1965. 533p. ML423 .R76 R58.

A footnoted life and works, with a list of the libretti, list of composes who worked with Romani, and his own worklist. Minor bibliography, no index.

274. Murata, Margaret K. "Rospigliosiana, ovvero gli equivoci innocenti." *Studi musicali* 1975: 130–143.

Rospigliosi wrote the texts for 11 operas staged in Rome. They are described here, with Roman sources for them. Attribution problems are discussed, and some are cleared up.

275. Murata, Margaret K. "Il carnevale a Roma sotto Clemente IX Rospigliosi." *RIM* 12 (1977): 83–99.

Rospigliosi was pope in 1668–1669. This is a detailed view of the events and festivals promoted by the pontiff, with descriptions of scenery, costumes, furnishings, dancing, and performers. The 1669 festival is credited by Murata with bringing on a resurgence of operatic life in Rome. Full documentation.

See also Murata (#446).

276. Honolka, Kurt. *Papageno: Emanuel Schikaneder, Man of the Theater in Mozart's Time.* Trans. Mary Wilde; ed. Reinhard G. Pauly. Portland, Ore.: Amadeus, 1990. 236p. ISBN 0-9313-4021-7. ML423 .S346 H613.

Schikaneder's career is presented in a rich cultural context, organized around the cities and theaters he worked in. The economic conditions of performers are discussed. Influences on Schikaneder, as well as synopses of his plays and libretti. Honolka raises the question: Is *Die Zauberflöte* great because of Schikaneder or in spite of him? Much on genesis and sources of the opera. Analysis of its libretto shows variants from both Viennese and Italian comic conventions. Worklist, bibliography, index.

See also Batley (#1333).

277. Schneider, Herbert, ed. *Correspondance d'Eugène Scribe et de Daniel Auber.* Sprimont, Belgium: Mardaga, 1998. 151p. ISBN 2-87009-505-8. PQ2425 .Z48 A4.

A collection of 90 letters, most of them published for the first time, between the librettist and composer. Their working practice is well displayed, with details of plans and revisions. They also discuss directors, artists, and the repertoire of the day. With 44 illustrations of persons mentioned, and an index of names and titles.

See also Pendle (#462).

278. Cavicchi, Adriano. "Verdi e Solera: Considerazioni sulla collaborazione per *Nabucco.*" In Atti (#1802) 1 (1966): 44–58.

A review of Solera's life and literary work and the genesis of *Nabucco.*

279. Freeman, Robert. "Apostolo Zeno's Reform of the Libretto." *JAMS* 21 (1968): 321–341.

"Zeno did not invent such ideas as the needs for more serious, more rational, and more readable libretti"; during his career (1695–1729) other librettists were doing those things too. Among them were Andrea Perucci, Alessandro Guidi, and Giulio Bussi. Contemporary accounts, including statements of Zeno himself, are cited. Indeed, Freeman's final estimate is that Zeno had "toxic effects" that kept "the musical-dramatic aspects of serious Italian opera in a lethargic condition for decades."

XII. Production

Bibliographies

280. Cowden, Robert H. "Acting and Directing in the Lyric Theater: An Annotated Checklist." *Notes* 30 (1974): 449–459.

   Consists of 111 entries, books and articles, in English, French, and German. As Cowden observes, the literature on these topics is thin, and many of the titles here are of only passing interest. The next items are among the more substantial contributions:

General Works

281. *NGDO* 3, 1106–1132, "Production," by Roger Savage, Barry Millington, and John Cox, is a useful survey of all production topics; with 25 illustrations and bibliography of about 200 items.

282. Central Opera Service, New York. *Opera Manual: A Handbook of Practical Operatic Information*. New York: Central Opera Service, 1956. 36p. MT955 .C4.

   Discusses about 500 "chamber operas" in terms of production requirements: voices needed and their types, sets, acts, duration, publisher. Most of the operas are little known.

283. Donington, Robert. *Opera and Its Symbols: The Unity of Words, Music, and Staging*. New Haven, Conn.: Yale U.P., 1991. 248p. ISBN 0-300-04713.4. ML1700 .D665.

   Takes strong issue with modern producers, who obstruct the perception of opera as "a great purveyor of archetypal images": "We do not want the director to stage what he may think the symbols mean. We just want him to stage the symbols." Donington explains those symbols most convincingly, for *Die Zauberflöte, Der Ring*, and *Parsifal*. The book is more than a critique of productions; it stands as the prime theoretical work on opera in the light of Carl Jung's description of the collective unconscious. Backnotes, musical examples, bibliography, and expansive index.

284. Eaton, Quaintance. *Opera Production: A Handbook*. Minneapolis: U. of Minnesota Press, 1961–1974. 2v. ISBN 0-8166-0689-7. MT955 .E25.

Detailed production information on some 700 operas and brief notes on another 150 in a supplement. Gives plot, duration, casting, publisher or other source of score, and much auxiliary guidance. The most important of the manuals.

285. Volbach, Walther R. *Problems of Opera Production*. 2nd ed. New York: Archon, 1967. xii, 218p. MT955 .V64.

First edition, 1953. Discussion of translations, staging, conductor, director, singers, designer, rehearsals, and administration. Review of modern productions. Minor bibliography, index.

286. Goldowsky, Boris. *Bringing Opera to Life: Operatic Acting and Stage Direction*. New York: Appleton-Century-Crofts, 1968. x, 424p. ISBN 0-13-083105-0. ML1700 .G738 B7.

Detailed directions for staging various standard operas, with diagrams covering all contingencies. Special attention to presentation of two arias: Cherubino's "No so più cosa son" and Leporello's "Il catalogo è questo." Index of operas.

287. *National Opera Association Catalog . . . of Contemporary American Operas*. Ed. Arthur Schoep. New York: National Opera Association, 1976. Looseleaf. ML128 .C4 N27.

Similar to Eaton (#284) in format but restricted to modern American works; includes many operas not described in Eaton or the other handbooks in this section.

288. *Opera in Context: Essays on Historical Staging from the Late Renaissance to the Time of Puccini*. Ed. Mark A. Radice. Portland, Ore.: Amadeus, 1998. 410p. ISBN 1-57467-032-8. MT95 O54.

Ten essays, including Malcolm S. Cole, "Mozart and Two Theaters in Josephinian Vienna"; Evan Baker, "Verdi's Operas and Giuseppe Bertoja's Designs at the Gran Teatro La Fenice, Venice"; and Evan Baker, "Richard Wagner and His Search for the Ideal Theatrical Space." Entered separately in this guide: Barbara Coeyman on Paris in the 17th century (#2267), Mark Radice on Purcell's theaters (#1522), Mark W. Stahura on the Haymarket (#2721), E. Douglas Bomberger on Berlin (#2364), Karin Pendle on the Salle le Peletier (#2299), and Helen Greenwald on Puccini (#1464). Indexed.

289. Sutcliffe, Tom. *Believing in Opera*. Princeton, N.J.: Princeton U.P., 1996. xv, 464p. ISBN 0-691-01563-5. ML1700 .S9485.

If you believe in opera, you will be able to assimilate its rendition in radical stagings. Directors responsible for those innovations since 1970 are discussed, including Peter Sellars, Steven Pimlott, Tim Hopkins, Richard Jones, David Alden, Patrice Chéron, Ruth Berghaus, Matthew Richardson, Graham Vick, and Peter Brook. Alfred Roller's 1910 essay on staging reform is given in English translation. Index; no bibliography.

290. Nagler, Alois Maria. *Misdirection: Opera Production in the 20th Century.* Trans. Johanna C. Sahlin. Hamden, Conn.: Archon, 1981. 134p. ISBN 0-208-01899-9. ML1700 .N33.

The original was *Malaise in der Opera* (Rheinfelden: Schäube, 1980). A sour view of Felsenstein, Rennert, Wieland Wagner, and all the moderns but interlaced with facts and perceptive observations. Also useful for summary stage histories of the operas examined: *Don Giovanni, Così fan tutte, Le nozze di Figaro, Fidelio, Der fliegende Holländer, Aida, Contes d'Hoffmann, Der Freischütz, Carmen,* and *Der Rosenkavalier.* Notes, name index.

291. Marek, George. "The Case of the Murdered Libretto." *OQ* 1-1 (Spring 1983): 3–7.

An entertaining excoriation of modern opera producers, especially Wieland Wagner and Walter Felsenstein.

See also Kornick (#2761).

Individual Producers and Directors

292. Beacham, Richard C. *Adolphe Appia: Artist and Visionary of the Modern Theatre.* Rev. ed. Philadelphia: Harwood Academic Publishers, 1994. xv, 307p. ISBN 3-7186-5507-1. PN2808 .A6B43.

First edition,1987, as *Adolphe Appia, Theatre Artist.* Following a useful preface, which presents a survey of the literature on Appia, there is a chronology of his works, a biography, and selected writings by the producer. With 51 illustrations and an expansive index.

293. Volbach, Walther R. *Adolphe Appia, Prophet of the Modern Theatre: A Profile.* Middletown, Conn.: Wesleyan U.P., 1968. xvii, 242p. PN2808 .A6 V6.

A wildly adulatory description of Appia's productions, especially of the *Ring* in Bayreuth and *Tristan* in Paris. Writings of his pupils are included. With 48 illustrations, backnotes, a bibliography of some 300 items, and index.

294. Neef, Sigrid. *Das Theater der Ruth Berghaus.* Frankfurt am Main: S. Fischer, 1989. 223p.

Not examined.

295. Bing, Rudolf. *5000 Nights at the Opera.* New York: Doubleday, 1972. 360p. ML429 .B613 A3.

A plain autobiography, without notes or reference features, giving little information about Bing's management of the Metropolitan Opera (1951–1972). No index. The next entry is more useful.

296. Bing, Rudolf. *A Knight at the Opera.* New York: Putnam, 1981. 287p. ISBN 0-399-12653-8. ML429 .B52 A33.

He really was a knight, having been thus honored in 1971. This review of his career at the Met is chatty and smug but it does offer some interesting letters to and from Maria Callas and documents revealing Bing's style in handling stage managers, TV people, unions, and, of course, singers. Includes a list of his

Metropolitan repertoire and all the artists who performed and a list of his new productions. Index of names and titles.

297. Blunt, Wilfrid. *John Christie of Glyndebourne*. New York: Theatre Arts, 1968. xiii, 303p. ML429 .C53 B6.

Concerns the founder of the Glyndebourne Opera (opened 1934) and his solution of numerous problems involved in making it one of the leading companies. Discussion of Rudolf Bing, the first manager; Carl Ebert, artistic director; Fritz Busch, conductor; and mezzo-soprano Kathleen Ferrier. Indexed.

298. Innes, Christopher D. *Edward Gordon Craig: A Vision of the Theatre*. Amsterdam: Harwood, 1998. xi, 340p. ISBN 90-5702-125-0. PN2598 C85 I56.

A revision of *Edward Gordon Craig* (New York: Cambridge U.P., 1983). Biography and documents, Craig's own writings, and a chronology of his productions (notably *Dido and Aeneas* and works by Handel). Backnotes, brief bibliography, and index.

299. Felsenstein, Walter. *Schriften zum Musiktheater*. Berlin: Henschelverlag, 1976. 575p. ML1700.1 .F44.

The author is best known for his innovative work as Intendant (manager) of the Komische Oper, Berlin. He gives general ideas on staging and particular approaches to a number of specific works. List of sources; chronology of works staged by him, 1926–1975; name index.

300. Felsenstein, Walter. *The Music Theater of Walter Felsenstein: Collected Articles, Speeches, and Interviews* . . . Ed. and annotated Peter Paul Fuchs. New York: Norton, 1975. xx, 188p. ISBN 0-393-03186-6. ML429 .F43 M9.

Felsenstein's writings on music theater in general and on such specific works as *Le nozze di Figaro, Don Giovanni,* and *Carmen.* Also interviews, and appraisals by seven scholars. Footnotes but no bibliography or index.

301. Friedrich, Götz. *Wagner-Regie*. Zurich: Atlantis Musikbuch, 1983. 240p. ISBN 3-254-00080-3. ML410 .W19 F65.

The director discusses his Wagner productions at various opera houses, with good illustrations. No footnotes or bibliography but with a name and title index.

302. Barz, Paul. *Götz Friedrich—Abenteuer Musiktheater: Konzepte, Versuch, Erfahrungen*. Bonn: Keil, 1978. 223p. ISBN 3-921591-04-X. ML3858 .B29

Descriptions, with poor black-and-white illustrations, of productions from 1959 to 1978. Interviews, stage plans, casts. Bibliography of writings by Friedrich, name and topic index.

303. *Opern—Zeiten: Entwürfe, Erfahrungen, Begegnungen mit Götz Friedrich: Eine Künstlerbiographie in 107 Beiträgen zum 65. Geburtstag*. Ed. F. Wilhelm Christians. Berlin: Propyläen, 1995. 304p. ISBN 3-5490-491-2. ML429 .F8 O64.

Brief essays by various writers on numerous productions; list of productions with casts, 1958–1995; list of awards. Photos—mostly black and white. No index.

304. Gallo, Fortune. *Lucky Rooster.* New York: Exposition, 1967. 304p. ML429 .G153 A3.

Gallo (whose name means "rooster" in Italian) founded the San Carlo Touring Company in 1909. His autobiography is not very informative about that important organization, being a tiresome gathering of anecdotes and invented conversations. No notes, index, or other reference features.

305. Gatti-Casazza, Giuilio. *Memories of the Opera.* New York: Scribner, 1941. xii, 326p. Reprint, New York: Vienna House, 1973. ISBN 0-9443-0022-5 (Vienna). ML429 .G17 A3.

The significant contributions of Gatti-Casazza to the establishment of the Met as a world-esteemed company remain to be adequately documented. His own account of that career (1908–1935) is vague and chatty, with invented conversations and too few facts. No notes, no bibliography. Index of names, titles, and topics.

306. Higgins, John. *The Making of an Opera: Don Giovanni at Glyndebourne.* New York: Atheneum, 1978. xiii, 272p. No ISBN. MT955 .H53.

An account of Peter Hall's rehearsals for the 4 June 1977 performance. It is interesting that the conductor, John Pritchard, did not appear on the scene until after Hall had done all the preliminary work. With index. The next item is similar.

307. Fay, Stephen. *The "Ring": Anatomy of an Opera.* London: Secker & Warburg, 1984. 218p. No ISBN. ML410 .W15 F4.

Hall's rehearsals for a Bayreuth production.

308. Hartmann, Rudolf. *Oper: Regie und Bühnenbild Heute.* Stuttgart: Fohlhammer, 1977. 267p. ML1700 .O61.

In English: *Opera* (New York: Morrow, 1972); in French: *Les grands opéras: Décor et mise en scène* (Paris: Vilo, 1977). Hartmann achieved world recognition for his productions at Munich, 1938–1967, and later in other European houses. This is a general essay on stage design, followed by illustrated accounts of specific productions dating from 1962 to 1976. Fine pictures; comments by other stage artists and producers. Appendix data on theaters he has worked in, from a production viewpoint. Bibliography of about 50 titles, no index.

309. Hartmann, Rudolf. *Richard Strauss: The Staging of His Operas and Ballets.* Trans. Graham Davies. New York: Oxford U.P., 1981. 280p. ISBN 0-19-520251-1. MT955 .H3332.

Originally *Richard Strauss: Die Bühnenwerke von der Uraufführung bis heute* (Munich: R. Piper, 1980). Interesting details on staging, with notes and good pictures. Bibliography of about 50 items, name and place index.

310. Irmer, Hans-Jochen. *Joachim Herz, Regisseur im Musiktheater.* Berlin: Henschelverlag, 1977. 218p. No ISBN. ML1700.1 .I71.

Chapters by various authors about Herz and Felsenstein and the Herz productions of Verdi, Wagner, Strauss, Mozart, and Handel. Index of his scenic designs but no general index.

311. Kranz, Dieter. *Der Regisseur Harry Kupfer: "Ich muss Oper machen": Kritiken, Beschreibungen, Gespräche.* Berlin: Henschelverlag, 1988. 310p. ISBN 3-3620-0291-9. MT95 .K840.

Interviews, performance reviews, and a chronology of productions. No bibliography or index.

312. Lewin, Michael. *Harry Kupfer.* Vienna: Europverlag, 1988. 471p. ISBN 3-2035-1024-3. ML429 .K9 A5.

A rounded view of Kupfer and his productions, including 10 interviews, excerpts from critical reviews, a chronology, and 243 illustrations. Indexes of titles and names, bibliography of about 300 items.

313. Liebermann, Rolf. *En passant par Paris: Opéras.* Paris: Gallimard, 1980. 457p. ML1727 .L716.

A splendid picture book, covering 55 productions given at the Paris Opéra. Liebermann was manager there from 1971 to 1980, after achieving fame as Intendant at Hamburg, 1959–1973. For each work treated here there are details of casting and staff, with perceptive commentaries. Some of the less common operas included are *Ariane et Barbe-Bleue, Erwartung, Intégrale, Marchand de Venise, Moses und Aron, Platée, Tom Jones,* and *Véronique.*

314. Lumley, Benjamin. *Reminiscences of the Opera.* London: Hurst & Blackett, 1864. xx, 448p. Reprint, New York: Da Capo, 1976. ISBN 0-306-70842-6 (Da Capo), ML429 .L95 A3.

As manager of Her Majesty's Theater, 1841–1852 and 1856–1859, Lumley was at the center of operatic life in London. This is a personal, emotional account of his activities (crises, mostly), involving the great composers and singers. Invented conversations impinge on credibility; no notes or index.

315. Mapleson, James Henry. *The Mapleson Memoirs, 1848–1888.* New York: Belford, Clarke, 1888. xi, 329p. Reprint, New York: Appleton-Century-Crofts, 1966.

Mapleson was an impresario in London, 1861–1889 (Drury Lane, Her Majesty's, Covent Garden), and then in America until 1897. This is a chatty, sometimes entertaining chronicle of his London adventures, often more imaginary than factual. The reprint is abridged and annotated by Harold Rosenthal and is much preferable to the original. It includes appendixes of interviews, peer observations, and a list of persons mentioned with brief identifications. A list of Mapleson's English premieres; name and title index.

316. Maretzek, Max. *Revelations of an Opera Manager in 19th-Century America.* New York: Dover, 1968. xxxi, 442p. ML429 .M32 A3.

This edition incorporates *Crotchets and Quavers* (1855) and *Sharps and Flats* (1890) and offers a new introduction by Charles Haywood plus an index. Maretzek was one of those colorful impresarios of the Golden Age, in continued confrontation with his "rapacious" singers, creditors, and tricky competitors. His account deals with a long period (1848–1890) in New York, where he managed the Academy of Music and other companies. Much of it is chatter and invented conversations, but useful information on personalities and conditions of the time is pervasive.

317. Braun, Edward. *Meyerhold: A Revolution in Theatre.* 2nd ed. Iowa City: U. of Iowa Press, 1995. 347p. ISBN 0-87745-514-7. PN2728 .M4 B72.

First edition, *The Theatre of Meyerhold* (London: Methuen, 1979). Russian director Vsevold E. Meierkhol'd was involved with spoken theater and opera. His career is thoroughly appraised here, to its grim conclusion in 1940, when he was executed for treason (later he was "rehabilitated"). Footnotes, bibliography of about 100 items, expansive index.

318. Leach, Robert. *Vsevold Meyerhold.* New York: Cambridge U.P., 1989. xiv, 223p. ISBN 0-521-26739-0. PN2728 .M4 L43.

A useful biography, with chronology of presentations and 75 black-and-white illustrations. Backnotes, good bibliography of about 100 items, index.

319. *Jean-Pierre Ponnelle, Arbeiten für Salzburg, 1968–1988.* Salzburg: Salzburger Festspiele, 1989. 128p. No ISBN. ML141 .S15 P66.

A photo book, with citations from reviews. Also a chronology and some information about Ponnelle.

320. Styan, J. L. *Max Reinhardt.* New York: Cambridge U.P., 1982. ISBN 0-521-22444-6. PN2658 .R4 S8.

A chronology of productions, with commentary, from 1900 to 1943. Backnotes, short bibliography, good index.

321. Rennert, Günther. *Opernarbeit: Inszenierungern 1963–1973.* Kassel: Bärenreiter, 1974. 263p. ISBN 3-7618-0432-6. ML3858 .R45.

A picture book of his stage designs, mostly from Munich, where he was Intendant from 1967 to 1976. Covers standard operas, plus some modern composers like Janáček and Penderecki—the latter represented by a wild naked scene from *Devils of Loudon.* No notes or index.

322. Littlejohn, David. "Reflections on Peter Sellars's Mozart." *OQ* 7-2 (Summer 1990): 6–36.

In addition to consideration of the Sellars productions, some pros and cons about the basic question of altering the original format of an opera.

323. Rumiantsev, Pavel Ivanovich. *Stanislavski on Opera.* Trans. and ed. Elizabeth Reynolds Hapgood. New York: Theatre Arts, 1975. x, 374p. ISBN 0-87830-132-1. ML429 .S8 R813.

Stanislavskii directed the new opera studio of the Bol'shoi Theater from 1918; in 1924 this became the Stanislavskii Opera Studio and in 1928 the Stanislavskii Opera Theatre. His influence on operatic acting was considerable, but this book—primarily comprising imaginary conversations in which the director gives advice on specific roles to various singers—does not do justice to him. Rumiantsev was a singer and director in most of Stanislavskii's productions. No bibliography, no index.

324. Skelton, Geoffrey. *Wieland Wagner: The Positive Skeptic*. London: Gollancz, 1971. 222p. ISBN 0-575-00709-5. ML429 .W135 S6.

   An adulatory, undocumented story of Richard Wagner's grandson, who was co-director at Bayreuth (with his brother Wolfgang Wagner) from the end of World War II until his death in 1966. His staging departed from emphasis on scenery and moved toward abstractions. Many good photos; list of productions, 1936–1966; bibliography of about 20 items; useful, expansive index of names and titles.

325. Haltrecht, Montague. *The Quiet Showman: Sir David Webster and the Royal Opera House*. London: Collins, 1975. 319p. ISBN 0-00211-1632. ML429 .W378 H19.

   A wandering account of Webster's career as manager of the Royal Opera (Covent Garden), 1945–1970. No notes, a weak bibliography of about 25 items, index of names and titles.

326. *Robert Wilson: The Theater of Images*. Ed. R. Stearns. New York: Harper, 1984. 158p. ISBN 0-06-015289-3. PN2287 .W494 R6.

   The catalogue of a 1980 exhibition in Cincinnati, including illustrations from *Einstein on the Beach*, stage directions, and a biographical sketch. No index.

327. Holmberg, Arthur. *The Theatre of Robert Wilson*. New York: Cambridge U.P., 1997. xix, 229p. ISBN 0-521-36492-2. PN2287 .W494 H65.

   Biographical notes, a chronology of productions (*Alceste, Die Zauberflöte, Lohengrin, Einstein on the Beach*), illustrations, and commentaries. Backnotes, bibliography, index.

Performance Practice

Authenticity

328. A useful overview of the "The Idea of Authenticity," by Stanley Sadie, appears in *Companion to Baroque Music* (#62), 435–445.

329. Jackson, Roland John. *Performance Practice, Medieval to Contemporary: A Bibliographic Guide*. Music Research and Information Guides, 9. New York: Garland, 1988. xxix, 518p. ISBN 0-8240-1512-6. ML128 .P235 J3.

   A valuable annotated bibliography of 1,392 books, parts of books, articles, and dissertations—all of them published 1960–1986. It is thus a continuation of Vinquist (#330) and also updates the bibliography in Donington (#335). Jackson updated his list in issues of *Performance Practice Review*. This book is arranged chronologically and topically within periods. For major composers there are long series of entries—for example, Handel, 22 items; Mozart, 34. Indexes of theorists, authors, and subjects.

330. Vinquist, Mary, and Neal Zaslaw. *Performance Practice: A Bibliography*. New York: Norton, 1971. 114p. ML128 .L3 V79.

   A gathering of some 1,450 items, arranged by author with brief annotations, with an awkward nonexpansive index. Most of the material deals with music before 1900. Supplements were published in *Current Musicology*, 1971 and 1973.

331. Brown, Howard Mayer, and Stanley Sadie. *Performance Practice.* New York: Norton, 1990. 2v. ISBN 0-3930-0208-9. ML457 .P44.

Material based on entries in *NG*. V.2, on the 17th century and after, covers topics germane to operatic studies: instruments, voices, improvisation, and so forth. Index. Will Crutchfield's contributions on vocal practice are of special interest (p.292–319; 424–458).

332. MacClintock, Carol. *Readings in the History of Music in Performance.* Bloomington: Indiana U.P., 1979. xii, 432p. ISBN 0-253-1449-57. ML457 .R28.

Extracts from writings by Monteverdi, Cavalieri, Marco da Gagliano, Thomas Campion, Giovanni Doni, Jacques-Bonnet Bourdelot, Charles de Sainte-Evremonde, Burney, and Charles de Brosses. No index.

333. Leppard, Raymond. *Authenticity in Music.* Portland, Ore.: Amadeus, 1989. 80p. ISBN 0-931340-20-9. ML457 .L46.

A thoughtful appraisal of the approaches to early music in modern performance, with a sensible balance reached: the musicological findings must be put into the context of what sounds best to our ears. As a conductor, Leppard tries to bring to the stage a performance that is not necessarily what the composer would have experienced in his own time but one that the composer would have preferred. Backnotes but no bibliography or index.

334. Dolmetsch, Arnold. *The Interpretation of Music of the 17th and 18th Centuries: Revealed by Contemporary Evidence.* London: Novello, 1915. Reprint, Seattle: U. of Washington Press, 1969. ISBN 0-295-78578-0. viii, 494p. ML467 .D65.

The classic pioneer study that opened the door to the early music/authenticity movement. Dolmetsch, an instrument maker and performer on numerous instruments, old and new, made an exhaustive examination of scores and writings to accompany his practical knowledge as a player.

335. Donington, Robert. *The Interpretation of Early Music.* 4th. ed. London: Faber & Faber, 1989. 768p. ISBN 0-571-04789-0. ML457 .D64.

First edition, 1963. The 1989 version is substantially the same as the 3rd edition, 1974. An elaboration of Dolmetsch (preceding entry), in the form of excerpts from Baroque-era theorists and extensive commentaries on them. Sections on style, ornamentation, tempo, dynamics, and a number of instruments. Important annotated bibliography, p.673–729. Donington also wrote a practical guide, in which vocal aspects get thorough attention: *A Performer's Guide to Baroque Music* (New York: Scribner, 1973).

336. Kivy, Peter. *Authenticities: Philosophical Reflections on Musical Performance.* Ithaca, N.Y.: Cornell U.P., 1995. xiv, 199p. ISBN 0-8014-3046-1. ML457 .K58.

Kivy is concerned that historical authenticity has come to dominate "reasons of the ear." He finds no philosophical "defense of historical authenticity in musical performance practice" and tries to impose "system and order" on the issue, with the aim of laying the "groundwork for future dialogue." In doing so, he brings up key questions: Why perform according to the supposed intentions of the composer at all? Why not let musicology establish musical texts, without the need to perform them? "An authentic performance continually and persistently draws attention to itself, to the medium: relatively transparent to its contemporaries, relatively opaque to us." "Historical authenticity should not . . . be pursued doggedly and single-mindedly to the end of collapsing performance into text." Bibliography, index.

337. Taruskin, Richard. *Text and Act: Essays on Music and Performance.* New York: Oxford U.P., 1995. 382p. ISBN 0-19-509437-9. ML157 .T37.

One of the 20 essays (published 1972–1994) in this volume had appeared in the *New York Times* (29 July 1990), attracting much attention for its critique of the authenticity movement. Taruskin holds that historical performance is in fact a creation of the present, based on contemporary aesthetic views. There is no definitive text, as Howard Mayer Brown (#331) and most other musicologists claim. Authenticity means that performers must be true to themselves, as well as to the composer.

338. Mertin, Josef. *Early Music: Approaches to Performance Practice.* Trans. Siegmund Levarie. New York: Da Capo, 1986. xv, 204p. ML457 .M4613.

Originally *Alte Musik: Wege zur Aufführungspraxis* (Vienna: Lafite, 1978). In the translator's words, a "highly subjective" approach to early music; Mertin, a conductor and organ builder as well as a musicologist, was a pioneer in the revival of baroque, renaissance, and medieval music. He believed that musical sense is a more reliable guide to historical performance than treatises and other documentation. But he was well aware of the research on authenticity, weaving it into his own presentation of "what a conductor must know" about notation, rhythm and meter, musical structures, sonorities, thorough bass, old instruments, and tuning/tempering of the organ and continuo instruments. He hoped to free musicians "from performance conditions of 1910, which continue to dominate the concert stage." The last chapter provides "analytic support for a practical performance" of Bach's *Magnificat*. Backnotes but no bibliography or index.

339. The journals *Historical Performance* (1988–) and *Performance Practice Review* (1988–1997) present further research and opinion in this controversial field. The *Review* has been replaced with an online *Performance Practice Encyclopedia,* <www.performancepractice.com>.

Editing

340. *NGDO* 2, 11–16, "Editing," by Ellen Rosand, Stanley Sadie, and Roger Parker, is a fine summary of the problems encountered in reconstructing old scores.

Ornamentation

341. There is a thorough survey in *NGDO* 3, 760–773, "Ornamentation," by Andrew V. Jones and Will Crutchfield. Many musical examples and a three-column bibliography. Another source, already mentioned, has good coverage for one period: *Companion to Baroque Music* (#62), 417–434, "Ornamentation," by David Fuller.

Instrumentation

342. Weaver, Robert. "The Orchestra in Early Italian Opera." *JAMS* 17 (1964): 83–89.

Although instrument playing became more elaborate and idiomatic during the 17th century, the role of the orchestra in opera diminished. Weaver does not accept the received explanation for this curiosity (economic restrictions prevented hiring larger numbers of players), holding for an aesthetic solution. As opera turned more to expression of emotions, the big brass orchestra became unsuitable. Composers preferred the "monochromatic string orchestra" as a setting for expressive singing.

343. Rose, Gloria. "Agazzari and the Improvising Orchestra." *JAMS* 18 (1965): 382–393.

In Agostino Agazzari's treatise *Del sonare sopra 'l basso con tutti li stromenti e dell'uso loro nel conserto* (1607), there is a distinction between foundation instruments that present the harmony and ornamental instruments that improvise above it. Rose suggests that the players of improvising instruments may have read from chord sequences in a short score that showed them the vocal parts and figured bass. Indeed, many scores for 17th-century operatic numbers present only a continuo, requiring the orchestra to invent the melodies.

344. Spitzer, John, and Neal Zaslaw. "Improvised Ornamentation in Eighteenth-Century Orchestras." *JAMS* 39 (1986): 524–577.

Who improvised, with which ornaments, and under what circumstances? The custom was more prevalent in Italy than elsewhere. German practice is the best documented. The "demise of improvised ornamentation is seen as a crucial step in the evolution of the orchestra as an institution. . . ."

345. Zaslaw, Neal. "Lully's Orchestra." In *Colloque* (#1127), 539–580.

Despite the significance now assigned to Lully's orchestra, "there are astonishingly few hard facts about his personnel." Zaslaw explores instrumental practice at opera, ballet, and concert. He disposes of some myths, notably the one about Lully stabbing himself fatally with a long baton. Between 1664 and 1674 "a fascinating new instrumentation had come into being . . . the earliest form of what later acquired the name orchestra." By orchestra, he means an ensemble based on doubled strings and winds, with stable instrumentation, and discipline. Lully's was the first to meet most of these criteria. With 26 plates.

Pitch

The name of any note, say "A," can be situated by musical notation on a page of score, but it cannot so easily be situated in the acoustic spectrum. The number of vibrations per second of a string or air column that produces written "A" has been a variable element over the centuries. Two recent essays on this difficult question, of obvious importance for authentic performance of opera:

346. Arthur Mendel. "Pitch in Western Music since 1500: A Reexamination." *AM* 50 (1978): 1–93.

     Mendel, one of the leading pitch scholars, here revises and updates his several earlier writings on the topic. He considers evidence for absolute pitches before 1834, for each instrument and voice range; and pitch in Bach, Mozart, and others. Pitch standards employed at various opera houses are compared; they show a general rise in pitch from 1829 (A = 434 at Paris Opéra) to 1878 (A = 446.8 at Vienna Staatsoper) but with many variants. In our own time the Paris pitch averages 447.2 during performances. Mendel cautions: "notions that the tendency of pitch standards has been continuously upward . . . are false."

347. Stratton, John. "Some Matters of Pitch." *OQ* 6-4 (Summer 1989): 49–60.

     In a convenient summary of the situation, directed at opera matters, Stratton deals with the historic pattern, concerns of singers, preferences of certain opera conductors, and the special questions raised by phonograph recordings. On the last-named point, see also "Pitch" in *Encyclopedia of Recorded Sound in the United States* (#434), 535–536.

Participants

Conductors

348. Gavazzeni, Giandrea. *La bacchetta spezzata*. Pisa: Nistri-Lischi, 1987. 234p. ML457 .G34.

     The author, music director at La Scala from 1965 to 1972, and also a conductor at the Metropolitan, offers interesting views of opera from the podium. Chapters on operatic conducting of Victor de Sabata, Arturo Toscanini, and Wilhelm Furtwängler are followed by Gavazzeni's own perspectives on operas of Verdi, Puccini, and Wagner. Phrase-by-phrase analysis and accounts of challenges posed by singers. Indexed.

349. Jensen, Luke. "The Emergence of the Modern Conductor in Nineteenth-Century Italian Opera." *Performance Practice Review* 4 (1991): 34–63.

     In the early 19th century the *violino principale* directed the orchestra. He had no full score but just his own part with cues for the other players and the singers. In France conducting with a baton emerged in the 1820s, over critical disapproval, and the baton became the norm at the Opéra by midcentury. In Italy the two approaches were continued together for some time. The article describes the cooperation between Verdi and two of the conductors who directed his works: Angelo Mariani and Emanuel Muzio; conductors were expected to prepare the premieres, and Italian conductors developed considerable authority over adjustments in the scores. The concentration of authority in the conductor began in Italy, along with the practice of placing the conductor between the orchestra and the audience. Gradually, in all countries, the growing complexity of 19th-century scores made it easier to conduct with a baton than with a violin bow.

Chorus

350. Grout, Donald Jay. "The Chorus in Early Opera." In *Festschrift Friedrich Blume* (#64), 151–161.

    Distinguishes between two uses of *coro* in 17th-century opera: it applied either to a chorus (more than one singer to a part) or to an ensemble (one singer to a part). Considers the role of the chorus in opera, its roots in Greek drama and 16th-century *intermedia*, and its changing function after 1620.

351. Cyr, Mary. "The Dramatic Role of the Chorus in French Opera: Evidence for the Use of Gesture, 1670–1770." In *Opera and the Enlightenment* (#91), 105–118.

    In the period covered, the chorus was divided into two groups, on either side of the stage. It remained on stage throughout the performance, with minimal movement if not total immobility (according to contemporary reports). But some illustrations suggest that chorus members "may have used simple dramatic gestures." Cyr comes to no conclusion on the point, but her essay is of interest for the contemporary documents and pictures it presents about staging practice.

See also Banducci (#663).

352. Mahling, Christoph-Hellmut. *Studien zur Geschichte des Opernchors.* Trossingen- Wolfenbüttel: Editio Intermusica, 1962. 360p. ML1700 .M1358.

    A reprint of the author's dissertation, U. of Saarbrücken. Traces the development of the chorus in opera from the 16th century to Wagner. Footnotes, bibliography, tables, no index.

353. De Venney, David P., and Craig R. Johnson. *The Chorus in Opera: A Guide to the Repertory.* Metuchen, N.J.: Scarecrow, 1993. 203p. ISBN 0-8108-2620-8. ML128 .C48 D47.

    A list of "nearly 600 choruses from 218 operas by 90 composers," arranged by composer, opera, and act. Performing forces are given, with duration, difficulty level, and comments. The authors followed Kobbé's plot book (#199), in which most choral numbers are mentioned. An interesting list of operas without choruses is included (although one of the withouts is *Pagliacci,* which does have a wonderful act 1 choral number). First-line index.

Singers and Singing

354. *NGDO* 4, 386–401, "Singing: A Bibliography," is an unsigned list of about 1,600 entries.

355. Reid, Cornelius L. *A Dictionary of Vocal Terminology: An Analysis.* New York: Joseph Patelson Music House, 1983. 457p. ISBN 0-915282-07-0. ML102 .V6 R4.

Θ A valuable and apparently unique glossary, defining and discussing some 1,200 terms. Some of the entries run to 10 or 12 pages, with examples from a wide spectrum of composition. Among the more familiar terms (Breathing, Head Voice) are found many that could be styled obscure (Abduct, Buccal, Lip Falsetto, Shouty Tone). The material on Placement is of special interest. Nine-page bibliography, name index.

356. Rosselli, John. *Singers of Italian Opera: The History of a Profession.* New York: Cambridge U.P., 1992. xvi, 272p. ISBN 0-521-41683-3. ML1460 .R68.

An economic history of the occupation, not a collective biography. The patronage system, castrati, training, problems of women singers, agents, audiences, and other marketing matters. Erudition and insight are pervasive. A notable section describes the struggle of women to be accepted on stage without becoming tainted in their personal lives. Although it claims to deal with "all those singers, members of the chorus as well as stars, who have sung Italian opera from 1600 to the present," the book is mostly about the years before 1850. Index of names and topics, backnotes, no bibliography.

357. Celletti, Rodolfo. *A History of Bel Canto.* Trans. Frederick Fuller. New York: Oxford U.P., 1991. 218p. ISBN 0-19-313209-5. ML1460 .C413.

Originally *Storia del belcanto* (1983). A narrative account of the style, which is defined by legato, *messa di voce,* equalization of registers, expressive use of ornaments, and "a voice limpid on the breath." Focus on the Baroque era, with attention to Rossini—the last bel canto composer—with material on romantic opera, verismo, and current revivals. *Semiramide* was the "last opera in a great Baroque tradition." Rossini hated the tenor high C, "screeching of a slaughtered chicken." A few footnotes, no bibliography, expansive index.

358. Dean, Winton. "The Performance of Recitative in Late Baroque Opera." In his *Essays on Opera* (#69), 78–90. Reprinted in *GL,* v.11.

Calls for recitative to be sung in *parlando* style, with free meter and tempo. The accompaniment needs to be flexible for this to happen. Dean prefers the so-called foreshortened cadence in the accompaniment, to the "delayed cadence" (see next entry). Primary sources and recent scholarship are examined and discussed. For historical background on the recitative, see Downes (#88).

359. Hansell, Sven Hostrup. "The Cadence in 18th-Century Recitative." *MQ* 54 (1968): 228–248.

Describes the two ways of performing the cadence: truncated (or "foreshortened" in Dean's terminology; see preceding entry) and delayed. The former was popular through the earlier 18th century, giving way gradually to the delayed manner. Quotations from treatises, musical examples, other documentary evidence.

360. Caswell, Austin B., ed. *Embellished Opera Arias. Recent Researches in the Music of the 19th and Early 20th Centuries, 7–8.* Madison, Wisc.: A-R Editions, 1989. xxxii, 219p. ISBN 0-89579-240-0. M2 .R23834 v.7–8.

An anthology of vocal scores from 1816–1860, consisting of 18 arias and four duets from 17 operas. More than half of the scores are from Rossini works; 15 are for female voice. Most of the material is taken from a Paris Conservatory method book published in 1849. These pieces were published in versions with embellishments, and that is how they appear here. They illustrate the ornamentation practice of leading singers. With source information and useful commentary.

361. Goldschmidt, Hugo. *Die italienische Gesangsmethode des XVII. Jahrhunderts und ihre Bedeutung für die Gegenwart.* 2nd ed. Breslau: Schlesische Buchdruckerei, 1892. vii, 137, 68p. Reprint, Hildesheim: Olms, 1997.

Describes techniques of singing, including ornamentation, as presented by writers in the 17th century. The 68-page appendix contains actual singing exercises.

362. Fortune, Nigel. "Italian 17th-Century Singing." *M&L* 35 (1954): 206–219.

Presents prefatory material from some 200 books of solo vocal music. The editors of these anthologies offered useful directions for interpretation, including use of falsetto, expressive gradations of volume, and rubato.

363. Goldovsky, Boris, and Arthur Schoep. *Bringing Soprano Arias to Life.* New York: Schirmer, 1973. iv, 326p. ISBN 0-911320-64-4. Reprint, Metuchen, N.J.: Scarecrow, 1990. ISBN 0-8108-2364-0. MT892 .G64.

A valuable, measure-by-measure analysis of 28 standard arias, offering guidance about vocal problems (including embellishments, rhythm, and tempo), the musical structure, staging and costume matters, and "actions of the aria." Character building is well treated, along with style, traditions, and translations. Musical examples, no index.

364. Keyser, Dorothy. "Cross-Sexual Casting in Baroque Opera: Musical and Theatrical Conventions." *OQ* 5-4 (Winter 1987–1988): 46–57.

A useful review of the casting of castrati, young boys in treble roles, women in male heroic roles, and women playing the roles of young boys. Considers the problem of modern productions that confront those conventions and finds no solution entirely satisfactory. Keyser objects to Paul Henry Lang's proposal, which is simply to transpose high parts down an octave and let men sing them. Things could get complicated in the 18th century, as Keyser demonstrates by recounting the bewilderment of Casanova when he encountered a woman thoroughly disguised as a castrato.

365. Giles, Peter. *The History and Technique of the Counter-Tenor: A Study of the Male High Voice Family*. Aldershot, England: Scolar Press; Brookfield, Vt.: Ashgate, 1994. xxiv, 459p. ISBN 0-8596-7931-4. ML1460 .G56.

Supersedes his *The Countertenor* (1982), although the earlier book is not mentioned in the later one. A valuable compendium of facts, including a historical summary, an account of the revival, recordings made 1904–1934, voice mechanism, registers and range, and the falsetto family. Appendixes treat Nicholas Morgan, Richard Elford, and John Saville in detail. With glossary of vocal terms and a good index; footnoted but without bibliography.

366. Rosselli, John. "The Castrati as a Professional Group and a Social Phenomenon, 1550–1850." *AM* 60 (1988): 143–179.

A thorough historical study and critical review of earlier literature. Attention to all contemporary documents gives an accurate picture of the phenomenon, which persisted for three centuries. The ambiguous attitude of the Catholic Church contributed to the longevity of the practice; indeed, castrati were heard in church more often than in opera during the 16th–18th centuries.

367. Ardoin, John. *Callas at Juilliard: The Master Classes*. New York: Knopf, 1987. 300p. ISBN 0-3945-6367-0. MT820 .C17.

Describes and illustrates with 950 musical examples how Maria Callas taught her interpretations of 75 arias.

368. Thomson, Virgil. *Music with Words: A Composer's View*. New Haven, Conn.: Yale U.P., 1989. x, 178p. ISBN 0-300-04505-0. ML1406 .T5.

A brief exposition (76p.) of Thomson's ideas about various elements of songwriting and singing, including the union of poetry and music, operatic writing, and coaching of singers. Examples of his own works, including three operas, take up the rest of the book. Expansive index.

Stage Designers

369. Atkinson, W. Patrick. *Theatrical Design in the Twentieth Century: An Index to the Photographic Reproductions of Scenic Designs*. Bibliographies and Indexes in the Performing Arts, 21. Westport, Conn.: Greenwood, 1996. 475p. ISBN 0-313-29701-0. PN2091 .S8 T47.

A useful resource, locating photos of some 3,000 stage works (plays, musicals, and operas). Arrangement is by title, with a designer index. The pictures are in English-language books and periodicals. *Aida* is represented by 14 different stage designs, *Siegfried* by 12, *Faust* by 35.

370. Friedman, Martin. *Hockney Paints the Stage*. New York: Abbeville, 1983. 227p. ISBN 0-89659-393-7. PN2096 .H57 F75.

The catalogue of an exhibition presented at the Walker Art Center, Minneapolis, 1983, consisting primarily of 250 fine illustrations. Hockney's designs were done for Glyndebourne and the Metropolitan; they include *The Rake's Progress*, *Die Zauberflöte*, and *L'enfant et les sortilèges*. Brief biography, interviews, and the artist's own accounts of some of his work. An appreciation by

Stephen Spender says that Hockney "translates music into visual images which are themselves musical." Indexed.

371. Wagner, Manfred. *Alfred Roller in seiner Zeit*. Salzburg: Residenz, 1996. 327p. ISBN 3-7017-0960-2. PN2096 .R65 W346.

A biography of Roller, whose work as a painter brought him first to designs for spoken drama, then to opera. Fine color reproductions of his paintings, posters, and stage scenes. Name index.

372. Svoboda, Josef. *The Secret of Theatrical Space: The Memoirs of Josef Svoboda*. Ed. and trans. Jarka Burian. New York: Applause Theater Books, 1993. 144p. ISBN 1-5578-3137-8. PN2096 .S9 A3.

A fine telling of Svoboda's busy career, which covered both spoken and operatic theater. With black-and-white pictures only, backnotes by Burian, a chronology of productions 1943–1992, and index.

373. Burian, Jarka. *The Scenography of Josef Svoboda*. Middletown, Conn.: Wesleyan U.P., 1971. xxii, 197p. ISBN 0-8195-4041-2. PN2096 .S9 B9.

The designer's life is presented, with his aesthetic principles and their embodiment in about 50 productions. Operas included (and illustrated in black-and-white pictures, with some stage plans) are by Janáček, Mozart, Puccini, Smetana, Wagner, Debussy, Weber, and Richard Strauss. Chronology of productions 1943–1971, quick bibliography, no index.

374. Burian, Jarka. *Svoboda: Wagner; Josef Svoboda's Scenography for Richard Wagner's Operas*. Middletown, Conn.: Weslyan U.P., 1983. x, 117p. ISBN 0-8195-5088-4. ML410 .W19 B9.

A discussion of Svoboda's productions, mostly at Covent Garden, Geneva, and Bayreuth. With 17 plates and 84 other illustrations, including stage plans. Notes, bibliography, no index.

Costumes

375. Van Witten, Leo. *Costuming for Opera: Who Wears What and Why*. Bloomington: Indiana U.P., 1981. 2v. Reprint, Metuchen, N.J.: Scarecrow, 1994. ISBN (Scarecrow) 0-8108-2744-1. MT955 .V36.

Costumes for 31 operas are discussed in this useful work and illustrated with period paintings and engravings. Glossary of costume terms.

Stage Effects

376. Two strong articles: "Machinery," by Edward A. Langhans, *NGDO* 3, 120–132, and "Lighting," *NGDO* 2, 1265–1277.

XIII. Philosophy and Theory of Opera

Philosophy rests on definitions. To define opera has proved troublesome; the concept appears to resolve into a polarity of drama-with-music on one end and music-with-drama on the other. "Prima la musica, poi le parole?" Or the opposite? Consider this definition from the *New Harvard Dictionary of Music* (#17): "A drama that is primarily sung, accompanied by instruments, and presented theatrically." And this from *NG* (#19): "The generic term for musical dramatic works in which the actors sing some or all of their parts." And: "A vocal work sung by characters who also use words and act their parts," from *Musical Morphology* (#398). There is a continuum suggested by the definitions, with the *NG* in a middle position, but few writers on the subject represent that central area. Whatever their titles and announcements, they cluster themselves around one or the other of the two poles: holding with drama as the meaning-giver, or with music. Music is seen, *au fond*, to be the support system for the text, or vice versa. One art swallows the other, as Susanne Langer puts it. The next entries in this guide are grouped around the two points.

Emphasis on Drama

377. Peri, Jacopo. *Le musiche sopra L'Euridice*. Florence, 1601.

This is the earliest opera for which a complete score has survived. In the foreword to the score, set to a text (published a year earlier) by Ottavio Rinuccini, Peri set down the ideas of the Florentine Camerata (see #2438ff.). They and he believed that the ancient Greeks and Romans "sang their tragedies throughout" in a form between song and speech and "following the passions." Quotations are from the translation in *Strunk, 659–662*.

378. Gluck, Christoph Willibald von. *Alceste*. Vienna: Giovanni Tomaso de Trattern, 1769.

In his dedication to the score, published two years after the premiere of the opera, Gluck explicated his views about "long disfigured" Italian opera and what he—with librettist Raniero Calzabigi—was doing to reform it. "I believed that my greatest labor should be devoted to seeking a beautiful simplicity . . . nor did I judge it desirable to discover novelties if . . . not naturally suggested by the situation and the expression." Music in support of the text, a return to Camerata principles. Quotations from *Strunk*, 932–934.

See also Algarotti (#2455).

379. Wagner, Richard. *Das Kunstwerk der Zukunft.* Leipzig, 1850.

Wagner's extensive writings on music drama (see #1981ff.) focus on his view of music as a factor in the drama, "the highest collective art work." But Wagner did not consider music as a handmaiden to the text. He saw music reaching its greatest potential in cooperation with the other arts. "The united sister arts will show themselves and bring their influence to bear, now collectively, now two at a time, now singly, as called for by the need of the dramatic action, the one determinant of aim and measure." Quotations from *Strunk,* 1,094–1,112.

380. Conrad, Peter. *A Song of Love and Death: The Meaning of Opera.* New York: Poseidon, 1987. 384p. ISBN 0-671-64353-3. ML1700 .C668.

The song is that of Orpheus, considered by Conrad to be the presiding myth throughout operatic history. Opera exists to express those Orphic love-death ideas. The approach is purely textual (no music is discussed): a study of libretti. Nothing is proved, and there are many forced associations. One reviewer, M. Owen Lee, described Conrad's method as a "sort of madness" through which "everything can be made to mean everything else."

381. Conrad, Peter. *Romantic Opera and Literary Form.* Berkeley: U. of California Press, 1977. vii, 185p. ISBN 0-5200-3258-6. ML2110 .C754.

An examination of Verdi, Wagner, Strauss, and some contemporaries in terms of their handling of story and literary sources of their plots. The underlying assumption—as in the previous entry—is that literary matters are the basic forces in opera. Conrad's terminology is inconsistent, and his efforts do not seem to advance his theories. Bibliography of about 50 items, name index.

382. Dahlhaus, Carl. "Drammaturgia dell'opera italiana." In Bianconi (#2428), 77–162.

Although focused on Italian practice, this is a significant contribution to operatic theory. Opera was created in the 17th century along with modern drama (Shakespeare and Racine) and should be examined in that context, not in the light of ancient Greek drama. The difference between drama and opera is that drama is articulated by verbal discourse, opera by scenic events. It is out of place to judge the dramatic quality of opera in terms of spoken drama. The form of classical tragedy is not relevant to the opera libretto, which has other purposes. In the Italian baroque it had to provide a vehicle for arias that displayed certain emotions (while making some sense as a story). In Italian opera of all periods, the musical realization is connected to whatever is onstage at the moment, apart from the textual narrative. It is anchored in the present, concerned with expressing affect. In both drama and opera, the text or story can be summarized, so it is a property and not the essence of the work (which can be experienced only in its own terms). Modern productions are thus wrongly conceived when they aim at making the story more realistic.

383. Hanning, Barbara. "The Influence of Humanist Thought and Italian Renaissance Poetry on the Formation of Opera." Ph.D. diss., Yale U., 1969. 374p.

384. Tomlinson, Gary. *Metaphysical Song: An Essay on Opera*. Princeton, N.J.: Princeton U.P., 1999. x, 192p. ISBN 0-691-00408-0. ML3858 .T66.

"Opera's history can be mapped and partitioned according to various supersensible realms it has brought into audible perception and the changing ways it has done so." Tomlinson connects opera with philosophy; it reflects the paradigmatic views of its time—in particular, views of the mind/body relation. Early opera had no unconscious; it was not yet dualistic. Philosophers looked for ways to make soul and substance one. Then the dualism of Descartes was accepted and expressed in absolute monarchs who shared human and divine attributes; they became central to operatic stories. Mozart, and comic opera generally, attacked that absolutism, forecasting Kant's subjectivity. Don Giovanni is a self that refuses to be transcended. Kant's worldview resonates in Verdi and his 19th-century contemporaries. Notes, expansive index.

385. Corse, Sandra. *Opera and the Uses of Language: Mozart, Verdi, and Britten*. Rutherford, N.J.: Fairleigh Dickinson U.P., 1987. 163p. ISBN 0-8386-3300-5. ML1700. C7.

"In opera, the aesthetic function of language is reduced in the text because it is redistributed to the music. Librettos are literary works in which the literary qualities have been to some extent stripped away, so they tend to emphasize the communicative function of language rather than its aesthetic function." Thus the "composer reinvents, with a different medium, the ambiguity and multiple relationships of literary texts." As this happens, "music often attempts to rescue and resurrect meaning, making meaning possible as a cooperative venture between music and text, composer and librettist, singer and audience." To demonstrate this thesis, Corse offers long program notes on six operas. *Le nozze di Figaro* goes smoothly, with partly acknowledged assistance from Siegmund Levarie (#1322), but trouble brews with the ever recalcitrant *Die Zauberflöte*. Music is there found to "undermine or contradict the text." Things are worse in *Falstaff*, where "the opera itself often works to subvert the meaning of Falstaff's words." Deconstruction seems forced here, outside its comfortable literary demesne. Sometimes music is said to do more than it really can, as in *Death in Venice*, where it is said to describe Aschenbach as "a person who is easily led by his emotions into irrational behavior." Musical examples, backnotes, bibliography, index.

386. Kerman, Joseph. *Opera as Drama*. 2nd ed. Berkeley: U. of California Press, 1988. xvii, 232p. ISBN 0-520-06273-6. ML3858 .K4.

First edition, 1956. This edition adds material on *Idomeneo*, a new chapter on operatic criticism, and revisions passim. Kerman gives to music "the central articulating function" and judges its quality by how well it "articulates the drama." Since drama in this context equals text, his view places music in the service/support role. Kerman's insistence that music "bears the ultimate responsibility for articulating drama" leads him to a favorable evaluation of composers who do best with that articulation (Monteverdi, Purcell, Gluck, Mozart, Verdi, Wagner, Debussy, Berg, and Stravinsky). Those whose music, however beautiful it may be, fails to articulate the text are condemned as "cynical" and "false." Puccini and Richard Strauss head that unhappy list. Even the select few are guilty at times of nonarticulating: Mozart nods in *Così fan tutte* and *Don Giovanni* ("dramatically cynical"). But Gluck is forgiven for making "Che farò senza Euridice" into a dance number instead of a sorrowful exhibit, the aria being "beyond grief." Whatever one may think of its philosophic underpinning, the book has perceptive studies of *Otello, Wozzeck,* and *The Rake's Progress* and a valuable analysis of *Tristan*'s last act. Index, no bibliography.

387. Schmidgall, Gary. *Literature as Opera.* New York: Oxford U.P., 1977. xi, 431p. ISBN 0-1950-2213-0. ML3858 .S348.

Examines the process of transforming a work of literature into an opera, following the idea that the literary quality of the original ought to be retained. Schmidgall is skeptical about current composers, who seek among inferior stage works for material. Backnotes, no bibliography, good expansive index of names, titles, and topics.

See also Donington (#283).

Gender Studies

The next entries fall into the drama-emphasis category, but they share a special concern for the way operatic texts depict women—and sometimes men. One gender study does fit into the music-emphasis group (#408).

388. Clément, Catherine. *Opera, or the Undoing of Women.* Trans. Betsy Wing. Minneapolis: U. of Minnesota Press, 1988. xviii, 201p. ISBN 0-8166-1653-1. ML2100 .C613.

Originally *L'opéra, ou la defaite des femmes* (Paris: B. Grasset, 1979). Patriarchal values pervade opera libretti, to the disadvantage of female characters. Clément is not much concerned with music, so she gives no credit to the splendid expressiveness of women singing; as reviewer Karin Pendle put it: "Opera heroines are often tormented and even slain in their male-dominated worlds; but the music in which their sufferings are expressed so often ennobles them that they appear heroic figures, not victims." One musical element is important: chromaticism, which has a seductive quality (Isolde, Carmen). Leitmotiv is a puzzle to Clément, at least in its function as a discloser of thoughts; she wonders "what would the 'thoughts' of a fictional character be?" Nevertheless, various operatic texts are intriguingly elucidated through a woman's eyes, and many insights emerge. For example, in the *Ring,* "mothers are the great sacrificial victims." Has it been noticed before, in the vast *Ring* literature, that the mothers are "just barely of some use for childbearing; after that they disappear"? Wing's translation is excellent, preserving the vivid diction of the original. Backnotes, bibliography, expansive index.

389. *En travesti*: *Women, Gender Subversion, Opera*. Ed. Corinne Blackmer and Patricia Juliana Smith. vi, 381p. New York: Columbia U.P., 1995. ISBN 0-231-10269-0. ML2100 .E6.

Essays that attempt to disclose various gender-based oddities in operas and opera composers. Topics include castrati and their roles, trouser roles, operas in which women sing duets with each other and those in which they do not, operas by declared or alleged homosexual composers or librettists, and even "opera itself" as an art form. The reviewer in *OQ* said that "most contributors . . . came to opera looking for queerness, and inevitably they found it." But another reviewer, in *JAMS,* was favorably disposed: "Although some may still want to argue against Reynolds' statement that 'everyone knows opera is about sex,' through the eloquent confessions in this volume I am convinced."

390. Koestenbaum, Wayne. *The Queen's Throat: Opera, Homosexuality, and the Mystery of Desire*. New York: Poseidon, 1993. 271p. ISBN 0-671-75457-2. ML429 .K74 A3.

An attempt to establish a "gay way of listening" to opera. The appealing mystery of the form is traced to the separation in puberty of the child and the mother, creating a "desiring subject who will spend the rest of his life in a quest for infantile wholeness." In listening to opera "we are the ideal mother . . . and the baby listening to the mother for signs of affection and attention." Thus the soprano fixation is accounted for. Includes a "pocket guide to [28] queer moments in opera," bibliography, and index.

391. McClary, Susan A. *Feminine Endings: Music, Gender, and Sexuality*. Minneapolis: U. of Minnesota Press, 1990. viii, 220p. ISBN 0-8166-1898-4. ML82 .M38.

Seeks out "sexual metaphors" and finds many. The cadential feminine ending is one, a woman's mad scene is another. "Excess" is a key concept; it always means something sexual in the subtext. The music sung by Carmen, for example, is marked by "chromatic excesses" and "her musical lines tease and taunt, forcing the attention to dwell on the . . . erogenous zones of her inflected melodies." Lucia's music is likewise "always given to excess." Lengthy considerations of *Bluebeard's Castle* and of Monteverdi's "construction of gender" are of interest. Backnotes, bibliography of 40p., index.

392. Hutcheon, Linda, and Michael Hutcheon. *Opera: Desire, Disease, Death*. Lincoln: U. of Nebraska Press, 1996. xvi, 296p. ISBN 0-8032-2367-6. ML1700 .H87.

An intriguing review of illnesses (explicit or implicit) in opera stories and connotations of specific diseases that contemporary audiences would have noted. Tuberculosis, for example, was believed to be caused by mental states and sexual indulgence until its correct infectious source was discovered in 1882. Syphilis is often in disguise, as in *Parsifal*. Discussion covers the pox, cholera, smoking, lesbian and gay elements, and even AIDS, for which no actual operatic specimen was available. Backnotes, expansive index.

393. Cavell, Stanley. *A Pitch of Philosophy: Autobiographical Exercises.* Cambridge, Mass.: Harvard U.P., 1994. xv, 196p. ISBN 0-6746-6980-0. B945 .C273 P58.

Includes a chapter, "Opera and the Lease of Voice," p.129–170, in which the meaning of opera is found in the roles women play and sing. Singing is a metaphor for female finding and losing the voice, so opera exhibits women's place in society. Gender issues are taken up in Mozart, Verdi, Wagner, and Debussy, and it becomes clear that Cavell is talking about text, not music.

394. Sala, Emilio. "Women Crazed by Love: An Aspect of Romantic Opera." Trans. William Ashbrook. *OQ* 10-3 (Spring 1994): 19–41.

Pursues the theme of madness among female characters through operas of the late 18th and 19th centuries, including *Nina* by Dalayrac, *Il pirata, I puritani, Anna Bolena, Lucia di Lammermoor,* and Catalani's *Edmea.*

395. Not used.

Emphasis on Music

396. Dahlhaus, Carl. *Esthetics of Music.* Trans. William W. Austin. New York: Cambridge U.P., 1983. xii, 115p. ISBN 0-521-1235-081. ML3845 .D18.

Originally: *Musikästhetik* (Cologne: Gerig, 1967). A fine review of (mostly German) thought, with imposing perceptions throughout. Interesting critique of Hanslick (#426). On opera specifically there is a short but important chapter (p.64–69). "Opera is a composite work, but not yet on that account a synthesis of all the arts. . . . The components have almost always been out of phase." Trying to get them into synthesis has been "something like an obsession—an *idée fixe*—in the history of opera." In the juncture of music, libretto, and staging matters, the text may play only a slight role. "More decisive than words, in opera, is the visible and palpable situation from which words grow." Novelty in opera may come from "the music as well as the text, scenery, or the relations among the various components." As for the temporal element: A performance is "contained in time," but the score "contains time." A melody is perceived as a totality in "now," though most of it is absent at this instant. We grasp details as part of an expected coherence.

See also next entry.

397. Dahlhaus, Carl. "What Is a Musical Drama?" *COJ* 1-2 (1990): 95–111.

Further thoughts on ideas introduced in #396, positing the value of musical form in the dramatic schema. "The teleological element is not very strong in opera, at least insofar as it consists of a configuration of affects, of extended lyrical elements—of arias, in short." However, "the fact that in opera, especially number opera, the teleological element remains—in comparison with the spoken genre—less prominent than the structural one is not a reason for denying the dramatic character of the form."

398. Levarie, Siegmund, and Ernst Levy. *Musical Morphology: A Discourse and a Dictionary.* Kent, Oh.: Kent State U.P., 1983. x, 344p. ISBN 0-87338-286-2. ML108 .L48.

This profound volume is a collection of stimulating essays that literally explain what music is and how it achieves its unique effects. Opera is dealt with in many of the essays, most cogently in "Opera," p.200–203. It is noted that the dilemmas of opera "can essentially be reduced to the difficulty of reconciling dramatic speed and literary clarity with a musical unfolding of forms. Because these two sets of postulates are incompatible, all operatic solutions have to be based on some sort of compromise." In practice, whatever composers and librettists have claimed and intended, opera became an alternation of literary and musical segments (obvious in the number opera, less so in Wagner). The authors do not assert a superiority of text over music or the opposite, but they observe that in such essential elements as characterization and overall unity of structure, it is the music that controls the events. Musical form (and other devices) may delineate a character, but the literary depiction of that character does not create a musical form. A text may have its own unity of events, but it does not hold that unity unless the musical elements, taking text into account, impose their own structure on the whole. Useful bibliography of some 250 items, expansive index.

399. Langer, Susanne K. *Feeling and Form: A Theory of Art Developed from "Philosophy in a New Key."* New York: Scribner's, 1953. xvi, 431p. BF458 .L28.

Langer's writings on aesthetics are of landmark significance. This book brings her ideas on all the arts into an elegant summary. A seminal belief is that when two or more arts combine in a single work, one of them assumes a primary role and assimilates the others; it bears the meaning for the entire work. For opera, music is the primary art: it "swallows" the text and the spectacle and creates whatever is valuable in the totality. In this respect, composers (except Mozart) have not been helpful with their public statements, and their claims for superiority of text must be disregarded. Music is motivated by text, not subordinated to it. "The *Gesamtkunstwerk* is an impossibility, because a work can exist in only one primary illusion, which every element must serve to create, support, and develop." That is what happened to Wagner's operas in spite of himself: they are music, and "what is left of his non-musical importations that did not undergo a complete change into music, is dross." (How this assimilation takes place is discussed in #418.)

400. Kivy, Peter. *Sound Sentiment: An Essay on the Musical Emotions, Including the Complete Text of "The Corded Shell."* Philadelphia: Temple U.P., 1989. xvi, 286p. ISBN 0-87722-641-5. ML3845 .K595.

Musical expressiveness is real: we actually hear certain emotive qualities in the music (apart from text). Music, like a face, can be expressive of an emotion (or feeling: the terms are equivalent here), and the better it does so, the more enjoyable it is. Emotive description of music is a valid analytic tool. Kivy emphasizes that while music is expressive of emotions, it does not arouse those emotions in the hearer; we respond to the expressiveness, although not with the same emotion that is portrayed (we hear a cry of pain; we feel sympathy, not pain). This is "cognitive speech theory" applied to music. Differing from Langer, Kivy says "music is expressive of individual, specifiable emotions." Put to the hard test of finding examples to demonstrate all this, Kivy has been unconvincing to many readers. For one thing, he is a theologian rather than a philosopher: one who begins with a belief and goes on to prove it true. He has no philosophic doubt that music can be "sad"—indeed much of the book is about sadness in music. How does it express sadness? By weeping figures, falling lines, "restless elements" like diminished triads, chromaticism, and above all by the minor key. These ubiquitous features take him only so far, however, and he has to grant that "a great deal of music bears no recognizable expressive character at all." Is the whole problem "trivial," in philosophic terms? One wonders, reading that "a musical composition can be expressive and bad, inexpressive and good." Numerous insights spark the volume, but there are many quirks to balance them, such as the finding of "brutality" in Beethoven's *Grosse Fuge,* then "vitality" or "energy" in it, and then "awesome angry beauty." [Not in minor, it cannot also be sad.]

A lengthy review of Kivy's ideas on musical representation: Douglas Dempster, "How Does Debussy's Sea Crash? How Can Jimi's Rocket Red Glare? Kivy's Account of Representation in Music," *Journal of Aesthetics and Art Criticism* 52–3 (Fall 1994): 415–428. Dempster is looking at Kivy's earlier book on the topic, *Sound and Semblance* (1984). He finds that despite "troubling counter evidence and vague formulation," Kivy in that book "has pointed us in the right direction."

401. Kivy, Peter. *Osmin's Rage: Philosophical Reflections on Opera, Drama, and Text.* Princeton, N.J.: Princeton U.P., 1988. xii, 303p. ISBN 0-91-07324-4. ML3858 .K53.

An absorbing effort to draw connections between opera in the 18th century and some psychological/philosophical texts of the period, in order to "provide new understanding" of Mozart and Handel. There are also new ideas on opera aesthetics, "new in the sense that they give us some new reasons to think those [previous] beliefs are true." Thoughts of Plato, Aristotle, and Girolamo Mei are applied to the work of the Camerata. Robert Donington's analysis of Monteverdi (#1245) is strongly disputed. Handel, in the da capo aria, represented the notion of obsession—the repetitions are not realistic in terms of the way people speak, but they convey the emotional *idée fixe*. The concept of realism cannot be taken, in opera, as meaning that operatic actions resemble ordinary human behavior or speech. But the da capo aria was replaced when psychological emotion-theory moved from Descartes (hard-wired, finite, fixed emotions) to associationism (fluid, rapidly changing). It was Mozart who replaced it, with the finale-ensemble. Mozart wrote for types, not characters: for sonorities, to be mixed like instruments of the orchestra. There is no use looking for emotional depths, however: "what music can't do, opera can't do." What music can do, and does do in opera, is take over the tensions of the text (which, as referring to the real world, are inherently unsolvable) and resolve them: this is the sense in which music serves the drama.

402. Kivy, Peter. *The Fine Art of Repetition: Essays in the Philosophy of Music.* New York: Cambridge U.P., 1993. x, 373p. ISBN 0-521-43462-9. ML3845 .K583.

Previously published essays, offering a cross section of Kivy's views on such topics as Platonism in music, authentic performance, "How did Mozart do it?," music and emotion, and discussions of Darwin, Kant, and Hanslick.

403. Leibowitz, René. *Les fantōmes de l'opéra. Essais sur le théâtre lyrique.* Paris: Gallimard, 1972. 393p. ML1700 .L43.

The point of opera is the creation of character and situation through purely musical means. Analyzes *Fidelio, Euryanthe, Don Carlos, Pique dame, Tosca, Pelléas et Mélisande,* and works of Monteverdi to demonstrate this. Interesting structural studies. Footnotes, no bibliography or index.

404. Lindenberger, Herbert Samuel. *Opera: The Extravagant Art.* Ithaca, N.Y.: Cornell U.P., 1984. 297p. ISBN 0-8014-1698-1. ML1700 .L56.

An intriguing view of opera, which "occupies a unique position in our culture: a form of high art distinctly more lofty in its modes of expression . . . whose adherents insist on treating it as a historically closed book, with no new chapters to be added." Lindenberger uses contemporary literary theory to illuminate problems about aesthetics, "commerce among genres," and the "fortunes of art in society." It must be said that this ambitious project never materializes, but many insights appear along the way. The libretto is perceived by the audience as a romance, without emotional values, as opposed to the text in a non-musical drama: torture, violence, and suffering are only a "spectacular entertainment." Richard Strauss wrote to Hofmannsthal that perhaps there is no such thing as a "true comic opera," because comic actions are not funny in opera—they represent what is funny. It is not laughter that the comic opera elicits, but "awe at the virtuosity and energy that mark both the process of composition and of performance."

Although most writing on opera centers on a "dramatic principle" and opposes mere musical display, we would not give up "vocal lustre and power" in performance for any dramatic skill or stylish production. No libretto is a predictor of success for the opera made from it. Strauss found the texts to *Die Meistersinger* and *Parsifal* "unspeakably boring." Lindenberger suggests that "the larger theme or dramatic action as a whole" is more important to the composer than the individual words, and all the listener wants is a "a series of connected events" with some plausibility. Indexed.

See also Lindenberger (#81).

405. Cone, Edward T. "The World of Opera and Its Inhabitants." In his *Music: A View from Delft* (#65), 125–138.

How does the world of opera differ from other dramatic worlds? Who lives there and what sort of life do they lead? In opera, singing takes the place of speech. The actors sing, but the characters do not—unless there is an actual song for the character to sing, like "Voi che sapete." Sometimes a song may take both parts, being speech and a song, as in "Un di felice" or "La donna è mobile." To understand opera, one must address such ambiguities. To be "real," songs are heard by others on stage, or form a basis for actions, like the parade after "Non più andrai." The ambiguity represents the conscious and subconscious aspects of the personality. In spoken drama a higher level of speech takes the role of operatic song, as in Shakespeare. "Sympathetic musings" on this fascinating exposition, by Ellen Rosand, appear in her "Operatic Ambiguities and the Power of Music," *COJ* 4-1 (March 1992): 75–80.

406. Katz, Ruth. *Divining the Powers of Music: Aesthetic Theory and the Origins of Opera*. New York: Pendragon, 1986. xi, 224p. ISBN 0-9187-2848-7. ML3858 .K32.

An intriguing application of philosophic issues to the history of opera. Katz doubts the usual reasons ascribed to the origin of opera, asserting the need to consider nonmusical factors. Why did the Camerata find acceptance? Because opera was seen as an expression of the power of music—an area of much speculation in that time of emerging scientific thought. Opera was "an ongoing laboratory" in which to test "the nature and boundaries of musical powers." There is a chapter on "social circles" where such ideas were debated toward the end of the 16th century, and there are interesting discussions of the place that the Camerata and similar groups had in the sociocultural context. Bibliography of about 250 items, name and topic index.

407. Poizat, Michel. *The Angel's Cry: Beyond the Pleasure Principle in Opera*. Trans. Arthur Denner. Ithaca, N.Y.: Cornell U.P., 1962. xiv, 220p. ISBN 0-8014-2388-0. ML1700 .P6513.

Originally *Opéra, ou le cri de l'ange* (Paris: Métailié, 1986). A psychoanalytic explanation of our desire for opera. Our "ecstatic pleasure in seeking to forget or deny . . . [our] fundamental attachment to language" is at the root. Poizat quotes Lacan: "There would be no music if language had not preceded it"; we want to return to the absence of language in our ancient past. [However, a current anthropologic view is that language originated in musical ritual.] An aria represents emotion and high feeling; recitative, a calm pleasure in the music. So an aria is "a cry" and Poizat's opera lover is one who is tortured by it ("I cried and cried"). Thus "the evolution of opera singing in general as a trajectory from speech to cry"—but only in female singing. "Male singing tends to re-emerge as pure speech." This murky philosophy does produce some interesting perspectives on male and female roles, castrati, travesti, and the like. Bibliography of about 150 items, expansive index.

408. Abel, Samuel D. *Opera in the Flesh: Sexuality in Operatic Performance*. Boulder, Colo.: Westview, 1996. xv, 235p. ISBN 0-8133-2900-0. ML1700 .A24.

Responds to Poizat (#407) and Koestenbaum (#390). Abel accepts Poizat's view of *jouissance* (which equates operatic pleasure and sexual pleasure) but wants it to be literal, not metaphoric. Opera, he says, is not simply like sex, it is sex; indeed, the orgasm is the model for describing operatic experience. Like McClary (#391), he is concerned with "excess" and its meaning. Text is not the bearer of these meanings; it is the music and the voice that are the seductive elements. Bibliography of about 200 items, expansive index.

409. Abbate, Carolyn. *"Unsung Voices": Opera and Musical Narrative in the Nine-teenth Century.* Princeton, N.J.: Princeton U.P., 1991. xvi, 288p. ISBN 0-691-09140-4. ML3838 .A2.

Music can be a dramatic narrative or a nonnarrative. The musical voice can "distance us from the sensual matter of what we are hearing." There is a voice act as well as a narrative act. What distinguishes a narrative from any story is that is says "once upon a time." In opera, narrative appears in scenes where a story is told by means of a song, clearly identified as such (cf. Cone, #405). Interesting perspectives on Wagner and Mozart illuminate this theory. Back-notes, bibliography of about 200 items, expansive index.

410. Robinson, Paul A. *Opera and Ideas: From Mozart to Strauss.* New York: Harper & Row, 1988. 279p. ISBN 0-0601-5450-0. ML1720 .R6.

Music, as well as text, does express some distinct ideas. Evidence is supplied for this view, which is hardly unusual but not recently popular. For example, in *Les troyens* there is, at crucial moments, a prominence of the instrumental bass, creating "an impression of forces at work . . . Those forces, I believe, are the impersonal laws of history, which carry the characters toward a destiny they don't fully understand." Further discussion touches on Mozart, Wagner, Strauss, Verdi, and Rossini. Robinson has difficulty locating purely musical idea communication, and nearly all the examples are textual as well. Bibliography, index.

411. Durante, Sergio. "Analysis and Dramaturgy: Reflections towards a Theory of Opera." In *Opera buffa* (#2141), 311–339.

Reviews recent theoretical approaches: Carl Dahlhaus, James Webster, and John Platoff. Asserts that the hierarchical relationships of music and drama are fluid, subject to change even within one set piece. "A musico-dramatic text embraces domains that, although apparently peripheral and often secondary for the music, can occasionally be located at the top of the ideal pyramid of significant elements. This need not imply an overevaluation of certain domains, or endanger the centrality of music in a discourse on opera."

412. Franklin, Peter. *The Idea of Music: Schoenberg and Others.* London: Macmillan, 1985. xv, 188p. ISBN 0-333-40028-3. ML3800 .F83.

The writings of Theodore Adorno are the starting point for essays on Pfitzner, Schoenberg, and Schreker. Adorno fostered the progressive artist, who would eliminate all clichés and destroy even the possibility of form. Twelve-tone technique can do this; it "enchains music by liberating it." Schoenberg is the ideal for Adorno, but only to a point; the 12-tone system itself becomes a form and must be abandoned. Franklin's section on Pfitzner's *Palestrina* is not about the music but about the story and what others said about it. A useful treatment of "Schreker's Decline" (p.139–160) finds in his music "stream of consciousness in the most profound sense." Franklin's language, like Adorno's, is in manifesto idiom. It "relies upon a consideration of ideas about music as much as upon the analytical or musicological study of specific works." Bibliography, index.

XIV. Analysis

413. Abbate, Carolyn, and Roger Parker. "On Analyzing Opera." In *Analyzing Opera* (#416), 1–24.

A valuable review of the problems and approaches to opera analysis. Special attention to macrostructure, unity, and Alfred Lorenz—with writers who followed or despised him. With 51 footnotes to mainstream analytical writing.

414. Dahlhaus, Carl. "Some Models of Unity in Musical Form." Trans. Charlotte Carroll Prather. *Journal of Music Theory* 19 (1975): 2–31.

An indispensable assessment of the place of "form theory" in contemporary thinking. In musical analysis it is now viewed as an optional tool, to be "rejected at any time if it does not prove useful." Schemata are "expedient means for a first conceptual approach to a work." Analysis is being modeled less on architecture than on literary theory (New Criticism), which finds form in an interplay among parts. Dahlhaus reviews the ideas of Ernst Kurth ("dynamics"), Alfred Lorenz ("rhythm in the large"), and Rudolph Réti ("developing variations"), but he is not sympathetic to any "search for a primary constituent which guarantees the unity and inner coherence of a work through its uninterrupted presence." Friedrich Blume's *Fortspinnung* theory looks at the process of joining unrelated independent elements "which become related through their placement/connection with one another."

415. Dahlhaus, Carl. "Zeitstrukturen in der Oper." *Musikforschung* 34–1 (1981): 2–11.

Time in opera differs from time in spoken drama: it is discontinuous, outside of real time—*Darstellungszeit*—(although recitative may resemble real time). In drama it is continuous, but tempo is more variable than in opera, more under the control of the actors. The counterpoint between real time and opera time creates a tension not present in spoken drama, and opera has another dimension of time in the running commentary made by the music (which is in present time). Drama is future-driven action; opera is present driven, focused on feelings of the moment, detached from future and past. Existing in the "absolute present"—*Dargestellten Zeit*—opera is not narrative at all. Elegant elucidations are presented for these ideas.

416. *Analyzing Opera: Verdi and Wagner.* Ed. Carolyn Abbate and Roger Parker. Berkeley: U. of California Press, 1989. ix, 304p. ISBN 0-520-06157-8. MT95 .A59.

Eleven significant papers that grew out of a 1984 conference at Cornell U. They include James A. Hepokoski, "Verdi's Composition of *Otello*: The Act II Quartet"; Joseph Kerman and Thomas S. Grey, "Verdi's Groundswells: Surveying an Operatic Convention"; Anthony Newcomb, "*Ritornello ritornato*: A Variety of Wagnerian Refrain Form"; Patrick McCreless, "Schenker and the Norns"; and these entered separately: Philip Gossett on the genesis of *Ernani* (#1877), Roger Parker on motives in *Aida* (#1868), Martin Chusid on tonality in *Rigoletto* (#1917), David Lawton on tonality in *Aida* (#1867), John Deathridge on the genesis of *Lohengrin* (#2022), Carolyn Abbate on opera as symphony (#2058), and Matthew Brown on Isolde's narrative (#2077). See also #413. Expansive index of names and topics.

417. Webster, James. "Understanding *opera buffa*: Analysis = Interpretation." In *Opera buffa* (#2141), 340–377.

Should be read with his #1288. Webster here takes a more open view toward operatic unity. "About the continuing centrality of analysis to operatic understanding there can be no doubt."

418. Marco, Guy A. "On Key Relations in Opera." *19thCM* 3 (1979): 83–88.

Proposes a path toward a general theory of operatic structure that includes tonal relations and the operating principles of the textual and visual components in the work. Follows Langer (#399): "When two arts are combined, one becomes the patterngiver for both, and it is on the basis of those patterns that the work's value may be judged. In the combination of music and text, the music gives the pattern . . . and takes the credit or blame for the result." But the laws of drama are not thereby set aside; opera "can hold in firm unity, over a time period of considerable magnitude, the diverse systems of norms which constitute dramatic and musical laws." It does so by taking those laws to general levels: approach and retreat, stress, balance, and reconciliation. Tonality is able to reflect such elements; the article endeavors to show how it does so.

XV. Critics and Criticism

General Works

419. Goldschmidt, Hugo. *Die Musikästhetik des 18. Jahrhundert und ihre Beziehung zu seinen Kunstschaffen.* Zurich: Rascher, 1915. 461p. Reprint, Hildesheim: Olms, 1968. ML3845 .G65.

   A narrative and analytic account of 18th-century criticism, based on theoretical writings. Opera is discussed extensively (p.263–450). Indexed.

420. Oliver, Alfred Richard. *The Encylopedists as Critics of Music.* New York: Columbia U.P., 1947. viii, 227p. ML1727 .O4.

   The role of the encyclopedists in the opera reform movement (they disagreed with Rameau, agreed with Gluck) and their critical philosophy in general. Music articles in the *Encyclopédie* are listed, along with sources cited in them. Also covers French music criticism before the encyclopedists and their later influence on European criticism. Bibliography of about 250 entries, general index.

421. Cowart, Georgia. *Origins of Modern Musical Criticism: French and Italian Music, 1600–1750.* Studies in Musicology, 38. Ann Arbor, Mich.: UMI Research, 1981. xi, 215p. ISBN 0-83571-166-8. ML3916 .C7.

   Based on the author's Ph.D. dissertation, Rutgers U., 1980. Traces the emergence of systematic music criticism, from the 17th-century disputes between so-called ancients and moderns to the Quarrel of the Buffoons. British and German contributions are noted, and the Lully-Rameau controversy is well covered. Footnotes, bibliography, index.

422. Kirchmeyer, Helmut. *Situatiionsgeschichte der Musik-kritik und des musikalischen Pressewesens in Deutschland.* Regensburg: Bosse, 1968–1972. 4v. ISBN 3-7649-2019-X. ML3915 .K57.

   Considers methods and principles of musical criticism and studies applications in 18th- and 19th-century Germany. The fourth volume deals with Wagner criticism. Bio-bibliography of critics, long extracts from contemporary newspaper and journal critiques, name index and list of source journals.

423. Haskell, Harry, ed. *The Attentive Listener: Three Centuries of Music Criticism*. Princeton, N.J.: Princeton U.P., 1996. xvii, 398p. ISBN 0-691-02641-6. ML55 .A88.

An anthology of critical writings from about 1700 to the present, taken from daily newspapers and periodicals. Among the critics represented are Addison, Ayrton, Chorley, Davison, Fétis, Castil-Blaze, Bellaigue, Hanslick, Korngold, Henderson, and Downes. Everything is translated into English. Bibliography, index.

424. Arundell, Dennis. *The Critic at the Opera*. London: Ernest Bonn, 1957. 424p. ML1731 .A74.

A collection of comments by critics from the 16th to the 20th century, with observations and notes. Bibliography of about 120 entries, in chronological order. Expansive index of names, titles, and topics; lists of theaters, works, singers, composers, and conductors.

Individual Critics

425. Aldrich, Richard. *Musical Discourse from the "New York Times."* New York: Oxford U.P., 1928. 305p. ML60 .A5.

The author was music editor of the *Times* from 1902 to 1923. He offers sophisticated comments on musical events, including opera; with interesting pieces on Jenny Lind and Adelina Patti.

426. Hanslick, Eduard. *Music Criticisms, 1846–99.* Trans. and ed. Henry Pleasants. Baltimore: Penguin, 1950. 313p. ML60 .H2492.

One of the most famous writers of musical criticism, Hanslick wrote for the Vienna *Presse* and *Neue freie Presse*. His novel concept that the value of music comes from its pure, nonreferential character (independent of program or dramatic text) is significant in the history of aesthetics. His views were applied harshly, however, and Wagner (a "referentialist") was among those to bear his scorn. Wagner turned him into Beckmesser. Most of the essays in this collection are about Wagner, but there are also opinions of Patti, Lilli Lehmann, *Otello,* and *Hansel und Gretel.*

427. Henderson, William James. *The Art of Singing.* New York: Dial, 1937. xvii, 509p. Reprint, Freeport, N.Y.: Books for Libraries, 1968. MT820 .H496 A8.

Includes *The Art of the Singer* (1906) and articles from the *New York Sun.* Henderson (1855–1937) was critic for the *Sun* and for the *New York Times*; his reviews of opera are of special value. Index of names and titles.

428. Hogarth, George. *Memoirs of the Opera in Italy, France, Germany and England.* 2nd ed. London: Richard Bentley, 1851. 2v. Reprint, New York: Da Capo, 1972. ISBN 0-306-70256-8. ML1700 .H72.

First edition, 1838: *Memoirs of the Musical Drama.* Hogarth (1783–1870) was critic for the London *Morning Chronicle* and *Daily News.* This collection includes important commentaries on Gluck and Piccinni, Mozart, *The Beggar's Opera,* and Jommelli, plus critiques on all the leading singers of the day. Engraved portraits, no index.

429. Klein, Hermann. *Thirty Years of Musical Life in London, 1870–1900*. New York: Century, 1903. xvii, 483p. ML285.8 .L8 K6.

Klein (1856–1934) wrote for the London *Sunday Times*. This collection has notes, portraits, and an excellent expansive index of names. There are essays of special interest on the de Reszkes, Patti, Sembrich, Lucca, Bispham, Melba (her debut), Schumann-Heink, Alvary, and Nordica.

430. Lonchampt, Jacques. *L'opéra d'aujourd'hui, journal de musique*. Paris: Éditions du Seuil, 1970. 301p. ML60 .L847.

Articles from *Le monde*, 1960–1970, covering performances in Paris and elsewhere in Europe. Useful for reviews of less common operas, including works of Honegger, Tomasi, Kosma, Landowski, Semenoff, etc.

431. Marcello, Benedetto. *Il teatro all moda*. Venice: Borghi de Belisania per A. Licante, ca. 1720.

A satirical and entertaining essay that sharply criticizes operatic practice of the time. Frequently translated. The most useful English rendition is "*Il teatro alla moda*," trans. Reinhard G. Pauly, *MQ* 34 (1948): 371–403; 35 (1949): 85–105, with valuable footnotes and helpful explanations. The same author has also written an important study: "Benedetto Marcello's Satire on Early 18th Century Opera," *MQ* 34 (1948): 222–233, which gives interesting material on stage devices and on other operatic satires of the period.

432. Porter, Andrew. *Music of Three More Seasons, 1977–1980*. New York: Knopf, 1981. 613p. ISBN 0-3945-1813-6. ML200.8 .N52 P9.

Interesting reviews by an English critic who wrote for the *New Yorker* magazine for several seasons of opera; these are all extracts from the magazine. Two earlier collections, *A Musical Season, 1972–1973* (1974), and *Music of Three Seasons, 1974–1977* (1978), are also of value.

433. Schmidgall, Gary. "Arcibrava, GBS!" *OQ* 14-4 (Summer 1998): 5–13.

A pleasing survey of reviews by George Bernard Shaw, "one of music history's wittiest, most exuberant and charmingly outrageous critics," who wrote for several London journals over a seven-year period. For all the originals, there is *Shaw's Music: The Complete Musical Criticism in Three Volumes*, ed. Dan H. Laurence (London: The Bodley Head, 1981).

Other critical collections are found under individual cities in Chapter XVIII.

XVI. Opera Recordings and Discography

This section is a guide to useful works of reference about opera recordings in audio and video formats.

434. *Encyclopedia of Recorded Sound in the United States*. Ed. Guy A. Marco; contributing ed. Frank Andrews. New York: Garland, 1993. xlix, 910p. ISBN 0-8240-4782-6. ML102 .S67 E5.

   The first extensive reference work to cover a wide range of topics in the area of recorded sound: history, terminology, technology, labels, performers, industry executives, and related subjects; with contributions by 32 specialists. "Opera Recordings," by Guy A. Marco and William Ashbrook (p.484–491) is a historical survey of recordings of single arias or numbers and of complete sets. There are separate articles on singers and conductors that identify their principal recordings and cite discographies about them. Bibliography of about 1,500 entries (full data); expansive index of names, firms, topics, and categories of performers.

435. *Rigler and Deutsch Record Index*. Washington: Association for Recorded Sound Collections, 1981–1983. 977 microfiches. Online through RLIN.

   An index to holdings of 78rpm discs in the New York Public Library, Yale U., Syracuse U., Stanford U., and the Library of Congress. Some 615,000 recordings are listed. The index offers access by composer, title, performer, and label. Details in *Duckles* 10.69.

436. Moses, Julian Morton. *Collectors' Guide to American Recordings, 1895–1925*. New York: American Record Collectors Exchange, 1949. 199p. Reprint, New York: Dover, 1977. ML156.2 .M67.

   Brief biographical information on about 225 performers, with more than 7,000 acoustic recordings made by them. Serial or matrix numbers, index by opera and instruments.

437. Blyth, Alan. *Opera on CD: The Essential Guide to the Best CD Recordings of 100 Operas*. 3rd ed. London: Kyle Cathie, 1994. viii, 211p. ISBN 1-8562-6139-5. ML156.4 .O6 B6.

First edition, 1992. Continues Blyth's critical listing of LP records: *Opera on Record* (London: Hutchinson, 1979–1984; 3v.). Despite the glib, journalistic style and the one-liners that sum up total performances, it is a useful presentation of the recorded repertoire, selecting preferred performances and "alternatives."

438. Bontinck-Küffel, Irmgard. *Opern auf Schallplatten, 1900–1962: Ein historische Katalog vollständiger oder nahezu vollständiger Aufnahmen . . .* Vienna: Universal, 1974. xv, 185p. ISBN 0-7024-0014-1. ML156.4 .O46 O61.

A fine survey of complete (or nearly complete) recordings of about 500 operas, with casts and full bibliographical detail. In composer order, without index.

439. Almquist, Sharon G. *Opera Mediagraphy: Video Recordings and Motion Pictures.* Music Reference Collection, 40. Westport, Conn.: Greenwood, 1993. xviii, 269p. ISBN 0-313-28490-3. ML158.6 .O6 O64.

A useful guide to videocassettes, motion pictures, or filmed stage versions of 156 operas. For each entry the cast is given, with timing, distributor, and citations to reviews. Indexes to singers, conductors, composers, and opera companies.

440. Almquist, Sharon G. *Opera Singers in Recital, Concert, and Feature Film: A Mediagraphy.* Music Reference Collection, 73. Westport, Conn.: Greenwood, 1999. xiv, 376p. ISBN 0-313-29592-1. ML158.4 .A46.

In this companion volume to the preceding item, Almquist lists 648 items under the names of singers. Material includes videocassettes, laser discs, feature films, and 16mm educational films. Each entry has a full description with contents and review citations. Indexes for conductors and pianists involved, as well as directors and producers. List of distributors.

441. Wlaschin, Ken. *Opera on Screen: A Guide to One Hundred Years of Films and Videos Featuring Operas, Opera Singers, and Operettas.* Los Angeles: Beachwood Press, 1997. viii, 628p. ISBN 1-888-32700-6. No call number in Library of Congress record.

Also available on CD-ROM. A useful list of materials in subject arrangement, covering such topics as castrati, divas, imaginary operas, operas based on movies, silent films of opera, and puppet opera. Entries for individual artists. Lists of television operas and scenes. Reviewers have noted numerous errors and omissions.

442. Scott, Michael. *The Record of Singing.* London: Duckworth, 1977. 2v. Reprint, Boston: Northeastern U.P., 1993. ISBN 0-684-15528-1. ML1460 .S34.

A knowledgeable account of singers who recorded in the acoustic period (to 1925), with photos. Recordings are mentioned, without discographical data. Name index.

443. Gruber, Paul. *The Metropolitan Opera Guide to Recorded Opera.* New York: Norton, for the Metropolitan Opera Guild, 1993. xv, 782p. ISBN 0-393-03444-5. ML156.4 .O46 M5.

A compilation of critical comments about "every complete recording made of 150 operas" by 71 composers. Although a few early sets were overlooked, this is the most thorough list of its kind. The 20 reviewers (British and American) quoted offer appraisals that range from sensible to bizarre, in the curious vocabulary of journalistic opera criticism. Expansive index of all the performers. The same author and publisher also issued *The Metropolitan Opera Guide to Opera on Video* (1997; xvi, 483p. ISBN 0-393-3045-366. ML158.6 .O6), which describes some 300 videos of about 150 operas, aiming for complete coverage of American releases. For each item the cast, conductor, and director are identified, and an evaluation is given. Index to all performers.

444. Croissant, Charles. *Opera Performances in Video Format: A Checklist of Commercially Released Recordings.* MLA Index and Bibliography Series, 26. Canton, Mass.: Music Library Association, 1991. xv, 121p. ISBN 0-9149-5443-1. ML1700 .C8.

Covers U.S. releases of videocassettes and laser discs of about 250 works. Casts are listed, with dates and locations of the recordings and citations to reviews. Indexes of titles, performers, and sites.

445. *Opera on Screen: Ein Projekt in Auftrag des Österreichischen Bundesministeriums für Wissenschaft und Forschung.* Vienna: IMZ, [1995?]. No ISBN. ML128 .O4 O647.

A composer list of some 3,200 entries for operas, operettas, and musicals on film and video. Bibliographic data are given for each title, with duration, cast, and date. Title and chronological indexes add to the value of this very useful compilation.

See also *NGDO* 2, 194–200: "Film," by Richard Evidon; and *Cinema et opéra*, a special issue of *ASO* 98 (1987).

XVII. Composers and Their Operas

The works cited in this chapter are concerned with specific operas or with several operas by one composer. By grouping them under composers' names, we can compare various approaches to each composer's output. In many instances the operas are discussed within a biographical context, so a number of biographies will be found; however, biographies that do not include substantial attention to operatic writing are in general omitted.

For those composers with extensive literature, there is a subdivision of the material as follows:

1. Editions
2. Thematic catalogues and worklists
3. Bibliographies and guides to resources
4. Dictionaries
5. Conferences
6. Collections of essays
7. Periodicals
8. Letters and documents
9. Prose works
10. Biographies
11. Special studies
12. Operas in general
    a. Production and reception
    b. Analysis
13. Individual works

These headings are used and modified or expanded as needed.

Two expressions are used frequently in the annotations to give the reader a tangible impression of the sort of approach taken by the authors. By far the most common approach to individual operas is the "program note." This term refers to the kind of general, nontechnical description that is usually found in the concert or opera program booklet: a plot synopsis, with background facts on the circumstances of the composer at work ("genesis"), some comments on the libretto vis-à-vis the original literary work, and perhaps some information about the premiere with its critical reception. If there is much said about later performances, the term is "performance history." Although a program note may be lengthy (even a whole book), it is accessible to nonspecialist readers; it is not footnoted and does not present original material.

In contrast to the program note, there is "analysis," which describes a work intensively with regard to its form, structure, harmonic and melodic elements, style, and technique. The analyst aims at specialized readers and endeavors to provide an original viewpoint that to some extent "explains" a work. Documentation of previous analyses (footnotes, bibliography) is a typical feature. Analysis may have diverse starting points or theoretical premises; indeed, specialists in analysis may be gathered under various headings or "schools," just as literary critics may be identified with distinctive labels.

Length of presentation does not distinguish a program note from an analysis, nor does the author's announced intention. Finally, it should be stressed that neither mode is superior sui generis; each may serve its purpose well or poorly, and both purposes are worthy. In scholarly writing, however, there is a clear trend away from program notes toward some kind of analysis, so a large proportion of the recent writing cited here will represent analytic approaches.

From the immense literature on major composers, only a handful of titles could be included. These are, for the most part, recent scholarly works, or "classic" studies, or works with strong bibliographic orientations (those that guide the reader to other writings). For lesser-known composers it has been necessary to select from what is available, but if a composer or opera is more thoroughly treated in *NGDO* or another encyclopedic source than in any monograph or journal articles, no entries appear.

Preference has been given to writing in English, French, German, Italian, and Spanish, but material in other languages is included as required by the circumstances.

Antonio Maria Abbatini (1609 [or 1610]–1677 [or 1679])

446. Murata, Margaret. *Operas for the Papal Court, 1631–1668.* Ann Arbor, Mich.: UMI Research, 1981. x, 474p. ISBN 1-8357-1122-6. ML1733.8 .R6 M97.

    Based on the author's dissertation (U. of Chicago, 1975). Attention is focused on Giulio Rospigliosi (see #274 and #275). Two of his texts were set by Abbatini: *Dal male il bene* (1654; with Marazzoli) and *La comica del cielo* (1668); both are analyzed from historical and stylistic viewpoints. Appendix of sources: manuscripts, library locations, editions, anthologies. Expansive index of names, titles, and topics; first-line index to arias. Bibliography of about 250 entries.

Adolphe Adam (1803–1856)

There is no recent writing of substance on Adam's operas. Plots, brief reports, and impressions are listed in:

447. Studwell, William E. *Adolphe Adam and Léo Delibes: A Guide to Research.* Garland Composer Resource Manuals, 5. New York: Garland, 1987. x, 248p. ISBN 0-8240-9011-X. ML134 .A34 S8.

    A thorough, annotated bibliography of writings on both composers. Adam's operas have 88 entries, but most are story summaries in books of opera plots. One older work is still useful:

448. Pougin, Arthur. *Adolphe Adam: Sa vie, sa carrière, ses memoires artistiques.* Paris: Charpentier, 1877. 370p. ML410 .A19 P8.

A documented biography, with worklist and descriptions of the compositions. Examples of Adam's work as a critic are included. No bibliography or index.

Agostino Agazzari (1578–ca.1640)

449. Johnson, Margaret F. "Aggazari's *Eumelio, a dramma pastorale.*" *MQ* 57-3 (July 1971): 491–505.

Although *Eumelio* (1606) was among the earliest Roman operas, it has received scant attention. It does have some interesting features, including "snatches of humor" and "well-developed musical and harmonic structures." Tonal centers underline dramatic action. Genesis and plot are given, with the suggestion that the opera deserves more study.

See also Rose (#343).

Isaac Albéniz (1860–1909)

450. Clark, Walter Aaron. *Isaac Albéniz: A Guide to Research.* Garland Composer Resource Manuals, 45. New York: Garland, 1998. xiii, 256p. ISBN 0-8153-2095-7. ML134 .A45 C53.

Citations to brief writings and reviews of the operas. The major account of the most successful stage work is Clark's own dissertation: "Spanish Music with a Universal Accent: Isaac Albéniz's Opera *Pepita Jiménez*" (U. of California, Los Angeles, 1992). It includes a detailed genesis study, musical analysis, and performance history and considers the importance of the work in the development of Spanish national opera. A catalogue of stage works is in an appendix. Indexed. A section on the opera is also found in:

451. Clark, Walter Aaron. *Isaac Albéniz: Portrait of a Romantic.* Oxford: Clarendon Press, 1998. xviii, 321p. ISBN 0-19-811636-X. ML410 .A33 C6.

A useful biography, with worklist and discussion of the compositions. *Pepita Jiménez* (1896) is well described (genesis, reception, analysis). There is also a thorough treatment of the unfinished trilogy on King Arthur, of which only *Merlin* (1886) was completed. Notes, strong bibliography of some 250 entries, expansive index.

Eugène D'Albert (1864–1932)

452. Pangels, Charlotte. *Eugen d'Albert: Wunderpianist und Komponist: Eine Biographie.* Zurich: Atlantis, 1981. 464p. ISBN 3-7611-0595-9. ML410 .A333 P3.

A life and works, with genesis of the operas, along with program notes and reception. Backnotes, worklist, name index, no bibliography.

453. Williamson, John. "Eugen d'Albert: Wagner and Verismo." *MR* 45 (1984): 26–46.

Wagnerian and Puccinian influences on *Tiefland* and *Liebesketten*. Analysis shows the treatment of motifs. The composer's problem, says Williamson, was that he was caught between styles.

Tomaso Albinoni (1671–1751)

454. Talbot, Michael. *Tomaso Albinoni: The Venetian Composer and His World.*
New York: Oxford U.P., 1990. viii, 308p. ISBN 0-19-315245-2. ML410
.A315 T37.

A strong biography, with 50 pages on the operas and serenatas. Libretti, program notes, and some technical observations. Only 6 of 81 operas survive
complete. Interesting perspectives on the "opera system" of the day, heavy
with financial and administrative intricacies. Worklist, modern editions, footnotes, brief bibliography, expansive index.

455. *Pimpinone: Intermezzi comici musicali* (1708), by Tomaso Albinoni, is v.43 of
RMBE. It is edited by Michael Talbot, who provides an extensive commentary,
including a catalogue of productions and an inventory of extant sources.

456. Talbot, Michael. "Tomaso Albinoni's *Pimpinone* and the Comic Intermezzo."
In *"Con che soavità"* (#2461), 229–248.

Talbot "draws heavily" on his preface to the *RMBE* edition but focuses here
on a 1709 Naples production, bringing out differences between Venetian and
Neapolitan practice. The work is "one of the few sets of comic intermezzi from
the first decade of the 18th century for which the music survives" and both the
composer and librettist (Pietro Pariati) are known. Footnotes identify the literature on the comic intermezzo.

Franco Alfano (1875–1954)

457. Gatti, Guido Maria. "Franco Alfano." *MQ* 9 (1923): 556–577.

An adulatory account written before Alfano's completion of *Turandot,* thus
able to focus on his own opera, *Risurrezione,* a sensation at its premiere
(1904). Also discussion of *Ombra di Don Giovanni* (1914) and *La leggenda di
Sakùntala* (1921).

Johann André (1741–1799)

In *GO: Belmont und Constanze,* v.6, and *Der Töpfer,* v.9.

Pasquale Anfossi (1727–1797)

458. Mattern, Volker. *"La finta giardiniera": Ein Vergleich der Vertonungen von
Pasquale Anfossi und Wolfgang Amadeus Mozart.* Laaber: Laaber, 1989.
551p. ISBN 3-8900-7111-2. MT95 .M278.

Compares the two operas, considering libretti, sources, story, premieres, characters and their music. Number-by-number analysis. Bibliography; no index.
Originally the author's Ph.D. dissertation, U. of Heidelberg, 1984.

459. Angermüller, Rudoph. "Die wiener Fassung von Pasquale Anfossis *Il curioso
indiscreto.*" In *I vicini di Mozart* (#90), v.1, 35–98.

Genesis, with attention to the question of libretto authorship: the usual attribution to Bertati is not supported by contemporary documents, and Giuseppe
Petrosellini is more likely. Reception history and much text with comments.

Mozart wrote two arias (KV 418 and KV 419) for soprano Aloisa Lange and a rondeau (KV 420) for Valentin Adamberger; these were heard in the production of *Il curioso* in Vienna, 30 June 1783.

George Antheil (1900–1959)

460. Whitesitt, Linda. *The Life and Music of George Antheil, 1900–1959.* Studies in Musicology, 70. Ann Arbor, Mich.: UMI Research, 1983. xxi, 351p. ISBN 0-8537-1462-4. ML410 .A638.

Avant-gardist Antheil was popular in Europe in the 1920s and from 1936 as a film composer in Hollywood. His opera *Transatlantic* (1930) is examined here: genesis, production, and reception, with commentary. Musical examples, index.

Dominick Argento (1927–)

461. Saya, Virginia Cotta. "The Current Climate for American Musical Eclecticism as Reflected in the Operas of Dominick Argento." Ph.D. diss., U. of Cincinnati, 1989. 266p.

Daniel François Esprit Auber (1782–1871)

Gustave is in *ERO,* v.31, and *La muette de Portici* is in *ERO,* v.30.

462. Pendle, Karin. *Eugène Scribe and French Opera of the Nineteenth Century.* Ann Arbor, Mich.: UMI Research, 1977. vi, 624p. ISBN 0-8357-1004-1. ML1727 .P398.

Librettist Scribe (see #277) wrote the texts for many composers, among them Auber. This book, based on the author's dissertation (U. of Illinois, 1970), has much detail on Auber's work, with special attention to *La muette de Portici* (1828). Extensive backnotes, bibliography of about 300 entries, expansive index of names, titles, and topics. An article drawn from this material, with the same title as the book, appeared in *MQ* 57-4 (October 1971): 535–561.

463. Schneider, Herbert. *Chronologisch-thematisches Verzeichnis sämtlicher Werke von Daniel François Esprit Auber.* Musikwissenschaftliche Publikationen, 1. Hildesheim: Olms, 1994. 2v. ML134 .A78 S36.

Not seen. Described in *Duckles* 6.16 as a classified thematic catalogue, generously supplied with publication and performance details of the dramatic works.

464. Schneider, Herbert. "Das Finale in den frühen *opéra-comiques* von D. F. E. Auber." In *Grétry et l'Europe* (#927), 167–190.

The structure of the finale differed, in the 18th century, between French *vaudeville* and operas of Germany and Italy. In the French style, "action and passions occupy the scene in turns" with no stops for recitatives. This can be seen in works of Leseur, Méhul, Cherubini, Berton, and Dalayrac, and in works not in French by Rossini and Mozart. Auber's finale style culminated in *Fra diavolo;* he gave growing importance to the act 3 finale. Measure-tabulations and five pages of musical examples.

465. Casini, Claudio. "Tre *Manon*." *Chigiana*, n.s., 8 (1972): 171–217.

Compares the settings by Auber, Massenet, and Puccini, concentrating on the first two. Cites the Wagnerian elements in Puccini's version.

466. Longyear, Rey Morgan. "D. F. E. Auber: A Chapter in the History of the *Opéra-comique*, 1800–1878." Ph.D. diss., Cornell U., 1957. 439p.

467. Longyear, Rey Morgan. "*La muette de Portici.*" MQ 19 (1958): 37–46.

Historical background for the story, plot and program notes, reception.

See also Pendle (#2299).

Jacques Auber (1689–1753)

La reine des Péris is in *FO, v.35.*

Pietro Auletta (1698–1771)

468. Walker, Frank. "*Orazio*: The History of a Pasticcio." MQ 38 (1952): 369–383. (Reprinted in *GL*, v.11.)

Disposes of earlier accounts of the performance history and establishes its premiere at Naples, 1737. It was revived anonymously in Florence in 1740 and in 1742, then in Venice in 1743 with a misattribution to Pergolesi. Further revivals and variants—which preserved little of the Auletta original—are scrupulously traced and compared. Walker concludes that "in the earlier part of the 18th century after an *opera buffa* had been in circulation for a few years nobody was at all sure whose it was, and only a fraction of the original music was left."

Johann Christian Bach (1735–1782)

469. *Johann Christian Bach, 1735–1782. The Collected Works.* Ed. Ernest Warburton. New York: Garland, 1989–1990. ISBN 0-8240-6050-4 (v.1; then consecutively). 48v. M3 .B119.

Facsimiles of 18th-century sources and new manuscript scores based on the best-available sources, without extensive critical comments. Informative introductions consider sources, genesis, and approach to textual problems. The final volume is a new thematic catalogue. These are the volumes with operatic material: v.1, *Artaterse;* v.2, *Catone in Utica;* v.3, *Alessandro nell'Indie;* v.4, *Orione;* v.5, *Adriano in Siria;* v.6, *Carattaco;* v.7, *Temistocle;* v.8, *Lucio Silla;* v.9, *La clemenza di Scipione;* v.10, *Amadis de Gaule,* and Gluck's *Orfeo* arranged by J. C. Bach; v.12, Single arias and overtures; v.14, *Endimione;* v.15, *Amor vincitore;* v.16, *Gioas, re di Giuda;* v.43–47, libretti.

470. Downes, Edward O. D. "The Operas of Johann Christian Bach as a Reflection of the Dominant Trends in *opera seria,* 1750–1780." Ph.D. diss., Harvard U., 1958. 1,145p.

471. Terry, Charles Sanford. *Johann Christian Bach.* 2nd ed. Oxford: Oxford U.P., 1967. lv, 373p. Reprint, with new foreword by H. C. Robbins Landon, Westport, Conn.: Greenwood, 1980.

First edition, 1929. A thorough examination of the compositions, along with a biographical account. For the operas: genesis, program notes, reception. Thematic catalogue, p. 193–361, and indexes of persons, places, and titles.

472. Warburton, Ernest. "A Study of Johann Christian Bach's Operas." Ph.D. diss., U. of Oxford, 1969.

Michael William Balfe (1808–1870)

473. Biddlecombe, George. *English Opera from 1834 to 1864, with Particular Reference to the Works of Michael Balfe.* Outstanding Dissertations in Music from British Universities. New York: Garland, 1994. xiii, 351p. ISBN 0-8153-1436-1. ML1731.4 .B5.

A revision of the author's Ph.D. dissertation, U. of London, 1990. Chapters 2 and 3 present a useful survey of the English 19th-century libretto. Then there are historic and analytic chapters on the operas of Balfe, William Vincent Wallace, Julius Benedict, and George Macfarren. Indexed.

Samuel Barber (1910–1981)

474. Hennessee, Don A. *Samuel Barber: A Bio-Bibliography.* Bio-Bibliographies in Music, 3. Westport, Conn.: Greenwood, 1985. 404p. ISBN 0-313-24026-4. ML134 .B175 H4.

A biographical section, then a worklist and list of writings about the composer. There are about 150 entries, mostly brief notices, on the operas. Name index.

475. Heyman, Barbara B. *Samuel Barber: The Composer and His Music.* New York: Oxford U.P., 1992. xviii, 586p. ISBN 0-19-506650-2. ML410 .B23 H5.

A valuable biographical narrative, enriched by Heyman's comments, plus perceptive observations on many of the compositions, with musical examples from them. *Antony and Cleopatra,* which was written for the opening of the new Metropolitan Opera House (1966), was a failure, not performed again until the 1991–1992 season in Chicago. Barber's views on the matter are given, along with a genesis and production account. *Vanessa* (1958) fared better; it is well covered here in 25 pages. Also a brief treatment of *A Hand of Bridge* (1959). Worklist, backnotes, index.

Francisco Asenjo Barbieri (1823–1894)

476. Casares, Emilio. *Francisco Asenjo Barbieri.* Madrid: Instituto Completense de Ciencias Musicales, 1994. 2v. ISBN 84-8048-065-3, 84-8048-80661. ML410 .B259 C373.

A well-documented life and works, bringing out Barbieri's dramatic concepts and structural designs. His most renowned works were *Jugar con fuego* (1851) and *Pan y toros* (1864). The composer's writings are reprinted, including his important *Istoria de la zarzuela* and *Crónica y memorias del teatro lírico español, 1829–63.* Worklist, good bibliography of about 150 items, indexes.

Béla Bartók (1881–1945)

Bartók's only opera was *A kékszakállu herceg vára* (1918), usually cited as *Duke Bluebeard's Castle* or simply *Bluebeard's Castle*. It is in *ASO* 149/150 (1992) and *ENOG* 44 (1991).

477. Antokoletz, Elliott. *Béla Bartók: A Guide to Research*. 2nd ed. Garland Composer Resource Manuals, 40. New York: Garland, 1997. xxxvii, 489p. ISBN 0-8153-2088-4. ML134 .B18 A7.

First edition, 1988. Consists of 1,200 numbered entries for writings by and about the composer, thoroughly annotated and indexed. About 50 items relate to *Bluebeard's Castle*.

478. Antokoletz, Elliott. "Bartók's *Bluebeard*: The Sources of Its Modernism." *College Music Symposium* 30–1 (Spring 1990): 75–95.

Historical sources of the opera, genesis, reception, and performance history. Detailed harmonic and structural analysis. Demonstrates how the work reflects the symbolism that had arisen in late-19th-century literature.

479. Heath, Mary Joanne Renner. "A Comparative Analysis of Dukas' *Ariane et Barbe-bleu* and Bartók's *Duke Bluebeard's Castle*." Ph.D. diss., Eastman School of Music, 1988. 219p.

480. Kroó, György. "*Duke Bluebeard's Castle*." *Studia musicologica* 1 (1961): 251–340.

A detailed account of all aspects of the opera: genesis, influences, and technical analysis.

481. Leafstedt, Carl. "Music and Drama in Béla Bartók's *Duke Bluebeard's Castle*." Ph.D. diss., Harvard U., 1994. 345p.

A revision of this dissertation has been announced for publication in 2000 by Oxford University Press.

482. Leafstedt, Carl. "Pelléas Revealed: The Original Ending of Bartók's Opera *Duke Bluebeard's Castle*." In *Bartók Perspectives,* ed. Elliott Antokoletz, et al. New York: Oxford U.P., projected for 2000.

Considers the revisions made by the composer after the premiere, especially in the concluding scene. The influence of Debussy, apparent in the original, was obscured in the alterations.

483. Leafstedt, Carl. "Bluebeard as Theater: The Influence of Maeterlinck and Hebbel on Balázs's Bluebeard Drama." In *Bartók and His World*, ed. Peter Laki, 119–148 (Princeton, N.J.: Princeton U.P., 1995. ISBN 0-691-00633-4. ML410 .B26 B272).

Examines the sources for the libretto by Béla Balázs, including folk and Oriental material. Symbolist Maurice Maeterlinck and philosopher Friedrich Hebbel were influential. A comparison of Maeterlinck's *Ariane* with *Bluebeard* is offered, and Hebbel's theories of drama are discussed.

484. Veress, Sándor. "*Bluebeard's Castle.*" *Tempo* 13 (1949): 32–38.

A psychological study of the characters, as demonstrated in the music; with micro- and macrostructural analysis.

See also McClary (#391).

Andrew Barton

The Disappointment is in *RRAM,* v.3. It is the earliest known American opera (1767), but there is no evidence that it was staged. Barton is a pseudonym; the work has been attributed to Thomas Forrest and also to John Leacock.

Jack Beeson (1925–)

485. Beeson, Jack. "The Autobiography of Lizzie Borden." *OQ* 4-1 (1986–1987): 15–42.

An interesting gathering of letters that passed between Beeson and librettist Richard Plant, in 1954–1963, as they developed the opera *Lizzie Borden*.

Ludwig Van Beethoven (1770–1827)

Editions

486. *Ludwig van Beethoven Werke*. Ed. Joseph Schmidt-Görg et al. Bonn: Beethoven Archiv, 1961–. M3 .B41 H5.

In progress; 28 volumes issued through 1999. *Fidelio* not yet published.

Thematic Catalogues and Worklists

487. Kinsky, Georg, and Hans Halm. *Das Werk Beethovens: Thematisch-bibliographisches Verzeichnis seiner sämtlichen vollendeten Kompositionen.* Munich: Henle, 1955. xxii, 808p. ML134 .B4 K56.

The standard worklist, generally used to identify Beethoven's compositions (with K numbers). Each entry has a thematic incipit and extensive information about the work and its sources, along with bibliographic references. Updated by:

488. Dorfmüller, Kurt. *Beiträge zur Beethoven-Bibliographie: Studien und Materialien zum Werkverzeichnis von Kinsky-Halm.* Munich: Henle, 1978. 452p. ISBN3-8732-8028-0. ML134 .B4 B42.

Bibliographies and Guides to Resources

489. *Beethoven Bibliography Database*. San Jose: San Jose State U., Ira F. Brilliant Center for Beethoven Studies.

An electronic file accessible through <www.sjsu.edu/music/beethoven>. As of 1998 consisted of about 7,000 entries; to be completed in the year 2004 with about 23,000 entries. A user's guide is available from the center.

Periodicals

490. *Beethoven Jahrbuch*, 1–, 1953–. Bonn: Beethoven Haus, 1953–. ML410 .B42 B763.

Continues *Neues Beethoven Jahrbuch* (1924–1942).

491. *Beethoven Forum*, 1–, 1992–. Lincoln: U. of Nebraska Press, 1–, 1992–. Irregular. ISSN 1059–5031. ML410 .B42 B416.

V.5, 1996, has miscellaneous material on *Fidelio*. One item is at #502.

Letters and Documents

492. *The Letters of Beethoven*. Ed. and trans. Emily Anderson. London: Macmillan, 1961. 3v. ML410 .B4 A217.

Described by Solomon (#494) as "a model of elegant translation and succinct annotation," this is a well-documented text with perceptive commentary. Index of works and list of the letters.

493. Johnson, Douglas, Robert S. Winter, and Alan Tyson. *The Beethoven Sketchbooks: History, Reconstruction, Inventory*. California Studies in 19th-Century Music, 4. Berkeley and Los Angeles: U. of California Press; New York: Oxford U.P., 1985. xx, 611p. ISBN 0-5200-4835-0. ML410 .B4 J66.

The definitive exploration of the numerous sketchbooks. Much *Fidelio* material appears in the books known as Landsberg 9, Dessauer, and Mendelssohn 15.

Biographies

494. Solomon, Maynard. *Beethoven*. 2nd ed. New York: Schirmer, 1998. xxii, 554p. ISBN 0-02-864717-3. ML410 .B4 S69.

First edition, 1977. The premier Beethoven biography and one of the most readable biographies of any composer. Solomon combines a keen musical approach with an accurate life story and penetrating psychological interpretation of the disturbed genius. He settles the doubts that have surrounded various episodes, such as the "immortal beloved," and the nephew, and indeed seems to explain all that can be explained. Backnotes, p.431–518, valuable bibliographic essay, p.486–518 (encompassing all previous writings), index of works, expansive general index.

Individual Works

Fidelio

ASO 10 (1977), COH (1996), ENOG 4 (1980), Rororo (1981).

495. Dean, Winton. "Beethoven and Opera." In *Essays* (#69), 123–163.

A valuable background study of Beethoven in Vienna and his operatic experiences there: operas he knew and liked, his early attempts to set various libretti, then to *Fidelio*. The 1805 premiere was a failure, but the 1814 revision was a success. Sources of the libretto, comparison of the versions, influences.

496. Hess, Willy. "Fünfzig Jahre im Banne von Leonore-Fidelio." *Beethoven-Jahrbuch* 9 (1973–1977): 167–184.

A summary of research on the opera, with special concern for the versions of 1805 and 1806, and differences between manuscript and printed editions. List of all writings on the opera by Hess (who has given it much attention).

497. Ruhnke, Martin. "Die Librettisten des *Fidelio*." In *Opern-studien: Anna Amalie Abert zum 65. Geburtstag,* ed. Klaus Hortschansky, 121–140 (Tutzing: Schneider, 1975; ISBN 3795- 20155-1; ML55 .A15).

Compares the 1805 and 1806 versions with a later libretto of 1814 and an earlier one of 1798.

498. Gossett, Philip. "The Arias of Marzelline: Beethoven as a Composer of Opera." *Beethoven Jahrbuch* 10 (1978–1981): 141–183.

Analyzes sketches for the aria, which opens the 1805 *Leonore,* and establishes a chronology of the versions. They finally resulted in "a mode of declamation appropriate for Marzelline's aria." Applies "linear reduction" to the drafts. Concludes that a "study of the sketches adds a wealth of associations and meanings" to study of the final form alone.

499. Albrecht, Theodore. "Beethoven's *Leonore*: A New Compositional Chronology Based on May-August 1804 Entries in Sketchbook Mendelssohn 15." *JM* 7 (1989): 165–190.

Offers "substantial (if sometimes speculative) evidence for a revised dating of Beethoven's early work . . . including *Leonore*." Events of 1804, including an incident related by one of the composer's pupils, plus dates of other sketches are considered. A new chronological table is provided for the contents of sketchbook Mendelssohn 15, drawing on facts developed by Tyson (#493).

500. Broyles, Michael. "Stylistic Dualism in Early Beethoven and the *Leonore* Challenge." *JM* 5 (1987): 419–447.

A study of the changes made by Beethoven in the three *Leonore* overtures, in the light of his other works of the time. He was learning that "the orchestra could be used in a poetic and dramatic manner independent of the classical symphonic approach."

501. Robinson, Paul. "*Fidelio* and the French Revolution." *COJ* 3-1 (March 1991): 23–48.

Finds a political interpretation that explicates the text and music. Freedom is the ideological center. The idea and word *Freiheit* are emphasized by musical climaxes. Freedom moves from "an unconstructed to a redeemed order" separated by the trumpet call in the middle of act 2. The French Revolution itself is symbolized.

502. Tusa, Michael C. "The Grave-digging Duet in *Leonore* (1805)." *Beethoven Forum* 5 (1996): 1–64.

Considers the surviving sketches for the 1805 version of *Fidelio* (then identified as *Leonore*), with focus on the duet (no. 14), "Nur hurtig fort, nur frisch gegraben." Examines "basic assumptions of the operatic world" and how the piece actually fits them. Searches for "the kinds of problems Beethoven posed for himself in the relatively unfamiliar role of opera composer." Concludes that his "basic operatic outlook was essentially that of his own time, one that sought an equilibrium between expressive urges and structural cohesion."

Vincenzo Bellini (1801–1835)

Thematic Catalogues and Worklists

503. Lippmann, Friedrich. "Bellini's Opern-Daten in Quellen." *Analecta musico-logica* 6 (1969): 365–397.

    A list of premieres with casts, giving manuscript and location information and citations to printed libretti. Extensive commentary.

Bibliographies and Guides to Resources

See #504.

Conferences

504. *Atti del Convegno Internationale di Studi Belliniani: Catania, 1985.*

    Not seen; information is from *NGDO* 1, 396. Consists of 17 papers presented at the conference. Among them: F. Giovale, "Ah, tu perdoni, 'quel pianto il dice': Note sul tema del sacrificio e del perdono nei libretti belliniani de Felice Romani"; Simon Maguire, "On the Question of Analysis in Bellini"; and Julian Budden, "La fortuna di Bellini in Inghilterra." There is also a review of Bellini studies in the form of a 30-page bibliographic essay.

Biographies

505. Adamo, Maria Rosario, and Friedrich Lippmann. *Vincenzo Bellini.* Turin: ERI, 1981. 576p. No ISBN. ML410 .B44 A5.

    In Italian. A thorough biography by Adamo (p.9–312), drawing on letters and primary sources, and study of the works by Lippmann (p.313–548). Lippmann offers genesis accounts, plots, program notes, and some technical notes. A particularly interesting section on the chronological development of Bellini's melodies. Footnotes, 200-item bibliography, poor nonexpansive index (more than 100 page references for *Norma*).

506. Brunel, Pierre. *Vincenzo Bellini.* Paris: Fayard, 1981. 431p. ISBN 2-213-00263-5. ML410 .B44 B89.

    A footnoted biography with some attention to the operas, concentrating on text; no musical examples. Worklist, bibliography of about 200 entries; index of names, titles, and topics.

507. Weinstock, Herbert. *Vincenzo Bellini: His Life and His Operas.* New York: Knopf, 1971. xx, 554, xxxvii p. ISBN 0-3944-1656-2. ML410 B44 W4.

    A fully documented life story, with good musical analysis of the operas, along with genesis accounts and reception histories. Weak bibliography and poor nonexpansive index.

508. Rosselli, John. *The Life of Bellini*. New York: Cambridge U.P., 1997. x, 184p. ISBN 0-521-46227-4. ML410 .B44 R77.

Although this is a popular-style brief story, it does have backnotes and good access through an expansive index. Some program notes on the operas.

Operas in General

509. *Vincenzo Bellini und die italienische "opera seria" seiner Zeit. Studien über Libretto, Arienform und Melodik*. Ed. Friedrich Lippmann. *Analecta musico-logica* 6 (1969). xii, 402p.

A special issue of the journal, consisting of important studies of the libretti, aria form, structure of the aria, and melodic style. Comparisons with work of Rossini, Donizetti, and other contemporaries. Discussion of sources, auto-graphs, early editions, etc. Bibliography of about 150 entries, some annotated. No index. A worklist is entered separately in this guide (#503).

510. Maguire, Simon. *Vincenzo Bellini and the Aesthetics of Early Nineteenth-Century Italian Opera*. Outstanding Dissertations in Music from British Universities. New York: Garland, 1989. 240p. ISBN 0-8240-2344-7. ML410 .B44 M3.

Originally the author's Ph.D. dissertation, U. of Oxford, 1985. He investigates early-19th-century poetry and European aesthetic thought, describing contem-porary Italian attitudes toward opera and emphasizing those that give Bellini's works their particular flavor. He also discusses orchestras and the bel canto tradition. Indexed.

511. Balthazar, Scott. "Evolving Conventions in Italian Serious Opera: Scene Struc-ture in the Works of Rossini, Bellini, Donizetti, and Verdi, 1810–1850." Ph.D. diss., U. of Pennsylvania, 1985. xvii, 595p.

512. *I teatri di Vincenzo Bellini*. Ed. Maria Rosario Adamo et al. Palermo: Nove-cento, 1986. 309p. No ISBN. ML410 .B44 T45.

Primarily a picture book (p.161–223), with portraits, stage sets, and posters, but also a detailed chronology of Bellini, program notes on 10 operas (by vari-ous authors), footnotes, and musical examples. No index or bibliography.

513. Greenspan, Charlotte. "The Operas of Vincenzo Bellini." Ph.D. diss., U. of California, Berkeley, 1977. 383p.

See also Celletti (#2473).

Individual Works

Beatrice di Tenda

ERO, v.5.

514. Brauner, C. S. "Textual Problems in Bellini's *Norma* and *Beatrice di Tenda*." *JAMS* 29 (1976): 99–118.

The composer's many changes and cuts are considered. Brauner does not always prefer the latest versions, giving reasons why the earlier manifestations were sometimes better.

I Capuleti e I Montecchi

ERO, v.3. Capuleti is sometimes seen with two t's, and the conjunction may be either "*e*" or "*ed.*"

515. Collins, Michael. "The Literary Background of Bellini's *I Capuleti ed I Montecchi.*" *JAMS* 35-3 (Fall 1982): 532–538.

Conjectures, convincingly, that the librettist Romani was not adapting Shakespeare at all but drawing on quite different versions of the romance. Useful bibliographical notes.

Norma

ASO 29 (1980), *COH* (1998), *ERO*, v.4.

516. Lippmann, Friedrich. "Lo stile belliniano in *Norma.*" In *Opera and Libretto I* (#220), 211–224.

Technical aspects of the music: psychology and form, drama, melody, rhythm, harmony, and dynamics.

See also Brauner (#514).

Il pirata

ERO, v.1.

517. Willier, Stephen. "Madness, the Gothic, and Bellini's *Il pirata.*" *OQ* 6-4 (Summer 1989): 7–23.

Ponders the obsession with mad scenes in early-19th-century opera and how the phenomenon related to the English gothic novel. Willier finds "extraordinary tensions and upheavals" in the era that may have led to such exotic entertainments. A gothic play, *Bertram,* was the source for *Il pirata;* it had a heroine's mad/death scene. Notes the similarity to *Lucia.* With 27 backnotes identifying relevant literature on gothic and madness on stage.

I puritani di Scozia

ASO 96 (1987).

518. Petrobelli, Pierluigi. "Bellini e Paisiello: Altri documenti sulla nascita dei Puritani." In *Il melodramma italiano dell'ottocento: Studi e ricerche per Massimo Mila,* 351–364 (Turin: Einaudi, 1977. ML1733.4 .M5).

Argues that Bellini kept Paisiello's works before him as a frame of reference while he planned *I puritani.* Discusses the early sketches.

519. Spina, Giuseppe. "Scott-Ancelot-Pepoli-Bellini: Genesi del libretto de *I puritani.*" *NRMI* 23 (1989): 79–97.

Walter Scott's *The Puritans of Scotland* is but dimly connected to the libretto: names of the characters are the same, and locations of the action, but little else. Other Scott works are found to have connections as well, but the most direct source was a play by J. A. F. Ancelot and J. Y. Bonface Saintine, *Têtes rondes et cavaliers* (1833). The similarities among these works are carefully laid out.

La sonnambula

ASO 178 (1997).

520. Degrada, Francesco. "Prolegomeni a una lettura della *Sonnambula*." In *Il melodramma italiano dell'ottocento: Studi e ricerche per Massimo Mila*, 319–350 (Turin: Einaudi, 1977. ML1733.4 .M5).

Genesis of the libretto and program notes on the music. Useful citations of earlier writings about the opera; 13 musical examples.

La straniera

ERO, v.2.

521. Lippmann, Friedrich. "Su *La straniera*." *NRMI* 5 (1971): 565–605.

Genesis, reception, and analysis. Finds more merit than most commentators have in this transition opera, citing some experimental ideas not repeated in Bellini's later works.

Georg Anton Benda (1722–1795)

Ariadne auf Naxos is in *GO*, v.4, and *Romeo und Julie* is in *GO*, v.5.

522. Garrett, Edith Vogl. "Georg Benda, the Pioneer of the Melodrama." In *Studies in Eighteenth-Century Music* (#73), 236–242.

Considers Benda "the most successful composer of modern melodrama" (which is a recitation accompanied by the orchestra). His *Medea* and *Ariadne auf Naxos* were praised by Mozart. Benda's orchestra engaged in word-painting; he "reveled in expressing pathos." Discusses the influence of the melodrama on *Die Zauberflöte, Fidelio, Der Freischütz,* and others.

523. Bauman, Thomas. "Benda, the Germans, and Simple Recitative." *JAMS* 34 (1981): 119–131.

Discusses an article published by Benda in 1783 or perhaps as early as 1776 (and reprints it in English). The controversy of that time in German opera was whether to keep spoken dialogue or switch to recitative in the Italian *seria* manner. Benda was opposed to simple recitative. A useful account of the aesthetic dispute is given, with full documentation.

524. Brückner, Fritz. *Georg Benda und das deutsche Singspiel*. Leipzig: Breitkopf und Härtel, 1904. Also in *SIMG* 5 (1903–1904): 571–621.

A detailed account of the emergence of *Singspiel*. Distinguishes between melodrama (opera) and monodrama (which puts music in a subsidiary, accompanying role). Benda's were monodrama. Descriptions of *Ariadne auf Naxos, Medea,* and several of his *Singspiele*. Program notes and performance histories, appendix of Benda's letters.

Richard Rodney Bennett (1936–)

525. Craggs, Stewart R. *Richard Rodney Bennett: A Bio-Bibliography*. Bio-Bibliographies in Music, 24. New York: Greenwood, 1990. 249p. ISBN 0-313-26179-2. ML134 .B4425.

A classified worklist, noting performances and writings about them.

Alban Berg (1865–1935)

No other composer has been the topic of so much important literature in the period immediately following his death. In view of the stunning complexity of the two operas, *Wozzeck* (1925) and *Lulu* (1937), it is all the more remarkable that an array of perceptive analysis took shape so quickly. A valuable survey of the literature is now available:

526. Simms, Bryan R. *Alban Berg: A Guide to Research*. Garland Composer Resource Manuals, 38. New York: Garland, 1996. xiii, 293p. ISBN 0-8153-2032-9. ML134 .B46 S56.

Consists of 1,064 annotated entries, selecting "less than half of all published writings on Berg," by omitting brief articles, reviews, and other minor pieces. There are 235 books and articles about *Wozzeck* and 163 about *Lulu*. Worklist, entries for Berg's own writings, biographical sketch, discussion of research trends, materials on the instrumental music, and indexes of authors, titles, and subjects.

Editions

527. Berg, Alban. *Sämtliche Werke*. Ed. Rudolph Stephan, for the Alban Berg Stiftung. Vienna: Universal, 1994–. M3 .B47.

V.1, *Wozzeck*; v.2, *Lulu*; neither published as of August 1999. Three volumes of other works have appeared.

Collections of Essays

528. *The Cambridge Companion to Berg*. Ed. Anthony Pople. New York: Cambridge U.P., 1997. xv, 304p. ISBN 0-521-56489-1. ML410 .B47 C38.

Consists of 13 essays, dealing with Berg's cultural environment, his place among 20th-century composers, his songs, and these on the operas: Anthony Pople, "The Musical Language of *Wozzeck*"; Douglas Jarman, "Secret Programmes" (a comparison of the formats of the sketches for the two operas); Patricia Hall, "Compositional Process in *Wozzeck* and *Lulu*: A Glimpse of Berg's Atonal Method"; and Judy Lochhead, "*Lulu*'s Feminine Performance."

529. *Alban Berg: Historical and Analytical Perspectives*. Ed. David Gable and Robert P. Morgan. New York: Oxford U.P., 1991. viii, 296p. ISBN 0-1931-1338-4. ML410 .B47 A777.

Of the 10 articles included, these are about the operas: Allen Forte, "The Mask of Tonality: Alban Berg's Symphonic Epilogue to *Wozzeck*"; Douglas M. Green, "A False Start for *Lulu*: An Early Version of the Prologue"; Claudio Spies, "Some Notes on the Completion of *Lulu*"; Patricia Hall, "Role and

Form in Berg's Sketches for *Lulu*"; and Leo Treitler, "The Lulu Character and Character of Lulu."

530. *The Berg Companion*. Ed. Douglas Jarman. Boston: Northeastern U.P., 1990. 301p. ISBN 1-55553-068-0. ML410 .B47 B53.

Four of the 13 essays in this anthology are about the operas: George Perle, "The First Four Notes of *Lulu*"; Derrick Puffett, "Berg and German Opera"; Patricia Hall, "The Sketches for *Lulu*"; Friedrich Cerha, "Some Further Notes on My Realization of Act III of *Lulu*."

See also Hall (#537).

Biographies

531. Reich, Willi. *The Life and Works of Alban Berg*. Trans. Cornelius Cardew. New York: Harcourt, Brace & World, 1965. 239p. ISBN 0-8443-0078-0. ML410 .B47 R3973.

Originally *Alban Berg: Leben und Work* (Zurich: Atlantis, 1963). Reich, a pupil of Berg's, has been regarded as his official biographer; this book includes a life story and edited versions of writings by Berg about *Wozzeck* and other works. Reich's own attempts at structural analysis seem rudimentary and oblivious to the studies by other scholars. Documented, with name and title index.

532. Redlich, Hans F. *Alban Berg: Versuch einer Würdigung*. Vienna: Universal, 1957. 393p. ML410 .B47 R37.

A much-abbreviated English translation: *Alban Berg: The Man and His Music* (London: Calder, 1957; 316p.). Redlich, in a pioneering study, uncovered new source material and offered a revision of Berg's *Wozzeck* lecture that differed from that of Reich. His analyses moved toward the sophistication of the next wave of scholars; had he not died before his revised edition could be completed, he might have had an important part in that wave.

533. Adorno, Theodor W. *Alban Berg, Master of the Smallest Link*. Trans. Juliane Brand and Christopher Hailey. New York: Cambridge U.P., 1991. xviii, 156p. ISBN 0-521-33016-5. ML410 .B47 A6313.

Originally *Alban Berg: Der Meister des kleinsten Übergangs* (Vienna: Lafite, 1968). A gathering of earlier writings by Adorno, with a few new sections. The analyses "mix technical observations on motivic matters with impressions and interpretations distinctive of Adorno" (Simms [#526], 180), who was Berg's student and friend from 1924. The composer's thoughts about his contemporaries are of interest. Indexed.

534. Jarman, Douglas. *The Music of Alban Berg*. Berkeley and Los Angeles: U. of California Press, 1979. xii, 266p. ISBN 0-5200-348-56. ML410 .B47 J37.

After brief attention to biography and documents, this outstanding study covers the music thoroughly. Discusses pitch organization, rhythm, and macrostructure as well as smaller structures (in this respect taking a broader view than Perle [#536]). Jarman acknowledges and builds on all earlier studies.

With 210 musical examples; worklist (including manuscripts and sketches, with locations); fine bibliography of about 150 items, fully described; expansive index of names, titles, and topics.

535. Carner, Mosco. *Alban Berg: The Man and the Work*. 2nd ed. London: Duckworth, 1983. xx, 314p. ISBN 0-7156-0769-3. ML410 .B47 C28.

First edition, 1975. The principal biography of Berg, including some musical analysis (most importantly of *Lulu*), with notes and musical examples. Perle's work appears to have been ignored. Worklist, bibliography (about 70 items), expansive index of names and titles.

Operas in General

536. Perle, George. *The Operas of Alban Berg*. Berkeley and Los Angeles: U. of California Press, 1980–1985. 2v. ISBN 0-520-03440-6; 0-520-04502-5. ML410 .B47 P45.

V.1: *Wozzeck*; v.2: *Lulu*. Perle, the leading authority on Berg's music, has been writing intriguing articles on the operas for 40 years. He offers extremely detailed analyses of pitch and structural organization in these works, as well as an acerbic review of what others have written about them. Perle steps away from the large-scale total-unity approach; he identifies the components of Berg's atonal universe and relates music to text at specific moments but does not find it worthwhile to seek unification of those components into a "single comprehensive system." Friedrich Cerha's completion of *Lulu* is discussed, and there are biographical matters as well. Bibliography of about 200 entries, index.

Individual Works

Lulu

ASO 181/182 (1998), COH (1991), Rororo (1985).

537. Hall, Patricia. *A View of Berg's "Lulu" through the Autograph Sources*. Berkeley and Los Angeles: U. of California Press, 1996. xi, 184p. ISBN 0-520-08819-0. ML410 .B57 H17.

An examination of the sketches; chronology of the autograph sources, interaction of role and form, Dr. Schön, the tone rows. Wondering why Berg's 12-tone music is so difficult to analyze, Hall concludes it is because of the "multiple levels of dramatic symbolism" and "the network of motivic and thematic coherence, the frequent tonal allusions." The composer manipulates the 12-tone method to accommodate those things, as well as tonality. Backnotes, bibliography, index. Based on the author's Ph.D. dissertation, Yale U., 1989.

538. Ertelt, Thomas F. *Alban Bergs "Lulu": Quellenstudium und Beiträge zur Analyse*. Alban Berg Studien, 3. Vienna: Universal, 1993. 220p. ISBN 3-7024-0208-X. MT100 .B5 E73.

A close study of the opera, based on Berg's manuscripts. Clarifies the relationship of the sources. Most of the book concerns materials about Dr. Schön and the variation interlude of act 3. Bibliography, no index.

See also Perle (#536, and in #530).

Wozzeck

ASO 36 (1981), COH (1989), ENOG 42 (1990), Rororo (1985).

539. Schmalfeldt, Janet. *Berg's "Wozzeck": Harmonic Language and Dramatic Design.* New Haven, Conn.: Yale U.P., 1983. xii, 281p. ISBN 0-3000-2710-9. MT100 .B57 S35.

A detailed study of pitch-class sets, especially those related to Marie and Wozzeck. With an explanation of set theory, bibliography (about 200 items), and index.

540. Treitler, Leo. "*Wozzeck* and the Apocalypse: An Essay in Historical Criticism." *Critical Inquiry* 3 (1976): 251–270.

Reprinted in Treitler's *Music and the Historical Imagination* (Cambridge, Mass.: Harvard U.P., 1989) and in *GL,* v.12. Examines the imagery of the biblical Apocalypse as found in Büchner's play and musically handled by Berg. Another study, not seen: David Fanning, "Berg's Sketches for *Wozzeck*: A Commentary and Inventory," *JRMA* 112 (1987): 280–322.

See also Perle (#536).

541. A steady source of new data and speculation on the operas is the *Newsletter of the International Alban Berg Society* (Durham, N.C.: The Society, 1968–).

Luciano Berio (1925–)

542. Osmond-Smith, David. *Berio.* Oxford Studies of Composers, 24. New York: Oxford U.P., 1990. 158p. ISBN 0-193-15478-1. ML410 .B4968 .O55.

A biography with technical analyses of the works; 28 pages on the theatrical compositions. Chronological worklist, bibliography of about 60 items, index.

543. Osmond-Smith, David. "*Nella festa tutto?* Structure and Dramaturgy in Luciano Berio's *La vera storia.*" *COJ* 9-3 (November 1997): 281–294.

Examines the choral textures and harmonics in "four festas," with technical analysis of the pitch sets.

544. Highton, Audrey Charlotte. "Performing Interpretation: Luciano Berio's *Un re in ascolto.*" D.M.A. diss., U. of Wisconsin-Madison, 1994. 165p.

See also *Oper heute* (#95).

Hector Berlioz (1803–1869)

Editions

545. Berlioz, Hector. *New Edition of the Complete Works.* Issued by the Berlioz Centenary Committee, London, in association with the Calouste Gulbenkian Foundation, Lisbon, under direction of Hugh Macdonald. Kassel: Bärenreiter, 1967–. ISBN varies. M3 .B52.

V.1: *Benvenuto Cellini*, 1995; v.2: *Les troyens*, 1967–70; v.3: *Béatrice et Bénédict*, 1980; v.8: *La damnation de Faust*, 1979, with supplement 1986. There are extensive notes and commentaries for each opera, in some cases in separate volumes. See also next entry.

Thematic Catalogues and Worklists

546. *Catalogue of Works of Hector Berlioz*. Ed. D. Kern Holoman. V.25 of the *New Edition* (#545).

Bibliographies and Guides to Resources

547. Langford, Jeffrey, and Jane Denker Graves. *Hector Berlioz: A Guide to Research*. Garland Composer Resource Manuals, 22. New York: Garland, 1989. xxi, 307p. ISBN 0-8240-4635-8. ML134 .B5 L3.

     A valuable survey of the Berlioz literature: 1,011 annotated entries. Also a worklist (keyed to the *New Edition* and to the earlier issue of complete works), author index, and expansive index of names and subjects.

548. Holoman, D. Kern. "The Present State of Berlioz Research." *AM* 47-1 (1975): 31–67.

     A lucid, learned summary of biographical and analytical studies, along with the important primary source materials. For a later review of the Berlioz literature by Holoman, see #555.

549. Hopkinson, Cecil. *A Bibliography of the Musical and Literary Works of Hector Berlioz*. 2nd ed. Tunbridge Wells, England: R. Macnutt, 1980. xix, 230p. ISBN 0-907180-00. ML134 .B5 H79.

     Not a true second edition but a facsimile reprint of the 1951 first edition, with additions and corrections. Keyed to the *New Edition* (#545). Gives all known manuscripts and editions in all countries, with detailed descriptions and locations; 22 plates, index.

Periodicals

550. *Berlioz Society Bulletin*, 1–, 1952–. London: Berlioz Society, 1952–. Quarterly. ML410 .B5 B547.

     A useful source for notices and reviews, as well as a number of essays on the operas.

Letters and Documents

551. Berlioz, Hector. *The Memoirs of Hector Berlioz* . . . Corrected ed. Trans. and ed. David Cairns. New York: Norton, 1975. ISBN 0-393-00698-0. ML410 .B5 A42.

     Aside from certain emendations, this is the same text as the first edition (London: Gollancz, 1969). It is a fine rendering of the composer's delightful and illuminating recollections, with full scholarly apparatus. The period covered is 21 March 1848 to 1 January 1865, during which he wrote *Les troyens* and *Béatrice et Bénédict* and experienced at least one trauma (a chapter begins: "Calamity—I become a critic"). Cairns holds that, despite the humor and romantic panache of the memoirs, they are basically accurate. "Errors and disputed points" are discussed, as are the sources. An appendix presents descriptions of Berlioz by his contemporaries; a glossary identifies persons mentioned and gives bio-sketches of them and also identifies places and institutions. Expansive index of names and titles.

552. Berlioz, Hector. *New Letters of Berlioz, 1830–1868*. With introduction, notes, and English translation by Jacques Barzun. New York: Columbia U.P., 1954. xxxi, 332p. Reprint, as "2nd ed.," Westport, Conn.: Greenwood, 1974. ISBN 0-8371-3251-7. ML410 .B5 A33.

A bilingual, annotated edition, with bibliography; no index. Several other collections of letters are described in Langford (#547), 39–45.

Prose Works

Berlioz wrote extensively as a critic and theorist, but only the work that relates to opera is considered here.

See also #893, on Gluck.

553. Murphy, Kerry. *Hector Berlioz and the Development of French Music Criticism*. Studies in Musicology, 97. Ann Arbor, Mich.: UMI Research, 1988. x, 295p. ISBN 0-8357-1821-2. ML3880 .M85.

Examines the early years of Berlioz as a critic, 1823–1837, and gives a complete list of his articles. The context of Parisian journalism and the music critics of the time are well described. The preferences of Berlioz were for Beethoven, Gluck, Weber, and Cherubini; he enjoyed grand opera more than *opéra comique*. Bibliography, index.

Biographies

554. Barzun, Jacques. *Berlioz and the Romantic Century*. 3rd ed. New York: Columbia U.P., 1969. 2v. ML410 .B5 B2.

First edition, 1950; second edition, 1956, was abridged and titled *Berlioz and His Century* (Cleveland: World; reprint, Chicago: U. of Chicago Press, 1982). A panoramic cultural history of the 19th century is offered as background for the Berlioz story. Genesis and reception accounts of the operas, chronology, bibliography/discography of 1,534 items, expansive name and topic index. This remains the standard biography.

555. Holoman, D. Kern. *Berlioz*. Cambridge, Mass.: Harvard U.P., 1989. 687p. ISBN 0-674-06778-9. ML410 .B5 H58.

A worthy successor to and perhaps replacement for Barzun (#554), considering both life and works in scholarly detail. Musical life in Paris, 1821–1869, is brought into vivid focus. Includes an interesting account of major performances of Berlioz works in concerts that he conducted. On the operas: genesis, reception, and technical descriptions. A chronological worklist gives library sources of manuscripts. The bibliography is in the form of an essay that reviews Berlioz research, updating #548. Backnotes, partly expansive index.

556. Macdonald, Hugh. *Berlioz*. Master Musicians. London: Dent, 1982. 261p. ISBN 0-460-03156-2. ML410 .B5 M13.

   A useful brief biography, presenting the results of latest scholarship. Macdonald is directing the issue of the complete works (#545). Bibliography, index.

See also #172.

Operas in General

557. Rushton, Julian. *The Musical Language of Berlioz*. New York: Cambridge U.P., 1983. xi, 303p. ISBN 0-521-24279-7. ML410 .B5 R87.

   A valuable analytic approach to the operas and other works, dealing specifically with each technical aspect: pitch, counterpoint, rhythm, melody, form, and instrumentation, taking Schenker principles as a ground. Lengthy analyses of sections from *Lélio, Benvenuto Cellini,* and *La damnation de Faust.*

558. Dickinson, A. E. F. "Berlioz' Stage Works." *MR* 31 (1970): 136–157.

   A general survey of the operas, including those left incomplete and those only planned.

559. Gräbner, Eric Hans. "Berlioz and the French Operatic Tradition." Ph.D. diss., York U. (England), 1967. 250p.

560. Langford, Jeffrey Alan. "The Operas of Hector Berlioz: Their Relationship to the French Operatic Tradition of the Early Nineteenth Century." Ph.D. diss., U. of Pennsylvania, 1978. 459p.

Individual Works

Béatrice et Bénédict

New Edition (#545), v.3.

561. Rushton, Julian. "Berlioz's Swan-Song: Towards a Criticism of *Béatrice et Bénédict*." *PRMA* 109 (1982–1983): 105–118.

   The adaptation from *Much Ado about Nothing* is discussed; it was "drastic, leaving very little of the original play." Also a light technical survey of the work.

Benvenuto Cellini

ASO 142 (1991), *New Edition* (#545), v.1.

562. Piatier, François. *Hector Berlioz "Benvenuto Cellini": Ou, le myth de l'artiste.* Paris: Aubier Montaigne, 1979. 137, [38]p. ISBN 2-700-70160-7. ML410 .B5 P44.

   Draws parallels between Berlioz and Cellini, then compares various versions of the opera. Analysis, along with reception history. Complete libretto, one-page bibliography, no index.

La damnation de Faust

ASO 22 (1979), *New Edition* (#545), v.8.

563. Reeve, Katherine. "The *Damnation of Faust,* or the Perils of Heroism in Music." In *Berlioz Studies,* ed. Peter Bloom, 148–188 (New York: Cambridge U.P., 1992; ISBN 0-521-41286-2; ML410 .B6 B57).

Reeve finds a new image of Faust in the opera, a romantic hero who is vulnerable in a society "at odds with its standards of good and evil." He is intellectually barren, politically ineffectual, and sexually impotent"—unworthy of Goethe's hero. His heroism consists merely in "inner suffering." At the end, "men and women are all victims." With 66 footnotes to the supporting literature.

564. Albright, Daniel. "Berlioz's *Faust*: The Funeral March of a Marionette." *Journal of Musicological Research* 13 (1993): 79–97.

This Faust is nihilistic, vehement but empty. He "struggles in vain to join in the symphonic texture of the music . . . he is exiled to a private plane of musical discourse." Goethe's vision of Faust is better depicted by Gounod.

Les troyens

ASO 128/129 (1990); COH (1988), *New Edition* (#545), v.2.

565. Macdonald, Hugh. "A Critical Edition of Berlioz's *Les troyens*." Ph.D. diss., U. of Cambridge, 1968. 4v.

The author is directing the issue of the *New Edition* (#545).

566. Goldberg, Louise. "*Les troyens* of Hector Berlioz: A Century of Productions and Critical Reviews." Ph.D. diss., U. of Rochester, 1974. 2v.

567. Goldberg, Louise. "Aspects of Dramatic and Musical Unity in Berlioz's *Les troyens*." *Journal of Musicological Research* 13 (1993): 99–112.

Explicates a tripartite structure, in which each section builds to a climax and events (musical and textual) are parallel to those in the other sections. The opera should not be thought of as "episodic" or without unity.

568. Cairns, David. "Berlioz and Virgil: A Consideration of *Les troyens* as a Virgilian Opera." *PRMA* 95 (1968–1969): 97–110. Reprinted in *GL*, v.12, and in *Responses: Musical Essays and Reviews,* by David Cairns, 88–110 (London: Secker & Warburg, 1973).

Shows relationships between the opera and the *Aeneid*. Berlioz expanded many situations that were only implied by Virgil, and he reordered events.

569. Lee, M. Owen. "The Exasperated Eagle and the Stoic Saint." *OQ* 2-4 (1984–1985): 76–84.

Considers the relationship of the story to Virgil's *Aeneid,* finding a number of allusions in the opera to scenes and symbols of the poem. Suggests that the connections are more intricate than has been noted previously.

Toussaint Bertin de la Doué (ca.1680–1745)

Le jugement de Paris is in *FO*, v.29.

Henri Montan Berton (1767–1844)

Silvie is in *FO*, v.60.

570. Robison, Carol Jeanne. "One-Act *Opéra-comique* from 1800–1810: Contributions of H.-M. Berton and Nicole Isouard." D.M.A. diss., U. of Cincinnati, 1986. 448p.

571. Taïeb, Patrick. "De la composition du *Délire* (1799) au pamphlet anti-dilettantes (1821): Une étude des conceptions esthétiques de H.-M. Berton." *RdM* 78 (1992): 61–107.

Le *délire* was one of the most successful *opéras-comiques* of Berton. In it he depicted madness by exaggerated harmony and orchestration. Then, 22 years later, turning against fashionable Italian opera, he wrote a pamphlet condemning such practices. Why this change of mind? Taïeb speculates about the reasons in the light of psychiatric theory of the time.

Ferdinando Bertoni (1725–1813)

572. Hansell, Sven H. "Ferdinando Bertoni's Setting of Calzabigi's *Orfeo ed Euridice*." In Muraro (#2576), 185–211.

Bertoni's most successful work was described by Loewenberg as "a rather clumsy imitation of Gluck's," but Hansell points out that Bertoni admitted his debt in a preface to the Vienna edition of the score (1783). There are indeed "striking similarities," which may have helped bring a favorable reception of Bertoni's version throughout Europe, though it faded after 1795. Hansell offers a scene-by-scene comparison of the two operas and finds that Bertoni comes out ahead in one or two places, e.g., the aria of Euridice, "Che fiero momento." He suggests that Bertoni's *Orfeo* could be as successful today as Gluck's Italian version of 1762.

Franz Adolf Berwald (1796–1868)

573. Berwald, Franz. *Sämtliche Werke = Complete Works*. Ed. by the Berwaldkommitten. Kassel: Bärenreiter, 1966–. M3 .B53 B5.

Includes the operas *Estrella de Soria* (v.17), *Jag gar i kloster* (v.19), and *Modehandlerskan* (v.20). Each volume has an introduction, synopsis, full score, and brief notes.

No substantive literature on the operas has been seen, apart from the following:

574. Sundström, Einar. "Franz Berwalds operor." *Svensk tijdskrift för musikforskning* 29 (1947): 16–62.

Genesis, reception, and analysis with musical examples of *Estrella di Soria* (1862) and *Drottningen av Golconda* (1864). Work on the lost opera, *Der verräther,* is described. Influences (Donizetti, Mozart, and Weber, primarily) are examined. Footnotes point to the other literature on these operas, all of it in Swedish.

575. Layton, Robert. *Franz Berwald.* London: A. Blond, 1959. 189p. ML410 .B63 L43.

Originally in Swedish (Stockholm, 1956). A popular account of life and works, with some attention (p.141–147) to the operas. Chronology, bibliography, worklist, no index.

Harrison Birtwistle (1934–)

576. Hall, Michael. *Harrison Birtwistle.* London: Robson, 1984. 186p. ISBN 0-85051-2703. ML410 .B644 H19.

A straightforward biography with worklist, composer's comments on certain works, and technical analysis. The operas *Punch and Judy* (1968), *Down by the Greenwood Side* (1969), and *Mask of Orpheus* (1986) are thoroughly examined. Bibliography, index.

577. Samuel, Rhian. "Birtwistle's *Gawain*: An Essay and a Diary." *COJ* 4-2 (July 1992): 163–178.

Technical comments on macrodesign, motives, and specific compositional devices. Also the diary entries of Samuel himself, who attended rehearsals in April and May 1991, before the premiere performance on 1 June.

Georges Bizet (1838–1875)

578. Dean, Winton. *Georges Bizet, His Life and Work.* 3rd ed. London: Dent, 1975. x, 306p. ML410 .B62 D28.

First edition, 1948. A popular biography, with program notes on the operas. Worklist, glossary of persons cited in the text, bibliography of about 100 items, name and title index.

579. Stricker, Remy. *Georges Bizet, 1838–1875.* Paris: Gallimard, 1999. 380p. ISBN 2-07-074803-0. ML410 .B65 S875.

A life story only, without musical analyses. Useful for genesis and extensive reception account of *Carmen.* Backnotes, worklist, bibliography of about 100 items, partly expansive index of names.

Individual Works

Carmen

ASO 26 (1980), COH (1992), ENOG 13 (1982). Recent literature is sparse. Two accounts of recent productions make an interesting comparison:

580. Koerth, Manfred. *Felsentein inszeniert "Carmen": Dokumentation.* Berlin: Akademie der Künste der Deutschen Demokratischen Republik, 1973. 127p. ML410 .B62 K6.

See #299 and #300 for material on Felsenstein, who was director of the Komische Oper, Berlin. This is an informative account of the entire preparation for performance.

581. Phillips, Harvey E. *The Carmen Chronicle: The Making of an Opera.* New York: Stein & Day, 1973. 288p. ISBN 0-8128-1609-9. ML410 .B62 P65.

Describes the planning of the Metropolitan production of 1972 by Goeran Gentele, who was killed before it could take place. Unfortunately, the book is in a chatty style, with invented conversations.

582. Furman, Nelly. "The Languages of Love in *Carmen.*" In *Reading Opera* (#218), 168–183.

The usual reading of the story centers on the victimization of Don José and his justified murder of the villainous Carmen. Furman reads it another way, as Carmen's story and her "struggle for freedom." For José love is "narcissistic eroticism," but for Carmen it is a bird in flight: it just happens. She loves love itself and its freedom.

583. Dean, Winton. "The True *Carmen*?" *Musical Times* 106 (1965): 846–855. Reprinted in *GL*, v.12.

Criticizes *Carmen: Kritische Neuausgabe nach den Quellen*, by Fritz Oeser, published by Bärenreiter. Oeser examines the sources, as well as Bizet's revisions (rejecting some). Dean finds the editor has made dubious changes and "has slighted Bizet's genius."

584. Huebner, Steven. "*Carmen* as *corrida de toros.*" *Journal of Musicological Research* 13 (1993): 3–29.

Carmen is "about male madness, and the transformation of José into an animal—in stark contrast to Escamillo, the other leading male and a 'true-life' matador." Carmen is also a matador, "without a sword"—she is impaled, and Escamillo is victorious. These ideas are realized in the music, which is subtly analyzed with micro- and macrotechniques. Most of the *Carmen* literature is cited in 35 footnotes.

585. Wright, Lesley A. "A New Source for *Carmen.*" *19thCM* 2-1 (July 1978): 61–69.

Examines the so-called censor's libretto; discusses variant readings and sources. A new "revision chronology" is proposed, in contrast to that in Fritz Oeser's edition (see #583). Useful references to earlier work.

586. Leicester, H. Marshall. "Discourse and the Film Text: Four Readings of *Carmen.*" *COJ* 6-3 (November 1994): 245–282.

Compares four motion picture versions of 1982–1983, by the directors Jean-Luc Godard, Carlos Saura, Peter Brook, and Francesco Rosi. Concentrates on the use of Bizet's music in the films, rather than on the Carmen story. Godard scarcely uses the music at all; Saura uses record playing to bring in the music; Brook actually presents the opera, but reduced and reconstituted. Rosi's version is a faithful rendition of the opera as staged.

See also McClary (#391).

La jolie fille de Perth

587. Westrup, Jack. "Bizet's *La jolie fille de Perth*." In *Essays* (#70), 157–170.

Discusses variants in the several published versions of the opera, which was first performed in 1867. Bizet's intentions have not been followed by these publications: he has been "maltreated by posterity." No other aspect of the opera is taken up.

Le pêcheurs de perles

ASO 124 (1989).

Boris Blacher (1903–1975)

588. Stuckenschmidt, Hans Heinz. *Boris Blacher.* Berlin: Bote & Bock, 1985. 64p. ISBN 3-7931-1391-4. ML410 .B66 S78.

Brief biography, an autobiographical sketch, worklist, and genesis of some of the operas.

Michel Blavet (1700–1768)

La jaloux corrigé is in *FO*, v.51.

589. La Laurencie, Lionel. "Deux imitateurs français des bouffons: Blavet et Dauvergne." *Année musicale* 2 (1912): 5–125.

A thorough discussion of Blavet's *La jaloux corrigé* (1752): genesis, program notes, musical examples, and reception (necessarily brief, as there were only six performances). Includes biographical information and extensive footnotes. On Dauvergne, the opera discussed is *Les troqueurs* (1753); it receives similar attention. The work was true *opéra-comique,* giving the *coup fatal* to the *comédie-vaudeville.*

Arthur Bliss (1891–1975)

590. Craggs, Stewart. *Arthur Bliss: A Bio-Bibliography.* Bio-Bibliographies in Music, 13. New York: Greenwood, 1988. 183p. ISBN 0-313-25739-6. ML134 .B62 C7.

Not much has been written on the operas. Craggs gives a dozen or so citations to brief treatments of *Olympians* and *Tobias.*

Marc Blitzstein (1905–1964)

591. Gordon, Eric A. *Mark the Music: The Life and Work of Marc Blitzstein.* New York: St. Martin's, 1989. xviii, 605p. ISBN 0-312-02607-2. ML410 .B6 G7.

A well-documented biography, with worklist by genre that offers valuable information about the compositions. Genesis, description, and reception for *The Cradle Will Rock* (1937) and other works of social significance. Expansive index.

592. Oja, Carol. "Marc Blitzstein's *The Cradle Will Rock* and Mass-Song Style of the 1930s." *MQ* 73 (1989): 445–475.

Considers the opera to be a direct descendant in spirit and sentiments of the workers' songs (mass songs) of the Depression era. Composers were trying then to appeal to the masses and to satisfy their own need for personal expression. Many such songs were written by members of the Composers Collective, of which Blitzstein was a member. He wrote such songs as "Into the Streets May First" (1934). *Cradle* is in fact a protest opera. Genesis and variants are discussed.

593. Dietz, Robert James. "The Operatic Style of Marc Blitzstein in the American 'Agit-prop' Era." Ph.D. diss., U. of Iowa, 1970. 475p.

Ernest Bloch (1880–1959)

594. Kushner, David. *Ernest Bloch: A Guide to Research.* Garland Composer Resource Manuals, 14. New York: Garland, 1988. xiii, 345p. ISBN 0-8240-7789-X. ML134 .B623 K9.

A worklist and 579 entries for literature about Bloch. Author, name, and subject indexes. The opera *Macbeth,* which was not a success, has a few brief descriptions.

John Blow (1649–1708)

595. Clarke, Henry Leland. "Dr. John Blow (1649–1708), Last Composer of an Era." Ph.D. diss., Harvard U., 1947. 4v.

François Adrien Boieldieu (1775–1834)

La dame blanche is in *ASO* 176 (1997).

596. Favre, Georges. *Boieldieu: Sa vie, son oeuvre.* Paris: Droz, 1944–1945. 2v. ML410 .B69 F35.

A scholarly biography, drawing on letters and documents. Plots and program notes for the operas, with handwritten musical examples that are difficult to decipher. Worklist (titles only, without details), bibliography, name index.

Arrigo Boito (1842–1918)

597. *Arrigo Boito: Musicista e letterato.* Ed. Giampiero Tintori. Milan: Nuove Edizioni, 1986. 199p. No ISBN. ML410 .B72 A77.

Eleven essays by various authors, covering Boito's life story, his work with Verdi, influence of Wagner, *Mefistofele,* and his letters. Amply illustrated, with worklist, but without index.

598. Nardi, Piero. *Vita di Arrigo Boito.* Verona: Mondadori, 1942. 753p. ML410 .B72 N2.

A revision, or reprint, came out in 1944; not seen. This is the standard biography, and since most of the considerable literature on Boito preceded it, it stands as a summary of scholarship. A scholarly work, with footnotes and expansive index. Operas receive program-note treatment.

599. *Arrigo Boito: Atti del Convegno Internazionale di Studi Dedicato al 150mo della Nascita di Arrigo Boito.* Florence: Olschki, 1994. vi, 598p. ISBN 88-2224-88-2. ML410 .B72 A76.

A gathering of 23 papers read at the conference, including several of special interest: Pierluigi Petrobelli, "Boito e Verdi"; Marcello Conati, "Il valore del tempo: Verdi e Boito, preistoria di una collaborazione"; Giovanella Cresci Marrone, "La 'romanità' del *Nerone*"; and Giovanni Morelli, "Qualcosa sul *Nerone*." Michele Girardi on *Falstaff* is entered at #1882. Name index.

600. Nicolaisen, Jay. "The First *Mefistofele*. *19thCM* 1 (1978) 221–232.

Despite a worthy libretto, the 1868 premiere was a disaster. Nicolaisen compares it with the revision for 1875, finding "compromises and concessions . . . to popular taste." The original was "sincere and determined."

601. Ashbrook, William. "Boito and the 1868 *Mefistofele* Libretto as a Reform Text." In *Reading Opera* (#218), 268–287.

It is a reform opera because it minimizes the number of arias and duets and the old structures of romantic opera. Boito placed "form over formula."

602. Brusa, Fillipo. "Il *Nerone* de Arrigo Boito." *RMI* 31 (1924): 235–443.

A thorough study, well documented. Detailed attention to the text, with a critique of its historical accuracy; technical analysis of the music.

Giovanni Bononcini (1670–1747)

Il Xerse is in *HS*, v.8.

603. Ford, Anthony. "Music and Drama in the Operas of Giovanni Bononcini." *PRMA* 101 (1974–1975): 107–120.

A general view of the operas in terms of structure. There were changes in the period away from the continuo aria toward more use of the orchestra and toward fewer aria numbers. Bononcini omitted the opening orchestral ritornello to carry on the action, as Handel did. He alternated textures and tempi to suggest extreme emotions. Text, music, mood, and character were always well matched.

604. Wolff, Hellmuth Christian. "Bononcini—oder die Relativität historischer Urteile." *Revue belge de musicologie* 11 (1957): 3–16.

A well-documented study of Bononcini's style and the context of his times. Useful comments on the writings of other scholars and quotations from them. Wolff observes that there is no thorough analysis of the operas. There is newer information in Wolff's chapter in *NOHM 5*.

605. Lindgren, Lowell. "The Three Great Noises 'Fatal to the Interests of Bononcini.'" *MQ* 61-4 (October 1975): 560–583.

Biographical background, with details on Bononcini's misguided activities in London after 1720.

606. Lindgren, Lowell. "I trionfi di Camilla." *Studi musicali* 6 (1977): 89–159.

A study of the libretto and music to Bononcini's *Il trionfo di Camilla* (1696). The text, by Silvio Stampiglia, was highly popular, being set 37 times in 70 years. Genesis, comparisons of versions, and an appendix list of Stampiglia's

Camilla productions, with full bibliographic descriptions of libretti and scores, as well as library locations. Lindgren's Ph.D. dissertation (Harvard U., 1972; xii, 1,049p.) is the most substantial treatise: "A Bibliographic Scrutiny of Dramatic Works Set by Giovanni and His Brother Antonio Maria Bononcini."

See also #947.

Giovanni Andrea Bontempi (1624–1705)

607. Engländer, Richard. "Die erste italienische Oper in Dresden, Bontempis *Il Paride in musica* (1662)." *Svensk tidskrift för musikforskning* 40 (1961): 119–134.

The opera was performed on 3 November and 13 November 1662, and the libretto was published in the same year. The opera is in reform style. Synopsis, musical examples, and some technical observations.

Alexander Borodin (1833–1887)

Prince Igor is in *ASO* 168 (1995).

608. Abraham, Gerald. *Borodin: The Composer and His Music.* London: Reeves, 1927. 205p. Reprint, New York: AMS, 1976. ISBN 0-404-1285-13. ML410 .B73 A4.

The only English biography, with genesis and program notes for the stage works (p.64–118).

609. *Alexander Borodin: Sein Leben, seine Musik, seine Schriften.* Musik konkret, 2. Berlin: Ernst Kuhn, 1992. 477p. ISBN 3-928864-03-3. ML410 .B74 A64.

A collection of 41 essays and translations from Russian scholars. They deal with the composer's life, his critical writings, works, sources, and memoirs of him by his contemporaries. On *Prince Igor* there are five essays, dealing with the text, genesis, and reception history. Worklist (titles in German), name index.

610. Bobeth, Marek. *Borodin und seine Oper "Fürst Igor": Geschichte, Analyse, Konsequenzen.* Berliner musikwissenschaftliche Arbeiten, 18. Munich: E. Katzbichler, 1982. 223p. ISBN 3-073970-48-1. ML410 .B74 B66.

A complete account of *Prince Igor,* including genesis, reception, and analysis. A *Leitmotiv* index is of special interest. Bibliography of about 120 entries, name index.

Rutland Boughton (1878–1960)

611. Hurd, Michael. *Rutland Boughton and the Glastonbury Festivals.* New York: Oxford U.P., 1993. xii, 415p. ISBN 0-19-81636-9. ML410 .B772 H9.

A revision of Hurd's *Immortal Hour: The Life and Period of Rutland Boughton* (London: Routledge & Kegan Paul, 1962). An adulatory biography, with genesis and some technical description of the operas. *Immortal Hour* was Boughton's 1914 opera. Worklist, musical examples, index.

Thomas-Louis Bourgeois (1676–1750)

Les amours déguisés is in *FO,* v.29.

George Frederick Bristow (1825–1898)

612. Gombert, Karl Erwin. "*Leonora* by William Henry Fry and *Rip van Winkle* by George Frederick Bristow: Examples of Mid-Nineteenth Century American Opera." D.A. diss., Ball State U., 1977. 264p.

Benjamin Britten (1913–1976)

Thematic Catalogues and Worklists

613. Mitchell, Donald, compiler. *Benjamin Britten: A Complete Catalogue of His Published Works*. Rev. ed. London: Boosey & Hawkes and Faber Music, 1973. 60p. Supplement, June 1978, 4p. No ISBN. ML134 .B85 B64.

   First edition, 1963. A fully descriptive worklist, in chronological order, with performance data and title index.

Bibliographies and Guides to Resources

614. Hodgson, Peter J. *Benjamin Britten: A Guide to Research*. Garland Composer Resource Manuals, 39. New York: Garland, 1996. 245p. ISBN 0-8153-1795-6. ML134 .B851 H63.

   An annotated bibliography of 91 books about Britten, with biographical notes, a description of the Britten-Pears Library in Aldeburgh, a worklist, and an author index. A separate list, not annotated, presents 266 theses and doctoral dissertations. Especially useful for contents listings of composite books.

615. *A Britten Source Book*. Ed. John Evans, Philip Reed, and Paul Wilson. Aldeburgh, England: The Britten Estate for the Britten-Pears Library, 1987. Corrected reprint, Aldershot, England: Scolar Press, 1988. 328p. ISBN 0-9511-9302-9. ML134 .B85 E9.

   A Britten chronology (128p.), list of his incidental music, discography, and topical bibliography of 3,273 titles. Hodgson (#614) provides an analysis of the bibliography by subject.

Collections of Essays

616. *The Britten Companion*. Ed. Christopher Palmer. London: Faber & Faber, 1984. 485p. ISBN 0-571-13168-9. ML410 .B853.

   A compilation of 36 essays, with a Britten chronology and two useful indexes. Contributors include John Evans, Christopher Headington, Donald Mitchell (seven pieces), and Christopher Palmer. Complete contents are in Hodgson (#614).

617. *The Cambridge Companion to Benjamin Britten*. Ed. Mervyn Cooke. New York: Cambridge U.P., 1999. xviii, 350p. ISBN 0-521-57384-4. ML410 .B86 C18.

   Consists of 17 essays, of which 5 are about the operas (entered separately in this guide). Backnotes, worklist, chronology, general index. No bibliography.

Biographies

618. White, Eric Walter. *Benjamin Britten: His Life and Operas*. 2nd ed. London: Faber & Faber, 1983. 322p. ISBN 0-571-18066-3. ML410 .B853 W4.

The publishers have chosen a confusing way of identifying various versions of this work. The first edition was 1948, a second edition appeared in 1954, and a clearly labeled third edition in 1970. So the new second is a further revision of the third. It is mainly a collection of program notes; in the author's words: "These little essays . . . lay no claim to offer musical analyses in depth." Useful chronology of published works and list of premieres. Good illustrations, weak bibliography of about 25 items, index of names, titles, and topics.

619. Carpenter, Humphrey. *Benjamin Britten: A Biography*. New York: Scribner, 1992. x, 677p. ISBN 0-684-19569-0. ML410 .B853 C37.

A subjective life story, emphasizing emotional matters (Britten is portrayed as a "perpetual child") and connecting those readings to compositional questions. Useful for behind-the-scenes depictions of the writing and producing of the operas and other works. Primary sources used. Worklist, strong indexes of titles, names, and topics.

620. Kennedy, Michael. *Britten*. Rev. ed. London: Dent, 1993. 355p. ISBN 0-460-86077-1. ML410 .B853 K45.

First edition, 1981. A useful life and works, if even more adulatory than average for a Britten book; the author wrote it "mainly as a celebration of the joy his music has brought me for over forty years." Worklist and discography.

Operas in General

621. Whittall, Arnold. *Britten and Tippett: Studies in Themes and Techniques*. 2nd ed. New York: Cambridge U.P., 1990. vii, 314p. ISBN 0-521-38501-6. ML390 .B853 W38.

First edition, 1982. A technical comparison of the works of the two composers, grounded in Schenker theory. Britten is found to employ "extended tonality and emancipation of the dissonance," while Tippett prefers "emancipation of the consonance" and a blurring of the line between "extended tonality" and "restricted atonality." Interesting, complex analyses. Bibliography, index.

622. Evans, Peter. *The Music of Benjamin Britten*. Rev. ed. London: Dent, 1989. 574p. ISBN 0-460-12607-5. ML410 .B853 E9.

First edition, 1979. A chapter on each work, presenting some technical analysis (notably for *Billy Budd*); but essentially this is a book of sophisticated program notes. More than 300 musical examples, worklist, bibliography of about 75 titles, name index.

623. Howard, Patricia. *The Operas of Benjamin Britten: An Introduction*. New York: Praeger, 1969. 236p. Reprint, Westport, Conn.: Greenwood, 1976. ISBN 0-214-66055-9 (Praeger). MT100 .B778 B7.

Synopsis and program notes for each opera (except *Death in Venice*, not yet written), with 102 musical examples. No bibliography, no index.

624. Herbert, David. *The Operas of Benjamin Britten: The Complete Librettos.* New York: Columbia U.P., 1979. xxx, 382p. Reprint, New York: New Amsterdam Books, 1989. ISBN 0-2310-48688 (Columbia), 0-941533-71-9 (New Amsterdam). ML 49 .B74 H5.

A useful handbook of the opera texts, with 140 plates that illustrate costumes and sets of the premieres. Includes some essays by librettists and designers. Bibliography of 13 items, good index of names, titles, and topics.

625. McDonald, Ellen. "Women in Benjamin Britten's Operas. " *OQ* 4-3 (Autumn 1986): 83–101.

Though Britten is regarded as a "champion of the oppressed," he did not recognize the oppression of women. He dealt with women as types, without "the full range of human qualities." The author's position is well supported by examples from the operas with leading female characters.

Individual Works

Albert Herring

626. Mitchell, Donald. "The Serious Comedy of *Albert Herring.*" *OQ* 4-3 (Autumn 1986): 45–59.

Britten has been accused of misjudgment for including a serious elegy (on the supposed death of Herring) at the end of his comedy. But Mitchell gives examples of operatic serious comedies, such as *Così fan tutte.* He finds intentional ambiguity in such works. In dealing with this discovery—not too clearly—he does offer a good summary of the opera's ideas and their musical expression.

627. Whittall, Arnold. "The Chamber Operas." In *Cambridge Companion* (#617), 95–112.

Technical analysis of *The Rape of Lucretia, Albert Herring,* and *The Turn of the Screw.* The three operas have a common theme, the vulnerability of innocence to corruption, but they take different perspectives on it.

Billy Budd

ASO 158 (1994), COH 1993.

628. Whittall, Arnold. "'Twisted Relations': Method and Meaning in Britten's *Billy Budd.*" *COJ* 2-2 (January 1990): 145–171.

Examines the characters of Budd and Vere in the story, with a "focus on one particularly significant musico-dramatic issue: how central aspects of the opera's denouement might best be understood in the light of Melville, the opera-maker's apparent intentions, and the composer's actual music." Cites writers who find suppressed homosexual desire by Claggart for Billy (e.g., Auden, E. M. Forster). The libretto makes Billy and Vere more heroic than the original story did. The musical analysis is of interest in itself, whether or not it demonstrates that with Britten "ambivalence got the better of certainty, pessimism of optimism."

629. Hindley, Clifford. "Eros in Life and Death: *Billy Budd* and *Death in Venice*." In *Cambridge Companion* (#617), 147–166.

   Both operas "are concerned with love between males." That attraction appears "in coded form" in *Billy Budd* because of the censorship of the times. But the later opera, appearing after the abolishment of censorship in 1968, is more open about it. Genesis and technical notes are given as well as this sexual aspect of the stories, but the homosexual idea is pervasive. Even the musical structure shows "different ways Claggart and Vere love Billy." And Hindley notes that Britten had described *Death in Venice* as "all that Peter [Pears] and I have stood for."

630. Boubel, Karen A. "The Conflict of Good and Evil: A Musical and Dramatic Study of Britten's *Billy Budd*." Ph.D. diss., U. of Wisconsin, 1985. 236p.

Death in Venice

COH (1987).

631. Evans, John. "*Death in Venice*: The Apollonian/Dionysian Conflict." *OQ* 4-3 (Autumn 1986): 102–115.

   The two sides of Aschenbach's nature are musically portrayed by key relations. The key of F is the Apollonian realm, and E is the opposing Dionysian. The tension between the realms is left unresolved at the end of the opera, as the orchestra sounds a high A above a G-sharp in the bass: "a question mark."

632. Evans, John. "Benjamin Britten's *Death in Venice:* Perspectives on an Opera." Ph.D. diss., U. of Wales, 1984.

633. Feldman, James. "The Musical Portrayal of Gustav von Aschenbach in Benjamin Britten's *Death in Venice*." Ph.D. diss., Kent State U., 1987. 255p.

634. Milliman, Joan Ann. "Britten's Symbolic Treatment of Sleep, Dream, and Death in His Opera *Death in Venice*." Ph.D. diss., U. of Southern California, 1977.

Gloriana

635. *Britten's "Gloriana": Essays and Sources*. Ed. Paul Banks. Aldeburgh Studies in Music, 11. Woodbridge, England: Britten Estate; Rochester, N.Y.: U. of Rochester Press, 1993. xi, 193p. ISBN 0-85115-340-2. ML410 .B853 B75.

   Seven studies, including a list of sources, accounts of genesis and reception, and a bibliography. Indexed. Contents in Hodgson (#614), 175–176.

636. Malloy-Chirgwin, Antonia. "*Gloriana*: Britten's 'Slighted Child.'" In *Cambridge Companion* (#617), 113–128.

   The opera was condemned at its premiere, during the coronation events of 1953 ("inharmonious and wearisome" was one comment), but only because of "misunderstanding and ignorance." Later performances were in fact better received. Genesis, including some of the correspondence between the composer and librettist William Plomer.

A Midsummer Night's Dream

637. Cooke, Mervyn. "Britten and Shakespeare: A Midsummer Night's Dream?" In *Cambridge Companion* (#617), 129–146.

Describes the libretto adaptation, which reduced the play to half its length, with resulting confusions in the story. For example, because of omissions, the lovers "go to bed unmarried, and the fairies conclude the work by blessing pleasures which are in fact illicit." Goes on to technical analysis, covering motifs, key symbolism, and formal elements. Finds musical and dramatic structures to have "equal status."

638. Bach, Jan Norris. "An Analysis of Britten's *A Midsummer Night's Dream.*" D.M.A. diss., U. of Illinois, 1971. 424p.

639. Godsalve, William H. L. *Britten's "A Midsummer Night's Dream": Making an Opera from Shakespeare's Comedy.* Madison, N.J.: Farleigh Dickinson U., 1995. 237p.

Based on the author's Ph.D. dissertation, U. of Saskatchewan, 1990. Genesis of the libretto, with an explanation of the omitted first Shakespeare scene; then musical analysis (motifs, tonal sets, vocal passages). Bibliography, index.

Owen Wingrave

ASO 173 (1996).

Paul Bunyan

640. Mitchell, Donald. *Benjamin Britten: "Paul Bunyan."* London: Faber & Faber, 1981. 96p. ISBN 0-591-15142-6. ML50 .B865 P3.

Text of W. H. Auden's libretto, with a genesis essay by Mitchell.

Peter Grimes

ASO 31 (1980), COH (1983), ENOG 24 (1983).

641. *The Making of "Peter Grimes."* Ed. Paul Banks. Rochester, N.Y.: U. of Rochester Press, 1996. 2v. ISBN 0-85115-632-0. ML96.5 .B74 P42.

V.1 is a reproduction of Britten's sketchbook; v.2 is a collection of essays, pictures of set designs, and miscellaneous documents.

642. Allen, Stephen Arthur. "'He Descended into Hell': *Peter Grimes,* Ellen Orford and Salvation Denied." In *Cambridge Companion* (#617), 81–94.

The story is derived from the poem "The Borough," by George Crabbe. In the poem Ellen Orford is only a spiritual essence, but in the opera she also loves Grimes. Allen analyzes her part in the opera from a technical viewpoint, with musical examples. Two "Ellen motifs" are identified.

643. Deavel, R. Gary. "A Study of Two Operas by Benjamin Britten: *Peter Grimes* and *Turn of the Screw.*" Ph.D. diss., Eastman School of Music, U. of Rochester, 1970. 344p.

644. Stallings, Bonnie L. "Diagetic Music in the Operas of Benjamin Britten: The Case of *Peter Grimes*." Ph.D. diss., U. of California at Los Angeles, 1994. xi, 220p.

645. Brett, Philip. "*Grimes* and *Lucretia*." In *Music and Theatre* (#68), 353–366.

    A consideration of Lucretia's sense of guilt, with its musical ramifications; comparison to *Peter Grimes*. Both operas illustrate the conflict between the individual and society.

The Rape of Lucretia

646. Mertz, Margaret Stover. "History of the Criticism and Sources of Benjamin Britten's *Rape of Lucretia*." Ph.D. diss., Harvard U., 1990. 326p.

647. *"The Rape of Lucretia": A Symposium*. Ed. Eric Crozier. London: John Lane, The Bodley Head, 1948. 101p. ML100 .B8.

    Not examined.

See also Brett (#645) and Whittall (#627).

The Turn of the Screw

648. Marsh, M. "*Turn of the Screw*: Britten and Piper's Operatic Fulfillment of Henry James' Novella." Ph.D. diss., U. of London, 1983.

649. Stimpson, Mansel. "Drama and Meaning in *The Turn of the Screw*." *OQ* 4-3 (Autumn 1986): 75–82.

    Britten's "finest opera" is popular but not well understood. One interpretation of its story is that the governess imagines it all, but Stimpson finds nothing in the opera to support this view. The explication offered is that Quint and Miss Jessel represent the awakening of sexual feelings in the children. For Miles there is the "corrupting" sense that his sexuality is homosexual, drawing him away from the governess toward Quint. The boy cannot cope with this discovery.

See also Deavel (#643) and Whittall (#627).

Ferruccio Busoni (1866–1924)

650. Roberge, Marc-André. *Ferruccio Busoni: A Bio-Bibliography*. Bio-Bibliographies in Music, 34. New York: Greenwood, 1991. xxix, 400p. ISBN 0-313-25587-3. ML134 .B94 R6.

    An annotated bibliography, with 121 entries about the four operas—mostly brief comments and program notes.

651. Beaumont, Antony [*sic*]. *Busoni the Composer*. Bloomington: Indiana U.P., 1985. 408p. ISBN 0-253-31270-1. ML410 .B9114 B37.

    A good resource for the operas and other works, giving genesis, reception, and technical notes on each. *Doktor Faust* has the most coverage, p.311–354. There are chapters on *Turandot* and *Arlecchino* as well. Worklist, bibliography (about 150 entries), general index, index of titles.

Francesca Caccini (1587–ca.1640)

652. Caccini, Francesca. *La liberazione di Ruggiero dall'isola d'Alcina*. Ed. Doris Silbert Smith. Smith College Music Archives, 7. Northampton, Mass.: Smith College, 1945. M1500 .C322 L5.

A piano-vocal score, with a 10-page introduction. This was the first opera by a woman; she was Giulio Caccini's daughter.

653. Raney, Carolyn. "Francesca Caccini, Musician to the Medici and Her *Primo libro* (1618)." Ph.D. diss., New York U., 1971. v, 240p.

Giulio Caccini (1546–1618)

654. Pirrotta, Nino. "Early Opera and Aria." In *New Looks* (#2429), 39–107.

A valuable discussion of the beginnings of opera, problems of form and definition, and the nature of the aria. Caccini's arias for *L'Euridice* (1600; the earliest opera for which complete music survives) are examined.

655. Pirrotta, Nino. "Temperaments and Tendencies in the Florentine Camerata." In his *Music and Culture in Italy from the Middle Ages to the Baroque*, 217–234 (Cambridge, Mass.: Harvard U.P., 1984; ML290.1 .P57).

A valuable study, generally minimizing the creativity of the Camerata. Caccini, the first monodist (in his solo madrigals) is well covered. It was his association with the Bardi group that brought them undeserved credit.

656. Giazotto, Remo. *Le due patrie di Giulio Caccini* . . . Florence: Olschki, 1984. vii, 89p. ISBN 88-222-3284-4. ML410 .C16 G44.

Facsimiles (29 plates) and discussions of 14 documents, relating to the Caccini family, from a private archive in Rome. Index, no bibliography.

657. Carter, Tim. "Giulio Caccini: New Facts, New Music." *Studi musicali* 16 (1987): 13–31.

New information from the Archivio di Stato, Florence, serves to clarify early stages in Caccini's career. A previously unknown solo song is given in score. Much of the new source material is from letters to and from Duke Cosimo de' Medici and his ambassador in Rome, Averardo Serristori.

Caccini's dedication to *L'Euridice* and his preface to *Le nuove musiche* (solo madrigals) are in *Strunk*. For material on the Camerata see #2440ff.

John Cage (1912–1992)

658. Kuhn, Laura Diane. "John Cage's *Europeras 1 & 2*: The Musical Means of Revolution." Ph.D. diss., U. of California at Los Angeles, 1992. 734p.

An extensive treatment of the *Europeras* appears in Lindenberger (#81).

Antonio Caldara (ca.1670–1736)

659. Kirkendale, Ursula. *Antonio Caldara: Sein Leben und seine venezianisch-römischen Oratorien*. Graz: Böhlaus, 1966. 406p. ML410 .C26 K6.

A revision of the author's Ph.D. dissertation, U. of Bonn, 1961. An Italian translation appeared in 1971 (Florence: Olschki). Caldara's biography is thoroughly examined, with passing attention to his operatic work (he was primarily a writer of oratorios). Footnoted, with bibliography but no index.

Robert Cambert (1628–1677)

Little has been written about Cambert, the first French opera composer. Two of his works, *Pomone* and *Les peines et les plaisirs de l'amour* are in *FO*, v.2.

André Campra (1660–1744)

In *FO*: *Le carvaval de Venise*, v.17; *Tancrède*, v.18; *Idoménée*, v.19; and *Ballet des âges*, v.20.

660. Barthelemy, Maurice. *André Campra (1660–1744): Étude biographique et musicologique*. Arles: Actes Sud, 1995. 334p. ISBN 2-7427-0002-1. ML410 .C2406 B28.

Supersedes his 1957 biography. A life story, with good detail on Campra's career at the Paris Opéra; genesis, program notes, and reception for the works presented. Some technical comments on *L'Europe galante* (1697). Notes, bibliography of primary and secondary sources (about 150 items), index.

661. Anthony, James R. "Printed Editions of André Campra's *L'Europe galante*." *MQ* 56-1 (January 1970): 54–73.

A facsimile publication of the 1724 full score (London: Gregg, 1967) is compared to the four earlier editions. Concentrates on relationships between the printer, Robert Ballard, and the composer.

662. Anthony, James R. "The Opera-Ballet of André Campra: A Study of the First Period of French Opera-Ballet." Ph.D. diss., U. of Southern California, 1964. 2v.

663. Banducci, Antonia. "Staging a *tragédie en musique*: A 1748 Promptbook of Campra's *Tancrède*." *Early Music* 21 (1993): 180–190.

A discussion of what may be "the earliest extant source of stage directions for a *tragédie en musique*, in the library at Versailles. It is a book of "over 120 manuscript prompt notes" for works performed at Versailles in 1748. Staging procedures are revealed, including machines, trapdoors, costumes, and actor movements. Some participation in the action by the chorus is indicated; on this matter, see also Cyr (#351).

664. Banducci, Antonia. "*Tancrède* by Antoine Danchet and André Campra: Performance History and Reception (1702–1764)." Ph.D. diss., Washington U., 1990. xiii, 409p.

665. Brown, Leslie Ellen. "The *tragédie lyrique* of André Campra and His Contemporaries." Ph.D. diss., U. of North Carolina, 1978. xvii, 365p.

Michele Carafa (1787–1872)

Le nozze di Lammermoor is in *IO–1810*, v.2.

Alfredo Catalani (1854–1893)

666. Gatti, Carlo. *Alfredo Catalani, la vita e le opere.* Milan: Garzanti, 1953. 250p. ML410 .C37 G3.

A life story, with program notes on the operas.

See also Nicolaisen (#2466).

Pier Francesco Cavalli (1602–1676)

667. Glover, Jane. *Cavalli.* London: Batsford, 1978. 191p. ISBN 0-71341-0078. ML410 .C37 G56.

A fine synthesis of what is known about the composer, whose operas were performed more than those of anyone else during his era. Biographical data are included, but operas are the main focus. Backnotes, musical examples, references to earlier scholarship. Bibliography has about 300 entries. List of all the operas, with dates, premieres, manuscript locations, and comments. Excellent index of names, titles, and topics.

Two older works remain useful for their detailed treatments:

668. Wellesz, Egon. "Cavalli und der Stil der venezianischen Oper von 1640–1660." *Studien zur Musikwissenschaft* 1 (1913): 1–103.

Extended excerpts in score, with perceptive structural analyses; consideration of choral writing, instrumentation, and aria style. Notes; no index.

669. Prunières, Henry. *Cavalli et l'opéra vénetien au XVIIe siècle.* Paris: Rieder, 1931. 120p. ML410 .C3913 P7.

A scholarly discussion of the period and of Cavalli's works, a few footnotes, extended musical examples, 40 pictures of scenes from productions. Bibliography of about 30 entries, no index.

670. Clinkscale, Martha Novak. "Pier Francesco Cavalli's *Xerse.*" Ph.D. diss., U. of Minnesota, 1970. 2v.

In v.2 there is a modern edition of the complete opera.

671. Rosand, Ellen. "Aria in the Early Operas of Francesco Cavalli." Ph.D. diss., New York U., 1971. x, 390p.

672. Rosand, Ellen. "Aria as Drama in the Early Operas of Francesco Cavalli." In Muraro (#2575), 75–96.

Shows "how Cavalli resolved the aria paradox by actually using arias *per se* (as closed forms) to develop, enhance, and define his musical dramas." For example, Daphne's aria in *Apollo* interprets her search for new modes of expression "by the sheer variety of its strophes" and her increased agitation by "gradual loss of patterns."

673. Rosand, Ellen. "Comic Contrast and Dramatic Continuity: Observations on the Form and Function of Aria in the Operas of Francesco Cavalli." *MR* 37 (1976): 92–105.

Contrasts serious and comic arias: they differ in musical and textual structures. The comic has sectional contrast "based on text form"; the serious has
continuity "based on text affect."

674. Jeffrey, Peter. "The Autograph Manuscripts of Francesco Cavalli." Ph.D. diss.,
Princeton U., 1980. 504p.

Friedrich Cerha (1926–)

675. McShane, Catherine Albertson. "The Music of Friedrich Cerha and an Analysis of His Opera *Der Rattenfaenger*." Ph.D. diss., U. of Texas, 1995. 426p.

Antonio (Pietro) Cesti (1623–1669)

Il pomo d'oro is in *RMBE,* v.42.

676. Schmidt, Carl B. "The Operas of Antonio Cesti." Ph.D. diss., Harvard U.,
1973. 2v.

With this massive work—1,721p.—Schmidt provided a documented biography and "a bibliographical scrutiny of all Cesti's operas." Sources, location,
stylistic analysis, worklist, bibliography. No index. Schmidt's later articles
offer condensed presentations of his research.

677. Schmidt, Carl B. "Antonio Cesti's *Il pomo d'oro*: A Re-examination of a
Famous Hapsburg Court Spectacle." *JAMS* 29 (1976): 381–412.

The date of the premiere was July 1668 rather than 1667 as given in standard
sources. New material, presumed lost, is discussed.

678. Wellesz, Egon. "A Festival Opera of the 17th Century." In his *Essays on
Opera,* trans. Patricia Keen, 54–81 (London: Dobson, 1950; ML1700.1
.W45).

Program notes and some technical comments on *Il pomo d'oro.*

679. Schmidt, Carl B. "Antonio Cesti's *La Dori*: A Study of Sources, Performance
Traditions, and Musical Styles." *RIM* 10 (1975): 455–498.

680. Pirrotta, Nino. "Le prime opere di Antonio Cesti." In *L'orchestra,* 153–181
(Florence: G. Barbera, 1954; ML455 .O64).

Establishes the sequence of Cesti's operas, demonstrating that the first was
Orontea (Venice, 1649). Discusses the libretti of the early works and compares
them to Cavalli's; concludes that Cesti favored music over plot and preferred
comic roles.

681. Holmes, William Carl. "*Orontea*: A Study of Change and Development in the
Libretto and Music of Mid-Seventeenth Century Italian Opera." Ph.D. diss.,
Columbia U., 1968. iv, 282p.

682. Holmes, William Carl. "Giacinto Andrea Cicognini's and Antonio Cesti's
Orontea, 1649." In *New Looks* (#2429), 172–219.

Lists and comments on the known libretti of the work, which was Cesti's first
opera and "one of the most widely performed in the 17th century." Discussion

of librettist Cicognini, who "concocted this new *dramma* from various and diverse ingredients." The result was a "romantic comedy in which characters from all stations of life . . . interact." With an interesting analysis of the emotional relationships among the characters.

683. Holmes, William Carl. "Yet Another *Orontea*: Further Rapport between Venice and Vienna." In Muraro (#2575), 199–225.

Concerns Cicognini's libretto and its settings by Cesti (1649), Francesco Ciriello (1654), Filippo Vismarri (1660), and—in French—by Paolo Lorenzani (1687). Cites all relevant literature on these composers and compares their settings. Shows how the Italian style of opera, especially the Venetian, "had been thoroughly integrated into the theatrical life of the imperial court at Vienna." Discusses the Cesti and Vismarri (Vienna) works from various perspectives: orchestra used, aria form, recitative, and scene structure. Cesti is found superior on all counts.

684. Heller, Wendy. "The Queen as King: Refashioning *Semiramide* for *seicento* Venice." *COJ* 5-2 (July 1993): 93–114.

Compares the 1667 Vienna version of Cesti's *La Semirami* with a revision of the libretto for Venice in 1670–1671, finding that the heroine had become en route "more powerful, more lascivious . . . more damaging to the men around her." The change reflects society's "growing insecurity about women's roles."

Petr Il'ich Chaikovskii. See Petr Il'ich Tchaikovsky.

Emmanuel Chabrier (1841–1894)

685. Myers, Rollo H. *Chabrier and His Circle*. London: Dent, 1969. xii, 178p. ISBN 0-460-3826-5. ML410 .C393 M9.

Biographical matter, then genesis, program notes, and reception of the operas, primarily *Le roi malgré lui*. Backnotes, short bibliography, index.

686. Pistone, Danièle. "Emmanuel Chabrier, Opera Composer." Trans. E. Thomas Glasow. *OQ* 12-3 (1996): 17–25.

Influences on Chabrier (mostly Wagner); innovations, such as "modal colorings."

George Whitefield Chadwick (1854–1931)

687. Yellin, Victor. "The Life and Operatic Works of George Whitefield Chadwick." Ph.D. diss., Harvard U., 1957. 308p. plus 113p. music.

Luciano Chailly (1920–)

688. Crest, Renzo. *Linguaggio musicale di Luciano Chailly*. Milan: G. Miano, 1993. 89p. No ISBN. ML410 .C47 C92.

A brief but useful assessment of the operas, in fairly nontechnical terms. Genesis and performance accounts, worklist, backnotes, discography, bibliography. No index.

Gustave Charpentier (1860–1956)

689. Delmas, Marc. *Gustave Charpentier et le lyrisme française*. Paris: Delagrave, 1931. 177p. ML410 .C5 D4.

     The most thorough study available of *Louise* (p.61–91) and *Julien* (p.92–115): analytic notes and reception accounts. Without bibliography or index.

690. Huebner, Steven. "Between Anarchism and the Box Office: Gustave Charpentier's *Louise*." *19thCM* 19-2 (Fall 1995): 136–160.

     How did *Louise* succeed at the Opéra-Comique, despite "subversive political undertones and . . . working class milieu"? Because it mythologized Paris and had a "propensity to encourage readings consonant with bourgeois morality." Detailed genesis, based on the composer's papers, and a close study of the opera from a social viewpoint.

Marc-Antoine Charpentier (1645/1650–1704)

In *FO*: *Le mariage forcé* and *Les arts florissans*, v.7, and *Médée*, v.8.
The recent interest in Charpentier is largely credited to the explorations of one scholar:

691. Hitchcock, H. Wiley. *Marc-Antoine Charpentier*. Oxford Studies of Composers, 23. New York: Oxford U.P., 1990. xi, 123p. ISBN 0-19-316411-2. ML410 .C42 H57.

     The first book in English about the composer. Biography, along with a valuable treatment of the stage works (p.94–115). Short descriptions and analytic comments about the pastorales, "operatic divertissements," and "tragedies." Works considered include *Celse martyr, David et Jonathas,* and *Médée.* Notes, bibliography, index.

692. Hitchcock, H. Wiley. *Les oeuvres de Marc-Antoine Charpentier: Catalogue raisonné*. La vie musicale en France sous les rois Bourbons. Paris: Picard, 1982. 419p. ISBN 2-7084-0084-3. ML134 .C425 H57.

     Front matter is in French and English. A biographical sketch, then a worklist in chronological order, with musical incipits, bibliographic information, sources, durations by section, secondary writings, discographies, and commentaries. There are 551 numbered compositions. Indexes of manuscripts (with *RISM* sigla) and performers; concordance with the listing for Charpentier in the *Catalogue du fonds de musique ancienne de la Bibliothèque Nationale* (1910–1914) by Jules Échorchville.

693. Hitchcock, H. Wiley. "*Les oeuvres de Marc-Antoine Charpentier*: Post-scriptum à un catalogue." *RdM* 70-1 (1984): 37–50.

     Reviews the state of scholarship on Charpentier and considers new editions and recordings. The most important writings are discussed, and lacunae in the literature are noted.

694. Cessac, Catherine. *Marc-Antoine Charpentier*. Paris: Favard, 1988. 604p. ISBN 0-931-3408-02. ML410 .C433.

     An English translation, by E. Thomas Glasow, has appeared (Portland, Ore.: Amadeus, 1995). A thorough examination of the life and works. For the operas, extensive genesis and reception studies, with program notes. *Saul* and *David et Jonathas* are especially well treated. Notes, bibliography of about 200 entries, and indexes of names and works.

695. Powell, John S. "Charpentier's Music for Molière's *Le malade imaginaire* and Its Revisions." *JAMS* 39-1 (Spring 1986): 87–142.

Charpentier's first major work for Paris (10 February 1673) and the only time he worked directly with Molière from concept to performance. Genesis details, explanation of the multiple versions of his score. All musical sources compared and tabulated.

See also #2227.

Carlos Chávez (1899–1978)

696. Parker, Robert L. *Carlos Chávez: A Guide to Research*. Garland Composer Resource Manuals, 46. New York: Garland, 1988. xi, 180p. ISBN 0-8153-2087-6. ML134 .C43 P37.

A thorough bibliography of 434 entries, including a worklist with full bibliographic details and manuscript locations, prose writings of Chávez, and the secondary literature. Also a useful biographical summary and commentary on compositional style. There are 14 entries on the stage works, but the only opera, *The Visitors,* has not attracted scholarly attention. Excellent indexing.

Luigi Cherubini (1760–1842)

697. Willis, Stephen. "Luigi Cherubini: A Study of His Life and Dramatic Music, 1795–1815." Ph.D. diss., Columbia U., 1975. 429p.

698. Willis, Stephen. "Cherubini: From *opera seria* to *opéra-comique*." In *Studies in Music* (#2462), 155–182.

Cherubini, widely acclaimed in his lifetime, revered by Beethoven and Mendelssohn, was nearly forgotten a hundred years later. Newly available sources are making a fresh study of his work possible. Willis explores the ideas and influences that transformed Cherubini from a writer of reform *serie* to a precursor of French grand opera. With *Ifigenia* (1788) he moved away from various clichés; with *Medée* (1797) he showed enhanced orchestration and vocality. But his style was not understood until the romantic era, when his works "would find their true place in music history." Appendix of his letters.

699. Selden, Margery. "The French Operas of Luigi Cherubini." Ph.D. diss., Yale U., 1951. xvii, 457p.

Individual Works

Éliza

700. Fend, Michael. "Literary Motifs, Musical Form and the Quest for the 'Sublime': Cherubini's *Éliza ou le voyage aux glaciers du Mont St. Bernard*." *COJ* 5-1 (March 1993): 17–38.

Discusses the contemporary mystique about the Alps as background for Cherubini's avalanche scene. Then analyzes the scene tonally and through motifs, seeking to explain "the overpowering effect of one sublime natural and moral event."

Lodoïska

701. Pencak, William. "Cherubini Stages a Revolution." *OQ* 8-1 (Spring 1991): 8–27.

Genesis and program notes on *Lodoïska,* which was performed 200 times in its first year, 1791. A prototypical rescue opera, it is said to have influenced *Fidelio.* Pencak identifies the slight literature on Cherubini in 31 footnotes.

Médée

ASO 68 (1984).

702. Ringer, Alexander. "Cherubini's *Médée* and the Spirit of French Revolutionary Opera." In *Essays in Musicology in Honor of Dragan Plamenac,* 281–299 (Pittsburgh: U. of Pittsburgh Press, 1969).

Genesis, social context, and program notes.

703. Fleischer, Tsippi. "Luigi Cherubini's *Médée* (1739): A Study of Its Musical and Dramatic Style." Ph.D. diss., Bar-Ilan U. (Israel), 1995. 371p.

Vincenzo Ciampi (ca. 1719–1762)

704. Sonneck, Oscar G. T. "Ciampi's *Bertoldo, Bertoldino e Cacasenno* and Favart's *Ninette à la cour*: A Contribution to the History of the Pasticcio." *SIMG* 12 (1911): 525–564.

Detailed genesis, analysis with many musical examples, comparison of different versions, and discussion of the two works in relation to parody. Sonneck finds that Egidio Duni had nothing to do with Favart's *Ninette,* contrary to earlier views.

Francesco Cilea (1866–1950)

Adriana Lecouvreur is in *ASO* 155 (1993).

705. D'Amico, Tomasino. *Francesco Cilea.* Milan: Curci, 1960. 162p. ML410 .C625 A51.

A useful life and works, with program notes and reception of the operas. The chapter on *Adriana Lecouvreur* (p.93–110) is a strong overview. Footnotes but no bibliography or index.

Domenico Cimarosa (1749–1801)

Il matrimonio segreto is in *ASO* 175 (1997).

706. Iovino, Robereto. *Domenico Cimarosa, operista napoletano.* Milan: Camunia, 1992. 247p. No ISBN. ML410 .I64 C63.

Life and works, with genesis and program notes on the operas, and a chronology. *Il matrimonio segreto* is adequately covered, p.131–154. Bibliography of some 50 items, no index.

707. Johnson, Jennifer Elizabeth. "Domenico Cimarosa (1749–1801)." Ph.D. diss., U. of Wales, 1976. 3v.

Includes a chronology of works and a thematic catalogue. Sources, genesis, and performance history for all the operas.

708. Lippmann, Friedrich. "Über Cimarosas *opere serie*." *Analecta musicologica* 21 (1982): 21–59.

Cimarosa's *opere buffe* are well known, but his serious operas are neglected, along with other Italian serious operas of the time. Lippmann lists 16 of them, with premiere information and comments. He then considers the libretti, form, and musical style in exemplary detail. With 16 extended musical examples.

709. Dietz, Hanns-Bertold. "Die Varianten in Domenico Cimarosas Autograph zu *Il matrimonio segreto* und ihr Ursprung." *Musikforschung* 31-3 (1978): 273–284.

Compares variants between the composer's autograph and the version used for the premiere in 1792; also compares other copies and editions.

Carlo Coccia (1782–1873)

Caterina di Giusa is in *IO–1810*, v.4.

Pascal Colasse (1649–1709)

Thétis et Pelée is in *FO*, v.10.

François Colin de Blamont (1690–1760)

Les festes greques et romaines is in *FO*, v.34.

Johann Georg Conradi (d.1699)

710. Buelow, George J. "Die schöne und getreue *Ariadne* (Hamburg, 1691): A Lost Opera by Johann Georg Conradi Rediscovered." *AM* 44 (1972): 108–121.

Reports on an anonymous manuscript in the Library of Congress of an opera called *Ariadne,* ascribed to Reinhard Keiser. Stylistic evidence indicates it is not by Keiser but by the "almost unknown" Conradi, Capellmeister of Hamburg Opera from 1690 to 1693. The manuscript "enables us to revise considerably our conception of opera in Hamburg in the late 17th century." With photocopies of the manuscript, music examples, and technical study of the score.

Aaron Copland (1900–1990)

711. Skowronski, JoAnn. *Aaron Copland: A Bio-Bibliography*. Bio-Bibliographies in Music, 2. Westport, Conn.: Greenwood, 1985. x, 273p. ISBN 0-313-24091-4. ML134 .C66 S55.

There is little scholarly literature on the operas. This bibliography locates reviews and brief commentaries.

712. Pollack, Howard. *Aaron Copland: The Life and Work of an Uncommon Man.* New York: Holt, 1999. xi, 690p. ISBN 0-8050-4909-6. ML410 .C756 P6.

The principal biography, uniting life and works in chronological arrangement. Music is discussed in detail but without musical examples. *The Tender Land* has genesis and program notes, p.469–478; *The Second Hurricane* is covered on p.303–310. Backnotes, strong bibliography of about 150 entries, expansive index.

713. Warrick, Kimberly Joanna. "A Stylistic Analysis of Aaron Copland's Two Operas: *The Second Hurricane* and *The Tender Land*." Ph.D. diss., U. of Northern Colorado, 1995. 154p.

Pietro Antonio Coppola (1793–1877)

La pazza per amore and excerpts from *Il postiglione di Longjumeaux* are in *IO–1810*, v.5.

Peter Cornelius (1824–1874)

714. Federhofer, Hellmut, and Kurt Oehl. *Peter Cornelius als Komponist, Dichter, Kritiker und Essayist*. Studien zur Musikgeschichte des 19. Jahrhunderts, 48. Regensburg: Bosse, 1977. 237p. ML410 .C77 P47.

A collection of 20 essays by various authors. These are on the operas: Egon Voss, "*Der Barbier von Bagdad* als komischer Oper"; Erwin Koppen, "*Der Cid* in thematologischer Sicht"; and Anna Amalie Abert, "Zu Cornelius' Oper *Gunlöd*."

715. Wagner, Günter. *Peter Cornelius: Verzeichnis seiner musikalischen und literarischen Werke*. Mainzer Studien zur Musikwissenschaft, 13. Tutzing: Schneider, 1986. 532p. ML134 .C67 A2.

A thorough worklist, with musical incipits, bibliographic data, locations, comments, and lists of secondary literature. Index.

716. Lawton, Orville Timothy. "The Operas of Peter Cornelius." Ph.D. diss., U. of Florida, 1988. 325p.

Francesco Corselli (ca.1702–1778)

717. Strohm, Reinhard. "Francesco Corselli's Operas for Madrid." In *Teatro y música* (#2667), 79–106.

The Italian composer joined the royal court of Spain, gaining, according to most music historians, "instant invisibility." But he was important, and his surviving works (*Farnace*, 1739, and *Achille in Sciro*, 1744) show the relevance of the Italian tradition to Spanish music and musical theater. Technical discussion with musical examples.

Cesar Cui (1835–1918)

718. Taruskin, Richard. "Kuchkism in Practice: Two Operas by Cui." In *Opera and Drama in Russia* (#2648), 341–426.

A valuable account of the Kuchka movement, which was based on the principle that music and text are equal. Actually the text was primary, since music had to correspond to its meaning, and operatic form depends on text. Genesis of *William Ratcliff*, with detailed analysis of music and libretto, music examples (some illegibly printed), performance information, and (negative) reception. Cui wrote his own, anonymous, review: that one was favorable. The study of that opera takes up most of the article, but there are 20 pages about *Angelo,* which also failed. Cui's attempts at Kuchkist opera were then abandoned, and he wrote number operas after that, only to have them poorly received as well. With 151 footnotes as a guide to the whole relevant literature.

Nicolas Dalayrac (1753–1809)

Nina ou la folle par amour and *Léon ou le château de Monténéro* are in *FO,* v.70.

719. *Nicolas Dalayrac: Musicien murétain, homme des lumières.* Muret: Société Nicolas Dalayrac, 1991. 112p. ISBN 2-909302-00-8.ML410 .D13 N63.

Papers from a 1990 colloquium held in Dalayrac's home city, Muret. Includes biographical material and two substantial contributions about the operas: Malou Haine, "Les opéras-comiques de Nicolas Dalayrac représentés au théâtre de Liège entre 1786 et 1835," and Dietmar Fricke, "Réception de l'opéra-comique de Nicolas Dalayrac en Allemagne: Le cas des *Deux petits savoyards.*" Indexed by name and topic, no bibliography.

720. Pendle, Karin. "A Working Friendship: Marsollier and Dalayrac." *M&L* 64 (1983): 44–57.

Benoît-Joseph Marsoller (1750–1817) was Dalayrac's librettist for 25 years and 20 operas, beginning with the successful *Nina* in 1786. Their collaboration was popular even during the Revolution, in which they were able to "represent the kind of continuity that made possible France's return to normal."

721. Charlton, David. "Motif and Recollection in Four Operas of Dalayrac." *Soundings* (Cardiff), 1978: 38–62.

Dalayrac made "a distinct contribution to the developing technique of motivic organization in opera." Analysis and musical examples are presented in support of this view. Variety is demonstrated in the motifs: they are sometimes reminiscent of a character's earlier appearance, and other times they unite similar situations or indicate unspoken thoughts.

Luigi Dallapiccola (1904–1975)

722. Dallapiccola, Luigi. *Selected Writings: V.1, Dallapiccola on Opera.* Ed. and trans. Rudy Shackelford. Musicians on Music, 4. London: Toccata Press, 1989. 291p. ISBN 0-907689-10-8. ML410 .C138 M17.

Autobiographical material and views on his work are blended in this fascinating volume. The composer lived through World War II and embodied its sad themes in such operas as *Il prigonero.* He talks about war, myth, Verdi, and Monteverdi (from whom he derived his own libretto for *Ulisse,* his best-known opera). Indexed.

723. Venuti, Massimo. *Il teatro di Dallapiccola.* Milan: Suvini Zerboni, 1985. ix, 151p. No ISBN. ML410 .D18 V46.

Good technical studies, with extended consideration of *Volo di notte, Job, Ulisse,* and *Marsia.* Discussion of Dallapiccola's aesthetics and theatrical writing. Detailed critical reception of the works. Bibliography of about 50 items, presenting a useful guide to the literature; name index.

724. Nicolodi, Fiamma. *Luigi Dallapiccola: Saggi, testimonianze, carteggio, biografia e bibliografia.* Milan: Suvini Zerboni, 1975. xiii, 171p. No ISBN .ML410 .D138 L8.

Life story, letters, essays, and writings about Dallapiccola and his work. Bibliography, index.

725. Nicolodi, Fiamma. *Parole e musica di Luigi Dallapiccola.* Rev. ed. Milan: Il Saggiatore, 1980. No ISBN. ML60 .D155.

First edition, as *Appunti, incontri,* 1970. A valuable compilation of the composer's writings, including his observations on the music of others as well as his own works. Long sections on *Ulisse, Canti de prigionia,* and *Job.* With 25 interviews, bibliography of 103 writings about Dallapiccola, expansive index.

726. Hess, Julia van. "Luigi Dallapiccolas Bühnenwerk *Ulisse.*" Ph.D. diss., U. of Cologne, 1993.

Walter Damrosch (1862–1950)

The Scarlet Letter is in *19CAMT,* v.16.

Aleksandr Sergeevich Dargomyzhskii (1813–1869)

727. Taruskin, Richard. "*The Stone Guest* and Its Progeny." In *Opera and Drama in Russia* (#2648), 249–340.

The opera (*Kammenyi gost',* 1872; completed by Cui) is "the very model of 'reformist' opera. No other music drama had ever so self-consciously and resolutely refused to be 'operatic,' not even Wagner's." The text of Pushkin's Don Juan play was virtually unaltered in the libretto; the composer literally set the play to music. A "melodic recitative" or "arioso" style is employed, with melody deemphasized; Tchaikovsky called it "an opera without music." Direct influence on Rimsky-Korsakov is noted, but in the end *The Stone Guest* did not affect mainstream practice in Russia. With extensive musical analysis, unfortunately accompanied by faded examples. There is also a discussion of *Rusalka* (1856, revived 1865), which was praised for its recitatives by Cui, leading Dargomyzhskii to elaborate the idiom in *The Stone Guest.* The 150 footnotes lead into the relevant literature.

Antoine Dauvergne (1713–1797)

Les troqueurs is in *FO,* v.51.
See also La Laurencie (#589).

Félicien David (1810–1876)

728. Achter, M. J. "Félicien David, Ambroise Thomas, and French *opéra-lyrique,* 1850–1870." Ph.D. diss., U. of Michigan, 1972. v, 341p.

Claude Debussy (1862–1918)

Bibliographies and Guides to Resources

729. Briscoe, James R. *Claude Debussy: A Guide to Research*. Garland Composer Resource Manuals, 27. New York: Garland: 1990. xxi, 504p. ISBN 0-8240-5795-8. ML134 .D26 B7.

Consists of a chronology, worklist, and 862 annotated entries that present the core literature on Debussy. Also a valuable section on the letters, including printed and manuscript collections and an index to all of them. With a general, nonexpansive index (to page numbers, not entry numbers) through which it is possible, if laborious, to track down some 150 writings about *Pelléas*.

730. Abravanel, Claude. *Claude Debussy: A Bibliography*. Detroit Studies in Music Bibliography, 29. Detroit: Information Coordinators, 1974. 214p. ISBN 0-911772-49-9. ML113 D483 no.29.

The most complete bibliography, with 1,854 books, articles, and dissertations noted. Full bibliographic data but no annotations. On *Pelléas*, we find a listing of premiere reviews from France, Germany, Austria, Czechoslovakia, and the U.S., then 142 writings about the work. Index of names.

Periodicals

731. *Cahiers Debussy*, 1–3, 1974–1976; n.s., 1–, 1977–. St.-Germaine-en-Laye: Centre de Documentation Claude Debussy, 1977–.

The only Debussy periodical, offering a wide range of brief notices and reports and occasional longer articles. Contents of all issues 1974–1987 are in Briscoe (#729), entry 123.

Biographies

732. Lockspeiser, Edward. *Debussy*. 5th ed. Rev. R. Langham Smith. London: Dent, 1980. 421p. ISBN 0-460-02192-2. ML410 .D28 L8.

First edition, 1936. The principal one-volume biography in English, based on the following item:

733. Lockspeiser, Edward. *Debussy: His Life and Mind*. London: Cassell, 1962–1965. 2v. Reprint, New York: Cambridge U.P., 1978. ISBN (Cambridge) 0-521-220563.X. ML410 .D28 L85.

The standard life and works, fully documented. Regarding *Pelléas* there is an extensive genesis, consideration of Wagner and other influences, and reception. Chronology, bibliography, index.

See also #2268, which includes an up-to-date section on Debussy by Roger Nichols.

Pelléas et Mélisande

ASO 9 (1977), COH (1989), ENOG 9 (1982).

734. Parks, Richard S. *The Music of Claude Debussy*. New Haven, Conn.: Yale U.P., 1989. xiv, 366p. ISBN 0-300-044439-9. ML410 .D28 P24.

A close technical study of Debussy's idiom, drawing on set theory and Schenkerian methods. Pitch-class analysis, drawing on Allen Forte's model, is especially fruitful in examining *Pelléas* (p.163–186), where it is found to underlie textual expression. Debussy "devised a new vocabulary of musical symbols." Backnotes, bibliography of about 150 items, expansive index.

735. Grayson, David A. "Waiting for Golaud: The Concept of Time in *Pelléas*." In *Debussy Studies,* ed. Richard Langham Smith, 26–50 (New York: Cambridge U.P., 1997; ISBN 0-521-46090-5; ML410 .D28 D39).

Stage time versus real time creates tensions in the opera. In act 1, scenes 1 and 2, the successive events may take place at the same time. An appendix presents a scene deleted by Maeterlinck before publication of the play, located in a manuscript in the Morgan Library; it would have been part of act 1.

736. Grayson, David A. *The Genesis of Debussy's "Pelléas et Mélisande."* Ann Arbor, Mich.: UMI Research, 1986. xiv, 342p. ISBN 0-8357-1674-0. ML410 .C28 G7.

Based on his Ph.D. dissertation, Harvard U., 1983. Considers the letters of the composer and other clues to his thinking as he dealt with the Maeterlinck play. Covers influences (e.g., Wagner), manuscripts, early editions, and other sources. Presents a reception account as well. Bibliography of some 250 items, index. One genesis aspect is elaborated in an article by Grayson: "The Libretto of Debussy's *Pelléas et Mélisande.*" *M&L* 66–1 (1985): 34–50.

737. Emmanuel, Maurice. *"Pelléas et Mélisande" de Debussy: Étude et analyse.* Paris: Mellottée, 1926. 224p. MT100 .D44 P28.

Analysis of structure, tonality, melody, and leading motives, with some genesis aspects.

738. Stirnemann, Kurt. *Zur Frage des Leitmotivs in Debussys "Pelléas et Mélisande."* Schweizer Beiträge zur Musikwissenschaft, 4. Bern: Haupt, 1980. 266p. ISBN 3-2580-2934-2. ML5 .S32 no.4.

Continues the leading motive analysis of Emmanuel, locating families of themes that are transformed in the course of the drama.

739. Abbate, Carolyn. "*Tristan* in the Composition of *Pelléas*." *19thCM* 5 (1981): 117–141. Reprint, *GL*, v.12.

Examines several manuscripts, revealing that early drafts are clearly connected to *Tristan*. Similarities are concentrated in the tryst scene of act 4, which has an evident dramatic twin in act 2 of *Tristan*. Specific Wagnerian quotations are pointed out, with reference to Holloway's work in this area (#740). Much convincing technical detail is presented. Abbate's analytic work is of great interest in itself, apart from the matter of Wagnerian influences.

740. Holloway, Robin. *Debussy and Wagner*. London: Eulenburg, 1979. 235p. ISBN 0-903873-26-5. ML410 .D28 H74.

Although Debussy wrote no theory of opera, "*Pelléas* fulfills better than any of Wagner's works the theoretical demands of *Oper und Drama*." Holloway explores musical and textual connections between *Tristan* and *Pelléas*, emphasizing that "Debussy is Wagnerian in a unique way." Musical examples display the relationships. No bibliography or index.

741. Youens, Susan Lee. "The Unseen Player: Destiny in *Pelléas et Mélisande*." In *Reading Opera* (#218), 60–91.

A speculation drawing on ideas of Schopenhauer. The protagonist of Pelléas is disclosed as "destiny."

Reginald De Koven (1859–1920)

The Highwayman is in *19CAMT*, v.15.

742. Krasner, Orly Leah. "Reginald De Koven (1859–1920) and American Comic Opera at the Turn of the Century." Ph.D. diss., City U. of New York, 1995. 551p.

Léo Delibes (1836–1891)

A thorough bibliography is in Studwell (#447): it presents 352 numbered entries. Items 267–348 are about operas. Nearly all the writing is brief and superficial.

743. Coquis, André. *Léo Delibes: Sa vie et son oeuvre, 1836–1891*. Paris: Richard-Masse, 1957. 166p. ML410 .D343 C8.

Life and works, with program notes and some technical treatment of the operas. Worklist, bibliography, no index.

744. Curzon, Henri de. *Léo Delibes: Sa vie et ses oeuvres (1836–1892)*. Paris: G. Legouix, 1926. 223p. ML410 .D343 C8.

A useful survey of the works, with program notes and technical comments on the operas.

745. Boston, Margie Viola. "An Essay on the Life and Works of Léo Delibes." D.M.A. diss., U. of Iowa, 1981. 96 leaves.

"Best and most sizeable English-language work on Delibes"—Studwell (#447). Genesis and reception accounts of the operas, with synopses. Also a strong worklist.

Individual Works

Lakmé

ASO 183 (1998).

746. Loisel, Joseph. *"Lakmé" de Léo Delibes: Étude historique et critique, analyse musicale*. Paris: P. Mellottée, 1924. 218p. ML410 .D4 L6.

Genesis, reception (with quotations from reviews), interpreters, and technical analysis with 133 musical examples.

747. Miller, Philip L. "The Orientalism of *Lakmé*." *Opera News* 6 (22 December 1941): 18–21.

A concise explication of the Oriental flavor in the opera, which is far from genuine but which audiences would understand as expressing the spirit of the exotic East.

748. Sharp, Stuart Walter. "The Twilight of French *opéra lyrique,* 1880–1900." D.M.A. diss., U. of Kentucky, 1975.

"Best English work on *Lakmé*"—Studwell (#447).

749. Cronin, Charles P. D., and Betje Black Klier. "Théodore Pavie's *Les babouches du Brahmane* and the story of Delibes's *Lakmé.*" *OQ* 12-4 (Summer 1996): 19–34.

Proposes the source of the opera to be Pavie's work and not, as supposed, Pierre Loti's *Rarahu.* Useful comments about other aspects of the work.

Frederick Delius (1862–1934)

750. *The Delius Companion.* Rev. ed. Ed. Christopher Redwood. London: Calder, 1980. 270p. ISBN 0-7145-3526-5. ML410 .D35 D44.

First edition, 1976. A handy gathering of life-and-works essays by various authors. One is "Delius as Composer of Opera" by Redwood. It gives genesis and program notes for *Koanga* and *A Village Romeo and Juliet.* Indexed.

751. Randel, William. "*Koanga* and Its Libretto." *M&L* 52 (1971): 141–156.

Extensive genesis account, program notes, description of the manuscript score, reception.

Henri Desmarets (1661–1741)

Didon is in *FO,* v.12, and *Iphigénie en Tauride* is in *FO,* v.21.

Paul Dessau (1894–1979)

752. *Paul Dessau von Geschichte gezeichnet: Symposion, Hamburg 1994.* Hotheim: Wolke, 1994. 206p. ISBN 3-923997-63-9. ML410 .D46 S94.

Of the 15 papers in this collection, two are on the operas: Gerhard Müller, "Zeitgeschichtliche Aspekte der *Lukullos*-Debatte"; and Gerd Rienäcker, "Utopien, Illusionen, Desillusionen in Paul Dessaus Oper *Leonce und Lena.*"

André Cardinal Destouches (1672–1749)

In *FO*: *Issé,* v.14; *Callirhoé,* v.15; *Les éléments,* v.16.

753. Kimbell, David R. B. "The *Amadis* Operas of Destouches and Handel." *M&L* 49 (1968): 329–346.

Genesis and detailed text comparison of the two works, bringing out differences between French tradition and the Italian/English traditions as exemplified in London, 1712–1715.

François Devienne (1759–1803)

Les visitandines is in *FO,* v.72.

Nicolas (Alexandre) Dezède (1740/1745–1792)

Blaise et Babet is in *FO,* v.67.

Karl Ditters Von Dittersdorf (1739–1799)

Die Liebe in Narrenhaus is in *GO*, v.15.

754. Riedinger, Lothar. "Karl von Dittersdorf als Opernkomponist." *Studien zur Musikwissenschaft* 2 (1914): 212–349.

A thorough examination of style and technique, with harmonic and structural analyses. Also a chronology of the operas, with premiere data, and a study of the libretti.

755. Horsley, Paul Joseph. "Dittersdorf and the Finale in Late Eighteenth-Century German Comic Opera." Ph.D. diss., Cornell U., 1988. xiv, 537p.

756. Tsai, Shunmei. "The Viennese *Singspiele* of Karl Ditters von Dittersdorf." Ph.D. diss., U. of Kansas, 1990. ix, 310p.

Gaetano Donizetti (1797–1848)

The recent outpouring of scholarly work on Donizetti points up the need for a major annotated bibliography. There is none at the moment, but a volume by James Cassaro in the Garland Composer Resource Manuals series is projected for 2000.

Editions

757. *Edizione critica delle opere di Gaetano Donizetti*. Ed. Gabriele Dotto and Roger Parker. Milan: Ricordi, 1991–. M1500 .D68 F276.

In progress. Operas seen as of December 1999: *Maria Stuarda* (1991) and *La favorite* (1997). See next entry.

758. Parker, Roger. "A Donizetti Critical Edition in the Postmodern World." In *Opera teatrale* (#765), 57–66.

A graceful discussion of editing old works, in general; then attention to Donizetti and problems of the new edition.

759. Saracino, Egidio. *Tutti i libretti di Donizetti*. Milan: Garzanti, 1993. 1,307p. ISBN 8-8114-1056-8. ML49 .C66 S2.

A basic compilation, giving the Italian text of each opera, without scholarly adornments.

Thematic Catalogues and Worklists

760. Lindner, Thomas. "An Integral Catalog of Donizetti's Operatic Works." *OQ* 14-3 (Spring 1998): 17–23.

An valuable inventory of the 64 operas that were complete and performed, in order by premiere date. Each is identified as *farsa, opera buffa, opera seria,* or *opera semiseria* and described as to number of acts, librettist, premiere date, and theater. Revisions, alternate titles, commentary. Appended lists take account of 10 unfinished operas, fragments, and *dubia;* 12 projected works; one false attribution; and some *scene liriche* and cantatas.

Bibliographies and Guides to Resources

761. Sacchiero, Valerio. "Contributo ad un catalogo donizettiano." In *Atti* (#764), v.2, 835–941.

    An inventory of Donizetti works in European libraries, including sacred and instrumental pieces as well as operas. Coverage: Italy, Belgium, Switzerland, Germany, Spain, France, U.K., Norway, Poland, Romania, and Sweden. Gives bibliographic descriptions and comments. More than 1,000 entries.

762. *Il Museo Donizettiano di Bergamo: Catalogo.* Rev. ed. Ed. Valeriano Sacchiero et al. Bergamo: Centro di Studii Donizettiani, 1969. 273p. ML136 .B38 M95.

    First edition, 1936. A description of materials in the Museo: autographs and manuscripts, music, letters, documents, artifacts, and pictures. With a table of operatic performances, 1946–1969. No index.

763. "Recordings." *OQ* 14-3 (Spring 1998): 103–208.

    A fine critical review by various scholars of the recorded operas, limited to in-print CDs.

See also #777.

Conferences

764. *Atti del I° Convegno Internazionale di Studi Donizettiani, 22–28 settembre 1975.* Bergamo: Azienda Autonoma di Turismo, 1983. 2v. No ISBN. ML410 .D68 C668.

    V.1, xl, 542p., 16 papers; v.2, p.543–1,053, 12 papers; no indexes. See #761, #775, #780, #785, #786, and #798.

765. *Opera teatrale di Gaetano Donizetti: Atti del Convegno Internaztionale di Studio, Bergamo, 17–20 settembre 1992.* Ed. Francesco Bellotto. Bergamo: Comune di Bergamo, 1993. 449p. ML410 .D68162.

    An important collection of 29 papers, dealing with the "Donizetti renaissance," textual problems, dramaturgy, vocal writing, and stage settings. Also reports from the Donizetti Society of London, the Centro di Studi Donizettiani di Bergamo, and the Freunde der Musik Gaetano Donizettis in Vienna. Appendix on Donizetti performances in Italian theaters during the first half of the 19th century, name index. See #758, #783, #784, #791, and #809.

Periodicals

766. *Donizetti Society Journal,* 1–, 1974–. London: Donizetti Society, 1974–. Irregular. ML410 .D7 A6. (Cited in this guide as *DSJ.*)

    Title varies: *Journal of the Donizetti Society.* Significant literature is found in every issue; only a selection of articles can be presented here. In addition to scholarly essays, there is news of Donizetti performances, recordings, and books.

767. *Studi donizettiani,* 1–4. 1962–1988. Bergamo: Secomandi, 1962–1988. ML410 .D56 A5.

Letters and Documents

768. Zavadini, Guido. *Donizetti: Vita, musiche, epistolario.* Bergamo: Istituto Italiano d'Arti Grafiche, 1948. xx, 1,019p. ML410 .D7 Z3.

    A biography, worklist, and 726 letters (of which 246 had not been previously published). Indexes of names and of the letters. See next two entries.

769. Barblan, Guglielmo, and Frank Walker. "Contributo all'epistolario de Gaetano Donizetti." *Studi donizettiani* 1 (1962): 1–150.

    Supplements the preceding item.

770. Chesi, Marcella. "Lettere indedite." *Studi donizettiani* 4 (1988): 7–120.

    About 100 letters, not in Zavadini. They include missives to and from the composer and some just about him. Footnoted, indexed.

Biographies

771. Ashbrook, William. *Donizetti and His Operas.* New York: Cambridge U.P., 1982. viii, 744p. ISBN 0-521-23526-X. ML410 .D68 A81 D6.

    The principal life and works, a much expanded revision of *Donizetti* (1965). The life story is brisk and documented. Each opera has a review of primary sources, synopsis, and program notes. Bibliography and index. Ashbrook and Julian Budden coauthored the *NG* article, reprinted in #2480.

772. Weinstock, Herbert. *Donizetti and the World of Opera in Italy, Paris, and Vienna in the First Half of the Nineteenth Century.* New York: Pantheon, 1963. xxii, 453p. ML410 .D7 W4.

    The standard older biography, thorough and footnoted. Genealogical tables, personal documents, and medical and legal documents are printed. Operas are described, with considerable background on the cities where they played. Donizetti's plan for a projected opera is discussed. Bibliography of about 150 items, index.

Operas in General

773. Dean, Winton. "Donizetti's Serious Operas." *PRMA* 100 (1973–1974): 123–141. Reprint, *GL*, v.12.

    Half of Donizetti's operas—and most of his mature works—are *opere serie.* Although "none is a flawless work of art," many could be "extremely moving in the theatre." An innovation was the slow cabaletta, appropriate to tragic arias; this idea was one that influenced Verdi.

774. Black, John. *Donizetti's Operas in Naples, 1822–1848.* London: Donizetti Society, 1982. 69, 51p. No ISBN. ML410 .C68 B62.

    Performance information on all the productions, in date order, including the number in each theater. Libretti, censorship, administration of the theaters. Contemporary sources used, but actual citations are lacking. Also a calendar of operas, by all composers, that were staged in Naples in the 1830s and 1840s. No bibliography or index.

See also #777.

775. Angermüller, Rudolph. "Il periodo viennese di Donizetti." In *Atti* (#764), v.2, 619–698.

Describes Vienna's opera seasons in 1842 and 1843 and Donizetti's activities there as Kammerkapellmeister (an appointment once held by Mozart). *Linda di Chamounix* and *Maria di Rohan* premiered at the Kärntnerthor and were well received. Critical notices are quoted extensively (p.647–695).

776. Croccolo, Enrico. *Donizetti a Lucca: Storia delle opere di Donizetti rappresentate a Lucca dal 1827 al 1858.* Lucca: G. Biagini, 1985. 118p. No ISBN. ML410 .D68 C93.

Reception of *Maria de Rohan, La favorita,* and *Roberto Devereux,* with much quotation from contemporary reviews. Also useful for the history of operatic life in Lucca. No notes, bibliography, or index.

777. *Donizetti e i teatri napoletani nell'ottocento.* Ed. Franco Mancini and Sergio Ragni. Naples: Electa, 1997. 256p. No ISBN. ML410 .D68 D665.

An exhibition catalogue with 20 essays. Topics include the first interpreters of Donizetti in Naples, the use of ballet, scenography, holdings of the Archivio Storico del Banco di Napoli, and Donizetti's letters regarding Naples. The most useful contribution is "Cronologia degli spettacoli (1822–1860)," by Monica Brindicci and Franco Mancini, 239–246. It complements Black's chronological approach (#774), being in title order. It also includes more of the smaller theaters. The book's bibliography, by Tiziana Grande, is also important, with full data given on some 600 titles.

778. Cronin, Charles. "The Comic Operas of Gaetano Donizetti and the End of the *opera buffa* Tradition." Ph.D. diss., Stanford U., 1993. 276p.

779. Jennings, Norman Lyle. "Gaetano Donizetti (1797–1848): The Evolution of His Style Leading to the Production of *Anna Bolena* in 1830." Ph.D. diss., Michigan State U., 1987. 343p.

780. Celletti, Rodolfo. "La vocalità di Donizetti." In *Atti* (#764), v.1, 107–147.

Vocalism in the bel canto period, and to some extent with Verdi, has two opposite modes: one goes with passionate/lyrical moments of the drama, and the other goes with moments of *gravità*. There is also an intermediate zone, where Donizetti had his best results. Celletti traces the composer's evolution as a writer for male and female voices, showing relationships to Rossini and Bellini. He gives attention to the mezzo-soprano, baritone, and bass voices as well as to the soprano and tenor. A thorough study by the leading authority on vocalism; with 69 musical examples.

781. Lippmann, Friedrich. "Die Melodien Donizettis." *Analecta musicologica* 3 (1966): 80–113.

Many musical examples are used to show similarities to Rossini, Bellini, and Verdi: cabalettas, expression of text emotion, rhythmic factors, harmonic background, chromaticism, and romantic tendencies. By 1835 Donizetti and Bellini had nearly identical melodic styles—one could hardly know who had written a given aria.

782. Black, John. "Cammarano's Libretti for Donizetti." *Studi donizettiani* 3 (1978): 115–131.

Not seen.

783. Commons, Jeremy. "De l'opera semi-seria." In *Opera teatrale* (#765), 181–193.

The *semi-seria,* an Italian adaptation of the *opéra-comique,* mixed singing with spoken dialogue and used contemporary themes and characters. *Opera buffa* was more fully "comic"; *semi-seria* had only some comedic elements. Social (not political) problems were addressed, leading on to *verismo.* Donizetti's *Emilia di Liverpool, Alina, Gianni da Calais,* and *Otto mesi* are discussed in this context. Both Donizetti and Bellini incorporated such themes into their serious operas to make the characters more empathetic to audiences, with the result that *semi-seria* was overshadowed, and the genre all but disappeared by 1842, the date of *Linda di Chamounix.* That was Donizetti's final work of *semi-seria,* after which he turned completely to tragedy.

784. Smith, Marion. "The *livrets de mise en scène* of Donizetti's Paris Operas." In *Opera teatrale* (#765), 371–391.

Examines the 11 staging manuals (*livrets*) by Louis Palianti, of Donizetti's French (or translated into French) operas. In general, the manuals grow more complex over time. They vary in style but have certain common features: all describe how scenes were to be "blocked," and many deal with set and costume. They refer to specific scenes and libretti. The main focus is on placement and movement of the characters, especially in recitative and ensembles; little is said about how the singers comport themselves in arias. Full descriptions and illustrations of the staging directions for three finales of *Les martyrs* at the Paris Opéra in 1840.

785. Zedda, Alberto. "La strumentazione nell'opere teatrale di Donizetti." In *Atti* (#764), v.1, 453–540.

An elaborate study of orchestral practice of Donizetti's time. His basic orchestra is described, along with special instruments used on occasion (harp, organ, tam tam, bells, guitar, etc.) His qualities as an orchestrator are examined, with reference to the instrumentation of specific numbers: overture, ensemble, cavatina, and so forth. Musical examples are used to demonstrate Donizetti's use of each instrument, and all the operas are analyzed from this aspect.

786. Zanolini, Bruno. "L'armonia come espressione drammaturgica in Gaetano Donizetti." In *Atti* (#764), v.2, 775–823.

An insightful discussion of formal and tonal procedures in Donizetti's Neapolitan period, with *Poliuto* (1848) analyzed in detail as an example. Other operas are involved as well. Modulations get special attention. The composer did not invariably keep one key through a number as Rossini did: he was more like Verdi, who was quite free in this regard. There were comments from the audience after the paper was read, with interesting views expressed on tonality in late-19th-century opera.

787. Walter, M. "Komponistorischer Arbeitsprozess und Werkcharacter bei Donizetti." *Studi musicali* 26 (1997): 445–518.

A valuable consideration of Donizetti's work habits. He began with much attention to the libretto; that part of his procedure has been well examined. Walter goes on to reconstruct the way the composer worked on the score itself. He composed at the piano, eight or nine hours a day; it was headwork, not inspiration. Unless he knew the orchestra that would be performing, he waited to orchestrate. He made no sketches for an overall plan and was ready to change anything to adjust to the needs of singers or the demands of censors. The article has 310 footnotes that lead to earlier writings on the composing process of Donizetti and of other composers.

See also Balthazar (#511).

Individual Works

L'ajo nell'imbarazzo

788. Watts, John. "*L'ajo nell'imbarazzo*." *DSJ* 1 (1974): 41–50.

Genesis, reception of the 1824 premiere, revision for Naples as *Don Gregorio* (1826). Full performance history, plot synopsis.

Anna Bolena

789. Gossett, Philip. "*Anna Bolena*" *and the Artistic Maturity of Gaetano Donizetti.* New York: Oxford U.P. , 1985. xvii, 183p. ISBN 0-1931-3205-2. ML410 .D68 G67.

An important study, rich with technical detail. Genesis, influence of Rossini, structural analysis, critical study of the compositional decisions. Comparisons between the manuscript and the final version. Musical examples, footnotes; no bibliography and no index.

Belisario

790. Ashbrook, William. "Popular Success, the Critics and Fame: The Early Careers of *Lucia di Lammermoor* and *Belisario*." *COJ* 2-1 (March 1990): 65–81.

The two premieres were within four months of each other. Their reception history is plotted, based on accounts in three contemporary journals. *Belisario* was better received at first but soon fell behind *Lucia*. Casting of the soprano roles is one probable reason.

Il campanello

791. Narici, Ilaria. "*Il campanello*: Genesi e storia di una farsa napoletana." In *Opera teatrale* (#765), 93–110.

A discussion of the background of the work, the time in which it was composed, and the relation between libretto and its literary sources; also premiere information. All research sources are described: autographs, manuscripts, and printed editions. With comments on the new critical edition of Donizetti's works and the editorial decisions involved.

Dom Sébastien

ERO, v.29.

Don Pasquale

ASO 108 (1988).

792. Rattalino, Piero. "Il processo compositivo nel *Don Pasquale* di Donizetti." *NRMI* 4 (1970): 51–68; 263–280.

Genesis: the sketches, modifications of the original libretto; various settings and melodies for the duet between Norina and the doctor in act 1. Instrumentation was changed after the premiere.

L'elisir d'amore

ASO 95 (1987).

Emilia di Liverpool

793. Commons, Jeremy. "*Emilia di Liverpool.*" *M&L* 40-3 (July 1959): 207–228.

A stage history, noting the various versions; it was not a successful work. Manuscripts, documents, and printed editions are compared. The revival in Liverpool, for the city's 750th anniversary, is described.

L'esule di Roma

794. Kaufman, Thomas G. "*L'esule di Roma*: A Performance History." *DSJ* 4 (1980): 104–109.

There were more than 60 productions in the 19th century. This is a chronology of 1828–1869, with casts, of performances in Italy, Spain, Eastern Europe, and Latin America.

La favorite (La favorita)

ERO, v.28.

795. Ashbrook William. "La composizione de *La favorita.*" *DSJ* 2 (1972): 13–27.

A detailed genesis account.

La fille du regiment

ASO 179 (1997).

796. Loveland, Karl. "Reading Donizetti's *La fille du regiment*: Genesis, Transformation, and Interpretations." Ph.D. diss., U. of Rochester, 1996. 337p.

Lucia di Lammermoor

ASO 55 (1983).

797. Smart, Mary Anne. "The Silencing of Lucia." *COJ* 4-2 (July 1992): 119–141.

The mad scene in a feminist context. Some critics regard Lucia's decline as "positive, even liberating" (Clément; Peter Conrad); she is "joyful, airy, and peaceful." Smart observes that the "same melismatic formulas occur in saner moments or in other operas, but in Lucia's mad scene they are longer and more frequent." As coloratura "becomes excessive, the device is marked and its uncanny significance emerges." There is some formal irregularity in the mad scene, but it ends with a cabaletta that is "almost startling in its formal regularity." The conclusion is that conflicting interpretations are the norm regarding madness. Lucia is clearly "defeated both by the forces of musical language and by the oppressive power of the plot." This attention to "excess" is also found in the study by McClary (#391).

798. Bortolotto, Mario. "Sul sestetto nell'opera *Lucia di Lammermoor.*" In *Atti* (#764), v.1, 51–60.

An interesting study of the sextet, identifying musical elements that form "objective correlatives" of the dramatic situation. One such element is the gradual slide toward metrical irregularity. Musical contrasts between the two parts of the ensemble also respond to shifts in the action.

See also Ashbrook (#790).

Lucrezia Borgia

799. Kaufman, Thomas G. "*Lucrezia Borgia*: Various Versions and Performance History." *DSJ* 5 (1984): 37–81.

Reception study, considering changes made for later performances and variant titles. Valuable chronology of performances, 1833–1902.

800. Guaricci, Joseph. "*Lucrezia Borgia.*" *DSJ* 2 (1975): 161–177.

Genesis, synopsis, technical notes with musical examples.

Maria di Rohan

801. Barblan, Guglielmo. "*Maria di Rohan.*" *DSJ* 2 (1975): 15–33.

Genesis, reception (it was enthusiastic), revisions in score and libretto. No musical analysis. Appendix by John Watts gives performance history, 1957–1974.

Maria Padilla

802. Parker, Roger. "*Maria Padilla*: Some Historical and Analytical Remarks." *DSJ* 5 (1984): 20–34.

Reception history; analysis of vocal aspects and overall structure.

803. Ashbrook, William. "Donizetti and Romantic Sensibility in Milan at the Time of *Maria Padilla.*" *DSJ* 5 (1984): 8–19.

Cultural background of Milan and its relation to the emotional and romantic aspects of the libretto.

Maria Stuarda

804. Commons, Jeremy, Patric Schmid, and Don White. "19th Century Performances of *Maria Stuarda.*" *DSJ* 3 (1977): 217–242.

Productions of 1835–1865 in various European houses, with changes in the score made for the different performances.

805. Watts, John. *"Maria Stuarda* in Performance." *DSJ* 1 (1974): 31–40; 3 (1977): 244–258.

Notes on 81 European performances, 1958–1977, in tabular form, with casts.

806. Brookens, Karen. "A Comparative Study of Thea Musgrave's *Mary Queen of Scots* and Gaetano Donizetti's *Maria Stuarda.*" D.M.A. diss., Arizona State U., 1997. 142p.

807. Ashbrook, William. *"Maria Stuarda*: The Libretto, Its Source, the Historical Background and Variants." *DSJ* 3 (1977): 97–105.

The source was an Italian version of Schiller's play. Modifications made in it by librettist Giuseppe Bardari are detailed. Considers the opera's relation to historical events and other 19th-century libretti on this story.

808. Cecchi, Paolo. "'Per rendere il soggetto musicabile': Il percorso fonte-libretto-partitura in *Maria Stuarda* e in *Marino Faliero.*" In *Opera teatrale* (#764), v.1, 229–275.

For *Maria Stuarda*: detailed genesis; literary source (Schiller), the librettist (Giuseppe Bardari); transformations of poetic elements. For *Marino Faliero*: the libretto by Emanuele Bidera and Agostino Ruffini, drawn from the tragedy by Delavigne, is shown to be more faithful to its source.

Marino Faliero

See Cecchi (#808).

Les martyrs

ERO, v.27.

809. Girardi, Michele. "Donizetti e il *grand opéra*: Il caso de *Les martyrs.*" In *Opera teatrale* (#765), 135–145.

Donizetti was the first composer commissioned to write a genuine *grand opéra.* This one is compared to *Les huguenots,* which had been a major early example of the genre and is shown to have clear influences on Verdi.

810. Allitt, John. *"Les martyrs* Revived." *DSJ* 2 (1975): 37–98.

Genesis, plot, program notes; with valuable appendixes of contemporary reviews and illustrations in 1840 and 1852. Also prints the French libretto.

Otto mesi in due ore

811. Bini, Annalisa. *"Otto mesi in due ore, ossia Gli esiliati in Siberia*: Vicende di un'opera donizettiana." *RIM* 22 (1987): 183–260.

Analysis of the libretto and the composer's modifications of the score for various performances. With two fragments in autograph and description of other sources.

Parisina

812. Barblan, Guglielmo. "Alla ribalta un'ottocentesca tragedia lirica: *Parisina d'Este* di Donizetti." *Chigiana* 21 (1964): 207–238.

Genesis, reception, analysis of structure and recurring themes.

Poliuto

813. Black, John. "Cammarano's Self Borrowings: The Libretto of *Poliuto*." *DSJ* 4 (1980): 89–103.

While composer self-borrowing has been well studied, librettist self-borrowing has not. Black uses *Poliuto* as a case study for it. (Cammarano made no secret of his practice.) Eight of the 15 set pieces in *Poliuto* were used in later works; these are carefully described.

See also Zanolini (#786).

Regina di Golconda

814. Mioli, Piero. "Da *Alina, regina di Golconda* a *Don Pasquale*: La prima buffa nel vocalismo donizettiano." *Studi donizettiani* 4 (1988): 127–161.

In contrast to Rossini, who made modest demands on the soprano voice, Donizetti gradually created the "prima donna assoluta," requiring agility and "canto di bravura." This development is tracked from *Alina* (1828) to *Don Pasquale* (1843).

Roberto Devereux

ERO, v.26.

815. Black, John. "*Elisabeth d'Angleterre, Il conte d'Essex,* and *Roberto Devereux.*" *DSJ* 5 (1984): 135–146.

A play by Jacques Ancelot, *Elisabeth d'Angleterre* (1829) was the source used by Cammarano for the *Roberto Devereux* libretto (1837). It was also used by Felice Romani for his libretto *Il conte d'Essex* (1833; music by Mercadante). Romani accused Cammarano of plagiarism. Black's comparison of the three texts demonstrates that Cammarano used Ancelot directly and did not steal anything from Romani.

Antonio Draghi (1634/1635–1700)

There is little recent writing about Draghi, who composed 170 works between 1662 and 1699.

816. Neuhaus, Max. "Antonio Draghi." *Studien zur Musikwissenschaft* 1 (1913): 104–192.

Gives the operas in chronological order, with casts, extended musical extracts, historical
context, and structural analysis. No index.

Paul Dukas (1865–1935)

Ariane et Barbe-Bleue is in *ASO* 149/150 (1992).

817. Suschitzky, Anya. "*Ariane et Barbe-Bleue*: Dukas, the Light, and the Well." *COJ* 9-2 (July 1997): 133–162.

Genesis; sources in Maeterlinck (Mélisande, after Pelléas, goes to Bluebeard and is again captive in a dark castle); use of Debussy's music. The article's focus is on the themes of light and dark. Ariane "lights the way out of the castle." She is a creature of a popular French image of the time, in which truth takes the form of a naked woman emerging from a dark well.

Egidio Duni (1708–1775)

In FO: *La peintre amoureux de son modèle* and *L'isle des faux*, v.52; *Les deux chasseurs et la laitière* and *La fée urgèle*, v.53.

818. Smith, K. M. "Egidio Duni and the Development of the *opéra-comique* from 1753 to 1770." Ph.D. diss., Cornell U., 1980. xiv, 348p.

See also Holmes (#1414).

Antonín Dvořák (1841–1904)

819. Dvořák, Antonín. *Complete Edition* = *Souborné vydáni*. Prague: Supraphon, 1955–. M3 .D93.

All the stage works to be included in v.1–13. Four have been seen: *The Jacobin, Rusalka, The Devil and Kate,* and *The Spectre's Bride.* Full scores, with words in Czech, German, and English. Brief information on sources and variants, in four languages.

820. Clapham, John. *Dvořák.* 2nd ed. New York: Norton, 1979. 238p. ISBN 0-3930-1204-2. ML410 .D9 C58.

A biography, with program notes on the operas. Bibliography of some 200 entries, worklist, chronology, name index.

821. Smaczny, J. A. "A Study of the First Six Operas of Antonín Dvořák." Ph.D. diss., U. of Oxford, 1989.

822. Schläder, Jürgen. "Märchenoper oder symbolisches Musikdrama? Zum Interpretations Rahmen der Titelrolle in Dvořáks *Rusalka.*" *Musikforschung* 34 (1981): 25–39.

Considers recent stagings in the light of the sources of the story: Hans Christian Anderson's *Little Mermaid* and Friedrich de la Motte Fouqué's *Undine.* Productions should not overemphasize the fairy-tale aspects.

Werener Egk (1901–1983)

823. Krause, Ernst. *Werner Egk: Oper und Ballett.* Wilhelmshaven: Heinrichshafen, 1971. 232p. ISBN 3-7959-0093-0. ML410 .E2 K9.

Genesis, plots, and technical notes on the operas, with musical examples. Worklist, discography, index.

824. *Werner Egk.* Ed. Alfred Boswald. Komponist in Bayern, 29. Tutzing: Schneider, 1997. 232p. ISBN 3-7952-0866-1. ML410 .E34 W47.

Essays by various authors. One is an extended treatment of the operas: Helga-Maria Palm-Beulich, "Welttheater in sieben Akten: AZu den Opern Werner Egks," 66–146. It offers genesis and technical analyses with musical examples. The book has a worklist, bibliography of about 60 entries, discography, and index.

Gottfried von Einem (1918–)

825. Rutz, Hans. *Neue Oper: G. von Einem und seine Oper "Dantons Tod."*
Vienna: Universal, 1947. 69p. MT100 .E35 R94.

    Essays by Rutz and four other scholars dealing with genesis, plot, musical
    analysis, and modern stagings of *Dantons Tod;* also the problems of modern
    opera in general. No index.

826. Rutz, Hans. "Danton's Death: Music Drama or Music Theater." *Musicology* 2
(1948): 188–194.

    The opera takes place on two separate planes: voice and orchestra. There is
    "hardly any thematic relationship" between them. But chorus and orchestra
    have a rare "thematic liaison" in the epilogue to scene 1. The orchestral music
    has no symphonic form: it has "only one tendency—the dramatic."

827. Schneider, Wolfgang. "From Drama to Libretto." *Musicology* 2 (1948): 182–
187.

    Genesis of *Dantons Tod,* which was based on a play by Georg Büchner. Librettist Boris Blacher had to condense the play, which had 29 scenes, and impose
    some order on its "formlessness of dramatic plan."

828. Reich, Willi. *"Der Prozess." MQ* 40 (1954): 62–76.

    A discussion of the premiere in Salzburg, 17 August 1953; with plot, program
    notes, and some musical examples with comments.

Hanns Eisler (1898–1962)

829. *Hanns Eisler Miscellany.* Compiled and ed. David Blake. Luxembourg: Harwood, 1995. xvi, 495p. ISBN 3-7186-5573-X. ML410 .E36 H225.

    A collection of 20 essays by various authors, including John Willett, "*Die
    Massnahme*: The Vanishing *Lehrstück*"; Eisler's "Notes on *Dr. Faustus*"; and
    Walter Mittenzwei, "On the *Faustus* Debate." The debate involved was about
    the place of art in East Germany's postwar social revolution. It all disheartened
    Eisler—he gave up composition and did not complete his Faust opera. The
    libretto is printed in the book, which also has a minor bibliography and index.

George Enescu (1881–1955)

The name is also seen as Enesco.

830. Malcolm, Noel. *George Enescu: His Life and Music.* London: Toccata, 1991.
320p. ISBN 0-907689-32-9. ML410 .E5 M2.

    The only English book on Enescu: a basic biography, with genesis and program notes on *Oedipe* (1936). Worklist, bibliography.

Ferenc Erkel (1810–1893)

831. Véber, Gyula. *Ungarische Elemente in der Opernmusik Ferenc Erkels.*
Bilthoven: Creyghton, 1976. 244p. ML410 .E77 V39.

    Not seen. Described in #77 as "useful background and detailed analysis of all
    the operas." Bibliography, index, summary in English.

832. Legány, Dezső. *Erkel Ferenc: Művei és korabeli történetük*. Budapest: Zen-eműkiadó, 1975. 143p. ISBN 963-330-061-4. ML410 .E77 L5.

In Hungarian, but the inventory of 77 works has data and facts that come across: premiere information, bibliographic descriptions, and library locations of manuscripts. Name index.

Manuel de Falla (1876–1946)

La vida breve is in *ASO* 177 (1997).

833. Chase, Gilbert, and Andrew Budwig. *Manuel de Falla: A Bibliography and Research Guide*. Garland Composer Research Manuals, 4. New York: Garland, 1986. 145p. ISBN 0-8240-8587-2. ML134 .F18 C5.

Consists of 385 annotated entries, which include a worklist and writings about Falla. Budwig has also provided a useful biographical summary of 40 pages. Operatic output is the subject of 64 entries, but most of them are reviews or brief notices. Indexes of titles, names, and authors.

834. Harper, Nancy Lee. *Manuel de Falla: A Bio-Bibliography*. Bio-Bibliographies in Music, 68. Westport, Conn.: Greenwood, 1998. 281p. ISBN 0-313-30292-8. ML134 .F19 H37.

A well-annotated bibliography of 798 entries but given in author order with poor indexing, so it is tedious to seek what has been written about the operas. It does not seem to add much to the preceding entry.

835. Budwig, Andrew. "Manuel de Falla's *Atlántida*: An Historical and Analytical Study." Ph.D. diss., U. of Chicago, 1984. 474p.

A valuable life story, based on private correspondence made available to Budwig by Falla's family, and a thorough analysis of *Atlántida*.

836. Ansermet, Ernest. "Falla's *Atlántida*." *Opera News*, 29 September 1962: 8–13.

A strong musical-dramatic analysis in a few pages.

837. Fernández Shaw, Guillermo. *Larga historia de "La vida breve."* Madrid: Revista de Occidente, 1972. 214p. ML410 .F16 F36.

A genesis study by the son of the librettist, drawing on correspondence between his father and the composer. The libretto is included. No attention to the music, no index.

838. Aubry, Jean. "*El retablo* by Manuel de Falla." *Chesterian* 34 (October 1923): 37–46.

Synopsis, with scene-by-scene musical analysis.

Gabriel Fauré (1845–1924)

839. Phillips, Edward R. *Gabriel Fauré: A Guide to Research*. Garland Composer Resource Manuals, 49. New York: Garland, 2000 [i.e., 1999]. xv, 429p. ISBN 0-8240-7073-9. ML134 .F29 P55.

A useful classified, annotated bibliography of 1,130 numbered entries and 18 master's theses. Stage works have 228 entries, but most of them are reviews and brief notices. Worklist, author index.

Charles-Simon Favart (1710–1792)

Ninette à la cour is in *FO*, v.50.

Vincenzo Fioravanti (1799–1877)

Il ritorno di Columella da Padova is in *IO–1810*, v.7.

Carlisle Floyd (1926–)

840. McDevitt, F. J. "The Stage Works of Carlisle Floyd." Ph.D. diss., Juilliard School, 1975.

841. Pollack, Howard. "The Reconstruction of *Jonathan Wade*." *OQ* 8-1 (Spring 1991): 62–83.

 The work was 80 percent revised after its unsuccessful 1962 premiere. The changes are described. Program notes on the revision, musical examples.

Lukas Foss (1922–)

842. Perone, Karen. *Lukas Foss: A Bio-Bibliography*. Bio-Bibliographies in Music, 37. New York: Greenwood, 1988. viii, 282p. ISBN 0-313-26811-8. ML134 .F58 P4.

 A useful worklist (in genre order), with critical commentaries cited. There are only a few entries about *The Celebrated Jumping Frog*.

Alberto Franchetti (1860–1942)

843. Mallach, Alan. "Alberto Franchetti and *Cristoforo Colombo*." *OQ* 9-2 (Winter 1992): 12–30.

 Genesis, program notes, reception, some biographical information.

See also Maehder (#2476).

François Francoeur (dit Le Cadet) (1698–1787)

Pirame et Thisbé and *Scanderberg,* both written with François Rebel, are in *FO*, v.36.

William Henry Fry (1813–1864)

844. Smith, Edwin. "William Henry Fry's *Leonora*." D.M.A. diss., U. of Kentucky, 1974. 311p.

845. Upton, William Treat. *William Henry Fry*. New York: Crowell, 1954. xv, 346p. Reprint, New York: Da Capo, 1974. ISBN 0-306-70625-3. ML410 .F965 U62.

 Leonora (1845) was the first opera by an American to be staged. Its genesis is well described here, with program notes and reception. Fry's *Aurelia the Vestal* (1841) is also discussed. With worklist, giving bibliographic details, but without footnotes. Expansive index.

See also Gombert (#612).

Johann Josef Fux (1660–1741)

846. *Johann Joseph Fux: Sämtliche Werke.* Ed. Hellmut Federhofer and Othmar Wessely. Graz: Akademische Druck und Verlagsanstalt; Kassel: Bärenreiter, 1959–. M3 .F97.

   In progress. Three volumes of series 5, the operas, have been seen: v.1, *Julo Ascanio;* v.2, *Pulcheria;* v.3, *Gli ossequi della notte.* These are full scores with introductions and critical notes, all in German.

847. Wellesz, Egon. *Fux.* New York: Oxford U.P., 1965. 54p. ML410 .F99 W45.

   Although not remembered as an opera composer, Fux did write 18 or 19 of them. This is a good introduction to the composer and his dramatic works. Program notes, with some technical comments, musical examples, footnotes.

848. Köchel, Ludwig Ritter von. *Johann Josef Fux.* Vienna: Alfred Hölder, 1872. 584, 185p. Reprint, Hildesheim: Olms, 1974. ML410 .F99 K77.

   An excellent scholarly study, still the principal biography after 13 decades. Documents, worklist, and annotated thematic catalogue (operas: p.127–147). Name and title index.

849. Meer, J. H. van der. *Johann Josef Fux als Opernkomponist.* Bilthoven: A. B. Creyghton, 1961. 3v. ML3410 .F99 M49.

   The only specific book about the operas, and a valuable one. Detailed analyses of text, ballet, aria, orchestra, etc., in 16 operas, with backnotes, bibliography (about 400 entries), and name index. V.3 consists of 91 extended musical extracts.

Baldassare Galuppi (1706–1785)

The first name is also seen as Baldassarre.

850. Bollert, Werner. *Die Buffo-Opern Baldassare Galuppis.* Bottrop: Postberg, 1935. 160p. ML410 .G16 B6.

   A documented, technical study of the arias, duets, recitative, choral numbers, instrumentation, and ballet. Comparison of different versions and extracts from contemporary critics. Bibliography of about 150 items, no index.

851. Piovano, Francesco. "Baldassare Galuppi: Note bio-bibliografiche." *RMI* 13 (1906): 676–726; 14 (1907): 333–365; 15 (1908): 233–274.

   A well-documented biography, then a thorough description of 114 operas. Premiere information, plots, and reception are given in detail The third segment corrects and adds to the material in the first two parts.

852. *Galuppiana 1985: Studi e ricerche. Atti del Convegno Internationale.* Ed. Maria Teresa Muraro and Franco Rossi. Quaderni della Rivista italiana di musicologia, 13. Florence: Olschki, 1986. viii, 342p. ML5 Q13.

   Consists of 17 papers from a conference held in Venice, 28–30 October 1985. The first, by Franco Rossi, is a useful bibliography of 133 Galuppi manuscripts in Venetian libraries. Material on the operas includes Claudio Gallico, "Da *L'Arcadia in Brenta* a *La diavolessa* di Goldoni e Galuppi: Una via alla riforma dell'opera italiana"; Reinhard Wiesend, "Baldassare Galuppi fra opera seria e opera buffa"; Stefan Kunze, "Per una descrizione tipologica della *Introduzione* nell'opera buffa del settecento e particolarmente nei drammi giocosi di Carlo Goldoni e Baldassarre Galuppi"; Maria Delogu, "Galuppi a Vienna: *Artaterse*"; Elena Sala di Felice, "Metastasio e Galuppi a Vienna"; and Dale E. Monson, "Galuppi, Tenducci, and *Montezuma*: A Commentary on the History and Musical Style of *opera seria* after 1750." The volume has a name index.

See also Heartz (#250) and other entries on Goldoni, who was one of Galuppi's librettists, and #1007.

Francesco Gasparini (1661–1727)

853. *Atti del Primo Convegno Internazionale.* Ed. Fabrizio della Seta and Franco Piperno. Quaderni della Rivista italiana di musicologia, 6. Florence: Olschki, 1981. 341p. ISBN 88-222-2988-6. ML5 .Q13.

Twenty papers from a conference held in Camaiore, 29 September–1 October 1978. Opera coverage includes Leopold M. Kantner, "Le opere di Francesco Gasparini a Vienna"; Reinhard Strohm, "Francesco Gasparini, le sue opere tarde e Georg Friedrich Händel" (see #854); and Lowell Lindgren, "Le opere drammatiche 'romane' di Francesco Gasparini (1689–1699)." The volume has name and composer indexes.

854. Strohm, Reinhard. "Francesco Gasparini's Later Operas and Handel." In *Essays on Handel* (#953), 80–92.

Originally in #853, in Italian. Concerns Gasparini in Rome, 1714–1727. His works influenced Handel, who knew *Tamerlano* (1711; revised as *Bajazet* in 1719); Handel's *Tamerlano* appeared in 1724, with evident borrowing. Another "partly derivative" Handel work was *Faramondo* (1738), drawn from Gasparini's opera of the same name (1720). Musical examples exhibit these relationships. Handel's other models—also with "a distinctively Roman basis"—were Bononcini and Stradella.

855. Strohm, Reinhard. "An Opera Autograph of Francesco Gasparini?" In *Essays on Handel* (#953), 106–121.

Originally in German, in *Hamburger Jahrbuch für Musikwissenschaft* 3 (1978). Examines an anonymous manuscript in the British Library (add. ms.14233), concluding that the arranger of the score for Milan appears to have been Gasparini. After Strohm had done this analysis, his conclusion was verified by the discovery of a letter written by Gasparini, showing the same handwriting.

Florian Gassmann (1729–1774)

856. Donath, Gustav. "Florian Gassmann als Opernkomponist." *Studien zur Musikwissenschaft* 2 (1914): 34–211.

A thorough, documented biography and full treatment of the works. List of operas, with premiere information and publication data, library locations of manuscripts, and detailed description of every work with musical examples. Pages 137–211 have extended excerpts.

Theobaldo Gatti (ca.1650–1727)

Scylla is in *FO*, v.23.

Pierre Gaveaux (1760–1825)

Léonore, ou l'amour conjugal is in *FO*, v.75.

George Gershwin (1898–1937)

Porgy and Bess is in *ASO* 103 (1987).

857. Rimler, Walter. *A Gershwin Companion: A Critical Inventory & Discography, 1916–1984*. Ann Arbor, Mich.: Popular Culture, Ink, 1991. xiv, 488p. ISBN 1-560-75019-7. ML134 .G29 R5.

A useful worklist, presenting all published and unpublished compositions by Gershwin in order of publication date. Information includes pre-CD discographies. Index of names and titles, another of recording artists.

858. Gilbert, Steven E. *The Music of Gershwin*. New Haven, Conn.: Yale U.P., 1995. xi, 255p. ISBN 0-300-06233-8. ML410 .G28 G46.

A useful technical study of the major works, in the context of Joseph Schillinger's composition method. *Porgy and Bess* has p.182–207. Tonal design is explored (the opera is in E major/minor). Backnotes, extended musical examples, bibliography of about 60 entries, expansive index.

859. Alpert, Hollis. *The Life and Times of "Porgy and Bess": The Story of an American Classic*. New York: Knopf, 1990. 354p. ISBN 0-39458339-6. ML410 .G268 A68.

A popular-style genesis-and-reception study, of interest for its coverage of European performances and the movie version. Undocumented quotations and invented scenarios detract from credibility. Bibliography of about 60 entries, expansive index.

860. Starr, Lawrence. "Toward a Reevaluation of Gershwin's *Porgy and Bess*." *American Music* 2–2 (Summer 1984): 25–37.

Answers various criticisms that have been leveled at the opera. Says the portrayal of black people is not condescending but authentic for its period. Prepares a formal plan for the work, with tonal structure and motifs (for those who said it was formless), and defends the effectiveness of the recitatives, noting that they should be sung lyrically instead of *parlando*—close to *arioso*.

861. Johnson, John Andrew. "Gershwin's American Folk Opera: The Genesis, Style, and Reputation of *Porgy and Bess*." Ph.D. diss., Harvard U., 1996. 915p.

862. Hamm, Charles. "The Theatre Guild Production of *Porgy and Bess*." *JAMS* 40–3 (Fall 1987): 495–532.

Reviews the performances and recordings that have claimed to present the complete opera, finding them all defective. Goes back to the 1935 Theatre Guild production with Gershwin involved, to find the authentic version. Examines Gershwin's original scores and compares them to various performances, noting cuts made. Hamm decides the 1935 manifestation is the best one and should be the one given today. He finds no formal design in the work and does not refer to Starr's efforts in disclosing one (#860).

863. Shirley, Wayne D. "Rotating *Porgy and Bess*." In *The Gershwin Style: New Looks at the Music of George Gershwin,* ed. Wayne Schneider, 21–34 (New York: Oxford U.P., 1999; xiv, 290p.; ISBN 0-19-509020-0; ML410 .G28 G38).

Shirley's essay, one of 12 in the volume, is an intriguing and ingenious examination of a set of four leaves, in Gershwin's hand, in the Library of Congress. The leaves show the Porgy motif in different versions. They are explained as efforts to implement Joseph Schillinger's "rotation" device for varying a theme; Gershwin had taken some composition lessons from him. With 33 notes.

Charles-Hubert Gervais (1671–1744)

Hypermnestre is in *FO,* v.31.

Jean-Claude Gillier (1667–1737)

Amphion is in *FO,* v.13.

Alberto Ginastera (1916–1983)

864. Storni, Eduardo. *Ginastera*. Madrid: Espasa-Calpe, 1983. 212p. ISBN 8–4239-5380-7. ML410 .G49 S88.

A straightforward biography, useful for reception accounts of *Don Rodrigo* and *Bomarzo*. No index.

865. Suárez Urtubey, Pola. *Alberto Ginastera*. Buenos Aires: Ediciones Culturales Argentinas, 1972. 162p. No ISBN. ML410 .G36 S9.

A biography, with micro- and macroanalysis of *Don Rodrigo*.

866. *Alberto Ginastera*. Ed. Friedrich Stangemacher. Bonn: Boosey & Hawkes, 1984. 122p. ISBN 3-8709-0204-3. ML410 .G49 A5.

Seven essays—in German—by various authors, three by Ginastera himself (about *Don Rodrigo* and *Bomarzo*). Malena Kuss has a fine technical study, "Symbol und Phantasie in Ginasteras *Bomarzo,*" giving micro- and macro-analysis but marred by inscrutable musical examples. The volume has a worklist, a bibliography of about 30 entries, and no index.

867. Kuss, Malena. "Type, Derivation, and Use of Folk Idioms in Ginastera's *Don Rodrigo*." *Latin American Music Review* 1 (1980): 176–195.

Finds this to be "the opera in which assimilation of native idioms of rural folk extraction takes place at the most basic and structural compositional level." The essay focuses on one such idiom, which is integrated into the basic 12-tone row as its first four-note segment, and on the structural role this segment plays throughout the work. Parallels to Berg's *Lulu* are pointed out.

Umberto Giordano (1867–1948)

Andrea Chenier is in *ASO* 121 (1989).

868. *Umberto Giordano.* Ed. Mario Morini. Milan: Sonzogno, 1968. 315, 119p. No ISBN. ML410 .G5 M86.

Ten essays by various writers on Giordano's style, orchestration, life, letters, and singers of his works. A valuable anthology of criticism by 23 scholars is included. List of premieres, chronology of life and works, discography, good bibliography (including newspaper reviews) of some 400 entries, indexes of titles and names.

869. *Umberto Giordano e il verismo. Atti del Convegno di Studi.* Ed. Mario Morini and Piero Ostali. Milan: Sonzogno, 1989. 174p. No ISBN. ML410 .G37 U734.

The conference, at Verona, 2–3 July 1986, yielded 25 informal papers. Name and title index.

Peggy Glanville-Hicks (1912–1990)

870. Hayes, Deborah. *Peggy Glanville-Hicks: A Bio-Bibliography.* Bio-Bibliographies in Music, 27. New York: Greenwood, 1990. x, 274p. ISBN 0-313-26422-8. ML134 .G52 H4.

A bibliography of 699 writings by Glanville-Hicks and 410 about her, with brief annotations. It is a challenge to find anything in this volume, which puts the entries in chronological order and has a very poor index. A worklist is included.

Philip Glass (1937–)

871. Glass, Philip. *Music by Philip Glass.* New York: Harper & Row, 1987. 222p. ISBN 0-0601-5823-9. ML410 .G398 A3.

A British edition was titled *Opera on the Beach* (London: Faber, 1988). Essentially a genesis account of *Einstein on the Beach* (1976) and *Akhnaten* (1984), disclosing the composer's strong concern with plot and visual elements. Full libretti are given, along with some musical examples in partly legible handwriting. The book also offers "revealing anecdotes" about Nadia Boulanger and Ravi Shankar, who helped Glass to formulate his views. Selective worklist, 1965–1987, expansive index.

872. Richardson, John. *Singing Archaeology: Philip Glass's "Akhnaten."* Middletown, Conn.: Wesleyan U.P., 1999. 294p. ISBN 0-8195-6317-X. ML410 .G54 R54.

The "central concern is to examine the complex and often troubled relationship between this music and earlier musical practices." Richardson also tries to answer the (apparently unanswerable) question: Why do the people who like Philip Glass's music like it? Genesis, reception, and a technical study of the micro and macro aspects are interesting, but the story drifts into Brechtian alienation, Akhnaten's "religious credo and its representation in music," and deep thoughts from Jacques Lacan and Julia Kristeva. Backnotes, expansive index. No bibliography, but the notes provide a good discursive guide to the literature on Glass.

873. Kostelanetz, Richard. *Writing on Glass: Essays, Interviews, Criticism.* New York: Schirmer, 1997. viii, 368p. ISBN 0-02-864657-6. ML410 .G398 W75.

A gathering of interviews with Glass and informal essays by 26 contributors about his work. The most useful contribution is Paul John Frandsen's on *Akhnaten.* Other operas discussed: *Einstein on the Beach,* by David Cunnigham; *Satharaha,* by Allan Kozinn; and *The Photographer,* by Robert C. Morgan.

874. Schwarz, K. Robert. *Minimalists.* London: Phaidon, 1996. 239p. ISBN 0-7148-3381-9. ML390 .S3976.

A study of eight composers, including two chapters on Glass. Genesis and long program notes on all the operas are of use. Worklists for the composers but no documentation. Expansive index.

Mikhail Ivanovich Glinka (1804–1857)

875. Brown, David. *Mikhail Glinka: A Biographical and Critical Study.* New York: Oxford U.P., 1974. 340p. ISBN 0-19-315311-4. ML410 .G56 B87.

A valuable, well-documented biography and introduction to the music. Includes extensive genesis and program notes on the operas (*Ruslan and Liudmila* has 50 pages). Worklist, minor bibliography (about 60 titles), name index.

876. Taruskin, Richard. "Glinka's Ambiguous Legacy and the Birth Pangs of Russian Opera." *19thCM* 1-2 (November 1977): 142–162.

Discusses the critical reception in Russia of Glinka's works and analyzes them in terms of the beginning of a national school of opera. With 70 footnotes, taking in the relevant literature.

877. Glinka, Mikhail Ivanovich. *Memoirs.* Trans. Richard B. Mudge. Norman: U. of Oklahoma Press, 1963. 264p. ML410 .G56 A22.

Glinka traveled widely, studied constantly, and met interesting people. The memoirs are given here in a well-documented annotated context, including a chronology of the life and performances of his works. No bibliography; index of names and titles.

878. Orlova, Aleksandra Anatol'evna. *Glinka's Life in Music: A Chronicle.* Trans. Richard Hoops. Russian Music Studies, 20. Ann Arbor, Mich.: UMI Research, 1988. xxiv, 823p. ISBN 0-8357-1864-6. ML410 .G55 O74.

A remarkable day-by-day account of Glinka's life, with references to all sorts of evidence and quotations from primary sources. Includes genesis details and reception accounts of the operas. Without bibliography (the notes throughout the text may serve); with indexes of persons and works.

See also several essays by Gerald Abraham, in his *Studies* (#2635) and *On Russian Music* (#2636). Readers of Russian will find an elaborate account of Glinka's music in v.1 of *Izbrannye trudy,* by Boris V. Asaf'ev (Moscow: Izd-vo Akademii Nauk SSSR, 1952–1957). A monograph by the same author, on the life and works, is also useful:

M. I. *Glinka* (Leningrad: Muzyka, 1950, reprinted 1978); about 90 pages are devoted *Ruslan and Liudmila*.

Christoph Willibald Gluck (1714–1787)

Editions

879. Gluck, Christoph Willibald. *Sämtliche Werke.* Ed. Gerhard Croll, for the Staatliches Institut für Musikforschung Presussischer Kulturbesitz, Berlin. Kassel: Bärenreiter, 1951–. M3 G63.

The operas, with critical commentaries, are in *Abteilung* 1, v.1–11; 3, v.1–26; 4, v.1–11. See #907 below.

Thematic Catalogues and Worklists

880. Wotquenne, Alfred. *Catalogue thématique des oeuvres de Chr. W. v. Gluck.* Leipzig: Breitkopf & Härtel, 1904. Trans. into German, Josef Liebeskind. Supplements in French and German, 1911. Reprint, Hildesheim: Olms, 1967. xi, 240p. ML134 .G56 W6.

Still useful; extended and corrected by Hopkinson (#882).

Bibliographies and Guides to Resources

881. Howard, Patricia. *Christoph Willibald Gluck: A Guide to Research.* Garland Composer Resource Manuals, 8. New York: Garland, 1987. xxiii, 178p. ISBN 0-8240-8451-9. ML134 .G56 H7.

An indispensable bibliography of 545 annotated entries, including a worklist, library holdings, biographical studies, and essays on individual works. With a convenient chapter on the reform opera and related genres. Indexes of works, authors, and names.

882. Hopkinson, Cecil. *A Bibliography of the Printed Works of C. W. von Gluck, 1714–1787.* Rev. ed. New York: Broude, 1967. xiv, 96p. ML134 .G58 H7.

First edition, 1959. Gives bibliographic descriptions of all the original scores, with locations, variants, and later publications (full scores and piano/vocals), including separate publications of individual arias. Updates Wotquenne's information (#880) and adds new items. Also a "comparative table of dates of editions" and a strong bibliography of about 120 entries. No index. Some corrections were noted in the review by François Lesure in *RdM* 43 (1967): 195.

883. Wortsmann, Stephan. *Die deutsche Gluck-Literatur.* Nuremberg: Koch, 1914. viii, 121p. ML410 .G51 W66.

A critical survey of German writing on Gluck up to 1914. Name index.

Conferences

884. *Kongressbericht Gluck in Wien. Wien, 12–16 November 1987.* Ed. Gerhard Croll and Monika Woitas. Gluck-Studien, 1. Kassel: Bärenreiter, 1989. 188p. ISBN 3-7618-0929-8. ML410 .G56 K82.

Consists of 22 papers, most of them very brief. Useful essays on the operas: Siegfried Mauser, "Musikalische Dramaturgie und Phänomene der Personencharakteristik in Glucks *Orfeo*"; Pierluigi Petrobelli, "La concezione drammatico-musicale dell'*Alceste*"; Bernd Baselt, "Zum Thema Händel und Gluck"; and László Somfai, "Die wiener Gluck-Kopisten—ein Forschungsdesiderat."

885. *Gluck e la cultura italiana nella Vienna del suo tempo. Chigiana*, n.s., 9/10 (1972–1973): 235–592.

An issue devoted to Gluck, with 24 papers from the conference in Siena, September 1973. Of interest: Julian Rushton, "From Vienna to Paris: Gluck and the French Opera"; Friedrich Sternfeld, "Gluck's Operas and Italian Tradition"; Francesco Degrada, "Aspetti Gluckiani nell'ultimo Hasse"; and Mercedes Viale Ferrero, "Appunti di scenografia settecentesca, in margine a rappresentazioni di opere in musica di Gluck e balli di Angiolini." Two papers on *Orfeo* are entered separately: Daniel Heartz (#906) and Michael Robinson (#908).

Periodicals

886. *Gluck Jahrbuch,* 1–4, 1913–1918. Berlin: Gluck Gesellschaft, 1913–1918. ML410 .G56 A18.

Only four issues were published, and most of the articles have been overtaken by later research.

Letters and Documents

887. Mueller von Asow, Hedwig, and Erich Hermann Mueller von Asow. *The Collected Correspondence of Christoph Willibald Gluck*. New York: Random House, 1962. xi, 239p. ML410 .G5 A46.

A well-annotated if poorly arranged gathering of materials, with source list and index of names, titles, and topics. Inaccuracies and omissions were pointed out in reviews by Winton Dean in *Musical Times* 103 (1962): 230–231, and Klaus Hortschansky in *Die Musikforschung* 17 (1965): 469–471.

Prose Works

Gluck's most renowned literary piece is the dedication to *Alceste* (#378).

Biographies

This major composer is without a full-scale modern biography. Some older volumes are of use:

888. Abert, Anna Amalie. *Christoph Willibald Gluck*. Munich: Bong, 1959. 288p. Reprint, Zurich: Büchergilde Gutenberg, 1960. ML410 G5 A55.

The standard life and works, with good descriptions of the operas. Worklist, minor bibliography, name index.

889. Cooper, Martin. *Gluck*. London: Chatto & Windus, 1935. xv, 293p. ML410 G5 C5.

Life and works, with good presentation of the composer's changing styles. Bibliography, worklist, index.

The likely author of the anticipated biography is not quite ready:

890. Howard, Patricia. *Gluck: An Eighteenth-Century Portrait in Letters and Documents*. New York: Oxford U.P., 1995. xiv, 271p. ISBN 0-19-81635-1. ML410 .G5 H668.

"Not a biography [but] a selection of material on which a biography might be based," this assemblage is highly valuable. It includes letters, reviews, and memoirs—almost none available before in English—arranged in chronological order with commentary. Bibliography of about 250 items, index.

Operas in General

891. Newman, Ernest. *Gluck and the Opera: A Study in Musical History*. London: Dobell, 1895. xx, 300p. Reprints, London: Gollancz, 1967; Westport, Conn.: Greenwood, 1976; New York: AMS, 1978. ISBN (Greenwood) 0-8371-8849-0. ML410 .G5 N3.

A valuable older study, including biography but concentrating on the operas. Genesis (letters quoted), program notes, reception. Accounts of the aesthetic theory and conventions of opera in Gluck's time are of interest. Footnoted but without bibliography. Worklist, index of names and topics.

892. Howard, Patricia. *Gluck and the Birth of Modern Opera*. New York: St. Martin's, 1963. 118p. ML410 G5 H6.

A general survey of the operas and their background; genesis, program notes, 40 musical examples. Useful list of the operas and ballets with premiere information. Minor bibliography, name index.

893. Berlioz, Hector. *Gluck and His Operas, with an Account of Their Relation to Musical Art*. Trans. Edwin Evans. London: Reeves, 1915. xiv, 167p. ML410 .B5 A543.

Essays on Gluck taken from *A travers chants, études musicales, adorations, boutades et critiques,* by Berlioz (Paris: Levy, 1862). Enlightened and perceptive reactions to *Orphée* (p.1–34) and *Alceste* (p.35–161), resulting from revivals of the operas in Paris, directed by Berlioz. Without notes, bibliography, or index.

894. Abert, Hermann. "Glucks italienische Opern bis zum *Orfeo*." *Gluck-Jahrbuch* 2 (1916): 1–25.

Argues that the early group of pre-*Orfeo* operas were influenced by Sammartini, while the next group may have been guided by Hasse. Anticipations of the reform operas are pointed out.

895. Kurth, Ernst. "Die Jugendopern Glucks bis *Orfeo*." *Studien zur Musikwissenschaft* 1 (1913): 193–277.

A thorough background study and technical analysis of 23 works produced from 1741 to 1760; reprinted from the 1908 edition of Gluck's works. Notes and extended musical examples.

896. Brown, Bruce Alan. *Gluck and the French Theatre in Vienna*. New York: Oxford U.P., 1991. xvii, 525p. ISBN 0-19-3164-15–9. ML1723.8 .V6 B76.

Between 1754 and 1764 a French troupe was in residence in Vienna, directed by Giacomo Durazzo, with Gluck as its music director, conductor, and composer. The Viennese French theater influenced Gluck in general and the reform operas in particular. Brown discusses the Viennese cultural context, the Burgtheater, economic and political conditions, Gluck's pantomime ballets, *Orfeo,* and the impact of Durazzo. One conclusion is that Gluck was less a reformer than one who rode the tides of change. Chronology, 1748–1765; list of Gluck's official positions in Vienna theaters; bibliography of some 300 items; index.

897. Haas, Robert. *Gluck und Durazzo im Burgtheater: Die "Opéra-comique" in Wien.* Vienna: Amalthea, 1925. 216p. ML1723.8 .V6 H13.

A major study of the development of comic opera in Vienna and Gluck's contributions to that repertoire. Extensive reference to contemporary sources. Index.

898. Nagler, Alois. "Gluck in Wien und Paris." *Maske und Kothurn* 1 (1955): 225–267. PN2004 .M36.

Considers 18th-century Gluck productions, beginning in 1753, bringing out the contributions of designers, choreographers, singers, and instrumentalists. A wide range of sources is cited and used to demonstrate the importance of those collaborators.

See also Heartz (#2134).

Individual Works

Alceste

ASO 73 (1985).

899. Sternfeld, Frederick W. "Expression and Revision in Gluck's *Orfeo* and *Alceste*." In *Essays Presented to Egon Wellesz* (#70), 114–129.

Compares the Vienna (1762, 1767) and Paris (1774, 1776) versions. There was an increased time dimension in the Paris (reform) operas: they had large scenes that could not be borrowed for other operas like the arias from number operas. But the Paris versions did have added numbers (dances, arias) that conflicted with the dramatic and tonal design. Sternfeld prefers the originals, while admitting to "several and substantial improvements" in the reform revisions.

900. Hastings, Margaret. "Gluck's *Alceste*." *M&L* 36 (1955): 41–54.

Considers variants in the source material of the Paris *Alceste,* other genesis matters, reception, and early stage history.

Iphigénie en Tauride

ASO 62 (1984); *FO,* v.63.

901. Landy, Rémy, and Pierre Peyronnet. "Dramaturgie textuelle et dramaturgie musicale." In *L'opéra au XVIIIe siècle* (#2251), 379–417.

A study of text problems and of how solutions were found by the composer and librettist in three 18th-century French operas: Rameau's *Hippolyte et Aricie,* Gluck's *Iphigénie en Tauride,* and Salieri's *Tarare.*

902. Dahlhaus, Carl. "Ethos and Pathos in Gluck's *Iphigenie auf Tauris.*" *Musik-forschung* 27 (1974): 289–300.

An imaginative perspective, drawing on the philosophic concepts of ethos (Apollonian) and pathos (Dionysian). Iphigenie represents ethos, and Orestes is pathos. Poised as he was between the baroque (pathos) and classical (ethos) eras, Gluck balanced these two elements in his music.

903. Cumming, Julie E. "Gluck's Iphigenia Operas: Sources and Strategies." In *Opera and the Enlightenment* (#91), 217–240.

The myth is traced from Euripedes to Racine, whose version was the source of the opera libretti of the 18th century. Pre-Gluckian settings had been made by Domenico Scarlatti, Caldara, Porpora, Sarti, Graun, Jommelli, Pasquini, Traetta, Galuppi, and others. There is discussion of some of these, indicating musical and dramatic borrowings. Gluck's versions of the recognition/sacrifice scene are detailed. All sources are described in extensive backnotes.

904. Rushton, Julian. "*Iphigénie en Tauride*: The Operas of Gluck and Piccinni." *M&L* 53-4 (October 1972): 411–430.

Gluck's version premiered in Paris in 1779, Piccinni's in 1781. The contrasting styles were at the heart of the Quarrel of the Buffoons (see #2257ff). Rushton makes a detailed comparison of the two settings, number by number, and declares Gluck the winner. Earlier literature is recalled through 20 footnotes.

See also Schmierer (#1415).

Orfeo ed Euridice

ASO 23 (1979), COH (1981), Rororo (1988).

905. La Laurencie, Lionel de. "*Orphée*" *de Gluck*. Paris: Mellottée, 1934. 349p. ML410 .G5 L3.

A discursive study of the Vienna and Paris versions, with genesis accounts and performance histories in Europe up to the 1920s. Also a consideration of the Orpheus myth in literature and opera. Gluck's *Orfeo*, says La Laurencie, is the oldest opera that is relevant to modern listeners.

906. Heartz, Daniel. "*Orfeo ed Euridice*: Some Criticisms, Revisions, and Stage-Realizations During Gluck's Lifetime." In *Gluck e la cultura* (#885), 383–394.

Examines critical responses to the Vienna premiere (1762) of Gluck's first version and later productions in London, Parma, Munich, and Stockholm. Considers revisions made in the score for those performances.

907. Finscher, Ludwig. "*Orphée et Euridice*": *Vorwort und kritischer Bericht*. Kassel: Bärenreiter, 1967. xxxviii, 367p.

Issued as part of the *Sämtliche Werke* (#879), v.1–6. A thorough history of the Paris version, with reviews reprinted, and of later performances to 1820. Questions of authenticity are taken up, regarding ballet sections and other elements.

908. Robinson, Michael. "The 1774 S. Carlo Version of *Orfeo*." In *Gluck e la cultura* (#885), 395–413.

   A good account of the production and of several others: Vienna, 1762; London, 1770 and 1771; Florence, 1771; and Naples, 1774. A table compares these productions bit by bit.

909. Brück, Paul. "Glucks *Orpheus*." *AfM* 7 (1925): 436–476.

   Compares the two versions, bringing about differences in declamation required by the change from Italian to French word-setting.

910. Gallarati, Paolo. *"L'Orfeo ed Euridice" di Gluck: Versione Viennese del 1762*. Turin: Giappichelli, 1979. 201p. ML410 .G5 G33.

   Depth analysis of the opera, placed in the context of contemporary works.

911. Loewenberg, Alfred. "Gluck's *Orfeo* on the Stage with Some Notes on Other Orpheus Operas." *MQ* 26 (1940): 311–339.

   Orpheus settings before Gluck; then reception and stage history of both Gluck versions up to 1939. Also a list of parodies of *Orfeo*.

912. Dalmonte, Rossana. "Ripensando a 'Che farò senza Euridice.'" In *Quaderni della Rivista italiana di musicologia* 32 (1994): 49–64.

   Eduard Hanslick (see #426) did serious damage to the idea of word supremacy in opera by writing a happy text to the music of Orfeo's tragic aria. Dalmonte makes a valiant effort to counter Hanslick, finding his parody does not fit Gluck's sorrow aspects, such as the descending tetrachord. A happy text would have had a different melody.

See also #899.

La recontre imprévue

913. Brown, Bruce Alan. "Gluck's *Recontre imprévue* and Its Revisions." *JAMS* 36 (1983): 498–518.

   Genesis, emphasizing changes made during rehearsals as revealed by manuscript sources.

Antonio Carlos Gomes (1836–1896)

914. Gomes Vaz de Carvalho, Itala. *Vida de Carlos Gomes*. 3rd ed. Rio de Janeiro: Noite, 1946. 247p. ML410 .G63 G63.

   First edition, 1935; an Italian translation appeared in the same year. The standard older biography, presenting a popular life story, some letters, and program notes on the operas. No footnotes, bibliography, or index.

915. Vetro, Gaspare Nello. *Antônio Carlos Gomes: Correspondências italianas*. Rio de Janeiro: Cátedra, 1982. 339p. ML410 .G63 A337.

   A translation from the original Italian, *Antonio Carlos Gomez: Carteggi italiani* (Milan: Nuove Edizioni, 1976). Essays by various writers, dealing with the composer's correspondence.

916. Vetro, Gaspare Nello. *Antônio Carlos Gomes: "Il guarany."* Parma: Tecno-grafica, 1996. 155p. ML410 .G63 A34.

    Reception history, especially in Italy, of Gomes's best-known opera. Includes a chronology of performances with casts. Without notes, bibliography, or index.

917. Ruberti, Salvatore. *"O guaraní" e "Colombo" de Carlos Gomes.* Rio de Janeiro: Laudes, 1972. 212p. ML410 .G63 R8.

    Extended program notes on the opera and the 1982 Columbus festival cantata, *Colombo.* No musical examples, notes, bibliography, or index.

François-Joseph Gossec (1734–1829)

Le pecheurs is in *FO*, v.59.

918. Dufrane, Louis. *Gossec: Sa vie, ses oeuvres.* Paris: Fischbacher, 1927. 267p. ML410 .G67 D86.

    A footnoted life and works. Worklist, program notes on the operas, name index.

Charles François Gounod (1818–1893)

Faust is in *ASO* 2 (1976), and *Roméo et Juliette* is in *ASO* 41 (1982).

There is a curious lack of scholarly writing on Gounod, whose *Faust* was once among the most produced operas worldwide. The standard biography dates from 1911:

919. Prod'homme, Jacques-Gabriel, and A. Dandelot. *Gounod: Sa vie et ses oeuvres.* Paris: Delagrave, 1911. 2v. Reprint, in 1v., Geneva: Minkoff, 1973. ISBN 2-8266-0051-6. ML410 .G7 P92.

    A well-documented life and works, with descriptions of the operas. Worklist, chronology, iconography, bibliography of about 120 titles, no index.

920. Harding, James. *Gounod.* New York: Stein & Day, 1973. 251p. ISBN 0-8128-1541-6. ML410 .G7 H4.

    A popular biography, without notes, together with program notes on the operas. Worklist of titles only, giving no information; name index.

921. Huebner, Steven. *The Operas of Charles Gounod.* New York: Oxford U.P., 1990. 314p. ISBN 0-19-315329-7. ML410 .G7 H8.

    A good account of Gounod's works, against a biographical backdrop. Detailed genesis for the operas; technical studies of melody, harmony, and form; and synopses. Musical examples and photographs. Descriptions of the four theaters and companies in mid–19th-century Paris. Bibliography, weak index.

922. Rustman, Mark M. "Lyric Opera: A Study of the Contributions of Charles Gounod." Ph.D. diss., U. of Kansas, 1986. vi, 456p.

See also Cooper (#66).

Carl Heinrich Graun (1704–1759)

See #947.

André Ernest Modeste Grétry (1741–1813)

La rosière de Salency is in *FO*, v.61, and *Richard Coeur de Lion* is in *FO*, v.62.

923. Jobe, Robert. "The Operas of André Ernest Modeste Grétry." Ph.D. diss., U. of Michigan, 1965. 311p.

924. Clercx, Suzanne. *Grétry, 1741–1813*. Brussels: La Renaissance du Livre, 1944. 139p. Reprint, New York: AMS, 1978. ML410 .G8 C62.

A perceptive life and works but not documented; also lacking musical examples and index.

925. Charlton, David. *Grétry and the Growth of "opéra-comique."* New York: Cambridge U.P., 1986. xii, 371p. ISBN 0-521-25229-X. ML410 .G83 C35.

A useful description of the operas, with technical analysis and musical examples. The political and musical context is well explored. Backnotes, minor bibliography, expansive index.

926. Pendle, Karin. "The *opéras-comiques* of Grétry and Marmontel." *MQ* 63-3 (July 1976): 409–434.

Discusses six operas written between 1768 and 1775 as illustrations of Grétry's maturing style. Marmontel was his librettist.

927. *Grétry et l'Europe de l'opéra-comique*. Ed. Philippe Vendrix. Liège: Mardaga, 1992. 389p. ISBN 2-87009-483-3. ML410 .G73 G73.

Sixteen essays by various authors. These are entered separately: M. Elizabeth Bartlet on Grétry in the Revolution (#928), Bruce Alan Brown on *opéra-comique* (#2246), David Charlton on a computer database of *opéra-comique* (#2247), Herbert Schneider on Auber (#464), and Manuel Couvreur on *folie* (#2250). The volume has a name index.

928. Bartlet, M. Elizabeth. "Grétry and the Revolution." In *Grétry et l'Europe* (#927), 47–112.

The composer's memoirs leave "a negative portrait of the Revolution." His operas of the 1790s were unsuccessful, although they are "worth further serious consideration." Grétry's complex political views are described, and there is a table of his operas from 1781 to 1803.

929. Culot, Paul, ed. *Le jugement de Midas* ... Brussels: Bibliothèque Royale Albert Ier, 1978. 89p. ML410 .G8 C9.

Facsimile of a contemporary score of the opera, with libretto. Reviews and other documents relating to the premiere in 1778 and relevant parts of the composer's memoirs.

930. Pendle, Karin. "*Les philosophes* and *opéra-comique*: The Case of Grétry's *Lucile*." *MR* 38 (1977): 177–191.

Diderot and his fellow *philosophes* favored this opera; their opinions are examined. Also program notes and some analysis of the work, discussion of its pivotal place in the change from trivial comic opera to the more serious style preferred by the savants. Citations to earlier literature.

931. Capelle, Irmlind. "Les méprises par ressemblance von Grétry und Lortzings *Die beiden Schutzen.*" In *"Opéra-comique" und ihr Einfluss* (#93), 347–361.

Was the 1786 Grétry work the basis for Lortzing's 1839 opera? *Les méprises* was not performed in Germany in the 1830s. But a play based on it was staged, and Lortzing had an acting part in it. Line-by-line comparison of the play with the Grétry libretto and a comparison of the two operatic settings.

932. Bartlet, M. Elisabeth. "Grétry, Marie-Antoinette, and *La rosière de Salency.*" *PRMA* 111 (1984–1985): 92–120.

Marie Antoinette, following her marriage to the future Louis XVI in 1770, exerted considerable influence over opera composers and style. She preferred the *comédie-italienne* to Lully and Rameau. Grétry was a favorite, and he prudently included "compliments to royalty and in particular to Marie-Antoinette" in his works. How he did that in *La rosière de Salency* is described. The musical content of the opera, along with a comparison of the original with later modifications, is analyzed as well.

933. Bonnert, Olivier H. "Autour des persans dans l'opéra au XVIIIe siècle." In *L'opéra au XVIIIe siècle* (#2251), 185–203.

Considers Rameau's *Les Indes galantes* and *Zoroastre,* Grétry's *Zémire,* and Salieri's *Tarare* from the viewpoint of their treatment of the Persian theme. The curious stereotype arose from the vogue for the exotic in the 18th century. Various composers exhibit diversity in their approach, but essentially they portrayed a remote world, not very Persian.

Louis Gruenberg (1884–1964)

934. Nisbett, Robert F. "Louis Gruenberg: His Life and Works." Ph.D. diss., Ohio State U., 1979. 441p.

Nisbett also published a quick overview, "Louis Gruenberg: A Forgotten Figure of American Music," in *Current Musicology* 18 (1974): 90–95.

935. Metzer, David. "A Wall of Darkness Dividing the World: Blackness and Whiteness in Louis Gruenberg's *The Emperor Jones.*" *COJ* 7-1 (March 1995): 55–72.

The libretto departs from the Eugene O'Neill play in its handling of racial depictions (changing the concept from colonialism to primitivism). This is demonstrated in the examination of various scenes and in the ending (suicide instead of massacre), but it is marred by the author's quirky search for a homosexual theme, both in the opera and in Lawrence Tibbett's renowned portrayal of the title role at the Metropolitan.

Pietro Alessandro Guglielmi (1728–1804)

936. Salvetti, G. "Un maestro napoletano di fronte alla riforma: l'*Alceste* di Pietro Alessandro Guglielmi." In *Napoli e il teatro* (#2534), 97–120.

Compares this *Alceste* (1769) with Gluck's (1767), finding that they diverge sharply in certain aspects, while representing the reform style. Guglielmi, with his librettist Giuseppe Parini, showed great flexibility in handling the dramatic exigencies. Their opera assigns distinct music to different personages. Guglielmi did not have Gluck's score.

937. Wolff, Hellmuth Christian. "Die komische Oper *La sposa fedele* (Venedig, 1767) von Pietro Guglielmi und ihre deutsche Singspiel Fassung als *Robert und Kalliste*." In Muraro (#2576), v.2, 123–145.

> Rossini regarded Guglielmi, along with Cimarosa and Paisiello, as his most significant predecessors, and Stendhal considered him the creator of *opera buffa*. *La sposa fedele* was successful in Venice, London, and elsewhere. A German libretto, entitled *Roert und Kalliste*, was used for a Berlin performance in 1775; it was something of a comic parody of the original. Comparison, musical examples.

Guglielmi wrote more than 80 operas, about 35 of them *serie* and the others *buffe*. The comic works are described in a Ph.D. dissertation by Kay M. Lipton, "The *opere buffe* of Pietro Alessandro Guglielmi in Vienna and Esterháza: Contributions to the Development of *opera buffa* between 1786 and 1793," U. of California at Los Angeles, 1995; 784p.

Jacques François Fromental Élie Halévy (1799–1862)

ASO 100 (1987); *ERO*, v.36.

938. Jordan, Ruth. *Fromental Halévy: His Life and Music, 1799–1862*. London: Kahn & Averill, 1994; New York: Limelight, 1996. xiv, 240p. ISBN (Limelight) 0-07910-079-6. ML410 .H17 J67.

> A basic biography, giving correspondence, with program notes and reception for the operas. Accuracy is not absolute; for example, as one reviewer noticed, "Eléazar" (hero of *La juive*) is consistently misspelled "Elazar." Bare worklist, backnotes, general index.

In Karin Pendle's study of Scribe/Auber (#462) there is some treatment of this now-neglected composer. He was of considerable interest to Richard Wagner, whose essay about him is in the *Gesammelte Schriften* (#1981), v.5, 35–55.

938a. Kaufman, Tom. "Jacques Fromental Halévy: More than a One-Opera Composer." *OQ* 15-4 (Autumn 1999): 660–676.

> He was "one of the leading figures in Parisian operatic life," composer of numerous successes. *La reine de Chypre* had 152 performances at the Paris Opéra in the 19th century (more than *Don Carlos* or *Les vêpres siciliennes*). The article has a useful chronology of Halévy's 34 stage works, with premiere information and casts.

939. Hallman, Diana R. "The French Grand Opera *La juive* (1835): A Socio-Historical Study." Ph.D. diss., City U. of New York, 1995. 573p.

See also Pendle (#2299).

George Frideric Handel (1685–1759)

His name is now usually written this way in English-speaking countries; it is the form that he himself used in England. German writers prefer Georg Friedrich Händel, the style still used by the Library of Congress.

Editions

940. Händel, Georg Friedrich. *Hällische Händel-Ausgabe*. Ed. Bernd Baselt and Walther Siegmund-Schultze, for the Georg-Friedrich-Händel Gesellschaft, Halle. Kassel: Bärenreiter, 1955–.

The operas are in series 2, v.1–14. Each appears in full score, with facsimiles and commentaries. This complete edition has been controversial from its inception, for reasons given in Dean's essay (#943). It is intended to replace the one edited by Friedrich Chrysander, issued 1858–1902.

Thematic Catalogues and Worklists

941. Baselt, Bernd. *Händel-Handbuch*. Kassel: Bärenreiter, 1978–. ML134 .H3 H3.

In progress. A valuable supplement to the *Ausgabe* (#940), consisting of a *Thematisch- systematisches Verzeichnis,* v.1–3; a collection of documents (#958), v.4; and a bibliography to be published as v.5. Stage works are in v.1.

For a brief, reliable list of works there is the compilation by Anthony Hicks in *The New Grove Handel* (#956). Earlier lists can now be disregarded.

Bibliographies and Guides to Resources

942. Parker-Hale, Mary Ann. *G. F. Handel: A Guide to Research*. Garland Composer Resource Manuals, 19. New York: Garland, 1988. xvii, 294p. ISBN 0-8240-8452-7. ML134 .H16 P37.

A second edition of this important guide is in progress. Parker-Hale sorts out the vast literature, presenting 938 critically annotated entries. Monographs and articles are listed in topical arrangement, with indexes of authors, compositions, and names. With a useful list of other Handel bibliographies, societies, journals, and reviews of the new *Ausgabe*.

943. Dean, Winton. "Scholarship and the Handel Revival, 1935–85." In *Tercentenary* (#950), 1–18.

An authoritative, critical review of principal writings. Observes that the Handel revival was not accompanied by major scholarship. Comments at length on the new *Ausgabe*: it had a dubious start, entirely in the hands of musicologists in the former DDR, and the first volumes were defective; but after reactions in British journals, an upgrading eventuated. Finally an international committee was established, and standards were raised. Indeed, all Handel scholarship grew in quality in the 1960s and 1970s. Principal titles are described.

944. Burrows, Donald, and Martha J. Ronish. *A Catalogue of Handel's Musical Autographs*. New York: Oxford U.P., 1994. xxxviii, 332p. ISBN 0-19-315250-9. ML134 .H24 B92.

An exhaustive, reliable inventory of manuscripts, with page-by-page tabulations and full bibliographic descriptions. Attention to physical condition, rather than to the music. All 112 known watermarks are shown and traced. More than 8,700 folios survive, most of them in the British Library and the Fitzwilliam Museum, Cambridge.

945. Burrows, Donald. "Sources, Resources and Handel Studies." In *Tercentenary* (#950), 19–42.

Describes the state of the art in "matters of source philology and source inter-pretation." "We need all of Handel's music, in the right keys, in the right order, and with the right words," or "any analysis will yield false results." Discusses Baselt's catalogue (#941), watermark research, the study of copyists, and the contents of manuscripts in Oxford and Hamburg. With 53 notes, identifying the relevant literature.

946. Smith, William C. *Handel: A Descriptive Catalogue of the Early Editions*. 2nd ed. Oxford: Blackwell, 1970. 378p. ML134 .H356.

First edition, 1960. Describes all printings during Handel's lifetime and those of special significance into the early 19th century. Information given includes text sources, singers named, and citations to advertisements. Expansive index.

947. *Handel Sources: Material for the Study of Handel's Borrowing*. Ed. John H. Roberts. New York: Garland, 1986. 9v. M1500 .S816 L88.

Nineteen sources: operas by Keiser, Gasparini, Giovanni Porta, C. H. Graun, Antonio Lotti, Alessandro Scarlatti, Bononcini, and Steffani are presented in facsimiles of contemporary manuscripts and printed editions. The series does not duplicate major sources that have already appeared in modern editions. Extensive commentaries by the editor cover the historical background and dis-cuss the actual borrowing that occurred. On the topic of Handel's borrowing, see Buelow (#976) and Roberts (#977).

See also #955.

Conferences

948. *Handel Collections and Their History*. Ed. Terence Best. New York: Oxford U.P., 1993. xvii, 252p. ISBN 0-1981-6299-5. ML410 .H13 H285.

Proceedings from a conference held at King's College, London, 24–26 Novem-ber 1990. Various scholars describe the collections of Hamburg, Malmesbury, Aylesford, Shaftesbury, Barrett Lennard, Chandos, Shaw-Hellier, Hall, and Santini. Also essays on the music paper used by Handel and his copyists in Italy and on early Handel editions. Indexed.

949. *Händel auf dem Theater: Bericht über die Symposien der Internationalen Händel-Akademie, Karlsruhe, 1986 und 1987*. Ed. Hans Joachim Marx. Laaber: Laaber, 1988. 225p. ISBN 3-8900-7146-5. ML410 .H13 H258.

A collection of 22 papers, dealing with such production topics as staging in Handel's time, contemporary staging, the castrato, and the performance differ-entiae of opera and oratorio.

Collections of Essays

950. *Handel, Tercentenary Collection.* Ed. Stanley Sadie and Anthony Hicks. Studies in Musicology, 99. Ann Arbor, Mich.: UMI Research, 1987. xi, 308p. ISBN 0-8357-1833-6. ML410 .H13 H257.

A splendid commemorative volume for the composer's 300th birthday. Of the 16 papers, these are cited elsewhere in this section: Winton Dean, on scholarship (#943); Donald Burrows, on resources (#945); George J. Buelow, on borrowing (#976); and John H. Roberts, also on borrowing (#977). Other entries on opera include Lowell Lindgren, "The Staging of Handel's Operas in London"; Duncan Chisholm, "New Sources for the Libretto of Handel's *Joseph*"; Elizabeth Gibson, "The Royal Academy of Music (1719–28) and Its Directors"; and Carole Taylor, "Handel's Disengagement from the Italian Opera." Index to the works cited, partly expansive general index.

951. *The Cambridge Companion to Handel.* Ed. Donald Burrows. New York: Cambridge U.P., 1997. xvi, 349p. ISBN 0-521-45425-5. ML410 .H13 C2.

A collection of 18 essays by various authors, together with a chronology, worklist, and index. Seven of the contributions are useful accounts of Handel's background in Germany, Italy, and London—covering theaters, concert life, and librettists. Two essays are entered separately in this guide: C. Steven La Rue on the aria (#969) and Winton Dean on production style (#974).

952. *Handel: A Celebration of His Life and Times.* Ed. Jacob Simon. London: National Portrait Gallery, 1985. 296p. ISBN 0-9040-1268-0. ML410 .H13 H19.

An elaborate catalogue of the exhibition held at the National Portrait Gallery, London, in 1985–1986. Shows portraits, manuscripts, documents, maps, engravings, a plan of Handel's house, musical instruments, and other iconographical material. Excellent descriptions and commentaries accompany the pictures.

953. Strohm, Reinhard. *Essays on Handel and Italian Opera.* New York: Cambridge U.P., 1985. x, 303p. ISBN 0-521-26428-6. ML410 .H13 S75.

Consists of 12 valuable essays in English, all but 1 translated from German; all have been previously published. Those relating to Handel are cited elsewhere in this section: #966, #972, #973, #983, and #988. There are two studies on Gasparini (#854, #855), one on Vinci (#1947), and one on Vivaldi (#1958).

Periodicals

954. Händel Jahrbuch, 1–6, 1928–1933; n.s., 1–, 1955–. Leipzig: Händel Gesellschaft, 1928–1933; 1955–. Annual. ML410 .H13 H13.

First series issued as *Veröffentlichungen der Händel Gesellschaft.*

955. *Göttinger Händel Beiträge,* 1–, 1984–. Kassel: Bärenreiter, 1984–. Irregular. ML410 .H13 G6.

Six volumes seen, issued 1984–1996; a seventh volume was unavailable. Useful bibliographies of writings about Handel have appeared: v.1 (1984), covering

1979–1983; v.2 (1986), covering 1984–1985; v.3 (1989), covering 1986–1987; v.4 (1991), covering 1988–1990; v.5 (1993), covering 1991–1992; v.6 (1996), covering 1993–1995. Not much about operas has been published in this journal. One useful study is Bernd Edelmann, "Die zweite Fassung von Händels Oper *Radamisto*," 3 (1969): 99–123.

Biographies

956. Dean, Winton. *The New Grove Handel*. New York: Norton, 1983. 185p. ISBN 0-393-30086-2. ML410 .H13 D24.

Reprint of the authoritative article in *NG,* with reliable worklist by Anthony Hicks.

957. Deutsch, Otto Erich. *Handel: A Documentary Biography*. New York: Norton, 1955. xiv, 942p. Reprint, New York: Da Capo, 1974. ML410 .H13 D47.

"All known and many hitherto unknown or overlooked documents" form the basis for this landmark work. Materials are reproduced in chronological order. Newspaper comments and notices are included. Partly annotated bibliography of about 1,500 entries; name, topic, and place index.

See also next entry.

958. *Dokumente zu Leben und Schaffen. Händel-Handbuch* (#941), v.4.

A revision of Deutsch (#957), presenting all known documents with concise commentaries in German. Much of the original was removed in the revision, however. The work received a harsh review by J. Merrill Knapp in *Göttinger Händel Beiträge* 3 (1989): 296–311.

959. Lang, Paul Henry. *George Frideric Handel*. New York: Norton, 1966. xviii, 731p. ML410 .H13 L26.

A semipopular study, written by a perceptive musicologist, sparsely footnoted and without bibliography. Lang shows special interest in cultural settings; his chapter on baroque opera is interesting from this viewpoint. Partly expansive index of names, titles, and topics.

960. Burrows, Donald. *Handel*. New York: Oxford U.P., 1994. xii, 491p. ISBN 0-02-870327-8. ML410 .H13 B94.

The new standard biography, presenting life and works interleaved. Handel's phases are taken as units: Germany, Italy, England. Program notes on the operas. Useful appendix material includes a calendar, worklist, and personalia. Footnotes, bibliography of some 200 entries, partly expansive index.

961. Hogwood, Christopher. *Handel*. London: Thames & Hudson, 1984. 312p. No ISBN. ML410 .H13 H66.

A lively, well-documented life and works, superbly illustrated. Good treatment of the operas (p.49–139), focusing on genesis and reception. Insightful comments throughout from this distinguished Handel interpreter. Chronology, bibliography of about 200 items, index.

Operas in General

962. Dean, Winton, and J. Merrill Knapp. *Handel's Operas, 1704–1726.* New York: Oxford U.P., 1987. V.1: xx, 751p. ISBN 0-193-15219-3. ML410 .H13 D37.

A projected second volume has not appeared. The most detailed and scholarly work on the mature operas of Hamburg, Italy, and London, using "every conceivable manuscript and relevant source." For each opera there is a study of the libretto, genesis, plot, reception, revisions, performance history, technical analysis, singers, and historical context. Handel's revisions and borrowings are explored, along with his connection between emotions and keys. Suggestions are given for modern staging, and various recent productions are described. The book is also a fine source of information on the general operatic scene. Fully documented, with brief bibliography and index.

963. Harris, Ellen. *Handel and the Pastoral Tradition.* New York: Oxford U.P., 1980. vii, 304p. ISBN 0-193-15236-3. ML410 .H13 H31.

Demonstrates that the tradition of pastoral drama strongly influenced Handel's work, variously according to the country he was in while composing. Good material on the pastoral dramas of Italy, Germany, and England; detailed attention to Handel's pastoral operas (*Florindo, Pastor fido, Acis and Galatea*); comprehensive chronology of Handel in Italy, 1706–1710. Useful tables of harmonic structures, including some in works of other composers. Bibliography of about 250 titles; index of names, titles, and topics.

964. Bianconi, Lorenzo. *I libretti italiani di Georg Friedrich Händel e le loro fonti.* Quaderni della Rivista italiana di musicologia, 26. Florence: Olschki, 1992. 2v. ISBN 88-222-3926-1. ML 5 .Q13.

Offers *"un testo pulito"* (a clean text) of the works from 1707 to 1741. The libretti are in Italian only; Bianconi notes that there is a satisfactory English collection (#965), although his gathering is in fact larger, since it includes pasticcios. The entire second volume is given to critical notes.

965. *The Librettos of Handel's Operas.* Ed. Ellen T. Harris. New York: Garland, 1988–1989. 13v. ISBN 0-8240-3863-0. ML49 .H13 H3.

A fundamental collection, presenting complete facsimiles of 71 libretti, including 42 premieres and 29 revisions. Rarities are included, such as the prompter's copy of *Radamisto* from the Victoria and Albert Museum and a hitherto unknown libretto for the 1732 *Giulio Cesare* revival. A general introduction in v.1 offers an overview of Handel's operatic career and a chronology of the operas (premieres and revivals under the composer's direction). Individual volumes have valuable commentaries and discussions of sources.

966. Strohm, Reinhard. "Handel and His Italian Opera Texts." In *Essays on Handel* (#953), 34–79.

Translation of an article that had appeared in *Händel-Jahrbuch,* 1975–1976. A concise summary of what had been discovered about these libretti at that time, citing recent references.

967. Eisenschmidt, Joachim. *Die szenische Darstellung der Opern Händels auf der Londoner Bühne seiner Zeit.* Berlin: Kallmeyer, 1940. 2v. ML5 .H25.

The nonmusical issues of performance: the London setting, Haymarket and Covent Garden theaters, singers, acting, production styles, and critical reception. All quotations are in German only. Notes, bibliography, no index.

See also Stahura (#2721).

968. Brainard, Paul. "Aria and Ritornello: New Aspects of the Comparison Handel/Bach." In *Bach, Handel, Scarlatti: Tercentenary Essays*, ed. Peter Williams, 21–33 (New York: Cambridge U.P., 1985; ISBN 0-521-25217-2; ML55 .B14).

Unlike Bach, Handel made subtle modifications in restatements of ritornellos. In many cases, the ritornello refers to musical or textual events from the first segment of the aria. Brainard also draws distinctions between the borrowing practices of the two composers.

969. La Rue, C. Steven. "Handel and the Aria." In *Cambridge Companion* (#951), 111–121.

A review of Handel's complex approach to the aria. In London he was able to "vary aria styles to suit specific dramatic contexts . . . [and] alternatively could suit the style to the specific singer." Considers the relation of oratorio aria to opera aria with Handel, finding that in the most effective examples of both he could "combine an abstract musical symbolism with an intense dramatic situation."

970. Celletti, Rodolfo. "Il virtuosismo vocale nel melodramma di Haendel." *RIM* 4 (1969): 77–101.

Points out that Handel was influenced in the development of his vocal style by Alessandro Scarlatti and Steffani. Through analysis of many examples, Celletti categorizes those influences, which related to extension of vocal ranges, higher tessitura, longer vocalizing passages, and increasingly varied figures.

971. La Rue, C. Steven. *Handel and His Singers: The Creation of the Royal Academy Operas, 1720–1728.* New York: Oxford U.P., 1995. xiii, 213p. ISBN 0-19-816315-0. ML410 .H13 L23.

Handel selected the singers for the 14 Royal Academy operas and wrote for their individual specializations. Among them were the castrato Senesino, Margherita Durastanti, Maria Maddalena Salvai, and Giuseppe Boschi. Handel's autographs are examined, revealing revisions made for specific character types. Notes, bibliography, index.

972. Strohm, Reinhard. "Towards an Understanding of the *opera seria*." In *Essays on Handel* (#953), 93–105.

Considers a number of reasons why modern Handel productions deviate from the composer's intentions, primarily from incomplete knowledge of texts and traditions but also because of modern theatrical conventions. It will help to recognize that Handel's early operas belong to the *opera seria* genre and to understand that genre. Its conditions were constantly shifting, and performances of a work differed as singers introduced new variations and scenes were changed to hold the interest of the audience. A new production that relied on an established score, which nobody could alter, "would have been something quite unthinkable." Handel's exhaustive planning included alterations.

973. Strohm, Reinhard. "Handel's *pasticci*." In *Essays on Handel* (#953), 164–211.

Originally in German in *Analecta musicologica* 14 (1974). Defines the genre and considers its London manifestations. Genesis, description, and reception of Handel's nine pasticcios, with an account of his revisions and extended musical examples. An appendix lists the sinfonias and arias of those works in chronological order, with names of singers and source information.

974. Dean, Winton. "Production Style in Handel's Operas." In *Cambridge Companion* (#951), 249–261.

Observes that "there can be no excuse for ignorance of how the operas were done in Handel's day, or for failing to take this into consideration for revivals in the modern theatre." Takes issue with much modern production, for its "self-indulgence and the urge to shock," and gives some horrible examples. "The crucial question—are the operas viable in the modern professional theatre in their own terms?—has too often been allowed to go by default."

975. "Kolloquium über aufführungspraktische Fragen bei Händel." *Händel-Jahrbuch* 12 (1966): 25–49.

A useful discussion about performance practice of the vocal music, with participation of Walther Siegmund-Schulze, Konrad Sasse, Percy Young, Alfred Mann, and Ernst Meyer.

976. Buelow, George J. "The Case for Handel's Borrowings: The Judgment of Three Centuries." In *Tercentenary* (#950): 61–82.

Aims "to review and evaluate the opinions of others about Handel's compositional practices." Notes that in writings of Germany in Handel's time "the concept of originality is rarely found." Indeed, originality as a value did not arise until the early 19th century. The earliest reference to Handel as one who appropriated large and small pieces of music by others is in 1722, in *Critica musica*, but the view expressed is that it is an honor to have one's music reworked by another. Buelow's survey of the literature on the topic of borrowing (or plagiarism, as some would have it) is excellent. He also considers what has been written about the Handel situation. He concludes that "at last Handel scholars have begun to see that the composer's extensive and manifold adaptations of his and other composers' works contain vital clues for defining the genius of his compositional craft and stylistic individuality."

977. Roberts, John H. "Why Did Handel Borrow?" In *Tercentenary* (#950), 83–92.

A number of answers to the title question have been given by other scholars: Handel responding to his unconscious needs, Handel weakened mentally by a paralytic stroke (1737) and thus unable to invent his own material, Handel taking music of others simply as a base for his improvisatory style. But recent research, summarized by Roberts, has disclosed much more borrowing than had been known in the years before the stroke. Other theories are disposed of, and Roberts puts forth his own—bold and cogent: Handel "had a basic lack of facility in inventing original ideas." So he gathered ideas as he heard them (even writing some fragments into his notebook) and put them to use. But "in his best music he always transformed his models radically and built from them structures that only he could have conceived."

Roberts has made another important contribution to this topic:

978. Roberts, John H. "Keiser and Handel at the Hamburg Opera." *Händel-Jahrbuch* 36 (1990): 63–88.

Reinhard Keiser directed the Theater am Gänsemarkt from 1703 to 1707, while a teenaged Handel played violin in the orchestra. Personal relationships between the two men—marked by Keiser's envy—are taken up. It was in Hamburg that Handel began his borrowings from Keiser's music.

See also #947 and #977.

Individual Works

Alcina

ASO 130 (1990).

979. Dean, Winton. "The Making of *Alcina*." In *"Con che soavità"* (#2461), 312–319.

Genesis, sources, and useful commentary on the most successful of Handel's later operas; it had 18 performances during the period 1735–1737.

Alessandro

980. King, Richard Glenn. "The Composition and Reception of Handel's *Alessandro* (1726)." Ph.D. diss., Stanford U., 1992. xv, 236p.

Almira

981. Fenton, Robin F. C. "*Almira* (Hamburg, 1705): The Birth of G. F. Handel's Genius for Characterization." *Handel-Jahrbuch* 33 (1987): 109–123.

Characterization results from "differentiation in function and musical realisation between recitative and aria." Responsibility for it shifted from the librettist to the composer by the end of the 17th century. *Almira* demonstrates Handel's skill in this area, and detailed analyses are offered to show how he did it. Fenton tends toward the fanciful, finding such things as "a welling of desire which is itself suggested in the rising melodic line and the modulation." With illegible musical examples.

Amadigi

982. Dean, Winton. "The Musical Sources for Handel's *Teseo* and *Amadigi*." In *Slavonic and Western Music: Essays for Gerald Abraham,* ed. Malcolm Hamrick Brown, 63–80 (New York: Oxford U.P., 1985; ISBN 0-8357-1594-9; ML55 .A18).

The two works, which were among the first five London operas, were "comparative failures." Only a few of the arias were published, thus manuscript copies are important—and they are numerous. Sources are collated here and displayed in tables.

Amadis

See: Kimbell (#753).

Ezio

983. Strohm, Reinhard. "Handel's *Ezio*." In *Essays on Handel* (#953), 225–231.

The unknown text-writer who adapted Metastasio's libretto (first performed to music by Pietro Auletta in Rome, 1729) for Handel greatly reduced the dialogue to accommodate the preference of London audiences for arias. With the story line thus dismembered, it was left to the music to express "more than what happens on the stage or stands in the text." Handel's way of doing so is analyzed by Strohm, and although the effects were technically praiseworthy, the "complexity and density of expression" may have been too much for the audiences. *Ezio* had only five performances.

Giulio Cesare

ASO 97 (1987).

984. Knapp, J. Merrill. "Handel's *Giulio Cesare in Egitto*." In *Studies in Music History: Essays for Oliver Strunk,* ed. Harold S. Powers, 389–403 (Princeton, N.J.: Princeton U.P., 1968; ML3797.1 .P69 S9).

Examines the four versions of the opera as performed in London between 1724 and 1732. Libretti and scores are compared through tabular presentation and placed in context of the characteristics of the work.

985. Monson, Craig. "*Giulio Cesare in Egitto*: From Sartorio (1677) to Handel (1724)." *M&L* 66 (1985): 313–343.

A considerable influence on Handel may have been exerted by the earlier work: the libretto, by Nicola Haym, seems to have been based on that of Francesco Bussani, and there are indications that Handel had Sartorio's music in mind.

Giustino

986. Strohm, Reinhard. "Vivaldi's and Handel's Settings of *Giustino*." In *Music and Theatre* (#68), 131–158.

Compares Vivaldi's *Giustino* (1724) to Handel's 1737 setting. Strohm says Handel knew the Vivaldi score. A number-by-number comparison shows close parallels in the texts. Musical relationships—more subtle—also suggest the influence of the earlier work.

Joseph

See #950.

Muzio Scevola

987. Rossi, Nick. "Handel's *Muzio Scevola*." *OQ* 3-3 (Autumn 1985): 17–38.

Paolo Rolli's libretto was used by Filippo Amadei, Giovanni Bononcini, and Handel. Reception at the Handel premiere in 1721 was good, but the opera was not performed after November 1722. Manuscripts and editions are described, and there are program notes on the opera.

Orlando

988. Strohm, Reinhard. "Comic Traditions in Handel's *Orlando*." In *Essays on Handel* (#953), 249–269.

Proposes that Handel's experience in Naples in 1729 coincided with his plan to produce *Orlando* in London. He was impressed by the comic intermezzi he saw there and by the singer Celestina Resse (later Gismondi), known as La Celestina. Having decided to introduce comic elements into the story, he advised his librettist Nicola Haym accordingly. Possibly La Celestina, who went to London to sing for Handel, influenced Haym in his work. But in the end it was Handel who created the "incredible combination of seemingly diverse ideas and images"—his "decisive answer to Baroque comedy," fusing the comic, tragic, rational, magical, and pastoral.

Poro

989. Cummings, Graham H. "The London Performances of Handel's Opera *Poro*." In *Konferenzbericht Halle: Probleme der Händelschen Oper,* 62–81 (Halle: Martin Luther Universität, 1982).

A full study of the libretto and Handel's adaptation of it for the 1736–1737 season in London. Discussion of cast; good documentation. Cummings studied the opera further in his Ph.D. dissertation, "Handel's *Poro*: An Edition and Critical Study," U. of Birmingham, 1984.

Radamisto

990. Knapp, J. Merrill. "Handel, the Royal Academy of Music, and Its First Opera Season in London (1720)." *MQ* 45 (1959): 145–167.

A valuable commentary on *Radamisto,* given in the first season of the academy, is part of this useful account of the London operatic scene. Notes that Handel was the chief musical figure at the academy from the outset, overshadowing Ariosto and Bononcini. Other productions of the season are described.

Rinaldo

991. Kubik, Reinhold. *Händels "Rinaldo": Geschichte, Werk, Wirkung.* Neuhausen-Stuttgart: Hänssler, 1982. 246p. ISBN 3-7751-0594-8. ML410 .H13 K8.

A thorough historical and technical study of the opera, covering the autograph, borrowings, alterations, and reception. Many tables, musical examples, and references. Bibliography, name index.

992. Price, Curtis. "English Traditions in Handel's *Rinaldo*." In *Tercentenary* (#950), 120–135.

Premiering on 24 February 1711, *Rinaldo* was Handel's first London opera. The influence of *The British Enchanters* (a "semi-opera" with a collaborative score) is examined and found significant. Resemblances of plot and scenic details are pointed out. For *Rinaldo* Handel had two librettists—one Italian, the other English. The Italian, Giacomo Rossi, wrote the first text, and Aaron Hill translated and adapted it. The adaptation drew not only on *British Enchanters* but also on the English stage traditions. As manager of the Queen's Theatre, Hill was also interested in enhancing the role of stage machinery, providing the kind of effects associated with the style of the English masque.

Rodrigo

993. Knapp, J. Merrill. "Handel's First Italian Opera: *Vincer se stesso è la maggior vittoria,* or *Rodrigo.*" *M&L* 62 (1981): 12–29.

   Rodrigo (Florence, 1707) had a libretto modeled on a 1699 work, *Il duello d'amore e di vendetta* (text by Francesco Silvani, music by Marc Antonio Ziani). The two operas are compared, and the relevant research is summarized. Notes that Handel at 22 was already "a practised Italianate musician."

Semele

ASO 171 (1996).

Serse (Xerxes)

994. Powers, Harold S. "Il *Serse* trasformato." *MQ* 47 (1961): 481–492; 48 (1962): 73–92. Reprint, *GL,* v.11.

   A valuable examination of the libretto, comparing the original version (Venice, 1654) with the Rome revision of 1694. A shift in emphasis from recitative to aria is noted. Bononcini's setting of the Rome libretto is compared with Handel's.

995. Dean, Winton. "Handel's *Serse.*" In *Opera and the Enlightenment* (#91), 135–167.

   The opera was a unique blend of farce, satire, and passion—not unlike the works of Mozart/Da Ponte. Borrowings from Bononcini's *Xerse* (1694) are analyzed, including the "melodic germ" of "Ombra mai fu." Handel greatly enhanced all his borrowings. With a lucid, technical study of music and drama. Appendix of sources and editions.

996. Osthoff, Wolfgang. "Haendels 'Largo' als Musik des goldenen Zeitalters." *AfM* 30 (1973): 175–189.

   Genesis of the famous aria "Ombra mai fu," considering poetic models. Settings of the text by Cavalli and Bononcini are examined and compared with Handel's.

997. "Kolloquium: Händels Oper *Xerxes* als Inszenierungsproblem." *Händel-Jahrbuch* 20 (1974): 22–65.

   A discussion of staging problems by Walther Siegmund-Schulze, Jens Peter Larsen, Reinhold Rüdiger, and other specialists.

Sosarme

998. Dean, Winton. "Handel's *Sosarme*: A Puzzle Opera." In *Essays on Opera* (#72), 115–147. Reprint, *GL*, v.11.

    Handel's operas present enough puzzles "to keep a posse of musicological detectives at work for years." *Sosarme* (1732) has a good share of unresolved questions: what was the original source of the libretto, who adapted it for Handel, why did Handel bother altering nearly all the names in the text, why did he cut so many recitatives, when did he do these things, and what exactly happened in 1734, when his company included only one of the 1732 cast and several of the other voices were of different pitch? Dean's responses to these queries are interesting and informative. He summarizes various wrong answers given in the past and also makes a critical estimate of the opera.

Tamerlano

999. Knapp, J. Merrill. "Handel's *Tamerlano*: The Creation of an Opera." *MQ 56* (1970): 405–430.

    Libretto genesis: comparison of Nicola Haym's text with its model by Agostino Piovene. The music of Gasparini, for the Piovene text, is compared with Handel's. How Handel and Haym worked together is illuminated by information in the musical autograph.

Teseo

See Dean (#982).

Howard Hanson (1896–1981)

1000. Perone, James E. *Howard Hanson: A Bio-Bibliography.* Bio-Bibliographies in Music, 47. Westport, Conn.: Greenwood, 1993. viii, 327p. ISBN 0-313-28644-2. ML134 .H173 P47.

    Hanson's *Merry Mount,* premiered at the Metropolitan Opera in 1934, has received little scholarly attention. Reviews and brief notices are cited in this volume.

Johann Adolf Hasse (1699–1783)

L'artigiano gentiluomo is in *RMCE*, v.9.

1001. Millner, Frederick A. *The Operas of Johann Adolf Hasse.* Studies in Musicology, 2. Ann Arbor, Mich.: UMI Research, 1979. xxi, 405p. ISBN 0-8357-1006-8. ML410 .H348 M65.

    A useful life and works, including for each opera: genesis, program notes, reception (with contemporary critiques quoted), performances by city. Worklist, backnotes, bibliography of about 100 items, expansive index of names, titles, and topics.

1002. "Johann Adolf Hasse und die Musik seiner Zeit." Ed. Friedrich Lippmann. *Analecta musicologica* 25 (1987): 1–520.

A journal issue devoted to 19 papers from a colloquium in Siena, 1983. Nine of the contributions relate to opera. These are the most useful: Martin Ruhnke, "Zum Rezitativ der *opera seria* vor Hasse"; Reinhard Wiesend, "Tonartendisposition und Rollenhierarchie in Hasses Opern"; and Gordana Lazarevich, "Hasse as a Comic Dramatist: The Neapolitan Intermezzi."

1003. *Hasse-Studien,* 1–, 1990–. Hamburg: Carus, 1990–. ML410 .H35 H38.

V.3, 1996, is the last one seen. A view of "Hasses Opern und die Gegenwart," by Reinhard Wiesend, is in v.1, 7–12. The article's footnotes cite the major Hasse literature and editions. A facsimile of the *Piramo e Tisbe* (it is spelled *Thisbe* on the title page) libretto (Vienna, 1768) is printed in v.3, along with two brief articles about the opera.

See also next entry.

1004. Degrada, Francesco. "Aspetti gluckiani nell'ultimo Hasse." *Chigiana* 29/30 (1975): 309–329. German translation as "Glucksche Aspekte in einem Spätwerk Hasses," *Hasse-Studien* 3 (1996): 5–23.

Piramo e Tisbe was a traditional Italian opera in its conception and structure, but it showed "progressive" elements as well—for example, the use of accompanied recitative as a means to continuity.

1005. Williams, David Richard. "Johann Adolf Hasse's *Attilio Regolo.*" D.M.A. diss., U. of Wisconsin, 1995. 614p.

1006. *Johann Adolf Hasse e Giammaria Ortes, lettere (1760–1783).* Ed. Livia Pancino. Brescia: Brepols, 1998. xv, 472p. ISBN 2-503-50705-0. ML410 .H35 A4.

In this interesting correspondence, Hasse provides much information about Venetian life, personalities, and opera. He talks about works he is composing and comments on Gluck and the reformists (he was not one of them). Good bibliography of some 300 entries, index.

1007. Heartz, Daniel. "Hasse, Galuppi, and Metastasio." In Muraro (#2576), v.1, 309–340.

Metastasio's libretto of *Artaterse* was set by Hasse (1730); the opera is analyzed by Heartz, with comments by contemporaries. The poet objected to liberties taken in a later setting, by Galuppi (1749). Charles Burney's comments on that dispute are given.

Joseph Haydn (1732–1809)

Editions

1008. Haydn, Joseph. *Werke.* Ed. Georg Feder, for the Joseph-Haydn-Institut Köln. Munich: Henle, 1958–.

Reihe 25 has the operas. They are published here without significant introductions or scholarly apparatus.

Thematic Catalogues and Worklists

1009. Hoboken, Anthony van. *Joseph Haydn: Thematisch-bibliographisches Werk-verzeichnis.* Mainz: Schott, 1957–1978. 3v. ML134 .H4 H68.

For each composition: dates, scoring, manuscripts and locations, editions, arrangements, thematic incipits, citations to Haydn's correspondence, and citations to secondary literature. Operas are in v.2. Since there is no title index, the effort of Anna-Lena Holm, *Index of Titles and Text Incipits to Anthony van Hoboken: "Joseph Haydn. Thematisch-bibliographisches Werkverzeichnis. 2, Vokalwerke."* (Strandvägen: Swedish Music History Archive, 1978), will be useful.

Bibliographies and Guide to Resources

1010. Grave, Floyd K., and Margaret G. Grave. *Franz Joesph Haydn: A Guide to Research.* Garland Composer Resource Manuals, 31. New York: Garland, 1990. xi, 451p. ISBN 0-8240-8487-X. ML134 .H272 G74.

A useful handbook, giving a fine biographical sketch, the history of Haydn research, a bibliography of 1,158 annotated entries, and a worklist. Author and subject indexes.

Continuing bibliographies appear in issues of *Haydn-Studien* (#1015).

Conferences

1011. *Haydn Studies: Proceedings of the International Haydn Conference, Washington, D.C., 1975.* Ed. Jens Peter Larson, Howard Serwer, and James Webster. New York: Norton, 1981. xvii, 590p. ISBN 0-393-95149-9. ML36 .I6024.

Two papers in this collection relate to opera: Georg Feder, "A Survey of Haydn's Operas," and Andrew Porter, "Practical Considerations in Modern Production." Interesting discussions follow each paper.

1012. *Joseph Haydn: Bericht über den Internationalen Joseph Haydn Kongress, Wien, Hofburg, 5–12 September 1982.* Ed. Eva Badura-Skoda. Munich: Henle, 1986. xviii, 641p. ML36 .I6025.

Not seen. Annotation in Grave (#1010), item 76, indicates that a number of papers present useful general material on Haydn documentation, bibliography, authenticity, and chronology.

1013. *Joseph Haydn: Tradition und Rezeption. Bericht über die Jahrestagung der Gesellschaft für Musikforschung, Köln, 1982.* Ed. Georg Feder, Heinrich Hüschen, and Ulrich Tank. Regensburg: Bosse, 1985. xvii, 266p.

Not seen. Annotation in Grave (#1010), item 78, says there are papers from a session on opera.

Collections of Essays

1014. *Haydn and His World.* Ed. Elaine R. Sisman. Princeton, N.J.: Princeton U.P., 1998. xiii, 474p. ISBN 0-691-05798-2, ML410 H4 H3.

Nine essays by various specialists, useful for material on originality, Haydn's library, and the Vienna musical scene. One contribution, by Rebecca Green, is specific to opera: "Representing the Aristocracy: The Operatic Haydn and *Le pescatrici.*" It shows how Haydn flattered his aristocratic audiences through textual adjustments (in this case of a Goldoni libretto) and gives a musical analysis of the opera, written for a wedding celebration at Esterháza in 1770.

Periodicals

1015. *Haydn-Studien,* v.1–, 1965–. Munich: Joseph Haydn Institut, 1965–. Irregular. ML410 .H4 A1 H29.

Valuable coverage of Haydn bibliography is presented in various volumes: A base list of 724 writings (about 50 on opera) appeared in 1974; writings of 1973–1983 appeared in 1985; those of 1984–1990 (1,255 entries, about 78 on opera) in 1986/1994. These bibliographies give full data on each item, and they are indexed by topic. A "Kolloquium über Haydns Opern," in 2:2 (May 1969): 113–118, gave a list of the operas with facts on the premiere and other background data, plus a useful inventory of the singing roles. Otherwise the *Studien* have presented only occasional short articles on the operas.

1016. *Haydn Yearbook = Haydn Jahrbuch,* v.1–, 1962–. Eisenstadt: Verein Internationale Joseph Haydn Stiftung, 1962–. Annual. ML410 .H4 H4.

Nothing of relevance to the operas was published until v.20, 1996, when a series of facsimiles of the libretti began to appear, with commentary by H. C. Robbins Landon.

Letters and Documents

1017. Landon, H. C. Robbins. *The Collected Correspondence and London Notebooks of Joseph Haydn.* London: Barrie & Rockliff, 1959. xxix, 367p. ML410 .H4 A3.

Annotated translations of about 350 letters and documents, with introduction and background commentaries and a bibliographical source catalogue. Other letters and Haydn materials published by Landon and others are cited in Grave (#1010), chapter 4.

Biographies

1018. Landon, H. C. Robbins. *Haydn: Chronicle and Works.* Bloomington: Indiana U.P., 1976–1980. 5v. ISBN 0-253-33700-3. ML410 .H4 L26.

The standard biography and critical study. Descriptions of the five volumes are in Grave (#1010), items 259–264. V.2 deals with opera at Esterháza, and v.3 includes a detailed account of *L'anima del filosofo.* There is also a brief version:

1019. Landon, H. C. Robbins, and David Wyn Jones. *Haydn: His Life and Music.*
Bloomington: Indiana U.P., 1988. 383p. ISBN 0-253-37265-8. ML410 .H4 L3.

An excellent condensation of #1018 with material from #1017 included. Biographical and critical chapters alternate. Technical analysis is limited. Bibliography, index.

1020. Larsen, Jens Peter. *The New Grove Haydn.* New York: Norton, 1982. 237p.
ISBN 0-393-01681-1. ML410 .H4 L3.

A valuable brief treatment with an up-to-date worklist (by Georg Feder), taken from *NG.* Classified bibliography of 400 items, index.

Operas in General

1021. Landon, H. C. Robbins. "The Operas of Handel." In *NOHM* 7, 172–199.

An authoritative critical discussion of the operas, in a biographical context.
Haydn's work is seen as a blend of Italian and Viennese traditions.

1022. Bartha, Dénes, and László Somfai. *Haydn als Opernkapellmeister.* Mainz:
Schott; Budapest: Verlag der Ungarischen Akademie der Wissenshaften, 1960.
470p. ML410 .H4 B245.

A bibliographic description of materials in the Esterháza opera collection of the Hungarian national library, focusing on those that pertain to Haydn's work as opera director. An informative chronicle of operatic life, 1776–1790, includes all performance aspects. Table of singers and instrumentalists for the period, a chapter on copyists, a review of paper and watermarks, and a catalogue of Haydn's insertion arias. Indexes of titles, roles, and aria text incipits.
Note #1024.

1023. Bartha, Dénes. "Haydn's Italian Opera Repertory at Esterháza Palace." In
New Looks (#2429), 172–219.

A new chronology of premieres conducted by Haydn from 1776 to 1790, with commentaries and citations to recent research. Relates activity in Esterháza to that in theaters of Vienna, Venice, and Naples.

1024. Harich, János. "Das Repertoire des Opernkapellmeisters Joseph Haydn in
Esterháza (1780–1790)." *Haydn Yearbook* 1 (1962): 9–110.

Offers corrections and additions to Bartha (#1022) and presents a new chronology with extensive commentary. Summary tables for each year. Lists of operas and composers, English-language summary.

1025. Feder, Georg, and Günter Thomas. "Dokumente zur Austattung von *Lo
speziale, L'infedeltà delusa, La fedeltà premiata, Armida* und anderen Opern
Haydns." *Haydn-Studien* 6–2 (November 1988): 88–115.

Describes all documents and contemporary accounts of the performances for the operas named. Also interesting details on financial records at Esterháza, including such items as the costs of costumes. With 184 footnotes, leading to all relevant research.

1026. Lippmann, Friedrich. "Haydns *opere serie*: Tendenzen und Affinitäten." *Studi musicali* 12 (1983): 301–331.

Considers Haydn's affinity for Italian types of serious opera to have been useful in forming his individuality as a musical dramatist. Criticizes modern critics who have found fault with Haydn for his Italianate tendencies.

1027. Lippmann, Friedrich. "Haydn und die *opera buffa*: Vergleiche mit italienischen Werken gleichen Textes." In *Joseph Haydn: Tradition* (#1013), 113–140.

The three comic operas by Haydn are compared with those of similar texts by Italian composers Piccinni, Cimarosa, and Paisiello. Haydn's settings tend to have more serious elements, less broad humor, and fewer *buffa* clichés.

1028. Lawner, George. "Form and Drama in the Operas of Joseph Haydn." Ph.D. diss., U. of Chicago, 1959. 241p.

1029. Hunter, Mary K. "Haydn's Aria Forms: A Study of the Arias in the Italian Operas Written at Esterháza, 1766–1783." Ph.D. diss., Cornell U., 1982. xv, 550p.

1030. Hunter, Mary K. "Haydn's Sonata-Form Arias." *Current Musicology* 37/38 (1984): 19–32.

Melodic and structural analysis of selected arias, comparing them to instrumental compositions. Despite the difference of media, there are strong similarities in such areas as thematic development.

1031. Hunter, Mary K. "Text, Music, and Drama in Haydn's Italian Opera Arias: Four Case Studies." *JM* 7 (1989): 29–57.

Takes two *buffa* arias and two *seria* arias and considers their form in relation to the dramatic situations involved. The serious roles seem more associated with the sonata form.

1032. Wirth, Helmut. *Joseph Haydn als Dramatiker: Sein Bühnenschaffen als Beitrag zur Geschichte der deutschen Oper.* Wolfenbüttel: Georg Kallmeyer, 1940. 197p. ML410 .H4 W5.

A wide-ranging study, dealing with opera background in Vienna, Italian influences, comparisons with Gluck, structure, style, characterization, and dramaturgy. Extensive lists of manuscripts, printed materials, and other sources.

1033. Badura-Skoda, Eva. "Haydns Opern: Anmerkungen zur Aufführungspraktischen Problemen der Gegenwart." *Oesterreichisches Musikzeitung* 37:3/4 (March–April 1982): 162–167.

Outlines the performance problems faced by today's directors and singers: the roles are as difficult to sing as Mozart's, tempo and dynamics are not established, ornamentation practice is not always clear, cadenzas have to be accommodated to the style of works in different periods. Haydn met similar challenges in his own productions.

1034. Steblin, Rita. "Key Characteristics and Haydn's Operas." In *Joseph Haydn: Bericht* (#1012), 91–100.

Examines ideas of Haydn's time about keys and their effects and relates those thoughts to actual practice in Haydn's works. Finds him to be flexible in such matters. With an interesting table of key characteristics as found in four contemporary composers.

1035. Clark, Caryl Leslie. "The *opera buffa* Finales of Joseph Haydn." Ph.D. diss., Cornell U., 1991. xi, 447p.

1036. Debly, Patricia Anne. "Joseph Haydn and the *dramma giocoso.*" Ph.D. diss., U. of Victoria, 1993. ix, 389p.

See also Heartz (#2134).

Individual Works

Armida

1037. Rice, John A. "Sarti's *Giulio Sabino,* Haydn's *Armida,* and the Arrival of *opera seria* at Esterháza." *Haydn Yearbook* 15 (1985): 181–198.

Opera seria, although popular elsewhere, was slow to reach Vienna, Paris, or Esterháza. *Giulio Sabino,* by Giuseppe Sarti (1781), was the first to be staged in Esterháza, in 1783. It is thoroughly discussed here and shown to have influenced Haydn's first effort in the genre, *Armida.*

1038. McClymonds, Marita P. "Haydn and the *opera seria* Tradition: *Armida.*" In *Napoli e il teatro* (#2534), 191–206.

Compares Haydn's setting of the story with versions of Anfossi, Jommelli, Sacchini, and Cherubini. Haydn's had the fewest stage effects and no ballet. He shared with those Italian composers a "formal and stylistic tradition," but many differences are found. Key relations and instrumentation are given special attention.

Il mondo della luna

1039. Thomas, Günter. "Observations on *Il mondo della luna.*" In *Haydn Studies* (#1011), 144–147.

A concise but varied approach to the opera, considering alternate versions, sources, later borrowings, and preparations for the premiere.

1040. Thomas, Günter. "Zu *Il mondo della luna* und *La fedeltà premiata*: Fassungen und Pasticcios." *Haydn-Studien* 2 (1969/1970): 122–126.

Offers evidence that the second version of *Il mondo* was the one performed at the premiere in 1777 and examines different settings of the same arias. Suggests that personnel changes required alterations in *La fedeltà.*

Orlando paladino

ASO 42 (1982).

La vera costanza

1041. Melkus, Eduard. "Haydn als Dramatiker am Beispiel der Oper *La vera costanza.*" In *Joseph Haydn: Bericht* (#1012), 256–276.

Praises the dramaturgy of the work and compares Haydn's theatrical craft with Mozart's. Argues that the Haydn operas are worthy to stand beside his instrumental masterpieces. Supports his views with diagrams, charts, and many musical examples.

1042. Walter, Horst. "On the History of the Composition and Performance of *La vera costanza.*" In *Haydn Studies* (#1011), 154–157.

Demonstrates that the opera was premiered in Esterháza in 1778, not in Vienna in 1776. The situation was obscured by a fire in Esterháza in 1779, destroying original performance materials.

Hans Werner Henze (1926–)

1043. Hochgesang, Deborah. "Die Opern Hans Werner Henzes im Spiegel der deutschsprachigen, zeitgenössischen Musikkritik bis 1966." Ph.D. diss., Hamburg U., 1993.

1044. Wagner, Hans-Joachim. "Studie zu *Boulevard solitude,* lyrisches Drama in sieben Bildern von Hans Werner Henze." Ph.D. diss., U. of Cologne, 1988.

See also Heister in #95.

Chevalier D'Herbain (ca. 1730/1734–1769)

Céline is in *FO*, v.47.

Victor Herbert (1859–1924)

1045. Waters, Edward N. *Victor Herbert: A Life in Music.* New York: Macmillan, 1955. 653p. Reprint, New York: Da Capo, 1978. ISBN 0-306-79502-7 ML410 .H62 W3.

A scholarly biography, though without bibliography. Worklist, premiere information, and publishers. Genesis and production of *Natoma* and *Madeleine.* Name and title index.

1046. Pearson, Edward Hagelin. "Victor Herbert's *Madeleine.*" *OQ* 13-4 (Summer 1997): 59–95.

Genesis, including negotiations between Herbert and Gatti-Casazza at the Metropolitan, where the opera premiered in 1914. Musical style is described: based on leading motives, with emphasis on drama instead of melody. Reception was poor: it had six performances and has not been revived at the Met. Better reviews came to the Chicago production of 1916 and a California staging in 1984, and since then there have been several performances.

Louis Joseph Ferdinand Hérold (1791–1833)

1047. Pougin, Arthur. *Hérold.* Paris: H. Laurens, 1906. 122p. ML410 .H56 P8.

This is the most recent work on the composer, who once occupied the first rank among French opera writers. *Zampa* (1831) was in the repertoire through the 19th century. Pougin offers a footnoted account of the life and works, with performance histories of the operas. Good plates and worklist; no bibliography or index.

Juan Hidalgo (ca. 1612–1685)

1048. Stevenson, Robert Murrell. "Espectáculos musicales en la España del siglo XVII." *Revista musical chilena* 27–121/122 (January–June 1973): 3–44. ML5 .R451.

One of the first great Spanish composers, Hidalgo produced the earliest surviving Spanish opera, *Celos aun del aire matan* (1660). This work is thoroughly discussed by Stevenson, in the context of a scholarly history of 17th-century opera and zarzuela; 168 footnotes point to the earlier literature of importance.

1049. Subirá, José. "*Celos aun del aire matan,*" *opera del siglo XVII*. Barcelona: Biblioteca de Catalunya, 1933. xxvii, 62p. M1503 .H62 C5.

A general study of the oldest known Spanish opera (1660), its genesis, and reception. It was Subirá who discovered the work and published it in the first modern edition. A later critical edition was prepared by Matthew D. Stroud (San Antonio: Trinity U.P., 1981). Pedro Calderón de la Barco was the librettist.

1050. Pitts, Ruth Landis. "Don Juan Hidalgo, Seventeenth-Century Spanish Composer." Ph.D. diss., Peabody College, 1968. 302p.

1051. Velez de Guevara, Juan. "*Los celos hacen estrellas.*" Ed. J. E. Varey and N. D. Shergold, music ed. Jack Sage. London: Tamesis, 1970. cxvii, 273p. ML1747.2 .V44.

The libretto and much of the music of the earliest known zarzuela (ca. 1662), with a useful commentary. Velez was the writer of the text, Hidalgo of the music.

Johann Adam Hiller (1728–1804)

Die Jagd is in *GO,* v.1.

Paul Hindemith (1895–1963)

1052. Hindemith, Paul. *Sämtliche Werke*. Ed. Kurt von Fischer and Ludwig Finscher, for the Hindemith Stiftung. Mainz: Schott, 1975–. M3 .H62 F6.

Full scores of the operas are in series 1, v.1–6, with brief introductions and some critical notes.

1053. Neumeyer, David. *The Music of Paul Hindemith*. New Haven, Conn.: Yale U.P., 1986. viii, 294p. ISBN 0-300-03287-0. ML410 .H685 N5.

A valuable technical analysis of Hindemith's works, set against a study of the composer's methods and principles as outlined in his *Craft of Musical Composition*. He discloses macrostructural designs as well as small-scale patterns, quotations, intervallic practices, and so forth. The major operas are well covered: *Cardillac,* p.168–183, and *Mathis der Maler,* p.85–109. Other stage works get brief comments. Bibliography of some 150 items, expansive index.

1054. D'Angelo, James P. "Tonality and Its Symbolic Association in Paul Hindemith's Opera *Die Harmonie der Welt*." Ph.D. diss., New York U., 1983. 599p.

1054a. Bruhn, Siglind. *The Temptation of Paul Hindemith: "Mathis der Maler" as a Spiritual Testimony.* Stuyvesant, N.Y.: Pendragon, 1998. xvii, 419p. ISBN 1-57647-013-X. ML410 .H685 B69.

A study of the Isenheim Altarpiece, by Mathis Grünewald, which inspired Hindemith, in an effort to disclose the full significance of the opera. Finds parallels in the lives of the painter and composer. The libretto is seen as representing spiritual crises in both lives. Bibliography, index.

1055. Cook, Susan C. *Opera for a New Republic: The "Zeitopern" of Krenek, Weill, and Hindemith.* Studies in Musicology, 96. Ann Arbor, Mich.: UMI Research, 1988. viii, 284p. ISBN 0-8357-1811-5. ML1729 .C66.

Cook defines *Zeitoper* as a satire on contemporary themes and technology; it emerged after World War II. American dance music and jazz were often incorporated. Attention focuses on Krenek's *Jonny spielt auf,* Weill's *Der Zar lässt sich photographieren,* and two works by Hindemith: *Hin und zurück* and *Neues vom Tage.* Genesis and performance histories (not much of that; the operas faded and had little influence). Well documented with statistics, production photos, and notes. Bibliography of about 400 items, index.

1056. Santore, Jonathan Conrad. "Dramatic Action, Motive Deployment, and Formal Structure in Hindemith's *Sancta Suxanna* and *Native Soil.*" Ph.D. diss., U. of California at Los Angeles, 1994. 2v.

E. T. A. Hoffmann (1776–1822)

1057. Hoffmann, Ernst Theodor Amadeus. *Ausgewählte musikalische Werke.* Ed. director Georg von Dadelsen. Munich: Schott, 1971–. M3.1 .H74 M9.

Not seen. V.1–3: *Undine;* v.4–5: *Die lustigen Musikanten;* v.6–8 (not yet published): *Liebe und Eifersucht.*

1058. Wilson, Richard L. "Text and Music in the Operas of E. T. A. Hoffmann." Ph.D. diss., U. of Southern California, 1988. 610p.

1059. Garlington, Aubrey S., Jr. "E. T. A. Hoffmann's *Der Dichter und der Komponist* and the Creation of German Romantic Opera." MQ 65 (1979): 22–47.

Hoffmann's *Der Dichter und der Komponist* (1813) and his other works are seen as blends of music and fantasy in which "the marvelous is the most indispensable element." Language and music function together as a higher language—the language of German romantic opera.

1060. Garlington, Aubrey S. Jr. "Notes on Dramatic Motives in Opera: Hoffmann's *Undine.*" MR 32 (1971): 136–145.

Discusses the concept of leading motive with examples from *Undine*: the characters think of situations, not of musical motives; the listeners translate the motives into those situations.

Gustav Holst (1874–1934)

1061. Short, Michael. *Gustav Holst: The Man and His Music.* New York: Oxford U.P., 1990. xiv, 530p. ISBN 0-19-314154-X. ML410 .H748 S6.

A useful life and works, well documented, with a worklist and a strong bibliography of some 500 entries. Technical analysis is treated topically (harmony, rhythm, form, etc.) in separate chapters, with considerations of various works in them. The operas are accounted for in this manner, rather than through individual accounts of each. Index.

Arthur Honegger (1892–1955)

1062. Halbreich, Harry. *Arthur Honegger.* Trans. Roger Nichols. Portland, Ore.: Amadeus, 1999. 677p. ISBN 1-57467-041-7. ML410 .H79 H313.

Originally *Arthur Honegger: Un musicien dans la cité des hommes* (Paris: Fayard, 1992). A documented life and works, with extended program notes on *Judith, Antigone,* and *L'aiglon* (composed with Ibert). Backnotes, worklist, quick bibliography, name index.

1063. Spratt, Geoffrey K. *The Music of Arthur Honegger.* Cork, Ireland: Cork U.P., 1987. xix, 651p. ISBN 0-9025-6134-0. ML410 .H79 S67.

Primarily a technical analysis of the nine dramatic works, with genesis and reception studies. The works are diagrammed and examined on macro and micro levels, with musical examples in full score. Spratt finds the "organic strength of the music" to result from the handling of motifs, not from tonal structure (which Honegger considered outmoded). Worklist, bibliography of about 400 items, index.

Engelbert Humperdinck (1854–1921)

Hänsel und Gretel is in *ASO* 104 (1987).

1064. *Engelbert Humperdinck zum 70. Todestag.* Ed. Eva Humperdinck and Jost Nickell. Siegburg: Franz Schmitt, 1992. 279p. ISBN 3-87710-153-4. ML410 .H9 A4.

A useful treatment of *Königskinder* takes up most of this book. Detailed genesis, with the composer's correspondence of 1894–1908. Facsimiles of programs and letters, footnotes, worklist.

Jacques Ibert (1890–1962)

1065. Failoni, Judith Weaver. "Tradition and Innovation in Jacques Ibert's Opera, *Persée et Andromède.*" Ph.D. diss., Washington U., 1995. 505p.

See also Halbreich (#1062).

Vincent D'Indy (1851–1931)

1066. Vallas, Léon. *Vincent D'Indy.* Paris: Michel, 1946–1950. 2v. ML410 .I7 V3.

A life and works, with genesis, reception, and technical notes on *Le chant de la cloche, Fervaal,* and *L'étranger.* The style, Wagnerian all the way, is analyzed in those terms. Musical examples, worklist and index, no bibliography.

Leoš Janáček (1854–1928)

Editions

1067. Janáček, Leoš. *Complete Critical Edition of the Works = Souborne kriticke vydani.* Ed. Jiří Vysloužil et al. Prague: Supraphon; Kassel: Bärenreiter, 1978–. M3 .J3 K6.

Although v.1–11 are designated for the stage works, none has been published. Other volumes in the series have full scores with critical commentaries (in Czech, German, English, French, and Russian). The edition is discussed in several essays of *Janáček* (#1069).

Bibliographies and Guides to Resources

1068. Mráček, Jaroslav. "The Reception of Leoš Janáček as Seen through a Study of the Bibliography: A Preliminary Report." In *Janáček* (#1069), 347–355.

A valuable bibliographic essay, citing the core literature.

Conferences

1069. *Janáček and Czech Music: Proceedings of the International Conference, St. Louis, 1988.* Ed. Michael Beckerman and Glen Bauer. Studies in Czech Music, 1. Stuyvesant, N.Y.: Pendragon, 1995. xi, 402p. ISBN 0-945-19336-4. ML410 .J18 J35.

Among the 32 papers, 5 are about opera. Two are entered separately in this section (#1077 and #1079). Three essays discuss the *Complete Critical Edition,* and one examines the writings about Janáček (#1068). The volume has a strong index.

Collections of Essays

1070. *Janáček Studies.* Ed. Paul Wingfield. New York: Cambridge U.P., 1999. Ca. 275p. ISBN 0-521-57357-2.

Not seen. According to the publisher's catalogue, the book has essays on opera, among other topics.

Letters and Documents

1071. Štědroň, Bohumir. *Leoš Janáček in Letters and Reminiscences.* Prague: Artia, 1946. 233p. ML410 .J18 A2 S8.

Also published in Czech (Prague: Panton, 1976) and German (Prague: Artia, 1955). An annotated collection of 230 letters and other writings by and about the composer. Worklist, index of names.

Biographies

1072. Vogel, Jaroslav. *Leoš Janáček: A Biography.* Rev. ed. London: Orbis; New York: Norton, 1981. 439p. ML410 .J18 V82.

First edition, in Czech, 1962; English translation (London: Hamlyn), 1962. A scholarly life and works, with detailed genesis and program notes on the operas. Worklist, indexes by name and title.

1073. Horsbrugh, Ian. *Leoš Janáček: The Field That Prospered.* New York: Scribner, 1981. 327p. ISBN 0-684-17443-X. ML410 .J18 H81.

A useful study, with footnotes, pictures, musical examples, and lengthy program notes on the operas. Premiere information and bibliographic data about the stage works are in an appendix. Expansive index of names and titles.

1074. Hollander, Hans. *Leoš Janáček: His Life and Work.* Trans. Paul Hamburger. New York: St. Martin's, 1963. 222p. ML410 .J18 H64.

A footnoted life and works, with about 30 pages of program notes on the operas. Worklist, with titles in Czech and English, and publication information. Partly expansive index of names and titles. The German translation by Kurt Honolka (Stuttgart: Belser, 1982) includes some updating of the text and bibliography and adds a chronology but omits the footnotes; its worklist has titles in Czech and German; its index is to names only.

Operas in General

1075. Ewans, Michael. *Janáček's Tragic Operas.* London: Faber & Faber, 1977. 284p. ISBN 0-571-10959-4. ML410 .J18 E9.

A German translation was published (Stuttgart: Reclam, 1981). Extended program notes on the major operas, with some analytical observations. Comments on the available editions and on the state of Janáček scholarship. Ewans cites the books he finds valuable, all of them in Czech. Expansive index of names, titles, and topics.

1076. Tyrrell, John R. "Janáček's Stylistic Development as an Operatic Composer, as Evidenced in His Revisions of the First Five Operas." Ph.D. diss., U. of Oxford, 1969. 2v.

1077. Tyrrell, John R. "Janáček's Recitatives." In *Janáček* (#1069), 3–19.

The composer's indication "recit" does not always call for traditional recitative. He was opposed to recitative in the old sense; he probably meant "speech melody," but it is never certain what his intention was.

1078. Tyrrell, John R. *Janáček's Operas: A Documentary Account.* Princeton, N.J.: Princeton U.P., 1992. xxv, 405p. ISBN 0-6910-9148-X. ML410 .J18 A4.

A chapter of analysis for each of the nine operas. Also letters and other writings of the composer, translated with commentaries. Bibliography, index.

Individual Works

The Cunning Little Vixen (Přihody lišky bystroušky)

ASO 84 (1986).

1079. Josephson, Nors. "Musical and Dramatic Organization in Janáček's *The Cunning Little Vixen.*" In *Janáček* (#1069), 83–91.

Shows through musical examples and scene-by-scene analysis the motivic permutations and organization in the opera. It is "based on a recurring intervallic matrix that is heralded at the very outset." D-flat major is the tonic; other principal tonal centers are A-flat minor, G-flat major, and E-flat major.

From the House of the Dead (Z mrtvého domu)

ASO 109 (1988).

Jenufa

ASO 102 (1987), ENOG 33 (1985).

Katya Kabanova (Kat'a Kabanová)

ASO 114 (1988), COH (1982), ENOG 33 (1985).

The Makropulos Affair (Věc Makropulos)

ASO 188 (1999), ENOG 33 (1985).

Niccolò Jommelli (1714–1774)

1080. McClymonds, Marita P. *Niccolò Jommelli: The Last Years 1769–1774.* Ann Arbor, Mich.: UMI Research, 1980. xix, 877p. ISBN 0-8357-1113-7. ML410 .J7 M14.

A thorough life and works, drawing on previously unpublished letters, including a useful account of Italian opera at the Portuguese court, 1750–1780 (with plans and pictures of the Ajuda and Tejo theaters in Lisbon), and stylistic explorations of the late operas and sacred music. An appendix offers a list of dramatic works by composers active in Portugal, 1755–1780, and another presents titles of works produced at the Portuguese court, 1752–1792. Good bibliography of about 200 entries and discussion of the major sources. Expansive index of names, titles, and topics. Some of this research was condensed for an article:

1081. McClymonds, Marita P. "The Evolution of Jommelli's Operatic Style." *JAMS* 33–2 (Summer 1980): 326–355.

Jommelli was much influenced by German music, even before his time in Stuttgart (1753–1769). His style changed slowly and logically over his career. After the German years he achieved final maturity and wrote some of his greatest operas.

1082. Abert, Hermann. *Niccolo Jommelli als Opernkomponist, mit einer Bibliographie.* Halle an der Saale: Niemeyer, 1908. 461p. ML410 .J755 A14.

A scholarly life and works, with sources identified (this constitutes the "Bibliographie" aspect of the book's title; there is no actual bibliography in it). Genesis and technical analysis of the operas, with a 64-page appendix of extended musical examples. Expansive index.

1083. Tolkoff, Audrey Lyn. "The Stuttgart Operas of Niccolò Jommelli." Ph.D. diss., Yale U., 1974. 431p.

See also Wilson (#258) and Henze-Döhring (#1307).

Scott Joplin (1868–1917)

Joplin's opera *Treemonisha* had no full-scale performance in his lifetime but was revived in 1972 by Robert Shaw in Atlanta, staged worldwide, and won a Pulitzer Prize. It has had no scholarly literature except for the dissertation noted below.

1084. Hebert, Rubye Nell. "A Study of the Composition and Performance of Scott Joplin's Opera *Treemonisha.*" D.M.A. diss., Ohio State U., 1976. 57p.

1085. Ping-Robbins, Nancy R. *Scott Joplin: A Guide to Research*. Garland Composer Resource Manuals, 47. New York: Garland, 1998. 419p. ISBN 0-8240-8399-7. ML134 .J75 P56.

   A varied guide to material about Joplin and ragtime, including 902 annotated entries for writings about him. For *Treemonisha* there are 77 items, mostly reviews and brief notices.

Reinhard Keiser (1674–1739)

1086. Zelm, Klaus. *Die Opern Reinhard Keisers. Studien zur Chronologie, Überlieferung und Stilentwicklung.* Musikwissenschaftliche Schriften, 8. Munich: Katzbichler, 1975. 246p. ISBN 3-87397-107-0. ML410 .K27 Z51.

   Inventory of sources and library locations; detailed analyses of aria, form, and scenic structure. Good plates and musical examples. Bibliography of about 150 entries, name index.

1087. Koch, Klaus-Peter. "Zu Reinhard Keisers Spätschaffen." *Händel-Jahrbuch* 36 (1990): 91–106.

   Keiser is reported to have written 118 operas, of which only 19 survive with music. Koch considers aria stye, structure, use of chorus, and output of different periods. He believes that the composer deserves more scholarly attention; the extant literature about him is traced in 58 footnotes.

1088. Arnn, John D. "Text, Music, and Drama in Three Operas by Reinhard Keiser." Ph.D. diss., Rutgers U., 1987. 592p.

1089. Brenner, Rosamond. "The Operas of Reinhard Keiser in Their Relationship to the Affektenlehre." Ph.D. diss., Brandeis U., 1968. 3v. Brenner also has an article, "Emotional Expression in Keiser's Operas," *MR* 33 (1972): 222–232.

1090. Melkus, Eduard. "Zur Aufführung von Keisers *Croesus* in Halle." *Händel-Jahrbuch* 36 (1990): 107–116.

   Croesus (1711) was revised for Hamburg in 1731. Melkus—who himself directed a revival in Halle—compares the two versions, with technical comments on structure, key, and aria style.

1091. Lamkin, Michael Deane. "*La forza del virtù oder Die Macht der Tugend* of Reinhard Keiser." Ph.D. diss., U. of Iowa, 1979. 685p.

See also Harris (#963) and Roberts (#947, #978).

Zoltán Kodály (1882–1967)

1092. Houlahan, Mícheál, and Philip Tacka. *Zoltán Kodály: A Guide to Research*. Garland Composer Resource Manuals, 44. New York: Garland, 1998. xiv, 611p. ISBN 0-8153-2853-2. ML134 .K64 T3.

An indispensable guide to the Hungarian and international literature, consisting of 1,457 thoroughly annotated entries. Worklist, with titles in original languages and English translations; chronology; biographical sketch; expansive indexes of authors/titles and compositions. There are only scattered references to the popular opera *Háry Janos*.

1093. Eősze, László. *Zoltán Kodály: His Life and Work*. Trans. István Farkas and Gyula Gulyás. New York: Belwin-Mills, 1962. 183p. ML410 .K732 E63.

Originally published in Hungarian, 1956. A basic life and works, with a chapter of program notes on the stage music (p.149–156).

Erich Wolfgang Korngold (1897–1957)

1094. Carroll, Brendan. "The Operas of Erich Wolfgang Korngold." Ph.D. diss., U. of Liverpool, 1975.

Ernest Krenek (1900–1991)

1095. Rogge, Wolfgang. *Ernest Kreneks Opern: Spiegel der zwanziger Jahre*. Wolfenbüttel: Möseler, 1970. 124p. ML410 .K77 R6.

A useful introduction to the composer's life, with some technical analysis of the works. No bibliography; index of names.

1096. Stewart, John L. *Ernest Krenek: The Man and His Music*. Berkeley: U. of California Press, 1991. xi, 445p. ISBN 0-520-07014-3. ML410 .K736 .S57.

Primarily a biography, with program notes on the music. Bibliography of about 400 items, index.

1097. Bowles, Garrett H. *Ernest Krenek: A Bio-Bibliography*. Bio-Bibliographies in Music, 22. Westport, Conn.: Greenwood, 1989. xiv, 428p. ISBN 0-313-25250-5. ML410 .K9 B6.

Krenek's greatly popular opera, *Jonny spielt auf*, lacks a scholarly literature. This book identifies the reviews and brief notices available.

See also Cook (#1055).

Friedrich Ludwig Aemelius Kunzen (1761–1817)

Das Fest der Winzer is in *GO*, v.11.

Michel de La Barre (ca.1675–1743 or 1744)

Le triomphe des arts is in *FO*, v.22.

Jean Benjamin de La Borde (1734–1794)

Annette et Lubin is in *FO*, v.59.

Louis La Coste (ca.1675–ca.1750)

Philomèle is in *FO*, v.24.

Pierre de La Garde (1717–1792)

Aeglé is in *FO*, v.47.

Elizabeth Jacquet de La Guerre (1639–1729)

Her *Céphale et Procris* (1694) was the first opera by a woman to be staged at the Paris Opéra.

1098. Borroff, Edith. *An Introduction to Elisabeth-Claude Jacquet de La Guerre.* Musicological Studies, 12. Brooklyn: Institute of Mediaeval Music, 1966. 180p. ML410 .L242 B7.

Musical and textual analysis with extended examples of *Céphale et Procris* (p.21–44) is part of this study of the composer. La Guerre displays "versatility of technique and style." Bibliography of about 50 items, no index.

Michel-Richard de Lalande (1657–1726)

In *FO*: *Ballet de la jeunesse*, v.9; *L'amour fléchy par la constance*, v.11; and *Les éléments*, v.16.

1099. Dufourcq, Norbert et al. *Notes et références pour servir à une histoire de Michel- Richard Delalande.* Paris: Picard, 1957. 356p. ML410 .L19 D86.

Documents, letters, notices, and reviews of performances; detailed worklist and thematic incipit catalogue. No bibliography or index.

See also #2227.

Édouard Lalo (1823–1892)

Le roi d'Ys is in *ASO* 65 (1984).

John Frederick Lampe (1703?–1751)

1100. Martin, Dennis Roy. "The Operas and Operatic Style of John Frederick Lampe (1703?–1751) with a Commentary and Critical Edition of His Most Important Work, *The Dragon of Wantley*." Ph.D. diss., U. of Iowa, 1979. 2v.

Stefano Landi (ca. 1590–ca. 1655)

His *Sant'Alessio* (1632) was the first opera on a historical subject. Landi had some stature as an operatic pioneer but is largely forgotten today. In Murata (#446) there is a treatment of *Sant'Alessio*, because the librettist was Rospigliosi. And Pirrotta's essay in *New Looks* (#2429) gives him some attention. There is also a dissertation:

1101. Carfagno, Simon A. "The Life and Dramatic Music of Stefano Landi, with a Transliteration and Orchestration of the Opera *Sant'Alessio*." Ph.D. diss., U. of California at Los Angeles, 1960. 2v.

Jean Marie Leclair (1697–1764)

Scylla et Glaucus is in *FO*, v.46.

1102. Zaslaw, Neal A. "Materials for the Life and Works of Jean Marie Leclair l'aîné." Ph.D. diss., Columbia U., 1970. 526p.

1103. Zaslaw, Neal A. "*Scylla et Glaucus*: A Case Study." *COJ* 4-2 (July 1992): 199–228.

Genesis, plot, reception (with full text of a review of the premiere), inventory of available sources. The opera appeared in 1746, just before the *querelle*, which prompted Zaslaw to give this interesting summary of critical controversies in French music:

Year	Conservative	Avant-garde
ca. 1673	Ancient music	Lully
ca. 1702	Lully	Italian music
ca. 1733	Lully	Rameau
ca. 1752	Lully and Rameau	Pergolesi, Rousseau
ca. 1774	Rameau	Gluck
ca. 1778	Gluck	Piccinni

Ferenc (Franz) Lehár (1870–1948)

Die lustige Witwe (The Merry Widow) is in *ASO* 45 (1982).

1104. Schönherr, Max. *Franz Lehár: Bibliographie zu Leben und Werk*. Vienna: Author, 1970. 161p. ML410 .L56.

Lists all books, articles, and other writings about the composer. Also gives corrected dates for all the operettas and discusses the place of music in Vienna during the years of World War II. Index.

1105. Gold, Edward. "Franz Lehar's Operettas: An Analysis." Ph.D. diss., New York U., 1993. 925p.

Jean-Baptiste Lemoyne (1751–1796)

1106. Rushton, Julian G. "An Early Essay in *Leitmotiv*: J. B. Lemoyne's *Electre*." *M&L* 52–4 (October 1971): 387–401.

The opera was a failure at the Académie Royale in 1782 but displays something of the "continuity and complexity of thematic cross reference which we tend to regard as Wagnerian." Musical examples and analysis of the motifs.

Leonardo Leo (1694–1744)

1107. Pastore, Giuseppe A. *Leonardo Leo*. Galatina: Pajano, 1957. 159p. ML410 .L575 P29.

Leo wrote 81 operas, none of which has received recent scholarly attention. This book offers a brief biography with backnotes and a list of the operas, with librettists and premiere data. No index, no bibliography.

1108. Hardie, Graham Hood. "Leonardo Leo (1694–1744) and His Comic Operas *Amor vuol sofferanza* and *Alidoro*." Ph.D. diss., Cornell U., 1973. vii, 289p.

Ruggero Leoncavallo (1857–1919)

Pagliacci is in *ASO* 50 (1983) and Rororo (1987).

1109. Sansone, Matteo. "The *verismo* of Ruggero Leoncavallo: A Source Study of *Paglicacci*." *M&L* 70–3 (August 1989): 342–362.

Leoncavallo wrote his own libretti. "If we analyze the composer's criteria for selecting and arranging his material, we gain an insight into the evolution (or rather, dissolution) of operatic *verismo* in the ten years between *Cavalleria rusticana* and *Tosca*." There is an interesting comparison of *Pagliacci* to an opera by Émile Pessard, *Tabarin* (1885).

Jean-François Lesueur (Le Sueur) (1760–1837)

La caverne is in *FO*, v.74; *Ossian ou les bardes* is in *ERO*, v.37.

1110. Mongrédien, Jean. *Jean-François Le Sueur: Contribution à l'étude d'un demi-siècle de musique française, 1780–1830*. Berne: P. Lang, 1980. 2v. ISBN 3-261046-945. ML410 .L59 M74.

A general biography with passing mention of the operas. Chapter endnotes, bibliography, name index.

1111. Mongrédien, Jean. *Catalogue thématique de l'oeuvre complète du compositeur Jean-François Le Sueur (1760–1837)*. Thematic Catalogues, 7. New York: Pendragon, 1980. xxviii, 434p. ISBN 0-9187-2812-6. ML134 .L46 M74.

Operas are well covered (p.45–219), with incipits for all arias and numbers in each. No bibliography or index.

György Ligeti (1923–)

1112. Richart, Robert W. *György Ligeti: A Bio-Bibliography*. Bio-Bibliographies in Music, 30. Westport, Conn.: Greenwood, 1991. xii, 188p.

Among the 729 entries (in author order) are many reviews and brief discussions of *Le grand macabre*.

1113. *Ligeti*. Ed. Enzo Restagno. Turin: ECT, 1985. xi, 265p. ISBN 88-7063-036-6. ML410 .L69 L72.

Essays by various authors; one is "Intorno al *Grand macabre*," by Piero Santi et al; it gives genesis and program notes.

1114. Burde, Wolfgang. *György Ligeti: Eine Monographie*. Zurich: Atlantis, 1993. 280p. ISBN 3-254-00184-2. ML410 .L64 B95.

A general life and works, with good coverage (p.217–244) of *Le grand macabre*: genesis, program notes, some technical observations. Remarkably small musical examples, backnotes, index, no bibliography.

1115. Floros, Constantin. *György Ligeti: Jenseits von Avantgarde und Post-Moderne.* Komponisten unserer Zeit, 26. Vienna: Lafite, 1996. 246p. No ISBN. ML410 .L64 F64.

> A well-documented biography, with a treatment of *Le grand macabre* (p.132–155): genesis, program notes and some technical notes, legible musical examples. Bibliography, index.

See also *Oper heute* (#95).

Franz Liszt (1811–1886)

1116. Saffle, Michael. *Franz Liszt: A Guide to Research.* Garland Composer Resource Manuals, 29. New York: Garland, 1991. xviii, 407p. ISBN 0-8240-8382-2. ML134 .L7 S2.

> Of the 1,084 annotated entries in this useful guide, just 3 are about Liszt's only opera, *Don Sanche.* (One is cited next.) Saffle also covers the well-known piano transcriptions of operatic material and the composer's plans for a Faust opera.

1117. Chantavoine, Jean. "Die Operette *Don Sanche*: Ein verloren geglaubtes Werk Franz Liszts." *Musik* 3–11 (1903–1904): 286–307.

A general description with musical examples.

Albert Lortzing (1801–1851)

1118. Subotnik, Rose R. "Lortzing and the German Romantics: A Dialectical Assessment." *MQ* 62 (1976): 241–264.

> Lortzing, who has been undervalued, aimed at unity of music and text on a grand scale. His success in Germany suggests that "society as a large collective force was as implicated in the creation of his repertory operas as was Lortzing himself." His great value was not self-expression but "stability required by a mass society." Subotnik's dissertation has more: "Popularity and Art in Lortzing's Operas: The Effects of Social Change on a National Operatic Genre" (Columbia U., 1973).

1119. Sanders, Ernest. "*Oberon* and *Zar und Zimmerman.*" *MQ* 40-4 (October 1954): 521–532.

> Notes that there is no "truly German counterpart of Italian opera." Of Lortzing, nothing is known outside Germany. New recordings of *Oberon* and *Zar und Zimmerman* were the basis for this article, which offers genesis/reception accounts of both works and summarizes the ideas on opera of both composers. The two operas are not really compared.

Antonio Lotti (1667–1740)

1120. Spitz, Charlotte. *Anotonio Lotti in seiner Bedeutung als Opernkomponist.* Leipzig: Noske, 1918. 114p. ML410 .L9 S7.

> A general biography, with attention and much praise for the operas. Based on the author's dissertation at Maximilians U., Munich. No index or bibliography.

Jean-Baptiste Lully (1632–1687)

Editions

1121. Lully, Jean-Baptiste. *The Collected Works*. Carl B. Schmidt, general editor. New York: Broude.

In progress, as announced in the Broude 1999 catalogue. Only one volume, of motets, has appeared (1996). The publisher has no plan to issue further volumes in the near future.

1122. Lully, Jean-Baptiste. *Oeuvres complètes*. Ed. Henri Prunières et al. Paris, 1930–1972. 11v.

Series discontinued. The operas *Cadmus et Hermione, Alceste,* and *Amadis* were published. Reprint announced in the Broude 1999 catalogue.

1123. Lully, Jean-Baptiste. *The "tragédies lyriques" in Facsimile*. Prefaces by François Lesure et al. New York: Broude, 1998–. M1500 .L95.

In progress. To include nine works. Four appeared in 1998: *Atys* (v.4), *Bellérephon* (v.7), *Persée* (v.9), and *Acis et Galatée* (v.14). Others to be issued are *Thésée, Proserpine, Phaëton, Roland,* and *Armide.*

1124. *The "livrets" of Jean-Baptiste Lully's "tragédies lyriques": A catalogue raisonné*. Compiled by Carl B. Schmidt. New York: Performers' Editions, 1995. xli, 633p. ISBN 0-9439-3050-2. ML134 .L92 S34.

Prints the *livrets* (libretti) for 15 operas, with indexes of performers, composers, librettists, printers, and cities.

Thematic Catalogues and Worklists

1125. Schneider, Herbert. *Chronologisch-thematisches Verzeichnis sämtlicher Werke von Jean-Baptiste Lully*. Mainzer Studien zur Musikwissenschaft, 15. Tutzing: Schneider, 1981. 570p. ML134 .L956 S3.

A worklist in date order, with musical incipits, information on manuscripts and printed sources, librettists, premiere facts, and citations of secondary literature. Supplemented by Bruce Gustafson, "The Lully Labyrinth: Cross References and Misattributions in the Lully Werke-Verzeichnis," *Notes* 44–1 (September 1987): 33–39; and Carl B. Schmidt, "Newly Identified Manuscript Sources for the Music of Jean-Baptiste Lully," *Notes* 44–1 (September 1987): 7–32.

Bibliographies and Guides to Resources

1126. *Lully Web Project*. Denton: U. of North Texas, 1997–.

Available at <www.library.unt.edu.> Gives a fact sheet for each work, including synopsis and performance history. The Lully bibliography includes master's theses.

Conferences

1127. *Jean-Baptsite Lully: Actes du Colloque = Kongressbericht, Saint Germain-en-Laye, Heidelberg, 1987*. Ed. Jérome de La Gorce and Herbert Schneider. Neue heidelberger Studien zur Musikwissenschaft, 18. Laaber: Laaber, 1990. 618p. ISBN 3-89007-211-9. ML410 .L84 L213.

A valuable collection of 35 papers on various aspects of Lully's work and influence. These are entered separately in this guide: Neal Zaslaw on Lully's orchestra (#345), James R. Anthony on Lully's airs (#1139), and Herbert Schneider on structure in Lully's scenes and acts (#1138). Other essays of interest on the operas: Patricia Howard, "The Positioning of Woman in Quinault's World Picture"; Volker Kapp, "Benserade, librettist de Lully et panégyriste du roi"; and Dietmar Fricke, "Molière et Lully: Une symbiose artistique sans suite?"

Collections of Essays

1128. *Lully, 1632–1687, tricentenaire*. Special issue of *Revue musicale* 398–399 (1987). 64p. ML5 .R47.

Consists of three papers by Henri Prunières: "Les premières ballets de Lully," "L'Académie Royale de Musique et le dance," and "La Fontaine et Lully." The third deals with the poet La Fontaine, who aspired to be Lully's librettist but was not accepted. Includes a useful discussion of libretto writing at the time, along with court intrigues.

1129. *Textes sur Lully et l'opéra français*. Ed. and introduction by François Lesure. Geneva: Minkoff, 1987. Various pagings. ISBN 2-82660-928-9. ML1727.3 .T35.

Reprints of: Charles Perrault, *Critique de l'opéra* (Paris: L. Billaine, 1674); Saint- Evremond, *Sur les opéras* (Paris: C. Barbin, 1684); and Antoine Louis Le Brun, *Théâtre lyrique avec une préface* (Paris: P. Ribou, 1712).

1130. *Jean-Baptiste Lully and the Music of the French Baroque: Essays in Honor of James R. Anthony*. Ed. John Hajdu Heyer. New York: Cambridge U.P., 1989. xiv, 328p. ISBN 0–521- 35263–0. ML410 .L95 J43.

A useful gathering of essays by various specialists. One paper is entered separately: Neal Zaslaw on the first opera in Paris (#2260). Lois Rosow's "How Eighteenth-Century Parisians Heard Lully's Operas: The Case of *Armide*" (see note at #1141) and Carl B. Schmidt's "The Geographical Spread of Lully's Operas during the Late Seventeenth and Early Eighteenth Centuries" are also of interest.

Biographies

1131. Couvreur, Manuel. *Jean-Baptiste Lully: Musique et dramaturgie en service du prince*. Brussels: Vokar, 1992. 454p. ISBN 2-8701-12005-2. ML410 .L95 C87.

A documented biography, with good accounts of the *querelle* and descriptions of the ballets, masques, and other stage works. Valuable bibliography of some 400 items, name and title index.

1132. Beaussant, Philippe. *Lully, ou le musicien du soleil.* Paris: Gallimard, 1992. 893p. No ISBN. ML410 .L95 B38.

Life story, then long accounts of *Psyché, Cadmus, Alceste, Thésée,* and *Armide.* For each there is genesis, program notes, musical examples, and some technical observations. Backnotes, worklist, bibliography, no index.

See also *New Grove French Baroque Masters* (#2227).

Operas in General

1133. Newman, Joyce. *Jean-Baptiste de Lully and His "tragédies lyriques."* Ann Arbor, Mich.: UMI Research, 1979. x, 266p. ISBN 0-8357-1002-5. ML410 .L95 N55.

As the first of the operatic "reformers," Lully created the distinctive French opera style, departing from the conventional Italian mode. Newman discusses the old and new traditions, gives biographical data, and then describes each of the operas in technical detail—music and libretto—with long musical examples. Footnotes, fine bibliography of about 400 items, expansive index of names, titles, and topics.

1134. Howard, Patricia. "The Operas of Jean-Baptiste Lully." Ph.D. diss., U. of Surrey, 1974.

1135. Schneider, Herbert. *Die Rezeption der Opern Lullys im Frankreich des ancien régime.* Mainzer Studien zur Musikwissenschaft, 16. Tutzing: Schneider, 1982. 394p. ISBN 3-79520-335-X. ML410 .L95 S24.

Much detail on the performances, revisions, and critical reception of the operas to the end of the 18th century. Manuscript and printed sources described. Valuable commentaries explore the French background for the operas. Bibliography, glossary.

1136. Wood, Caroline. *Music and Drama in the "tragédie en musique," 1673–1715: Jean- Baptiste Lully and His Successors.* Outstanding Dissertations in Music from British Universities. New York: Garland, 1996. xii, 391p. ISBN 0-8153-2450-2. ML1717 .W666.

Originally the author's Ph.D. dissertation, U. of Hull, 1981. Includes sections on the first 40 years of French opera; Lully at the Académie; recitative by Lully and later composers and similar treatment of aria, ensemble, and chorus; orchestra, libretto, and special effects. Bibliography of about 80 entries, index.

1137. Rosow, Lois. "Making Connections: Thoughts on Lully's Entr'actes." *Early Music* 21–2 (May 1993): 231–239.

The entr'acte was not just filler but essential to the drama: it represented the activity of the story that was supposed to occur between acts. Events were recalled, and a bridge—musical and emotional—was forged. Examples from *Roland* and *Armide.*

1138. Schneider, Herbert. "Strukturen der Szenen und Akte in Lullys Opern." In *Colloque* (#1127), 77–98.

Form and tonal structure of scenes from Monteverdi, Cesti, and Alessandro Scarlatti, which were models for Lully's plans. He modified the earlier approach by giving greater emphasis to tonal connections in the shaping of scenes. He usually based the musical form on the dramatic form of the text, but at times the musical form was developed more independently. Schneider also points to philosophical and political associations Lully made with his formal designs.

1139. Anthony, James R. "The Musical Structure of Lully's Operatic Airs." In *Colloque* (#1127), 65–76.

An examination of some 600 airs for solo voice in the 13 *tragédies en musique*. Anthony classifies them as dialogue airs, monologue airs, dance songs, and maxim airs; these types are defined. Most of the airs, in all categories, are in binary form; others are in rondeau or ternary form. But in the monologue type, the rondeau predominates. A table clarifies these distinctions.

1140. Howard, Patricia. "Lully and the Ironic Convention." *COJ* 1 (1989): 139–153.

Considers "a relationship between style and situation in a practice which appears to belong exclusively to the French stage, which was initiated by Lully, and which, half a century after his death, seems to have been forgotten." The idea is that Lully's arias carry coded messages—for example, the bass voice in a doubled continuo air = a rejected lover. Destouches, Campra, and even Rameau used similar devices.

See also Howard (#267).

Individual Works

See also items noted at #1122, #1123, and #1132.

Amadis

FO, v.6.

Armide

FO, v.6.

1141. Rosow, Lois. "Lully's *Armide* at the Paris Opéra: A Performance History, 1686–1766." Ph.D. diss., Brandeis U., 1981. xiv, 716p.

An article based on this research is in #1130.

1142. Torrefranca, Fausto. "La prima opera francese in Italia? (*L'Armida* di Lully, Roma, 1690)." In *Musikwissenschaftliche Beiträge: Festschrift für Johannes Wolf zu seinem sechzigsten Geburtstag*, ed. W. Lott et al., 191–197 (Berlin: Breslauer, 1929; ML55 .M97).

Although Ademollo (#2568) lists a performance of *L'Armida* at the Tor di Nona (Tordinona) in 1690, no contemporary evidence supports him, and no libretto has been seen for the Italian version. A French libretto has survived, with a wax stain on one page, suggesting it was taken to a performance.

Torrefranca suggests that the opera was privately performed, for a French audience, and not publicly staged.

Atys

ASO 94 (1987), *FO*, v.3.

Ballet de flore

FO, v.1.

Le bourgeois gentilhomme

FO, v.1.

Cadmus et Hermione

1143. Burgess, Geoffrey Vernon. "Ritual in the *tragédie en musique* from *Cadmus et Hermione* (1673) to *Zoroastre* (1749)." Ph.D. diss., Cornell U., 1998. xxxviii, 744p.

Les festes de l'amour et de Bacchus

FO, v.2.

Persée

FO, v.5.

Psyché

1144. Turnbull, Michael. "A Critical Edition of *Psyché*: An Opera with Words by Thomas Corneille and Philippe Quinault, and Music by Jean-Baptiste Lully." Ph.D. diss., U. of Oxford, 1981.

The author's name is given as T. M. Turnbull.

1145. Turnbull, Michael. "The Metamorphosis of *Psyché*." *M&L* 64 (1983): 12–24.

The transformation was from the 1671 *tragédie ballet* to the 1678 *tragédie en musique*. The opera was an improvement over the ballet in terms of dramatic ideals but was not fully successful in character portrayal.

Le triomphe de l'amour

FO, v.4.

Bruno Maderna (1920–1973)

1146. Fearn, Raymond. *Bruno Maderna*. Contemporary Music Studies, 3. New York: Harwood Academic Publishers, 1990. xv, 367p. ISBN 3-7186-5011-8. ML410 .M22 F43.

A brief biography with extended consideration of the works, including *Don Perlimpin, Hyperion,* and *Aria*. Descriptions and technical analyses, with many musical examples (some illegible). Detailed worklist, two-page bibliography, index.

Gian Francesco Majo (1732–1770)

Ifigenia in Tauride is in *RMCE,* v.46. See also Henze-Döhring (#1307).

1147. Di Chiera, David. "Life and Operas of Gian Francesco di Majo." Ph.D. diss., U. of California at Los Angeles, 1962. 2v.

Marin Marais (1656–1728)

Alcione is in *FO,* v.25.

1148. Milliot, Sylvette, and Jérome de La Gorce. *Marin Marais.* Paris: Fayard, 1991. 288p. ISBN 2-213-02777-3. ML410 .M31 M65.

   The life story, a review of the instrumental works, and a long section (p.154–256) on the *tragédies en musique.* Genesis, synopses, and program notes for *Alcide, Ariane et Bacchus, Alcyone,* and *Sémélé.* Bibliography of about 150 items, name index.

1149. Thompson, Clyde H. "Marin Marais, 1656–1728." Ph.D.diss., U. of Michigan, 1956. 2v.

1150. Renken, Alice Brin. "Marin Marais's *Alcione*: An Edition with Commentary." Ph.D. diss., Washington U., 1981. 328p.

Marco Marazzoli (1602/1608–1662)

See Murata (#446), Witzenmann (#1174), and Zaslaw (#2260).

Heinrich August Marschner (1795–1861)

1151. Palmer, A. Dean. *Heinrich August Marschner, 1795–1861: His Life and Works.* Ann Arbor, Mich.: UMI Research, 1980. xx, 591p. ISBN 0-8357-1114-5. ML410 .M35 P3.

   A thorough study, with references to all previous literature. Includes biographical treatment (lists of letters, archival inventory); synopses, program notes, sources, and bibliography for each opera; illustrations of productions; stylistic commentary. Bibliography of about 600 books, journal and newspaper articles, and other writings. Index of names and titles.

Vicente Martin y Soler (1754–1806)

1152. Link, Dorothea Eva. "The Da Ponte Operas of Vicente Martin y Soler." Ph.D. diss., U. of Toronto, 1991. 353p.

1153. Platoff, John. "A New History for Martin's *Una cosa rara.*" *JM* 12 (1994): 85–115.

   A useful review essay, considering the 1990 Henle Verlag edition of the score and libretto, and a CD of 1991. The opera was an early success, then forgotten. Synopsis; technical comments on the style, with musical examples; comparison to *Le nozze di Figaro.*

Jean-Paul Egide Martini (= Johann Paul Ágid Schwarzendorf, 1741–1816)

Henry IV is in *FO,* v.64.

Bohuslav Martinů (1890–1959)

1154. Halbreich, Harry. *Bohuslav Martinů: Werkverzeichnis, Dokumentation, und Biographie.* Zurich: Atlantis, 1968. 384p. ML410 .M39 H2.

The most useful life and works. For the 16 operas there is information on the premieres (with casts), instrumentation, plot, and program notes. The worklist is alphabetical, with titles in Czech and German. Annotated bibliography of about 25 entries, index.

1155. *The Stage Works of Martinů.* Ed. Rudolf Pečman. Prague: Czechoslovak Music Information Centre, 1967. 235p. ML410 .M284 .S77.

Consists of 15 papers, in German or English, given at a colloquium in Brno, 1966. Topics include a comparison of Martinů and Janáček and studies of the operas *Les larmes de Couteau, Die Stimme des Waldes, Juliette, Grieschische Passion,* and *Ariadne.* Without bibliography or index.

1156. *Bohuslav Martinů: Anno 1981.* Ed. Jítka Brabcová. Prague: Česká Hudební Společnost, 1990. 339p. ISBN 80-900070-31. ML410 .M284 B67.

Consists of 47 brief papers given at a conference in Prague, 26–28 May 1981. Three are about opera: Rudolf Vonásek, "Gesang und Schauspielkunst in den Opern von Bohuslav Martinů"; Karel Risinger, "Einfachheit und Modernität im *Miafest der Brünnlein*"; and Eva Vítová, "Zur Tradition der Inszenierung von Bohuslav Martinůs Opern auf der Bühne des Staatstheaters in Brno."

Pietro Mascagni (1863–1945)

Collections of Essays

1157. Morini, Mario, ed. *Pietro Mascagni.* Milan: Sonzogno, 1964. 2v. ML410 .M294 M6.

A comprehensive musicological view of the composer, including a collection of criticisms (Hanslick, Torchi, Abbiati, Pizzetti, and others); letters and documents; biography; an impressive list of premieres and important productions of all 15 operas in all principal cities, with casts; an immense bibliography, giving full information on about 1,000 publications; and a discography for every aria. Elaborately footnoted, index of names and titles.

Conferences

1158. *Puccini e Mascagni. Giornata di Studi.* Lucca: Pacini, 1996. 160p.

Not examined; information is from Fairtile (#1437), entry 680. Consists of eight papers from a conference in Viareggio on 3 August 1995. Parallels between the works of the two composers are discussed, among them exotic settings, their modernism, and the "*malinconia erotica del settecento.*"

Another collection of conference papers (Livorno, 1985) was not examined. See also #1162, #1163, and #1164.

Biographies

1159. Stivender, David. *Mascagni: An Autobiography Compiled, Edited, and Translated from Original Sources.* White Plains, N.Y.: Pro/Am Music Resources, 1988. xvi, 372p. ISBN 0-912483-06-7. ML410 .M29 A3.

Since this book was favorably reviewed in OQ and *Choice,* it is included in this guide. It is a weird blend of invented first-person narrative and imaginary conversations, drawn in a manner not well explained from writings by Mascagni and other materials. Let the reader judge its value. Bibliography and index.

Individual Works

Cavalleria rusticana

ASO 50 (1983), Rororo 1987.

1160. Sansone, Matteo. "Verga and Mascagni: The Critics' Response to *Cavalleria rusticana.*" *M&L* 71-2 (May 1990): 198–214.

The two leaders of literary *verismo* were Giovanni Verga and Luigi Capuana. They aimed at truth, spontaneity, and restraint, under a philosophic cloud of pessimism. Music in the *verismo* operas increased the emotional aspects of the stories, emphasized exotic settings, and sought to raise the love/jealousy syndrome to a universal level.

1161. Favia-Artsay, Aida. "Did Mascagni Write *Cavalleria?*" *OQ* 7-2 (Summer 1990): 83–89.

It was his only successful opera and like none of his others. Favia-Artsay speculates, on the basis of a remark by her voice teacher (from the Milan Conservatory, where Mascagni had studied), that "Mascagni did not write *Cavalleria,* Ponchielli did. Everybody at the conservatory knew about it." Ponchielli was the professor, Mascagni the student; Ponchielli died as Mascagni left the school. Could it be that the older man had loaned the younger his sketches for an opera and did not get them back? No response has been seen to Favia-Artsay's query.

1162. *Cavalleria rusticana, 1890–1990: Cento anni di un capolavoro.* Ed. Piero Ostali and Nandi Ostali. Milan: Sonzogno, 1990. 209p. No ISBN. ML410 .M2698 C28.

Consists of 12 brief papers given at a conference held in Livorno in September 1990. They deal with the *verismo* aspect, other "rustic" operas, and reception. An appendix presents interesting critical views of the opera by 13 writers of 1890–1982. Name index, title index.

Iris

1163. *Mascagni e l'"Iris" fra simbolismo e floreale. Atti del 2° Convegno di Studi su Pietro Mascagni.* Ed. Mario Morini and Piero Ostali. Milan: Sonzogno, 1989. 113p. No ISBN. ML410 .M2698 M37.

Consists of 10 papers from a conference in Livorno, 7–8 May 1988. They deal with genesis, harmony and color, vocal aspects, and reception. Name and title index.

Il piccolo Marat

1164. *"Il piccolo Marat"*: *Storia e rivoluzione nel melodramma verista. Atti del 3°
Convegno di Studi su Pietro Mascagni.* Ed. Piero Ostali and Nandi Ostali.
Milan: Sonzogno, 1990. 141p. No ISBN. ML410 .M19 C66.

Consists of 10 papers from a conference in Livorno, 9–10 June 1989. They
deal with dramaturgical and scenic aspects, the musical language, and the relation between the opera and the historical-patriotic tradition of the time in
Italy. Name and title index.

For material on *Guglielmo Ratcliff* and *Parisina* see Maehder in *Reading Opera*
(#2476).

Jules Massenet (1842–1912)

Le roi de Lahore and *Hérodiade* are in *ASO* 187 (1998).

1165. Irvine, Demar. *Massenet: A Chronicle of His Life and Times.* Seattle: Author,
1974. 483p. (Typescript.) ML410 .M41 I72.

Biography, letters, genealogy—a good footnoted introduction to the composer's life. Then, for 27 operas, plots, premiere data and reviews, and editions. Table of Paris performances, 1867–1915. Bibliography of about 100
items, worklist, expansive index of names.

1166. Harding, James. *Massenet.* London: Dent, 1970. 229p. ISBN 460-03928-8.
ML410 .M41 H1.

A popular biography, with program notes on the operas. Worklist, list of the
operas with premiere casts and other facts. Bibliography of about 100 items,
name and title index.

1167. Finck, Henry T. *Massenet and His Operas.* London: John Lane, 1910. 245p.
ML410 .M41 F4.

Much detail on performance history makes this older book worth consulting.
It also includes biographical information and a good expansive index but is
not documented.

Individual Works

Le Cid

ASO 161 (1994).

Don Quichotte

ASO 93 (1986).

Esclaramonde

ASO 148 (1992).

Griselda

ASO 148 (1992).

Manon

ASO 123 (1989).

1168. Loisel, Joseph. *Manon de Massenet: Étude historique et critique, analyse musicale*. Paris: Mellotée, 1922. 170p. MT100 .M26 M2.

> Not examined.

See also Casini (#465).

Thaïs

ASO 109 (1988).

Werther

ASO 61 (1984).

Johann Mattheson (1681–1764)

1169. *New Mattheson Studies*. Ed. George J. Buelow and Hans J. Marx. New York: Cambridge U.P., 1983. xiv, 495p. ISBN 0-521-25115-4. ML55 .M327 N5.

> A useful collection of 23 papers, in German or English, given at a symposium in Wolfenbüttel in 1981. Topics include the place of Mattheson's work in the context of his times, the composer's ideas on performance, and the uncertain relationship between him and J. S. Bach. An essay by Buelow deals with *Affektenlehre* (finding no formal system of them); one by Hans Wilhelm Eckardt is on Hamburg during Mattheson's period there. The Mattheson manuscripts had been thought lost in the bombing of Hamburg during World War II, but Hans Joachim Marx reports on many that survived.

1170. Cannon, Beekman C. *Johann Mattheson, Spectator*. Yale Studies in the History of Music, 1. New Haven, Conn.: Yale U.P., 1947. xi, 244p. Reprint, New Haven: Archon, 1968. ISBN (Archon) 0-20800-311-8. ML423 .M43 C3.

> The Hamburg background, a Mattheson biography, and a survey of his numerous critical writings. Detailed, annotated worklist. Footnotes, bibliography of about 100 items, index.

1171. Buelow, George J. "An Evaluation of Johann Mattheson's Opera *Cleopatra* (Hamburg, 1704)." In *Studies in Eighteenth-Century Music* (#73), 92–107.

> Of Mattheson's 15 operas, only 1 has survived in complete score; it is in the Library of Congress. Buelow finds the music "worthy of his greatest contemporaries, Keiser and Handel." He describes the aria style in detail and prints one in full. The music follows Mattheson's theory of key characteristics: C major being rude, bold, and joyful; C minor sweet; D major harsh (good for alarms and war scenes); E major sounding like "despair and sadness"; and so on. Tonal design is discussed, as is influence on Handel, with whom Mattheson—so the story goes—had a duel during a performance of *Cleopatra,* as they disputed who should be playing when on the harpsichord.

Simon Mayr (1763–1845)

1172. Balthazar, Scott L. "Mayr, Rossini, and the Development of the Early *concertato* Finale." *JRMA* 116 (1991): 236–266.

Mayr was one of the now obscure composers who shaped the transition (in 1795–1815) from *opera seria* to 19th-century *melodramma*. The *concertato* finale of the penultimate act of serious opera is found in Mayr and was already developed before Rossini used it (and got credit for inventing it).

1173. Shaheen, Ronald Thomas. "Neoclassic Influences in the Two Versions of Giovanni Simone Mayr's *Lodoiska*." Ph.D. diss., U. of California at Los Angeles, 1996. xviii, 665p.

Domenico Mazzocchi (1592–1663)

1174. Witzenmann, Wolfgang. "Domenico Mazzocchi, 1592–1663: Dokumente und Interpretationen." *Analecta musicologica* 8 (1970): 1–282.

An issue of the journal is devoted to this scholarly biography based on the author's Ph.D. dissertation, U. of Tübingen, 1970. All the works are discussed, including the opera *La catena d'Adone* (1626), his best-known composition.

Virgilio Mazzocchi (1597–1646)

Like his brother, Domenico, Virgilio is remembered for one successful opera, *Chi soffre speri* (1637); see Bianconi (#2449).

Étienne Nicolas Méhul (1763–1817)

1175. Pougin, Arthur. *Méhul: Sa vie, son génie, son caractère.* Paris: Fischbacher, 1889. 309p. Reprint, Geneva: Minkoff, 1973. ISBN 2-8266-0104-0. ML410 .M49 P8.

There was a second edition (not seen) in 1893 of this dependable biography. Well footnoted, with extensive quotations from correspondence. Detailed accounts of performances but nothing about the music itself. Chronological list of the operas, with premiere dates and theaters. No bibliography or index.

1176. Strobel, Heinrich. "Die Opern von E. N. Méhul." *ZfM* 6 (1923–1924): 362–402.

Plots, program notes, and some technical comments, with 38 musical examples.

1177. Cordes, Robert de. "Étienne Nicolas Méhul's *Euphrosine* and *Stratonice*: A Transition from *comédie mêlée d'ariettes* to *opéra-comique*." Ph.D. diss., U. of Southern California, 1979.

1178. Bartlet, M. Elizabeth. "Étienne Nicolas Méhul and Opera during the French Revolution, Consulate, and Empire: A Source, Archival, and Stylistic Study." Ph.D. diss., U. of Chicago, 1982. 5v.

1179. Bartlet, M. Elizabeth. "A Newly Discovered Opera for Napoleon." *AM* 56 (1984): 266–296.

The opera *Les troubadours* was written for the marriage of Napoleon and Marie-Louise in 1810, but was not performed. There was a delay in completion of the work, and by the time it was ready, Napoleon had decided against further festivities. The music is thoroughly described, along with the curious background events.

Four operas are in *ERO*: *Euphrosine et Coradin,* v.38; *Ariodante,* v.39; *Uthal,* v.40; and *Joseph,* v.41. Two others are in *FO*: *Stratonice,* v.72, and *Mélidore et Phrosine,* v.73.

Felix Mendelssohn (1809–1847)

1180. Schünemann, Georg. "Mendelssohns Jugendopern." *ZfM* 5 (1922–1923): 506–545.

Covers *Die wandernden Komödianten, Die beiden Pädagogen, Die Soldaten-liebschaft,* and *Die beiden Neffen,* along with three scenes from an incomplete *Lustspiel.* Technical comments with extended musical examples.

1181. Warrack, John. "Mendelssohn's Operas." In *Music and Theatre* (#68), 263–297.

Genesis, program notes, and reception of the operas, with footnotes to sources and the slight secondary literature. The composer's gifts "matured too early for him . . . to adapt them to novel forms and ideas"—so his youthful works were in *Singspiel* form, and he did not succeed in the new romantic genres.

Gian Carlo Menotti (1911–)

1182. Grieb, Lyndal. *The Operas of Gian Carlo Menotti, 1937–1972: A Selective Bibliography.* Metuchen, N.J.: Scarecrow, 1974. 193p. ISBN 0-8108-0743-2. ML134 .M533 G7.

A useful annotated list of more than 1,000 writings about Menotti, including books, articles, dissertations, and newspaper notices. Also a biographical sketch and worklist, with premiere data and editions. Name index.

1183. Marriott, Richard John. "Gian Carlo Menotti: Total Musical Theatre; A Study of His Operas." Ph.D. diss., U. of Illinois, 1975. 274p.

1184. Ardoin, John. *The Stages of Menotti.* Garden City, N.Y.: Doubleday, 1985. 255p. ISBN 0-385-14938-7. ML410 .M52 A85.

A well-illustrated gathering of detailed program notes and synopses of all the operas. Interviews with the composer illuminate the discussions. Chronology, discography, bibliography, and expansive index of names, titles, and topics.

1185. Wlaschin, Ken. *Gian Carlo Menotti on Screen: Opera, Dance, and Choral Works on Film, Television, and Video.* Jefferson, N.C.: McFarland, 1999. 186p. ISBN 0-7864-0608-9. ML410 .M52 W6.

A useful list of visuals. *The Telephone* has had 14 screen versions and has been telecast in 10 countries; *The Medium* has had 14 screen versions. Index of titles and artists, bibliography of about 150 items.

There is no satisfactory biography. John Gruen's often cited *Menotti: A Biography* (New York: Macmillan, 1978) is superficial and undocumented.

Saverio Mercadante (1795–1870)

In *IO–1810*: *Elisa e Claudio* and excerpts from *L'apoteosi d'Ercole*, v.14; *Il giuramento*, v.18; *Elena da Feltre*, v.20; *Il bravo*, v.21; and *La vestale*, v.22.

1186. Kaufman, Tom. "Mercadante and Verdi." *OQ* 13-3 (Spring 1997): 41–56.

   Most comments about Mercadante's music are uninformed; Kaufman holds that much of it is worthy of comparison with Verdi's. Among the writers chastised are Julian Budden, Francis Toye, and Michael Rose (in *NGDO*). Kaufman refutes claims that Mercadante kept Verdi from performing in Naples. Tables of performances of selected works by both composers are given, showing that Mercadante was more popular up to 1900, when the tide shifted. Musical examples from many operas, with interesting discussions, and 26 footnotes to the other secondary literature.

1187. Bryan, Karen McGaha. "An Experiment in Form: The Reform Operas of Saverio Mercadante." Ph.D. diss., Indiana U., 1994. 2v.

André Messager (1853–1929)

1188. Wagstaff, John. *André Messager: A Bio-Bibliography*. Bio-Bibliographies in Music, 33. New York: Greenwood, 1991. xv, 188p. ISBN 0-3132-5736-1. ML134 .M5359 .W3.

   The listing includes many reviews and notices for the stage works.

Giacomo Meyerbeer (1791–1864)

1189. *Giacomo Meyerbeer: A Life in Letters*. Ed. Heinz Becker and Gudrun Becker. Trans. Mark Violette. Portland, Ore.: Amadeus, 1989. 215p. ISBN 0-931340-19-5. ML410 .M61.

   A well-annotated presentation of 116 letters, dealing with genesis and production of his operas and his always favorable views on other composers. Useful biographical section, worklist, bibliography, index.

1190. Döhring, Sieghart, and Arnold Jacobshagen. *Meyerbeer und das europäische Musiktheater*. Laaber: Laaber, 1998. x, 514p. ISBN 3-89007-410-3. ML410 .M606 M61.

   A collection of 27 papers presented at a 1991 symposium. These are the most useful: Jean Mongrédien, "Les débuts de Meyerbeer à Paris: *Il crociato in Egitto* au Théâtre Royal Italien"; Knud Arne Jürgensen, "The 'Ballet of the Nuns' from *Robert le diable* and Its Revival"; Marta Ottlová, "Oper und Traum: *Le pardon de Ploërmel*"; Albert Gier, "*L'africaine* und die Ideologie des Kolonialismus"; Robert I. Letellier, "History, Myth and Music in a Theme of Exploration: Some Reflections on the Musico-Dramatic Language of *L'africaine*"; Jürgen Schläder, "Die Sterbeszene der Sélika: Zur Dramaturgie des Finales in Meyerbeers *L'africaine*"; Fabrizio della Seta, "Un aspetto della ricenzione di Meyerbeer in Italia: Le traduzioni dei *grands opéras*"; and Andrew Everett, "Meyerbeer in London." Indexed.

1191. Frese, Christhard. *Dramaturgie des grossen Opern Giacomo Meyerbeer.* Berlin: Lienau, 1970. 308p. No ISBN. ML410 .M61 F65.

Extended program notes, with some technical observations, on *Robert le diable, Les huguenots, Le prophète,* and *L'africaine.* Backnotes, bibliography of some 100 items but no index.

1192. Becker, Heinz. "Zwischen Oper und Drama: Zu Meyerbeers Konzeption der dramatischen Szene." In *Wagner Symposium* (#1973), 86–94.

Meyerbeer moved from the formal number opera to the freer romantic style, displaying increasing creativity in orchestration. He had been impressed by *Rienzi.* Although he did not abandon the singer-dominated style, he adapted it to dramatic purposes.

1193. Conati, Marcello. "Quasi un mistero: Il silenzio italiano sui *grand-opéra* di Meyerbeer." *NRMI* 33–2 (April–June 1999): 157–170.

Roberto il diavolo (1831) was not staged in Italy until 1840 and *Gli ugonotti* (1836) not until 1841. The delay was due to the lack of preparedness in most Italian theaters for Meyerbeer's scenic requirements, vocal types, and orchestration. Only Florence, where the premieres took place, was equipped to deal with French grand opera: it was indeed a center of new ideas. This article is to continue in a later issue of *NRMI.*

See also Cooper (#66).

Individual Works

Excerpts from five early operas are in *IO–1810,* v.23.

L'africaine

ERO, v.24.

1194. Roberts, John Howell. "The Genesis of Meyerbeer's *L'africaine.*" Ph.D. diss., U. of California, Berkeley, 1977. 233p.

1195. Cruz, Gabriela. "Laughing at History: The Third Act of Meyerbeer's *L'africaine.*" *COJ* 11-1 (March 1999): 31–76.

The opera is a "rather fictionalized account of Vasco da Gama's first sea voyage to India." Disregard for historical fact is offset by what Cruz calls "concern with and use of historical narrative." Genesis of the opera is explored and found to have been focused on the literary figure of Radamastor. All sources are described. The conclusion is that the "textual and musical components of the ballad challenged established modes of comprehension in opera." There is also a summary of the reception of the work.

See also #1190.

Il crociato in Egitto

ERO, v.18. See also #1190.

1196. Everist, Mark. "Meyerbeer's *Il crociato in Egitto*: *Mélodrame,* Opera, Orientalism." *COJ* 8-3 (November 1996): 215–250.

Genesis, with attention to the heretofore unknown source of the libretto. Everist says it was *Les chevaliers de Malte,* a *mélodrame* of 1813 by Jean-Antoine-Marie Monperlier, Jean- Baptiste Dubois, and Hyacinthe Albertin. Following a comparison of play and libretto, there is a study of Orientalism, race, religion, liberty, and licentiousness, all having a part in the work.

L'etoile du nord

ERO, v.22.

Les huguenots

ASO 134 (1990), *ERO,* v.20.

1197. Walter, Michael. *Hugenotten-Studien.* Frankfurt: Lang, 1987. iv, 260p. ISBN 3-8204-9866-4. ML410 .M606 W23.

Genesis, text, reception, and scene-by-scene analysis—an excellent handbook for the opera. Backnotes, bibliography of some 200 entries, no index.

1198. Mitchell, Michael Kenneth. "Melodrama and the Illusion of Tragedy in Meyerbeer's *Les huguenots.*" Ph.D. diss., U. California at Santa Barbara, 1994. 407p.

Le pardon de Ploermel

ERO, v.23. See also #1190.

Le prophète

ERO, v.21.

1199. Gibson, Robert Wayne. "Meyerbeer's *Le prophète*: A Study in Operatic Style." Ph.D. diss., Northwestern U., 1972. 226p.

1200. Armstrong, Alan. "Gilbert-Louis Duprez and Gustave Roger in the Composition of Meyerbeer's *Le prophète.*" *COJ* 8-2 (July 1996): 147–165.

Discusses the rising power of the star singer in the Paris Opéra in the 1830s and 1840s. Meyerbeer and others revised to satisfy certain singers; the two tenors of the article title influenced alterations in *Le prophète.* These revisions are discussed, along with the opera's genesis.

See also Pendle (#2299).

Robert le diable

ASO 96 (1985), *ERO,* v.19. See also #1190.

Darius Milhaud (1892–1974)

1201. Drake, Jeremy. *The Operas of Darius Milhaud.* Outstanding Dissertations from British Universities. New York: Garland, 1989. 439p. ISBN 0-8240-0192-3. ML410 .M674 D7.

Milhaud wrote 16 operas, all of which are examined in this valuable work. Genesis, plot, libretto studies, formal analysis, and reception accounts are given. Drake finds no large-scale harmonic organization, because of the modal basis of the composer's idiom. Instead there are long, slowly unfolding melodic lines. Reproduced from the typescript of Drake's dissertation at the U. of Oxford, the print version suffers from scarcely legible musical examples. Strong bibliography, no index.

1202. Rosteck, Jens. "Darius Milhauds experimenteller Beitrag zur französischen Literaturoper am Beispiel der Claudel-Vertonung *Christophe Colomb* und *L'Oresteia d'Eschyle.*" Ph.D. diss., Freie U., Berlin, 1993.

Jean-Joseph Cassanéa de Mondonville (1711–1772)

In FO: *Carnaval du Parnasse,* v.48, and *Titon et l'aurore,* v.49.

Stanislaw Moniuszko (1819–1872)

Halka and *The Haunted Manor* are in ASO 83 (1986).

1203. Maciejewski, B. M. *Moniuszko: Father of Polish Opera.* London: Allegro, 1979. 155p. No ISBN. ML410 .M74 M2.

Genesis, program notes, and synopses for six operas; *Halka* gets the most attention. Some of the composer's letters are extracted, but the book is not footnoted, and there is no bibliography. Name index.

Pierre Alexandre de Monsigny (1729–1817)

In FO: *Le roy et le fermier* and *On ne s'avise jamais de tout,* v.57, and *Le deserteur,* v.58.

Michel Pignolet de Montéclair (1667–1737)

In FO: *Les festes de l'été,* v.32, and *Jephté,* v.33.

Claudio Monteverdi (1567–1643)

Editions

1204. Monteverdi, Claudio. *Opera omnia.* Ed. Biblioteca Statale Civica di Cremona and Scuola di Paleografia e Filologia Musicale Pavia. Cremona: Fondazione Claudio Monteverdi, 1970–. M3 .M78.

The operas are in volumes 8, 16, and 17. Other editions of the operas are listed in Adams (#1206), 31–33. Critical articles about the various editions are summarized in Adams, p.228–245.

Thematic Catalogues and Worklists

1205. Stattkus, Manfred H. *Claudio Monteverdi: Verzeichnis der erhaltenen Werke.* Bergkamen: Stattkus, 1985. 183p. ML134 .M66 .S72.

A worklist, with identification of manuscript and printed sources. With indexes of titles, subtitles, incipits, editors, and publishers. Chronology of printed issues, bibliography.

Bibliographies and Guides to Resources

1206. Adams, K. Gary, and Dyke Kiel. *Claudio Monteverdi: A Guide to Research.* Garland Composer Resource Manuals, 23. New York: Garland, 1989. xviii, 273p. ISBN 0-8240-7743-1. ML134 .M66 A5.

Consists of 878 annotated entries in classified arrangement, covering background materials for Monteverdi studies, his life, works, and the modern revival materials. Worklist, indexes of authors, proper names, and compositions.

1207. Abert, Anna Amalie. *Claudio Monteverdis Bedeutung für die Entstehung des musikalischen Dramas.* Darmstadt: Wissenschaftliche Buchgesellschaft, 1979. 103p. ISBN 3-5340-7614-1. ML410 .M7 A14 C6.

Discusses the state of research since 1920 on the life and works and comments on the editions. A valuable essay, marred by incomplete data on the writings cited. Name index.

See also Fabbri (#1217).

Conferences

1208. *Congresso Internazionale sul Tema Claudio Monteverdi e il Suo Tempo.* Ed. Raffaello Monterosso. Verona: Valdoneza, 1969. 638p. ML410 .M77 C6.

Consists of papers from the conference held in Venice, Mantua, and Cremona, in May 1968. The essay by Nino Pirrotta, "Teatro, scene e musica nelle opere di Monteverdi," is entered in its English translation at #1225. Francesco Degrada, on the libretto, is at #1236. Most of the congress was concerned with nonoperatic topics.

1209. *International Congress on Performing Practice in Monteverdi's Music.* Ed. Raffaello Monterosso. Cremona: Fondazione Claudio Monteverdi, 1995. 283p. ISBN 88-86288-25-5. ML410 .M664 I572.

The conference was held at Goldsmith's College, University of London, in 1993. Of the 13 papers, 3 were on opera: Walter Pass, "Monteverdi's *Il ritorno d'Ulisse in patria*"; Nigel Rogers, "Some Thoughts on Monteverdi's *Orfeo* and a Suggested Alternative Ending"; and Anthony Pryer, "Authentic Performance, Authentic Experience, and *'pur ti miro'* from *Poppea*." Indexed.

1210. "Convegno Internationale di Studi Monteverdiani." *RIM* 2–2 (1967): 201–389.

This issue of the journal contains papers presented at the conference, Siena, 28–30 April 1967. Among those about opera: Andrea della Corte, "Aspetti del 'comico' nella vocalità teatrale di Monteverdi"; Anna Maria Abert, "Monteverdi e lo sviluppo dell'opera"; Anna Mondolfi Bossarelli, "Ancora intorno al codice napoletano della *Incoronazione di Poppea*"; and Hellmuth Christian Wolff, "L'influsso di Monteverdi sull'opera veneziana."

Collections of Essays

1211. *The Monteverdi Companion*. Ed. Denis Arnold and Nigel Fortune. New York: Norton, 1968. 328p. ISBN 0-393-33636-0. ML410 .M7 A75.

Eleven essays by various authors, including Robert Donington on *Orfeo* (#1245) and Janet E. Beat, "Monteverdi and the Opera Orchestra of His Time." Index.

1212. *The New Monteverdi Companion*. Ed. Denis Arnold and Nigel Fortune. London: Faber & Faber, 1985. 353p. ISBN 0-571-13148-4. ML410 .M77 N5.

An update of #1211 with most articles carried over, with revisions. The Donington and Beat studies are omitted. Two new pieces deal with opera: Iain Fenlon, "The Mantuan Stage Works," and Jane Glover, "The Venetian Operas." Denis Arnold and Nigel Fortune revised the bibliography they prepared for the earlier volume. Index.

1213. Harnoncourt, Nikolaus. *Der musikalische Dialog: Gedanken zu Monteverdi, Bach, und Mozart*. Salzburg: Residenz, 1984. 304p. ISBN 3-7017-0372-8. ML60 .H337.

A collection of short essays by Harnoncourt. The operas *Orfeo, Il ritorno d'Ulisse*, and *L'incoronazione di Poppea* are examined in terms of authentic performance. Without footnotes or bibliography.

1214. Chafe, Eric. *Monteverdi's Tonal Language*. New York: Schirmer, 1992. xviii, 442p. ISBN 0-02-870495-9. ML410 .M77 C4.

Important essays by Chafe, on technical aspects of the compositions. There are separate entries in this guide for studies on *L'incoronazione di Poppea* (#1239) and *Orfeo* (#1244). Backnotes, valuable bibliography of some 150 items, title index, general index.

Letters and Documents

1215. *The Letters of Claudio Monteverdi*. Trans. with introduction by Denis Stevens. New York: Cambridge U.P., 1980. 443p. ISBN 0-05-212359-1. ML410 .M7 A2 S82.

All the known letters, translated for the first time into English. (The standard collection in Italian is by Domenico de' Paoli, *Claudio Monteverdi: Lettere, dediche, e prefazioni* [Rome, 1973].) Stevens covers the years 1601–1643 with 126 letters, notes, and comments. Points of difference in translation, or text, between the present edition and previous versions of the letters are not generally clarified—or even mentioned. Index.

Biographies

1216. Schrade, Leo. *Monteverdi: Creator of Modern Music.* New York: Norton, 1950. 348p. Reprint, New York: Da Capo, 1979. ML410 .M7 S37.

A scholarly life story, the first important biography in English, which helped to bring about the Monteverdi revival. It has little about the music except for a useful background chapter on *Orfeo*. Bibliography of about 150 entries, index of names, titles, and topics.

1217. Fabbri, Paolo. *Monteverdi.* Trans. Tim Carter. New York: Cambridge U.P., 1994. 350p. ISBN 0-521-35133-2. ML410 .M77 F2.

Originally in Italian (Turin: EDT, 1985). The English edition is rather condensed, being primarily a documentary life story; the Italian original (460p.) had stronger discussions of the music. Useful review of the literature on Monteverdi from the 17th century on. Worklist, bibliography, name index.

1218. De' Paoli, Domenico. *Monteverdi.* Milan: Rusconi, 1979. 592p. ML410 .M77 P35.

A well-documented life and works, with useful background chapters on the Italian madrigal, the Camerata, and music at St. Mark's basilica. Detailed worklist, chronology of Monteverdi's life, maps, photographs of important locations, and other pictorial material. The compositions are discussed in nontechnical style, with musical examples. Bibliography, title index, name index.

1219. Leopold, Silke. *Claudio Monteverdi und seine Zeit.* Laaber: Laaber, 1982. 368 p. ISBN 3-9215-1872-5. ML410 .M77 L5.

A fine biography with emphasis on the music, which is carefully described. Useful chronology of Monteverdi and the period, bibliography, name index.

1220. Redlich, Hans F. *Claudio Monteverdi: Life and Works.* Trans. Kathleen Dale. New York: Oxford U.P., 1952. 204p. Reprint, Westport, Conn.: Greenwood, 1970. ISBN 0-8371-4003-X. ML410 .M77 R432.

Originally *Claudio Monteverdi: Leben und Werk* (Olten: Otto Walter, 1949). There are new chapters in the English version and other expansions and revisions. The book is an important contribution by a major scholar on the composer. In addition to biography and description of the works, there is guidance for modern performances and editions. Backnotes, worklist, chronology, bibliography, name index.

1221. Tomlinson, Gary. *Monteverdi and the End of the Renaissance.* Berkeley: U. of California Press, 1987. xii, 280p. ISBN 0-520-05348-6. ML410 .M77 T7.

A useful background treatment of the Italian cultural scene, with writings of numerous scholars of the time presented. Monteverdi's life and works are placed in that context, the compositions taken in chronological order, and evaluated. Title index, general index.

See also *New Grove Italian Baroque* (#2459).

Operas in General

All the operas are in ENOG 45 (1992).

1222. Abert, Anna Amalie. *Claudio Monteverdi und das musikalische Drama.* Lipp-
stadt: Kistner & Siegel, 1954. 354p. ML410 .M7 A14.

Valuable technical accounts of the operas, with musical examples and footnotes. Bibliography of about 200 items, name index.

1223. Glover, Jane. "The Venetian Operas." In *The Monteverdi Companion* (#1211),
288–315.

Examines the differences in style between the first opera, *Orfeo,* and the later
works, *Il ritorno d'Ulisse* and *L'incoronazione di Poppea.* Particular points of
change involve dramatic format, harmony and melody, and orchestral requirements. Includes extended descriptions of musical and dramatic elements.

1224. Pirrotta, Nino. "Monteverdi and the Problems of Opera." In *Music and Culture* (#2443), 235–253.

Originally in Italian, in *Studi sul teatro veneto fra rinascimento ed età barocca,*
ed. Maria Teresa Muraro (Florence: Olschki, 1971), trans. Harris Saunders.
An important study of influences on Monteverdi's operas, including a detailed
comparison of *Orfeo* with Peri's *Euridice.* Lesser-known works are also taken
up, with explanation of their impact on Monteverdi.

1225. Pirrotta, Nino. "Theater, Sets and Music in Monteverdi's Operas." In *Music
and Culture* (#2443), 254–270.

Originally in Italian, in *Congresso Internazionale* (#1208), translated here by
David Morgenstern. A study of the opera premieres in terms of the halls and
modes of presentation. The uncertain venue of the *Il ritorno d'Ulisse* premiere
is assigned to the SS. Giovanni e Paolo theater, and a sketch of the theater's
floorplan is included.

1226. Harnoncourt, Nikolaus. *The Musical Dialogue: Thoughts on Monteverdi,
Bach, and Mozart.* Trans. Mary O'Neill. Ed. Reinhard G. Pauly. Portland,
Ore.: Amadeus, 1989. 220p. ISBN 0-931340-08-X. ML60 .H337.

Originally *Der musikalische Dialog: Gedanken zu Monteverdi, Bach und
Mozart* (Salzburg: Residenz, 1984). Analyses of performance problems by a
leading practitioner of the authentic performance movement. The essays are
variable in length and approach. Monteverdi's operas take up p.121–144.
Without notes, bibliography, or index.

1227. McClary, Susan. "Constructions of Gender in Monteverdi's Dramatic Music."
COJ 1 (1989): 203–223.

An intriguing examination focused on *Orfeo* and *L'incoronazione di Poppea*
in the context of altered views about women in the 17th century. Women were
associated with eroticism and seen as a threat to men unless controls were
placed on them. But "traditional hierarchies of authority were subjected to
extraordinary questions during this period of doubt and shifting alliances."
Footnotes are a guide to most of the current feminist approaches to music.

1228. Cancelled entry.

Individual Works

Arianna

ENOG 45 (1992).

1229. Porter, William V. "Lamenti recitativi da camera." In *"Con che soavità"* (#2461), 73–110.

> Monteverdi produced three settings of Ariadne's lament, "Lasciatemi morire," for accompanied solo voice: (1) in the opera *Arianna* (1608; music lost); (2) an independent piece for chamber players (published 1623); and (3) a spiritual work with Ariadne's words reworked and assigned to the Virgin Mary (published 1640). Porter discusses these, concentrating on the chamber works. Extensive footnotes cover the entire literature on all the Monteverdi versions.

1230. Rosand, Ellen. "The Descending Tetrachord: An Emblem of Lament." *MQ* 65 (1979): 346–359. Reprint, *GL,* v.5.

> Looks at the reasons for the association, in the mid–17th century, between the idea of lamentation and the descending minor tetrachord. Gives background of the lament and takes up notable examples, among them the one in Monteverdi's *Arianna*. It is not an aria with a standard structure; rather, it flows with the shape of the text. "Fully aware of the dramatic possibilities in the tetrachord, Monteverdi deliberately and irregularly contradicts the strong implications of the pattern . . . by employing suspensions, syncopation, and phrase overlapping, he creates affective dissonances." Earlier laments of Francesco Cavalli are contrasted with Monteverdi's. The tetrachord formula was carried forward to Purcell, Handel, and Bach. Musical examples, footnotes to the relevant literature.

L'incoronazione di Poppea

ASO 115 (1988), ENOG 45 (1992).

1231. Osthoff, Wolfgang. "Die venezianische und neapolitanische Fassung von Monteverdis *Incoronazione di Poppea*." *AM* 26 (1954): 88–113.

> Compares the two manuscripts in detail. Both have to be taken into account in the search for an authentic score.

1232. Fenlon, Iain, and Peter N. Miller. *The Song of the Soul: Understanding "Poppea."* RMA Monographs, 5. London: Royal Musical Association, 1992. viii, 96p. ISBN 0-94785-404-5. ML410 .M8 F37.

> An exploration of Tacitism, Senecan neostoicism, and the neostoicism of the Incogniti. Holds that Venetian intellectual life "explains far more of the detail of both the libretto and the score . . . than has been recognized." The opera is much more than a celebration of the triumph of Amor: it is a celebration of *constantia*. That principle is embodied in Drusilla (who thus appears to be the protagonist).

1233. Rosand, Ellen. "Monteverdi's Mimetic Art: *L'incoronazione di Poppea*." *COJ* 1 (1989): 113–137. Reprinted in #74.

Notes that "certain dramatic situations are well suited to portrayal in terms of the contrast between speech and song," and that "certain emotional states, happiness or exuberance, translate naturally into song because the character feels like singing." The melodic line expresses feelings in different ways: a "wandering irresolute melodic line, like that of Ottone, knows not where it goes." Erratic rhythm portrays Ottone's heartbeat in the opening of act 2, scene 2. Similar examples of word-painting are cited. But in *Poppea*, "music does not imitate text; it co-opts its function in the representation of feeling."

1234. Chiarelli, Alessandra. "*L'incoronazione di Poppea o Il Nerone*: Problemi di filologia testuale." *RIM* 9 (1974): 117–151.

A summary of the author's dissertation, U. of Bologna, 1973. She compares the Venetian and Neapolitan manuscripts in great detail, collating all sources.

1235. Heller, Wendy. "Tacitus Incognito: Opera as History in *L'incoronazione di Poppea*." *JAMS* 52-1 (Spring 1999): 39–96.

The earliest known account of Nero's affair with Poppea Sabina was in the *Annals* of Tacitus. The suicide of Seneca is portrayed by Tacitus as a moral victory in the neostoic tradition, but in Venice the event was reinterpreted. The Accademia degli Incogniti sided with "political pragmatism rather than moral censure, with civic virtue rather than withdrawal and solitude, and with the fulfillment of natural instincts rather than their suppression." Thus the problematic ending of the opera is explained, in terms of contemporary values. The article also takes up the role of women in 17th-century Venice and the evidence of male homosexuality in the opera (Nero is alleged to have been homosexual, and a passage in the Nerone/Lucano duet is found to be erotic in its melodic/harmonic elements, "the musical representation of the sexual climax"). These ideas are intricately worked out, and 114 footnotes lead to the relevant literature.

1236. Degrada, Francesco. "Gian Francesco Busenello e il libretto della *Incoronazione di Poppea*." In *Congresso Internazionale* (#1208), 81–102.

Biography and background of Busenello and aspects of the *Poppea* libretto. His text, dark and pessimistic, was altered by Monteverdi to give a more positive, Christian perspective.

1237. Covell, Roger David. "Monteverdi's *L'incoronazione di Poppea*: The Musical and Dramatic Structure." Ph.D. diss., U. of New South Wales, 1977.

1238. Curtis, Alan. "La Poppea *impasticciata*." *JAMS* 42-1 (Spring 1989): 23–54.

Stylistic and historic evidence indicates that Monteverdi did not write all the music. Suggests that Francesco Sacrati was probably another composer involved. See next entry.

1239. Chafe, Eric. *Monteverdi's Tonal Language* (#1214), chapters 13, 14, and 15.

These parts of the book are concerned with *Poppea*. Chafe takes up the tonal language, and the "two symmetrical points of allegorical culmination, the first Seneca's otherworldly victory, fulfilled in his death, and the second very much a worldly victory, celebrating life and love, regardless of the absence of virtue."

Musical relationships "constitute a thread of allegorical meaning" linking the two scenes of doubtful authorship (as per Curtis, #1238) with others that are surely by Monteverdi. So it may be that Monteverdi did conceive the whole opera but, being unable to finish, "communicated aspects of his intent" to one or more of the young composers in his circle.

Chafe looks at "the allegorical dimension and its derivation from the libretto." That dimension is expressed in the music, where there is a "dialectic relationship of the modal/hexachord and major/minor tonal systems." Modal = virtue and traditional values; key = fortune. For example, Poppea's eroticism is portrayed by "major/minor cadential inflections, reiterated phrygian sigh figures, the mixture of swift-paced triple-meter lines with drawn-out, languid cadences."

1240. Osthoff, Wolfgang. *Das dramatische Spätwerk Claudio Monteverdi*. Tutzing: Schneider, 1960. 267p. ML410 .M77 O8.

Originally the author's dissertation, U. of Heidelberg, 1954. A technical study of *Poppea* and *Il ritorno d'Ulisse,* with attention to structure, ostinato, walking bass lines, and the use of instrumental interludes. Footnotes, bibliography, index of names and subjects.

1241. Rosand, Ellen. "Seneca and the Interpretation of *L'incoronazione di Poppea.*" *JAMS* 38 (1985): 34–71.

Identifies Seneca as the protagonist and suppports the claim with a study of the music assigned to him. Relates the libretto to the Roman play *Octavia,* ascribed to Seneca.

1242. Day, Christine J. "The Theater of SS. Giovanni e Paolo and Monteverdi's *L'incoronazione di Poppea.*" *Current Musicology* 25 (1978): 22–38.

Describes the theater in Venice where the *Poppea* premiere took place and gives details on the flying machine and the sets.

1243. Salvetti, Guido. "Alcuni criteri nella rielaborazione ed orchestrazione dell'*Incoronazione.*" In "Convegno" (#1210), 332–340.

Compares performances of the work by Gaetano Cesari (1907), Giacomo Benvenuti (1937), and Giorgio F. Ghedini (1953 and 1965). Finds the two earlier productions more faithful to the Venetian manuscript with regard to instrumentation.

Orfeo

ASO 5 (1976), COH (1986), ENOG 45 (1992), Rororo (1988).

1244. Chafe, Eric. *Monteverdi's Tonal Language* (#1214), chapter 7.

After a description of the "regulating framework," explains how tonal correspondences involve symmetrical and other large-scale patterns. The tonal language of *Orfeo* is analyzed; it shows a tension between "allegorical and contingent."

1245. Donington, Robert. "Monteverdi's First Opera." In *The Monteverdi Companion* (#1211), 257–276.

Donington is an advocate of Jungian analysis, and he applies the approach to characters and situations in the opera. He also describes motivic relationships and the means of achieving unity. Kivy (#401) is one of those who disputes Donington's approach to *Orfeo*.

1246. Fenlon, Iain. "Monteverdi's Mantuan *Orfeo*: Some New Documentation." *Early Music* 12 (1984): 163–172.

A series of letters—most of them not previously published—between Francesco and Ferdinando Gonzaga helps to clarify questions about the text and premiere. In the first letter (1607), Francesco said he would have a play with music performed at the carnival. Ferdinando sent him a singer for it, a castrato named Giovanni Gualberto, who sang in the premiere. Some reasonable suppositions are possible regarding the room of the performance. Fenlon amplified on this matter in an essay in the COH on *Orfeo*.

1247. Allorto, Riccardo. "Il prologo dell'*Orfeo*: Nota sulla formazione del recitativo monteverdiano." In *Congresso Internazionale* (#1208), 157–168.

Compares the prologue to those in Peri and Caccini. Finds Monteverdi's to be in a style that resembles that of his fourth and fifth books of madrigals.

1248. Müller, Reinhard. *Der "stile recitativo" in Claudio Monteverdis "Orfeo."* Münchner Veröffentlichungen zur Musikgeschichte, 38. Tutzing: Schneider, 1984. 126p. ISBN 3-795-20414-3. MT100 .M72 M8.

A revision of the author's dissertation, U. of Munich, 1978. It is a thorough analysis of the treatment of text in the opera. The role of the continuo also receives extensive attention. Footnotes, bibliography, index of names and subjects.

1249. Cammarota, Lionello. "L'orchestrazione dell'*Orfeo* di Monteverdi." In Muraro (#2575), 21–40.

Considers modern editions in the light of Monteverdi's indications for instrumentation and finds the need for greater fidelity to his intentions.

Il ritorno d'Ulisse in patria

ASO 159 (1994).

1250. Goldschmidt, Hugo. "Claudio Monteverdis Oper: *Il ritorno d'Ulisse in patria*." *SIMG* 9 (1907–1908): 570–592.

An analysis and appraisal, characterizing Monteverdi as the leading opera composer of his time. He attained mastery in this opera.

1251. Rosand, Ellen. "Iro and the Interpretation of *Il ritorno d'Ulisse in patria*." *JM* 7-2 (Spring 1989): 141–164.

Iro, the beggar in *Il ritorno*, is the Arnaios of Homer, his role greatly expanded. In the opera he has a "strangely protracted" lament scene. His role is semicomic at first, then increasingly desperate and depressed, leading to madness and suicide. None of this is in Homer, so why here? Rosand proposes a binary opposition of sense and reason in the opera. "Iro's body, representing the weakness of the flesh, is in effect set against the moral strength, the chaste love, of Penelope." The opera is compared to *Poppea*: both examine issues of chaste and unchaste love. But the music does not distinguish between these loves—indeed, "it could actually be exchanged." Music represented human passion, "whatever its source." For another view, see the next item.

1252. Carter, Tim. "'In Love's Harmonious Consort'? Penelope and the Interpretation of *Il ritorno d'Ulisse in patria.*" *COJ* 5-1 (March 1993): 1–16.

Finds no puzzle in *Il ritorno*; Carter brushes away Rosand's interpretation (previous item). The moral of the opera is the reward for "Patience, the power of love over time and fortune." Penelope's refusal to sing rather than speak is one of the most striking features, "exposing the dramatic and aesthetic dilemmas that lie at the very heart of the opera." Her enclosure in the palace is shown by her enclosure in a joyless world of recitative. In the happy ending she does sing "the most stunning aria in the opera." Thus constancy is celebrated above all.

See also Osthoff (#1290).

Douglas Moore (1893–1969).

1252a. Weitzel, H. "A Melodic Analysis of Selected Vocal Solos in the Operas of Douglas Moore." Ph.D. diss., New York U., 1971.

Jean-Joseph Mouret (1682–1738)

Les festes de Thalie and *Les amours de Ragonde* are in *FO*, v.30.

1253. Viollier, Renée. *J.-J. Mouret, le musicien des grâces, 1682–1738.* Paris: Floury, 1950. 236p. ML410 .M94 V8.

Life and works, with genesis, program notes, and reception of the operas. Worklist, musical examples, bibliography, no index.

1254. *Jean-Joseph Mouret et le théâtre de son temps: Actes des Journées d'Études . . .* Aix-en-Provence: CAER, 1983. 177p. ISBN 2-8266-0860-6. ML410 .M94 J4.

Six papers presented at a conference in Aix-en-Provence, 28–29 April 1982. One is on opera: Gérard le Coat, "L'expression des affects chez Jean-Joseph Mouret: *Le triomphe des sens* come étude de cas." It describes the use of melodic, harmonic, dynamic, and "syntactic" means to expression. The book also has a worklist by François Gervais.

Wolfgang Amadeus Mozart (1756–1791)

Editions

1255. Mozart, Wolfgang Amadeus. *Neues Ausgabe sämtlicher Werke.* Kassel: Bärenreiter, 1955–. M3 .M9392.

Issued by the Internationale Stiftung Mozarteum Salzburg. All the stage works have been published, in series 2. For a description see *Mozart Compendium*

(#1269). An inventory of 19 earlier collected editions is in Hastings (#1259), 29–30.

1256. *The Librettos of Mozart's Operas*. Ed. Ernest Warburton. New York: Garland, 1992. 7v. ISBN (v.1) 0-8153-0108-1. ML49 .M83 W4.

V.1–4, printed librettos from premieres; v.4, revivals; v.5, pasticcios to which Mozart contributed; v.6–7, earlier texts that were set later by Mozart.

Thematic Catalogues and Worklists

1257. Köchel, Ludwig, Ritter van. *Chronologisch-thematisches Verzeichnis sämtlicher Tonwerke Wolfgang Amadeus Mozarts . . .* 6th ed. Ed. Franz Gieglin, Alexander Weinmann and Gerd Sievers. 1,024p. Wiesbaden: Breitkopf & Härtel, 1964. ML134 .M9 A3.

First edition, 1862. The standard list, source of the identifying K-numbers. Works are in chronological order, with melodic incipits and references to sources and modern editions. Indexes to titles and first lines, general index. The next entry is a necessary adjunct:

1258. Zaslaw, Neal, and Fiona Morgan Fein. *The Mozart Repertory: A Guide for Musicians, Programmers, Researchers*. Ithaca, N.Y.: Cornell U.P., 1991. 157p. ISBN 0-8014-9937-2. ML134 .M9 M83.

Zaslaw will edit the next revision of Köchel's *Verzeichnis*. This book gives supplementary entries and information to the 1964 edition and gives connections to the *Neues Ausgabe* (#1255). Material is in classified order, without index.

Bibliographies and Guides to Resources

1259. Hastings, Baird. *Wolfgang Amadeus Mozart: A Guide to Research*. Garland Composer Resource Manuals, 16. New York: Garland, 1989. xx, 411p. ISBN 0-8240-8347-4. ML134 .M9 H34.

A useful gathering of annotated citations to the principal secondary literature about Mozart (1,120 entries), plus various reference lists: Mozart's pupils, his patrons, 150 characters in the operas, organizations devoted to him (arranged by city), and libraries/archives (also by city). A dictionary of Mozart's contemporaries, with connections to him noted, covers 1,400 persons. Author and name indexes.

1260. Angermüller, Rudolph, and Otto Schneider. *Mozart-Bibliographie . . .* Kassel: Bärenreiter, 1976–. (Title varies.) ML5 .M617; ML134 .M9 A588.

First issued as part of the *Mozart Jahrbuch 1975;* then as a separate publication, each covering a five-year period of writings (four years in the latest volume). More than 14,000 books and articles are included, in author order, with full bibliographic data but without annotations. The 1992–1995 bibliography (published 1998) has 3,947 entries. Index of persons, places, topics, and works.

Prior to the Angermüller series, bibliographies had been issued in volumes of the *Mozart Jahrbuch*. Rudolf Elvers and Géza Rech compiled the first one, covering 1945–1950 for the 1951 volume. (Elvers noted that there had been no Mozart bibliographies published since 1930.)

See also *RISM* A, 1, supplement (#11), which is an inventory of Mozart works published before 1800.

1261. Freitag, Wolfgang. *Amadeus and Company: Mozart im Film.* Vienna: Umbruch, 1991. 286p. ISBN 3-9006-0212-3. ML410 .M95 F86.

An annotated list of about 70 films that include Mozart's music, even Hollywood adaptations of it (e.g., *Vertigo*), issued since 1923. Index of names.

Conferences

1262. "Colloquium: Mozart und Italien. Rome, 1974." *Analecta musicologica* 18 (1978): 1–318.

Consists of 19 papers, of which 8 are on the operas. Two are entered separately: Pierluigi Petrobelli on *Don Giovanni* in Italy (#1311) and Wolfgang Witzenmann on manuscripts of *Die Zauberflöte* (#1342). No bibliography or index.

1263. *Mozartanalyse im 19. und frühen 20. Jahrhundert. Bericht über die Tagung Salzburg 1996.* Ed. Gernot Gruber and Siegfried Mauser. Schriften zur musikalischen Hermeneutik, 6. Laaber: Laaber, 1999. 194p. ISBN 3-89007-339-5. ML410 .M95 M692.

An interesting collection of papers presented at the conference, offering analytic studies by various classic theorists: Tovey, Riemann, Schenker, Kurth, Halm, and by genre. One essay is about operatic criticism: Silke Leopold, "*Idomeneo* und andere: Drei kurze Überlegungen zur Analyse Mozartscher Opera im 19. Jahrhundert." The authors summarized are Johann Friedrich Reichardt, Alexander Oulibicheff, Otto Jahn, Hanslick, and Karl Grunsky.

Periodicals

1264. *Mozart Jahrbuch,* 1–, 1950–. Salzburg: Internationale Stiftung Mozarteum, 1950–. Annual. ML5 .M77.

Supersedes the *Neues Mozart Jahrbuch,* 1–3, 1941–1943 (Regensburg, 1941–1943) and the original *Mozart Jahrbuch,* 1–3, 1923–1929 (Munich, 1923–1929).

1265. *Acta Mozartiana,* 1–, 1954–. Augsburg: Deutsche Mozart Gesellschaft, 1954–. Quarterly. ML410 .M95 A6.

1266. *Mozart Studien,* 1–, 1992–. Tutzing: Schneider, 1992–. Irregular. ML410 .M95 M9035.

V.4 (1995) is devoted to textual studies and aria form of the operas. It includes a table of the aria types in the Italian operas. V.6 (1997) includes articles on the Mozart-Da Ponte collaborations (#1283), the ensembles in *Don Giovanni*, French translations of the operas, comic elements in *La finta semplice,* and the character of Count Almaviva.

1267. *Mitteilungen der Internationalen Stiftung Mozarteum,* 1– 1952–. Salzburg: Internationale Stiftung Mozarteum, 1952–. Quarterly. ISSN 0541-2331.

Collections of Essays

1268. *Wolfgang Amadè Mozart: Essays.* Ed. Stanley Sadie. New York: Oxford U.P., 1996. xvii, 512p. ISBN 0-19-816443-2. ML410 .M95 W885.

Essays by various authors, including 15 about the operas: Tim Carter, "Mozart, Da Ponte and the Ensemble: Methods in Progress?"; Jessica Waldoff and James Webster, "Operatic Plotting in *Le nozze di Figaro*"; John Platoff, "Catalogue Arias and the 'Catalogue Aria'"; Bruce Alan Brown, "Beaumarchais, Paisiello and the Genesis of *Così fan tutte*"; Caryl Clark, "Recall and Reflexivity in *Così fan tutte*"; Daniel Heartz, "When Mozart Revises: The Case of Guglielmo in *Così fan tutte*"; Dorothea Link, "*L'arbore di Diana*: A Model for *Così fan tutte*"; Christoph- Hellmut Mahling, "'. . . New and Altogether Special and Astonishingly Difficult': Some Comments on Junia's Aria in *Lucio Silla*"; Federico Pirani, "Operatic Links between Rome and Vienna, 1776–1790"; Andrew Dell'Antonio, "'*Il compositore deluso*': The Fragments of *Lo sposo deluso*"; Neal Zaslaw, "Waiting for *Figaro*"; Julian Rushton, "'. . . *Hier wird es besser seyn—ein blosses Recitative zu machen* . . .': Observations on Recitative Organization in *Idomeneo*"; Marita P. McClymonds, "The Great Quartet in *Idomeneo* and the Italian *opera seria*"; Konrad Küster, "An Early Form in Mozart's Late Style: The Overture to *La clemenza di Tito*"; and Don Neville, "From Simplicity to Complexity in *La clemenza di Tito*." Footnoted, no bibliography, partly expansive index.

1269. *The Mozart Compendium: A Guide to Mozart's Life and Music.* Ed. H. C. Robbins Landon. New York: Schirmer, 1990. 452p. ISBN 0-02-871321-4. ML410 .M95 M875.

Essays by 24 specialists cover a wide range of Mozart material: sources, collected editions, musical life in cities (Salzburg and Vienna) and countries (France, England, Netherlands, Germany, and Italy), and Mozart in literature (Mörike, Bernard Shaw, Pushkin, E. T. A. Hoffmann, Kierkegaard). The volume is marred by a weak bibliography and very poor index (not expansive; some 500 entries under "Vienna").

Biographies

1270. Einstein, Alfred. *Mozart: His Character, His Work.* Trans. Arthur Mendel and Nathan Broder. New York: Oxford U.P., 1945. 492p. ML410 .M9 E4.

A thoughtful examination of Mozart's life, with general observations on the music. Program notes on the operas, p.383–472. Worklist, name index.

1271. Deutsch, Otto Erich. *Mozart: A Documentary Biography, 1756–1791.* Trans. Eric Blom, Peter Branscombe, and Jeremy Noble. Stanford, Calif.: Stanford U. Press, 1965. 680p. ISBN 0-8047-2333-0. ML410 .M95 D4782.

Originally *Mozart: Dokumente seines Lebens* (Kassel: Bärenreiter, 1961). The principal biography, concentrating on the person, drawn from a wide range of contemporary source materials. Worklist, bibliography, index. *Addenda und Corrigenda* by Joseph Heinz Eibl was issued by the same publisher in 1978. See next entry.

1272. Eisen, Cliff. *New Mozart Documents: A Supplement to O. E. Deutsch's Documentary Biography.* Stanford, Calif.: Stanford U. Press, 1991. xvii, 192p. ISBN 0-8047-1955-1. ML410 .M95 D48.

This is "not a completion" of the documentary work but "an attempt to explore systematically a number of previously overlooked sources, principally newspapers and other periodicals of the 18th century." Materials are organized chronologically according to the events they describe. Everything is in English translation only. List of sources consulted, general index, title index.

Letters and Documents

The numerous publications of this material are cited with comments in Hastings (#1259), 71–73. A specialist in the physical characteristics of the autographs has an important contribution:

1273. Tyson, Alan. *Mozart: Studies of the Autograph Scores.* Cambridge, Mass.: Harvard U.P., 1987. 381p. ISBN 0-6745-8830-4. ML410 .M9 T95.

A collection of 18 essays, all but one previously published, which approach the scores through study of paper, inks, methods of copyists, and other internal evidence. Tyson is able to authenticate and date the manuscripts and to clarify questions about them. Four of the pieces are about operas; they are entered separately in this section: #1294 on *Clemenza,* #1300 on *Così fan tutte,* and #1320 and #1321 on *Figaro.* Backnotes, indexes.

Operas in General

1274. Dent, Edward Joseph. *Mozart's Operas: A Critical Study.* 2nd ed. London: Oxford U.P., 1947. 276p. ML410 .M9 D32.

First edition, 1913. The intention of the new edition was to appeal more to "the general reader rather than . . . the musicologist." However, the original edition was not highly technical either; both editions offer sensible program notes, without analysis. Expansive index of names and titles.

1275. Kunze, Stefan. *Mozarts Opern.* Stuttgart: Reclam, 1984. 685p. ISBN 3-15-00326-6. ML410 .M9 K94.

An imposing tome, to be sure, with 175 musical examples and 38 pictures, but the extensive commentaries on the operas do not add to previous knowledge. In a sense, Kunze diminishes earlier research in his citations by concentrating strongly on German scholarship and neglecting essential English language writings. Weak bibliography; name index.

1276. Heartz, Daniel. *Mozart's Operas.* Ed. Thomas Bauman. Berkeley: U. of California Press, 1990. 363p. ISBN 0-520-06862-9. ML410 .M9 H2.

A valuable collection of 16 essays by Heartz, 6 of them newly published, and 2 new essays by Bauman. These are entered separately in this section: Heartz on the genesis of *Le nozze di Figaro* (#1323), on sources of *Così fan tutte* (#1304), on parallels between *La clemenza di Tito* and *Die Zauberflöte* (#1296), and on the overture to *La clemenza di Tito* (#1298); and Bauman on instrumental music in *Die Zauberflöte* (#1336) and on *Die Entführung aus dem Serail* (#1314). The volume also has genesis studies of *Idomeneo, Le nozze di Figaro,* and *Don Giovanni*; two further essays on *Don Giovanni* (the ballroom scene, the sextet); "Setting the Stage for *Figaro,*" "Mozart's Tragic Muse," "Mozart and His Italian Contemporaries," and "Three Schools for Lovers, or '*Così fan tutte le belle.*'" List of works cited, expansive index of names and topics.

1277. Angermüller, Rudolph. *Mozart's Operas.* Trans. Stewart Spencer. New York: Rizzoli, 1988. 295p. ISBN 0-8478-0993-5. ML410 .M9 A813.

Originally *Mozart: Die Opern von der Uraufführung bis heute* (Frankfurt am Main: Propylaen, 1988). A luxurious coffee-table book with fine illustrations and useful commentary. Nearly every page has at least one picture, many of them in color, many showing modern staging. Genesis, program notes, and reception are presented for even the lesser-known operas, in popular style with little documentation. Weak index.

1278. Kaiser, Joachim. *Who's Who in Mozart's Operas: From Alfonso to Zerlina.* Trans. Charles Kessler. London: Weidenfeld & Nicolson, 1987. 212p. ISBN 0-02-873380-0. ML410 .M95 K23.

Originally *Mein Name ist Sarastro* (Munich: Piper, 1984). Detailed accounts, in popular style, of 56 characters from seven operas, with speculations about their motivations and personalities as suggested by the texts. Musical matters are not taken up. Backnotes, expansive index.

1279. Brophy, Brigid. *Mozart the Dramatist: The Value of His Operas to Him, to His Age, and to Us.* Rev. ed. New York: Da Capo, 1988. 332p. ISBN 0-306-80389-5. ML410 .M9 B818.

First edition, 1964. This is a reissue with a few alterations. Brophy studies the texts of the operas, with passing attention to the music. The centerpiece of the book is her examination of the Masonic and mythological bases for *Die Zauberflöte.* She also deals at length with *Don Giovanni,* taking gender-based and Freudian approaches. There is an overall concern with 18th-century intellectual life and its manifestation in the operas. Footnoted, bibliography, no index.

1280. Allanbrook, Wye Jamison. *Rhythmic Gesture in Mozart: "Le nozze di Figaro" and "Don Giovanni."* Chicago: U. of Chicago Press, 1983. 396p. ISBN 0-2260-1403-7. ML410 .M9 A73.

An imaginative study of movement, including questions of tempo and meter, and use of dances. The motions of the singers fall into standard patterns (*topoi*) and reveal the character being portrayed. Specific meters have their own affects (i.e., duple = exalted passions, triple = terrestrial passions). Dances have their special meanings; the minuet, for example, standing for elegance and refinement. Allanbrook goes through both operas, finding such patterns and explicating them. A Mozart opera, she says, is "a momentary proportioning of musical styles." Backnotes, expansive index, no bibliography.

1281. Nagel, Ivan. *Autonomy and Mercy: Reflections on Mozart's Operas*. Trans. Marion Faber and Ivan Nagel. Cambridge, Mass.: Harvard U.P., 1991. 148p. ISBN 0-674-05477-6. ML410 .M9 N1313.

Originally *Autonomie und Gnade: Über Mozarts Opern* (Munich: Carl Hanser, 1988). Seeks the "guiding idea of Mozart's mature operas." It is discovered in the shift from domination (monarchy) to freedom (equality, especially of men and women). Critical reactions to the book have praised it as "the standout book of the Mozart year" and one "to be read by anyone to whom Mozart's operas are important" or condemned it as "not worth reading" and a "political and philosophical ramble." Certainly the concepts are sufficiently general to fit into various theories. Numerous factual errors muddy the waters further. No bibliography or index.

1282. Steptoe, Andrew. *The Mozart–Da Ponte Operas: The Cultural and Musical Background to "Le nozze di Figaro," "Don Giovanni," and "Così fan tutte."* New York: Oxford U.P., 1988. 273p. ISBN 0-19-313215-X. ML410 .M95 S79.

Argues that "Mozart's operas can only be understood within the social and musical context in which they were composed" but presents no real connections between the context and the opera. Nor is there—despite the title of the book—much said about Da Ponte. Nevertheless, there is a useful summary analysis of the works, with focus on the ensembles, presenting tonal diagrams and other technical approaches. Key structure in *Così fan tutte* is well displayed. Footnotes, short bibliography, expansive index.

1283. Kunze, Stefan. "Mozart und Da Ponte: Eine glückliche Begegnung zwischen Textdichter und Komponist?" *Mozart Studien* 6 (1996): 15–29.

Text also in Italian. Considers the relationship between composer and librettist, which had to be more than just congenial and cooperative; after all, there have been many such pairs without special results. And Da Ponte worked with other composers, producing no masterpieces. What is needed is in-depth study of prosody, verse structure, rhythm, expressiveness, text, and, above all, the scenic dimension. Examples show how Mozart composed a scene in such a way as to exhibit character.

1284. Lühning, Helga. "Mozart als Regisseur." *Mozart Studien* 3 (1993): 91–113.

Although the concept of director was still taking shape in the 18th century, Mozart played that role; the article explains how he did it. One way was for the music to compel certain stage actions, so that no director had to explicate them. For instance, in dialogue arias, stage actions are conditioned by the presence or absence of the person being addressed or by direct address to the audience. Mozart indicates through rhythmic and metric configurations how a text is to be interpreted. Dance and orchestra are other "directing forces."

1285. Noske, Fritz. *The Signifier and the Signified: Studies in the Operas of Mozart and Verdi*. The Hague: Nijhoff, 1977. viii, 418p. Reprint, New York: Oxford U.P., 1990. ISBN (Oxford) 0-19-81620-14. ML1700.1 .N897.

An interesting attempt to apply semiotic critical method to the operatic genre. Noske finds the "musical figure of death," "ironic signs," and other devices to indicate mood and situation. He studies "relationships, coherence, and continuity" in the operas. Unity is not found in formal design but in process, especially the unfolding of melody. Aside from the thesis being pursued—which could be more clear in premise and execution—there are good musical analyses of the operas, with references to earlier literature. No bibliography, however. Name and title index.

1286. Federhofer, Hellmut, et al. "Tonartenplan und Motivstruktur (Leitmotivtechnik) in Mozarts Musik." *Mozart-Jahrbuch* 1973–1974: 82–144.

A wide-ranging discussion by a working party, considering tonal design and other unifying devices. Contributors are László Somfai, Janos Liebner, Daniel Heartz, Frederich Neumann, Georg Feder, and Gernot Gruber. Not indexed.

1287. Moberly, Robert B. *Three Mozart Operas: "Figaro," "Don Giovanni," "The Magic Flute."* London: Gollancz, 1967. 303p. MT100 .M91 M69.

A sophisticated critique of the libretti, with some allusions to the music. Moberly moves line-by-line through the texts, with illuminating and often entertaining results. For instance, there is the story of Figaro measuring the room, which is told here in remarkable depth. The scene-order puzzle of *Figaro,* act 3 is less clearly expounded, based on the idea that the composer and librettist casually shifted the order to accommodate a performer's need for a costume change. (See Tyson, #1320.) Indexed.

See also #1325.

1288. Webster, James. "Mozart's Operas and the Myth of Musical Unity." *COJ* 2-2 (July 1990): 197–218.

Taking Kunze (#1275) as a point of departure, Webster disputes the necessity of text to give shape to the music. Musical events in an aria would be clear and ordered even disregarding the words. He is also concerned about the customary reliance on instrumental forms as a basis for analyzing opera. The sonata form is actually rare in Mozart. Kunze, Steptoe and others follow this practice, building on Abert (#1306) and Levarie (#1322). Why think of numbers as key related when they are separated by recitatives, and by long stretches of time? Is D major the dominant or tonic in the opening of *Figaro*? In fact, Webster finds that the whole notion of unity in Mozart's operas "leads to absurd results" and that unity has an "irrelevance to opera now seems obvious." However, see his "Understanding *opera buffa*" (#2141).

1289. Webster, James. "The Analysis of Mozart's Arias." *Mozart Studies* 2 (1997): 101–199.

Aria types, the role of the orchestra, textual and musical "parameters," aria as drama. Detailed studies of eight major arias. Believes arias to be equal in importance to ensembles.

1290. Osthoff, Wolfgang. "Mozarts Cavatinen in ihre Tradition." In *Helmuth Osthoff zu seinem 70. Geburtstag,* 139–177 (Tutzing: Schneider, 1969; ML55 .H48).

A historical review of the cavatina form, covering Jommelli, Galuppi, Hasse, and Gluck. Examples from Mozart demonstrate his approaches.

1291. Neumann, Frederick. *Ornamentation and Improvisation in Mozart.* Princeton, N.J.: Princeton U.P., 1986. xii, 301p. ISBN 0-691-9123-4. ML410 .M9 N26.

Study of the appoggiatura, grace note, trill, diminutions, and other devices, with numerous musical examples from the operas. Neumann suggests alternative readings of certain arias and recitatives, based on the typical improvisatory practice of Mozart's time. Footnotes, expansive index, no bibliography.

1292. Engel, Hans. "Die *finali* der Mozartschen Opern." *Mozart Jahrbuch* 5 (1954): 113–134.

Considers the keys, characters, and mood structure in the finales of 20 operas. A useful table shows the opening and closing keys of the works. With comments on earlier writers who had covered some of the ground (Abert, Levarie, et al.), and 33 footnotes identifying the significant literature.

1293. Gruber, Gernot. *Mozart and Posterity.* Trans. R. S. Furness. London: Quartett, 1991. ix, 277p. ISBN 1-55553-194-6. ML410 .M9 G8713.

Originally *Mozart und die Nachwelt* (Salzburg: Residenz, 1985). An elaborate reception history of all the works, in chronological order. Backnotes, bibliography, and a fine index that allows search under opera titles.

See also Heartz (#251, #2134), Kivy (#401), and material on Da Ponte (#241ff.).

Individual Works

La clemenza di Tito

ASO 99 (1987), COH 1991.

1294. Tyson, Alan. "*La clemenza di Tito* and Its Chronology." *Musical Times* 156 (1975): 221–225, 227. Reprinted in #1273.

Analysis of paper discloses the sequence in which the numbers were written.

1295. Lühning, Helga. "Zur Entstehungsgeschichte von Mozarts *Titus.*" *Musikforschung* 27–3 (July–September 1974): 300–318.

Detailed genesis, using all sources and sketches. References to previous literature are in 87 footnotes.

1296. Heartz, Daniel. "*La clemenza di* Sarastro: Masonic Beneficence in the Last Operas." In *Mozart's Operas* (#1276), 255–275.

Much on the Masonic background but of greater interest for its discovery of parallels between *La clemenza di Tito* and *Die Zauberflöte.* Numerous insights on this aspect and many others in the two operas.

1297. Heartz, Daniel. "Mozart and His Italian Contemporaries: *La clemenza di Tito*." *Mozart Jahrbuch* 21 (1978–1979): 275–293.

Examines various settings of Metastasio's libretto.

1298. Heartz, Daniel. "The Overture to *La clemenza di Tito* as Dramatic Argument." In *Mozart's Operas* (#1276), 319–341.

In several Mozart operas, some "late or even final musical gesture in the work became . . . the nucleus of the overture." *Clemenza* demonstrates this more than any other: the overture is "a compendium of musical ideas from passages throughout the drama." These passages are not simply melodies but harmonic, rhythmic, or melodic fragments.

1299. Durante, Sergio. "Mozart and the Idea of *vera opera*: A Study of *La clemenza di Tito*." Ph.D. diss., Harvard U., 1993. 479p.

Così fan tutte

ASO 131/132 (1990), COH 1995, Rororo (1984).

1300. Tyson, Alan. "Notes on the Composition of Mozart's *Così fan tutte*." *JAMS* 37 (1984): 356–401. Reprinted in #1273.

There is little documentation from which to derive a genesis for the opera, but the autograph, sketches, and printed libretto of 1790 provide some information. The sequence of the writing is revealed in part by study of the paper used (watermarks, numbering of the sheets, and so on).

1301. Steptoe, Andrew. "The Sources of *Così fan tutte*: A Reappraisal." *M&L* 62 (1981): 281–294.

The libretto is of uncertain origin: an invention of Da Ponte or an adaptation from ? The plot is a "fusion of two traditional stories . . . developed in the light of current stage fashions." Those stories (*topoi*) were the wager theme and the Procris myth; the latter was exhibited in the *Decameron* and Shakespeare's *Cymbeline*. The Viennese context of the times (antisentimental) gave shape to the libretto.

1302. Levarie, Siegmund. "Das Fermaten-Motiv in *Così fan tutte*." *Mitteilungen der Internationalen Stiftung Mozarteum* 43-3/4 (November 1995): 37–40.

During the opera a rhythmic pattern consisting of a dotted quarter note held (fermata) followed by an eighth note and quarter note is heard 44 times. These instances are examined closely and found to have a common ground in the story, because they occur in times of conflict between what is said and what is real: an ambivalence of feeling or ironic contrast. The pattern is not limited to any melodic structure. It is a rhythmic leitmotiv. See next entry.

1303. Glasow, E. Thomas. "*Così fan tutte*'s Sexual Rhythmics." *OQ* 11-4 (1995): 17–29.

Independently of the preceding study, Glasow sets out to deal with the fermatas in *Così*. He counts 153 of them, 48 in the finale of act 2. These fermatas are in various rhythmic patterns, not just in the pattern that concerned

Levarie. Glasow finds them to have been "often specifically gender related." Feminine codes were the "fluttery, upbeat (female) syncopation" and the "sensuous, triple-meter melodic line and soft female cadences." The downbeat stood for male assertiveness. Some interesting ideas—but no explanation of the fermata emerges.

1304. Heartz, Daniel. "Citations, Reference, and Recall in *Così fan tutte*." In *Mozart's Operas* (#1276), 229–253.

Commenting on Steptoe (#1301), Heartz says that Goldoni's libretto, *Le pescatrici* (1752), should be added to the possible sources for *Così*. Then he notes various musical references in the opera, to the *Figaro* overture, to *Entführung*, to *Idomeneo*. Along the way he offers many insights about everything else that happens.

1305. Goehring, Edmund J., Jr. "The Comic Vision of *Così fan tutte*: Literary and Operatic Traditions." Ph.D. diss., Columbia U., 1993. 317p.

See also #1268.

Don Giovanni

ASO 24 (1979) and 172 (1996), COH (1981), ENOG 18 (1983), Rororo (1981).

1306. Abert, Hermann. *Mozarts "Don Giovanni."* Trans. Peter Gellhorn. London: Eulenberg, 1976. 138p. MT100 .M91 A18.

Originally published as part of Abert's 1924 edition of Otto Jahn's Mozart biography. It is well known as an early example of close analysis of opera. Today it reads more like a graceful, erudite, semitechnical program note. Abert was given to romantic phrases, such as "with terrible force this music storms across the heights and depths of human fortune"; and "it leads us into a world so sublime that the heart stands still." With a few short musical examples.

1307. Henze-Döhring, Sabine. "*Opera seria, opera buffa,* und Mozarts *Don Giovanni*." *Analecta musicologica 24 (1986): 1–274.*

A journal volume in two parts, the first made up of writings on several composers, the second containing essays on dramaturgy in *Don Giovanni*. Included in part 1: "Musikalische Exposition des Hauptkonflikts: Niccolò Jommellis *Attilio Regolo*," "Transparenz des dramatischen Entwicklungsprozesses: Niccolò Jommellis *Armida abbandonata*," "Vom Affekt zum 'Gefühl': Gian Francesco de Majos *Ipermestra* und *Adriano in Siria*," "Mozarts *Idomeneo*," "Exposition und Integration verschiedener *caratteri* beim frühen Piccinni," "Musikalisches 'In-Szene-Setzen' phantastischer Handlungsmomente beim frühen Paisiello," "Exposition musikalisch-dramatischer Zusammenhänge durch Integration der 'Nummern': Paisiellos *Il barbiere di Siviglia*," "Anfänge musikalisch-szenischen Gestaltens: Paisiellos *Il re Teodoro in Venezia*," and "Dan Finale des IV. Aktes von Mozarts *Le nozze di Figaro*."

On *Don Giovanni* (p.136–260) Henze-Döhring presents a measure-by-measure description of the work. Although musical as well as textual elements are carefully identified, the result is a long microstructural study, with little attention to macrostructure. Indeed, the author has trouble finding the formal dividers, wondering, for example, where the exposition ends. Ultimately, the dramatic conception of the opera lies in the unification of *opera buffa* and *opera seria*.

1308. Küster, Konrad. " '*Voglio far il gentiluomo*': Zu den dramatischen Strukturen in Mozarts *Don Giovanni*." *Mozart Studien* 1 (1992): 91–111.

Two worlds in conflict: Don Giovanni has his destiny to work out, while bringing distress to the persons he encounters. Mozart's key selections and structure underline this polarity.

1309. Levarie, Siegmund. "*Don Giovanni*'s Three Women." *Spotlight* (New York: New York City Opera Guild; early summer 1989): 5–7.

A brief, perceptive character study of the Don, drawn from story and music. Answers such questions as: Why did he choose the contradance for his round with Zerlina? Whose fib is revealed by a deceptive cadence?

1310. Waldoff, Jessica. "*Don Giovanni*: Recognition Denied." In *Opera buffa* (#2141), 286–307.

Applying Aristotle's concept of the discovery/recognition moment does not seem to work out in this story. The protagonist—Waldoff assumes it is Don Giovanni—fails to recognize the true state of affairs, and he is omitted from the affirmation of the finale.

1311. Petrobelli, Pierluigi. "*Don Giovanni* in Italia: La fortuna dell'opera ed il suo influsso." In "Colloquium" (#1262), 30–51.

The first Italian performance did not take place until 1811, in Rome. There were difficulties for Italian orchestras in playing the score, and indeed the orchestra in the Rome premiere did a poor job of it. Special concerns came up in the act 1 finale, with its simultaneous scoring for three instrumental groups. (Nevertheless, Petrobelli observes that orchestras were handling Haydn and Beethoven symphonies without unusual problems.) Voice types in Italy were not easily matched to Mozart's characters either. Many cuts were made in the score for Italian performances, to accommodate these instrumental and vocal challenges. Audiences were another obstacle to acceptance of *Don Giovanni* and other Mozart operas: they did not find as much melody there as they like, and too much "harmony." (While such responses may seem unsophisticated, they were shared by Bellini, Donizetti, and Verdi—all of whom concentrated their interest on the ensemble work.) With a list of 35 Italian productions, 1811–1871.

1312. Kierkegaard, Søren. *Either/Or*. Trans. and ed. Howard Vincent Hong. Princeton, N.J.: Princeton U.P., 1987. 2v. ISBN 0-691-07315-5; 0-691-07316-3. B4373 .E61 H7.

Originally published in Danish (Copenhagen, 1843). An essay concerns *Don Giovanni*: "The Immediate Stages of the Erotic: Or the Musical Erotic." The philosopher's idiom is an elusive, flowery one but in places absorbing. "Don Juan constantly hovers between being the idea, that is to say, energy, life—and being the individual. But this hovering is a musical trembling." Only music can express Don Juan, since music has "the epic quality that can go on as long as it will, since one can constantly let it begin again . . . and hear it over and over again." It is the same with the Don's seductions: "he constantly finishes, and constantly begins again." For him, a seduced woman is dangerous because she has moved to a "consciousness which Don Giovanni does not have." His power cannot be expressed in words; only music can give us a conception of it. This nameless force is the exuberant joy of life. If Don Giovanni is portrayed as trying hard, against serious obstacles, he becomes reflective, a planner, *verbal*; but the musical Don has no plan and meets no resistance.

1313. Brown, Kristi Ann. "A Critical Study of the Female Characters in Mozart's *Don Giovanni* and *Die Zauberflöte*." Ph.D. diss., U. of California, Berkeley, 1997. 262p.

See also #2141.

Die Entführung aus dem Serail

ASO 59 (1984), COH (1988), Rororo (1983).

1314. Bauman, Thomas. "Coming of Age in Vienna: *Die Entführung aus dem Serail*." In *Mozart's Operas* (#1276), 65–87.

Considers how Mozart interpreted the Viennese operatic scene in 1781, as indicated by his letters to his father. (The preferred composers there were Paisiello, Salieri, and Gluck.) Genesis, traced mostly in the letters, analysis, and many useful observations follow. "Like all Mozart's operas, the *Abduction* was a child of circumstance" but also related to the "parallel emotional coming of age Mozart experienced in his first 16 months in Vienna."

1315. Osthoff, Wolfgang. "Comicità alla turca, musica classica, opera nazionale: Osservazioni sulla *Entführung aus dem Serail*." In *Opera and Libretto II* (#221), 157–174.

Mozart intended to write an opera that could represent Germanic ideals and also please Viennese audiences. His use of so-called Turkish elements represented the barbaric strain in humanity, overcome by the gentle, classical aspect that was to characterize German national opera. With an interesting explication of how Mozart achieves the Turkish mood.

La finta giardiniera

1316. Angermüller, Rudolph. "Wer war der Librettist von *La finta giardiniera*?" *Mozart-Jahrbuch* 1976–1977: 1–120.

Argues that the supposed librettist, Raniero Calzabigi, did not in fact write the text. Suggests, on the basis of recently discovered material, that the real author was Abate Giuseppe Petrosellini. (This conclusion has been generally accepted.)

Idomeneo

ASO 89 (1986), COH (1993), Rororo (1988).

1317. Hirschberg, Jehoash. "Formal and Dramatic Aspects of Sonata Form in Mozart's *Idomeneo*." *MR* 38 (1977): 192–210.

An analysis of the arias and ensembles. They show how Mozart, in his operas, was shifting from the da capo form (which he hardly used after 1780) to something closer to sonata form. Not exactly sonata form, however: "The arias in *Idomeneo* contain no development sections, so that the process of growth and development is centered in the recapitulation and its relation to the exposition." Table of the arias and tonal scheme.

1318. Heartz, Daniel. "The Great Quartet in Mozart's *Idomeneo*." *Music Forum 5* (1980): 233–256.

A close examination of the act 3 quartet, considering all musical and textual elements. Heartz explains how they all blend into a dramatic unity, with tonalities at the core: "The E-flat of the quartet represents the most formidable challenge to the primacy of the keynote D. Its unholy alliance with A creates a dissonance that must be resolved on every level, from the fermata chords in the second part of the quartet to the eventual resolution of the whole drama on the dual plateaux of penultimate B-flat and of the ultimate D major triumph."

1319. *Mozart Jahrbuch* 1973–1974. Issue on *Idomeneo*.

Includes Daniel Heartz, "Idomeneus Rex," Gustav Rudolf Sellner, "Grundlagen zur Aufführung des *Idomeneo* in Salzburg 1973," Margaret Dietrich, "Wiener Fassungen des *Idomeneo*," and detailed discussions by working groups of the tonal plan and motivic structure of the opera and of vocal and instrumental elements.

See also Heartz (#1276) and Böhmer (#2407).

Lucio Silla

ASO 139 (1991). See also #1268.

Mitridate

ASO 54 (1983).

Le nozze di Figaro

ASO 135/136 (1990), COH (1988), ENOG 17 (1982), Rororo (1981).

1320. Tyson, Alan. "*Le nozze di Figaro*: Lessons from the Autograph Score." *Musical Times* 122 (1981): 456–461. Reprinted in #1273.

Takes issue with Moberly (#1325) regarding what Mozart intended as the order of scenes in act 3. Finds no documents to support Moberly's ordering, while evidence from paper study suggests he is wrong. The musical evidence, in terms of key sequence, is ambiguous.

1321. Tyson, Alan. "Some Problems in the Text of *Le nozze di Figaro*: Did Mozart Have a Hand in Them?" *JRMA* 112–1 (1986–1987): 99–131. Reprinted in #1273.

While "careful scrutiny of the well-preserved *Figaro* autograph can yield much information as to how it was put together," other useful clues "perhaps to the changes that Mozart himself was induced to make in it, can come from a careful study and comparison of the many *Abschriften*." These are the copyists' full scores, in which changes by Mozart (and others?) were made as needed after the autograph was done. Tyson describes 13 of them.

1322. Levarie, Siegmund. *Mozart's "Le nozze di Figaro": A Critical Analysis.* Chicago: U. of Chicago Press, 1952. 268p. Reprint, New York: Da Capo, 1969. ISBN 0-306-70897-3. MT100 .M78 L4.

The starting point for technical studies of *Figaro,* this is an outstanding example of structural analysis. Tonal design is central—the opera is a binary structure in D major—but all dramatic and musical elements are brought into a convincing unity. Nevertheless, the author concludes that "a complete analysis is neither possible nor desirable. Even if all the virtues could be verbalized, their finite sum would ever fall short of the totality of the work."

1323. Heartz, Daniel. "Constructing *Le nozze di Figaro.*" In *Mozart's Operas* (#1276), 77–98.

Genesis, drawn largely from Da Ponte's memoirs. As they wrote, both composer and librettist had to bear in mind the extant competition, Paisiello's popular *Il barbiere di Siviglia* (which had the same characters and even a love aria by Rosina, comparable to "Porgi amor"). Comparisons are made in detail, including tonal schemes. Heartz presents a tonal plan for *Figaro* that is much like Levarie's (who is not mentioned) but without the macrostructural description.

1324. Abbate, Carolyn, and Roger Parker. "Dismembering Mozart." *COJ* 2 (1990): 187–195.

A study of the opening duettino, usually regarded as a perfect example of words, action, and music in higher unity. But the words resolve the tension first, before the tonal resolution (D to G) occurs. Other examples are given of closure in music but not in text and vice versa. The authors question whether the classical analysis, which assumes a correspondence between words and music, is appropriate. (However, it may be noted that musical resolution is not limited to tonal cadence; indeed, Levarie's explication of this scene relies more on changes in melodic character.)

1325. Moberly, Robert, and Christopher Raeburn. "Mozart's *Figaro*: The Plan of Act III." *M&L* 46 (1965): 134–136.

Concerns the question of number ordering. "Dove sono" was originally intended to come between the count's aria and the sextet; so the order was number 17–19a–19b ("Dove sono")-18-20. But there was one singer for two roles, Bartolo and Antonio, and time was needed for a costume change, so the shift in order was made. The result is not satisfactory, since it does not leave time enough for the offstage trial during the count's aria. Other plot disturbances are cited. The same ideas are taken up in #1287.

1326. Allanbrook, Wye Jamison. "Pro Marcellina: The Shape of *Figaro,* Act IV." *M&L* 63 (1982): 69–82.

Disapproves of the customary cuts of numbers 24 and 25, since they contribute significantly to the plot and musical structure.

1327. Ruf, Wolfgang. *Die Rezeption von Mozarts "Le nozze di Figaro" bei die Zeitgenossen.* Beihefte zum Archiv für Musikwissenschaft, 16. Wiesbaden: Steiner, 1977. 148p. ISBN 3-515-02408-5. ML55 .A67 v.16.

Compares the reception to that of Paisiello's *Il re Teodoro in Venezia.*

1328. Noske, Fritz. "Social Tensions in *Le nozze di Figaro*." *M&L* 50–1 (January 1969): 45–62.

The opera has "no message: it does not propagate reform of the social order. Mozart only registers the social climate, without taking sides." See next entry.

1329. Brophy, Brigid. "*Figaro* and the Limitations of Music." *M&L* 51 (1970): 26–36.

Disputes those, like Noske (#1328), who find a social theme in the opera and see no erotic desire in the count, only his wish to act like a nobleman. In any case, the class matter is in the libretto only; music cannot express it. Our concept of operatic characters is drawn from the words and dramatic action—the music of course reflects this. Melodic characterization is really mood painting.

See also #1268.

Die Zauberflöte

ASO 1 (1976) and 101 (1987), COH (1991), ENOG 3 (1980), Rororo (1982).

1330. Schneider, Otto. "*Die Zauberflöte* in der Literatur: Ein bibliographisches Überblick." *Österreichische Musikzeitschrift* 22–8 (August 1967): 458–464.

An annotated list of 300 writings on the opera, useful despite a crowded narrative format.

1331. Eckelmeyer, Judith A. *The Cultural Context of Mozart's "Magic Flute": Social, Aesthetic, Philosophical.* Lewiston, N.Y.: E. Mellen, 1991. V.1: viii, 329p. ISBN 0-7734-9642-4. ML410 .M95 E19.

A second volume was not seen, but it is described in the first as consisting of three appendixes: a libretto of the opera; a letter from Gottfried van Swieten to Joseph II with a reply; and the text of a Masonic writing by Christian Rosenkreuz, who gave his name to the Rosicrucians. V.1 explains the importance of these sources, then goes on to describe the opera in detail with both text and musical structure in mind. The libretto is "a message of struggle toward a better world, a regenerated and transformed society." Musically, the work is "an enormous sonata, consisting of the usual exposition, development, and recapitulation." (See also next entry.) With a line-by-line account of Mozart's changes to the Schikaneder libretto.

1332. Eckelmeyer, Judith A. "Structure as a Hermeneutic Guide to *The Magic Flute.*" *MQ* 72-1 (Spring 1986): 51–73.

Considers key progession in the overture as an intrinsic part of the opera. Tries to align events to illustrate dialectic form; e.g., act 2 contains a clear synthesis of thesis and antithesis sections. This idea is pressed into sonata-allegro form, and a schematic table is worked out. Eckelmeyer gives some interesting binary relations of plot, similar to those of Levarie in *Figaro* (#1322).

1333. Batley, E. M. *A Preface to "The Magic Flute."* London: Dennis Dobson, 1969. 175p. SBN 234-77205-0 [*sic*: an early form of ISBN]. ML410 .M95 B33.

Good background chapters on Viennese popular theater and the growth of German *Singspiel,* with attention to Schikaneder's role. Then a chapter on the disputes over authorship of the libretto and a chapter on its unifying features. Schikaneder's shifting fortunes as a manager of the Freihaustheater (1789–1801) and the Theater an der Wien (1801–1804; he was later assistant there until 1806) are recounted. The authorship question turns on the claim of Brigid Brophy (#1279) that the libretto was a collaboration with Karl Ludwig Giesecke—Brophy following Otto Jahn and Edward Dent in this matter. Batley disputes the claim, bringing forth the two Schikaneder biographers, both asserting sole authorship for him, and also on the grounds of Giesecke's lack of requisite talent—his art being one of plagiarism only. Getting into the plot, Batley deals exhaustively with the problematic characters of the Queen of the Night and Sarastro, who appear to undergo transformations. He says the queen is "dual, but not contradictory": she is a widow and mother "on the human plane" but also self-centered and neglectful of maternal duties. Her good qualities are steadily diminished until her only function is to symbolize darkness and evil. Sarastro's bad side is exhibited early on (he is a kidnapper, after all), but he comes to symbolize honor and truth.

1334. Freyhan, Michael. "Toward the Original Text of Mozart's *Die Zauberflöte.*" *JAMS* 39 (1986): 355–380.

In 1814 publisher Simrock "rejected the autograph version in common use in favor of another text. That manuscript source came from Konstanze, who had it available only 23 days before her husband's death." Quality is arguably superior to that of the autograph, and Simrock used it until 1862. Contemporary sources are carefully examined from this perspective.

1335. Chailley, Jacques. "*La flute enchantée*": *Opéra maçonnique.* Paris: Robert Laffort, 1968. 342p. Reprint, Paris: Éditions d'Aujourd'hui, 1975. ML410 .M8 C43.

An English translation, "*The Magic Flute*": *Masonic Opera,* was made by Herbert Weinstock (New York: Knopf, 1971). A long account of the libretto, bringing out every possible Masonic symbol. Index of names, titles, and topics.

1336. Bauman, Thomas. "At the North Gate: Instrumental Music in *Die Zauberflöte.*" In *Mozart's Operas* (#1276), 277–297.

Considers various interpretations of the libretto, such as Chailley's, and finds that most overlook the music. So Bauman intends to bring "at least one portion of Mozart's music into recent interpretations . . . in particular into ideas about Pamina and Tamino as co-equal, merged personalities." In a valuable study, he explains how Mozart established the orchestra as a distinct "persona" and how multilayered interpretations of the music are called for, just as in the libretto. For instance, in Pamina's aria in act 2, the orchestral ritornello "derives a psychological subtext from key verbal phrases" and may also echo Tamino's thoughts. The overture fits in to the "rich store of symbolic meanings" in the opera, offering "a musical narrative of contrapuntally conjoined personalities who are developed and shaped by their common experience."

1337. Levarie, Siegmund. "Two Fairy-Tale Operas: A Comparison." *OQ* 7-1 (Spring 1990): 7–11.

The operas are *Die Zauberflöte* and *Die Frau ohne Schatten*. The latter was imagined by its creators, Richard Strauss and Hugo von Hofmannsthal, to share the atmosphere of the former. Although a comparison of the two libretti would seem to favor the acclaimed Hofmannsthal over the much maligned Schikaneder, "*Die Frau ohne Schatten . . .* remains woefully defective when compared to *Die Zauberflöte.*" Both stories hinge on the triumph of love over serious trials. But *Die Frau ohne Schatten* gives no demonstration of love until the final scene, where triumph is extolled; in fact, the "Emperor and Empress never sing together, never act together, and (with the exception of a short pantomime in the Empress' dream) never appear on the stage together." This contrasts with the gradual, "artful unveiling of love" between Pamina and Tamino. Motivation for the change of character by Barak's wife in the Strauss work is not offered and is thus unconvincing. Nor is there justification for the punishment of the nurse, whose behavior had been exemplary. Finally, there is the Emperor's inactivity: "to be loved, one has to do something," but he "remains unrelated and insipid throughout." Other loose ends are pointed out, completing a rare case in the opera literature; indeed, are there any other instances of harsh critiques leveled at Hofmannsthal?

1338. Levarie, Siegmund. "Papageno und Pamina." *Mitteilungen der Internationalen Stiftung Mozarteum* 35–1/4 (July 1987): 103–105.

Discusses parallels between Papageno and Tamino, but a more subtle relationship is found between Papageno and Pamina. Their duet, one of the loveliest in the opera, is in the tonic E-flat—the only appearance of the key, except for the *Bildnisarie*, between the overture and the finale. From similar experiences the two have basically different outcomes: she reaches maturity, he parodies her with light and foolish songs as she sings of her separation from Pamino. The key scheme elucidates this. "The layers of this magic opera seem to be endless."

1339. Godwin, Jocelyn. "Layers of Meaning in *The Magic Flute*." *MQ* 65 (1979): 471–492.

A libretto study, finding a higher level of meaning than the usual Masonic symbols: it is the opera as a "historical allegory of esoteric organizations in the

Christian world, colored by the particular history of postmedieval Freemasonry, but applicable to others as well." A further layer has a Jungian base: Pamina is Tamino's "anima," and Monostatos is Papageno's (and/or Sarastro/s) "shadow," while the story as a whole is a search for "individuation." Sarastro is the archetype of the wise man, a symbol of the integrated self.

1340. Horwath, Peter. "Symbolism in *Die Zauberflöte*: Origin and Background of the Symbolism of 'Sevenfold,' 'Mighty,' and 'All-Consuming Sun Disk.'" *OQ* 8-3 (Autumn 1991): 58–86.

A useful discussion of Viennese Masonic history, which emphasized male superiority over women, mixed with fear of women's wiles. The septagram refers to the Grand Lodge of Austria (there were seven regional lodges). The dying king's bequest of the sun disk to Sarastro signifies his relinquishment of absolute power—or the yielding of secular to spiritual power. With 67 footnotes to the relevant literature.

1341. Waldoff, Jessica. "The Music of Recognition: Operatic Enlightenment in *The Magic Flute*." *M&L* 75 (1994): 214–235.

Recognition scenes are frequent in 18th-century opera (indeed, in all opera). They develop a new awareness in the minds of the protagonist, as per Aristotle's *Poetics*. This opera is about light and dark: movement toward the light of knowledge. The recognition scene occurs in the finale to act 1 (number 8), as Tamino converses with the priest. [It may be noted that this "recognition" comes too early in the work to be Aristotelian. And is Tamino the protagonist?]

1342. Witzenmann, Wolfgang. "Zu einigen Handschriften des *Flauto magico*." In "Colloquium" (#1262), 55–95.

Manuscripts of the Italian version of the opera cast some light on the slow reception of *Die Zauberflöte* in Italy. Witzenmann examines the Italian sources in Dresden, Milan, Naples, Florence, and Rome and compares them to the published Italian libretti of 1794 and 1816. Three Italian translations are also compared. A major concern in Italy was the spoken dialogue in the opera, which was modified to accompanied recitative for performance there, as late as the 20th century. All the sources are described in great bibliographic detail with references to the total literature in 118 footnotes.

See also Moberly (#1287), Heartz (#1296), and Brown (#1313).

Thea Musgrave (1928–)

1343. Hixon, Donald. *Thea Musgrave: A Bio-Bibliography.* Bio-Bibliographies in Music, 1. Westport, Conn.: Greenwood, 1984. 187p. ISBN 0-313-23708-5. ML134 .M967 H6.

An annotated bibliography that includes several hundred reviews and notices of *Mary Queen of Scots, The Decision,* and *The Voice of Ariadne.*

Modest Petrovich Musorgsky (1839–1881)

The name is also transliterated Mussorgsy or Musorgskii.

Editions

1344. *Modest Petrovich Musorgskii. Polnoe akademicheskoe sochineni = Complete Works.* Ed. Eugenii Levasev and Giorgii Vasil'evich Sviridov, for the Institute of the Russian Federation for the Study of the Arts. Moscow: Muzyka; Mainz: Schott, 1989–. M3 .M982.

In progress. All the operas are to appear in series 1, v.1–11. The only one seen is *Boris Godunov,* in v.2, parts 1 and 2 (1996). It is a full score of the 1869 version, with extensive critical notes and introduction in Russian and English. Information includes a discussion of editing problems, description of the autographs, discrepancies between full and vocal scores of the original version, stage directions, historical and literary comments, and text of the libretto. Name index.

Collections of Essays

1345. *Musorgsky: In Memoriam, 1881–1981.* Ed. Malcolm Hamrick Brown. Ann Arbor, Mich.: UMI Research, 1982. 337p. ISBN 0-8357-1295-8. ML410 .M97 M98.

Essays by various specialists, including Richard Taruskin, Malcolm Hamrick Brown, Boris Schwarz, Maria Schneerson, Alexandra Orlova, Robert Oldani, and Gerald Abraham. Topics covered: life, style, individual works. "Editions of *Boris Godunov,*" by Oldani, gives library locations of all the manuscripts and describes the composer's piano-vocal score, the Rimsky-Korsakov version, and the modern edition of Lloyd-Jones (#1354). The study by Orlova and Schneerson examines the *Boris* libretto in terms of its emergence from Pushkin's play and a history by Karamzin. Expansive index of names, titles, and topics.

1346. Taruskin, Richard. *Musorgsky: Eight Essays and an Epilogue.* Princeton, N.J.: Princeton U.P., 1993. xxxiv, 415p. ISBN 0-691-09147-1. ML410 .M983 T19.

Includes important studies, entered separately, of Serov and Musorgsky (#1349), the two versions of *Boris* (#1355), folk song in *Boris* (#1356), genesis of *Khovanshchina* (#1357), and a view of *Sorochintsi Fair* (#1358). Also in the book: "Handel, Shakespeare, and Musorgsky" and "Folk Texts in *Boris Godunov.*" All except the one on *Sorochintsi Fair* are reprints of earlier publications. Expansive index.

Biographies

1347. Orlova, Alexandra. *Musorgsky's Days and Works: A Biography in Documents.* Trans. and ed. Roy J. Guenther. Ann Arbor, Mich.: UMI Research, 1983. 650p. ISBN 0-8357-1234-5. ML410 .M97 O7.

Originally in Russian (Moscow, 1963). A documentary chronicle, drawing on all sources: letters, diaries, newpaper articles, and writings of contemporaries. Includes details of genesis and production for the operas. Bibliographic references, index.

Operas in General

1348. Emerson, Caryl. "Musorgsky's Libretti on Historical Themes: From the Two *Borises* to *Khovanshchina*." In *Reading Opera* (#218), 235–267.

Covers much of the same ground as Taruskin (#1355), with new material on *Khovanshchina*. Considers various contemporary and later revisionist critiques of the opera and looks for evidence of progressive social themes in it. Musorgsky began with "a *kuchkist* passion for verisimilitude," then became more flexible. In *Khovanshchina* the reality is focused on each character's sense of time and of the past; all are bound by fate.

1349. Taruskin, Richard. "Serov and Musorgsky." In *Eight Essays* (#1346), 96–122.

"Musorgsky rejected Serov but all his works accepted him." Many similarities are identified, some that may be borrowings (including principal scenes in *Boris*). Much of Musorgsky's style can be traced to Alexander Serov's works. Taruskin presents a vivid view of "the tumultuous world of St. Petersburg musical politics" of the mid–19th century.

Individual Works

Boris Godunov

ASO 27/28 (1980) and 191 (1999), ENOG 11 (1982), Rororo (1982).

1350. Fulle, Gerlinde. *Modest Mussorgskijs "Boris Godunov": Geschichte und Werk, Fassungen und Theaterpraxis*. Wiesbaden: Breitkopf und Härtel, 1974. 357p. ISBN 3-7651-0078-1. ML410 .M97 F84.

The libretto in all versions; performances and reception in Western Europe, 1913–1971. Good documentation throughout, with 600 footnotes and a bibliography of about 250 items. Musical examples, no index.

1351. Emerson, Caryl, and Robert William Oldani. *Modest Musorgsky and Boris Godunov: Myths, Realities, Reconsiderations*. New York: Cambridge U.P., 1994. xiii, 339p. ISBN 0-521-36193-1. ML410 .M97 E43.

A valuable examination of genesis, ideology, the 1874 revision (preferred to the 1869 original), reception, performance history, and interpretation. Musical analysis, with examples, is technical. The historical Boris is described, and literary sources are detailed. Changes to the opera by Rimsky-Korsakov and the new orchestration by Shostakovich are discussed. Backnotes, good bibliography of about 150 items, index.

1352. Oldani, Robert William. "Musorgsky's *Boris* on the Stage of the Maryinski Theater: A Chronicle of the First Production." *OQ* 4-2 (Summer 1986): 75–92.

The production took place on 27 January 1874 (old calendar) in St. Petersburg. Genesis, description of the cuts that reduced the duration from 3 hours and 15 minutes to 2 hours and 20 minutes, reception (hostile critics, enthusiastic audience).

1353. Carr, Maureen A. "Keys and Modes, Functions and Progressions in Musorgsky's *Boris Godunov.*" Ph.D. diss., U. of Wisconsin-Madison, 1972. 4,104p.

The dissertation is in nine volumes. V.1, text of the opera; v.2–6, orchestral score and analysis; v.7–9, charts, tables, and a literal translation.

1354. Lloyd-Jones, David. *Boris Godunov: Critical Commentary and Musical Appendices.* London: Oxford U.P., 1975. 70p. plus 200p. facsimiles and music. ISBN 0-19-337699-7. M1500 .M98 B872.

This is v.2 of a *Boris* set; the first volume has the full score, edited by Lloyd-Jones. The complete texts of the 1869 and 1872 versions are given, with extensive commentary on them, on genesis, and on sources.

1355. Taruskin, Richard. "Musorgsky vs. Musorgsky: The Versions of *Boris Godunov.*" In *Eight Essays* (#1346), 201–290.

An exhaustive review of the 1869 and 1872–1874 versions of the opera, disclosing that they are not variants of one plan but two distinct entities based on different concepts of opera. In 1869 fidelity to the text was primary; in 1872 there was a more casual relation to the Pushkin source, plus a whole new final scene not in Pushkin at all.

1356. Taruskin, Richard. "*Slava!*" In *Eight Essays* (#1346), 300–312.

More than a dozen Russian folk songs (words and/or music) are found in *Boris,* and other numbers are original but folklike. *Slava!* is the only folk song that appears with both words and music in the coronation scene. The song's place in Russian Christmas and New Year observations is discussed. It acquired a civic and ceremonial character, which was Musorgsky's context for it. Taruskin also notes the use of the song by other composers.

Khovanshchina

ASO 57/58 (1983), ENOG 48 (1994).

1357. Taruskin, Richard. "The Power of the Black Earth: Notes on *Khovanshchina.*" In *Eight Essays* (#1346), 313–327.

Background on the reign of Peter the Great and the *streltsy* revolts on which *Khovanshchina* is focused. Genesis; the work was left unfinished at the composer's death in 1881. His views on the "Old Believers" were not made clear, but Rimsky-Korsakov treated them as unworthy reactionaries as he completed the opera.

Sorochintsi Fair (Sorochinskaia iarmaka)

1358. Taruskin, Richard. "*Sorochintsi Fair* Revisited." In *Eight Essays* (#1346), 328–394.

Musorgsky completed only a little over half of the opera, which was based on a Gogol story of the same name. The composer abandoned work on it, then returned in earnest in 1877. His plan for the structure is given, with letters he wrote at the time. A technical analysis of the work, with musical examples, is offered, in a rich context of Russian aesthetic disputes of the period and the composer's efforts to adapt to prevailing views.

Otto Nicolai (1810–1849)

Il templario is in *IO–1810,* v.26.

1359. Konrad, Ulrich. *Otto Nicolai (1810–1849): Studien zu Leben und Werk.* Sammlung Musikwissenschaftlichen Abhandlungen, 73. Baden-Baden: V. Koerner, 1986. 449p. ISBN 3-87320-573-4. ML55 .S2 v.73.

Life and works, with letters, worklist, good bibliography of sources and expansive name and title index. Very little said about the operas.

Carl Nielsen (1865–1931)

1360. Miller, Mina F. *Carl Nielsen: A Guide to Research.* Garland Composer Resource Manuals, 6. New York: Garland, 1987. xvi, 245p. ISBN 0-8240-8569-8. ML134 .N42 M5.

An extensively annotated bibliography of 401 writings, many in Danish. Nielsen's operas *Saul and David* and *Maskarade* have about 50 entries, mostly reviews and brief notices. Indexes of titles, names, authors.

1361. Balzer, Jürgen. "The Dramatic Music." In *Carl Nielsen Centenary Essays,* ed. Jürgen Balzer, 75–101. Copenhagen: Nyt Nordisk Forlag-Arnold Busck, 1965. 130p. ML410 .N625 B3.

Program notes with some technical observations on the operas. This seems to be the only study of them published in a common language.

1362. *The Nielsen Companion.* Ed. Mina F. Miller. Portland, Ore.: Amadeus, 1995. x, 666p. ISBN 1-57467-004-2. ML410 .N67 N66.

A collection of 23 essays by various writers, 7 by Miller. There are only passing references to the opera *Maskarade.* Useful bibliography of 250 entries, index.

Luigi Nono (1924–1990)

1363. Stenzl, Jürg. *Luigi Nono.* Reinbeck bei Hamburg: Rowohlt, 1998. 158p. ISBN 3-4915-0582-7. ML410 .N81 S82.

A handy fact book, including a biography, chronology, worklist, discography, and bibliography. For each opera there is a genesis account and details of performances. Indexed.

1364. Taibon, Mateo. *Luigi Nono und sein Musiktheater.* Vienna: Bühlau, 1993. 206p. ISBN 3-205-98067-0. ML410 .N81 T13.

Interesting background on Italian music theater after World War II; biography of Nono; then chapters on *Intolleranza 1960, Al gran sole,* and *Prometeo.* Genesis of each, with analyses of text and music, staging matters, and press reactions. Worklist, discography, good bibliography of about 75 entries, no index.

1365. Gilbert, Janet Monteith. "Dialectic Music: An Analysis of Luigi Nono's *Intolleranza.*" D.M.A. diss., U. of Illinois, 1979. 154p.

Jacques Offenbach (1819–1880)

1366. Faris, Alexander. *Jacques Offenbach*. New York: Scribner, 1980. 273p. ISBN 0-684-16797-2. ML410 .O41 F3.

> A straightforward biography, with backnotes and program notes for the operas. Table of stage works, 1839–1881, giving librettists and premiere information. Worklist of the nonstage works, by genre. Pictures and musical examples, bibliography of about 120 entries. Expansive index of names, titles, and topics.

1367. Hawig, Peter. *Jacques Offenbach: Facetten zu Leben und Werk*. Beiträge zur Offenbach-Forschung, 2. Cologne: Dohr, 1999. 311p. ISBN 3-925366-57-1. ML410 .O3 H395.

> A biography set in the context of culture under Napoleon III, with a useful survey of research about the composer and desiderata for scholarship. Extended coverage of reception. Bibliography, 177 numbered items arranged by opera, name index.

Individual Works

La belle Hélène

ASO 125 (1989).

Les contes d'Hoffmann

ASO 25 (1980), Rororo (1984).

1368. Eisenberg, Anna. "Jacques Offenbach: *Hoffmanns Erzählungen*. Analyse der szenischen Bearbeitung." Ph.D. diss., U. of Cologne, 1974. 380p.

La périchole

ASO 66 (1984).

Giovanni Pacini (1796–1867)

In *IO–1810*: *Il barone di Dolsheim*, v.29; *L'ultimo giorno di Pompei*, v.32; *Il corsaro*, v.34; and *Saffo* (with excerpts from *Furio Camilla*), v.36.

1369. Lippmann, Friedrich. "Giovanni Pacini: Bemerkungen zum Stil seiner Opern." *Chigiana* 24 (1967): 111–124.

> Pacini wrote 90 stage works from 1813 to 1867. Style is romantic *seria*. Libretti are comparable in quality to those of Rossini, Donizetti, and Verdi; music is worthy of comparison to Bellini. Many works, such as *Saffo*, are worthy of revival. Musical examples, technical observations.

Ferdinando Paër (1771–1839)

1370. Minardi, Gian Paolo. "Paër semiserio." In *I vicini di Mozart* (#90), 343–358.

> *Griselda* (1797) was his earliest *semiseria* (Italian equivalent of the *opéra-comique* in the late 18th century); it is analyzed here, with a genesis account. Other operas in the genre are also examined: *Camilla* (1799), *I fuorusciti di Firenze* (1802), and the culminating *Leonora* (1804).

Giovanni Paisiello (1740–1816)

1371. Hunt, Jno Leland. *Giovanni Paisiello: His Life as an Opera Composer.*
National Opera Association Monograph Series, 2. New York: National Opera
Association, 1975. vii, 88p. No ISBN. ML410 .P14 H8.

The author's name is given here as it appears on the title page. A footnoted
biography, with a chronology and a worklist. Genesis and reception of the
operas. Paisiello's years in Russia are of interest. Backnotes, brief bibliography; without index.

1372. Corte, Andrea della. *Paisiello.* Turin: Bocca, 1922. 352p. ML410 .P149 C82.

The standard older biography, with program notes for major operas. No bibliography; name index.

1373. Robinson, Michael F., and Ulrike Hofmann. *Giovanni Paisiello (1740–1816):
A Thematic Catalogue of His Works.* Thematic Catalogues, 15. Stuyvesant,
N.Y.: Pendragon, 1989–1994. 2v. ISBN 0-918728-75-4; 0-945193-60-2.
ML421 .P195 A3.

V.1: Dramatic works; v.2: Nondramatic works. A valuable compilation,
including incipits for all numbers in the operas, library locations, and comments on productions. Indexed.

1374. Piperno, Franco. "L'anima pazza per amore, ossia il Paisiello contrafatto." In
Opera and Libretto I (#220), 137–148.

Considers newly discovered manuscripts in Chioggia of Paisiello's arias from
Nina osia la pazza per amore (1789) and compares them with the original version.

1375. Scherliess, Volker. "*Il barbiere di Siviglia*: Paisiello and Rossini." *Analecta
musicologica* 21 (1982): 100–128.

Rossini's work was a failure in its premiere, while Paisiello's was one of the
most popular operas of the day. Genesis of both: revisions; manuscripts and
sources; technical comparison, especially of metric features.

1376. Goldin, Daniela. "*Il barbiere di Siviglia* da Beaumarchais all'opera buffa." In
Muraro (#2576), v.2, 323–348.

Paisiello's librettist, Giuseppe Petrosellini, eliminated the nuances of the original play, rushing on to action elements. He assumed the audience would know
the play, and merely gave tags of it to show where the plot was. Cesare
Sterbini, librettist for Rossini, was much more faithful to Beaumarchais and
also more imaginative in defining the characters. He maintained the tensions
of the original text.

See also Ruf (#1327).

Carlo Pallavicino (1630–1688)

The name also appears as Pallavicini, and the birthdate is in doubt.

1377. Smith, Julian. "Carlo Pallavicino." *PRMA* 96 (1969–1970): 57–71.

A brief biography with background on the times. Useful comments on the style, with musical examples. Connections to all earlier studies are made via 43 footnotes.

1378. McKee, Richard M. "A Critical Edition of Carlo Pallavicino's *Il Vespasiano*." Ph.D. diss., U. of North Carolina, 1989. 810p.

See also Henze-Döhring (#1307 and #2575).

Horatio Parker (1863–1919)

1379. Kearns, William K. *Horatio Parker, 1863–1919*. Composers of North America, 6. Metuchen, N.J.: Scarecrow, 1990. xvii, 356p. ISBN 0-8108-2292-X. ML410 .P17 K43.

Parker was among the leading composers and teachers (Charles Ives was among his pupils) of his time. His opera *Mona* was performed at the Metropolitan in 1912. This is a well-documented biography with program notes and musical examples, a worklist, bibliography, library holdings, and index.

Bernardo Pasquini (1637–1710)

1380. Crain, Gordon F. "The Operas of Bernardo Pasquini." Ph.D. diss., Yale U., 1965. 2v.

See also #2576.

Krzysztof Penderecki (1933–)

1381. Schwinge, Wolfram. *Krzysztof Penderecki: His Life and Works: Encounters, Biography, and Musical Commentary*. Mainz: Schott, 1989. 290p. ML410 .P2673 .S413.

First edition, in German (Stuttgart: Deutsche Verlags Anstalt, 1979; 2nd German edition, *Begegnungen, Lebensdaten, Werkkommentare* [Mainz: Schott, 1994; ISBN 3-7957-0265-8]). Life and works, with good technical analysis of the operas *Verlorene Paradis, Teufel von Loudon,* and *Ubu Rex*. Illustrations from modern stagings, where nudity seems pervasive. Worklist, backnotes, name index.

John Christopher Pepusch (1667–1752)

1382. Kidson, Frank. *"The Beggar's Opera": Its Predecessors and Successors*. Cambridge: Cambridge U.P., 1922. 109p. ML1731.3 .K46.

Pepusch composed only a part of the music for John Gay's very popular *Beggar's Opera* (1728); most of the score consisted of adapted folk songs or borrowings from other composers. This study takes up the sources, early publications, and critiques of productions. Includes a synopsis and pictures. No notes or bibliography; expansive index of names and titles.

1383. Schultz, William Eben. *Gay's "Beggar's Opera": Its Content, History, and Influence*. New Haven, Conn.: Yale U.P., 1923. xxiii, 407p. Reprint, New York: Russell & Russell, 1967. PR3473 .B6 S5.

A valuable account of the opera's sources, reception in Britain and the U.S., and further performance history. Realism and morality issues are discussed, as is the influence of the opera. Primary materials are described. Footnotes, bibliography of about 100 items, index.

1384. Cook, Donald F. "The Life and Works of Johann Christoph Pepusch (1667–1752), with Special Reference to His Dramatic Works and Cantatas." Ph.D. diss., King's College, London, 1983.

1385. Williams, J. G. "The Life, Work and Influence of J. C. Pepusch." Ph.D. diss., U. of York, 1976.

See also discussions of the opera in Hogarth (#428) and Aldrich (#425).

Giovanni Battista Pergolesi (1710–1736)

Editions

1386. Pergolesi, Giovanni Battista. *Complete Works = Opere complete*. Ed. Barry S. Brook, Francesco Degrada, and Helmut Hucke. Stuyvesant, N.Y.: Pendragon, 1986–. M3 .P475.

Two of the operas have appeared: *Adriano in Siria* and *Livietta e Tracollo*. For information on this and other Pergolesi editions, see Paymer (#1389), 19ff.

Thematic Catalogues and Worklists

1387. Paymer, Marvin E. *Giovanni Battista Pergolesi, 1710–1736: A Thematic Catalogue of the "Opera omnia" with an Appendix Listing Omitted Compositions*. Thematic Catalogues, 1. New York: Pendragon, 1977. 99p. ISBN 0-918728-01-0. ML134 .P613 A35.

An important contribution, which disposes of most of the works that had been attributed to Pergolesi: only 30 of the 148 compositions in the 1939–1943 collected edition are authentic. The new edition (#1386) will remedy these errors. With musical incipits and an index locator to help find them.

1388. Hucke, Helmut. "Pergolesi: Probleme eines Werkverzeichnisses." *AM* 52-2 (1980): 195–225.

A useful study of sources involved in preparing an authentic worklist, with references to earlier literature in 239 footnotes. Hucke is one of the editors of the new complete edition.

Bibliographies and Guides to Resources

1389. Paymer, Marvin E., and Hermine W. Williams. *Giovanni Battista Pergolesi: A Guide to Research*. Garland Composer Resource Manuals, 26. New York: Garland, 1989. xvi, 190p. ISBN 0-8240-4595-5. ML134 .P613 P6.

A valuable information source on the composer, featuring 489 annotated entries (61 on the operas) that cover the literature. Also a worklist, inventory of editions, and a biographical summary. Author and title indexes.

1390. Schlefer, James R. "Inventory of Sources for the Music of Giovanni Battista Pergolesi in Catalogues of Libraries, Private Collections, and Exhibitons." 1985. (Typescript.)

A survey prepared for the Pergolesi Research Center, City U. of New York, and available there. Described in Paymer (#1389), item 114.

Conferences

1391. *G. B. Pergolesi (1710–1736): Note e documenti raccolti in occasione della settimana celebrativa (15–20 settembre 1942)*. Ed. Sebastiano Arturo Luciani. Siena: Ticci, for the Accademia Musicale Chigiana, 1942. 102p. ML390 .S56.

Thirteen papers are separately described in Paymer (#1389), item 89.

1392. *Pergolesi Studies = Studi pergolesiani. Proceedings of the International Symposium*. Stuyvesant, N.Y.: Pendragon, 1986. 2v. ISBN 0-918728-79-7. ML410 .P29 P47.

One volume on each of the two conferences, Jesi (Italy), 1983, and New York, 1986. Contents available through Paymer (#1389), item 88. One paper is entered at #1397.

Collections of Essays

1393. *Il caso Pergolesi*. Ed. Barry S. Brook and Marvin Paymer. Bergamo: Bolis, 1985. 189p.

Not seen. Eight essays are described in Paymer (#1389), item 87.

1394. *Pergolesi*. Ed. Francesco Degrada et al. Naples: Sergio Città, 1986. 237p. No ISBN. ML410 .P44 P83.

A collection issued to observe the 250th anniversary of Pergolesi's death. Most of the essays are about biographical and background matters. Excellent photographs of cities, theaters, and other sites relevant to the composer. Bibliography of about 150 entries, worklist, no index.

Biographies

1395. Radiciotti, Giuseppe. *Giovanni Battista Pergolesi*. Milan: Fratelli Treves, 1935. 300p. ML410 .P43 R123.

First edition, 1910. A German translation: *Giovanni Battista Pergolesi: Leben und Werk* (trans., enlarged, and rev. Antoine E. Cherbuliez [Zurich: Pan, 1954]). A scholarly life and works, with program notes on the operas. Footnotes, worklist, bibliography of about 250 titles, name index.

Individual Works

L'Olimpiade

IO–1640, v.34.

La serva padrona

1396. Folena, Gianfranco. *Il linguaggio della "Serva padrona."* In Muraro (#2576), v.2, 1–20.

Librettist Gennaro Federico used a colloquial Italian text in his earlier *Lo frate 'nnamorato,* but he did not write dialect in *La serva padrona.* Nevertheless, he was able to delineate the fairly complex character of Serpina through nuances of linguistic idiom, which Pergolesi matched with musical inventiveness.

1397. Piperno, Franco. "Gli interpreti buffi di Pergolesi: Note sulla diffusione de *La serva padrona.*" In *Pergolesi Studies* (#1392), 166–177.

Describes productions of 1733 and 1752 and lists 61 other performances with casts and other facts about them.

Jacopo Peri (1561–1633)

1398. Peri, Jacopo. *Euridice.* Ed. Howard Mayer Brown. Madison, Wisc.: A-R Editions, 1981. ISBN 0-89579-137-4. M2 .R29 v.36–37.

The vocal score of *Euridice* (1600), the earliest opera for which music has survived. The editor has added a preface, critical comments, and notes on prior writings.

1399. Brown, Howard Mayer. "How Opera Began: An Introduction to Jacopo Peri's *Euridice* (1600)." In *The Late Italian Renaissance,* ed. Eric Cochrane, 401–443 (New York: Harper & Row, 1970). Reprint, *GL,* v.11.

A useful review of ideas held by Italian musicians in the 16th century regarding Greek music. Many believed that contemporary music should be modeled on the Greek in order to achieve the expressive quality that Greek music apparently had. Brown's discussion centers on the Camerata, a group active in Florence in the 1570s to 1590s. Music written by Camerata members before 1600 had no special "effective expression"—it was typical courtly entertainment. But with *Euridice* there were new techniques for expressing emotion: "dissonance treatment, sudden shifts of harmony, so-called forbidden music intervals, ametrical rhythms, striking juxtapositions—purely formal and highly emotional scenes, and control of musical shape and phrase length." These devices were best suited to the portrayal of sadness and grief. Peri was less successful in depicting happy feelings.

1400. Palisca, Claude. "Aria in Early Opera." In *Festa musicologica: Essays in Honor of George J. Buelow,* 257–270 (Stuyvesant, N.Y.: Pendragon, 1995; ML55 .B84).

The prologue to Peri's *Euridice* is not a recitative, according to the definition in Peri's preface. It is an aria in the "16th-century sense: a melodic formula for singing stanzas adhering to a constant poetic form." Palisca calls it an "archaic aria." Other nonrecitative numbers include strophic songs that "later in the 17th century might have been called arias" and madrigal. Such genres are neither recitative nor arias as we think of those forms.

1401. Carter, Tim. "Jacopo Peri (1561–1633): His Life and Works." Ph.D. diss., U. of Birmingham, 1980.

1402. Carter, Tim. "Jacopo Peri." *M&L* 61 (1980): 121–135.

Much information is packed into this article, based on the author's dissertation. Peri's life and his changing fortunes are described, with the genesis of *Euridice* (which was not a success). With 66 footnotes to the earlier literature.

1403. Carter, Tim. "Jacopo Peri's *Euridice* (1600): A Contextual Study." *MR* 43 (1982): 83–103.

The opera is "far more carefully composed than is commonly assumed" and has many links with the 16th century. Peri drew on many sources for the recitative: improvisatory practices, madrigal techniques, a smattering of Greek theory, and ideas of the Camerata.

1404. Sonneck, Oscar G. T. "*Dafne*, the First Opera: A Chronological Study." *SIMG* 15 (1913–1914): 102–110.

Caccini is not mentioned in Rinuccini's dedicatory preface, and Caccini does not allude to *Dafne* in his writings. Nor do other writers connect Caccini with *Dafne*. Sonneck thinks that Peri composed the music for the 1600 and 1604 performances. He doubts that any Caccini music for *Dafne* was performed anywhere before 1602. The only musical setting preserved is by Jacopo Corsi.

1405. Sternfeld, Frederick W. "The First Printed Opera Libretto." *M&L* 59 (1978): 121–138.

It is *Dafne* (1598), by Peri and Rinuccini. Sternfeld describes the manuscript and three printed libretti; one, newly discovered in the New York Public Library, appears to be the earliest (for the 1598 performance).

See also material on the Camerata and early Florentine opera, at #2439ff. Peri's foreword to the printed *Euridice* is in *Strunk*.

Emile Pessard (1843–1917)

See Sansone (#1109).

Hans Erich Pfitzner (1869–1949)

1406. Toller, Owen. *Pfitzner's "Palestrina": The "Musical Legend" and Its Background.* [London ?]: Toccata Press, 1997. ISBN 0-907689-248. ML410 .P48 T65.

Genesis, scene-by-scene program notes with technical observations. Footnotes, bibliography of about 50 items, name and topic index.

1407. Lee, M. Owen. "Pfitzner's *Palestrina* : A Musical Legend." *OQ* 4-1/2 (Spring 1986): 54–60.

The composer called his opera a "musical legend." It "deals freely with historical facts" but is "fundamentally true." Program note, some reception—the opera "has not won the public."

1408. Williamson, John. *The Music of Hans Pfitzner.* New York: Oxford U.P., 1992. xiv, 382p. ISBN 0-19-816160-3. ML410 .P32 W5.

Life and works, with letters. Chapter 5 on *Palestrina* (p.126–205) has genesis, synopsis, and musical analysis (motifs, dissonance treatment, key associations). Worklist, notes, bibliography of some 200 items, expansive index of names and titles.

1409. *Symposium Hans Pfitzner, Berlin 1981.* Ed. Wolfgang Osthoff. Tutzing: Schneider, 1984. 243p. ISBN 3-7952-0434-8. ML410 .P48 S98.

Two of the essays are about the opera: Benrhard Adamy, "Das *Palestrina*—Textbuch als Dichtung," and Stefan Kunze, "Zeitschichten in Pfitzners *Palestrina*" (a technical analysis).

See also Franklin (#412).

François André Danican Philidor (1726–1795)

In *FO*: *Tom Jones*, v.53; *Blaise le savetier*, v.54; *Le sorcier*, v.54; and *Ernelinde*, v.56.

1410. Carroll, C. M. "François André Philidor: His Life and Dramatic Art." Ph.D. diss., Florida State U., 1960. 2v.

Niccolò Piccinni (1728–1800)

Atys is in *FO*, v.65.

1411. Cametti, Alberto. "Saggio cronologico delle opere teatrali (1754–1794) di Nicolò Piccinni." *RMI* 8 (1901): 75–100.

A useful review of all source material on Piccinni, with locations of manuscripts and modern editions; 139 bibliographic entries in date order.

1412. Rushton, Julian. "Theory and Practice of Piccinnisme." *PRMA* 98 (1971–1972): 31–46.

Both Piccinni and Gluck attempted to depart from the old French style but to keep freedom of structure with "Italianate" music. Piccinni's French operas are as dramatic as Gluck's. He preferred regular meter, while Gluck used varied tempi to show conflicts in aria situations. Piccinni was something of a "Gluckiste." "Piccinisme" was "a trend, an atmosphere"—not a school. It lacked a composer of substance.

1413. Liggett, Margaret M. "A Biography of Niccolò Piccinni and a Critical Study of His *La Didone* and *Didon*." Ph.D. diss., Washington U. of St. Louis, 1977. 437p.

1414. Holmes, William C. "Pamela Transformed." *MQ* 38 (1952): 581–594.

Samuel Richardson's novel *Pamela* (1740) was translated into Italian in 1744 and made into a play by Goldoni as *Pamela nubile* (1750). In 1756 Goldoni turned the play into a libretto as *La buona figliola*, and it was set to music by Egidio Duni in 1757. That effort was not notable, but when Piccinni took the same text in 1760 he achieved fantastic success. *La Cecchina (La buona figliola)* was "the most popular *opera buffa* of the 18th century." In 1767 it was the first Italian opera performed in English in Britain, at Covent Garden. [It was also the first opera staged in Africa and in Asia.] Holmes notes the changes in story and character through the various versions.

1415. Schmierer, Elisabeth. "Piccinni's *Iphigénie en Tauride*: '*chant périodique*' and Dream Structure." *COJ* 4-2 (July 1992): 91–118.

Piccinni's arias represent the form ideal of his time, referred to as *chant périodique*. He was more concerned with "the shape of an entire aria" than with strictly musical procedures. Schmierer compares a scene from this opera with the parallel scene in Gluck's setting. The two operas were the focus of the *querelle* (see #2257ff. and Rushton, #904). Another comparison of the Gluck-Piccinni versions is in Francesco Degrada, "Due volti di Ifigenia," *Chigiana* 32 (1975): 165–233.

1416. Allroggen, Gerhard. "Piccinnis *Origille*." *Analecta musicologica* 15 (1975): 258–297.

A long synopsis of the comic opera, premiered at the Teatro Nuovo, Naples, in 1740. Technical observations on aria form, orchestral music, and key relations, with extended musical examples.

See also Henze-Döhring (#1307).

Ildebrando Pizzetti (1880–1968)

1417. Pizzetti, Bruno. *Ildebrando Pizzetti: Cronologia e bibliografia*. Parma: La Pilotta, 1980. 531p. No ISBN. ML410 .P7 P7.

A detailed life chronology, with a thorough worklist. References to reviews of performances and other notices. Name index.

1418. Gatti, Guido Maria. *Ildebrando Pizzetti*. Trans. David Moore. London: D. Dobson, 1951. 124p. ML410 .P7 G2.

First Italian edition, 1934; second edition (Turin: Parovia, 1955). A life and works, with p.15–61 on the operas. Genesis and program notes, with some technical comments and musical examples. Worklist, bibliography, no index.

1419. Santi, Piero. "Il mondo della *Dèbora*." *Rassegna musicale* 32 (1962): 151–168.

Genesis of the opera *Dèbora e Jaéle,* with technical notes on the music.

Carlo Francesco Pollarolo (ca. 1653–1722)

1420. Termini, Olga Ascher. "Carlo Francesco Pollarolo: His Life, Time, and Music, with Emphasis on the Operas." Ph.D. diss., U. of Southern California, 1970. 728p.

1421. Termini, Olga Ascher. "Carlo Francesco Pollarolo: Follower or Leader in Venetian Opera?" *Studi musicali* 8 (1979): 233–272.

Late baroque Italian opera had a stylistic change, from Venetian to the Neapolitan tradition. The complete picture of the transition is missing because individual composers need to be studied. Pollarolo is among the neglected. Termini offers "a corrected biography and an overview of Pollarolo's operatic style." His music shows "pre-Neapolitan traits" in the late period: fewer but more elaborate arias and alternation between secco recitative and aria.

Nicola Antonio Porpora (1686–1768)

1422. Robinson, Michael F. "Porpora's Operas for London, 1733–1736." *Soundings* 2 (1971–1972): 57–87.

Sources, libretti, analysis, and comparisons with Handel. Porpora wrote "opera of the nobility."

1423. Walker, Frank. "Chronicle of the Life and Works of Nicola Porpora." *Italian Studies* 6 (1951): 29–62.

A well-documented summary of Porpora's life, then a critique of the sources and earlier secondary literature (much of it is unreliable). Despite the title, this article is a narrative, not a chronology. List of operas and librettists, including premiere information.

Giovanni Porta (1690?–1755)

Numitore is in *HS*, v.4.

Francis Poulenc (1899–1963)

1424. Keck, George Russell. *Francis Poulenc: A Bio-Bibliography*. Bio-Bibliographies in Music, 28. New York: Greenwood, 1990. xi, 304 p. ISBN 0-313-25562-8. ML134 .P87 K3.

Among the entries in this bibliography are about 50 citations to reviews and brief notices on the operas. Index.

1425. Daniel, Keith W. *Francis Poulenc: His Artistic Development and Musical Style*. Studies in Musicology, 52. Ann Arbor, Mich.: UMI Research, 1982. 390p. ISBN 0-8357-1284-2. ML410 .P787 D3.

A valuable life and works, with technical analysis of the compositions. One chapter (p.282–312) is about the stage works. Poorly reproduced musical examples are a problem. Chapter endnotes, important bibliography of some 800 titles, worklist, expansive general index.

1426. Kipling, Diane Yvonne. "Harmonic Organization in *Les mamelles de Tirésias* by Francis Poulenc." Ph.D. diss., McGill U., 1995. 239p.

Sergei Sergeevich Prokofiev (1891–1953)

Biographies

1427. Robinson, Harlow. *Sergei Prokofiev: A Biography*. New York: Viking, 1987. xiv, 573p. ISBN 0-670-80419-3. ML410 .P865 R55.

A useful life and works, well documented, with a worklist (titles in English only) and chronology. Program notes and reception for the operas, but there is not much about music here. Good bibliography of about 125 entries, expansive index of names, titles, and topics.

1428. Nestyev, Israel. *Prokofiev.* Trans. Florence Jonas; foreword by Nicolas Slonimsky. Stanford, Calif.: Stanford U.P., 1960. 528p. ML410 .P865 N4.

Originally in Russian (Moscow, 1957). A well-documented life story and program notes on the works. An anti-Western point of view is pervasive but does not bias the facts. Worklist in chronological order, with dates of premieres and publishers. Expansive name and title index.

1429. Prokofiev, Sergei Sergeevich. *Prokofiev by Prokofiev: A Composer's Memoir.* Ed. David H. Appel. Trans. Guy Daniels. Garden City, N.Y.: Doubleday, 1979. xii, 370p. ISBN 0-385-09960-6. ML410 .P865 A315.

Originally in Russian: *Avtobiografiia* (Moscow: Sov. Kompozitor, 1973). The English version of this youthful daily journal is considerably abridged. Notes, expansive index of names and titles.

Operas in General

1430. McAllister, Margaret. "The Operas of Sergei Prokofiev." Ph.D. diss., Cambridge U., 1970.

Individual Works

The Gambler (Igrok)

1431. Robinson, Harlow. "Dostoevsky and Opera: Prokofiev's *The Gambler.*" MQ 70 (1984): 96–108.

Considers the libretto in relation to the Dostoevsky novel. Prokofiev first discussed the idea in 1914 and had the orchestra score done by 1917, but the revolution interrupted plans and there was no performance until 1929 in Brussels. The libretto follows the source closely, but the concept of the story is treated in a "strongly satirical" way.

Maddalena

1432. Wierzbicki, James. "*Maddalena*: Prokofiev's Adolescent Opera." OQ 1-1 (Spring 1983): 17–35.

Written in 1911, the work was not performed until 1979 (on BBC radio) and not staged until 1981. In America it was first heard in St. Louis, 1982. The article covers genesis, program notes, and reception. Nine musical examples and some technical comments.

The Love for Three Oranges (Liubov k trem apelsinam)

ASO 133 (1990).

1433. Taruskin, Richard. "From Fairy Tale to Opera in Four Moves (Not So Simple)." In *Opera and the Enlightenment* (#91), 299–307.

The opera is an adaptation from Carlo Gozzi, but it can be traced to a Neapolitan collection of folk and fairy tales of 1634. The Gozzi revision of the old tale is described. Vsevold Meierkhol'd, theater director in St. Petersburg, made a play of it in 1914 and gave it to Prokofiev in 1918 as the composer was coming to America. Prokofiev set it for the Chicago Opera and conducted the premiere on 30 December 1921. The libretto is compared to Meierkhol'd's text.

War and Peace (Voina i mir)

1434. Volkov, Anatolii. *"Voina i mir" Prokof'eva*. Moscow: Muzyka, 1976. 135p.

The abstract reads: "A monograph based on manuscript materials which deals with the operatic heritage of the composer. Discusses some general problems of dramaturgy and musical form; considers the variants in the overall composition of the opera and the general meaning of the changes. The formal design of the music is examined."

1435. Brown, Malcolm Hamrick. "Prokofiev's *War and Peace*: A Chronicle." *MQ* 63 (1977): 297–326.

Genesis, which dates to 1935. The libretto was sketched in 1941 and the piano score completed in 1942. The composer's own description of revisions made up to 1943 is given. The work was a great success in 1946–1947, with 105 performances. Then government objections led to more changes in 1949–1950 and new success in 1953—but the composer died without hearing the last revised version.

Giacomo Puccini (1858–1924)

Thematic Catalogues and Worklists

1436. Hopkinson, Cecil. *A Bibliography of the Works of Giacomo Puccini, 1858– 1924*. New York: Broude Brothers, 1968. xvii, 77p. ML134 .P94 H7.

A valuable annotated worklist, showing variant editions. Appendixes give lists of extant manuscripts, dedicatees, performances at leading houses to 1965 (the Opéra-Comique is the winner, with 3,862 performances of his operas). Ricordi plate numbers as well as textual variants in *Madama Butterfly* are also included.

See also Scherr (#1487).

Bibliographies and Guides to Resources

1437. Fairtile, Linda B. *Giacomo Puccini: A Guide to Research*. Garland Composer Resource Manuals, 48. New York: Garland, 1999. ISBN 0-8153-2033-7. ML134 .P94 F35.

An indispensable handbook for Puccini studies, centered on a bibliography of 720 books, articles, dissertations, and conference papers. Detailed, critical annotations are provided, citing scholarly disagreements as well as connections. Arrangement is classified, bringing together writings on each opera and other topics. Contents of 30 collective volumes are listed, and Puccini institutions are described. The review of Puccini studies, 1884–1997 (p.21–31) is an excellent introduction to the field. Discography, videography, index of names (note: references in the index are to page numbers, not item numbers).

1438. Greenwald, Helen M. "Recent Puccini Research." *AM* 65 (1993): 23–50.

A useful guide to Puccini scholarship, presenting major writings in 10 categories. Disputes over the importance and value of the operas began as they were first appearing and have continued into a second century. Greenwald's authoritative commentary is not well supported by the bibliographical style of entry, which gives only initials instead of first names of authors and omits publishers from imprint data for books.

Conferences

1439. *Esotismo e colore locale nell'opera di Puccini. Atti del Primo Convegno Internazionale sull'Opera di Giacomo Puccini.* Ed. Jürgen Maehder. Pisa: Giardini, 1985.

The theme of exoticism is traced by 19 papers, not only about *Turandot* but also on *Manon Lescaut, Madama Butterfly,* and *La fanciulla del West.* Contents in Fairtile (#1437), item 669.

1440. Cancelled entry.

1441. *Giacomo Puccini: L'uomo, il musicista, il panorama europeo. Atti del Convegno Internationale di Studi . . . Lucca, 25–29 novembre 1994.* Ed. Gabriella Biagi Ravenni and Carolyn Gianturco. Lucca: Libreria Musicale Italiana, 1997. xii, 596p. ISBN 88-7096-166-4. ML410 .P97 C668.

Consists of 27 papers from the conference. Separate entries appear in this section for Julian Budden on leading motives (#1460), Helen Greenwald on rhythm (#1463), William Ashbrook on revisions of *Butterfly* (#1480), Suzanne Scherr on genesis of *Manon Lescaut* (#1486), Deborah Burton on Tristanisms in *Tosca* (#1494), Michele Bianchi on unity in *Il trittico* (#1497), Kii-Ming Lo on drafts of *Turandot* (#1504), and Harold Powers on tonal relations in *Turandot* (#1507). Other papers are listed in Fairtile (#1437), item 682.

Fairtile gives contents of many other conferences in her "Collective Volumes" chapter.

Collections of Essays

1442. *The Puccini Companion.* Ed. William Weaver and Simonetta Puccini. New York: Norton, 1994. 436p. ISBN 0-393-02930-1. ML410 .P89 W3.

Consists of 18 essays. These are entered separately in this section: William Weaver on the heroines (#1461), Arthur Groos on the genesis of *Butterfly* (#1481), Leonardo Pinzauti on *Il trittico* (#1500), and William Ashbrook on *La rondine* (#1489). Other papers are listed in Fairtile (#1437), item 677.
A number of other collections are listed, with contents, in Fairtile's chapter, "Collective Volumes." Included there are Puccini volumes of *ASO*, COH, and ENOG, as well as issues of *Quaderni pucciniani* (next entry).

Periodicals

1443. *Quaderni pucciniani,* v.1–, 1982–. Milan: Istituto di Studi Pucciniani, 1982–. Irregular. ML410 .P97Q33.

Four volumes have been seen: 1982, 1985, 1992, and 1996. Contents of all four are in Fairtile (#1437), items 664, 672, 676, and 681.

Letters and Documents

1444. Gara, Eugenio, with assistance of Mario Morini. *Carteggi pucciniani.* Milan: Ricordi, 1958. xxii, 744p. ML410 .P89 A3.

More than 900 letters from, to, and about Puccini; well annotated, sometimes censored. Without index.

1445. *Puccini: 276 lettere inedite: Il fondo dell'Accademia d'Arte a Montecatini Terme.* Ed. Giuseppe Pintorno. Milan: Nuove Edizioni, 1974. 223p. ML410 .P89 A36.

A collection of letters from 1899 to 1924, many of them short and without musical reference, but others with useful comments on opera publications and performances. Chronology, glossary of persons, name index.

1446. *Pucccini com'era.* Ed. Arnaldo Marchetti. Milan: Curci, 1973. 495p. ML410 .P89 A35.

A good selection of 473 letters, to and from, with commentary. Some facsimiles and other illustrations. Content is both musical and otherwise, including the first publication of three letters from Puccini's lover, Josephine von Stängel. Name index.

1447. *Letters of Giacomo Puccini: Mainly Connected with the Composition and Production of His Operas.* Rev. ed. Ed. Giuseppe Adami. Trans. Ena Makin. London: Harrap, 1974. 341p. ISBN 1-245-52422-3. ML410 .P89 A2.

Originally *Giacomo Puccini epistolario* (Milan: Mondadori, 1928). Adami was librettist for three of the operas, so many of these letters (those to Adami) concern genesis matters. A running commentary puts the missives into context, and the translator adds interesting footnotes. Index of addressees, general index.

Biographies

1448. Carner, Mosco. *Puccini: A Critical Biography.* 2nd ed. London: Duckworth, 1974. xvi, 520p. ISBN 0-7156-0795-2. ML410 .P89 C3.

First edition, 1958; this edition is really a somewhat augmented reprint. A further revised reprint was also issued: New York: Holmes & Meier, 1992. It is a respectable biography, with footnotes and quotations from the letters. Criticized by Fairtile and others for an armchair Freudian interpretation of certain operas. There are plots and program notes, with occasional technical observations. Bibliography of about 60 titles, name and title index.

1449. Casini, Claudio. *Giacomo Puccini.* Turin: UTET, 1978. xi, 595p. No ISBN. ML410 .P89 C339.

Primarily a life story, and a good one; well documented and thoughtful. Comments on the operas are sometimes original, but there is no technical analysis. Worklist (with casts of premieres), bibliography of about 150 items, index.

1450. Girardi, Michele. *Puccini: L'arte internationale di un musicista italiano.* Venice: Marsilio, 1995. 512p. ISBN 88-317-5818-7. ML410 .P97 G52.

An English translation, by William Ashbrook, has been announced. It is a routine biography but conveys interesting perceptions on the operas (genesis, structure, vocal writing, revisions). Strong worklist, bibliography, index.

1451. Greenfield, Howard. *Puccini*. New York: Putnam, 1980. 299p. ISBN 0-399-12551-5. ML410 .P89 C73.

A popular life story, drawn mostly from the letters (about 200 of them newly published) but without direct documentation. Includes comments on earlier biographies, none of which appears satisfactory to Greenfield. Bibliography of about 150 works. Index of names, theaters, and titles, partly expansive.

1452. Marchetti, Leopoldo. *Puccini nelle immagini*. Milan: Garzanti, 1949. 205p. No ISBN. ML88 .P9 M3.

A fine picture book, with photos of locations and performance materials, facsimiles of letters, pages from autograph scores of the operas, a family tree, and other images.

Operas in General

1453. Ashbrook, William. *The Operas of Puccini*. New York: Oxford U.P., 1968. xv, 269p. MT100 .P95 A8.

Program notes on all the operas, with footnotes and musical examples. Sources are discussed. Bibliography of about 60 entries, index of names and titles.

1454. Osborne, Charles. *The Complete Operas of Puccini*. New York: Atheneum, 1982. 279p. ISBN 0-689-1184-3. ML410 .P89 O8.

Genesis, program notes, and synopses, with 72 musical examples and a name index. Not without its odd opinions, such as "*Tosca* is popular with audiences not because of the quality of its music, but because its melodramatic plot is tautly constructed and its three leading roles give their interpreters ample opportunity to shine vocally."

1455. Greenwald, Helen M. "Dramatic Exposition and Musical Structure in Puccini's Operas." Ph.D. diss., City U. of New York, 1991. xxviii, 340p.

1456. Bögel, Hartweg. *Studien zur Instrumentation in den Opern Giacomo Puccinis*. Tübingen: H. G. Vogler, 1978. 245p. No ISBN. MT100 .P79 B6.

A valuable examination of Puccini's orchestration, considering many technical aspects. The means of achieving local color and atmosphere are well described. Sketches are checked for instrumental indications. Music examples, facsimiles, bibliography.

1457. Anders, Michael F. Musical and Dramatic Structure in the Finales of the Operas of Giacomo Puccini." Ph.D. diss., Ohio State U., 1997. xii, 232p.

1458. Celletti, Rodolfo. "Vocalità dell'opera pucciniana." In *Critica pucciniana*, 35–51 (Lucca: Comitato Nazionale per le Onoranze a Giacomo Puccini nel Cinquantanerario della Morte, 1976; ML 410 .P89 C934).

A useful technical analysis of the vocal writing, with consideration of French influences, delineations of melody types, and descriptions of writing for different voice types.

1459. Carner, Mosco. "The Exotic Element in Puccini." *MQ* 22-2 (January 1936): 45–67.

Examines *Butterfly, La fanciulla del West,* and *Turandot* to find the rhythmic, melodic, harmonic, and instrumental features that contribute to their exoticism.

1460. Budden, Julian. "La dissociazione del *Leitmotiv* nelle opere di Puccini." In *Giacomo Puccini* (#1441), 452–466.

In Puccini's hands the *Leitmotiv* is made flexible: "a prism that emits various colors in accord with the way it is placed, changing meaning along with the instrumentation; there is no time in his operatic style for long Wagnerian ruminations."

1461. Weaver, William. "Puccini's Manon and His Other Heroines." In *Puccini Companion* (#1442), 111–121.

Women in the Puccini stories are rather alike, given to exaggerated hopes and a poor grip on reality. They are only "superficially moral," and they die unredeemed. Turandot is an exceptional case—still standing at the end.

1462. Martino, Daniele A. *Catastrofe sentimentali: Puccini e la sindrome pucciniana.* Turin: Edizioni di Torino, 1993. 141p. ISBN 88-7063-185-0. ML410 .P97 M377.

Each opera is found to have a perfect blend of sentiments, conflicts, suffering, and catharsis: that is the syndrome. (Martino discovers the same combination in the works of other composers as well, so it might as well be the "opera syndrome.") He also looks for gender stereotyping and notes that the heroines are similar, except for Turandot, who is thus classed as "superwoman": "la donna inesistente." Backnotes, name and title index.

1463. Greenwald, Helen M. "Character Distinction and Rhythmic Differentiation in Puccini's Operas." In *Giacomo Puccini* (#1441), 495–515.

Rhythm and meter are dramatic and structural devices that "shape the parameters of scenes, delineate characters, and even express the cultural and psychological roots of the drama." This study focuses on the women. Their first entrances nearly all have "rhythmic punctuation." It gets complicated: in *Butterfly,* where Puccini "juxtaposes the anapest (typical of Japanese music) with other metric and formal configurations to define the respective sexual and psychological milieux of Cio-Cio San and Pinkerton." There is also attention to waltzes and other dances.

1464. Greenwald, Helen M. "Realism on the Opera Stage: Belasco, Puccini, and the California Sunset." In *Opera in Context* (#288), 279–296.

Introduction of electric lighting was a major factor in production, contributing to realism by clarifying time, place, and mood. Producer/playwright/director David Belasco (1853–1931), a pioneer of modern staging, was sensitive to lighting effects, and so was Puccini. They worked together on *La fanciulla del West*. Greenwald describes the results in that opera and lighting effects in other Puccini works. The relationship of such effects to tonality is explored.

1465. Santi, Piero. "Tempo e spazio ossia colore locale in *Bohème, Tosca,* e *Madama Butterfly.*" In *Esotismo* (#1439), 83–97.

How the composer deals with the passage of time: it is not a pattern but differs with each opera. The sense of time in the female characters is distorted in times of crisis.

1466. Ferrando, Enrico Maria, ed. *Tutti i libretti di Puccini*. Milan: Garzanti, 1984. 619p. No ISBN. ML49 .P75 F5.

All the final versions of the texts, with genesis of each, and information about the authors. There is a useful essay on Puccini's revisions. No index.

1467. Petrocchi, Giorgio. "L'opera di Giacomo Puccini nel giudizio della critica." *RMI* 45–1 (1941): 40–49.

Considers scholarly opinions on the operas, including the negative views of Fausto Torrefranca and Ildebrando Pizzetti [Joseph Kerman had not yet arrived on the scene] and more enlightened appraisals—many by non-Italians.

See also the useful discussion of Puccini, especially the early operas, in Nicolaisen (#2466).

Individual Works

La bohème

ASO 20 (1979), COH 1986, ENOG 14 (1982), Rororo (1981).

1468. Maisch, Walter. *Puccinis musikalische Formgebung, untersucht an der Oper "La bohème."* Neustadt: Schmidt, 1934. 90p. ML3995 .M23 P97.

This seems to be the earliest technical analysis of a Puccini score; it was originally the author's dissertation. Maisch devises an elaborate micro- and macro-analysis, taking a Lorenzian tonality approach (see #2002). Musical examples, diagrams, and footnotes but no bibliography or index.

1469. Maehder, Jürgen. "Paris-Bilder: Zur Transformation von Henry Murgers Roman in den Bohème-Opern Puccinis und Leoncavallos." *Jahrbuch der Opernforschung* 2 (1986): 109–176.

An Italian translation appeared in *NRMI* 24–3/4 (July-December 1990): 402–455. A detailed double-genesis, concentrating on the two libretti drawn from the same novel. Musical sketches and libretto drafts are discussed, with facsimiles.

1470. Goldin, Daniela. "Drammaturgia e linguaggio della *Bohème* di Puccini." In *La vera Fenice: Librettisti e libretti tra sette e ottocento*, 335–374 (Turin: Piccola Biblioteca Einaudi, 1985; ML2110 .G64).

Libretto genesis, explaining how Luigi Illica turned the text by Henry Murger into operatic material. The Leoncavallo version is compared to Puccini's. Poetic and syntactical elements are discussed.

1471. Atlas, Allan. "Mimi's Death: Mourning Puccini and Leoncavallo." *JM* 14–1 (Winter 1996): 52–78.

A comparison of the Puccini and Leoncavallo settings, based on dramatic theory, attempting to demonstrate why Puccini's version is more emotionally effective.

Edgar

1472. "Puccini giovane a Milano: L'opera *Edgar* e le composizioni giovanili."

Quaderni pucciniani 3–1 (1992).

Eight papers about *Edgar*, from a conference at La Scala, 2 February 1990. The opera premiered there 100 years earlier. Topics include genesis, libretto, the context of the times in Italy, and the act 4 prelude. Contents in Fairtile (#1437), item 676.

See also #2466.

La fanciulla del West (Girl of the Golden West)

ASO 165 (1995).

1473. Rinaldi, Mario. *Giacomo Puccini: "La fanciulla del West."* Guide musicali, 3. Milan: Istituto di Alta Cultura, 1943. 100p.

Not seen; information is from Fairtile (#1437). Cultural context, genesis, and program notes with some technical observations. Reception of the American and Italian premieres.

1474. Atlas, Allan W. "Belasco and Puccini: 'Old Dog Tray' and the Zuni Indians." *MR* 75–3 (Fall 1991): 362–397.

Looks for source of the aria in act 1, "Che faranno i vecchi miei," formerly misidentified as the American song "Old Dog Tray." The melody is actually drawn from a Zuni Indian sun dance.

1475. Atlas, Allan W. "'*Lontano-tornare-redenzione*': Verbal *Leitmotives* and Their Musical Resonance in Puccini's *La fanciulla del West*." *Studi musicali* 21–2 (1992): 359–398.

The three words quoted in the title of the article recur in the opera, acting as "verbal *leitmotives*." They function as themes in the reversal of character experienced by Minnie.

1476. Atlas, Allan W. "Multivalence, Ambiguity and Non-Ambiguity: Puccini and the Polemicists." *JRMA* 118–1 (1993): 73–93.

Takes up the currently popular analytic terms of "multivalence" and "ambiguity," showing (through examples from *Manon Lescaut* and *La fanciulla del West*) that the concepts are not necessarily linked. Operas may indeed have formal structure, which may be based on tonal relations.

1477. Dotto, Gabriele. "Opera Four Hands": Collaborative Alterations in Puccini's *Fanciulla*." *JAMS* 42 (March 1989): 604–624.

Arturo Toscanini conducted the world premiere at the Metropolitan Opera House in December 1910. His score has been located and found to contain alterations he made for the performance. Puccini accepted the changes, which appear in the published score. Dotto discusses the changes.

See also #1464.

Gianni Schicchi; see *Il trittico*

Madama Butterfly

ASO 56 (1983), *ENOG* 26 (1984).

1478. Smith, Julian. "A Metamorphic Tragedy." *PRMA* 106 (1979–1980): 105–114.

Reprinted in *ENOG* 26 (1984). Discusses the failure of the 1904 premiere and the subsequent changes made in three revisions. Finds that the character of Butterfly is much the same in all versions, but Pinkerton and his wife are considerably altered.

See also #1480.

1479. Berg, Karl Georg Maria. "Das Liebesduett aus *Madama Butterfly*: Überlegungen zur Szenendramaturgie bei Giacomo Puccini." *Musikforschung* 38–3 (July-September 1985): 183–194.

Seeks a large formal structure in the act 1 love duet, finding an arch (ABA), comparable to that of "Mi chiamano Mimì." Proposes that this form emphasizes the vulnerability of the two women.

1480. Ashbrook, William. "Reflections on the Revisions of *Madama Butterfly*." In *Giacomo Puccini* (#1441), 159–168.

A description of the revision made after the failed premiere—one that differs considerably in its conclusions from Smith's (#1478). Ashbrook finds that the changes "affected our perception of Cio-Cio San." Puccini eliminated a comic drinking song and many racial slurs, and in general "tightened up the score" in ways that emphasized Cio-Cio San as a tragic figure. Kate's role was reduced at the same time.

1481. Groos, Arthur. "Lieutenant F. B. Pinkerton: Problems in the Genesis and Performance of *Madam Butterfly*." In *Puccini Companion* (#1442), 169–201.

Discusses the four published versions of the opera in the light of the literary sources, focusing on the problematic character of Pinkerton.

1482. Groos, Arthur. "Return of the Native: Japan in *Madama Butterfly*; *Madama Butterfly* in Japan." *COJ* 1-2 (July 1989): 167–194.

Puccini's efforts to produce a Japanese atmosphere were affected by his theatrical wish for the exotic. In Japan, for which Groos gives a performance history, the opera is interpreted in various ways to present a more favorable picture of the national character.

1483. Groos, Arthur. "*Madama Butterfly*: The Story." *COJ* 3-2 (July 1991): 125–158.

Identifies the real-life naval officer, William B. Franklin, who was apparently the model for Pinkerton. Justifies Pinkerton's behavior to some extent by describing the Japanese practice of allowing foreign men to marry in the country on a temporary basis.

1484. Atlas, Allan W. "Crossed Stars and Crossed Tonal Areas in Puccini's *Madama Butterfly*." *19thCM* 14-2 (Fall 1990): 186–196.

An ingenious and unusual approach to tonal relations, in which certain keys have affirmative connotations for given characters and other keys have negative connotations for them. For example, G-flat major is affirmative for Butterfly ("Un bel di") but negative for Pinkerton. There is also a structural plan for the opera as a whole. Atlas and Roger Parker (*19thCM* 15-3 [Spring 1992]: 229–234) disagreed over these ideas.

1485. Ross, Peter. "Elaborazione leitmotivica e colore esotico in *Madama Butterfly*." In *Esotismo* (#1439), 81–110.

Discovers Wagnerian-type leading motives that evolve with the dramatic situation, and shows how Puccini varied them while preserving an exotic atmosphere.

See also Bögel (#1456).

Manon Lescaut

ASO 137 (1991).

1486. Scherr, Suzanne. "The Chronology of Composition in Puccini's *Manon Lescaut*." In *Giacomo Puccini* (#1441), 81–110.

Examines the full score autograph fair copy and finds moments "where Puccini struggled with the emerging new style which was to blossom more fully in *La bohème*." He was in transition "from a style based on the extended scene to the new temporal aesthetic." Genesis, important structural analysis, and an interesting evaluation of the composer: what distinguished him from his contemporaries was a "balance of intensities" and "dramatic pacing."

1487. Scherr, Suzanne. "Editing Puccini's Operas: The Case of *Manon Lescaut*." *AM* 62–1 (January–April 1990): 62–81.

A useful description of the manuscripts and published versions of the opera, which was Puccini's most revised work. Publishing practices of the G. Ricordi firm at the time also need to be considered in preparing any modern edition. A table of all known editions corrects and expands Hopkinson (#1436).

1488. Scherr, Suzanne. "Puccini's *Manon Lescaut*: Compositional Process, Stylistic Revision, and Editorial Problems." Ph.D. diss., U. of Chicago, 1993.

La rondine

1489. Ashbrook, William. "*La rondine*." In *Puccini Companion* (#1442), 244–264.

Genesis, and three revisions, carefully explored.

Suor Angelica; see *Il trittico*

Il tabarro; see *Il trittico*

Tosca

ASO 11 (1977), *COH* (1985), *ENOG* 16 (1982).

1490. Winterhoff, Hans-Jürgen. *Analytische Untersuchungen zu Puccinis "Tosca."* Kölner Beiträge zur Musikforschung, 72. Regensburg: Bosse, 1973. 136p. ISBN 3-7649-2088-2. ML410 .P89 W788.

A musical and dramatic analysis of the opera's structure and leading motives. Shows how the music distinguishes between the world of Scarpia and that of Tosca and Cavaradossi. Bibliography, no index.

1491. Nicasio, Susan Vandiver. *Tosca's Rome: The Play and the Opera in Historical Perspective*. Chicago: U. of Chicago Press, 1999. ca. 344p. ISBN 0-226-57971-9. Not seen.

1492. Burton, Deborah. "An Analysis of Puccini's *Tosca*: A Heuristic Approach to the Unifying Elements of the Opera." Ph.D. diss., U. of Michigan, 1995. 538p.

1493. Burton, Deborah. "The Real Scarpia: Historical Sources for *Tosca*." *OQ* 10-2 (Winter 1993–1994): 67–86.

Using contemporary sources, Burton describes the historical environment for the opera, including likely real-life models for the principal characters. There was indeed a performance of a *Te Deum* in Rome, in the period of the story, to celebrate the battle of Marengo (incorrectly reported, in life and in the opera, to have been a defeat for Napoleon).

1494. Burton, Deborah. "*Tristan, Tosca* (e Torchi)." In *Giacomo Puccini* (#1441), 127–145.

Notes several quotations from Wagner in the Puccini operas, some of them first observed by Luigi Torchi in a 1900 article. Goes on to explain how the *Tristan "Liebesruhe Motiv"* is the musical base on which *Tosca* is constructed. Identifies motives and their Wagnerian development into full structures.

1495. Schoffman, Nachum. "Puccini's *Tosca*: An Essay in Wagnerism." *MR* 53–4 (November 1992): 268–290.

A table of *Tosca's* 25 musical motives, showing all their appearances and their interrelationships. The author concludes that many are Wagnerian in concept and function.

1496. Atlas, Allan W. "Puccini's *Tosca*: A New Point of View." In *Studies in the History of Music 3: The Creative Process*, 247–273 (New York: Broude, 1992; ML1 .S899).

Another imaginative approach to macrostructure by Atlas (see #1484), finding tonal relations as the basis for the large design. Unfortunately for this analysis, and for so many like it, it runs into inconsistencies and disruptions of the plan. The author is therefore required to explain those departures as special instances of some kind: signs of emotional crisis, in this case.

Il trittico (= Il tabarro, Suor Angelica, and *Gianni Schicchi)*

ASO 82 (1985).

1497. Bianchi, Michele. "Il 'caso *Trittico*': Vitalità della morte e declino della vita."
In *Giacomo Puccini* (#1441), 214–229.

Earlier writers found nothing to unify the three works into a trilogy (although
Mosco Carner had suggested they were like the three books of the *Divina commedia*). Bianchi notes that the three plots are involved with a death that has
already occurred. Another common theme was one that obsessed Puccini: old
age and lost youth.

1498. Leukel, Jürgen. *Studien zu Puccinis "Il trittico."* Musikwissenschaftliche
Schriften, 18. Munich: Musikverlag Emil Katzbichler, 1983. 172p. ISBN 3-
87397-117-8. MT100 .P97 L5.

After a consideration of the one-act opera genre, turns to the genesis of *Il trittico,* with many quotes from Puccini's letters. Also a musical analysis. No
index. The book is based on the author's dissertation, Frankfurt U., 1980.

1499. Greenwald, Helen M. "Puccini, *Il tabarro,* and the Dilemma of Operatic
Transposition." *JAMS* 51–3 (Fall 1998): 521–558.

A landmark study that takes on "one of the most entangled and contentious
issues of opera analysis." Most evidence suggests that composers in the 19th
century normally transposed arias for the benefit of singers as needed, usually
down a half step. Some scholars think this practice showed indifference to
tonal relations and tonal macrostructure, but others believe that the composer
simply changed to an alternative plan, incorporating the alteration. Greenwald
cites all the relevant literature in her copious footnotes, which form a valuable
bibliographic essay. Her analysis of the opera from the tonal point of view is
elaborate and convincing. She concludes that the "study of tonal conduct
within an opera ought not, then, to be hamstrung by prescribed goals defined
only by structures frozen in a Classical aesthetic." With a "more sophisticated
view" of these matters, one can "explore with greater if still discreet confidence a musical justification for Puccini's alterations as well as those reforged
ideas of other opera composers."

1500. Pinzauti, Leonardo. "Giacomo Puccini's *Trittico* and the Twentieth Century."
In *Puccini Companion* (#1442), 228–243.

Finds the genesis of the opera to be involved with the deaths of publisher
Giulio Ricordi (1912) and Arrigo Boito (1918), leading to a sense of alienation
in the composer's outlook. That feeling, blended with the new modernism,
produced the style of the work.

1501. Greenwald, Helen M. "Verdi's Patriarch and Puccini's Matriarch: 'Through
the Looking Glass and What Puccini Found There.'" *19thCM* 17-3 (Spring
1994): 220–236.

Finds similarities of structure and symbolic relationships between a scene from
Verdi's *Don Carlos* (Philip II and the Grand Inquisitor) and *Suor Angelica.*

Parental anguish is combined with authoritarian anger in both cases. Musical examples and diagrams display the parallels in the scores.

Turandot

ASO 33 (1981), ENOG 27 (1984).

1502. Ashbrook, William, and Harold Powers. *Puccini's "Turandot": The End of the Great Tradition*. Princeton Studies in Opera. Princeton, N.J.: Princeton U.P., 1991. x, 193p. ISBN 0-691-09137-4. ML410 .P89 A7.

The tradition seen as coming to a close was Italian *melodramma*. A thorough technical analysis is offered, along with textual elements, a genesis account, and reception/performance history. This important book is the starting point for *Turandot* studies. Bibliography of about 100 entries, index.

1503. Maehder, Jürgen. "Studien zum Fragmentcharakter von Giacomo Puccinis *Turandot*." *Analecta musicologica* 22 (1984): 298–379.

Translated and reprinted in *Quaderni pucciniani* 2 (1985), *Esotismo* (#1439), and ENOG 27 (1984). A valuable, thorough examination of Franco Alfano's ending of the work occasioned by the death of Puccini (and Liu, in the opera). All the relevant sketches and letters by Puccini, the correspondence of Casa Ricordi, and Alfano's other compositions are studied. Then there is a detailed analysis of the Alfano completion, along with Arturo Toscanini's abridgment of it. Maehder takes a favorable view of Alfano's accomplishment. Facsimiles and musical examples.

1504. Lo, Kii-Ming. *"Turandot" auf der Opernbühne*. Perspektiven der Opernforschung, 2. Frankfurt: Peter Lang, 1996. 491p. ISBN 3-631-42578-3. ML1700 .P4 v.2.

An exhaustive review of the *Turandot* story in Chinese myth and a discussion of Chinese language and music as related to it. The European literary sources are described as well, along with music written for them; seven other operas on the tale are discussed. Genesis of the Puccini version includes some of his previously unpublished letters to librettist Renato Simoni and three versions of the libretto. Bibliography, no index. A shorter account is in the next entry.

1505. Lo, Kii-Ming. "Giacomo Puccini's *Turandot* in Two Acts: The Draft of the First Version of the Libretto." In *Giacomo Puccini* (#1441), 239–258.

The opera was planned to have three acts. The composer's first version of the libretto shows a long first act, but the final libretto shows it divided into two acts. By the end of 1921, Puccini had decided to make it three acts. Lo describes all the changes made to reach the final form of the opera and discusses Puccini's compositional methods. A letter by Puccini, dated 8 February 1921, includes the little verse "Bevi una tazza di caffè di notte! Vedrai, non dormi! E pensi a Turandotte!" That end-rhyme should have settled the vexing puzzle of how to pronounce the name of the opera, but it did not (see Casali, #1508).

1506. Korfmacher, Peter. *Exotismus in Giacomo Puccinis "Turandot."* Cologne: Dohr, 1993. 243p. ISBN 3-925366-13-4. ML410 .P97 K84.

A history of the myth and its manifestations in Europe, connected to a genesis of the opera. The emphasis is on explicating the exotic atmosphere of the score and of other scores at the time. Bibliography, index.

1507. Powers, Harold S. "Dal padre alla principessa: Riorientamento tonale nel finale primo della *Turandot*." In *Giacomo Puccini* (#1441), 259–280.

Comments on the Atlas-Parker controversy (#1484) about composer transpositions and their impact on tonal design. Powers disagrees with both of them but favors the view that the composer knew what he was doing. In *Turandot,* Puccini transposed the finale of act 1 from G major/E minor to G-flat major/E-flat minor. In doing so, he realigned one relationship and strengthened two others, making a stronger link to the enigma scene of the second act. He did not annul the role of the tonal design he had written originally but subordinated that design to another consideration, so that the finale to act 1 is still part of the tonal web but *in modo diverso*. The change was in no way casual. Later thoughts by Powers on the transposition issues are in #2475.

1508. Casali, Patrick Vincent. "The Pronunciation of *Turandot*: Puccini's Last Enigma." *OQ* 13-4 (Summer 1997): 77–92.

Why is the final "t" silent in all the early recordings? Rosa Raisa—who created the title role—clearly said in a 1962 interview that it had to be silent, claiming both Puccini and Toscanini had said so. Casali says Puccini's contemporaries all agreed on the silent "t." But in a 1961 Metropolitan performance and recording the "t" is sounded. It is also heard in later recordings and in German-language recordings of all periods. The essay offers a tabulation of the silent and sounded "t" in recorded performances. Puccini's verse (#1505) is not mentioned.

Le villi

1509. Budden, Julian. "The Genesis and Literary Source of Giacomo Puccini's First Opera." *COJ* 1-1 (March 1989): 79–85.

Offers a summary of the story on which the work seems to have been based, Alphonse Karr's story *Le Willis,* and presents a genesis account. Librettist Ferdinando Fontana made a one-act opera of it, and Puccini set it in accord with the paradigmatic Italian style of the time, more Germanic than melodic.

Daniel Purcell (1660–1717)

1510. Barstow, Robert Squire. "The Theatre Music of Daniel Purcell." Ph.D. diss., Ohio State U., 1968. 2v.

Daniel was the brother of Henry Purcell.

Henry Purcell (1659–1695)

Editions

1511. *The Works of Henry Purcell.* Ed. Margaret Laurie et al. London: Novello, 1959–1979. 32v. M3 .P98 1959.

Operas published: v.3, *Dido and Aeneas*; v.12, *The Fairy Queen*; v.19, *The Indian Queen* and *The Tempest*; v.26, *King Arthur*. These are revised versions of earlier publications, except for *Dido*, which was a new edition (1979). Each work has an introduction, list of sources, and notes to the score. *An Index to the Works of Henry Purcell as Published by the Purcell Society*, by Alan Smith, appeared in 1970.

Thematic Catalogues and Worklists

1512. Zimmerman, Franklin B. *Henry Purcell 1659–1695: An Analytical Catalogue of His Music*. London: Macmillan, 1963. xxiv, 575p. ML134 .P95 Z72.

Described by the compiler as "a fairly complete list of Purcell's complete works and their main sources." It has cross-references and an inventory of manuscripts and other sources. Musical incipits are given for all movements of the compositions.

Bibliographies and Guides to Research

1513. Zimmerman, Franklin B. *Henry Purcell: A Guide to Research*. Garland Composer Resource Manuals, 18. New York: Garland, 1989. xi, 333p. ISBN 0-8240-7786-5. ML134 .P95 Z55.

A valuable presentation of secondary literature on Purcell, annotated and arranged by the author with a classified list of topics. Also a worklist, long list of editions, and a substantial biographical sketch. Index of names, titles, and topics.

Conferences

1514. *Performing the Music of Henry Purcell*. Ed. Michael Burden. New York: Oxford U.P., 1996. xvii, 302p. ISBN 0-19-816442-4. ML410 .P93 P4.

Consists of 16 papers (7 of them on the operas), most of them from a 1993 conference at Oxford. The opera items are Michael Burden, "Purcell Debauch'd: The Dramatick Operas"; Richard Semmens, "Dancing and Dance Music in Purcell's Operas"; Andrew H. Walkling, "Performance and Political Allegory in Restoration England: What to Interpret and When"; Ruth-Eva Ronen, "Of Costume and Etiquette: Staging in the Time of Purcell"; Roger Savage, "Calling Up Genius: Purcell, Roger North, and Charlotte Butler"; Julia Muller and Frans Muller, "Purcell's *Dioclesian* on the Dorset Garden Stage"; and Lionel Sawkins, "*Trembleurs* and Cold People: How Should They Shiver?" A useful eight-page review of this collection, by Robert Shay, appeared in *Journal of Seventeenth-Century Music* 4–1 (1998).

Collections of Essays

1515. *Henry Purcell (1659–1695): Essays on His Music*. Ed. Imogen Holst. New York: Oxford U.P., 1959. 136p. ML410 .P98 .H76.

Nine essays by various authors. Two relate to the operas: Imogen Holst, "Purcell's Librettist, Nahum Tate," and Michael Tippett, "Our Sense of Continuity in English Drama and Music." Tippett observes that "failing an English opera composer as such, Purcell is all there is." He offers interesting Langerian observations on *Dido*.

1516. *The Purcell Companion.* Ed. Michael Burden. London: Faber & Faber, 1995. x, 504p. ISBN 0-931340-93-4. ML410 .P93 P86.

Eleven essays by various scholars.Three are on operatic matters: Edward A. Langhans, "The Theatrical Background"; Roger Savage, "The Theatre Music"; and Robert Savage, "Producing *Dido and Aeneas*: An Investigation into Sixteen Problems" (entered at #1524).

Biographies

1517. Keates, Jonathan. *Purcell: A Biography.* London: Chatto & Windus, 1995. x, 304p. Reprint, Boston: Northeastern U.P., 1996. ISBN (Northeastern) 1-55553-287-X. ML410 .P93 K4.

A personalized life story, with program notes on the operas. Backnotes, expansive index, no bibliography.

1518. Zimmerman, Franklin B. *Henry Purcell, 1659–1695: His Life and Times.* 2nd ed. Philadelphia: U. of Pennsylvania Press, 1983. xxxvi, 473p. ISBN 0-8122-7869-0. ML410 .P93 Z5.

First edition, 1969. The standard life and works, fully documented, well illustrated, with bibliography and index.

See also *New Grove North European* (#170).

Operas in General

1519. Moore, Robert Etheridge. *Henry Purcell and the Restoration Theatre.* London: Heinemann, 1961. xv, 223p. Reprint, Westport, Conn.: Greenwood, 1974. ISBN (Greenwood) 0-8371-7155-5. ML410 .P93 M6.

A documented account of the stage works in program-note style, with musical examples. No bibliography. Name, title, and topic index.

1520. Price, Curtis. *Henry Purcell and the London Stage.* London: Cambridge U.P., 1984. 380p. ISBN 0-521-23831-5. ML410 .P93 P7.

A scholarly, analytic work, with good documentation and musical examples. Considers the sources and music for more than 50 plays as well as the operas and gives a comprehensive picture of the London theatrical milieu. Bibliography of about 150 modern writings, index.

1521. Squire, W. Barclay. "Purcell's Dramatic Music." *SIMG* 5 (1903–1904): 489–564.

A valuable gathering of data on 54 plays to which Purcell contributed vocal or instrumental music. Sources of each, their dates according to various scholars, and what is known of the musical numbers.

1522. Radice, Mark A. "Theater Architecture at the Time of Henry Purcell and Its Influence on His 'Dramatick Operas.'" In *Opera in Context* (#288), 73–94.

London's only "opera house" in Purcell's time was the Dorset Garden Theatre. His stage works of the 1690s were given there. Its architecture and elaborate machinery are described and illustrated.

Individual Works

Dido and Aeneas

ASO 18 (1978).

1523. Harris, Ellen T. *Henry Purcell's "Dido and Aeneas."* New York: Oxford U.P., 1987. xii, 184p. ISBN 0-19-315253-3. ML410 .P93 H3.

An account of the research undertaken by Harris as she prepared a revision of the score (published by Oxford U.P. in 1988). Considers the sources, libretto and its literary tradition, editions, reception, and performance history. Technical analysis includes studies of declamation and the ground bass. Useful bibliography of primary and secondary sources, index.

1524. Savage, Roger. "Producing *Dido and Aeneas.*" *Early Music* 4 (1976): 393–406.

Reprinted in 1516 and 1525. Reviews modern ideas on staging the work and considers "16 problems" to be solved in the process, such as choice of edition, decor, "who dances what?" and even "Is Dido a virgin queen at the start and when does intimacy take place?" The essay is reprinted in the next item.

1525. Purcell, Henry. *Dido and Aeneas.* Ed. Curtis Price. Norton Critical Score Series. New York: Norton, 1986. 277p. ISBN 0-393-02407-5. M1500 .P98 D76.

A reprint of the old Purcell Society score (1878) with a critical edition of the original libretto (of which only one copy is known to exist). Valuable background essay by Price, covering the allegory and sources, and an account of early performances, by Margaret Laurie. Some contributions by George Bernard Shaw are included, as well as material by Andrew Porter, Jack Westrup, Robert E. Moore, Edward Dent, and Roger Savage (his #1524 reprinted). No index or bibliography.

Dioclesian

1526. Muller, Julia. *Words and Music in Henry Purcell's First Semi-Opera, "Dioclesian": An Approach to Early Music through Early Theatre.* Studies in the History and Interpretation of Music, 28. Lewiston, N.Y.: E. Mellen, 1990. viii, 507p. ISBN 0-88946-495.2. ML410 .P93 M8.

Bibliographic description of sources, provenance of the play and opera, line-by-line study of the text, scenes and machines, productions. The libretto (1690) was adapted by Thomas Betterton from a play of the same name by John Fletcher and Philip Massinger. Good bibliography of about 400 items, no index.

The Fairy Queen

1527. Mandinian, Edward. *Purcell's "The Fairy Queen" as Presented by the Sadler's Wells Ballet and the Covent Garden Opera: A Photographic Record with the Preface to the Original Text, and a Preface by E. J. Dent, and Articles by Constant Lambert and Michael Ayrton.* London: Lehmann, 1948. 96p. PR3671 .S6 A6448 M3.

The title speaks for itself. No index.

1528. Savage, Roger. "The Shakespeare-Purcell Fairy Queen: A Defense and Recommendation." *Early Music* 1 (1973): 200–221.

The opera is based on Shakespeare's *A Midsummer Night's Dream*. Weber's *Oberon* followed the same play, and Savage compares the two approaches. He also gives useful suggestions for performing the Purcell work, holding to the style of Purcell's time.

King Arthur

ASO 163 (1995).

1529. Charleton, David. "*King Arthur*: A Dramatick Opera." *M&L* 64 (1983): 183–192.

A close analysis of text and music, with a study of the sources.

Sergei Vasil'evich Rachmaninoff (1873–1943)

1530. Palmieri, Robert. *Sergei Vasil'evich Rachmaninoff: A Guide to Research*. Garland Composer Resource Manuals, 3. New York: Garland, 1985. xvii, 335p. ISBN 0-8240-8996-0. ML134 .R12 P3.

An outstanding handbook, including 375 annotated entries for the literature (in Russian as well as the usual languages) for the secondary literature. Also a worklist, an inventory of the Rachmaninoff performing repertoire, 12 illustrations, and indexes of authors, names, subjects, and titles. Titles of works cited are in Russian (Library of Congress transliteration) and English. The only completed operas are *Aleko* (1893), *The Miserly Knight* (1906), and *Francesca da Rimini* (1906). The literature about them is nearly all in Russian, summarized in Palmieri's entries. One English book has some coverage of the operas:

1531. Norris, Geoffrey. *Rakhmaninov*. London: Dent, 1976. 211p. ISBN 0-460-03134-7. ML410 .R12 N67.

A documented life and works, with worklist, chronology, bibliography, and name index. Some discussion of the operas. Norris also wrote a short article in program-note style about *Aleko*, "Rakhmaninov's Student Opera," *MQ* 59 (July 1973): 441–448.

1532. Martyn, Barrie. *Rachmaninoff: Composer, Pianist, Conductor*. Aldershot (England): Scolar, 1990. 584p. ISBN 0-85967-809-1. ML410 .R12 M17.

The principal life and works in English, based on archival Russian materials. *Aleko* has program notes, p.57–64. Chapter endnotes, token bibliography, name and title index.

Pietro Raimondi (1786–1853)

Il ventaglio is in *IO–1810*, v.40.

Jean-Philippe Rameau (1683–1764)

Editions

1533. *Jean-Philippe Rameau. Opera omnia.* Ed. director Sylvie Bouissou. Paris: G. Billaudot, 1996–. M3 .R171.

In progress; projected 44v. Series 4 will include all the dramatic works in 31v. Published: *Les surprises de l'amour* (1996), *Achante et Céphise* (1998), and *Zoroastre* (1998). Each volume has a scholarly introduction in French and English, with discussion of editorial variants, sketches, versions, cuts, and textual matters. When possible, each edition is based on a source of the first performance.

1534. *Jean-Philippe Rameau: Oeuvres complètes.* Paris: Durand, 1895–1924. Reprint, New York: Broude, 1968. 18v. in 20. M3 .R25 B754.

All the stage works included. Each volume has extensive commentaries in French, including production statistics as well as editorial issues.

Bibliographies and Guides to Research

1535. Foster, Donald. *Jean-Philippe Rameau: A Guide to Research.* Garland Composer Resource Manuals, 20. New York: Garland, 1989. xii, 292p. ISBN 0-8240-5645-0. ML134 .R14 F7.

A valuable annotated bibliography of 711 entries, with a useful background essay on Rameau research. Material on the Rameau revival is grouped separately. Indexes of names, authors, and titles.

Conferences

1536. *Jean-Philippe Rameau: Colloque International Organisé par la Société Rameau, Dijon, 21–24 septembre 1983: Actes.* Ed. Jérome de La Gorce. Paris: Champion, 1987. 605p. ISBN 2-85203-029-2. ML410 .R2 J43.

Consists of 42 papers from the conference. Contents are in Foster (#1535), item 701. Neal Zaslaw on the operatic apprenticeship is entered here at #1540. Other operatic essays include Jacques Morel, "*Hippolyte et Aricie* de Rameau et Pellegrin dans l'histoire du mythe de Phèdre"; Jacques van den Heuvel, "*Platée,* opéra-bouffe de Rameau au milieu du XVIIIe siècle"; Nicholas McGegan and Gina Spagnoli, "Singing Style at the Opéra in the Rameau Period"; Christian Berger, "Ein *tableau* des *Principe de l'harmonie*: *Pygmalion* von Jean-Philippe Rameau"; and Nathalie Lecomte, "Les divertissements dans les opéras de Rameau."

Collections of Essays

1537. Beaussant, Philippe, ed. *Rameau de A à Z.* Paris: Fayard, 1983. 399p. ISBN 2-21301-277-6. ML410 .R2 R35.

Information in dictionary arrangement about the composer and his works, prepared by 23 authors. Entries include names of persons, places, characters in the operas, titles of musical and theoretical works, terms, and instruments. Each opera has an entry, some of them extensive (*Dardanus* has 4½ pages). Opera worklist (giving 18th-century performances), bibliography of about 150 titles.

Biographies

1538. Girdlestone, Cuthbert. *Jean-Philippe Rameau: His Life and Work*. 2nd ed. London: Cassell, 1969. 631p. ML410 .R17 G5.

First edition, 1957. Remains the standard full-scale biography, covering life and all the works, with extensive comparisons to Gluck and Lully. Well documented, with bibliography of some 200 titles, indexing by names, subjects, and titles. Some addenda were incorporated into the author's French translation (Paris: Desclée de Brouwer, 1983). Girdlestone also wrote the Rameau articles for *NG* and *MGG*.

See also *New Grove French Baroque* (#2227).

Operas in General

1539. Dill, Charles. *Monstrous Opera: Rameau and the Tragic Tradition*. Princeton, N.J.: Princeton U. Press, 1998. xx, 197p. ISBN 0-691-044443-0. ML410 .R2 D57.

Tries to identify the "complex relationship between works, composer, and audience." The result is a genesis study, with technical notes, comments on dramatic conditions, and notices of critical opinion by contemporaries. Backnotes, good bibliography of sources, expansive index.

1540. Zaslaw, Neal. "Rameau's Operatic Apprenticeship: The First Fifty Years." In *Jean-Philippe Rameau* (#1536), 23–50.

A gathering of information from archival documents, contemporary notices, Rameau's own writings, and secondary sources, with indications of reliability for each source. The article is a valuable "preliminary outline for a documentary biography." This period of the composer's life, during which he absorbed dramatic music in Paris and began his own career there, has not been carefully studied.

1541. Masson, Paul-Marie. *L'opéra de Rameau*. Paris: H. Laurens, 1930. 594p. Reprint, New York: Da Capo, 1972. ISBN 0-306-70262-2. ML410 .R17 M41.

One of the classic music biographies, still valuable after 70 years. Considers life and works, with footnotes, musical examples, and technical analyses of *l'expression dramatique et ses moyens*. The transition period from Lully to Rameau is carefully explored, then all the stage types, Rameau's libretti, arias, ensembles, and dances. Bibliography of about 250 books, worklist with manuscript locations, name index.

1542. Ahnell, Emil G. "The Concept of Tonality in the Operas of Jean-Philippe Rameau." Ph.D. diss., U. of Illinois, 1957. 269p.

1543. Brundrett, Grant A. "Rameau's Orchestration." Ph.D. diss., Northwestern U., 1962. 496p.

1544. Sadler, Graham. "Rameau and the Orchestra." *PRMA* 108 (1981–1982): 47–68.

A useful account of the composer's instrumentation practice and the orchestral forces employed at the Paris Opéra in his time. Each instrumental group is discussed separately.

Individual Works

Les Boréades

1545. Bouissou, Sylvie. "*Les Boréades* de J.-Ph. Rameau: Un passé retrouvé." *RdM* 69 (1983): 157–185.

Using manuscript evidence, the author establishes the work's completion date as 1763, a year earlier than had been supposed. It was rehearsed but not staged in Rameau's lifetime. Cast, chorus, and orchestra are reconstructed from the manuscript lists of performers. The article was followed by a full-scale study in the author's dissertation, "Jean-Philippe Rameau: *Les Boréades*" (U. of Paris, 1986).

1546. Térey-Smith, Mary. "Jean-Philippe Rameau: *Abaris* ou *Les Boréades*: A Critical Edition." Ph.D. diss., U. of Rochester, 1971. 2v.

Castor et Pollux

1547. Jullien, Adolphe. "Rameau: Ses débuts et son opéra *Castor et Pollux*." In *Musique: Mélanges d'histoire et de critique musicale et dramatique,* by Adolphe Jullien, 122–142 (Paris: Librairie de l'Art, 1896; ML270.1 .J94).

The performance and publication history of the opera. For a long period, Rameau's works were misunderstood and undervalued, and he suffered unfavorable comparisons to Lully.

1548. Dill, Charles. "The Reception of Rameau's *Castor et Pollux* in 1737 and 1754." Ph.D. diss., Princeton U., 1989. xi, 323p.

Dardanus

FO, v.40.

1549. Beaussant, Philippe. "*Dardanus*" *de Rameau*. Collection opéra. Paris: Albin Michel, 1980. 121p. ML410 R2 B35.

Historical background, genesis, program notes, and description of the early productions.

1550. Dacier, Émile. "L'opéra au XVIIIe siècle: Les premières représentations du *Dardanus* de Rameau (novembre–decembre 1739)." *Revue musicale* 3 (1903): 163–173.

A detailed reception study, quoting manuscript and printed sources. A performance list is included.

1551. Legrand, Raphaelle. "*Dardanus* de Jean-Philippe Rameau: La première version de 1739." Ph.D. diss., U. of Tours, 1991. 2v.

Les fêtes de Ramire

FO, v.4.

Les fêtes d'Hébé

FO, v.39.

1552. Cyr, Mary. "Rameau's *Les fêtes d'Hébé*." Ph.D. diss., U. of California, Berkeley, 1975. 2v.

Hippolyte et Aricie

1553. Graf, Georg. *Jean-Philippe Rameau in seiner Oper "Hippolyte et Aricie": Eine musikkritische Würdigung.* Wädenswil (Switzerland): Villiger, 1927. 170p. ML410 .R17 H7G7.

A publication of the author's dissertation, U. of Basel, 1927. Identified by Foster (#1535) as "the earliest book-length study of an opera by Rameau." It deals with the libretto and gives an analytical description of the music, number by number, with examples.

See also #1536.

Les Indes galantes

ASO 46 (1982); *Chefs,* v.34.

1554. Leclerc, Hélène. "*Les Indes galantes* (1735–1952): Les sources de l'opéra-ballet . . ." *Revue d'histoire du théâtre* 5 (1953): 259–285.

A description of the premiere and a reception study of the early productions; also an account of the Paris revival in 1952. Costumes and stage effects are described and illustrated from contemporary documents.

Les paladins

FO, v.44.

1555. Wolf, Robert Peter. "Jean-Philippe Rameau's *comédie lyrique* 'Les paladins' (1760): A Critical Edition and Study." Ph.D. diss., Yale U., 1977. 2v.

Pigmalion

FO, v.42. See also #1536.

Platée

FO, v.42; *Chefs,* v.35. See also #1536.

La princesse de Navarre

FO, v.41.

1556. Sawkins, Lionel. "Rameau's Last Years: Some Implications of Rediscovered Material at Bordeaux." *PRMA* 111 (1984–1985): 66–91.

Reports on a previously unknown score and parts of the opera, used in a Bordeaux performance in 1763. Collates all known sources and draws new conclusions about performance practice, Rameau's scoring, and dance numbers. Facsimiles, musical examples, tables.

Zoroastre

Chefs, v.36.

1557. Rice, Paul F. "Mid-Eighteenth Century Changes in French Opera: The Two Versions of Rameau's *Zoroastre.*" *Recherches sur la musique française classique* 21 (1983): 128–144.

A study based on the author's dissertation, U. of Victoria, 1981. Rice compares the 1749 and 1756 versions, finding that the latter has more *ariettes* and more segmentation of the text, leading to the future French opera style.

Maurice Ravel (1875–1937)

L'heure espagnole and *L'enfant et les sortilèges* are in *ASO* 127 (1990).

François Rebel (1701–1775)

Pirame et Thisbé and *Scanderberg,* both written with François Francoeur, are in *FO,* v.36.

Jean Féry Rebel (1666–1747)

Ulysse is in *FO,* v.22.

Johann Friedrich Reichardt (1752–1814)

Ino and *Die Geisterinsel* are in *GO,* v.4.

Luigi Ricci (1805–1859)

Chiara di Rosembergh is in *IO–1810,* v.42, and *Un'avventura di Scaramuccia* is in *IO-1810,* v.44.

Nicolai Rimsky-Korsakov (1844–1908)

1558. Seaman, Gerald R. *Nikolai Andreevich Rimsky-Korsakov: A Guide to Research.* Garland Composer Resource Manuals, 17. New York: Garland, 1988. xxxi, 377p. ISBN 0-8240-8466-7. ML134 .R57 S4.

An indispensable handbook, especially so for those not comfortable with Russian. Seaman's 1,305 annotated entries are mostly of Russian writings. Includes a worklist, with titles in Russian and English, and full information on performances, editions, and locations of sources. Indexes of authors, titles, and topics.

In the present guide, entries are limited to those in Western languages.

Biographies

1559. Rimsky-Korsakov, Nicolai. *My Musical Life.* Trans. Judah A. Joffe. New York: Knopf, 1924. xxiv, 389p. ML410 .R45 A3.

The complex history of publication and translation of this diary is set forth in Seaman (#1558), item 180. It is an important document for the study of Russian music as well as a fine resource on the genesis and circumstances of the composer's own works.

1560. Iastrebtsëv, Vasilii Vasil'evich. *Reminiscences of Rimsky-Korsakov.* Trans. and abridged by Florence Jonas. New York: Columbia U.P., 1985. xv, 578p. ISBN 0-2310-5260-X. ML410 .R45 I151.

Originally published in Russian (Petrograd, 1917) and in a revised, abbreviated edition (Moscow, 1959–1960); the latter was the basis for the English translation. Seaman describes the author as "A Russian Boswell," whose journal recorded his almost daily meetings with the composer, giving a "unique insight into Korsakov's life, his home environment, his compositions, their rehearsal and performance, and his creative plans." The English version has a foreword by Gerald Abraham and an index. In it the transliteration used is Vasily Yastrebtsëv.

See also *New Grove Russian Masters 2* (#2643).

Operas in General

1561. Gilse van der Pals, Nikolai. *N. A. Rimsky-Korsakow: Opernschaffe: Nebst Skizze über Leben und Werken.* Leipzig: W. Bessel, 1929. vii, 691p. Reprint, Hildesheim:Olms, 1977.

Genesis, libretto, and musical analysis of the 15 operas. Without bibliography or index.

1562. Griffiths, Steven. *A Critical Study of the Music of Rimsky-Korsakov, 1844–1890.* Outstanding Dissertations in Music from British Universities. New York: Garland, 1989. 432p. ISBN 0-8240-0197-4. ML410 .R55 G75.

A publication of the author's dissertation, U. of Sheffield, 1982. Most of the book is about instrumental works; only four operas were completed in the period studied. For those (*Maid of Pskov, May Night, Snowmaiden,* and *Mlada*) there are program notes, genesis accounts, and some literary/musical analysis. Brief bibliography, 118 pages of musical examples, no index.

Individual Works

Christmas Eve (Noch pered)

1563. Taylor, Philip. *Gogolian Interludes: Gogol's Story "Christmas Eve" as the Subject of the Operas by Tchaikovsky and Rimsky-Korsakov.* London: Collets, 1984. iv, 264p. ISBN 0-912483-22-9. PG3332 .N5 T39.

Both libretti are given in English, with the genesis of each opera. There is analysis of both works and an appendix giving contemporary documents and critical views.

The Golden Cockerel (Zolotoi petushok)

1564. Abraham, Gerald. "Satire and Symbolism in *The Golden Cockerel.*" *M&L* 52 (1971): 46–54.

Genesis, literary sources (which include Washington Irving), censorship and its impact, and an examination of the characters. Concludes there is political satire in the opera but no deeper symbolism.

See also Abraham in *Studies* (#2635).

The Invisible City of Kitezh (Skazanie o nevidimom gradie Kitezhie)

ASO 162 (1994), with *Sadko*.

See Abraham in *Studies* (#2635).

The Maid of Pskov (Pskovitianka)

1565. Abraham, Gerald. "*Pskovityanka:* The Original Version of Rimsky-Korsakov's First Opera." *MQ* 54 (January 1968): 58–73.

    The opera was drawn from a play by Lev Alexandrovich Mey; it was first composed as a song, then as an opera. Genesis and sketch plans composed for the early and final versions. Abraham finds the final version preferable.

See also Abraham, *Studies* (#2635), and Taruskin in *Russian and Soviet Music* (#2640).

May Night (Maiskia noch')

See Abraham, *Studies* (#2635).

Mlada

See Abraham, *On Russian Music* (#2636).

Mozart and Salieri (Motsart i Sal'eri)

See Taruskin, *Opera and Drama* (#2648).

Sadko

ASO 162 (1994), with *The Invisible City of Kitezh*.

The Snow Maiden (Snegurochka)

1566. Getteman, H. "*Sniegourotchka,* opéra de M. Rimsky-Korsakoff." *Revue musicale* 8 (1908): 137–143; 179–187; 213–216.

    Genesis, folk song sources, reception, and musical analysis. Also discussion of the libretto and of the differences between *Snow Maiden* and contemporary German music.

See also Abraham, *Studies* (#2635).

The Tale of Tsar Saltan (Skazka o Tsare Saltane)

See Abraham, *On Russian Music* (#2636).

The Tsar's Bride (Tsarskaia nevesta)

See Abraham, *Studies* (#2635).

Rinaldo di Capua (ca. 1705–ca. 1780)

1567. Gallico, Claudio. "Rinaldo da Capua, 'Zingara' o 'Bohémienne.'" In Muraro (#2576), v.1, 425–436.

Discusses various versions of *La zingara* (1753), which grew from two inter-mezzi of 1751. Sorts out three scores with the name *La bohémienne* and gives tabular comparisons of them with *La zingara*. [Rinaldo di Capua is the form of the composer's name given in most sources. It is also seen as Rinaldo da Capua.]

Luigi Rossi (1597–1653)

1568. Ghislanzoni, Alberto. *Luigi Rossi.* Milan: Bocca, 1954. 321p. ML410 .R832 G42.

A scholarly life story, with footnotes and documents. Useful thematic cata-logue of 388 works, including individual arias. Some musical examples but lit-tle actual discussion of the music. No bibliography or index.

See also Murata (#446) for a discussion of the opera *Il palazzo incantato*.

Michelangelo Rossi (ca. 1600–1656)

See Murata (#446) for a discussion of the opera *Erminia sul Giordano*.

Gioachino Antonio Rossini (1792–1868)

The name is also spelled Gioacchino. The considerable literature on Rossini lacks a bibliographic guide. One of the Garland Composer Resource Manuals, by Denise Gallo, is in preparation. Some of the entries below were derived from her draft mater-ial.

Editions

1569. Rossini, Gioachino. *Edizione critica delle opere di Gioachino Rossini.* Ed. Fondazione Rossini, Pesaro. Milan: Ricordi, 1979–. M3 .R67.

In progress. *Sezione 1: Opere teatrali* is projected for 42 volumes. For each opera there is a score and critical commentary by the editor, consisting of an inventory of sources and a measure-by-measure description with musical examples. Without extensive notes, bibliography, or index. Full contents are in the *Bollettino* 37 (1997).

Conferences

1570. *Gioachino Rossini, 1792–1992: Il testo e la scena. Convegno Internazionale di Studi, Pesaro, 25–28 giugno 1992.* Ed. Paolo Fabbri. Pesaro: Fondazione Rossini, 1994. xvi, 701p. No ISBN. ML410 .R8 G57.

Consists of 31 papers from the conference. They deal with Rossini's epoch, the contemporary stage, text and libretto, and Rossini in Paris. These are of partic-ular interest: Charles S. Brauner, "'No, no, Ninetta': Observations on Rossini and the Eighteenth-Century Vocabulary of *opera buffa*"; Marco Beghelli, "La retorica del melodramma: Rossini, Chiave di volta"; Sieghart Döhring, "Rossini nel giudizio del mondo tedesco"; Emilio Sala, "All ricerca della *Pie voleuse*" (sources for *La gazza ladra*); and M. Elizabeth Bartlet, "Staging French Grand Opera: Rossini's *Guillaume Tell*." Two essays are entered separately: Cesare Questa and Renato Raffaelli on *Otello* (#1591) and Janet Johnson on Rossini as theater director (#1575).

Periodicals

1570a. Centro Rossiniano de Studi. *Bollettino,* 1–, 1955–. Pesaro: Fondazione Rossini, 1955–. Irregular. ML5 .C42.

Biographies

1571. Radiciotti, Giuseppe. *Gioacchino Rossini: Vita documentata; opere ed influenza su l'arte*. Tivoli: Chicca, 1927–1929. 3v. ML410 .R8 R22.

A classic life and works, the basis for much of the later writing on Rossini. Fully documented, elegantly illustrated, with worklist, letters, and genesis studies for the operas. Extensive program notes but no technical analysis. The development of the composer's style is well delineated, along with an assessment of his place in music history. Bibliography, name index.

1572. Rognoni, Luigi. *Gioacchino Rossini*. 3rd ed. Turin: Einaudi, 1977. 559p. ML410 .R8 R73.

First edition, 1956. A valuable biography, with ample notes and musical examples. Program notes on the operas and a good study of the overtures. Worklist, compiled by Philip Gossett, gives premiere data, editions, and comments. The bibliography of some 300 titles is intended to supplement that of Radiciotti. Index of names, titles, and topics.

1573. Weinstock, Herbert. *Rossini: A Biography*. New York: Knopf; London: Oxford U.P., 1968. xviii, 560p. ML410 .R8 W35.

A footnoted account of the composer's life and times, with program notes for each opera. Includes the text of his will, the contract for *Il barbiere di Siviglia*, and other documents. Chronological worklist of the operas, with premiere information. Bibliography of about 600 items, name and title index.

1574. Osborne, Richard. *Rossini*. The Master Musicians. London: Dent, 1986. 330p. ISBN 0-460-03179-1. ML410 .R8 O9.

A useful life and works, documented and reflective of current research. Chronology, worklist, bibliography of about 150 items (conveniently arranged by composition covered), index of names and titles.

1575. Johnson, Janet. "Rossini, Artistic Director of the Théâtre Italien, 1830–1836." In *Gioachino Rossini, 1792–1992* (#1570) 599–622.

Not seen; information from Gallo (see note at head of this Rossini section). Counters earlier opinion that Rossini was an inactive director, offering new documentation as evidence of his continuous participation in casting, selection of works for performance, and reconstituting the orchestra under a new conductor.

See also *New Grove Masters of Italian Opera* (#2480).

Operas in General

1576. Gossett, Philip. "The Operas of Rossini: Problems of Textual Criticism in Nineteenth-Century Opera." Ph.D. diss., Princeton U., 1970. 2v.

1577. Gossett, Philip. "Gioachino Rossini and the Conventions of Composition." *AM* 42 (1970): 48–58. Reprint, *GL,* v.8.

Evidence indicates Rossini had very little time between receipt of the libretto and the premiere (one month for *Cenerentola*), and no sketches survive from his Italian period (1818–1822), with only two fragments from Paris. Gossett concludes that Rossini wrote the final full score directly, probably beginning with main lines, voices, and bass. One reason he could write so quickly was that he used the same patterns (conventions), whatever the libretto was about.

1578. Gossett, Philip. "Le sinfonie di Rossini." *Bollettino* 13 (1979) 7–123.

Text in Italian and English. It is a detailed study of the overtures, with tabular comparisons of characteristics and 77 examples. The archetypal Rossini overture is defined by melodic, harmonic, and instrumental elements. Essentially it consists of a slow section, a quick main exposition section, a short modulation, and recapitulation. Both the exposition and recapitulation conclude in crescendos and cadences. The form changed in terms of structural and dramatic features over the composer's career. Abridged as "The Overtures of Rossini," *19thCM* 3-1 (July 1979): 3–31.

1579. Celletti, Rodolfo. "Origini e sviluppi della coloratura rossiniana." *NRMI* 5 (1968): 872–919.

Explains and illustrates the development of all technical devices for the different voice types. The composer gradually wrote more of the ornamentation that singers had been improvising. The so-called reform of florid singing has not been supported by the practice of singers: "I cantanti hanno gaiamente continuato a interpolare." The study was also published in *Analecta musicologica* (see #2473).

1580. Lippmann, Friedrich. "Per un esegesi dello stile rossiniano." *NRMI* 2 (1968): 813–856.

A perceptive account of unique elements—especially melodic typology—in Rossini's style, with musical examples and good footnote references to earlier analysis.

1581. Balthazar, Scott. "Rossini and the Development of Mid-Century Lyric Form." *JAMS* 41 (1988): 102–125.

Although Bellini has been generally credited with devising the typical aria form of the mid 19th century, Rossini played a substantial role Indeed, his first examples preceded Bellini's by about 10 years. This so-called lyric form is A A' B A (or C). Each phrase of music sets two lines of text, and full text lines are not repeated until the coda.

See also #511.

Individual Works

Aureliano in Palmira

1581a. Two useful articles appeared in OQ 15-1 (Winter 1999): Thomas Lindner, "Rossini's *Aureliano in Palmira*: A Descriptive Analysis," 18–32, and Tom Kaufman, "A Performance History of *Aureliano in Palmira*," 33–38.

Il barbiere di Siviglia (The Barber of Seville)

ASO 37 (1981), ENOG 36 (1985).

1582. Everist, Mark. "Lindoro in Lyon: Rossini's *Le barbier de Séville*." *AM* 64 (1992): 50–85.

The libretto was rewritten in French, and changes were made in the score as well, for the Lyon performance (1821). The alterations are described.

See also Scherliess (#1375) and Goldin (#1376).

La cenerentola

ASO 85 (1986), ENOG 1 (1980).

1583. Zedda, Alberto. "Problemi testuali della *Cenerentola*." *Bollettino* 5 (1971): 29–51.

A genesis study, with useful citations to earlier writing about the opera.

1584. Rogers, Stuart W. "*Cenerentola* a Londra." *Bollettino* 37 (1997): 51–68.

A performance history of London productions.

Le Comte Ory

ASO 140 (1991); *ERO*, v.16.

Elisabetta, regina d'Inghilterra

ERO, v.7.

La gazza ladra

ASO 110 (1988).

Guillaume Tell (William Tell)

ASO 118 (1989); *ERO*, v.17.

1585. Baggioli, Andrea. "Le fonti letterarie di *Guillaume Tell*." *Bollettino* 37 (1997): 5–50.

Compares the literary sources: texts by Michel-Jean Sedaine and Antoine-Marie Lemierre.

1586. Cametti, Alberto. "Il *Guglielmo Tell* e le sue prime rappresentazioni in Italia." *RMI* 6 (1899): 580–592.

A narrative account of the opera's successful arrival in Italy, beginning in Lucca, 1831.

1587. Berlioz, Hector. "*Guillaume Tell.*" *Gazette musicale de Paris* 1 (1834): 326–327+.

The perceptive observations of Rossini's fellow composer are translated in *Strunk*.

1588. Bartlet, M. Elizabeth, ed. "*Guillaume Tell*" *di Gioacchino Rossini: Fonti iconografiche.* In collaboration with Mauro Bucarelli. Pesaro: Fondazione Rossini, 1996. xxvi, 200p.

Not seen.

L'italiana in Algeri

ASO 157 (1994).

Maometto II (Le siège de Corinthe)

The French name was for the Paris revision. ASO *81 (1985);* ERO, *v.11.*

Mosé in Egitto (Moïse et Pharaon)

The French name was for the Paris revision. Both versions are in *ERO,* v.9 and v.15.

1589. Conati, Marcello. "Between Past and Future: The Dramatic World of Rossini in *Mosé in Egitto* and *Moïse et Pharaon.*" *19thCM* 4 (1980): 32–47.

The two works are seen as independent of each other. The Italian version (1818) is more coherent and balanced than the French (1827) and not at all inferior. But *Moïse* formed a transition between 18th-century *opera seria* and 19th-century *melodramma;* it was a milestone in Rossini's career.

Otello

ERO, v.8.

1590. Klein, John W. "Verdi's *Otello* and Rossini's." *M&L* 45 (1964): 130–145.

All praise for Verdi and negation for Rossini. Mostly about characterization, but Klein also accuses Rossini and his librettist (Francesco Beria di Salsa) of ignoring Shakespeare. However, Klein seems not to realize that Shakespeare was not their direct source: they used French and Italian adaptations, which varied considerably from the original. See next item.

1591. Questa, Cesare, and Renato Raffaelli. "I due finali di *Otello.*" In *Gioachino Rossini* (#1570), 182–203.

Not seen; information from Gallo (see note at head of this Rossini section). Explains that the libretto was drawn from Shakespearean adaptations by Jean-François Ducis and Giovanni Carlo Cosenza. Both had light endings, which Rossini followed for the 1820 revival in Rome.

Ricciardo e Zoriade

ERO, v.10.

Semiramide

ASO 184 (1998); *ERO,* v.13.

Le siège de Corinthe (see *Maometto II*)

Il signor Bruschino

1592. Radiciotti, Giuseppe. "*Il signor Bruschino* ed il *Tancredi* di G. Rossini." *RMI* 27 (1920): 231–266.

Genesis for both operas and program notes with musical examples. For *Tancredi* there is a detailed performance history, 1813–1862.

Tancredi

1593. Gossett, Philip. "The Tragic Finale of *Tancredi.*" *Bollettino* 10 (1976): 9–172.

Text in English and Italian. The finale was introduced for the revival in Ferrara, 1813. Its music had disappeared but was found (in manuscript) in a private collection. Gossett analyzes it, with extended musical examples. This article was also published separately by the Fondazione Rossini, Pesaro, 1977.

Il turco in Italia

ASO 169 (1996).

1594. Mila, Massimo. "*Il turco in Italia,* manifesto di dolce vita." *NRMI* 2–5 (September–October 1968): 857–1,071.

A protracted program note, with discussion of the production history and critical reception of the work over the years. Good footnoting identifies all the earlier literature on the opera.

See also Radiciotti (#1592).

Il viaggio a Reims

ASO 140 (1991).

1595. Johnson, Janet. "A Lost Rossini Opera Recovered: *Il viaggio a Reims.*" *Bollettino* 17 (1983): 5–112.

Text in English and Italian. A reconstruction of nine numbers of the score, using five sources. Rossini borrowed much of the music from *Le Comte Ory.* Musical examples and commentary, performance history.

Zelmira

ERO, v.12.

Jean-Jacques Rousseau (1712–1778)

The philosopher was also a musical theorist and the composer of *Le devin du village* (1752), a successful *intermède,* which has a critical edition in *FO,* v.50.

1596. Arnheim, Amalie. "*Le devin du village* von Jean-Jacques Rousseau und die Parodie *Les amours de Bastien et Bastienne.*" *SIMG* 4 (1902–1903): 686–727.

The opera is a pastorale, in form and content. Genesis, technical analysis with 25 pages of musical examples, reception, and place in history of French music.

Rousseau was at the center of the *Querelle* (see #2257ff.). His views on music and art are well explicated in:

1597. Robinson, Philip E. J. *Jean-Jacques Rousseau's Doctrine of the Arts*. Bern: P. Lang, 1984. iv, 520p. ISBN 3-2610-3379-7. PQ2056 .A38 R6.

Music is the primary partner in opera. Mixtures of speech and music, as in the *opéra-comique*, are ridiculous. But then recitative, which avoids the speech element, tends to be boring. Rousseau overcame his early distaste for Italian music but admired the French composers as well: he praised all in his *Dictionnaire de musique*. It may have been personal animosity toward Rameau that influenced Rousseau's eventual turn against the French. Robinson's review is complemented by a strong bibliography of some 150 entries, but it lacks an index.

Joseph-Nicolas-Pancrace Royer (1705–1755)

Zaide is in *FO*, v.45.

Anton Rubinstein (1829–1894)

There is no substantive literature except in Russian. A valuable bibliography, with worklist, by Richard Taruskin is in *NGDO* 4, 80–84.

Antonio Sacchini (1730–1786)

Oedipe à Colonne is in *FO*, v.69.

1598. Thierstein, E. A. "Antonio Maria Gasparo Sacchini and His French Operas." Ph.D. diss., U. of Cincinnati, 1974. 209p.

1599. Schlitzer, Franco. *Antonio Sacchini: Schede e appunti per una sua storia teatrale*. Siena: [Ticci], 1955. 77p. ML410 .S1 S34.

Life and works, with letters. Worklist gives performance details and writings about each opera. No index.

1600. Tozzi, Lorenzo. "Il *Renaud* di Antonio Sacchini: Genesi di una metamorfosi." *Chigiana* 32–12 (1975): 225–263.

Genesis, with emphasis on the novelty of *Renaud* compared to earlier operas by Sacchini. This was no longer a simple gathering of arias but a dramatic work, a true *tragédie-lyrique*. Long musical examples, with technical comments.

Joseph Boulogne, Chevalier de Saint-Georges (1739–1799)

L'amant anonyme is in *FO*, v.66.

Camille Saint-Saëns (1835–1921)

Samson et Dalila is in *ASO* 15 (1978).

1601. Locke, Ralph P. "Constructing the Oriental 'Other': Saint-Saëns' *Samson et Dalila*." *COJ* 3-1 (March 1991): 261–302.

The European image of the Oriental woman was as an odalisque or concubine: she was voluptuous and vulnerable but potentially dangerous. European women could not be portrayed that way on stage, but "Eastern" women were acceptable with those qualities. The Oriental man was seen as cruel and despotic. These characterizations are applied to the opera and found to fit well.

Antonio Salieri (1750–1825)

Les danaïdes is in *FO,* v.68; *Der Rauchfangskehrer* is in *GO,* v.14.

1602. Rice, John A. *Antonio Salieri and Viennese Opera.* Chicago: U. of Chicago Press, 1998. xx, 648p. ISBN 0-2267-1125-0. ML410 .S14 R534.

A study of the works, in rich musical and political context. Genesis, reception, chronology of the operas, all with full documentation. "Mozart and Salieri" (p.459–492) addresses their relationship; Rice concludes that they were rivals, but there is no evidence of inimical activity by either. Bibliography of 400 primary and secondary sources, expansive index.

1603. Swenson, Edward Elmgren. "Antonio Salieri: A Documentary Biography." Ph.D. diss., Cornell U., 1974. xii, 408p.

1604. Angermüller, Rudolph. *Antonio Salieri: Sein Leben und seine weltliche Werke.* Munich: Katzbichler, 1971–1974. 3v. ISBN 3-87397-016-3, 3-87397-019-8, 3-87397-021-X. ML410 .S16 A7.

A valuable work, based on the author's dissertation (U. of Salzburg, 1970). It gives great detail on the operas and their performance histories. All numbers of all the operas are described, with reference to sources. Earlier research is covered in a thorough bibliographic essay. The third volume comprises documents. Index of names, places, and titles.

1605. Braunbehrens, Volkmar. *Maligned Master: The Real Story of Antonio Salieri.* Trans. Eveline L. Kanes. New York: Fromm International, 1993. 276p. ISBN 0-88064-140. ML410 .S143 B713.

A straightforward life story, with some special effort to clear Salieri's name after the calumnies of the movie *Amadeus*. Program notes on the operas, backnotes, bibliography of some 150 items, index of names and titles.

1606. Angermüller, Rudolph. "Salieri—Opern in Esterháza." *Chigiana* 36 (1979): 87–99.

Haydn produced or planned to produce five Salieri works: *La scuola de' gelosi; La fiera in Venezia; Axur, re d'Oramus; La grotta di Trofonio;* and *La secchia rapita.* These are discussed in detail, with attention to plot, performance history, and changes made in them by Haydn. *La scuola de' gelosi* was particularly successful, with 23 performances in 1780–1781. Relationship between the two composers is also considered. Salieri's sonnet about Haydn, in Italian, is reproduced in the article.

1607. Walton-Myers, Edith Hays. "Antonio Salieri's *La cifra*: The Creation of a Late 18th-Century Opera." Ph.D. diss., Northwestern U., 1977. 365p.

See also Landy (#901) and Bonnert (#933).

Joseph-François Salomon (1649–1732)

Medée et Jason is in *FO,* v.28.

Giovanni Battista Sammartini (1701–1775)

1608. Jenkins, Newell, and Bathia Churgin. *Thematic Catalogue of the Works of Giovanni Battista Sammartini: Orchestral and Vocal Music.* Cambridge, Mass.: Harvard U.P., 1976. 315p. ISBN 0-674877-357. ML134 .S189 J52.

> Includes information on the operas: premiere dates and places, casting, and instrumentation. Many thematic excerpts (30 are from *L'Agrippina*); manuscript sources and library locations. Comments on publication history, references to secondary literature. An expansive index of names and titles concludes this useful handbook.

1609. Jenkins, Newell. "The Vocal Music of Giovanni Battista Sammartini." *Chigiana* 32 (1977): 277–309.

> The three operas—*Memet, L'ambizione superata dalla virtù,* and *L'Agrippina*— are thoroughly analyzed. The discussion is related to elaborate tonal-structure diagrams.

Giuseppe Sarti (1729–1802)

1610. Scarpatta, Umberto. "Un opera pietroburghese: Il *Castro e Polluce*." In *Giuseepe Sarti, musicista faentino: Atti del Convegno Internazionale, Faenza, 25–27 novembre 1983,* 93–112 (Modena: Mucchi, 1983; ML410 .S18 C66).

> This is the only useful contribution on opera of the 19 papers in the volume. It gives genesis, a list of all the numbers in the opera with their instrumentation, and a formal analysis. The earlier literature on Sarti is identified with 21 footnotes.

Alessandro Scarlatti (1660–1725)

Editions

There is no collected edition. Modern publications of individual operas are listed in Vidali (#1611), 193–197. The principal series is issued by Harvard U.P., "The Operas of Alessandro Scarlatti"; this series is cited below as *OAS.*

Bibliographies and Guides to Resources

1611. Vidali, Carole F. *Alessandro and Domenico Scarlatti: A Guide to Research.* Garland Composer Resource Manuals, 34. New York: Garland, 1993. xxi, 132p. ISBN 0-8240-59452-5. ML134 .S218 V5.

> A valuable handbook on both composers. For Alessandro Scarlatti there is an annotated bibliography of 457 items, plus a description of modern editions and facsimile issues. Individual numbers in the Harvard series (*OAS)* are described, with references to reviews. Indexes of authors, names, and titles.

Biographies

1612. Dent, Edward J. *Alessandro Scarlatti: His Life and Works.* 2nd ed. London: Edward Arnold, 1960. 252p. Reprint, St. Clair Shores, Mich.: Scholarly Press, 1976. ML410 .S218 D3.

First edition, 1905. This edition includes footnotes by Frank Walker.The only full-length biography in English, it is a plain life and works, with program notes on selected operas and 94 musical examples. Worklist with library locations. No bibliography, expansive index of names and titles.

See also *New Grove Italian Baroque Masters* (#2459).

Operas in General

1613. Grout, Donald Jay. *Alessandro Scarlatti: An Introduction to His Operas.* Berkeley: U. of California Press, 1979. vii, 154p. ML410 .S22 G7.

Consists of lectures given in 1976, with some footnotes added. They offer a casual presentation of the life, style, reputation, and contemporaries of Scarlatti. Grout notes that only 30–35 of the operas survive in "salvageable" form. He edited the series of critical editions issued by Harvard (*OAS*). With an appendix of musical examples and a good index of names, titles, and topics; no bibliography.

1614. Lorenz, Alfred Ottokar. *Alessandro Scarlattis Jugendoper: Ein Beitrag zur Geschichte der italienischer Oper.* Augsburg: Benno Filser, 1927. 2v. ML410 .S22 L7.

An important study of the works written through 1697. Technical discussions cover micro- and macrostructural elements. There are 401 musical examples in v.2, including 135 complete numbers. A chronological list of the operas is in v.1.

1615. Morey, Carl Reginald. "The Late Operas of Alessandro Scarlatti." Ph.D. diss., Indiana U., 1965. 312p.

Individual Works

La caduta de' decemviri

OAS, v.6.

Il Ciro

1616. Jones, Gaynor G. "Alessandro Scarlattis *Il Ciro.*" *Hamburger Jahrbuch für Musikwissenschaft* 3 (1978): 225–237.

Examines 18th-century libretti based on Cyrus of Persia, including the one by Scarlatti. Performance histories (with biographical information on the singers) and research problems encountered with this material.

Il Dafni

HS, v.7.

1617. Sartori, Claudio. "*Il Dafni* di Alessandro Scarlatti." *RMI* 45 (1941): 176–183.

Discusses the three libretti on Dafni by Scarlatti (dating from 1700, 1701, and 1715) and gives performance information; also comments on two other settings, of 1709. Brings out similarities and differences in these texts.

Gli equivoci nel sembiante

OAS, v.7.

1618. D'Accone, Frank A. *The History of a Baroque Opera: Alessandro Scarlatti's "Gli equivoci nel sembiante."* Monographs in Musicology, 3. New York: Pendragon, 1985. x, 187p. ISBN 0-918728-21-5. ML410 .S22 D15.

A thorough account of the premiere performance (Rome, 1679), with much attention to the libretto and to performance history. Well documented, with sources reproduced.

La Griselda

OAS, v.3.

1619. Grout, Donald Jay. "The Original Version of Alessandro Scarlatti's *Griselda.*" In *Essays on Opera* (#72), 103–114.

Describes the alterations made in the manuscript score by Scarlatti, perhaps before the opera's premiere.

Marco Attilio Regolo

OAS, v.2.

Massimo Puppieno

OAS, v.5.

Mitridate Eupatore

1620. Westrup, Jack. "Alessandro Scarlatti's *Il Mitridate Eupatore* (1707)." In *New Looks* (#2429), 133–150.

A discussion, based on the Paris manuscript, of instrumentation, harmony, and interpretative questions. Cites errors in the published edition.

Il Pompeo

HS, v.6.

La principessa fedele

OAS, v.4.

La Statira

OAS, v.9.

1621. Holmes, William C. *"La Statira" by Pietro Ottoboni and Alessandro Scarlatti: The Textual Sources, with a Documentary Postscript.* Monographs in Musicology, 2. New York: Pendragon, 1983. vii, 92p. ISBN 0-918728-18-5. ML410 .S22 H6.

> A comparison of the printed libretto with a working autograph and an examination of both texts in the context of four surviving copies of the score. Variants and corrections are explicated. Documents of 1690 about the opera are reproduced. In the course of this scholarly analysis, the circumstances of opera production in Rome are exhibited.

Telemaco

IO–1640, v.23.

Tigrane

OAS, v.8.

1622. Collins, Michael. "An Introduction to Alessandro Scarlatti's *Tigrane.*" In *Essays on Music* (#67), 82–102.

> Genesis, libretto sources, reception history, and program notes, with discussion of the four surviving manuscripts.

1623. Pauly, Reinhard G. "Alessandro Scarlatti's *Tigrane.*" *M&L* 35 (1954): 339–346.

> Describes the surviving score, which includes stage directions. It seems to be from a later performance, not from the premiere, since the role of Tigrane appears to have been transposed for a castrato.

Arnold Schoenberg (1874–1951)

This is the spelling preferred by the composer in his later years; however, the Library of Congress retains Schönberg, as do most German writers.

Editions

1624. Schönberg, Arnold. *Sämtliche Werke.* Ed. Rudolf Stephan, for the Akademie der Kunste, Berlin. Mainz: Schott; Vienna: Universal, 1966–. No ISBN. M3 .S36.

> In progress. *Abteilung* 3 is for stage works. *Von heute auf morgen* has been published (1972–1974; 2v.), and so has *Moses und Aron* (1977–1980; 3v.) These are orchestra scores, with extensive critical apparatus in German and English.

Biographies

1625. Reich, Willi. *Schoenberg: A Critical Biography.* Trans. Leo Black. London: Longman, 1971. xi, 268p. ISBN 0-582-12753-X. ML410 .S283 R43.

> Originally *Schönberg, oder der konservative Revolutionär* (Vienna: Molden, 1968). A general life and works, footnoted, with program notes on the operas. Worklist in the translation has titles in English only; in the German edition

they are in German. No information is provided about the compositions listed. Bibliography of about 25 books, name index.

1626. Newlin, Dika. *Schoenberg Remembered: Diaries and Recollections (1938– 76)*. New York: Pendragon, 1980. x, 369p. ISBN 0-9187-2814-2.

When Newlin was Schoenberg's student, 1938–1941, she kept detailed diaries that are rich with the composer's presence. She continued the diaries into 1976, with more emphasis on her own ideas, which are of great interest. Bibliography, index.

Individual Works

Erwartung

1627. Buchanan, Herbert H. "A Key to Schoenberg's *Erwartung*." *JAMS* 20 (1967): 434–449.

Rejects the standard view that *Erwartung* is atonal and athematic; finds both tonal and thematic elements, both related to one of the composer's early songs, "Am Wegrand," op.6, no.6 (1905). Identifies motivic cells that help to provide cohesion. Musical examples and references to earlier literature.

1628. Garcia Laborda, José Maria. *Studien zu Schoenbergs Monodram "Erwartung," Op. 17*. Laaber: Laaber, 1981. 363p. ISBN 3-9215-18547. MT100 .S45 G3.

Genesis and background, with a close micro- and macroanalysis; scholarly and thorough. The 453 backnotes are poorly supported by a weak bibliography of about 90 items with incomplete data. Other problems are the lack of an index and the inscrutable handwritten musical examples.

1629. Budde, Elmar. "Arnold Schönbergs Monodrama *Erwartung*: Versuch einer Analyse der ersten Szene." *AfM* 36 (1979): 1–20.

Two approaches to the work: emotional expression and musical structure. Music is analyzed by "traditional methods and categories." Includes consideration of earlier studies by Carl Dahlhaus and Anton Webern.

1630. Lessem, Alan Philip. *Music and Text in the Works of Arnold Schoenberg: The Critical Years, 1908–1922*. Ann Arbor, Mich.: UMI Research, 1979. 247p. ISBN 0-8357-0994-9. ML410 .S283 L47.

A general examination of "expressionism, drama and music" that includes detailed studies of *Erwartung* and *Die glückliche Hand*. Extensive notes and musical examples. Bibliography of about 200 items. Expansive index of names, titles, and topics.

See also Franklin (#412).

Die glückliche Hand

1631. Steiner, Ena. "The 'Happy' Hand: Genesis and Interpretation of Schoenberg's *Monumentalkunstwerk*." *MR* 41 (1980): 207–222.

Genesis; parallels to the work of his friend, the painter Kandinsky; letters. Nothing said about the music itself.

1632. Crawford, John C. "*Die glückliche Hand*: Schoenberg's *Gesamtkunstwerk*." *MQ* 60 (1974): 583–601.

A study of "artistic influences," then of aesthetic aims and their realization in the work. Kandinsky had the greatest impact, along with Wagner's leading motives, and Strindberg. The work had special influence on Alban Berg.

See also #1630.

Moses und Aron

ASO 167 (1995).

1633. Wörner, Karl Heinrich. *Schoenberg's "Moses und Aron."* Trans. Paul Hamburger. London: Faber & Faber, 1963. 208p. ML410 .S28 W613.

Originally *Gotteswort und Magie* (Heidelberg: Schneider, 1959). This is a thorough historical and technical study, offering details of the tone rows as well as a chronicle of productions, with fine photos. Emphasis is on the religious ideas of the text. The libretto in German/English is given in full, with musical examples. Bibliography of about 30 entries, index of names, titles, and topics.

1634. Lewin, David. "*Moses und Aron*: Some General Remarks and Analytical Notes for Act 1, Scene 1." *Perspectives of New Music* 6 (1967): 1–17. Reprint, *GL*, v.12.

Analysis of pitch structure, dramatic structure, texture, pitch/drama relations, and metric elements.

1635. Cooper-White, Pamela. *Schoenberg and the God-Idea: The Opera "Moses und Aron."* Studies in Musicology, 83. Ann Arbor, Mich.: UMI Research, 1985. xii, 339p. ISBN 0-8357-1647-3. ML410 .S283 W45.

A valuable revision of the author's Harvard dissertation. Genesis, bringing out the stages of composition and the composer's religious thought. Versions of the text are compared, and compositional techniques (the tone row) are explicated. Characterization and leading motives are covered. Analytical diagrams make all this accessible. Notes, good bibliography of about 40 entries, expansive index. The only difficulty given to the reader is in the minuscule reproduction of some full-score examples.

1636. Hair, G. "Schoenberg's *Moses und Aron*." Ph.D. diss., U. of Sheffield, 1973.

1637. Davison, Stephen. "Of Its Time, or Out of Step? Schoenberg's *Zeitoper, Von heute auf Morgen*." *Journal of the Arnold Schoenberg Institute* 14–2 (1991): 271–298.

Technical analysis of the set and pitch-class structure, macrostructure, and dramatic form.

Franz Schreker (1878–1934)

1638. Hailey, Christopher. *Franz Schreker, 1878–1934: A Cultural Biography.* New York: Cambridge U.P., 1993. xx, 433p. ISBN 0-521-39255-1. ML410 .S288 H3.

Gives the Viennese and Berlin background of Schreker and his struggles—as a
Jew—with Nazism. He was the "most frequently performed opera composer
of his generation" until Hitler's social decrees forced him to retire; he died a
broken man. He was not revisited after the war: his students had dispersed,
and his works remained unperformed. The negative opinions of Theodore
Adorno had much influence. Hailey believes that the compositions deserved
better, and he finds much of value in the operas as he discusses them. Genesis
and analysis, with reception of *Die ferne Klang*. Worklist, good bibliography
(some 30 items, by and about), expansive index of names, titles, cities, and topics.

1639. *Franz Schreker Symposium*. Ed. Elmar Budde and Rudolf Stephan. Berlin:
Colloquium Verlag, 1980. 141p. ISBN 3-767-8052-43. ML410 .S235 F8.

Consists of nine papers given at a meeting in Berlin, 6–8 October 1978. Three
concern operas: Rudolf Stephan, "Anmerkungen zur Oper *Das Spielwerk*" (a
comparison of the 1912 and 1919 versions); Christopher Hailey, "Zur Entstehungsgeschichte der Oper *Christophorus*" (genesis, variant versions compared); and Wolfgang Molkow, "Die Rolle der Kunst in den frühen Opern
Franz Schrekers."

1640. Franklin, Peter R. "Style, Structure and Taste: Three Aspects of the Problem of
Franz Schreker." *PRMA* 109 (1982–1983): 134–146.

Looks at 1908–1916, the period of Schreker's first successes. The composer
blended radical innovation with sentimental clichés. Franklin leans to subjective descriptions, such as "we can only approach the work's summatory overture as a psychological case-study in which we become involved at our peril."
Program notes on *Der ferne Klang* and *Die Gezeichneten*, with musical examples and some technical observations.

1641. Franklin, Peter R. "Distant Sounds—Fallen Music: *Der ferne Klang* as a
'Woman's Opera.'" *COJ* 3-2 (1991): 159–172.

Franklin says it is not a gender opera, unless as a stereotype of "masculine
fears and fantasies," but a failed or transitional experiment in modernism.
Musical examples appear, but the discussion is really about the text.

1642. Neuwirth, Gosta. *Die Harmonik der Oper "Der ferne Klang" von Franz
Schreker*. Regensburg: Bosse, 1972. 256p. ISBN 3-7649-2056-4. MT100 .S38
N5.

Genesis, sources, harmony, form, tonality—all in a useful scene-by-scene
analysis. Bibliography, name index. Based on the author's dissertation, Freie
Universität, 1968.

1643. Brzoska, Matthias. *Franz Schrekers Oper "Der Schatzgräber."* Beihefte zum
Archiv für Musikwissenschaft, 27. Stuttgart: Franz Steiner, 1988. 209p. ISBN
3-515-04850-2. ML55 .A67 v.27.

Genesis, structure, drama and character, performance history. Musical examples with technical analysis. Bibliography of about 100 items, no index.

See also Franklin (#412).

Franz Peter Schubert (1797–1828)

Editions

1644. Schubert, Franz. *Neue Ausgabe sämtlicher Werke*. Editorial directors, Walther Dorr and Arnold Feil, for the Internationale Schubert-Gesellschaft, Tübingen. Kassel: Bärenreiter, 1964–. No ISBN. M3 .S38.

In progress. Series 2, the stage works, has published *Des Teufels Lustschloss* (1989; 2v.), *Der vierjährige Posten* (1992), *Fernando* (1992), *Alfonso und Estrella* (1993–1995; 3v.), and *Die Zauberharfe* (1995). Each volume has a full score, facsimiles, and critical comments in German only.

Collections of Essays

1645. *Cambridge Companion to Schubert*. Ed. Christopher Gibbs. New York: Cambridge U.P., 1997. xii, 340p. ISBN 0-521-48229-1. ML410 .S3 C18.

Consists of 16 essays, just 1 on opera: Thomas Denny, "Schubert's Operas: The Judgment of History?" It includes program notes for *Fierrabras*.

1646. *Schubert Studies: Problems of Style and Chronology*. Ed. Eva Badura Skoda and Peter Branscombe. New York: Cambridge U.P., 1982. xiv, 369p. ISBN 0-521-22606-6. ML410 .S3 S2996.

A collection of 14 essays, with only 1 general study of the operas: Elizabeth Norman McKay, "Schubert as a Composer of Operas." It deals with influences, genesis and reception, and gives plots with program notes.

Biographies

1647. McKay, Elizabeth Norman. *Franz Schubert: A Biography*. New York: Oxford U.P., 1996. xvi, 362p. ISBN 0-19-816523-4. ML410 .S3 M34.

A footnoted life and works, with program notes on the operas. With an indifferent bibliography and a partly expansive index. McKay's other book (next entry) is preferable for information on the operas, but this one is a competent background study.

Operas in General

1648. McKay, Elizabeth Norman. *Franz Schubert's Music for the Theater*. Tutzing: Schneider, 1991. 412p. ISBN 3-7952-0664-2. ML410 .S26 M14.

Genesis, reception, and program notes on the operas, with 89 musical examples. No footnotes; weak bibliography; name index. McKay's dissertation also dealt with the operas: "The Stage Works of Schubert, Considered in the Framework of Austrian Biedermeier Society." U. of Oxford, 1962.

1649. Hoorickx, P. Reinhard van. "Les opéras de Schubert." *Revue belge de musicologie* 28/30 (1974–1976): 238–259.

A list of the 10 complete operas and 11 that are incomplete, plus 16 arias. Brief descriptive comments, with just two reference footnotes.

1650. Brown, Maurice J. E. "Schubert's Two Major Operas—A Consideration of the Possibility of Actual Stage Productions." *MR* 20 (1959): 104–118.

Gives extended program notes on *Fierrabras* and *Alfonso und Estrella*. [Both operas did get produced but only in concert versions, on radio, or by university groups. No full-scale professional performance has been noted.]

1651. Cunningham, George R. "Franz Schubert als Theaterkomponist." Ph.D. diss., Albert-Ludwigs-U. (Freiburg), 1974. 223p.

1652. Citron, M. J. "Schubert's Seven Complete Operas: A Musico-Dramatic Study." Ph.D. diss., U. of North Carolina, 1971. viii, 169p.

1653. Wischusen, Mary Ann. "The Stage Works of Franz Schubert: Background and Stylistic Influences." Ph.D. diss., Rutgers U., 1983. 769p.

Robert Schumann (1810–1856)

Genoveva is in *ASO* 71 (1985).

1654. *Schumann: A Symposium.* Ed. Gerald Abraham. London: Oxford U.P., 1952. vi, 319p. Reprint, Westport, Conn.: Greenwood, 1977. ML410 .S4 A6317.

Includes Abraham's essay, "Dramatic Music," p.260–282. It gives program notes and some musical examples.

1655. Siegel, Linda. "A Second Look at Schumann's *Genoveva.*" *MR* 36 (1975): 17–41.

Believes that the work would be worth reviving if performed according to the "spirit of the opera and the directions of the composer." Genesis, reception, musical examples with technical comments.

1656. Abert, Hermann. "Robert Schumann's *Genoveva.*" *Zeitschrift der International Musikgesellschaft* 11 (1910): 277–289.

Considers the opera "an important document not only for an understanding of Schumann's own art, but also for the development of modern opera." Genesis, technical analysis, *Leitmotiven.*

Georg Caspar Schürmann (1672–1751)

1657. Schmidt, Gustav Friedrich. *Die frühdeutschen Oper und die musikdramatische Kunst Georg Caspar Schürmanns.* Regensburg: Bosse, 1933–1934. 2v. ML410 .S28 S35.

A documented life and works, with letters; descriptions and locations of libretti; technical analysis; performance data; and chronological worklist of 150 items. Name and title index.

Joseph Schuster (1748–1812)

Der Alchymist is in *GO*, v.5.

Heinrich Schütz (1585–1672)

1658. Skei, Allen B. *Heinrich Schütz: A Guide to Research*. Garland Composer Resource Manuals, 1. New York: Garland, 1981. xxxi, 186p. ISBN 0-8240-9310-0. ML134 .S412 S5.

An important annotated bibliography of 632 entries in classified order, with author and title indexes. Gives only four citations to *Dafne* (1627), the first opera with a German libretto. There are no substantial studies.

See also Giraud (#228).

Anton Schweitzer (1735–1787)

Alceste is in *GO*, v.3.

Alexander Serov (1820–1871)

Operas in General

1659. Abraham, Gerald. "The Operas of Serov." In *Essays Presented to Egon Wellesz* (#70), 171–184.

Genesis, reception, and musical examples with technical notes. In theory, Serov was Wagnerian, but *Judith* (1863) is an Italian-style opera; it was successful despite critical condemnation by V. V. Stasov. *Rogneda* (1865) was another popular work, also non-Wagnerian.

See also Richard Taruskin's valuable overview in *NGDO* 4, 321–325.

Individual Works

Judith (Iudith)

1660. Taruskin, Richard. "'This Way to the Future': The Case of Serov's *Judith*." In *Opera and Drama in Russia* (#2648), 33–78.

That Serov's operas are no longer staged is partly due to V. V. Stasov's torrent of negative writing about them. Stasov was Wagnerian, and although Serov was of the same persuasion, *Judith* was in the Italian manner. Some Wagnerian elements occurred, nevertheless, such as a few leading motives. Production details are given, with synopses of *Judith, Rogneda,* and *Power of the Fiend (Vrazh'ia sila)*. The Russian secondary literature is cited in 126 footnotes. Taruskin added to the discussion of *Judith* in his *Musorgksy* (#1346).

Rogneda

1661. Taruskin, Richard. "*Pochvennichestvo* on the Russian Operatic Stage: Serov and His *Rogneda*." In *Opera and Drama in Russia* (#2648), 79–140.

Now "about as thoroughly forgotten as an opera can become," *Rogneda* was a popular success at its premiere, 27 October 1865, and was performed 70 times in the next five years. It was connected to the nationalist spirit in art of the time, represented by the *Pochvenniki,* centered on Dostoevsky. Taruskin gives a lucid summary of this movement—which faded in the mid-1860s—and its impact on the genesis of the opera. In the end, *Rogneda* is an Italian-style number opera, with arias, songs, and dances. Musical examples and analysis bring out all the aspects, and 120 footnotes guide the reader to the Russian primary and secondary literature.

Power of the Fiend (= Power of Evil; Vrazh'ia sila)

1662. Taruskin, Richard. "Drama Revealed through Song: An Opera after Ostrovsky." In *Opera and Drama in Russia* (#2648), 141–248.

The opera was Serov's "most original, most unified, most authentic achievement," both nationalistic and realistic. Genesis: the work was apparently completed by his wife after Serov died on 20 January 1871. Detailed study of folk song elements and full technical analysis with (hard-to-read) musical examples. Reception account (mixed) and 160 valuable footnotes to the Russian primary and secondary literature. The person alluded to in the title of this article was Alexander Nikolevich Ostrovsky, playwright and librettist.

Roger Sessions (1896–1985)

1663. Olmstead, Andrea. *Roger Sessions and His Music.* Ann Arbor, Mich.: UMI Research, 1985. xvii, 218p. ISBN 0-8357-1633-3. ML410 .S473 O4.

A life and works, with some coverage of the opera *Montezuma* (p.125–138): genesis, production, reception, and program note; no analysis. Bibliography, indexes.

1664. Mason, Charles. "A Comprehensive Analysis of Roger Sessions' Opera *Montezuma.*" D.M.A. diss., U. of Illinois, 1982.

1665. Laufer, Edward C. "Roger Sessions' *Montezuma.*" *Perspectives of New Music* 4–1 (1965): 95–108.

Serial techniques described: the set is four unordered trichords.

See also Stevenson (#2115).

William Shield (1748–1829)

The comic opera *The Poor Soldier* (1783), by Shield and John O'Keeffe (or O'Keefe), is in *RAM*, v.6. It is described as "the most popular afterpiece in the late eighteenth-century theater."

Dmitrii Dmitrievich Shostakovich (1906–1975)

1666. *Shostakovich: The Man and His Music.* Ed. Christopher Norris. Boston: Marion Boyars, 1982. 233p. ISBN 0-8531-5502-X. ML410 .S53 S5.

"The Operas," by Norris (p.105–124), has program notes and guidance to other literature through 27 footnotes.

1667. Shostakovich, Dmitrii Dmitrievich. *Testimony: The Memoirs of Dmitrii Shostakovich.* Trans. Antonia W. Bouis. New York: Harper & Row, 1979. xli, 289p. ISBN 0-0601-4476-9. ML410 .S53 A3.

Of interest for background on the upheavals in Russia over *Lady Macbeth*. Includes a chronological worklist, all in English. Expansive index of names and titles.

Updated biographical and bibliographical material is in *The New Grove Russian Masters 2* (#2643).

Individual Works

Lady Macbeth of Mtensk District (Ledi Makbet Mtsenskago uezda)

ASO 141 (1991).

1668. Emerson, Caryl. "Back to the Future: Shostakovich's Revision of Leskov's *Lady Macbeth of Mtensk District*." *COJ* 1-1 (1989): 59–78.

> Genesis and place of the work in Russian cultural history. "The opera can be seen as defending the virtuous martyrdom implicit in a 'woman's lot,' against attempts to parody that tradition."

1669. Brown, Royal S. "The Three Faces of Lady Macbeth." In *Russian and Soviet Music* (#2640), 245–252.

> An immediate success at its premiere (Leningrad, 22 January 1934) but soon submerged in angry negative reaction, notably in *Pravda*. Objections included the sexual theme and the extraordinary musical depiction of (offstage) intercourse. The composer revised the work as *Katerina Ismailova* in 1956 (premiere 1963), greatly reducing the erotic components. Brown describes the revision and also another version in a 1935 piano score.

The Nose (Nos)

1670. Fay, Laurel E. "The Punch in Shostakovich's *Nose*." In *Russian and Soviet Music* (#2640), 229–244.

> Genesis, the Gogol story on which it is based, and brief comments on the musical idiom, which is "non-tonal and non-lyrical." The cast is huge: 78 solo singing roles and nine spoken roles; more than 200 rehearsals were required for the premiere in 1930. It was a success, receiving 16 performances, but politically unacceptable, so it then went unstaged in Russia until 1974. There were some productions outside Russia in the 1960s.

Bedřich Smetana (1824–1883)

Operas in General

1671. Large, Brian. *Smetana*. London: Duckworth, 1970. xvii, 473p. ML410 .S63 L4.

> Biography and genealogy, plus a good introduction to all the operas. Separate chapters on *Bartered Bride, Dalibor, Two Widows, The Kiss, The Secret,* and *The Devil's Wall*. Style is program note, but primary sources are cited and there is some technical commentary. An appendix gives detailed comparisons of the five versions of *Bartered Bride* and the three versions of *Two Widows*. With 26 plates, 112 musical examples, chronological worklist, and expansive index of names and titles.

1672. Jiranek, Jaroslav. *Smetanova operni tvorba.* Prague: Supraphon, 1984–1989. ML410 .S63 J57. 6v.

Readers of Czech will find this monumental compilation informative. It includes a full account of each opera (genesis, libretto, production, and reception), with detailed technical analysis. Bibliographies, name indexes.

Individual Works

The Bartered Bride (Prodaná nevěsta)

1673. Abraham, Gerald. "The Genesis of *The Bartered Bride.*" *M&L* 28 (1947): 36–49.

Genesis, revisions, sketches, reception, and technical observations. Special attention given to the sextet.

1674. Pražák, Premysl. *Smetanova "Prodaná nevěsta": Vznik a osudy díla.* Prague: Lidová Demokracie, 1962. 329p. MT100 .S53 P9.

A study of the genesis and libretto, with useful list of performances by country. No musical examples, no index.

Dalibor

1675. Clapham, John. "Smetana's Sketches for *Dalibor* and *The Secret.*" *M&L* 61 (1980): 136–146.

Describes sketchbook material and variants that the composer introduced over time. His sketching method changed between the two operas, from fuller to less complete ideas written down.

The Secret (Tajemství)

See #1675.

Ethel Smyth (1858–1944)

1676. Abromeit, Kathleen A. "Ethel Smyth, *The Wreckers,* and Sir Thomas Beecham." *MQ* 73 (1989): 196–211.

Background on Smyth and her picturesque efforts to get her opera produced. This finally happened in Leipzig (in German translation) in 1906 and was well received. After another performance, in Prague, Thomas Beecham finally agreed to conduct it at Covent Garden, but Smyth said, "He wrecked it."

Harry T. Somers (1925–).

1677. Cherney, Brian. *Harry Somers.* Canadian Composers, 1. Toronto: U. of Toronto Press, 1975. xii, 185p. ISBN 0-8020-5325-4. ML410 .S6864 C5.

Somers's "most important achievement" is the opera *Louis Riel.* It receives a 10-page discussion here: genesis, reception, technical notes. Worklist, bibliography, index.

John Philip Sousa (1854–1932)

El capitan is in *19CAMT,* v.14.

Louis Spohr (1784–1859)

1678. Brown, Clive. *Louis Spohr: A Critical Biography.* New York: Cambridge U.P., 1984. xi, 364p. ISBN 0-521-23990-7. ML410 .S7 B8.

Life and works, with substantial attention to the operas: plots, genesis, musical examples, and technical observations. Backnotes, bibliography of primary and secondary materials, expansive index.

Gasparo Spontini (1774–1851)

The first name is also seen as Gaspare. Three operas are in *ERO: La vestale,* v.42; *Fernand Cortez,* v.43; and *Olympie,* v.44.

1679. Ghislanzoni, Alberto. *Gasparo Spontini: Studio storico-critico.* Rome: Edizione dell'Ateneo, 1951. 281p. ML410 .S76 G45.

A footnoted biography, with about 50 photographs. Program notes and some technical comments on the operas. No bibliography; name index.

1680. Fragapane, Paolo. *Spontini.* 2nd. ed. Bologna: Sansoni, 1983. 466p. ML410 .S76 F7.

First edition, 1954. A useful well-documented biography, with a bibliographic essay that describes the earlier Spontini literature (most of it very early). Program notes on the operas. Worklist, giving publishers or library locations and instrumentations. Bibliography, name index.

1681. Libby, Dennis Albert. "Gasparo Spontini and His French and German Operas." Ph.D. diss., Princeton U., 1969. 2v.

Agostino Steffani (1654–1728)

La lotta d'Hercole con Archelao is in *HS,* v.9.

1682. Baxter, W. H. "Agostino Steffani: A Study of the Man and His Work." Ph.D. diss., Eastman School of Music, U. of Rochester, 1957. 472p.

1683. Croll, G. "Agostino Steffani (1654–1728): Studien zur Biographie, Bibliographie der Opern und Turnierspiele." Ph.D. diss., U. of Münster, 1960.

1684. Keppler, Philip. "Agostino Steffani's Hannover Operas and a Rediscovered Catalogue." In *Studies in Music History: Essays for Oliver Strunk,* ed. Harold Powers, 341–355 (Princeton, N.J.: Princeton U.P., 1968).

Discusses stage works presented in Hanover, 1679–1697, the nine operas of that period attributed to Steffani (six are said to be definitely genuine), and a manuscript catalogue of the operas located by the author in the Hannover Landesbibliothek "in a mislabelled cardboard box."

1685. Marles, Candace. "Opera as *instrumentum regni*: Agostino Steffani's *Enrico Leone.*" *OQ* 11-1 (1984–1995): 43–78.

The opera (1689) was "profoundly affected" by the political circumstances of its production: that context is the subject here. *Enrico Leone* was the first of Steffani's six operas for Hanover, and Duke Ernst August influenced it strongly. He suggested the subject and was represented by the mythic hero. Text and arias glorify his qualities. Musical numbers are described, with examples.

1686. Marles, Candace. "Music and Drama in the Hanover Operas of Agostino Steffani (1654–1728)." Ph.D. diss., Yale U., 1991. xii, 356p.

Stephen Storace (1763–1796)

1687. Girdham, Jane Catherine. "Stephen Storace and the English Opera Tradition of the Late Eighteenth Century." Ph.D. diss., U. of Pennsylvania, 1988.

Alessandro Stradella (1639–1682)

1688. Gianturco, Carolyn, and Eleanor McCrickard. *Alessandro Stradella (1639–1682): A Thematic Catalogue of His Compositions*. Thematic Catalogues, 16. Stuyvesant, N.Y.: Pendragon, 1990. 325p. ISBN 0-945193-05-X. ML134 .S89 A25.

A valuable compilation of data about the prolific Stradella, covering about 300 authentic and extant vocal works, in addition to instrumental material. The main task of the compilers was to clean up the mangled worklist of Remo Giazotto in his 1962 biography of Stradella: it seems that it was embellished with fake documentation and led to vast misconceptions about the composer's output. Gianturco and McCrickard offer complete accounts of the authentic works, including incipits of many arias of all the operas and source information. A useful name list includes about 400 librettists, poets, patrons, and opera characters. Well indexed.

1689. Gianturco, Carolyn. "The Operas of Alessandro Stradella (1644–1682)." Ph.D. diss., U. of Oxford, 1970. 2v.

Note that the composer's birthdate was later found, by Gianturco, to be 1639 rather than 1644; see previous entry, and the next entry, based on the dissertation.

1690. Gianturco, Carolyn. *Alessandro Stradella: 1639–1682: His Life and Music*. New York: Oxford U.P., 1994. xiv, 333 p. ISBN 0-19-8161-387-1. ML410 .S87 G45.

The chapter on theater music, including five operas, gives plots and technical notes. Footnotes, bibliography of about 250 items, expansive index.

1691. Jander, Owen H. "The Works of Alessandro Stradella Related to the Cantata and the Opera." Ph.D. diss., Harvard U., 1962. 512p.

Johann Strauss, Jr. (1825–1899)

Significant literature is lacking. The complete edition includes critical notes:

1692. Strauss, Johann (Sohn). *Gesamtausgabe*. Ed. Fritz Racek et al., for the Johann Strauss-Gesellschaft, Vienna. Vienna: Doblinger, 1967–. M3 .S89 G5.

Series 2, v.1–19, covers the stage works. Published: v.3, *Die Fledermaus;* v.9, *Eine Nacht in Venedig*.

Richard Strauss (1864–1949)

Bibliographies and Guides to Resources

1693. Ortner, Oswald. *Richard Strauss Bibliographie.* Vienna: C. Prachner, 1964–1973. 2v. ISBN 3-8511-91102. ML134 .S93 O77.

> V.1, 1882–1944; v.2, 1944–1964. A thorough bibliography of 3,463 items, hailed by Del Mar (#1698) as "absolutely complete." Topical arrangement (each opera has a separate section), then chronological. For books the publishers and pagination are given; for articles the pagination is not always included. Each volume has a name/title/topic/place index.

Collections of Essays

1694. *Richard Strauss and His World.* Ed. Bryan Gilliam. Princeton, N.J.: Princeton U.P., 1992. xi, 425p. ISBN 0-691-09146-3. ML410 .S896 R44.

> Consists of 12 essays by various scholars. Two are about *Daphne*: Bryan Gilliam, "*Daphne*'s Transformation," and a selection of letters between Strauss and librettist Joseph Gregor. The other operatic item is Paul Bekker, "*Elektra*: A Study." Indexed.

1695. *Richard Strauss: New Perspectives on the Composer and His Work.* Ed. Bryan Gilliam. Durham, N.C.: Duke U.P., 1992. ISBN 0-8223-1207-7. ML410 .S896 R56.

> A collection of 10 essays by various scholars. Three are on operatic matters: Reinhold Schlotterer, "Ironic Allusions to Italian Opera in the Musical Comedies of Richard Strauss"; Lewis Lockwood, "The Element of Time in *Der Rosenkavalier*"; and Bryan Gilliam, "Strauss's *Intermezzo*: Innovation and Tradition." Indexed.

Periodicals

1696. *Richard Strauss-Blätter,* 1–, June 1971–. Vienna: Internationale Richard Strauss Gesellschaft, 1971–. Irregular. ML410 .S93 R518.

> Publisher varies. A new (semiannual) series began with numbering from 1–, in June 1979. The earlier series, which ended December 1978, had articles in both German and English, in parallel columns. The *Neue Folge* articles are in either German or English, without translations. The content has been primarily short notices, discographies, and bibliographies, with feature articles of a few pages in length. *RILM* 10–4 (1976): 516, 612–613, gives complete contents of v.1–8. Material of research interest is entered separately below.

Letters and Documents

1697. Brosche, Günter, and Karl Dachs. *Richard Strauss Autographen in München und Wien: Verzeichnis.* Tutzing: Schneider, 1979. xv, 378p. ML134 .S83 B87.

> An inventory of manuscripts and letters, arranged by library, in Munich and Vienna; full bibliographic descriptions. Also 31 letters printed in full for the first time.

See also #255.

Biographies

1698. Del Mar, Norman. *Richard Strauss: A Critical Commentary on His Life and Works.* London: Barrie & Rockliff, 1969–1973. 3v. ISBN 0-8019-5700-1. ML410 .S93 D35.

The standard biography, with footnotes, quoted letters, and documents. Lengthy program notes on the operas, with particular detail for *Ariadne* and *Die Frau ohne Schatten.* Worklist gives titles in English only and very little information (e.g., omits publishers). Discography has label numbers only. Bibliography of about 70 titles, expansive index of names and titles.

1699. Kennedy, Michael. *Richard Strauss: Man, Musician, Enigma.* New York: Cambridge U.P., 1999. xvi, 451p. ISBN 0-521-58173-7. ML410 .S93 K46.

Supersedes his *Richard Strauss* (New York: Schirmer, 1996). The first major biography since Del Mar's, focusing on the personality, which he finds enigmatic. The composer's relationship with the Nazis is explored; it was tricky on both sides, since Strauss had a Jewish daughter-in-law. Music is not much discussed. Backnotes, minor bibliography, expansive index.

1700. Schuh, Willi. *Richard Strauss: A Chronicle of the Early years, 1864–1898.* Trans. Mary Whittall. New York: Cambridge U.P., 1982. 555p. ISBN 0-521-24104-9. ML410 .S93 S38 R52.

Originally *Richard Strauss: Jugend und frühe Meisterjahre. Lebenschronik, 1864–1898* (Zurich: Atlantis, 1976). Useful for background only, as there are only passing references to the major operas, all of which were written after the period covered. Weak bibliography, expansive index of names and titles.

1701. Wilhelm, Kurt. *Richard Strauss: An Intimate Portrait.* Trans. Mary Whittall. New York: Rizzoli, 1989. 312p. ISBN 0-8478-1021-6. ML410 .S896 W541.

Originally *Richard Strauss persönlich: Eine Bildbiographie* (Munich: Kindler, 1984). A collection of excellent illustrations with a sensible commentary, which includes attention to the reception of the operas by critics and cartoonists. Views of the composer's private life are of interest, as are numerous quotations by him. Chronology; index of topics, titles, and names of persons in his life. No footnotes or bibliography (sources of the photos are not identified).

Operas in General

1702. Abert, Anna Amalie. *Johann Strauss: Die Opern.* Hannover: Friedrich, 1972. 133p. ML410 .S93 A52.

Technical analysis of each opera, in terms of libretto, compositional process, harmonic and melodic materials. Many long musical examples. Also a life chronology. No footnotes; bibliography of about 60 entries. No index.

1703. Mann, William. *Richard Strauss: A Critical Study of the Operas.* London: Cassell, 1964. 402p. MT100 .S93 M28.

Also in German: *Richard Strauss: Das Opernwerk,* trans. Willi Reich (Munich: Beck, 1967). Plots and program notes for all the stage works. Bibliography of about 75 items, expansive index of names and titles.

1704. Osborne, Charles. *The Complete Operas of Richard Strauss*. London: O'Mara, 1988. vi, 248p. ISBN 0-948397-51-9. ML410 .S93 O31.

A popular-style consideration of genesis, reception, and synopses with program notes. No footnotes; token bibliography, index.

1705. Schlötterer, Roswitha. "Zum Gesangstil in den Opern von Richard Strauss." *Richard Strauss-Blätter* 36 (December 1996): 52–82.

Considers four singing styles: *secco* recitative, accompanied recitative, aria, and ensemble, giving the composer's ideas on their performance. He used them freely out of their traditional historical contexts.

1706. Jefferson, Alan. "Richard Strauss's Operas Performed in Great Britain." *Richard Strauss-Blätter* 15 (June 1986): 104–179.

Updates an earlier list in *The Operas of Richard Strauss in Great Britain, 1910–63* (London: Society for Theatre Research, 1963), covering here 1910–1985. Chronology, casts, programs.

See also #255, #309, and #1695.

Individual Works

Die ägyptische Helena

1707. Lesnig, Günther. "70 Jahre *Die ägyptische Helena*." *Richard Strauss-Blätter* 38 (December 1997): 3–67.

Unsuccessful at first, the opera gained popularity and has had more than 350 performances worldwide. This is a detailed chronicle of them, with casts.

Arabella

ASO 170 (1996), COH 1989, ENOG 30 (1985).

1708. Bogosavljević, Srdan. "Hofmannsthal's 'Mythological' Opera *Arabella*." In *Theatre and Performance in Austria from Mozart to Jelinek,* ed. Ritchie Robertson and Edward Timms, 73–80 (Edinburgh: Edinburgh U.P., 1993; PN 2611 .T48).

"*Arabella* is a myth of conservative restoration." In 1927 Hofmannsthal was concerned about growing liberalism in Austria and wanted to show the country as the "quintessence of European consciousness." This idea became involved with the Slavs, seen by the poet as "natural" people in the Austrian family. Thus the opera hero is Mandryka, a Slav who dominates the story.

1709. Prochazka, Thomas. "60 Jahre *Arabella* an der Wiener Staatsoper." *Richard Strauss-Blätter* 30 (December 1993): 53–83.

Traces the vacillating fortunes of the opera through reviews and contemporary documents. Recent public opinion is divided. Critics seem to be concentrating on the staging rather than the music.

1710. Lesnig, Günther. "50 Jahre *Arabella* an der Wiener Staatsoper." *Richard Strauss-Blätter* 9 (June 1983): 77–89.

Without overlapping the previous entry, lists the casts of all performances in chronological order.

Ariadne auf Naxos

ASO 77 (1985).

1711. Daviau, Donald G., and George J. Buelow. *The "Ariadne auf Naxos" of Hugo von Hofmannsthal and Richard Strauss.* Chapel Hill: U. of North Carolina Press, 1975. 269p. ISBN 0-8078-8080-9. ML410 .S93 D35.

A scholarly study of the shaping of the libretto (correspondence, revisions) and of the music. Technical discussion of tonality and structure, with musical examples. Bibliography of about 450 titles, no index.

1712. Gräwe, Karl Dietrich. "Sprache, Musik und Szene in *Ariadne auf Naxos* von Hugo von Hofmannsthal und Richard Strauss." Ph.D. diss., Ludwig-Maximilians-U. (Munich), 1969. 357p.

1713. Forsyth, Karen. *"Ariadne auf Naxos" by Hugo von Hofmannsthal and Richard Strauss.* New York: Oxford U.P., 1982. viii, 291p. ISBN 0-19-815536-0. ML50 .S93 A62 F7.

A thorough background treatment, based on the author's Oxford dissertation. Genesis, revisions, critical reception. Detailed analysis of the *Vorspiel*. Hofmannsthal's previously unpublished notes, playbills, musical examples, footnotes. Bibliography of about 90 items, expansive index of names, titles, and topics. More on the genesis is in Richard Kuhns, "The Rebirth of Satyr Tragedy in *Ariadne auf Naxos*," *OQ* 15-4 (Autumn 1999): 435–448.

1714. Erwin, Charlotte Elizabeth. "Richard Strauss's *Ariadne auf Naxos*: An Analysis of Musical Style Based on a Study of Revisions." Ph.D. diss., Yale U., 1976. 265p.

1715. Lesnig, Günther. "70 Jahre *Ariadne auf Naxos.*" *Richard Strauss-Blätter* 26 (December 1991): 54–102.

Details on some 400 performances at the Wiener Staatsoper to 1991. This is a revision of the author's earlier list, in the same journal, 18 (December 1987).

Capriccio

ASO 152 (1993).

1716. Wilhelm, Kurt. *Fürs Wort brauche ich hilfe: Die Geburt der Oper "Capriccio" von Richard Strauss und Clemens Kraus.* Munich: Nymphenburger, 1988. 352p. ISBN 3-4850-0568-1. ML410 .S896 W5.

Genesis, sketches, revisions, scene-by-scene description, reception of the premiere. Then an account of the Kraus performance at the Bayerische Staatsoper, 28 October 1942. With 97 facsimiles and 73 photos (8 in color). Name index.

1717. Lesnig, Günther. "50 Jahre *Capriccio.*" *Richard Strauss-Blätter* 28 (December 1992): 29–78.

Since its premiere in 1942, the opera has become one of the most performed by any composer. This chronology of performances, with casts, has useful photos of theater programs from many countries.

Daphne

1718. Birkin, Kenneth. *"Friedenstag" and "Daphne"*: *An Interpretative Study of the Literary and Dramatic Sources of Two Operas by Richard Strauss*. Outstanding Dissertations in Music from British Universities. New York: Garland, 1989. 321p. ISBN 0-8240-0186-9. ML410 .S93 B48.

Originally the author's dissertation, U. of Birmingham, 1983. Genesis, showing that the two works were planned to be a double bill, presenting a view of peace among men and a view of peace between man and nature. Correspondence between the composer and two librettists (Stefan Zweig and Joseph Gregor), technical analysis. Bibliography, no index.

1719. Gilliam, Bryan Randolph. "Richard Strauss's *Daphne*: Opera and Symphonic Continuity." Ph.D. diss., Harvard U., 1984. 324p. See also Gilliam's essay in 1694.

1720. *Richard Strauss-Blätter* 3 (1972) was a special issue on *Daphne*.

Elektra

ASO 92 (1986), COH 1990, ENOG 37 (1988).

1721. Gilliam, Bryan Randolph. *Richard Strauss's "Elektra."* New York: Oxford U.P., 1991. xiv, 265p. ISBN 0-19-313214-1. ML410 .S9 G54.

Primarily a genesis study, detailing the two years of work by the composer and Hofmannsthal. Also structural analysis and reception. Index.

1722. Lesnig, Günther. "75 Jahre *Elektra*." *Richard Strauss-Blätter* 12 (December 1984): 33–64.

Chronology of worldwide performances, with casts.

1723. Kramer, Lawrence. "*Fin-de-siècle* Fantasies: *Elektra*, Degeneration, and Sexual Science." *COJ* 5-2 (July 1993): 141–165.

A deconstructionist treatment of the work, seeking a "feminist understanding." Kramer finds misogyny in operas of the period but also "their possible subversions of it." In *Elektra* there is a "striking instance of the simultaneous workings of participation and subversion." Strauss privileges Elektra's subjectivity while giving her "atavistic traits—animalism, uncleanliness, sensual cruelty, erotic perversity, amorality, automatism"—which deny her that subjectivity. Apart from such observations, the article is useful for detailed micro- and macroanalysis of the music.

1724. Enix, Margery. "A Reassessment of *Elektra* by Strauss." *Indiana Theory Review* 2–3 (Spring 1979): 31–38. ML1 .I4.

The opera is not progressive but "a conservative work for its time." It is traditional in harmonic procedures and tonal syntax, with a clear tonal center. The 20 *Leitmotiven* are harmonically conceived, and most of the opera is diatonic rather than chromatic.

1725. Kaplan, Richard Andrew. "The Musical Language of *Elektra*: A Study in Chromatic Harmony." Ph.D. diss., U. of Michigan, 1985. 190p.

1726. Hawkins, Jocelyn Hunter. "Hofmannsthal's *Elektra*: The Play and the Opera." Ph.D. diss., Indiana U., 1974. 326p.

1727. McDonald, Lawrence Francis. "Compositional Procedures in Richard Strauss' *Elektra*." Ph.D. diss., U. of Michigan, 1976. 196p.

1728. Dinerstein, Norman Myron. "Polychordality in *Salome* and *Elektra*: A Study of the Application of Reinterpretation Technique." Ph.D. diss., Princeton U., 1974. 170p.

1729. Adams, Nancy Ruth. "*Elektra* as Opera and Drama." Ph.D. diss., U. of Pennsylvania, 1989. 312p.

See also #1694.

Feuersnot

1730. Morris, Christopher. "What the Conductor Saw: Sex, Fantasy, and the Orchestra in Strauss's *Feuersnot*." *Journal of Musicological Research* 16–2 (1996): 83–110.

The noteworthy segment in the second opera (1901) by Strauss is an offstage love scene, in which a "combination of orchestral music and stage lighting represent a sexual encounter between characters discreetly silenced and hidden from view." Critics objected to the verisimilitude achieved. Morris analyzes all the elements to explain "how this libidinal exchange [is] conveyed in music." [A similar instance in Shostakovich's *Lady Macbeth* has already been cited (1669)]. Also a general plot and musical study of the work.

Die Frau ohne Schatten

1731. Konrad, Claudia. "*Die Frau ohne Schatten* von Richard Strauss: Studien zur Rezeptionsgeschichte." Ph.D. diss., U. of Hamburg, 1987.

1732. Konrad, Claudia. *"Die Frau ohne Schatten" von Hugo von Hoffmansthal und Richard Strauss: Studien zur Genese, zum Textbuch, und zur Rezeptionsgeschichte.* Hamburger Beiträge zur Musikwissenschaft, 37. Hamburg: K. D. Wagner, 1988. vi, 393p. ISBN 3-889-7904-02. ML423 .H715 K82.

Sources, fairy opera in general, place of this one in the work of Hoffmansthal, premiere reception and performance history, in cultural and political context. Foreign press reactions are of interest. Footnotes, bibliography of about 600 items, no index.

1733. Knaus, Jakob. *Hofmannsthals Weg zur Oper "Die Frau ohne Schatten."* Berlin: de Gruyter, 1971. 151p. ISBN 3-11-001865-9. ML423 .H74 K6.

Originally the author's dissertation (Zurich, 1971). A detailed study of the play and libretto, interactions between author and composer (many letters), the compositional process. Long footnotes, musical examples. Other operas are considered as well. Bibliography of about 120 entries, name index.

1734. Pantle, Sherrill Jean Hahn. "*Die Frau ohne Schatten* by Hugo von Hofmannsthal and Richard Strauss: An Analysis of Text, Music, and Their Relationship." Ph.D. diss., U. of Colorado, 1976. 310p.

1735. Lesnig, Günther. "75 Jahre *Die Frau ohne Schatten*." *Richard Strauss-Blätter* 32 (December 1994): 3–83.

A chronology of 1,300 performances worldwide since 1919. Many photos and house programs.

1736. Hörr-Szalay, Peter. "*Die Frau ohne Schatten* an der Wiener Staatsoper: 80 Jahre im Spiegel der Presskritik." *Richard Strauss-Blätter* 41 (June 1999): 3–27.

An inventory of critical writings about the Vienna performances.

1737. *Richard Strauss-Blätter* 2 (1971) was a special issue on the opera.

See also Levarie (#1337).

Friedenstag

1738. Axt, Eva-Maria. "Musikalische Form als Dramaturgie . . . in der Oper *Friedenstag* von Richard Strauss und Joseph Gregor." Ph.D. diss., Technische U. (Berlin), 1988.

See also Birkin (#1718).

Guntram

1739. Lesnig, Günther. "100 Jahre *Guntram*". *Richard Strauss-Blätter* 31 (June 1994): 3–33.

Genesis, production, and reception of the first Strauss opera (1894). It is now forgotten, and there was not even a centennial performance anywhere. However, there were performances in New York, Milan, and Munich in the 1980s. The article chronicles all performances over the century.

Intermezzo

See #1695.

Der Rosenkavalier

ASO 69/70 (1984), COH 1986, ENOG 8 (1981).

1740. Schuh, Willi. *Der Rosenkavalier: Fassungen, Filmszenarium, Briefe.* Frankfurt: Fischer, 1972. 349p. ISBN 3-10-031533-2. ML410 .S93 A47.

The complete German libretto (1910) is given, with a full discussion of its genesis and several variants, including the author's typescript. Staging directions and diagrams. Correspondence among the many persons concerned with the opera, from 1905 to 1945. Description, with photos, of Robert Wien's 1926 film. Fine plates, bibliography, lists of editions, libretti, and letters, but no index to it all.

1741. Hartlieb-Wallthor, Artur. "Die Personen im *Rosenkavalier*." *Richard Strauss-Blätter* 30 (December 1993): 35–52.

Tries to identify real-life persons behind the characters. The Marschallin was probably Countess Althan; Octavian may have been a member of the Rofranos, an ancient Austrian noble family.

1742. Hartlieb-Wallthor, Artur. "80 Jahre *Der Rosenkavalier*." *Richard Strauss-Blätter* 21 (June 1989): 17–27.

Not a chronology, like those of Lesnig, but an overview in narrative style. The *Blätter* has not published a detailed performance history of the opera.

1743. Jefferson, Alan. "Tonality of the Rose." *Richard Strauss-Blätter* 25 (June 1991): 26–47.

A rather simplified approach to tonal structure of the opera, without diagrams or details.

See also #1695.

Salome

ASO 47/48 (1983), COH (1989), ENOG 37 (1988).

1744. Gilman, Sander L. "Strauss and the Pervert." In *Reading Opera* (#218), 306–327.

Holds that composers choose libretti in part out of cultural considerations and implications of historical and national contexts. The context for *Salome* included Oscar Wilde's great popularity in Germany, with the division of opinion about his trial and homosexuality itself. Some writers linked sexual perversion to the Jews, both being "anti-natural." Wilde's life and his play were both regarded as perverted. Salome is not homosexual but is a "sexual hysteric"; Herod has the "Jewish" quality of incestuous sexuality. But only Eastern Jews were typecast this way. Modern, liberal Jews were in fact the ideal audience Strauss wrote for, and those liberated Jews did accept the opera. Music is not discussed. A dissertation also takes up the Semitic problem: Anne M. Seshadri, "Richard Strauss, *Salome*, and the 'Jewish Question.'" Ph.D. diss., U. of Maryland, 1998. vi, 350p.

1745. Boulay, Jean-Michel. "Monotonality and Chromatic Dualism in Richard Strauss's *Salome*." Ph.D. diss., U. of British Columbia, 1992.

Die schweigsame Frau

1746. Lesnig, Günther. "60 Jahre *Die schweigsame Frau*." *Richard Strauss-Blätter* 34 (December 1995): 57–110.

Not a great success, the opera has had just 67 performances worldwide. Lesnig gives a chronology of them with programs and photos.

Igor Stravinsky (1882–1971)

Letters and Documents

1747. Stravinsky, Igor. *Selected Correspondence.* London: Faber & Faber, 1982–1985. 3v. ISBN 0-571-11724-4. ML410 .S932 A395.

An annotated selection of letters by and to the composer. The correspondence with W. H. Auden, librettist for *The Rake's Progress,* gives some insights into the collaborative process. Expansive index of names and titles.

Biographies

1748. White, Eric Walter. *Stravinsky: The Composer and His Works.* 2nd ed. London: Faber & Faber, 1979. 656p. ISBN 0-571-04923-0. ML410 .S932 W58.

A strong scholarly biography, with footnotes and documents. Includes program notes on the stage works. Chronological worklist, with titles in English only. Catalogue of manuscripts (1904–1952) in Stravinsky's possession. Good annotated bibliography of about 100 entries, including special issues of journals. Name and title (English only) index.

1749. Taruskin, Richard. *Stravinsky and the Russian Tradition: A Biography of the Works through "Mavra."* Berkeley: U. of California Press, 1996. 2v. ISBN 0-520-07099-2. ML410 .S932 T38.

A monumental work of biography and musical analysis, offering vast detail and complete documentation. Taruskin's insights into the music are perceptive and imaginative. *Mavra* is the topic of chapter 19 of v.2. Later volumes will take up the major stage works.

1750. Craft, Robert. *Stravinsky: Glimpses of a Life.* New York: St. Martin's, 1992. xv, 416p. ISBN 0-312-08896-5. ML410 .S932 C85.

This "half biography and half musical commentary" consists of 15 previously published essays and 10 new ones. Craft's close association with Stravinsky allowed him to see "glimpses" closed to the rest of the world, and he offers a revealing (often unflattering) account of the composer's personal life. On the musical side there is a valuable genesis study of *Oedipus rex,* and there are perceptive analyses of *Histoire du soldat* and several instrumental works. Expansive index.

Operas in General

1751. Schouvaloff, Alexander, and Victor Borovsky. *Stravinsky on Stage.* London: Stainer & Bell, 1982. 226p. ISBN 0-85249-604-4. ML410 .S932 S37.

An attractive volume of photographs, many in color, showing major productions worldwide. Also premiere data, including casts, and synopses. Index of theaters, names, and titles.

1752. Lederman, Minna. *Stravinsky in the Theatre.* New York: Pellegrini & Cudahy, 1949. 228p. Reprint, New York: Da Capo, 1975. ML410 .S932 L47.

Discusses all the stage works and gives table of premieres for major cities. Operas included are *Rossignol, Histoire du soldat, Mavra,* and *Oedipus rex.*

An extensive bibliography by Paul Magriel of more than 600 titles is the finest feature of the book: it lists books and articles about each work and provides abstracts for book entries. No index.

1753. Albright, Daniel. *Stravinsky: The Music Box and the Nightingale.* Newark: Gordon & Breach, 1990. vii, 87p. ISBN 2-88124-295-2. ML410 .S9 A6.

Although Stravinsky stated that music is unable to express anything but itself, Albright finds certain ideas in his music. In many works Stravisnky places two systems in opposition: nature (the nightingale) and art (the music box). He illustrates the artificiality of both. Interesting analyses of several works, including a detailed study of *The Rake's Progress*: genesis, philosophical and allegorical aspects. Bibliography, no index.

1754. Walsh, Stephen. *The Music of Stravinsky.* London: Routledge, 1987. 317p. ISBN 0-4150-0198-6. ML410 .S932 W2.

A perceptive, analytic approach to the music, with reference to other studies. Chapter 10 is on *The Rake's Progress*: it covers genesis and technical matters. Bibliography of about 200 items, expansive index.

1755. Dahlhaus, Carl. "Strawinskijs episches Theater." *Beiträge zur Musikwissenschaft* 23 (1981): 163–186.

A close study of the dramatic form in all the operas and theater pieces, with a useful excursus into terminology.

Individual Works

Mavra

See Taruskin (#1749).

Oedipus rex

ASO 174 (1996).

The Rake's Progress

ASO 145 (1992), COH (1982), ENOG 43 (1991), Rororo (1987).

1756. Hunter, Mary. "Igor and Tom: History and Destiny in *The Rake's Progress*." OQ 7-4 (1990–1991): 38–52.

Puzzles over leading motives in the opera. There is one made from Bach's name: what does it mean? Other motives are found to be without "distinctive characteristics, personalities, or other inherent meanings." Hunter finds a "relationship to the texts set to them," however, and accepts passages as motives even with the notes changed or out of order. Some are associated with "larger questions of destiny and death" and "an analogy between Tom's personal fate and Stravinsky's sense of his specifically musical destiny."

1757. Carter, Lee Chandler. "The Progress in *The Rake's Progress*." Ph.D. diss., City U. of New York, 1995. x, 179p.

See also Walsh (#1754).

Jean-Baptiste Stück (1680–1755)

The name is also seen without the umlaut. *Méléagre* is in *FO,* v.26.

Arthur Seymour Sullivan (1842–1900)

1758. Dillard, Philip H. *How Quaint the Ways of Paradox! An Annotated Gilbert and Sullivan Bibliography.* Metuchen, N.J.: Scarecrow, 1991. viii, 208p. ISBN 0-8108-2445-0. ML134 .S97 D5.

A topical arrangement of 530 books, articles, and dissertations. Includes biographies of both men, production accounts, and works of criticism and analysis. Also a list of 526 scores and collections of libretti. Name and title index.

1759. Dillard, Philip H. *Sir Arthur Sullivan: A Resource Book.* Lanham, Md.: Scarecrow, 1996. xiii, 428p. ISBN 0-8108-3157-0. ML410 .S95 D56.

Chronology, dictionary of persons associated with Sullivan, theaters, biographical data, worklist, discography. Bibliography of about 350 items, title and first-line index, name index.

1760. Ledbetter, Steven, and Percy Young. *Arthur Sullivan: The Operas.* New York: Broude, 1994–.

Projected to be 10v., of which one is published: *Trial by Jury.* It concerns genesis, autograph, reception, and the characters of the opera. The libretto is given with notes and the full score with notes and variants. Documentation is thorough.

1761. Stedman, Jane W. *W. S. Gilbert: A Classic Victorian and His Theatre.* New York: Oxford U.P., 1996. xix, 374p. ISBN 0-19-816174-3. PR4715 .G4 S8.

A documented life story, with genesis accounts of the operas, giving great detail on *The Mikado.* Working methods of Gilbert and Sullivan well described. Bibliography of about 150 items, partly expansive index.

1762. Jacobs, Arthur. *Arthur Sullivan: A Victorian Musician.* 2nd ed. Portland, Ore.: Amadeus, 1992. xv, 494p. 0-931-34051-9. ML410 .S95 J28.

First edition, 1984. A plain life story, with little direct notice of the music. Bibliography, index.

1763. Bradley, Ian. *The Complete Annotated Gilbert and Sullivan.* New York: Oxford U.P., 1996. xiv, 1,197p. ISBN 0-19-876503-X. ML49 .S9 A1.

Consists of 13 libretti, amply footnoted to clarify the text. Variant texts are given, with historical notes.

1764. Dixon, Geoffrey. *The Gilbert and Sullivan Concordance: A Word Index to W. S. Gilbert's Libretti for the Fourteen Operas.* New York: Garland, 1987. 2v., 1,877p. ISBN 0-8240-8505. ML49 .S9 A2.

A quoted context is given for each occurrence of every word in the texts, together with its location. This is not only the first Gilbert and Sullivan concordance but the only word index to any composer's libretti. Probably its main value is as a guide to quotations.

1765. Joseph, Tony. *The D'Oyly Carte Opera Company, 1875–1982: An Unofficial History*. Bristol: Bunthorne, 1994. xi, 388p. ISBN 0-9507-9221-1. ML1731.8 .L72 D75.

A well-documented narrative of the company founded by Richard D'Oyly Carte. He brought Gilbert and Sullivan together for their first success, *Trial by Jury*, in 1875 and produced all their other operas. After years of financial difficulties, the organization folded in 1992. Backnotes, 43 illustrations, bibliography of about 120 items, name and title index. No chronology (see #1767).

Two older books are still of value:

1766. *Crowell's Handbook of Gilbert & Sullivan*. Ed. Frank Ledlie Moore. New York: Crowell, 1962. 264p. MT100 .S9747 M7.

Historical and biographical essays on Gilbert, Sullivan, Richard D'Oyly Carte, the Savoy Company, etc. Synopses and program notes on each opera. Chronology, list of the roles, first lines and famous lines, themes and texts. Bibliography of about 35 items, annotated. No index.

1767. Rollins, Cyril, and R. John Witts. *The D'Oyly Carte Opera Company in Gilbert & Sullivan Operas: A Record of Productions, 1875–1961*. London: Michael Joseph, 1962. 186, xxvi p. ML1731 .R85.

All British, American, and Canadian productions of the company are described, with photos and details about persons and events. Index of actors, actresses, composers, librettists, administrators, titles, and theaters.

1768. A website describes the major collection of Gilbert and Sullivan materials in the Morgan Library (New York): <www.nyu.edu/pages/curator/gs/>.

Franz Xaver Süssmayr (1766–1803)

Der Spiegel von Arkadien is in *GO*, v.17.

Karol Szymanowski (1882–1937)

1769. Michalowski, Kornel. *Karol Szymanowski: 1882–1937: Bibliografia 1967–1991; Dyskografia 1981–1991*. Krakow: Musica Lagellonica, 1993. 2v. ISBN 83-7099-001-0. ML134 .S95 M62.

A useful classified bibliography, including newspaper articles and reviews: 1,630 numbered entries. The discography has 203 items. The opera *Król Roger* has about 90 entries. Author and title indexes.

1770. Wightman, A. "The Music of Karol Szymanowski." Ph.D. diss., U. of York, 1972.

1771. Chylinska, Teresa. *Karol Szymanowski: His Life and Works*. Trans. John Glowacki. Los Angeles: U. of Southern California School of Music, distributed by Pendagon, 1993. 355p. ISBN (Pendragon) 1-916545-00-8. ML410 .S98 C55.

Not seen.

Deems Taylor (1885–1966)

1772. Brody, Elaine. *"The King's Henchman*: Fifty Years Later." *Notes* 34–2 (December 1977): 319–322.

The premiere at the Metropolitan Opera was 17 February 1927. The opera had 14 performances over three seasons. Brody discusses it in the light of a letter by Taylor that described his intentions for the work and gave his views on the function of opera.

Petr Il'ich Tchaikovsky (1840–1893)

Various Roman alphabet spellings (transliterations) of the name are common. The Library of Congress now accepts Tchaikovsky in place of Chaikovsky, with the first names as shown here.

Editions

1773. Tchaikovsky, Peter Ilich. *New Edition of the Complete Works = Novoe polnoe sobranie sochinenii.* Ed. Ljodmila Z. Korabel'nikova et al. Moscow: Muzyka; Mainz: Schott, 1993–. M3 .C42.

In progress. V.1–21 will include all the stage works.

Biographies

1774. Brown, David. *Tchaikovsky: A Biographical and Critical Study.* New York: Norton, 1978–1991. 4v. ISBN 0-393-07535-2. ML410 .C4 B87.

A strong life and works, with extensive material on the operas. For each there is genesis and background information, synopses, program notes, and technical observations. Many musical examples and thorough documentation with primary sources. Name and title index.

See also *New Grove Russian Masters 1* (#2642) and Richard Taruskin's valuable entry in *NGDO* 4, 662–672.

Operas in General

Program notes on all the operas appear in Abraham, *Slavonic and Romantic Music* (#2634).

Individual Works

Eugene Onegin (Evgenii Onegin)

ASO 43 (1982), *ENOG* 38 (1988), Rororo (1985). See also Abraham, *On Russian Music* (#2636).

The Queen of Spades (Pique dame; Pikovaia dama)

ASO 119/120 (1989).

The Smith (Kuznets Vakula)

See Taylor (#1563).

Georg Philipp Telemann (1681–1767)

Don Quichotte auf der Hochzeit des Comacho is in *RMBE,* v.64.

1775. Ottzenn, Curt. *Telemann als Opernkomponist: Ein Beitrag zur Geschichte der Hamburger Oper.* Berlin: Ebering, 1902. 88p. ML410 .T2 O9.

Program notes on *Der geduldige Sokrates, Sieg der Schönheit, Damon, Pimpinone, Adelheid, Miriways, Emma und Eginhard, Flavius Bertaridus,* and *Don Quichotte.* Name index.

1776. Peckham, Mary Adelaide. "The Operas of Georg Philipp Telemann." Ph.D. diss., Columbia U., 1972. iv, 303p.

1777. Ruhnke, M. "Telemanns Hamburger Opern und ihre italienischen und französischen Vorbilder." *Hamburger Jahrbuch für Musikwissenschaft 5* (1981): 9–27.

Technical descriptions and examination of sources for *Flavius Bertaridus, Miriways, Sieg der Schönheit, Der geduldige Sokrates, Damon,* and *Orpheus.*

See also *New Grove North European* (#170).

Ambroise Thomas (1811–1896)

1778. Rogeboz-Malfroy, Elisabeth. *Ambroise Thomas, temoin du siècle 1811–1896.* Besançon: Éditions Cêtre, 1994. 327p. ISBN 2-8782-3098-1. ML410 .T475 R72.

A useful life and works, with description of each opera. Premiere data given, including cast, and details on later productions. Synopses, lists of musical numbers, and technical observations. Footnotes, bibliography of about 250 items, name index.

See also Achter (#728).

Virgil Thomson (1896–1989)

1779. Meckna, Michael. *Virgil Thomson: A Bio-Bibliography.* Bio-Bibliographies in Music, 4. New York: Greenwood, 1986. xiv, 203p. ISBN 0-313-25010-3. ML134 .T43 M4.

A useful list of 195 musical and literary works by Thomson and 288 citations to literature about him. About 40 items are reviews or brief notices of *Four Saints in Three Acts.*

1780. Sundman, Alexandra Gail. "The Making of an American Expatriate Composer in Paris." Ph.D. diss., Yale U., 1999. 2v.

1781. Ward, Kelly M. "An Analysis of the Relationship between Text and Musical Shape . . . in *Four Saints in Three Acts* by Virgil Thomson." Ph.D. diss., U. of Texas, 1978. 387p.

Michael Tippett (1905–1998)

ENOG 29 (1985) covers all the operas.

1782. Theil, Gordon. *Michael Tippett: A Bio-Bibliography.* Music Reference Collection, 21. New York: Greenwood, 1989. xii, 344p. ISBN 0-313-24270-4. ML134 .T5 T5.

A useful guide to reviews and notices on the operas.

1783. Kemp, Ian. *Tippett: The Composer and His Music.* New York: Oxford U.P., 1987. xi, 516p. ISBN 0-9038-7323-0. ML410 .T59 K32.

A life and works, with good technical analysis of *The Midsummer Marriage, King Priam,* and *The Knot Garden.* Bibliography, index.

1784. White, Eric Walter. *Tippett and His Operas.* London: Barrie & Jenkins, 1979. 142p. ISBN 0-214-20573-8. ML410 .T595 W58.

Synopses, premiere data, and program notes for four operas (*New Year* was not yet written). Letters from Tippett to White, regarding *The Midsummer Marriage,* are quoted extensively. Without notes, musical examples, or bibliography. Index of names, titles, and topics.

1785. Scheppach, Margaret A. *Dramatic Parallels in Michael Tippett's Operas: Analytical Essays on the Musico-Dramatic Techniques.* Studies in the History and Interpretation of Music, 22. Lewiston, N.Y.: Mellen, 1990. viii, 184p. ISBN 0-88946-447-2. ML410 .T59 S325.

Technical studies of the five operas, in search of meaning and messages. The musical analyses are basic but clear. Bibliography, no index.

1786. Jones, Richard Elfyn. *The Early Operas of Michael Tippett: A Study of "The Midsummer Marriage," "King Priam," and "The Knot Garden."* Lewiston, N.Y.: Mellen, 1996. ISBN 0-7734-8816-2. ML410 .T59 J79.

Detailed technical analyses, with backnotes, 152 musical examples, and name index.

1787. Dickinson, A. E. F. "Round about *The Midsummer Marriage.*" *M&L* 37 (1956): 50–60.

Program note, with a search for unifying features. Finds "notable gaps in continuity and distracting infelicities of language" and that "proportions appear debatable," but the "composer has found the right musical means for his ends."

1788. *Tippett Studies.* Ed. David Clarke. New York: Cambridge U.P., 1999. xv, 232p. ISBN 0-521-59205-4. ML410 .T59 T59.

A collection of essays by various authors. Includes Arnold Whittall, "'Is There a Choice at All?' *King Priam* and Motives for Analysis"—a highly technical study of harmonic elements—and Rowena Pollard and David Clarke, "Tippett's *King Priam* and the 'Tragic Vision'"—genesis, Tippett's philosophy of death and his interpretation of Aristotle's catharsis, technical analysis.

Tommaso Traetta (1727–1779)

1789. Riedlbauer, Jörg. *Die Opern von Tommaso Trajetta.* Studien und Materialen zur Musikwissenschaft, 7. Hildesheim: Olms, 1994. ix, 585p. ISBN 3-487-09798-2. ML410 .T76 R6.

"Trajetta" is the spelling on the title page. The book is based on the author's dissertation, Regensburg U., 1990. It gives a brief life story, then a section on each opera: program notes with some musical examples and technical comments. Footnotes, thematic catalogue (with incipits of the arias), bibliography of some 200 items (only a few actually about Traetta), index of names and places.

1790. Cantrell, Byron. "Tommaso Traetta and His Opera *Sofonisba.*" Ph.D. diss., U. of California at Los Angeles, 1957. 256p.

Ignaz Umlauf (1746–1796)

Die schöne Schwesterin is in *GO*, v.13.

Ralph Vaughan Williams (1872–1958)

1791. Butterworth, Neil. *Ralph Vaughan Williams: A Guide to Research.* Garland Composer Resource Manuals, 21. New York: Garland, 1990. x, 382p. ISBN 0-8240-7746-6. ML134 .V3 B9.

A useful handbook of varied information, including a detailed worklist and discography. The main section consists of 564 annotated entries for the secondary literature, in classified arrangement; 64 items relate to the stage works—nearly all of them synopses and brief notices. General index, index of works, and index of artists on the cited recordings.

1792. Day, James. *Vaughan Williams.* 3rd ed. New York: Oxford U.P., 1998. xiii, 343p. ISBN 0-19-816632-X. ML410 .V3 D4.

First edition, 1961. Life and works, with a chapter on the operas (p.157–173), giving genesis and program notes. Worklist, bibliography of about 100 items, expansive index.

1793. Reber, William Francis. "The Operas of Ralph Vaughan Williams." D.Mus. diss., U. of Texas, 1977. 536p.

1794. Meares, Stanley. *"Pilgrim's Progress." British Music Society Journal* 5 (1983): 1–26.

A musical analysis, with critical comments.

1795. Forbes, Anne-Marie. "Motivic Unity in Ralph Vaughan Williams' *Riders to the Sea.*" *MR* 44 (1983): 234–245.

Identifies 23 motives, in four "families," and relationships among them. The situation is nicely clarified with diagrams.

Giuseppe Verdi (1813–1901)

To keep this section within reasonable bounds, a number of citations to items in Harwood (#1800) are made instead of full bibliographic entries. Indeed, this coverage of Verdi material is best viewed as a representative sample of important writings in different areas of Verdi scholarship. The reader will find all these areas greatly enriched in Harwood's bibliography.

Editions

1796. Verdi, Giuseppe. *The Works = Le opere.* Ed. Philip Gossett et al. Chicago: University of Chicago Press; Milan: Ricordi, 1983–. M3. V48.

A definitive new edition, in progress. Series 1, operas, to be 31v. These have appeared (1999): *Nabucco, Ernani, Luisa Miller, Rigoletto, Il trovatore, Alzira,* and *La traviata.* For each work there is a score and extensive critical commentary in English, covering sources, variants, and measure-by-measure annotations. Volumes are footnoted but without bibliographies or indexes.

Thematic Catalogues and Worklists

1797. Chusid, Martin. *A Catalogue of Verdi's Operas.* Hackensack, N.J.: J. Boonin, 1974. xi, 201p. ISBN 0-913574-05-8. ML134 .V47 C5.

The standard list, containing much useful material: premiere dates and casts, autographs, early scores, locations of sources, arias and numbers of each work with alternatives and variants from different versions, and inventories of full scores and piano-vocal scores. Bibliography of about 180 entries. Name index with identifiers ("tenor," "librettist").

1798. Hopkinson, Cecil. *A Bibliography of the Works of Giuseppe Verdi, 1813–1901.* New York: Broude, 1973–1978. 2v. ISBN 0-8450-7004-5. ML134 .V47 H6.

An attempt to record all editions in all formats of all the works of Verdi. Gives musical incipits, publishing histories, locations, plate numbers, bibliographic descriptions, and commentaries. Hopkinson notes omissions in Chusid's catalogue (previous entry), wondering why they were not selected; but others (e.g., next entry, and Andrew Porter in *The Verdi Companion* [#1806]) have called attention to lacunae in Hopkinson's supposedly complete list. The bibliographer's dilemma is vividly presented: if you are selective, they will wonder about your criteria; if you try to be comprehensive, they will always find something you left out.

1799. Bartoli, Maria Adelaide Bacherini. "Aggiunte, integrazioni, e rettifiche alla *Bibliography of the Works of Giuseppe Verdi* di Cecil Hopkinson: Edizioni verdiane nella Biblioteca Nazionale Centrale di Firenze." *Studi verdiani* 4 (1986–1987): 110–135.

Addenda and corrigenda for #1798, noting materials in the Florence national library that were overlooked by Hopkinson.

Bibliographies and Guides to Resources

1800. Harwood, Gregory. *Giuseppe Verdi: A Guide to Research.* Garland Composer Resource Manuals, 42. New York: Garland, 1998. xxx, 396p. ISBN 0-8240-4117-8. ML134 .V47 H37.

An essential handbook for Verdi studies, centered on 1,036 thoroughly annotated entries for the secondary literature. Other useful lists include literary sources for the operas, alternative titles associated with the operas, a chronology, a worklist, and biographical notices on persons connected with the composer. Indexes of authors, editors, translators, and an expansive index of topics. Regular bibliographic listings in *Studi verdiani* (#1811) and *Verdi Newsletter* (#1812) will serve to update Harwood.

1801. Kämper, Dietrich. "Das deutsche Verdi-Schriftum: Hauptlinien der Interpretation." *Analecta musicologica* 11 (1972): 185–197.

Reviews the German writings on Verdi from the earliest notice in 1843. Skepticism prevailed before Hermann Abert. Wagnerian influences are a pervasive concern (Wagner himself wrote nothing about Verdi).

Conferences

1802. *Atti del I° (II° etc.) Congresso Internazionale di Studi Verdiani* . . . Parma: Istituto di Studi Verdiani, 1969–. ML36 .C769.

Proceedings for these conferences have been published under the title *Atti*: 1 (1966, Venice); 2 (1969, Verona, Parma, Busseto) on *Don Carlos*; 3 (1972, Milan). Descriptions and contents in Harwood (#1800), items 224–226.

1803. *Verdi's Middle Period, 1849–1859: Source Studies, Analysis, and Performance Practice.* Ed. Martin Chusid. Chicago: U. of Chicago Press, 1997. xii, 436p. ISBN 0-226-10658-6. ML410 .V4 V354.

Papers given at the International Verdi Congress, Belfast, March 1993. Contents in Harwood (#1800), item 235.

1804. "Colloquium Verdi-Wagner, Rome 1969: Bericht." Ed. Friedrich Lippmann. *Analecta musicologica* 11 (1972): 1–342.

This issue of the journal presents 19 papers from the conference. Four are cited separately: Ziino (#1968), Kämper (#1801), Dahlhaus (#2007), and Celletti (#1845).

Other congress reports are entered under individual operas.

Collections of Essays

1805. Martin, George. *Aspects of Verdi.* New York: Dodd, Mead, 1988. xiv, 304p. ISBN 0-396-08843-0. ML410 .V4 M264.

A valuable collection of Martin's essays, including some revisions of material published previously. Contents in Harwood (#1800), item 244.

1806. *The Verdi Companion.* Ed. William Weaver and Martin Chusid. New York: Norton, 1979. 366p. ISBN 0-393-01215-8. Reprint, London: Gollancz, 1980. ML410 .V4 V295.

Essays (some previously published) by various scholars on Verdi and politics, Verdi and his impresarios and publishers, his librettists, his treatment of the voice, and his obscure contemporaries. The most useful contribution is the selective bibliography by Andrew Porter: a critical inventory that is truly critical. There is also a long chronology of Verdi, p.255–324. Further contents in Harwood (#1800), item 248.

1807. Petrobelli, Pierluigi. *Music in the Theater: Essays on Verdi and Other Composers.* Trans. Roger Parker and William Drabkin. Princeton, N.J.: Princeton U.P., 1994. ix, 192p. ISBN 0-691-09134-X. ML410 .V2 P28.

Eleven essays, eight of them on Verdi. Contents in Harwood (#1800), item 378.

1808. Parker, Roger. *Leonora's Last Act: Essays in Verdian Discourse.* Princeton, N.J.: Princeton U.P., 1997. xii, 187p. ISBN 0-691-01557-0. ML410 .V4 P155.

Eight essays, two of them previously published. Five are entered separately: #1853, #1883, #1887, #1902, and #1941.

Periodicals

1809. *Verdi: Bollettino dell'Istituto di Studi Verdiani* 1–, 1960–. Parma: Istituto di Studi Verdiani, 1960–. Irregular. ML410 .V4 V3.

Title varies. Most numbers focus on one opera. Individual issues are noted below under their operas. Contents of all numbers from 1960 to 1989 are in Harwood (#1800), p. xxv.

1810. *Quaderni* 1–, 1963–. Parma: Istituto di Studi Verdiani, 1963–. Irregular. ML410 .V4 I8 Q3.

Numbers are devoted to specific operas. Individual issues are noted below under their operas. Contents of numbers 1–5 are in Harwood (#1800), p. xxv.

1811. *Studi verdiani* 1–, 1982–. Parma: Istituto di Studi Verdiani, 1982–. Irregular. ML410. V53 574.

Last one seen, v.12 (1997). Volumes have useful bibliographies of current writing on Verdi, by author, with subject indexing; there were 186 entries in v.12. Also discographies.

1812. *Verdi Newsletter* 1–, 1976–. New York: American Institute for Verdi Studies, 1976–. Irregular. ML5 .V4 A64.

Title varies. Each issue has a bibliography of new publications, including dissertations and journal articles, reviews of books, and notices of worldwide performances. Issues 9–10 include a description of the New York University Verdi Archive.

Letters and Documents

1813. Cesari, Gaetano, and Alessandro Luzio. *I copialettere di Giuseppe Verdi.* Milan: n.p., 1913. Reprint, Bologna: Forni, 1968. xx, 759p. ML410 .V4 A3.

The *copialettere* are Verdi's correspondence notebooks, in which he drafted and copied his letters. Cesari presents 398 letters with commentaries. Criteria for the selection are not given, and unexplained chronological gaps are found. Eccentric suppressions and various inaccuracies cloud the value of this important resource. Index of names, titles, and topics. It is best to avoid the English translation by Charles Osborne of 293 of these letters (see #1820).

See also #246.

1814. Luzio, Alessandro. *Carteggi verdiani*. Rome: Accademia Nazionale dei Lincei, 1935–1947. 4v. ML410 .V4 A42.

Letters, documents, and facsimiles generally adding to previously published material. Well indexed by name and title of composition. Full description in Harwood (#1800), item 29.

1815. *Verdi: The Man in His Letters*. Ed. Franz Werfel and Paul Stefan. Trans. Edward O. D. Downes. New York: L. B. Fischer, 1942. 469p. Reprint, New York: Vienna House, 1973. ISBN 0-8443-0088-8. ML410 .V4 A385.

Originally *Giuseppe Verdi Briefe* (Berlin: Paul Zsolnay, 1926). A selection from the *Copialettere* and the *Carteggi veridani* for the period 1880–1901, with brief comments. Expansive index of names, topics, and places.

1816. *The Verdi-Boito Correspondence*. Trans. William Weaver. Chicago: U. of Chicago Press, 1994. lxiv, 321p. ISBN 0-226-85304-7. ML410 .V4 A4.

Originally *Carteggio Verdi-Boito*, ed. Mario Medici and Marcello Conati (Parma: Istituto di Studi Verdiani, 1978). A scholarly edition, presenting 301 letters with extensive commentaries. Indexed by name, date, place, and composition title. Further information in Harwood (#1800), item 46. The English translation conceals the curious fact that Boito invariably addresses Verdi in the most formal style (*Lei*), while Verdi addresses him with the semiformal *voi*.

1817. *Carteggio Verdi-Ricordi 1880–1881*. Ed. Pierluigi Petrobelli, Marisa Di Gregorio Casati, and Carlo Matteo Mossa. Parma: Istituto di Studi Verdiani, 1988. xxiv, 347p. ISBN 88-85065-06-8. ML410 .V4 A4.

Presents 246 letters and telegrams, with commentaries. The main topic is the revision of *Simon Boccanegra,* which premiered in 1881 at La Scala. Indexed by writers, names, titles, places, and institutions. Further information in Harwood (#1800), item 80.

1818. *Carteggio Verdi-Ricordi 1882–1885*. Ed. Franca Cella, Madina Ricordi, and Marisa Di Gregorio Casati. Parma: Istituto Nazionale di Studi Verdiani, 1994. xxii, 540p. ISBN 88-85065-11-2. ML410 .V4 A4 1994b.

A collection of 346 documents, many published for the first time. Topics include operas in progress (*Otello* and the *Don Carlos* revision) and the recently produced revision of *Simon Boccanegra*. Indexed by writers, names, titles, places, and institutions. A continuation volume, for 1886–1888, was announced but has not been seen.

1819. Jensen, Luke. *Giuseppe Verdi and Giovanni Ricordi, with Notes on Francesco Lucca: From "Oberto" to "La traviata."* New York: Garland, 1989. ix, 456p. ISBN 0-8240-5616-7. ML410 .V4 J46.

Revision of the author's dissertation, New York U., 1987. Includes letters, contracts and documents (among them the *libroni*—internal ledgers of the Ricordi firm), and full discussion of their context. The publisher Lucca was a competitor of Ricordi's, engaged by Verdi for three operas when he and Ricordi were out of sorts. Among the interesting aspects of this study is information about Verdi's working habits. No index.

1820. Gossett, Philip. Review of Charles Osborne, *Letters of Giuseppe Verdi. MQ* 59–4 (1973): 633–639.

Criticizes the Osborne translation of the *copialettere,* citing "an enormous number of errors in translations and commentary." "Blatantly false translations abound in large measure, and Osborne seems unaware of even the most accessible Verdi literature."

1821. Conati, Marcello. *Encounters with Verdi.* Trans. Richard Stokes. Ithaca, N.Y.: Cornell U.P., 1984. 417p. ISBN 0-575-03349-5. ML410 .V4 I753.

Originally *Interviste e incontri con Verdi* (Milan: Emme, 1981). Published also as *Interviews and Encounters with Verdi* (London: Gollancz, 1984). Consists of 50 contributions by authors from various countries, narrating visits and meetings with the master. Footnotes, bibliography of about 250 items, index of names and titles.

Biographies

1822. Baldini, Gabriele. *The Story of Giuseppe Verdi: "Oberto" to "Un ballo in maschera."* Trans. and ed. Roger Parker. New York: Cambridge U.P., 1980. xx, 296p. ISBN 0-521-22911-1. ML410 .V48 B1363.

Originally *Abitare la battaglia: La storia di Giuseppe Verdi* (ed. Fedele D'Amico; Milan: Garzanti, 1970). A biographical account interwoven with discussions of the operas, mostly from a literary point of view. Parker adds a useful preface and reference footnotes.

1823. Budden, Julian. *Verdi.* Rev. ed. London: Dent, 1993. xi, 404p. ISBN 0-460-86111-5. Reprint, New York: Schirmer, 1996. ISBN 0-02-864616-9. ML410 .V4 B9.

First edition, 1985. A useful life and works, including a chronology, worklist, biographical dictionary of friends and associates, bibliography, and name index.

1824. Kimbell, David R. B. *Verdi in the Age of Italian Romanticism.* New York: Cambridge U.P., 1981. ix, 703p. ISBN 0-521-23052-7. ML410 .V4 K5.

A valuable account of the cultural and political scene into the 1850s and Verdi's relationship to it. Genesis and analysis of the early operas (from *Oberto,* 1839, to *La traviata,* 1853) in that romantic context; attention to censorship and business aspects. Backnotes, musical examples, and many documents. Also sections on the arias, ensembles, recitatives, orchestration, and so on. Weak bibliography: important items are missing, and incomplete data are given for the 100 or so entries. Expansive index of names, topics, and titles.

1825. Mila, Massimo. *La giovinezza di Verdi.* 2nd ed. Musica e musicisti, 1. Turin: ERI, 1978. 541p. ML410 .V48 M59.

First edition, 1958. A valuable account of Verdi's life and works to 1853. Biography and analyses of the operas are interwoven. Detailed worklist, indexes of names and titles.

1826. *Verdi: A Documentary Study.* Comp., ed., and trans. William Weaver. London: Thames & Hudson, 1977. 256p. ISBN 0-500-01184-2. ML410 .V4 V29.

A fine assemblage of 118 illustrations, 54 in color—pages from scores, pictures of documents, and of all Verdi's persons and places, sets, and costumes. Also an annotated selection of letters. Index of names and titles.

1827. Pauls, Birgit. *Giuseppe Verdi und das Risorgimento: Ein politischer Mythos im Prozess der Nationenbildung.* Berlin: Akademie Verlag, 1996. 353p. ISBN 3-05-003013-5. ML410 .V4 P18.

Based on the author's dissertation, U. of Frankfurt, 1996. A revisionist view of Verdi's long-acclaimed role in the Italian unification movement, finding the so-called political messages of the operas illusory. There were social themes in the texts, however, and Verdi as a person did take part in political life (he served as a senator). The whole Risorgimento movement is carefully presented. Bibliography, name index.

1828. Phillips-Matz, Mary Jane. *Verdi: A Biography.* New York: Oxford U.P., 1993. xxx, 941p. ISBN 0-19-313204-4. ML410 .V4 P43.

A strong life and works, the longest in English, drawing on archival and little-known sources. Family background and youth are stressed, as well as Verdi's relationships with women. Verdi's composing is approached from a business viewpoint. The book is scholarly and sensible, without dramatization.

1829. Basevi, Abramo. *Studio sulle opere di Verdi.* Florence: Tofani, 1859. xi, 324p. ML410 .V53 B3.

Consists of 20 chapters, one on each opera up to *Aroldo.* Determines that Verdi was an eclectic composer who drew upon the styles of Rossini, Donizetti, the French school, and even (in *Simon Boccanegra*) the German school. Expansive index. See Powers (#1852) and Parker (#1853) for discussions related to Basevi's book.

See also *NGDO* 4, 932–953, the most up-to-date biography, by Roger Parker, and *New Grove Masters of Italian Opera* (#2480), a fine study by Andrew Porter.

Operas in General

1830. Budden, Julian. *The Operas of Verdi.* Rev. ed. New York: Oxford U.P., 1992. 3v. ISBN 88-7063-038-2; 88-7063-042-0; 88-7063-058-7. ML410 .V4 B88.

First edition, 1973–1981. This edition is only slightly altered; in fact, Budden refers to it in the preface as a reprint. Some corrections are made passim, and there is some updating in the notes. It remains the most satisfactory commentary on the operas, presenting historical and technical viewpoints in great detail, with ample reference to earlier research. Strong sections explicate the opera scene of Verdi's time. Relevant letters are given (in English only). The operas are analyzed, with about 1,000 musical examples to illustrate the arguments. On the negative side, Budden reveals a blind spot toward macroanalysis (tonal, structural), which leaves him uncertain about an opera's formal plan. And the bibliography—unchanged from the first edition—is a disappointing array in the *New Grove* style: articles unpaginated, authors identified by initials instead of full names, and lack of publishers for book entries. Name, title, and topic indexes.

1831. Parker, Roger. *Studies in Early Verdi (1832–1844): New Information and Perspectives on the Milanese Musical Milieu, and the Operas from "Oberto" to "Ernani."* Outstanding Dissertations in Music from British Universities. New York: Garland, 1989. 232p. ISBN 0-8240-2020-0. ML410 .V4 P157.

The *Oberto* discussion examines Verdi's autograph score. Other topics include the libretto of *Un giorno di regno,* the early performance history of *Nabucco,* and the influence of singers in *I lombardi.* An extract is cited under *Ernani* (#1878).

See also Gerhard (#2272).

Libretti

1832. Lavagetto, Mario. *Quei più modesti romanzi: Il libretto nel melodramma di Verdi.* Milan: Garzanti, 1979. 205p. ML410 .V4 L33.

The texts are examined from many viewpoints: dramaturgy, characterization, plot structure, and linguistic/prosodic elements. Various librettists are discussed and compared. Bibliography, no index.

1833. Parker, Roger. "On Reading Nineteenth-Century Opera: Verdi through the Looking Glass." In *Reading Opera* (#218), 288–305.

Observes that "we can espouse no 'ideal' way in which words and music will make drama together, and that we should be careful not to approach the issue with unconscious or *a priori* assumptions, to see things in terms of 'improvement' from one composer, period, or national school to another." Nevertheless, comparisons will have their way, and Parker does see Verdi as losing creative energy as he moved from the traditional libretto. Boito's skillful texts sustained the composer then and refueled his creativity.

1834. Van, Gilles de. *Verdi's Theater: Creating Drama through Music.* Trans. Gilda Roberts. Chicago: U. of Chicago Press, 1998. x, 424p. ISBN 0-226-14369-14. ML410 .V4 V26.

Originally *Verdi: Un théâtre en musique* (Paris: Fayard, 1992). A useful account of Verdi's developing ideas about dramaturgy. His work is compared with that of his contemporaries. The way his libretti took shape is closely analyzed. Name and title indexes.

Production and Reception

1835. Martin, George. *Verdi at the Golden Gate: Opera and San Francisco in the Gold Rush Years.* Berkeley: U. of California Press, 1993. xxii, 321p. ISBN 0-520-08123-4 ML1711.8 .S2 M37.

Eight Verdi operas were staged in San Francisco in the 1850s, gaining favorable reactions. This is a detailed account of the reception, in the context of operatic life on the West Coast. Much information is included about theatrical life in San Francisco, with data on the individual houses and lists of premieres. A table shows later Verdi productions in the city, up to 1899. Expansive index.

1836. Conati, Marcello. "Prima le scene, poi la musica." *Studi musicali* 26 (1997): 519–541.

It was "organic" with Verdi to plan—from the first sketches—for the spectacle of an opera, along with the words and music. He worked on all aspects at once. Examples of his directions for various operas are given to illustrate this point, especially in *Simon Boccanegra*.

1837. Conati, Marcello. *La bottega della musica: Verdi e La Fenice*. Milan: Il Saggiatore, 1983. 452p. No ISBN. ML410 .V4 C67.

A thorough discussion of the composer's negotiations with the Venetian opera house La Fenice. Archival materials in the house library are described and used for the study. More than 350 letters or documents are photocopied and indexed. The operas premiered at La Fenice were *Ernani, Attila, Rigoletto, La traviata,* and *Simon Boccanegra*.

1838. Petrobelli, Pierluigi, et al. *"Sorgete! Ombre serene!" L'aspetto visivo dello spettacolo verdiano*. 2nd ed. Parma: Istituto Nazionale di Studi Verdiani, 1996. 200p. ISBN 88-85065-123-9. ML141 .P2 V476.

The catalogue of an exhibition on scenography and costume in Verdi productions, including modern stagings. More than 100 illustrations, with extensive commentaries and documentation. Useful list of 29 scenographers and some facts about them, as well as a bibliography of about 100 entries on visual aspects of Verdi productions. Valuable introductory essay, discussing the composer's involvement with these matters.

1839. Rosen, David. "The Staging of Verdi's Operas: An Introduction to the Ricordi *disposizioni sceniche*." In *Report of the 12th Congress of the International Musicological Society, Berkeley, 1977,* ed. Daniel Heartz and Bonnie Wade, 444–453 (Kassel: Bärenreiter, 1981; ML26 .I62).

The production books (*disposizioni sceniche*) gave detailed instructions for staging matters and are thus a valuable guide to performance practice of the time. Verdi gave his approval to these books, so they are also a guide to his intentions. Rosen believes he was primarily interested in realism and "visual magnificence." The book presents an inventory of the production books—and some French equivalents, used in Verdi works—and their locations, with bibliographic detail.

Analysis: Harmony

1840. Vlad, Roman. "Alcune osservazioni sulla struttura delle opere di Verdi." In *Atti* (#1802), v.3, 495–522.

Not so much about structure, as the article title suggests, but about harmony at the microlevel. Vlad disputes the common view that Verdi was conservative in harmonization. He gives examples to show progressive tendencies—from *Rigoletto* on—for instance, chromaticism, modality, and free treatment of dissonance.

1841. Vlad, Roman. "Anticipazioni nel linguaggio armonico verdiano." *Rassegna musicale* 21 (1951): 237–245.

Describes harmonic practices of Verdi that anticipate later practice: polytonality, modality, dissonance treatment, unusual modulations, and so on. Such techniques appear early and are found throughout Verdi's works, so they could not have originated as Wagner imitations.

1842. Pizzetti, Ildebrando. "Contrappunto e armonia nell'opera di Verdi." *Rassegna musicale* 21 (1951): 189–200.

An overview of Verdi's harmonic and contrapuntal practice, finding more sophistication in it than has been generally credited to him. A close look at the harmonies of a *Rigoletto* aria points out the subtleties.

Analysis: Melody and Voice

1843. Wedell, Friedrich. *Annäherung an Verdi: Zur Melodik des jungen Verdi und ihren musiktheoretischen und ästhetischen Voraussetzungen.* Kieler Schriften zur Musikwissenschaft, 44. Kassel: Bärenreiter, 1995. xix, 344p. ISBN 3-7618-1259-0. ML290.4 .W43.

Originally the author's Ph.D. dissertation, Kiel U., 1995. Summarizes a number of treatises on melody that would have been known to Verdi, then sees to what extent he attended to them. Wedell then compares Verdi's melodic practice to that of Bellini and Donizetti. Without index.

1844. Crutchfield, Will. "Vocal Ornamentation in Verdi: The Phonographic Evidence." *19thCM* 7 (1983–1984): 3–54.

Studies more than 1,200 early Verdi recordings and gives transcriptions of 207 examples by 74 singers. A valuable analysis of these performances enhances understanding of improvised ornamentation and cadenzas by singers contemporary with the composer, including some who had worked with him. Biographical summaries on the singers, discographical information.

1845. Celletti, Rodolfo. "Lo stile vocale di Verdi e di Wagner." *Analecta musicologica* 11 (1972): 328–341.

Verdi and Wagner gave similar roles to tenors, sopranos, and mezzos but a variety of roles to baritones. In Wagner the soprano and tenor are heroic voices (*Heldentenor*). Bellini began the "massacre" of the voice by raising the tessitura about a third. Verdi then increased orchestral accompaniments, requiring louder singing. His *tenore di grazie* evolved into the *tenore di forza*. Otello is his only *Heldentenor*. Wagner departed from the traditional vocality in *Tristan* and *Siegfried*—presenting a wider range and quick moves from one vocal area to another. Isolde and Kundry are the novel sopranos (Kundry is something of a Rossinian soprano). In sum, the major difference between the approaches of the two composers is in their handling of the text.

1846. Edwards, Geoffrey, and Ryan Edwards. *The Verdi Baritone: Studies in the Development of Dramatic Character.* Bloomington: Indiana U. Press, 1994. x, 193p. ISBN 0-253-31949-8. ML410 .V4 E3.

Goes through the leading baritone roles in seven operas and explains—in extended program notes—how their character is displayed through musical means. What it seems to amount to is that Verdi followed the story. Backnotes, bibliography, no index.

1847. Andre, Naomi Adele. "Azucena, Eboli, and Amneris: Verdi's Writing for Women's Lower Voices." Ph.D. diss., Harvard U., 1996. ix, 430p.

Analysis: Rhythm

1848. Noske, Frits R. "Verdi and the Musical Figure of Death." In *Signifier* (#1285), 171–214.

A chapter devoted to the idea that death in opera is frequently associated with the anapest. Noske finds examples from Lully through Berlioz and notes Verdi's use of the device, especially in *Macbeth*.

1849. Rosen, David. "Meter, Character, and *tinta* in Verdi's Operas." In *Verdi's Middle Period* (#1803), 339–392.

Observes the different moods engaged by Verdi's use of various triple meters: 3/8, 3/4, and 6/8. During the middle period, 3/8 was more common. The distinction is always important for expressing the situation and should not be passed over by performers.

1850. Marvin, Roberta Montemorra. "Aspects of Tempo in Verdi's Early and Middle Period Italian Operas." In *Verdi's Middle Period* (#1803), 393–411.

Verdi's autograph scores show growing attention to details of tempo markings; he began including metronome indications with *Attila* and continued using them. Tempo designations in many of the operas are arrayed and discussed.

Analysis: Form

1851. Budden, Julian. "Problems of Analysis in Verdi's Works." In *Nuove prospettive* (#1916), 125–129.

A brief, pessimistic look at the search for unifying features in the operas: all approaches present great obstacles. Tonal structure seems invalid, since most of the operas end in a key other than the one in which they begin. Thematic development is not much pursued. Motivic unity is also scarce.

1852. Powers, Harold S. "*La solita forma* and 'The Uses of Convention.'" *AM* 59 (1987): 65–90.

Revises an essay that had appeared in *Nuove prospettive* (#1916). Takes issue with other scholars who have expressed themselves on the unity issue, especially Budden (#1830, #1851) and Gossett (#246). Powers looks for answers in dramatic issues rather than in musical demands. Verdi achieved effects by deviating from patterns that the audience was expecting (*solite forme*). Suggests that Verdi was influenced in these matters by the writings of Abramo Basevi (#1829). See also Parker (#1808) and next item.

1853. Parker, Roger. "*Insolite forme*, or Basevi's Garden Path." In *Leonora's Last Act* (#1808), 42–60.

Summarizes and criticizes Powers's article (#1852). How did the audience develop the expectations that Powers says Verdi manipulated? Basevi is not a reliable guide to this area, and Powers is wrong to accept his views. Parker doubts that audiences were aware of the standard forms or the departures from them.

1854. Jablonsky, Stephen. "The Development of Tonal Coherence as Evidenced in the Revised Operas of Giuseppe Verdi." Ph.D. diss., New York U., 1973. 465p.

The author's imaginative approach was to compare original and revised versions of 12 pairs of musical numbers taken from six pairs of operas. He found that there was increased tonal coherence and more logical connection among key centers in the revisions.

1855. Lawton, David. "Tonality and Drama in Verdi's Early Operas." Ph.D. diss., U. of California, Berkeley, 1973. 2v.

The operas up to and including *Rigoletto* are examined from the viewpoint of tonal structure, both micro- and macrolevels. Up to *Macbeth,* Verdi may have changed keys to satisfy singers; thus, tonal design was obscured. But he did not make such alterations thereafter, so his intentions are clear. Various devices are identified: referential use of keys, repeated series of keys in cadential patterns, and the shaping of large forms through key relations. Although convincing answers are not found here—for example, Lawton is unable to determine a key center for *Rigoletto;* he seems to find it in a mystic point between D major and D-flat major—the questions raised are stimulating and the analyses are exacting. See also the author's #1867 and #1911.

1856. Moreen, Robert Anthony. "Integration of Text Forms and Musical Forms in Verdi's Early Operas." Ph.D. diss., Princeton U., 1975. 338p.

A unique approach, examining the "relationship of the prosodic form of the libretti of Verdi's operas to the musical and dramatic shape of the operas." Finds that the division of the numbers of the early operas, and other patterns in them, grow out of poetic-structural demands. Both micro- and macrolevel consequences are discussed in the works through *La traviata.*

1857. Pagannone, Giorgio. "Aspetti della melodia verdiana: Periodi e barform a confronto." *Studi verdiani* 12 (1997): 48–66.

Discusses the function in Verdi of ternary (ABA, AABA, or *periodo*) and binary (AAB, or barform) structures in arias. Barform was used to heighten dramatic movement, often with a change of key. With 35 extensive footnotes to the related literature and musical examples from many operas.

1858. Webster, James. "To Understand Verdi and Wagner We Must Understand Mozart." *19thCM* 11 (1978): 175–193.

A view developed later in #1288, that the search for unity in operas is not working and that other approaches are needed. Summarizes recent efforts at macroanalysis of Verdi's works.

1859. Gable, David. "Mode Mixture and Lyric Form in the Operas of Giuseppe Verdi." Ph.D. diss., U. of Chicago, 1997. 2v.

1860. Van, Gilles de. "La notion de *tinta*: Mémoire confuse et affinités thématiques dans les opéras de Verdi." *RdM* 76 (1990): 187–198.

The concept of *tinta* refers to a sense of unity that emerges in a work when various elements are appropriately melded. Those elements may include motivic affinities, melodic similarities, tonalities, and resemblances in orchestration. Such associations are felt by the listener, but only analysis can disclose them. Van illustrates his understanding of the concept by examining act 2, scene 2, of *La forza del destino.*

Analysis: Instrumentation

1861. Harwood, Gregory W. "Verdi's Reform of the Italian Opera Orchestra." *19thCM* 10 (1986–1987): 108–134.

The development of Verdi's ideas on size, balance, and seating arrangements for the orchestra, in part influenced by practice at the Paris Opéra.

Analysis: Choral Writing

1862. Engelhardt, Markus. *Die Chore in den frühen Opern Giuseppe Verdis.* Würzburger musikhistorische Beiträge, 11. Tutzing: Schneider, 1988. 374p. ISBN 3-7952-0551-4. ML410 .V4 E49.

A publication of the author's Ph.D. dissertation, U. of Wurzburg. It is a thorough study of Verdi's varied use of the chorus. Topics covered include function of the choral number in the larger work, text and musical form, musical style, and performance practice. Expansive index of names and titles.

Individual Works

Materials on each opera are grouped as follows: genesis and documents, analysis, and performance history.

Aida

ASO 4 (1976; 1993), *ENOG* 2 (1980), Rororo (1985).

1863. Busch, Hans. *Verdi's "Aida": The History of the Opera in Letters and Documents.* Minneapolis: U. of Minnesota Press, 1978. lv, 688p. ISBN 0-8166-0798-2. ML410 .V4 V312.

An impressive gathering of letters, contracts, sketches, stage directions, drawings, and other documents, spanning 23 years. All materials are annotated and unified into a result "as vivid and enthralling as a novel" (Julian Budden's review). Includes original production notes by Verdi, Giulio Ricordi, and Franco Faccio. Bibliography of 250 items, expansive index to the letters, index of names, titles, and topics.

1864. *Genesi dell' "Aida" con documentazione indedita.* Ed. Saleh Abdoun. *Quaderni* 4 (1971): 1–189.

This issue of *Quaderni* observed the centenary of *Aida*'s premiere with letters and documents about the event and genesis of the opera. Material from the

Cairo Opera archives was published for the first time. Also a performance history, 1871–1881, and fine illustrations of scenery and costumes. Indexes of documents, cities, and names.

1865. Kitson, John Richard. "Verdi and the Evolution of the *Aida* Libretto." Ph.D. diss., U. of British Columbia, 1985. 2v.

1866. Petrobelli, Pierluigi. "Music in the Theater (à propos of *Aida,* Act III)." In *Music in the Theater* (#1807), 113–126.

Describes and discusses the opening scene of act 3, seeking the dramatic language of the opera. The methodology is largely semiotic, following the ideas of Frits Noske (#1285).

1867. Lawton, David. "Tonal Systems in *Aida,* Act III." In *Analyzing Opera* (#416), 262–275.

Describes the tonal structure of the act, showing how it combines with motivic relationships to produce a unified whole. The key progression is a double cycle, moving from G major through F major to D-flat major/minor, the final key of the opera.

1868. Parker, Roger. "Motives and Recurring Themes in *Aida.*" In *Analyzing Opera* (#416), 222–238.

It is the "most nearly Wagnerian of Verdi's operas" but has fewer, more easily identifiable motives. They are employed with subtlety; for example, the Aida theme refers only to her uncertain love for Radames; it is not in the act 4 tomb scene, where her love is final. The interweaving and variations of this theme are remarkable (and so is this analysis).

See also Gossett (#246).

Un ballo in maschera (A Masked Ball)

ASO 32 (1981–1982), ENOG 40 (1989). *Verdi 1* (1960) offers various approaches (one is at #1869). An exchange of ideas on the opera's tonal macrostructure appeared in *19thCM*: Siegmund Levarie, "Key Relations in Verdi's *Un ballo in maschera,*" 2 (1978–1979): 143–147; Joseph Kerman, "Viewpoint," ibid., 186–191; Guy A. Marco, "On Key Relations in Opera" (#418); and a last word by Levarie, *19thCM* 3 (1979): 88–89. In synopsis: Levarie offers an explication of *Ballo*'s macrostructure based on the interplay of dramatic situations and key patterns; Kerman takes issue with the basic notion and with details of execution; Marco looks at a basis for a general theory of operatic structure that stems from key relations; Levarie sums up with a statement distinguishing his own "ontic" (being) orientation from Kerman's "gignetic" (becoming) position. The debate was pursued by Roger Parker and Matthew Brown in "Motivic and Tonal Interaction in Verdi's *Un ballo in maschera,*" *JAMS* 36-2 (Summer 1983): 243–265. They present some useful schematics that elucidate many structural features but find themselves unable to discover any tonal or motivic patterns that unify the entire work. They conclude with murky grumbles about the danger of "organicism." See also Siegmund Levarie, "A Pitch Cell in Verdi's *Un ballo in maschera,*" *Journal of Musicological Research* 3 (1981): 388–409.

1869. Corte, Andrea della. "Saggio di bibliografia delle critiche al *Ballo in maschera.*" *Verdi* 1–3 (1960): 1,165–1,197.

Discusses critiques and reviews and reprints segments of them, covering the history of performances from the premiere to the 1950s.

See also #1934.

Il corsaro

Quaderni 1 (1963) consists of several articles on the opera.

Don Carlos

ASO 90 (1986; 1990), ENOG 46 (1992).

1870. Günther, Ursula. "La genèse du *Don Carlos,* opéra en cinq actes de Giuseppe Verdi, représenté pour la première fois a Paris le 11 mars 1867." *RdM* 58 (1972): 16–64; 60 (1974): 87–158.

A thorough genesis, based partly on newly discovered sources. The composer's changes and corrections are discussed; rehearsals are inventoried. References to previous writings are cited in 286 footnotes. Various disagreements with Anthony Porter (#1872) are explored. It is curious that Budden (#1830, v.2) makes only four passing references in footnotes to this monumental research.

1871. Günther, Ursula. "La genèse de *Don Carlos* de Verdi: Nouveaux documents." *RdM* 72 (1986): 104–117.

Describes material not available for her earlier study: parts of an autograph manuscript located in the library of the Paris Opéra and some illustrative items. Another supplement appeared as "Zur Revision des *Don Carlos*: Postscriptum zu Teil II," *Analecta musicologica* 19 (1979): 373–377.

1872. Porter, Andrew. "The Making of *Don Carlos.*" *PRMA* 98 (1971–1972): 73–88.

Genesis, with discussion of Verdi's intentions for the (French) production: he wanted to infuse the *grand opéra* genre with heightened characterization, dramatic shape, and "warmth."

See #1870.

1873. Chusid, Martin. "The Inquisitor's Scene in Verdi's *Don Carlos*: Thoughts on the Drama, Libretto, and Music." In *Studies in Musical Sources* (#74), 505–534.

Presents multiple viewpoints on the scene: prosodic, harmonic, and Verdi's alternative ideas for the opening.

See also Noske (#1285), 294–308.

1874. Gualerzi, Giorgio. "Un secolo di *Don Carlos.*" In *Atti* (#1802), v.3, 494–504.

Performance history, 1867–1969.

I due Foscari

1875. Petrobelli, Pierluigi. "Osservazioni sul processo compositivo in Verdi." *AM* 43 (1971): 125–142.

Examines draft fragments for *I due Foscari* and the sketch for *Rigoletto*, to explain Verdi's specific changes in the final versions of both works. Concludes that the sketch is a concentrated nucleus of the musical ideas; those ideas expand into the revised score. Petrobelli supplemented these observations in "L'abbozzo di Busseto e la creazione musicale in Verdi," *Biblioteca '70 3* (1973): 17–32.

Ernani

Although *Ernani* "has provoked the most scholarly study of any of Verdi's earliest operas" (Harwood), none of the opera guide series has yet covered it.

1876. *"Ernani" ieri e oggi: Atti del Convegno Internazionale di Studi, Modena, Teatro San Carlo, 9–10 dicembre 1984*. Ed. Pierluigi Petrobelli. In *Verdi* 4 (1987).

The conference papers take up this issue of *Verdi*. One of them is a genesis study: "Gli anni di *Ernani*," by Gustavo Marchesi, 19–42.

See also #1879.

1877. Gossett, Philip. "The Composition of *Ernani*." In *Analyzing Opera* (#416), 27–55.

An Italian translation appeared in #1876. Genesis, with revisions described and alterations in the autograph score. Various clues point to the nature of the closing trio in the original version (not extant).

1878. Parker, Roger. "Levels of Motivic Definition in Verdi's *Ernani*." *19thCM* 6 (1982–1983): 141–150.

The evident attempt by Verdi to underscore certain moments of love and honor with melodic motives was not fully successful. The reason is that the motives are neither sufficiently distinctive nor repeated often enough to establish themselves in the drama. However, motives do help to unify a part of act 1. Parker finds internal coherence in the use of a "recurring melodic contour, the rising sixth from dominant to mediant." He feels it is "unfortunate that a good deal of the close analytic work of recent years has concerned itself with the contentious topic of overall key relationships" instead of motivic study.

1879. Conati, Marcello. *"Ernani di Verdi: Le critiche del tempo—alcune considerazioni."* In *"Ernani" ieri e oggi* (#1876), 207–272.

Prints 31 reviews from 1844 to1847, then lists 200 performances with full descriptions. The opera was a success from the beginning.

Falstaff

ASO 87 (1986), COH 1983, ENOG 10 (1982), Rororo 1986.

1880. Cone, Edward T. "The Old Man's Toys: Verdi's Last Operas." In *Music: A View from Delft* (#65), 114–133.

Stravinsky said that in *Otello* and *Falstaff* subtlety has replaced melodic inspiration; *Falstaff* is "a meaningless puppet show, written for an old man's amusement." Cone disagrees, finding in the late works "not less invention, but more." Melodies no longer repeat themselves into arias but develop and recur in the orchestra as needed. In fact, Verdi's early works have arias that are "diluted," "containing much less music than their own space. So he learns concentration." As in Wagner, these are orchestral arias, not sung; but sung phrases contribute to the unfolding of the complete dramatic line. This is a principle of late Beethoven as well.

1881. Hepokoski, James A. "The Compositional History of Verdi's *Falstaff*: A Study of the Autograph Score and the Early Editions." Ph.D. diss., Harvard U., 1979. 2v.

1882. Girardi, Michele. "Fonti francesi del *Falstaff*: Alcuni aspetti di drammaturgia musicale." In *Arrigo Boito* (#599), 395–430.

A French translation of the Shakespeare plays seems to have been Boito's source for the *Falstaff* libretto. His copy of the translation, by François-Victor Hugo, shows underlined passages that occur in the libretto, plus annotations indicating how the two relevant plays might be related in shaping the character of Sir John.

1883. Parker, Roger. "*Falstaff* and Verdi's Final Narratives." In *Leonora's Last Act* (#1808), 100–125.

A kaleidoscopic presentation of "an opera that constantly plays with ambiguous, multivalent musical gestures."

1884. Sabbeth, Daniel Paul. "Principles of Tonal and Dramatic Organization in Verdi's *Falstaff*." Ph.D. diss., City U. of New York, 1976. 234p.

Some of this work had been anticipated in Sabbeth's article in *Atti* (#1802), v.3. He finds that the final fugue is a unifying motive of the opera and that the entire work possesses three levels of tonal organization. Tonal movement is diatonic, and large-scale motions take the place of traditional numbers.

La forza del destino

ASO 126 (1989), *ENOG* 23 (1983). *Verdi* 2 (1961–1966) has several articles on the work (two are cited below).

1885. Marchesi, Gustavo. "Gli anni della *Forza del destino*." *Verdi* 2–4/5/6 (1961–1966): 17–42; 713–744; 1,505–1,542.

Genesis and first performance, focused on Verdi letters.

1886. Holmes, William C. "The Earliest Revisions of *La forza del destino*." *Studi verdiani* 6 (1990): 55–98.

Reconstructs the revisions from materials in the Kirov Library in the city of the premiere, St. Petersburg, and a score Verdi prepared for another performance, in Madrid. Most revisions were minor, but in act 3 there were extensive changes.

1887. Parker, Roger. "Leonora's Last Act: *La forza del destino.*" In *Leonora's Last Act* (#1808), 61–99.

> The opera (premiere 1862) was revised in 1869 for La Scala. Parker uses this revision as a springboard for interesting views on revisions in general. Are they improvements, based on a composer's growing maturity, or should the original be regarded as the perfect inspiration? Wonders about Cone's contention (in #1926) that Verdi's revisions moved toward "tonally unified structures." *Forza* was in E major, but the revision starts in E major and ends in A-flat major. What Verdi did was "merely replace one set of connections with another"; he was not "reconstituting some organic mass."

1888. Petrobelli, Pierluigi. "More on the Three 'Systems': The First Act of *La forza del destino.*" In *Music in the Theater* (#1807), 127–140.

> The systems are dramatic action, verbal organization, and music. Their interactions in act 1 are persuasively demonstrated by Petrobelli. For instance, the first *scena finale* uses sonata form with key words occurring at principal junctures.

1889. Corte, Andrea della. "Saggio di bibliografia delle critiche alla *Forza del destino.*" *Verdi* 2–6 (1966): 1,863–1,906.

> Citations and extracts from reviews and critiques of the opera, from premiere days to the 1960s.

Jérusalem/I lombardi

I lombardi (1843) was revised for Paris as *Jérusalem* (1847); the French version was later translated into Italian as *Gerusalemme. Quaderni* 2 (1963) presents varied material about the work.

1890. Kimbell, David R. "Verdi's First *rifacimento*: *I lombardi* and *Jérusalem.*" *M&L* 60 (1979): 1–36.

> A detailed account of the changes made for the French production, from simple carryovers to substantial innovations. Kimbell believes that not all the adjustments were made to please Parisian audiences; some of the changes reflect the composer's growing maturity.

Luisa Miller

ASO 151 (1993).

1891. Senici, Emanuele. "Verdi's *Luisa,* a Semiserious Alpine Virgin." *19thCM* 22-2 (Fall 1998): 144–168.

> The original play, by Schiller, had a town locale, but librettist Cammarano moved it to the Alps. This is "not a trivial detail" but is "at the core *Luisa Miller*'s musico-dramatic construction and cultural signification." An alpine setting was often used in opera to symbolize purity of the heroine. Verdi here and elsewhere "investigated ambience as a means of exploring generic mixture."

Macbeth

ASO 40 (1982), *ENOG* 41 (1990).

1892. Rosen, David, and Andrew Porter. *Verdi's "Macbeth": A Sourcebook*. New York: Norton, 1985. 527p. ISBN 0-393-95073-5. ML410 .V4 V35.

"In part a collection of papers delivered at the Fifth Institute of Verdi Studies, 1977" (Danville, Ky.). Includes a piano-vocal score from 1847 and essays by many leading Verdians (Chusid, Degrada, Weaver, Budden, Conati, Porter, etc.). Bibliography and index of names, topics, and works. Among the important inclusions are a performance history, a table of revisions, and illustrations of the original costumes.

1893. Goldin, Daniela. "Il *Macbeth* verdiano: Genesi e linguaggio di un libretto." *Analecta musicologica* 19 (1979): 336–372.

A fine review of previous writings (130 notes) makes this genesis account particularly useful. The source for the libretto was Carlo Rusconi's translation from Shakespeare.

1894. Degrada, Francesco. "Lettura di *Macbeth* di Verdi." *Studi musicali* 6 (1977): 207–267.

A well-documented genesis, with texts of letters, libretto alterations by Piave, and references to earlier literature.

1895. Osthoff, Wolfgang. "Die beiden Fassungen von Verdis *Macbeth*." *AfM* 29 (1972): 17–44.

Genesis, with program notes and musical examples; comparison of the original version with the revision for Paris in 1865.

1896. Antokoletz, Elliott. "Verdi's Dramatic Use of Harmony and Tonality in *Macbeth*." *In Theory Only* 4 (November–December 1978): 17–28.

Notes the importance of the pitch cell c/d-flat in the foreground or background as a symbol of murder and guilt.

1897. Chusid, Martin. "Evil, Guilt and the Supernatural in Verdi's *Macbeth*: Toward an Understanding of the Tonal Structure and Key Symbolism." In *Sourcebook* (#1892), 249–260.

The keys of E and B-flat are found to represent two levels of supernatural, respectively: a lesser and a more powerful realm. Other keys are associated with Macbeth himself, Scotland, and murder/guilt.

1898. Sabbeth, Daniel. "On the Tonal Organization of *Macbeth II*." In *Sourcebook* (#1892), 261–269.

Identifies some of the harmonic devices that create special effects: mixture of major and minor, lowered sixth of the scale, and associations of keys with characters and ideas.

I masnadieri

1899. Marvin, Roberta Montemorra. "Verdi's *I masnadieri*: Its Genesis and Early Reception." Ph.D. diss., Brandeis U., 1992. 2v.

The most important study of the opera, including all known letters and documents, a performance history (1847–1852) with reprints of articles, and a discussion of changes made by censors. Marvin has also written a number of articles, for which see Harwood, p.243–244.

Nabucco

ASO 86 (1986; 1991; 1994).

1900. Cancelled entry.

1901. Parker, Roger. "The Exodus of *Nabucco*." In *Studies in Early Verdi* (#1831), 111–141.

A performance history, with casts and survey of the reviews. Parker notes that the famous chorus was not singled out at the time as especially notable. See next item.

1902. Parker, Roger. "*Va pensiero* and the Insidious Mastery of Song." In *Leonora's Last Act* (#1808), 20–41.

Links with the Risorgimento have given the opera great external significance. The chorus *Va pensiero* was sung at Verdi's funeral. But no reliable pre–1848 evidence indicates that it was any sort of rallying cry for Italian independence. The piece "moved fairly uneventfully through a historical period of great political tension" and only later "emerged as the representative of that period."

See also #278.

Oberto

1903. *Kimbell, David.* "Poi . . . diventò l'Oberto." M&L 42 (1971): 1–7.

Genesis: the opera was a revision of the earlier work called *Rocester*. The autograph and 1839 libretto are compared.

1904. Parker, Roger. "The Autograph Score of *Oberto, Conte di San Bonifacio*." In *Studies in Early Verdi* (#1831), 64–82.

Supports Kimbell's view that the opera was a refashioned *Rocester*. A thorough account of the revisions and the compositional process is given.

Otello

ASO 3 (1976; 1990), COH (1987), ENOG 7 (1981), Rororo (1981).

1905. Busch, Hans. *Verdi's "Otello" and "Simon Boccanegra" (Revised Version) in Letters and Documents.* New York: Oxford U.P., 1988. lx, 891p. ISBN 0-19-313207-9. ML410 .V4 V36.

A valuable compilation of 656 letters and numerous other documents dealing with the genesis of *Otello* and the revision of *Simon Boccanegra*. Among the interesting materials are production books, complete with diagrammed stage directions compiled by Ricordi and the first Iago, Victor Maurel. There is also a reception account. Bibliography and index.

1906. Hepokoski, James A. "Boito and F.-V. Hugo's 'Magnificent Translation': A Study in the Genesis of the *Otello* Libretto." In *Reading Opera* (#218), 34–59.

Concludes, after a study of the alternatives, that Boito's libretto was most indebted to the French translation of François-Victor Hugo of 1860. In addition to Hugo's text, his comments resonated with Boito, who may have developed Iago's character in part as a consequence of them. The Italian stage traditions for the Shakespeare play are also taken into account.

1907. Noske, Frits. "*Otello*: Drama through Structure." In *Essays on Music* (#67), 14–47, and in *Signifier* (#1285), 133–170.

Compared to Shakespeare, the Verdi-Boito personages are "flat." Interest in the work is sustained by the dramatic impact of specific situations. Noske speculates about who the protagonist is: Iago seems to be the central character of the plot, but Otello is central in the drama.

1908. Fairtile, Linda B. "Verdi's First 'Willow Song': New Sketches and Drafts for *Otello*." *19thCM* 19 (1995–1996): 213–230.

The new material is in the New York Public Library: it contains sketches and a continuity draft for act 4 through the "Ave Maria" and sketches for the act 1 "Brindisi." The text and music of the "Willow Song" are completely different in these documents from the final version. Fairtile suggests that Verdi abandoned his initial setting and asked Boito for a new version.

1909. Coe, Doug. "The Original Production Book for *Otello*: An Introduction." *19thCM* 2 (1978–1979): 148–158.

The production books indicate Verdi's intentions for staging and should be followed in modern performances.

1910. Archibald, Bruce. "Tonality in *Otello*." *MR* 35 (1974): 23–28.

An imaginative approach to tonal structure, taking the key of F major as the tonic of act 1, from which prior and later keys are said to "radiate" in the form of a star.

1911. Lawton, David. "On the *bacio* Theme in *Otello*." *19thCM* 1 (1977–1978): 211–220.

Approaches the *bacio* theme through Schenkerian analysis, finding that the tonalities are a microversion of the tonal form of the entire opera. Keys are associated with Otello's conflicts: C major with his downfall, E major with his triumphs, and D-flat major with his loving nature.

1912. Parker, Roger, and Matthew Brown. "*Ancora un bacio*: Three Scenes from Verdi's *Otello*." *19thCM* 9 (1985–1986): 50–61.

Having reviewed analytical results of other writers (Budden, Noske, Lawton), the authors offer their own perspectives. Coherence in the love scene is achieved through recurring harmonic and melodic elements, and the return of the *bacio* theme at the end of the opera is a culmination of many melodic and harmonic relationships.

1913. Hepokowski, James A., and Mercedes Viale Ferrero. *"Otello" di Giuseppe Verdi*. Milan: Ricordi, 1990. 324p. ISBN 88-7592-085-0. ML410 .V4 H48.

Genesis, the first production and its staging (from the Ricordi *disposizioni sceniche),* including attention to the costumes at La Scala and in Rome and Paris. Color reproductions of scenery sketches are a valuable feature.

1914. Bergeron, Katherine. "How to Avoid Believing (While Reading Iago's *"Credo")*." In *Reading Opera* (#218), 184–199.

A semiotic approach, citing "conflicts" in the text of the aria, which encourage new readings. The pleasure of it lies in its resistance to easy reading, its thwarted expectations. The text mixes free verse and end rhymes. The orchestra gives "mixed signals." The aria is neither recitative nor traditional aria. A crisis of identity for Iago is thus indicated, and his pronouncements present two distinct "I's": one who believes, one who names. This conflict is not resolved, but Iago's final laugh moves beyond the words and music "toward a definitive view of the text as mockery."

See also Cone (#1880).

Rigoletto

ASO 112 (1988), ENOG 15 (1982), Rororo (1982). *Verdi* 3 (1969–1982) is mostly concerned with *Rigoletto*. One article of importance:

1915. Marchesi, Gustavo. "Gli anni del *Rigoletto*." *Verdi* 3 (1969–1982): 1–26; 849–875; 1,517–1,543.

An elaborate genesis, featuring Verdi letters. Considers the character of the duke in the opera and his possible real-life counterpart.

1916. *Nuove prospettive nella ricerca verdiana. Atti del Congresso Internazionale in Occasione della Prima del "Rigoletto" in Edizione Critica, Vienna, 12–13 marzo 1983.* Ed. Marisa Di Gregorio Casati and Marcello Pavarani. Parma: Istituto di Studi Verdiana; Milan: Ricordi, 1987. xii, 137p. ISBN 88-85065-03-1. ML410 .V4 C68.

Summaries of 10 papers are given by Harwood (#1800), item 231.

1917. Chusid, Martin. "The Tonality of *Rigoletto*." In *Analyzing Opera* (#416), 241–261.

Identifies D-flat major—the key of Monterone's curse—as the tonic, but distant keys (D, B, E) dominate act 3. Chusid has no explanation for this, other than an extramusical one: events in the plot. He gives an elegant analysis of "Caro nome" and the quartet, showing the parallel harmonic progressions. Also notes that Verdi's drafts present increasing clarity of tonal relationships.

1918. Lawton, David. "Tonal Structure and Dramatic Action in *Rigoletto*." *Verdi* 3-9 (1982); 1,559–1,581.

The keys of D-flat major and D major and their related tonalities are the basis of the opera's structure.

1919. Veinus, Abraham, and John Clarke Adams. "*Rigoletto* as Drama." In *Atti* (#1802), v.3, 464–494.

Considers the proper goals for modern productions, following Verdi's ideas for the premiere and performance traditions since that time.

1920. Corte, Andrea della. "Saggio di bibliografia delle critiche al *Rigoletto*." Ed. and completed by Marcello Conati. *Verdi* 3–9 (1982): 1,634–1,772.

Reviews and critiques drawn from various writings about the opera are summarized, with some direct quotations.

1921. Gualerzi, Giorgio. "Il cammino dell'opera." *Verdi* 7//8/9 (1969–1982): 147–176; 980–1,014; 1,588–1,633.

A detailed reception study, using the writings of singers and critics.

Simon Boccanegra

ASO 19 (1979; 1994), ENOG 22 (1983). *Atti* (#1802), v.4, is primarily about it.

1922. Osthoff, Wolfgang. "Die beiden *Boccanegra*: Fassungen und der Beginn von Verdis Spätwerk." *Analecta musicologica* 1 (1963): 70–89.

A technical comparison of the two versions, with footnotes and musical examples.

1923. Detels, Claire Janice. "Giuseppe Verdi's *Simon Boccanegra*: A Comparison of the 1857 and 1881 Versions." Ph.D. diss., U. of Washington, 1982. vi, 221p.

Harwood (#1800), item 883, cites two short spin-off articles from this study.

1924. Noske, Frits R. "*Simon Boccanegra*: One Plot, Two Dramas." In *Signifier* (#1285), 215–240.

Finds the revision to be completely different dramatically from the original, although the plot remains as it was. The relationship between events and emotion is enhanced. With a tabular comparison of the two versions.

1925. Sopart, Andreas. "Giuseppe Verdis *Simon Boccanegra* (1857 und 1881): Eine musikalisch-dramaturgische Analyse." *Analecta musicologica* 26 (1988): 1–213.

This issue of the journal is devoted to Sopart's study, the most elaborate of the comparisons between the two versions.

1926. Cone, Edward T. "On the Road to *Otello*: Tonality and Structure in *Simon Boccanegra*." *Studi verdiani* 1 (1982): 72–98.

The revision reinforces the tonal structure of the work, which is focused on a circle of keys a major third apart. Dramatic development is enhanced by the stronger harmonic basis. (Note Parker's comments, in #1887.)

1927. Neuls-Bates, Carol. "Verdi's *Les vêpres siciliennes* (1855) and *Simon Boccanegra* (1857)." Ph.D. diss., Yale U., 1970. 2v.

Considers the two cited operas as harbingers of Verdi's new style, exhibited in *Un ballo in maschera*.

1928. Conati, Marcello, and Natalia Grilli. *"Simon Boccanegra" di Giuseppe Verdi.* Milan: Ricordi, 1993. 263p. ISBN 88-7592-359-0. ML410 .V4 C675.

A variety of viewpoints on the staging and performance history of the opera. Facsimiles of the original libretti (1857 and 1881) are presented, with the *disposizione scenica* of 1881. Well illustrated with drawings of scenery and costumes and contemporary engravings.

Stiffelio (Aroldo)

The unsuccessful *Stiffelio* (1850) was revised as *Aroldo* (1857).

1929. *Tornando a "Stiffelio." Atti del Convegno Internazionale di Studi, Venezia, 17–20 dicembre 1985.* Ed. Giovanni Morelli. Quaderni della Rivista italiana di musicologia, 14. Florence: Olschki, 1987. xv, 380p. ISBN 88-22-23484-7 ML410 .V4 T62.

Papers from the conference, dealing with genesis, the libretto, technical observations on the music, reception, and the transformation into *Aroldo*. Harwood (#1800), item 234, cites the more significant essays. This is one of them:

1930. Chusid, Martin. "Apropos *Aroldo, Stiffelio,* and *Le pasteur,* with a List of 19th-Century Performances of *Aroldo.*" In *Tornando* (#1929), 281–303. Reprinted in *Verdi Newsletter* 144 (1986): 15–28.

A thorough comparison of the two works and the source of the libretto, *Le pasteur,* by Emile Souvestre, in its stage adaptation by Eugène Bourgeois. Includes performance histories of both operas (88 productions), suggesting that neither was a total failure. All documents relating to the works are described.

1931. *"Stiffelio."* Ed. Mario Medici and Marcello Pavarani. *Quaderni* 3 (1968): 1–157.

The entire issue of *Quaderni* consists of essays on the opera. Harwood (#1800), item 902, cites them.

La traviata

ASO 51 (1983; 1993), ENOG 5 (1981), Rororo (1983).

1932. *Violetta and Her Sisters: The Lady of the Camellias: Responses to the Myth.* Ed. Nicholas John. London: Faber & Faber, 1994. x, 305p. ISBN 0-5711-6665-2. NX652 D86 V66 or HQ117 .V565.

Essays about courtesans, by various authors. Genesis, staging, and character of Violetta in *La traviata* are thoroughly studied (p.217–303). No index.

1933. Chusid, Martin. "Drama and the Key of F Major in *La traviata.*" In *Atti* (#1802), v.3, 89–121.

Suggests that F major is a key that Verdi associated with happy love scenes, at least from around the time of *La traviata.* Chusid gives examples from many of the operas.

1934. Della Seta, Fabrizio. "Il tempo della festa: Su due scene della *Traviata* e su altri luoghi verdiani." *Studi verdiani* 2 (1983): 108–146.

Sonata form is said to be the structural base of the first act. In the second act, the author finds parallels to the opening of *Rigoletto* and the finale of *Un ballo in maschera*.

1935. Della Seta, Fabrizio. "Varianti (d'autore e non) ne *La traviata*." In *Napoli e il teatro* (#2534), 417–435.

Discusses a number of scenes and the minor changes (e.g., adding or deleting a measure) by Verdi after the premiere. These alterations have not always been observed in performance. Della Seta justifies the variants.

Il trovatore

ASO 60 (1984; 1990), ENOG 20 (1983), Rororo (1986).

1936. Mossa, Carlo Matteo. "La genesi del libretto del *Trovatore*." *Studi verdiani* 8 (1992): 52–103.

A valuable exploration of the text and its sources, with correspondence, drafts, and the autograph libretto. Controversy developed between Cammarano and Verdi over the characterization of Azucena, with the composer's ideas prevailing upon the death of the librettist.

1937. Lawton, David. "*Le trouvère*: Verdi's Revision of *Il trovatore* for Paris." *Studi verdiani* 3 (1985): 79–119.

Political, legal, and financial considerations behind the revision are described, as well as the alterations themselves. Some of the changes might be included in modern stagings.

1938. Petrobelli, Pierluigi. "Per un' esegesi della struttura drammatica del *Trovatore*." In *Atti* (#1802), v.3, 387–407. English trans. William Drabkin, in *Music Analysis* 1 (1982): 129–141.

The dramatic structure is forged from various musical devices such as rhythmic motives, melodic figurations, and sonorities. There is less characterization here than in Verdi's other operas of the period. Footnotes give a good review of the earlier literature. See next entry.

1939. Drabkin, William. "Characters, Key Relations, and Tonal Structure in *Il trovatore*." *Music Analysis* 1 (1982): 143–153.

Takes as starting point the Petrobelli study (previous entry), giving it in translation, then elaborates on matters of key. Finds a dual polarity around E minor, which moves toward G major or C major according to the circumstances of the plot. See next entry.

1940. Greenwood, Joanna. "Musical and Dramatic Motion in Verdi's *Il trovatore*." *Jahrbuch für Opernforschung* 2 (1986): 59–73.

A totally different structural picture, drawn from Schenkerian analysis, is developed here from that of Drabkin/Petrobelli, which Greenwood disputes. There is a useful summary of the numerous approaches to tonal structure in Verdi.

1941. Parker, Roger. "Leonora's Last Act: *Il trovatore.*" In *Leonora's Last Act* (#1808), 168–187.

Considers certain poor matches between words and music in Verdi, focusing on Leonora's aria "D'amor sull'ali rosee," suggesting that such "uneasy disjunctions" may be their "customary state of existence." Speculates that "part of the reason for this aria's effect lies precisely in the gaps that increasingly emerge between its words and it music." Leonora's vocal liberation pulls against the strictures of the "juggernaut called plot."

Les vêpres siciliennes (I vespri siciliani)

ASO 75 (1985).

1942. Budden, Julian. "Varianti nei *Vespri siciliani.*" *NRMI* 6 (1972): 155–181.

Genesis and revisions, and a discussion of reception—which became increasingly unfavorable.

1943. Vlad, Roman. "Unità strutturale dei *Vespri siciliani.*" In *Il melodramma italiano dell'ottocento: Studi e ricerche per Massimo Mila*, 43–90 (Turin: Einaudi, 1977; ML1733.4 .M5).

Finds formal coherence in the opera based on recurrence of melodic motives.

See also Neuls-Bates (#1927).

Alexei Nikolaevich Verstovskii (1799–1862)

1944. Abraham, Gerald. "The Operas of Alexei Verstovsky." *19thCM* 7 (1984): 326–335.

Askold's Tomb (Askold'ova mogila) (1835) was the earliest Russian opera to achieve any lasting success and was the first to be staged in the U.S. (1869). Abraham gives a general description, with musical examples.

Heitor Villa-Lobos (1887–1959)

1945. Appleby, David P. *Heitor Villa-Lobos: A Bio-Bibliography.* Bio-Bibliographies in Music, 9. New York: Greenwood, 1988. xiv, 358p. ISBN 0-313-25346-3. ML134 .V65 A7.

There is no research literature on the operas. This bibliography cites some reviews and short notices.

Leonardo Vinci (1696–1730)

1946. Meikle, Robert Burns. "Leonardo Vinci's *Artaterse*: An Edition with an Editorial and Critical Commentary." Ph.D. diss., Cornell U., 1970. 656p.

1947. Strohm, Reinhard. "Leonardo Vinci's *Didone abbandonata* (Rome 1726)." In *Essays on Handel* (#953), 213–224.

Genesis, the libretto by Metastasio, borrowings, technical analysis. Vinci's music "is determined by words, rhymes, and phrase-shapes."

1948. Markstrom, Kurt Sven. "The Operas of Leonardo Vinci, Napoletano." Ph.D. diss., U. of Toronto, 1993. v, 356p.

Filippo Vitali (ca. 1600–1653)

1949. Pruett, James W. "The Works of Filippo Vitali." Ph.D. diss., U. of North Carolina, 1962. 2v.

Antonio Vivaldi (1678–1741)

Bibliographies and Guides to Resources

1950. Talbot, Michael. *Antonio Vivaldi: A Guide to Research*. Garland Composer Resource Manuals, 12. New York: Garland, 1988. xlv, 197p. ISBN 0-8240-8386-5. ML134 .V7 T34.

A valuable annotated bibliography of 432 entries, plus a thorough study of the four catalogues of Vivaldi's works (by Mario Rinaldi, Marc Pincherle, Antonio Fanna, and Peter Ryom). Also useful inventories of manuscripts, libraries, societies, and Vivaldi scholars. General index.

Collections of Essays

1951. *Opera and Vivaldi*. Ed. Michael Collins and Elise K. Kirk. Austin: U. of Texas Press, 1984. 398p. ISBN 0-292-70746-0. ML1703 .O63.

Consists of 21 essays by various specialists "derived from the Dallas Opera Vivaldi Symposium" of 1980; *Orlando* was produced at that time. Contributions of interest include Eric Cross, "The Relationship between Text and Music in the Operas of Vivaldi," and John W. Hill on *Orlando* (1960). Name index.

Periodicals

1952. *Quaderni vivaldiani*, 1–, 1980–. Florence: Olschki, 1980–. Irregular. ML410 .V82.

An important journal of scholarly studies. Some of the valuable material on opera is in v.1 (1980): Francesco Degrada, "Vivaldi e Metastasio: Note in margine a una lettura dell'*Olimpiade*"; Gianfranco Folena, "Prima le parole, poi la music: Scipione Maffei poeta per musica e *La fida ninfa*"; and Maria Teresa Muraro and Elena Povoledo, "Le scene della *Fida ninfa*: Maffei, Vivaldi, e Francesco Bibiena." V.2 (1982) includes Bruno Brizi, "Gli *Orlandi* di Vivaldi attraverso i libretti," and Franco Fino, "Le tre *Griselde*: Appunti su Goldoni librettista di Vivaldi." The same volume has nine essays on social and intellectual conditions of the opera composer in Vivaldi's time. V.3 (1982) has "I libretti vivaldiani," ed. Anna Laura Bellina et al. It gives detailed bibliographic descriptions of 76 libretti, with facsimiles, as well as indexes of persons and arias. V.4 (1988) includes Martin Steinebrunner, "*Orlando furioso*: Vom Epos zur Oper"; Anna Laura Bellina et al., "Il pasticcio *Bajazet*"; and Michael Collins on the orchestra in Vivaldi operas (see #1957)." V.6 (1991) has a Vivaldi chronology. V.10 (1998) has Antonio Fanna and Michael Talbot, "Cinquant'anni di produzioni e consumi della musica dell'età ci Vivaldi, 1947–1997," and various essays on opera revivals in the late 20th century.

Biographies

1953. Talbot, Michael. *Vivaldi*. Rev. ed. New York: Schirmer, 1993. 237p. ISBN 0-02-872665-0. ML410 .V82 T34.

First edition, 1978. This revision introduces corrections, new endnotes, and updated appendixes. The first English-language life and works, also published in Italian and German. With worklist, bibliography, and index. Talbot also wrote the Vivaldi chapter for *New Grove Italian Baroque Masters* (#2459), which has the reliable Peter Ryom worklist. The scores of 21 operas have survived, not all complete. Although they are relatively little studied—by Talbot or other specialists—they are "vital and imaginative."

Operas in General

1954. Cross, Eric. *The Late Operas of Antonio Vivaldi, 1727–1738*. Ann Arbor, Mich.: UMI Research, 1981. 2v. ISBN 0-8357-1158-7. ML410 .V82 C8.

Background material on Venice and the *opera seria;* then detailed technical examination of the Vivaldi works, emphasizing *Griselda*. Attention to characterization and overall structure. Chronology of operas, with casts and notes. V.2 is made up of musical examples. Bibliography of about 150 entries; expansive index of names, titles, and topics; separate index of works.

1955. *Antonio Vivaldi: Da Venezia all'Europa*. Ed. Francesco Degrada and Maria Teresa Muraro. Milan: Electa, 1978. 161p. No ISBN. ML410 .V82 A85.

Consists partly of papers given at a conference in Venice, 1978. One is:

1956. Garbero, Elvira. "Drammaturgia vivaldiana: Regesto e concordanza dei libretti." In *Antonio Vivaldi* (#1955), 111–153.

A careful chronological inventory of the libretti, presenting for each a list of the characters and their interpreters, plots, and staging directions, as well as miscellaneous facts as appropriate and available.

1957. Collins, Michael. "L'orchestra nelle opera teatrali di Vivaldi." In *Quaderni vivaldiani* 4 (1988): 285–312.

Compares the accompaniments to arias as written by Vivaldi, Handel, and their contemporaries. The "dominant tendency" was toward more dense yet less intrusive accompaniments.

1958. Strohm, Reinhard. "Vivaldi's Career as an Opera Producer." In *Essays on Handel* (#953), 122–163.

This important article also appeared in *Antonio Vivaldi: Teatro musicale, cultura, società* (Florence: Olschki, 1982). By 1739 Vivaldi, having written 94 operas, "was almost primarily an opera composer." But research is showing that in many of those works he acted rather as a producer and arranger than as a composer: an impresario. A tabular presentation shows his role in the operas he produced. With a list of his singers (and brief biographies), his librettists, the operas he produced by other composers, his pasticcios, and the collaborative compositions. An extensive chronological commentary on the productions (1713–1739) is of special value.

Individual Works

La fida ninfa

See #1952.

Il Giustino

See Strohm (#986).

Griselda

1959. Hill, John W. "Vivaldi's *Griselda.*" *JAMS* 31 (1978): 53–82. Reprinted in *GL,* v.11.

Genesis, showing the adaptation by Goldoni of the original libretto by Apostolo Zeno and the source in Boccaccio. The singer Anna Giro had some influence over the alterations, and the article deals with her contribution and career.

See also #1952.

L'Olimpiade

See #1952.

Orlando

1960. Hill, John W. "Vivaldi's *Orlando*: Sources and Contributing Factors." In *Opera and Vivaldi* (#1951).

Genesis, identifying all literary and musical sources. The libretto (after Ariosto) was by Grazio Braccioli, whose text had been set by Giovanni Alberto Ristori and produced by Vivaldi in Venice with some numbers of his own. In later versions, more of the music was by Vivaldi, and in 1727 he wrote a new score. This is all sorted out clearly by Hill.

See also #1952.

Tamerlano (Bajazet)

1961. Cross, Eric. "Vivaldi and the Pasticcio: Text and Music in *Tamerlano.*" In *"Con che soavità"* (#2461), 275–311.

Vivaldi's choice of material was sometimes a result of the singer involved or the stimulus of a similar dramatic situation. He borrowed from himself and other composers. Useful diagrams illustrate how certain singers came to dominate in various settings (getting more arias and more time on stage). Footnotes to the relevant pasticcio literature.

See also #1952.

Georg Joseph Vogler (1749–1814)

In *GO*: *Der Kaufmann von Smyrna,* v.8, and *Lampedo,* v.9.

Georg Christoph Wagenseil (1715–1777)

1962. Vetter, Walther. "Italienische Opernkomponisten um Georg Christoph Wagenseil: Ein stilkundlicher Versuch." In *Festschrift Friedrich Blume* (#64), 363–374.

Notes that Northerns (Germans) have always been attracted to the Southern (Italian) opera idiom. Metastasio's work was an example of widely diffused Italian art: his *Olimpiade* was set by Caldara, Pergolesi, Galuppi, and others from the South, and also by Gassman, Hasse, and Wagenseil (in 1749). Vetter comments on the various settings, concluding that Wagenseil's is less Italianate than the others, being more on the German line to Gluck.

Richard Wagner (1813–1883)

It is said that the literature about Wagner is greater than that on any other musician. A bibliography prepared before his death already had more than 10,000 items in it (#1965). There is no recent guide to those writings, although periodic bibliographies appear in Wagner serials. None of the Wagner websites checked in 1999 provided substantive bibliographic information. The selection of materials that follows is intended to be a representation of old and new research, illustrating the variety of approaches that have been taken by scholars to the music dramas.

Editions

1963. Wagner, Richard. *Sämtliche Werke*. Ed. Carl Dahlhaus et al. Mainz: Schott, 1975–. M3 .W13.

A publication of the Gesellschaft zur Förderung der Richard-Wagner Gesamtausgabe. Full scores, with elaborate commentaries and critical apparatus (in German and English), and bibliographies have been issued for *Rienzi* (5v.), *Der fliegende Holländer* (2v.), *Tannhäuser* (4v.), *Tristan und Isolde* (3v.), *Die Meistersinger* (3v.), *Das Rheingold* (2v.), *Die Götterdämmerung* (3v.), *Parsifal* (3v.), and *Lohengrin* (2v.). Additional volumes have presented documents appertaining to *Rienzi*, the *Ring*, and *Parsifal*. The last volume seen was a collection of Wagner's transcriptions from other composers: *Bearbeitungen*, v.20, IIA (1999).

Thematic Catalogues and Worklists

1964. Deathridge, John, Martin Geck, and Egon Voss. *Wagner Werk Verzeichnis (WWV): Verzeichnis der musikalischen Werke Richard Wagners in ihre Quellen*. Mainz: Schott, 1986. 607p. ISBN 3-7957-2201-2. ML134 .W2 D28.

Text in German; introduction in German and English. An indispensable inventory of Wagner's compositions. It is "not simply a list of finished autographs, important manuscript copies, first editions and printed copies, [but] also encompasses the entire range of sources relevant to the composition of a work and its first performance." Musical incipits are given and secondary literature cited. Index of names and places.

Bibliographies and Guides to Resources

1965. Oesterlein, Nikolaus. *Katalog einer Richard Wagner-Bibliothek.* Leipzig: Breit-kopf und Härtel, 1882. 4v. Reprint, Wiesbaden: Sändig, 1970. ISBN 2-500-21920-9. ML134 .W134 O29.

Consists of 10,180 numbered entries: the writings of Wagner himself (includ-ing letters and documents as well as prose works) and most of what was writ-ten about him and his music during his lifetime. Covers translations, photos and portraits, books, articles, reviews of performances, etc. Some of the book entries are annotated, and periodical articles are summarized. Name index in each volume.

1966. *Internationale Wagner-Bibliographie, 1944-1945-.* Ed. Herbert Barth. Bay-reuth: Edition Musica, 1956–. 56p. ML134 .W134 I6.

Continuations, ed. Herbert Barth, or by his son Henrik: 1956–1960 (142p.); 1961–1966 (99p.); 1967–1978 (173p.). Publisher varies. These are selective lists of writings in French, German, and English, grouped by language, with name indexes. Special features appear in the various volumes; e.g., 1945–1955 has an international discography, performance statistics for the Wagner operas by major opera companies, and descriptions of important collections; 1956–1960 includes performance data for all the Bayreuth Festival performances from 1876 to 1960 with names of all singers in each role.

1967. Borchmeyer, Dieter. "Wagner Literature: New Light on the Case of Wagner." *Wagner* 12–3 (Sept. 1991): 51–74.

Not seen. The abstract in *RILM* describes it as a "critical evaluation of the state of Wagner literature in Germany in the 1980's."

1968. Ziino, Agostino. "Rassegna della letteratura Wagneriana in Italia." *Analecta musicologica* 11 (1972): 14–135.

A valuable, exhaustive survey of Italian writing about Wagner, which is "povera non come quantità ma come qualità." Most of the publications in Italy have been polemics, listeners' guides, and biographies; original research and systematic analysis are rare. The earliest critical writing came after the *Lohengrin* performance in Bologna (1871), but there were anti-Wagnerian authors in the 1850s. Support for Wagner developed in the 1870s; headed by Filippo Filippi. He and others began to see the complexities of design in the music and began to accept the role of the orchestra as carrier of melody. Luigi Torchi, in the 1890s, was the first to treat Wagner objectively. Arnold Bona-ventura distinguished between Wagner the theoretician (weak) and Wagner the composer (great). After 1913 there was less interest in Wagner, with the turn against "romantic decadence." Long quotations and useful commentaries, 371 footnotes, and bibliography in date order from 1861 to 1970.

Dictionaries

1969. Bauer, Hans-Joachim. *Richard Wagner-Lexikon.* Bergisch Gladbach (Ger-many): G. Lübbe, 1988. 608p. ISBN 3-7857-0495-X. ML410 .W2 B344.

A useful dictionary of about 1,000 entries, covering persons connected to Wagner, the operas, opera characters, archives, theaters, and other topics. With a name index, in dauntingly small print.

1970. Lewsey, Jonathan. *Who's Who and What's What in Wagner.* Brookfield, Vt.: Ashgate, 1997. xiii, 350p. ISBN 1-8592-8280-6. ML410 .W2 L497.

A breezy dictionary of characters, things, and events in the operas, with much space given to synopses. No index.

1971. Hodson, Phillip. *Who's Who in Wagner: An A-to-Z Look at His Life and Work.* New York: Macmillan, 1984. 182p. ISBN 0-02552030-X. ML410 .W19 H64.

A useful book, intended only "for the most general audience," but of wider application. Consists of entries, in alphabetical order, for persons, characters (including such categories as ambassadors, apprentices, and the like), works, topics, objects in the operas (such as the ashtree in Hunding's cottage), places as settings, and places in Wagner's life. No bibliography or index.

1972. Mander, Raymond, and Joe Mitchenson. *The Wagner Companion.* New York: Hawthorn, 1978. x, 265p. ISBN 0-8015-8356-X. ML410 .W13 M27.

Production histories with good illustrations, glossary of the names of characters, discography of all complete recordings in print. Name and title index, weak bibliography. Note that #1974 has the same name.

Conferences

1973. *Wagnerliteratur—Wagner Forschung: Bericht über das Wagner-Symposium, München, 1983.* Ed. Carl Dahlhaus and Egon Voss. Mainz: Schott, 1985. 239p. ISBN 3-7957-2202-0. ML410 .W231 W22.

Consists of 21 papers from the 1983 conference. Three are entered separately: Friedrich Lippmann on Wagner's early influences (#2017), Reinhard Strohm on the overtures (#2016), and Heinz Becker on Meyerbeer (#1192). Other entries of special interest are Martin Grego-Dellin, "Wagners Bild in der Literature," Stefan Kunze, "Dramatische Konzeption und Szenenbezug in Wagners *Tannhäuser*," and Oswald Georg Bauer, "Das *Tannhäuser*-Bacchanal." The volume has an expansive name index.

Collections of Essays

1974. *The Wagner Companion.* Ed. Peter Burbidge and Richard Sutton. New York: Cambridge U.P., 1979. 462p. ISBN 0-521-2287-9. ML410 .W13 W137.

Essays by various scholars, dealing with the genesis of the operas, *Leitmotiven* and some of the less obvious elements of the musical language, the music drama as a total work of art, and so on. Robert Bailey makes an important contribution with "The Method of Composition," continuing the line of thought in his "Siegfrieds Tod" article (see #2045). A useful study by Geoffrey Skelton on the founding of Bayreuth is also worth noticing, but most of the content of this volume is derivative or otherwise unsatisfying. Backnotes, bibliography of about 350 entries (incomplete data), expansive index of names and subjects. Note that #1972 has the same title.

1975. *Wagner Handbook*. Ed. Ulrich Müller and Peter Wapnewski. Trans. John Deathridge. Cambridge, Mass.: Harvard U.P., 1992. xv, 711p. ISBN 0-674-94530-1. ML410 .W231 R55.

Originally *Richard Wagner-Handbuch* (Stuttgart: Alfred Kröner, 1986). A collection of essays by various specialists, grouped in 23 topical sections. Coverage includes biographical views, Wagner research (a useful survey by John Deathridge, with some defense of the maligned Alfred Lorenz), genesis and reception studies, Wagner in literature and film, individual works, his influences (by Carl Dahlhaus), and the prose writings. Indexes of compositions and prose writings, expansive general index. Bibliography of some 500 items is of limited use because of incomplete data presented.

1976. *The Wagner Compendium: A Guide to Wagner's Life and Music*. Ed. Barry Millington. New York: Schirmer, 1992. 431p. ISBN 0-02-871359-1. ML410 .W23 .W12.

An interesting gathering of 18 essays by various scholars. Among the topics: a chronology, a who's who of Wagner's contemporaries, the German historical background, the intellectual climate, the musical background. Wagner as a person (appearance, family, character, money, women, dealings with publishers), myths and legends (one is that the Wagner bibliography is the largest of any musician—but this revisionist negation is not supported with data), Wagner's opinions, the sources for Wagner research, a Wagner glossary (with some uncommon terms: *Kunstreligion, Naturmotiv,* quadratic melody, *Wahn*), melodic style, composing method, Wagner as librettist, program notes on the operas (nothing new—40 pages could have been saved), the prose works, orchestration, performance practice, reception and influence. The highlight of the volume is a strong bibliographic essay (p.402–410), topically divided. Christopher Wintle's summary of analytic schools and landmarks is especially valuable. Stewart Spencer's overview of research laments the lack of an adequate bibliography of writings on Wagner, the deficient editions of his prose works and letters, and the lack of a focal point in any significant scholarly journal. (Spencer does not cite *Wagner* [#1978], but editor Millington adds a note about it.) This bibliographic summary is connected, unfortunately, to yet another of those bibliographies with incomplete publication information (about 600 items). Expansive index.

Periodicals

1977. *Richard Wagner Jahrbuch*. Leipzig, 1906–1913. Successor to *Richard Wagner Jahrbuch*. Stuttgart, 1886 (one volume published).

1978. *Wagner*. 1–, 1980–. London: Wagner Society, 1980–. 3 per year. ISSN 0963-3332.

Frequency and place of publication vary. Footnoted articles and useful book reviews. The London Wagner Society also issues *Wagner News* (6 per year; ISSN 0263-3248), which gives an international calendar of events, reviews of books and recordings, and other notices.

1979. *Wagner News*. 1–, September–December, 1977–. Chicago: Wagner Society of America, 1977–. Irregular.

> Notices of events and miscellaneous information, focused on the U.S.

Letters and Documents

1980. Wagner, Richard. *Selected Letters of Richard Wagner*. Trans. and ed. Stewart Spencer and Barry Millington. New York: Norton, 1988. 1,030p. ISBN 0-393-02500-4. ML410 .W2 A317.

> A collection of about 500 letters, drawn from the 10,000 or so extant letters, with commentaries. In chronological sequence, with good historical background essays. The selection of material illustrates the composer's personality and his approach to composition. With a fine index.

Prose Works

Wagner's writings have attracted much scholarly attention. A collective publication was issued under his own direction (#1981) . Wagner's life as told by himself is inscribed in two works: *Mein Leben* (Munich: Bruckmann, 1911; 2v.), best presented in Martin Grego-Dellin's critical edition (Munich: List, 1969; 2v.), which covers the years 1813–1864; and *Das braune Buch,* published in complete form under the editorship of Joachim Bergfeld (Zurich: Atlantis, 1975) and in English translation by George Bird, as *The Diary of Richard Wagner, 1865–1882: The Brown Book* (London: Cambridge U.P., 1980). Contents of *The Brown Book* include diary entries for 1865–1868 and sketches for works—some later completed, like *Parsifal,* others abandoned—with philosophic notes and miscellaneous telegraphic comments. The English version has 202 footnotes and an index of names, topics, and titles.

1981. Wagner, Richard. *Gesammelte Schriften und Dichtungen*. Leipzig: Breitkopf und Härtel, 1871–1873. 9v. PT2551 .W35.

> A revised edition with an additional volume appeared in 1883. Wagner supervised the original and revised versions. Reprints in 1887 and 1897 were identified as the third and fourth editions. The next issue with new material was the *Sämtliche Schriften und Dichtungen,* ed. Hans von Wolzogen and Richard Sternfeld (1911; 12v.). This edition was translated into English by W. A. Ellis as *Richard Wagner's Prose Works* (London: Kegan Paul, Trench, & Trübner, 1883–1899; 8v). Details on the contents of these editions are summarized clearly by Nicolas Slonimsky (#165). The *NG* account could hardly be more obscure.

There have been some useful presentations of Wagner's ideas in topical/historical formats:

1982. Wagner, Richard. *Wagner on Music and Drama: A Compendium of Richard Wagner's Prose Works*. Selected and arranged by Albert Goldman and Evert Sprinchorn. Trans. H. Ashton Ellis. New York: Dutton, 1964. 447p. ML410 .W1 A134.

> Described in the introduction as "an integrated presentation of the whole of Wagner's thought by means of an arrangement of key pieces in passages drawn

from many sources . . . fitted together so that they can be read as continuous systematic exposition." The concept is reasonably well implemented, but the effort is diminished by the paucity of notes and lack of an index.

1983. Hürlimann, Martin. *Richard Wagner in Selbstzeugnissen und im Urteil der Zeitgenossen*. Zurich: Manesse, 1972. 412p. ML410 .W2 H89.

Offers Wagner's opinions and recollections of events in contrast with views by contemporary critics and musicians (Schumann, Berlioz, Hanslick, etc.), as well as observations by Minna and Mathilde. Weak bibliography; name and title index.

1984. Glass, Frank W. *The Fertilizing Seed: Wagner's Concept of the Poetic Intent*. Studies in Musicology, 63. Ann Arbor, Mich.: UMI Research, 1983. xi, 320p. ISBN 0-8357-1396-2. ML410 .W29 G54.

Glass provides a service by distinguishing between Wagner's early (in *Oper und Drama*) and later views. His ideas did change: "In later writings, music and gesture seem to receive more emphasis than formerly; poetry less." But the fundamental idea of *Oper und Drama* was constant: "that poetic intent incites the musical response and calls it forth as drama." Backnotes, bibliography of about 100 items, expansive index of names, titles, subjects.

1985. Borchmeyer, Dieter. *Richard Wagner: Theory and Theatre*. Trans. Stewart Spencer. New York: Oxford U.P., 1991. xx, 423p. ISBN 0-19-315322-X. ML410 .W2 B62.

Originally *Das Theater Richard Wagners* (Stuttgart: Reclam, 1982). The composer's views on artist and audience, opera in the context of Nietzsche's *Birth of Tragedy* and other philosophical writings, and dramaturgy (the ideas set against actual practice in the operas). Borchmeyer minimizes Wagner's less attractive concepts, such as his anti-Semitism. Bibliography of about 100 entries and expansive index.

1986. Rather, L. J. *Reading Wagner: A Study in the History of Ideas*. Baton Rouge: Louisiana State U.P., 1990. xii, 349p. ISBN 0-8071-1557-6. ML410 .W29 R23.

An interesting account of Wagner's thinking on various issues and its connections to ideas of the times. Descriptions of his library and reading habits; his poetry (considered better than most people believe); his views on animals, Christianity, Jews, love, and women. Social relationships were central in his thoughts and appear to have been expressed musically through tonal associations. The Oedipus and Ring myths are analyzed and found to have "close structural relationships." Bibliography of about 350 items, expansive index.

1987. Grey, Thomas S. *Wagner's Musical Prose: Texts and Contexts*. New York: Cambridge U.P., 1995. xix, 397p. ISBN 0-521-41738-4. ML410 .W29 G84.

An important, complex approach to many themes: Wagner and absolute music, gender issues, form in the operas, the endless melody, the leitmotiv, delirium and death, denouements, etc. Bibliography, index.

Biographies

1988. Newman, Ernest. *Life of Richard Wagner*. New York: Knopf, 1933–1946. 4v. Reprint, New York: Cambridge U.P., 1976. ML410 .W1 N52.

A well-documented, interesting life story. Quotations from letters and other materials are given in English translation only. The bibliography is poor, but the expansive index of names, titles, and topics in each volume is useful.

1989. *The New Grove Wagner*. Ed. Carl Dahlhaus and John Deathridge. New York: Norton, 1984. 226p. ISBN 0-393-30092-7. ML410 .W1 D4.

A brief account, revised from the *NG* article, valuable for encompassing all newer research and for the strong worklist.

1990. Westernhagen, Curt von. *Wagner*. 2nd ed. Zurich: Atlantis, 1979. 601p. ISBN 3-7611-0287-9. ML410 .W1 W52.

In English as *Wagner: A Biography,* trans. Mary Whittall (New York: Cambridge U.P., 1978. 2v.). First edition, 1968. A scholarly work, citing letters and primary documents. Detailed life chronology, plain worklist. Meager bibliography, and name index only (the English translation has a good expansive index of names and titles). Problems with the book are that it does not account for much recent scholarship, although it does advance beyond Newman in some respects (such as the coverage of Cosima's diaries), and that it is frequently unreliable regarding facts. Compared with Newman's detached manner, Westernhagen is more than a little adulatory about his subject.

Of a fairly large number of shorter biographies published in recent years, a few may be mentioned:

1991. Chancellor, John. *Wagner*. Boston: Little, Brown, 1978. x, 310p. ISBN 0-316-13622-0. ML410 .W1 C43.

An adequate narrative in short, informal format, with a few footnotes. A life chronology is the main reference feature. Weak bibliography, expansive index of names and titles.

1992. Watson, Derek. *Richard Wagner: A Biography*. London: Dent, 1979. 352p. ISBN 0-460-03166-X. ML410 .W1 W338.

A general work, without footnotes, presenting a dispassionate view of Wagner's personality. Considerable commentary on the prose writings; nothing about the music. Appendix of biographical sketches about persons mentioned. Weak bibliography, partly expansive index of names and titles.

1993. Taylor, Ronald. *Richard Wagner: His Life, Art and Thought*. London: Paul Elek, 1979. 285p. ISBN 0-2364-0071-X. ML410 .W13 T24.

A good introduction: sympathetic to Wagner but not adulatory. Strong in background matters, such as the revolution of 1848 and its consequences, Bavarian politics, and the like.

1994. Gutman, Robert W. *Richard Wagner: The Man, His Mind, and His Music.* New York: Harcourt, 1968. xx, 490p. ML410 .W1 G83.

The author states his purpose: "to see Wagner in terms of ideas—of cultural history." He aims at nonspecialists, however, and offers what is essentially a chronological life story, without reference footnotes and dominated by discussion of the prose writings. Gutman is uneasy in the face of macrostructural questions about the music: "one can feel, not demonstrate, the strength of his formal logic." The Lorenz demonstrations are "protracted and tortuous." Excellent bibliography of about 500 items, expansive index.

A useful supplement to the regular biographies:

1995. Mack, Dietrich, and Egon Voss. *Richard Wagner: Leben und Werk in Daten und Bildern.* Frankfurt: Insel, 1978. 271p. ISBN 345-8320-342. ML410 .S196 R51.

A picture book, consisting of 206 plates with commentaries. Shows Wagner's scores, manuscripts, places, programs, and persons. Good detailed chronology and list of the prose works. No index.

1996. Wagner, Cosima. *Cosima Wagner's Diaries.* Ed. and annotated Martin Grego-Dellin and Dietrich Mack. Trans. with an introduction by Geoffrey Skelton. New York: Harcourt Brace Jovanovich, 1977–1978. 2v. ISBN 0-15-122635-0. ML410 .W11 C5253.

The original was *Cosima Wagner: Die Tagebücher, 1869–1877, 1878–1883* (Munich: Piper, 1976–1977). Her daily jottings concern domestic matters to some degree but also bring hundreds of vignettes of her husband and his remarks—giving a highly personal impression of his contorted character and extravagant biases. The English version benefits from scholarly annotations by Skelton. List of works cited, name index.

Operas in General

Production and reception

1997. Osborne, Charles. *The World Theater of Wagner: A Celebration of 150 Years of Wagner Productions.* New York: Macmillan, 1982. 224p. ISBN 0-02-594050-3. MT100 .W2082.

An illustrated narrative account of productions in major cities of the world, with biographical sketches of important individuals involved. Name and title index.

1998. Petzet, Michael, and Detta Petzet. *Die Richard Wagner Bühne König Ludwigs II.* Munich: Prestel, 1970. 840p. ML410 .W11 P5.

Documents of the Munich premieres and early stagings of nine operas there, and of *Parsifal* at Bayreuth, with much production detail. The views of King Ludwig are summarized, and there is a presentation of miscellaneous correspondence and essays. With 771 fine plates. Name index.

1999. Millington, Barry, and Stewart Spencer. *Wagner in Performance.* New Haven, Conn.: Yale U.P., 1992. x, 214p. ISBN 0-300-05718-0. ML410 .W19 W12.

Consists of 10 essays by various writers, including material on performance practice, reception of Wagner in Vienna, conducting Wagner, Bayreuth, "America's Wagner cult," and Wagner on record. Backnotes, expansive index, no bibliography.

2000. Jung, Ute. *Die Rezeption der Kunst Richard Wagners in Italien.* Regensburg: Bosse, 1974. 524p. ISBN 3-7649-2076-9. ML410 .W1 J95.

A thorough description of productions at Bologna, La Scala, and elsewhere in Italy, with critical reception and other contemporary writing about the music. Extends from early performances to the 1960s. Excellent footnotes lead into the entire relevant literature, which is enumerated in a 700-item bibliography (marred by incomplete information). Partly expansive index of names, titles, and topics.

2001. Bauer, Oswald Georg. *Richard Wagner: Die Bühnenwerke von der Uraufführung bis heute.* Frankfurt: Propyläen, 1982. 288p. ISBN 3-549-06658-9. ML410 .W19 B38.

Presents illustrated production histories for all the music dramas, emphasizing German theaters. Bibliography of about 75 entries on production matters, index of names and places. An English translation was issued: *Richard Wagner: The Stage Designs and Productions from the Premieres to the Present* (New York: Rizzoli, 1983).

Material on the Bayreuth Festival is entered at #2370ff.

Analysis

2002. Lorenz, Alfred Ottokar. *Das Geheimnis der Form bei Richard Wagner.* Berlin: Hesse, 1924–1933. 4v. Reprint, Tutzing: Schneider, 1966. ML410 .W22 L86.

V.1, *Der Ring des Nibelungen;* v.2, *Tristan und Isolde;* v.3, *Die Meistersinger;* v.4, *Parsifal.* The seminal work on macroanalysis of the operas. Lorenz pioneered the concept that large-scale works are built from the same formal patterns as small works: that the simple ABA and AAB forms are found, extended over long time spans, in operatic structures. His ideas and his imaginative application of them to the Wagner music dramas continue to arouse controversy. Modern scholarship is turning away from Lorenzian analytic technique, while leaving open the question of some kind of structure in large works. A fairly positive position has been taken by Donald J. Grout: "One may not choose to follow Lorenz in every detail, and it would certainly be in order to question some of his interpretations of the basic formal schemes; but taken as a whole, it is impossible in the face of his demonstration not to be convinced of the essential orderliness, at once minute and all-embracing, of the musical cosmos of the *Ring,* as well as of *Tristan, Die Meistersinger,* and *Parsifal.* It is an orderliness not derived at second hand from the text, but inhering in the musical structure itself" (#78, p.474). One scholar who modeled his approach on Lorenz is Siegmund Levarie (cf. #1322). Negative appraisals appear in Dahlhaus (#2042) and Bailey (#2045). See also Abraham (#2055*), Coren (#2057), Parker and Brown (#1868*), and the next entry.

2003. Newcomb, Anthony. "The Birth of Music out of the Spirit of Drama: An Essay in Wagnerian Formal Analysis." *19thCM* 5 (1981): 38–66.

A fine overview of scholarship concerning form in the operas. The work of Lorenz, a "seemingly indigestible lump," was in part broken down by Carl Dahlhaus, Guido Adler, August Halm, and Ernst Kurth. Analysts find form in grand design, procedure, or extramusical mood. Tension results as the demands of one of these meet the demands of another. Lorenz overestimated tonality and motivic evolution at the expense of "projection through musical but not traditional functional-tonal means." Dahlhaus and other modern analysts have failed "to consider the linear prolongations and chord connections of functional tonality as valid in Wagner over sizeable stretches of music." Finally, Newcomb states that the "essence of Wagnerian form lies in its ambiguity and incompleteness."

2004. Newman, Ernest. *The Wagner Operas.* New York: Knopf, 1949. xii, 724p. Reprint, Princeton, N.J.: Princeton U.P., 1991. MT100 .W2 N53.

British title: *Wagner Nights.* Detailed program notes and technical observations on all the post-*Rienzi* works. Much attention to the leitmotiv, illustrated by many musical examples (198 of them for the *Ring*). Does not attempt structural analysis. No bibliography; index of names and titles.

2005. Dahlhaus, Carl. *Wagners Konzeption des musikalischen Dramas.* Regensburg: Bosse, 1971. 124p. ISBN 3-764-920-610. ML410 .W13 D13.

A useful introduction to Wagner's intentions regarding music drama; form and motives in the *Ring* (taking up micro- and macrostructure, with attention to Lorenz, who is denounced as unconvincing; however, see next entry); and the music as drama. Footnotes, no index.

2006. Dahlhaus, Carl. *Richard Wagner's Music Dramas.* Trans. Mary Whittall. New York: Cambridge U.P., 1979. 161p. ISBN 0-521-22397-0. ML410 .W13. D153.

Originally *Richard Wagners Musikdramen* (Velber: Friedrich, 1971). Excellent essays on the motives and structures of the operas, relying much on the Lorenzian idea of large forms based on the AAB and ABA principles. Considerable character analysis of Siegfried, Brünnhilde, and others, done with great insight. No footnotes, bibliography, or index. Other writings by Dahlhaus reveal his several imaginative approaches to form in opera: #396, #397, #414, #415, #2041, #2042, and the next entry.

2007. Dahlhaus, Carl. "Wagners dramatisch-musikalischer Formbegriff." *Analecta musicologica* 11 (1972): 290–301.

"Form" is an equivocal term in music. It may refer to the theoretical element and/or to the aesthetic (feeling) element. To Wagner, form was more the latter: that is what he wrote about. *Melodie* is also an aesthetic concept with Wagner, not a music-theoretical term; it refers to the extended feeling-tone of the work rather than to the usual sense of melody. Motives, in Wagner's writings, were supposed to make a total art form, not a tonal architecture. The architecture analogy breaks down in the music anyway, since there are no clear segments to stop and examine, like building blocks, at least not after the early operas. Dahlhaus criticizes Lorenz for discovering such large segments (periods) where they do not exist. But no other satisfactory theory of form in the music drama has been proposed. The great problem in making such a theory will be in understanding the details of the work.

2008. Bailey, Robert. "The Evolution of Wagner's Compositional Procedure after *Lohengrin.*" *Proceedings of the Eleventh Congress of the International Musicological Society, Copenhagen, 1972,* 240–245 (Copenhagen: Hansen, 1974; ML26 .I61).

Considers changes in the interrelations between drafts and final full scores. Beginning in 1856, with *Siegfried,* Wagner added second drafts before going to the full score.

2009. Lavignac, Albert. *Music Dramas of Richard Wagner and His Festival Theatre in Bayreuth.* New York: Dodd, Mead, 1898. 515p. MT100 .W2 L4.

A useful compilation of motivic occurrences in each opera, shown in harmonized musical examples. No index.

2010. Redlich, Hans F. "Wagnerian Elements in Pre-Wagnerian Opera." In *Essays* (#70), 145–156.

Wagner admitted being influenced by several composers, including Carl Loewe (1796–1869) and Albert Lortzing (1801–1851). He had a persistent interest in certain specific operas: Auber's *La muette de Portici* (1828), Spohr's *Jessonda* (1823), and Marschner's *Hans Heiling* (1833). In *La muette* the mute heroine required the orchestra to express her feelings, and her bridal procession was the "blueprint" for the one in *Lohengrin. Jessonda* had an influence on *Die Meistersinger,* and *Hans Heiling* had a profound influence on *Die Walküre, Tannhäuser,* and other works. Redlich appends musical examples to demonstrate these connections, but it must be said that the similarities may not be solid enough to make his case.

2011. Adorno, Theodor W. *In Search of Wagner.* Trans. Rodney Livingstone. [Manchester?]: NLB, 1981. 159p. ISBN 0-86091-037-7. ML410 W23 A241.

Originally *Versuch über Wagner* (1952). Adorno's mixture of Marxist philosophy and perceptive musicality was long regarded as significant to Wagner criticism. Today it may seem more like a curiosity. Adorno regarded Wagner as a "dilettante" whose works fail to achieve any artistic or social value. His approach and language can be indicated by a few quotes: "Wagner draws his productive force from an irreducible contradiction, and wrests a progressive constructiveness from the regressive moment of gesture. This goes as far beyond mere subjective expression as it cancels and preserves it in the double Hegelian sense." "Wagner's hostility to standard forms ends in absurdity." "In sacrificing the fairy-tale to what has existed from time immemorial, Wagner's work allows itself to be appropriated by bourgeois ideology." Adorno does provide some good insights into some musical areas, like instrumentation. Indexed.

2012. Nietzsche, Friedrich. *The Birth of Tragedy and the Case of Wagner.* New York: Vintage, 1967. 223p. B3313 .G42 E55.

This is one of many translations and editions of Nietzsche's views on the composer, first his friend, then his enemy. They met in 1868 when the philosopher was 24, and Wagner impressed him greatly. He became an advocate of Wagnerian theory, and his *Geburt der Tragödie aus dem Geiste der Musik* (1870–1871) was at first criticized as Wagner propaganda. But the value of that treatise lies in its analysis of Greek tragedy; the Wagner section is a minor supplement. When Wagner's theater in Bayreuth opened in 1876, Nietzsche became skeptical—he found the Bayreuth atmosphere grandiose—and he turned against the composer (*Der Fall Wagner,* 1888). He had thought Wagner was Dionysian but found he was only romantic. An article by Mark Berry, "Nietzsche's Critique of Wagner," *Wagner* 20–1 (January 1999): 38–48, is a useful commentary. Another recent study, Joachim Köhler's *Nietzsche and Wagner,* trans. Ronald Taylor (New Haven, Conn.: Yale U.P., 1998), was not seen.

2013. Gloede, Wilhelm. "Zur Verhältnis zwischen den Anfangs und den Endtonarten in Wagners Musikdramen." *Musica* 38 (1984): 429–432.

How to explain that most of Wagner's operas end in a key other than the opening key? Many have wondered this, and nobody has devised a satisfactory answer. Gloede observes that some of those operas have a closing key one step higher than the start key, and there is a change from minor to major (*Tristan, Walküre, Siegfried*), but the pattern is not explicable on musical grounds. Indeed, Gloede concludes that any answer to the tonal design question must have the text as a component.

2014. Petty, Jonathan Christian, and Marshall Tuttle. "The Genealogy of Chaos: Multiple Coherence in Wagnerian Music Drama." *M&L* 79 (1998): 72–98.

Explores the use of key-association and tonal relations to respond to the multiple demands of narrative coherence, fidelity to myth, and "psychologizing." With 106 notes to related writings, including many recent ones.

2015. Nattiez, Jean-Jacques. *Wagner Androgyne: A Study in Interpretation.* Trans. Stewart Spencer. Princeton, N.J.: Princeton U.P., 1993. xx, 359p. ISBN 0-691-09141-2. ML410 .W13 N3513.

Describes the intellectual world in which Wagner worked, then his changing ideas on the relation of poetry and music—which were reflected by the changing relations between men and women in the operas (there was a shift from male to female domination). Nattiez attacks current critical method, especially deconstruction; he accepts multiple interpretations but says that some can be false. He does not go far into gender issues. A question remains about the term "androgyne" in the title of the book. The author admits "difficulty in explaining Wagnerian androgyny . . . partly because we do not have a clear theory of what it is." Nattiez applies the term widely, to bisexuals, homosexuals, heterosexuals, and cross-dressers, and as a linguistic paradox.

2016. Strohm, Reinhard. "Gedanken zu Wagners Opernouvertüren." In *Wagnerliteratur* (#1973), 69–84.

The overtures have not been much studied as separate pieces but considered as integral parts of their operas. Strohm examines Wagner's writings about the overture and discusses those of *Rienzi, Der fliegende Holländer*, and *Tannhäuser*. Influences, notably that of Mendelssohn, are discussed, with musical examples and technical observations.

See also Abbate (#2062).

Individual Works

Die Feen

2017. Lippmann, Friedrich. "*Die Feen* und *Das Liebesverbot,* oder die Wagnerisierung diverser Vorbilder." In *Wagnerliteratur* (#1973), 14–46.

It is generally accepted (and acknowledged by Wagner) that the early operas were influenced by Beethoven, Weber, Marschner (*Die Feen*), Rossini, and Bellini (*Das Liebesverbot*), but specific illustrations of that influence have not been offered. Lippmann gives parallel musical examples showing how Wagner adapted arias and duets from the other composers, transforming their ideas with greater chromaticism and harmonic richness.

Der fliegende Holländer (The Flying Dutchman)

ASO 30 (1980), ENOG 12 (1982), Rororo (1982).

2018. Machlin, Paul Stuart. "Genesis, Revisions and Publications History of Wagner's *Flying Dutchman*." Ph.D. diss., U. of California, Berkeley, 1975. 233p.

Machlin also has a useful article: "Wagner, Durand, and *The Flying Dutchman*: The 1852 Revisions of the Overture," *M&L* 55-4 (October 1974): 410–428.

2019. Barker, Frank Granville. "*The Flying Dutchman*": *A Guide to the Opera*. London: Barrie & Jenkins, 1979. 159p. ISBN 0-2142-0655-6. ML410 .W23 B25.

Various perspectives on the opera, in a popular style: genesis, story, reception, productions, illustrations. A German-English libretto is included. No music examples and not much said about the music. Without index.

Das Liebesverbot

2020. Engel, Hans. "Über Richard Wagners Oper *Das Liebesverbot*." In *Festschrift Friedrich Blume* (#64), 80–91.

Genesis, with quotations from Wagner and study of the sources; technical discussion including early *Leitmotiven* in the work, tonal structure of the finale to act 1 (which Engel compares to finales in Auber and Bellini), and musical examples.

2021. Williams, Simon. "Wagner's *Das Liebesverbot*: From Shakespeare to the Well-Made Play." *OQ* 3-4 (Winter 1985–1986): 56–69.

Wagner was the first to set *Measure for Measure*, which he did with a poor German translation. His reason was that it glorified "free sensuality." The adaptation is studied, and the plot is shown to deteriorate into a series of incidents with weak characterization. Wagner himself condemned the work as "a sin of my youth." Music is not discussed in the article.

See also Lippmann (#2017).

Lohengrin

ASO 143/144 (1992), *ENOG* 47 (1993), *Rororo* (1989).

2022. Deathridge, John. "Through the Looking Glass: Some Remarks on the First Complete Draft of *Lohengrin*." In *Analyzing Opera* (#416), 56–91.

> One of the special interests of Deathridge is the Wagner sketches, which "have not had the critical attention they deserve" (see also his #2033 and #2046); most scholarship is now analysis. Furthermore, "posterity has tended to treat them roughly"—e.g., only 14 of the 21 sheets in the composition sketch of *Lohengrin* (May–July 1846) survive. (After this article was completed, another sheet was located, according to an editorial note.) Deathridge discusses all the sheets and details Wagner's revisions in the light of his written thoughts of the time. A table shows three versions of the Elsa/Lohengrin duet in act 3, scene 3: verse draft, first complete draft, and final. Material that was necessary for plot coherence was cut by Wagner from Ortrud's speech in the same scene.

2023. Cramer, Thomas. "*Lohengrin,* Edition und Untersuchung." Habilitation-schrift, Karlsruhe U., 1971. 598p.

Die Meistersinger von Nürnberg

ASO 116/117 (1989), *COH* (1994), *ENOG* 19 (1983), *Rororo* (1981).

2024. Mey, Curt. *Der Meistergesang in Geschichte und Kunst.* 2nd ed. Leipzig: H. Seeman, 1901. xvi, 392p. Reprint, Walluf: Sändig, 1973. ISBN 3-500-27350-5. ML183 .M61.

> A general study of the Meistersingers in history and art, with a long section (p.271–390) on the opera. Covers poetic and metrical form, appearance of motives, text problems, sources, and other aspects. No index.

2025. McDonald, William E. "Words, Music, and Dramatic Development in *Die Meistersinger*." *19thCM* 1-3 (March 1978): 246–260.

> A useful examination of the story and personages, most interesting for a character appraisal of Hans Sachs.

2026. Komow, Ray. "The Genesis and Tone of *Die Meistersinger*." Ph.D. diss., Brandeis U., 1991. vi, 455p.

2027. Komow, Ray. "The Structure of Wagner's Assembly of the Mastersingers' Guild." *Journal of Musicological Research* 13 (1993): 185–206.

> The structure of the scene "reflects a process in which form-dictating factors phase in and out of synchronization. Factors tend to be synchronous when only the masters are portrayed and asynchronous when Walther is involved . . . Wagner manipulated the degree of formal coalescence to suggest disintegration or cohesion and, in so doing, to serve as a tool for dramatic characterization" (from the author's abstract).

Parsifal

ASO 38/39 (1982), COH (1981), ENOG 34 (1986), Rororo (1984).

2028. Geck, Martin, and Egon Voss. *Dokumente zur Entstehung und ersten Auf-führung des Bühnenweihfestpiels "Parsifal."* Richard Wagner. Sämtliche Werke, 30. Mainz: Schott, 1970. 261p. ML410 .W145 G44.

Presents the source material on the opera: the musical and prose sketches and the documents concerning the 1862 performances. Index.

2029. Bauer, Hans-Joachim. *Wagners "Parsifal": Kriterien der Kompositiontechnik.* Berliner musikwissenschaftliche Arbeiten, 15. Munich: Katzbichler, 1977. 338p. ISBN 3-8739-7045-7. ML410 .W2 B345.

A useful survey of various musical elements in the work: *Leitmotiven,* melodic structure, rhythmic structure, instrumentation, and harmony. Many citations to Lorenz, not always in agreement, and to Ernst Kurth. Musical examples in full score, poorly reproduced; bibliography of about 100 items; no index.

2030. Kindermann, William. "Wagner's *Parsifal*: Musical Form and the Drama of Redemption." *JM* 4 (1986): 431–446; 5 (1987): 315–316.

Finds the analyses by Lorenz to be "almost always artificial." It is more promising to identify "tonal pairings": two keys and the tension between them for dramatic effect. In *Parsifal,* the keys of A-flat and C are the basis of organi-zation for much of the Grail music.

2031. Unger, Max. "The Cradle of the *Parsifal* Legend." *MQ* 18 (1932): 428–442.

Considers the Persian source of the tale. The epics were brought to France by the Crusaders and were translated into French. The original story is summa-rized and compared to that of Wolfram von Eschenbach. Montsalvat is equated with a castle, still standing, in Persia (Iran) near the Lake of Hamun.

2032. Emslie, Barry. "Woman as Image and Narrative in Wagner's *Parsifal*: A Case Study." *COJ* 3-2 (July 1991): 109–124.

Kundry "exposes the powerful and irreconcilable narrative and thematic con-tradictions on which *Parsifal* rests." The real agenda of the opera is a "ratio-nale for masculine sexual and social freedom without loss of the dominant male's high moral and social status."

See also Groos (#2067).

Rienzi

2033. Deathridge, John. *Wagner's "Rienzi": A Reappraisal Based on a Study of Sketches and Drafts.* Oxford: Clarendon Press, 1977. xvii, 199p. ISBN 0-19-816131-X. ML410 .W132 D28.

Based on the author's Oxford dissertation (1974). A thorough discussion of all sources: sketches, drafts, fragments (with clear distinctions among cate-gories—a fine approach to terminological consistency), and their library loca-tions. Comparison of the draft with the 1844 vocal score of Gustav Klink. All previous literature is considered; there are 199 backnotes in the main text and

29 more in the appendix. German passages are not translated. Bibliography of about 75 entries, name and title index.

Der Ring des Nibelungen: The Cycle

2034. *New Studies in Richard Wagner's "The Ring of the Nibelung."* Ed. Herbert Richardson. Lewiston, N.Y.: Edwin Mellen, 1991. viii, 189p. ISBN 0-88946-445-6. ML410 .W2 N49.

Nine papers given at a symposium in Seattle in 1987, many taking up unusual aspects of the cycle: William O. Cord, "On Dwarves and Giants and Wagner's *Ring*"; John Daverio, "Wagner's *Ring* as 'Universal Poetry'"; Richard Justin, "Darwin, Marx, Wagner: Dialectical Materialism in the *Ring*"; John C. Long, "The Rhinemaidens of the Waste Land: T. S. Eliot's *Waste Land* and Richard Wagner's *Ring of the Nibelung*"; Robert C. Martin, "Wagner's *Ring*: A Doorway to Perception"; William E. Grim, "Did Wagner Create Hitler? Reflections on the Influence of the *Ring* on Modern German History"; Ruth Koheil and Herbert Richardson, "Why Brünnhilde Is the True Hero of the *Ring* Cycle: An Analysis of Her Psychological Development"; and two that are entered separately: Sandra Corse on authority (#2051) and Brian Henderson on *Finnegans Wake* (#2052).

2035. Cord, William H. *An Introduction to Richard Wagner's "Der Ring des Nibelungen": A Handbook*. Athens: Ohio U. Press, 1983. 163p. ISBN 0-8214-0648-5. ML410 .W1 A289.

A convenient general introduction in popular style, giving sensible program notes on each opera. No musical examples or analysis. Chronological table for Wagner's works, with dates of literary sources, sketches, premieres, etc. Discography of complete recordings, bibliography of about 150 English-language writings. No index.

2036. Holman, J. K. *Wagner's "Ring": A Listener's Companion and Concordance*. Portland, Ore.: Amadeus, 1996. 440p. ISBN 1-57467-014-X. ML410 .W22 H65.

A useful handbook of varied information, dealing with the myth, story, genesis, characters, language, and staging. Identification of 145 motives and a concordance of key words (in English translation only) that leads to text locations for each appearance. Also long comments on the recordings. Backnotes and index.

2037. Donington, Robert. *Wagner's "Ring" and Its Symbols: The Music and the Myth*. Rev. ed. New York: St. Martin's, 1974. 342p. ML410 .W15 D6.

First edition, 1963. German translation as *Richard Wagners "Ring des Nibelungen" und seine Symbole: Musik und Mythos* (Stuttgart: Reclam, 1976). One of the most controversial books in opera literature. Donington presents an ingenious interpretation of the story and characters in psychoanalytic (mostly Jungian) terms. For instance, Fricka is said to personify Wotan's superego. Provocative musical analyses follow from the author's premises; there are 91 examples of motives with discussion. Annotated bibliography of about 150 items. Index of names, characters, themes, and topics. See also Donington's *Opera and Its Symbols* (#283).

2038. Cumrow, Robert C. "The *Ring* Is a Fraud: Self, Totem, and Myth in *Der Ring des Nibelungen*." *OQ* 1-1 (Spring 1983): 107–125.

An effective deconstructive essay that points out numerous inconsistencies between plot events and symbolic intentions.

2039. Cooke, Deryck. *I Saw the World End: A Study of Wagner's "Ring."* New York: Oxford U.P., 1979. 360p. ISBN 0-193153-81. ML410 .W15 C77.

The theme of this book is the mythological base for the story. The approach includes serious attention to Wagner's intentions, as well as the resulting "overt meaning." Cooke—who died before completing the work—examines the characters and their motivations, relating all to the sagas. He reviews the previous literature very critically, taking issue with Donington in particular. A rudimentary bibliography, expansive index of names, titles, topics, and characters.

2040. Lee, M. Owen. *Wagner's "Ring": Turning the Sky Around.* New York: Summit, 1990. 120p. ISBN 0-671-70773-6. ML410 .W15 L3.

Based on the author's intermission radio talks during Metropolitan Opera broadcasts. These are elegant essays on various aspects of the operas, aimed at a general audience but of interest to anyone for their insights. Bibliography, no index.

2041. Dahlhaus, Carl. "Tonalität und Form in Wagners *Ring des Nibelungen*." *AfM* 40-3 (1983): 165–173.

Considers the Lorenz and Halm approaches to the tonality concept. Then concludes that tonality is a dependent variable, a function of form just as form is a function of tonality.

See also Dahlhauss's other writings on the topic of form, noted at #2006, and the next entry.

2042. Dahlhaus, Carl. "Formprinzipien in Wagners *Ring des Nibelungen*." In *Beiträge zur Geschichte der Oper,* ed. Heinz Becker, 95–129 (Regensburg: Bosse, 1969; reprint, *GL,* v.12).

Finds major weaknesses in the analyses of Lorenz (#2002), including the basic concept of poetic/musical period—which can have, in Lorenz, as few as 14 measures or as many as 840 measures. This 1:60 ratio indicates that such a period has no validity as a formal element. The Lorenz barform is likewise of such variety in its dimensions as to become meaningless. These views are supported by numerous examples.

2043. Westernhagen, Curt von. *The Forging of the "Ring."* Trans. Mary Whittall. New York: Cambridge U.P., 1976. viii, 248p. ISBN 0-521-21293-6. ML410 .W15 W1583.

Originally *Die Entstehung des "Ring"* (Zurich: Atlantis, 1973). An important study of Wagner's sketches—more than 800 pages of them—with all passages

compared with final versions of the scores. Modifications are dated and analyzed. Bibliography of works consulted, name index.

2044. Magee, Elizabeth. *Richard Wagner and the Nibelungs.* New York: Oxford
U.P., 1991. 230p. ISBN 0-19-816190-5. ML410 .W25 M34.

A useful account of the mythological sources and Wagner's adaptations of
them. His reading was voluminous, of the stories themselves and of contemporary scholarship about them. The result was an interpretation that blended his
views with the romantic train of thought in Germany. With 211 footnotes to
support all aspects of the study, minor bibliography, expansive index.

2045. Bailey, Robert. "The Structure of the *Ring* and Its Evolution." *19thCM* 1-1
(July 1971): 48–61.

A fine account of the composer at work. Consideration of tonal planning in
terms of associative keys and macrostructure, presenting an anti-Lorenzian
approach. An earlier contribution by Bailey, "Wagner's Musical Sketches for
Siegfrieds Tod," in *Studies in Music History: Essays for Oliver Strunk,* ed.
Harold Powers, 439–494 (Princeton, N.J.: Princeton U.P., 1968), clarifies the
relation between sketches and the final version of *Siegfrieds Tod*—Wagner's
early name for the *Ring*—and parallel segments of the *Ring* sketches and last
version. One of Bailey's observations—about the time interval between
Siegfried and *Götterdämmerung*—inspired a most interesting study by Kenneth G. Chapman: "Siegfried and Brünnhilde and the Passage of Time in Wagner's *Ring,*" *Current Musicology* 32 (1981): 43–58.

2046. Deathridge, John. "Wagner's Sketches for the *Ring*: Some Recent Studies."
Musical Times 118 (May 1977): 383–389.

Primarily a commentary on the work of Westernhagen (#2043), with attention
to analyses by Robert Bailey and others. He faults Westernhagen for claiming
to have examined all the sketches, observing that certain categories were omitted. Deathridge had made a useful contribution in this regard by defining the
diverse types of drafts and sketches in the Wagnerian sources. See his article,
"The Nomenclature of Wagner's Sketches," *PRMA* 101 (1974–1975), and his
book on *Rienzi* (#2033). He concludes that no study has yet presented a totally
convincing account of how the *Ring* evolved.

2047. Corse, Sandra. *Wagner and the New Consciousness: Language and Love in
the "Ring."* Madison, N.J.: Fairleigh Dickinson U.P., 1990. 209p. ISBN 0-
8386-3378-1. ML410 .W25 C82.

Corse's deconstructive approach to the text is effective: she demonstrates that
"Wagner's ideology of the annihilation of the self for the good of all remains
unconvincing." Trying to create a hero to exemplify the power of love, Wagner
fell into "patriarchical stereotypes of male self aggrandizement. So the last part
of the *Ring* remains a confusing work." Backnotes, minor bibliography,
expansive index.

2048. Shaw, George Bernard. *The Perfect Wagnerite: A Commentary on the
Niblung's [sic] Ring.* London: Richards, 1898. xviii, 151p. MT100 .W25 S53.

This older commentary is still of interest, perhaps mostly for its style and vigor. It offers a clever socialist interpretation, aimed at general readers. Without notes or index.

2049. *The Threat to the Cosmic Order: Psychological, Social, and Health Implications of Richard Wagner's "Ring of the Nibelung."* Ed. Peter Ostwald and Leonard S. Zegans. Madison, Conn.: International Universities Press, 1997. xii, 190p. ISBN 0-8326-6528-3. ML410 .W2 T53.

Consists of 11 essays by various authors, taking up themes indicated by the title of the book: Leonard S. Zegans, "Richard Wagner's Cosmology: Self-Deception, Realization, and the Destruction of Nature"; Robert W. Gutman, "A Passion to Command and Demand"; Alessandra Comini, "The Visual Wagner: Environments, Icons, and Images"; David Clay Large, "Richard Wagner and the Problem of German Identity"; George H. Pollock, "Notes on Incest Themes in Wagner's *Ring* Cycle"; Eric A. Plaut, "Dwarfs, Giants, Dragons, and Other Body Distortions in Wagner's Operas"; Gunter B. Risse, "Health and Medicine in Wagner's Germany, 1820–1890"; Fritz C. Redlich, "The Impact of Richard Wagner on Adolf Hitler"; Thomas S. Grey, "Sickness or Redemption? Wagnerism and the Consequences"; and David Littlejohn, "Panel Discussion on Performance, Interpretation, Staging and Audience Response to the *Ring*."

2050. Levin, David J. *Richard Wagner, Fritz Lang, and the Nibelungen: The Dramaturgy of Disavowal.* Princeton Studies in Opera. Princeton, N.J.: Princeton U.P., 1998. xi, 207p. ISBN 0-6910-2621-1. ML410 .W2 L48.

Considers the reworking of the Nibelung myth by Wagner and analyzes Fritz Lang's 1924 film of the epic. Backnotes, bibliography, index.

2051. Corse, Sandra. "The Voice of Authority in Wagner's *Ring*." In *New Studies* (#2034), 19–38.

An unusual perspective on the text, based on the premise that *Leitmotiven* occur verbally as well as musically. They take the form of recurring statements, quotations of one person by another, and of "embedded narrations" that point to past events. Corse merges this idea with theories of linguist M. M. Bakhtin. One of his ideas is that people quote one another with varying degrees of exactitude and concentration: the fully accurate, focused quotation is reserved for authoritative voices. In the *Ring* there is no real authoritative voice to demand the respect of exact quotation with no comment by the quoter; Wotan's authority is undermined as his words are mixed with musical motives that do not support them. The decline of his power through the cycle is shown by the diminished weight given to his words as repeated by others.

2052. Henderson, Brian. "The *Ring* and the *Wake*." In *New Studies* (#2034), 55–88.

Just as James Joyce based the structure of *Ulysses* on the *Odyssey,* he modeled (according to Henderson) *Finnegans Wake* on the *Ring*. Joyce was fascinated by the Old Norse *Edda* and sagas, and that interest infused his final novel in many ways, from overall structure to characterization and diction. Many specific parallels are noted.

See also Lindenberger (#81).

Der Ring des Nibelungen: Das Rheingold

ASO 6/7 (1976; 1992), ENOG 35 (1985).

2053. Knapp, J. Merrill. "The Instrumentation Draft of Wagner's *Das Rheingold*."
JAMS 30-2 (Summer 1977): 272–295.

Describes and discusses the Wagner manuscript at Princeton U. in the light of
materials at Bayreuth. Compares the format and details with the full score.
Useful footnote references on the terminology of drafts and on the validity of
the collections of Wagner letters.

2054. Darcy, Warren. *Wagner's "Das Rheingold."* New York: Oxford U.P., 1996. xv,
259p. ISBN 0-19-816266-9. MT100 .W26 D33.

A valuable musical and textual analysis, concentrating on genesis: sketches
and drafts. Endeavors to make "a theoretical framework with which the opera
can be meaningfully analyzed." Comments on earlier analyses and utilizes the
methods of both Lorenz and Schenker in explaining tonal structure and unity.
Rhythmic and motivic elements are thoroughly explored as well. Bibliography,
index.

Der Ring des Nibelungen—Die Walküre

ASO 12/13 (1977; 1993), ENOG 21 (1983).

2055. Jenkins, John Edward. "The *Leitmotiv* 'Sword' in *Die Walküre*." Ph.D. diss.,
U. of Southern Mississippi, 1978. 160p.

See also Gerald Abraham, *A Hundred Years of Music* (3rd ed., Chicago: Aldine,
1964), where there is a readable technical introduction to Wagnerian procedures, with
detailed analyses—following Lorenz closely—of *Die Walküre*.

Der Ring des Nibelungen: Siegfried

ASO 14 (1977; 1993), ENOG 28 (1984).

2056. McCreless, Patrick Phillip. *Wagner's "Siegfried."* Ann Arbor, Mich.: UMI
Research, 1981. 248p. ISBN 0-8357-1361-X. ML410 .W15 M35.

Based on the author's dissertation, U. of Rochester, 1981. A thorough analysis
of the work's genesis and musical structure at micro- and macrolevels. With 85
notes to the earlier literature, bibliography of about 125 entries, and expansive
index of names, titles, and topics.

2057. Coren, Daniel Henry. "A Study of Richard Wagner's *Siegfried*." Ph.D. diss., U.
of California, Berkeley, 1971.

A curious effort to show that "the *Ring* is not a vast organic entity" but a collection of internally unified discrete scenes. Coren has strongly negative views
of the Lorenz school (Levarie's approach to *Le nozze di Figaro* [#1322] is classified as "wrong-headed"), but his own attempts at analysis are, in fact, rather
Lorenzian.

Der Ring des Nibelungen: Götterdämmerung

ASO 16/17 (1978; 1993), ENOG 31 (1985).

2058. Abbate, Carolyn. "Opera as Symphony: A Wagnerian Myth." In *Analyzing Opera* (#416), 92–124.

Disputes the common view that the Wagner operas are symphonic, in the sense of being unified as absolute music. Blames Lorenz for this myth, finding it "fantastic and rather silly" to discover "sonatas, adagios, and rondos . . . lurking within *Tristan* or the *Ring*." Goes through Wagner's statements on symphony (in *Zukunftsmusik*), in which he expressed his bond to Beethoven. Then analyzes the last scene in act 2 of *Götterdämmerung* and seems not to know what to say about it. The scene is not symphonic; indeed, it is "inimical to 'symphonic' ideals" because of the "droning, intrusive recurrences of untransformed motivic cells." There are "certain harmonic, linear, tonal, rhythmic, and instrumental events that are musically unseemly, even incoherent." But as she proceeds through the piece, Abbate finds "gestures that at first are intrusive, illogical, unreconciled with what precedes and follows them are gradually assimilated and finally consumed in engendering the 'symphonic' musical juggernaut of the finale . . . the anti-symphonic principle, one that twists music to serve the meaning of words it accompanies, yields to the symphonic principle that addresses conventional musical canons of closure, coherence, motivic interrelationship" giving the "symphonic principle the final word."

2059. Wintle, Christopher. "The Numinous in *Götterdämmerung*." In *Reading Opera* (#218), 200–234.

"Numinous," in Michael Tippett's terminology, means a relating of the marvelous to the everyday. Wintle looks at Siegfried's funeral march from this point of view. It is a lament and a paean. The numinous highlight occurs when the dead hero raises his hand. Although the study begins with a focus on these textual turns, it develops into a thoroughly musical, interesting, and primarily tonal analysis.

2060. Kinderman, William. "Dramatic Recapitulation in Wagner's *Götterdämmerung*." *19thCM* 4 (1980): 101–112.

Concerns act 3, scene 2, the episode prior to Siegfried's moments of revelation before his death—a segment that has been overlooked by analysts, e.g., Lorenz. The scene is shown to be in a tonal framework of E major and C minor/major, with various intricacies. Wagner's method involved setting large sections on "the tension between two tonal centers."

Tannhäuser

ASO 63/64 (1984), ENOG 39 (1988), Rororo (1986).

2061. Abbate, Carolyn. "The Parisian 'Venus' and the 'Paris' *Tannhäuser*." *JAMS* 36-1 (Spring 1983): 73–123.

The two versions discussed are those of Dresden (1845; revised 1845–1847) and Paris (1861). What is now known as the Paris version is what was given in

Munich in 1867 and in Vienna in 1875. Differences are analyzed closely, with details of the revision process. Full of valuable insights into the compositional act and into structural questions. All important editions and secondary literature are cited in 42 footnotes. Texts of 11 letters are in an appendix. A fuller treatment of this research is in Abbate's dissertation, "The 'Parisian' *Tannhäuser*" (Princeton U., 1984).

2062. Abbate, Carolyn. "Erik's Dream and Tannhäuser's Journey." In *Reading Opera* (#218), 129–167.

The dream of Erik in *Der fliegende Holländer* and Tannhäuser's narrative are common romantic types, found more often in spoken drama than in opera. Story telling or dream telling requires coherence in the text, contrary to the repeats and out-of-order material of the aria form. Sometimes recitative is used for the story, but usually—before 1850—narratives were simply avoided in opera. Erik's dream particularizes the generality of Senta's preceding ballad; Senta understands, listening to the dream story, what will occur. The dream tale is an intrusion into the order of the opera up to that point. Tannhäuser's narrative begins in formal structure, then dissolves into "musical anarchy."

2063. Strohm, Reinhard. "Dramatic Time and Operatic Form in Wagner's *Tannhäuser*." *PRMA* 104 (1977–1978): 1–10.

A perceptive study of what might be called "real time" (not Strohm's term) as opposed to operatic time, in this work and in operas in general. Spoken drama "proceeds mainly along the time lapse required by speech," but opera has another layer of "musically organized time" over it. Only recitative is in real time. The general tendency (as per Dahlhaus) in opera is toward "expansion of moments." *Tannhäuser* is exceptional in its adherence to real time, so that events take place as they might in spoken drama. Even the interval between acts 1 and 2 corresponds to the time needed for the situation in the next scene to develop. During arias, action is continuing. Only the act 3 prelude departs from the pattern, distorting real time to take in the entire pilgrimage.

2064. Hopkinson, Cecil. *"Tannhäuser": An Examination of 36 Editions*. Tutzing: Schneider, 1973. 48p. ISBN 3-7952-0122-5. ML410 .W235 N8.

Wagner wrote the libretto in 1843 and the music in 1844; the premiere took place in Dresden, 1845. Many printings of the work followed. Hopkinson gives bibliographic descriptions and locations of 36 publications, the last from 1892. Facsimiles, notes, comments, quotes from Wagner.

See also #1973.

Tristan und Isolde

ASO 34/35 (1981), ENOG 6 (1981).

2065. Bailey, Robert. "The Genesis of *Tristan und Isolde* and a Study of Wagner's Sketches and Drafts for the First Act." Ph.D. diss., Princeton U., 1969. 390p.

The author's abstract states that he was able to derive "the full story of how *Tristan* was put together act by act." He also offered a contribution toward "a new musical and dramatic analysis of the first act."

2066. Bartels, Ulrich. *Analytisch enstehungsgeschichtliche Studien zu Wagners "Tristan und Isolde" anhand der Kompositionsskizze des zweiten und dritten Aktes.* Cologne: Studio, 1995. 3v. ISBN 3-8956-4009-3. ML410 .W15 B27.

Not seen. Presents text, sketches, and facsimiles.

2067. Groos, Arthur. "Appropriation in Wagner's *Tristan* Libretto." In *Reading Opera* (#218), 12–33.

The libretto was first published in Leipzig in 1859, one year before the score and six years before the Munich premiere. Wagner's view of the Tristan romance as told by Gottfried von Strassburg was very negative. He used it only as a stimulus, changing it from an external telling of events to an internal account of feeling. In this respect his pronouncements in *Oper und Drama* matched his actual compositional method. Groos labels Wagner's approach to the original story as "appropriation" rather than adaptation. The article concludes with a similar study of *Parsifal*.

2068. Zuckerman, Elliott. *The First Hundred Years of "Tristan."* New York: Columbia U.P., 1964. xiv, 235p. ML410 .W1 Z8.

Deals with various topics: sources of the music and of the legend, the impact of early performances, Nietzsche, influence on symbolist poets and novelists, 20th-century analytic approaches. An appendix gives the premiere dates of *Tristan* and the other operas in major cities. Notes but no bibliography. Expansive index of names, titles, and topics.

2069. Knapp, Raymond. "The Tonal Structure of *Tristan und Isolde*: A Sketch." *MR* 45 (1984): 11–25.

The macroproblem for analysts is that the three acts end in three keys: C major, D major, and B major. How does this tonal motion support the drama? Knapp works out a plan that is based on the tonalities of the prelude, where the elements occur "in a modulating but tonally focussed theme" of love moving to death. Although the original puzzle is left unsolved, there are interesting observations here. Support is offered for Mitchell's analysis of the "Tristan chord" (#2075).

2070. McKinney, Bruce. "The Case against Tonal Unity in *Tristan.*" *Theory and Practice* 8 (1983): 62–67.

The "case" is essentially based on Wagner's statements, not on the musical conditions in the opera, but the author does stress that "dissonances are not allowed to resolve," which limits the element of tonality in the structure.

2071. Burnstein, L. Poundie. "A New View of *Tristan*: Tonal Unity in the Prelude and Conclusion to Act I." *Theory and Practice* 8 (1983): 15–42.

While the analytic tradition assigns the prelude to the key of A minor, Burnstein reads it in "C major alone," holding that A does not resolve any significant harmonic tensions and thus cannot be the tonic.

2072. Kinderman, William. "Das 'Geheimnis der Form' in Wagners *Tristan und Isolde.*" *AfM* 40 (1983): 174–188.

Generally follows Lorenz, although Kinderman takes the tonic of the opera to be the closing B major (for Lorenz the tonic was E major, B major being its dominant). The central key is established in the opening sounds of the work, as the "Tristan chord" resolves into B major (for Lorenz the prelude is in A minor, closing with a bridge to C minor for the opening scene; the Tristan chord is read in A minor with the B chord as its dominant of the dominant).

2073. Dahlhaus, Carl. "*Tristan*—Harmonik und Tonalität." *Melos/Neue Zeitschrift für Musik* 4 (1978): 215–219.

Wagner's *Leitmotiven* were harmonic as well as melodic. The Tristan chord recurs in act 3, scene 1; and that return gives support to the identification of the key in the opening of the opera, which is A minor. The composer anticipated the moment in the third act as he penned the prelude.

2074. Jackson, Roland. "*Leitmotiv* and Form in the *Tristan* Prelude." *MR* 36 (1975): 42–53.

Takes the approach that Wagner's formal design is made of "an ever changing succession of musical ideas, each flowing directly into the next." This may not seem like an advance over the earlier analyses, which Jackson discusses, by Newman, Lavignac, Lorenz, and Mitchell.

2075. Mitchell, William J. "The *Tristan* Prelude: Techniques and Structure." *Music Forum* 1 (1969): 162–203.

The most exhaustive and generally the most accepted analysis of the *Vorspiel*. Such studies have had a rich history, already sufficient in the 1920s for Lorenz (#2002) to critique them. There has been intense disagreement, even on the basic point of labeling the chords; the reason is that a chromatic work must relate individual chords to a broad context. Mitchell tries "to find an embracing structure by means of linear-harmonic analytic procedures." In the *Tristan* chord, he reads the note A as a "dependent passing tone" and the G-sharp as the "principal tone." Bar one and its upbeat are tonic—so the prelude begins in F major and moves to E in measure 3. (The argument appears to equate key with chord.)

2076. Kurth, Ernest. *Selected Writings.* Trans. and ed. Lee A. Rothfarb. New York: Cambridge U.P., 1991. 253p. ISBN 0-521-35522-2. MT6 .K995 E75.

This convenient gathering includes material from three books by Kurth: *Grundlagen des linearen Kontrapunkts* (1917), *Romantische Harmonik und ihre Krise in Wagners "Tristan"* (1920; 2nd ed. 1923), and *Bruckner* (1925). The second work is of greatest interest to modern scholars. Kurth's idea of romantic harmony centered on the individual chord, which is heard three ways at once: as a solitary absolute sonority, or as successor to the preceding chord, and in relation to the central tonic harmony. During the romantic period, there was a move toward progression effects, connecting two chords, and in "the delight in the sonic appeal itself." Progressions of chords whose roots are separated by diminished fifths, augmented fourths, and other altered intervals became acceptable. Large-scale tonal relations were no longer primary, but the basic pillars remained in the music, so that large units could still express a single key. Such wide-ranging designs must be sought on a case-by-case basis in the romantic compositions; the influence of music drama "extended tonal closure less and less over large cohesive passages." In Wagner, however, tonal development expands to large dimensions, in which "individual original chords of a cadence are transformed into core structures around which entire chord groups unfold." Large-scale cadential relations of the pillars emerge through the "restlessness and wealth of the digressions." And—of special interest to the Lorenzian tonic of *Tristan*—the tonic in these expanded forms is often suppressed. This volume has an excellent introduction, footnotes, outlines of the three books, a strong bibliography of about 100 entries, and an expansive index. Rothfarb has done everything possible to make this difficult writing accessible.

2077. Brown, Matthew. "Isolde's Narrative: From *Hauptmotiv* to Tonal Model." In *Analyzing Opera* (#416), 180–201.

Brown asks, how did Wagner construct "episodes that are internally unified yet still promote the continuity and coherence of the whole?" The narrative is taken as a case study for dealing with this question. Brown disagrees with Lorenz and Bailey (#2065) regarding its form: they both stress the "tonal coherence" of the episode, but Lorenz does not deal with the chromaticism of the second part, and Bailey does not determine "hierarchies among secondary key areas." Brown's own approach is Schenkerian: "to show that each *Hauptmotiv* or form of a *Hauptmotiv* serves a specific formal function and that each articulates distinct voice leading spans and motivic complexes."

William Walton (1902–1983)

2078. Smith, Carolyn. *William Walton: A Bio-Bibliography*. Bio-Bibliographies in Music, 19. New York: Greenwood, 1988. 246p. ISBN 0-313-23591-9. ML134 .W25 S6.

There is no research writing about the Walton operas, but this bibliography provides some guidance to the brief notices and reviews. Arrangement is by author.

2079. Craggs, Stewart R. *William Walton: A Source Book*. Aldershot, England: Scolar Press; Brookfield, Vt.: Ashgate, 1993. xiii, 333p. ISBN 0-85967-934-9. ML134 .W25 A13.

A useful handbook, including a descriptive worklist (manuscripts and first editions), bibliography of writings about Walton, and a discography. Reviews and brief notices on the operas are cited. Craggs also prepared *William Walton: A Catalogue* (2nd ed.; New York: Oxford U.P., 1990; ML134 .W25 A13), in which letters and documents are noted in the entries for each work.

Robert Ward (1917–)

2080. Kreitner, Kenneth. *Robert Ward: A Bio-Bibliography.* Bio-Bibliographies in Music, 17. New York: Greenwood, 1988. 173p. ISBN 0-313-25701-9. ML134 .W26 K9.

The bibliography section has 373 writings by and about Ward, with an index of interviews. Notices and reviews of the operas are included. With a worklist and index.

Carl Maria von Weber (1786–1826)

Editions

2081. Weber, Carl Maria. *Musikalische Werke: Erste kritische Gesamtausgabe.* Ed. H. J. Moser et al. Augsburg, Cologne: Benno Filser, 1926–[1933]. Reprint, New York: Broude, 1977. M3 .W37.

This project, which would have been the only complete edition of Weber, ceased after issuing three volumes. Only early works are included.

Thematic Catalogues and Worklists

2082. Jähns, Friedrich Wilhelm. *Carl Maria von Weber in seine Werken. Chronologischthematisches Verzeichniss seiner sämtlichen Compositionen.* Berlin: Schlesinger, 1871. 476p. ML134 .W37 A2.

This excellent compilation is still the standard worklist. It is fully documented and includes extensive commentaries.

Bibliographies and Guides to Resources

2083. Henderson, Donald G., and Alice H. Henderson. *Carl Maria von Weber: A Guide to Research.* Garland Composer Resource Manuals, 24. New York: Garland, 1990. xxiii, 385p. ISBN 0-8240-4118-6. ML134 .W39 H4.

A useful handbook of 883 entries for writings by and about Weber, all annotated, in topical arrangement. Expansive index of names and places.

Prose Works

2084. Weber, Carl Maria von. *Sämtliche Schriften.* Ed. Georg Kaiser. Berlin, Leipzig: Schuster & Löffler, 1908. 585p. ML410 .W3 A34.

The standard German edition of Weber's extensive writings, covering his autobiographical sketch and numerous critiques of performances and performers and works. Insights and perceptive opinions are everywhere. Important commentary, name index.

2085. Weber, Carl Maria von. *Writings on Music.* Ed. John Warrack. Trans. Martin Cooper. New York: Cambridge U.P., 1981. 402p. ISBN 0-521-22892-1. ML410 .W3 A37.

A valuable collection of reviews, articles, and open letters to journals. Biographical glossary, footnote comments, name index.

2086. Hsu, Dolores Menstell. "Weber on Opera: A Challenge to Tradition." In *Studies in Eighteenth-Century Music* (#73), 297–309.

A summary of Weber's writings on opera, most of them from newspapers in Prague and Dresden from 1813 to 1820. His likes and dislikes are made clear, as well as the embodiment of his ideas in *Der Freischütz*. The ideal for him was a perfect balance among music, drama, dance, scenery, and costumes. His writings enhanced public acceptance of German opera. With 20 footnotes to the earlier literature.

Biographies

2087. Warrack, John Hamilton. *Carl Maria von Weber.* 2nd ed. Cambridge: Cambridge U.P., 1976. 411p. ISBN 0-521-21354-1 ML410 .W3 W26.

First edition, 1968. A German translation of that edition appeared as *Carl Maria von Weber: Eine Biographie* (Hamburg: Claassen, 1972). A valuable life story, citing major documents, letters, and other primary sources; bibliographic essay on the sources and on critical studies. Program notes on the six major operas, with attention to genesis and reception. Worklist; a chapter (in the revised edition only) on Weber's style and historical significance. A poor bibliography detracts from the utility of this work: it has about 100 incomplete entries, many of them trivial, and omits important writing, such as the Gras dissertation (#2096). Index of names, titles, and places. Warrack is also the author of the Weber section of *New Grove Early Romantic Masters* (#172).

Operas in General

2088. Jones, Gaynor G. "Backgrounds and Themes of the Operas of Carl Maria von Weber." Ph.D. diss., Cornell U., 1972. 369p.

2089. Moser, Hans Joachim. *Geschichte der deutschen Musik von Auftreten Beethovens bis zur Gegenwart.* 5th ed. Stuttgart: Cotta, 1930. 3v. ML275 .M68.

There is a useful overview of Weber's stage works in "Die romantische Oper," v.3, 72–129. Moser's commentary, including comparisons with the operas of contemporary composers, is always perceptive.

Individual Works

Die drei Pintos

2090. Weber, Carl Maria von. *Die drei Pintos,* as completed by Gustav Mahler. Ed. James L. Zychowicz. Madison, Wisc.: A-R Editions. 2v. 0-89579-423-3.

Described as "forthcoming" in the A-R 1999 catalogue. The opera was intended to be a comic counterpart to *Die Freischütz* but was left unfinished. Mahler completed and conducted it in 1888. The new edition "includes the complete libretto with English translation, an introduction, and critical apparatus," according to the announcement.

2091. Laux, Karl. "In Erinnerung gebracht: *Die drei Pintos.*" *Musikbühne* 76 (1976): 89–105.

A well-documented genesis, with description of the work.

Euryanthe

ASO 153 (1993).

2092. Tusa, Michael C. *Euryanthe and Carl Maria von Weber's Dramaturgy of German Opera.* New York: Oxford U.P., 1991. 293p. ISBN 0-19-315325-4. ML410 .W3 T9.

A thorough, documented study of the work and its place in the development of romantic opera. Genesis, sources, synopsis, and technical examination of the style. Some attention to macrostructure and key relations. The weak index hampers use. A fuller treatment appeared as the author's dissertation:

2093. Tusa, Michael C. "Carl Maria von Weber's *Euryanthe*: A Study of Its Historical Context, Genesis, and Reception." Ph.D. diss., Princeton U., 1983. 600p.

2094. Tusa, Michael C. "Richard Wagner and Weber's *Euryanthe.*" *19thCM* 9–3 (Spring 1986): 206–221.

Considers the influence of the work on Wagner's early operas. Technical analyses reveal many similarities with passages in *Die Feen, Die Hochzeit, Tannhäuser,* and *Lohengrin.* Tusa is careful not to make a case for influences out of mere examples of common practice in the period. Some parallels between *Der Freischütz* and *Der fliegende Holländer* are also discussed.

2095. Tusa, Michael C. "Weber's *Grosse Oper*: A Note on the Origins of *Euryanthe.*" *19thCM* 8–2 (Fall 1984): 119–124.

Genesis in detail, in the light of the poor reception of *Der Freischütz;* considers how much that adverse reaction determined the totally different style of *Euryanthe* and decides it was not a factor, since the second work was being planned even before the first was finished.

Der Freischütz

ASO 105 (1988), Rororo (1981).

2096. Gras, Alfred H. "A Study of *Der Freischütz* by Carl Maria von Weber." Ph.D. diss., Northwestern U., 1968. 321p.

An intriguing, Lorenzian analysis, blending poetic and musical approaches. Tonal structure is explored. Gras notes that although the opera is not much performed outside of Germany, it did have 475 performances in that country during 1956–1960.

2097. Pahlen, Kurt. *Carl Maria von Weber: "Der Freischütz."* Munich: Wilhelm Goldmann, 1982. 272p. ISBN 3-4423-3044-0. ML410 .W37 P141.

A useful overview of the work, with libretto, genesis, reception, and a discography of 10 complete recordings.

2098. Abert, Hermann. "Carl Maria von Weber und sein *Freischütz. Jahrbuch der Musikbibliothek Peters* 33 (1926): 9–29.

The opera needs to be evaluated independently of its supposed place as a precursor of Wagner; it has great inventiveness and strong musical form. Abert reviews the state of Weber scholarship, finding little to praise.

See also Bomberger (#2364).

Oberon

ASO 74 (1985).

2099. Gallarati, Paolo. "Grammatica dell'esotismo nell'*Oberon* de Weber." In *Opera and Libretto II* (#221), 175–198.

Weber used numerous devices to give an impression of exotic otherness. Timbre, rhythm, ornaments, dynamics, and an ambiguous tonal or modal base all take part. The fluid melodies, "which know no straight line," are on the road to Wagner.

Kurt Weill (1900–1950)

Die Dreigroschenoper (*The Three Penny Opera*) is in COH (1990) and Rororo (1987); *Aufstieg und Fall der Stadt Mahagonny* is in *ASO* 166 (1995).

2100. Kowalke, Kim H. *Kurt Weill in Europe.* Ann Arbor, Mich.: UMI Research, 1979. 600p. ISBN 0-8357-1076-9. ML410 .W395 K7.

A valuable, scholarly examination of the early Weill (to 1935), concentrating on biographical and background matters. Some attention to *Dreigroschenoper* and *Mahagonny*. Worklist through 1935, including literary writings; extensive bibliography of more than 300 entries; expansive index of names, titles, and topics. Based on the author's Ph.D. dissertation (Yale U., 1977). Kowalke has edited two useful collections of essays: *A New Orpheus* (New Haven, Conn.: Yale U.P., 1986) and *A Stranger Here Myself* (Hildesheim: Olms, 1993). Contents are on the website <www.kwf.org>, which is maintained by the Kurt Weill Foundation, New York. The website describes the new *Kurt Weill Edition* (one volume published: a facsimile of *Die Dreigroschenoper*), gives a worklist, calendar of events, and a good bibliography that includes many dissertations.

2101. Drew, David. *Kurt Weill: A Handbook.* Berkeley: U. of California Press, 1987. 480p. ISBN 0-5200-5839-9. ML134 .W4 A2.

A useful compilation, including a chronological, annotated thematic worklist (with individual song titles). Sources, documents, manuscripts, and commentary are given. The distinction between autograph and manuscript is not always made clear, and there are subjective excursions plus some mind reading involved. Weill's American work gets less attention, and his Broadway musicals are minimized. This is not a biography. Indexed.

2102. Jarman, Douglas. *Kurt Weill: An Illustrated Biography.* Bloomington: Indiana U.P., 1982. 160p. ISBN 0-253-14650-X. ML410 .W395 J37.

A life and works, with emphasis on musical commentaries on the compositions. Also a chronological worklist and a bibliography of about 80 books and articles; backnotes and index.

2103. Kilroy, David Michael. "Kurt Weill on Broadway: The Postwar Years (1945–1950)." Ph.D. diss., Harvard U.P., 1992. 527p.

2104. Schebera, Jürgen. *Kurt Weill: An Illustrated Life.* Trans. Caroline Murphy. New Haven, Conn.: Yale U.P., 1995. xi, 381p. ISBN 0-300-06055-6. ML410 .W395 S3513.

Originally *Kurt Weill, 1900–1950: Eine Biographie in Texten, Bildern, und Dokumentation* (Wiesbaden: Breitkopf und Härtel, 1990). A well-documented, chronologically ordered biography, with program notes on the stage works. The collaboration with Berthold Brecht is described in detail (p.89–180), and the Broadway "operas" are well covered (p.310–337). With backnotes, bibliography of about 300 items, and expansive index.

See also Cook (#1055).

Peter Winter (1754–1825)

Leonardo und Blandine is in *GO*, v.10.

Ernst Wilhelm Wolf (1735–1792)

Die Dorfdeputierten is in *GO*, v.2.

Ermanno Wolf-Ferrari (1876–1948)

2105. *Ermanno Wolf Ferrari.* Ed. P. Hamann et al. Tutzing: Schneider, 1986. 164p. ISBN 3-7952-0481-X. ML410 .W85 E65.

A gathering of eight essays by various authors and a worklist. On the operas: Robert Maxym, "Gedanken zu Wolf-Ferraris Opern: Aus der Praxis eines Dirigenten," and Anton Würz, "Ermanno Wolf-Ferrari als Opernmeister." Bibliography, name index.

Riccardo Zandonai (1883–1944)

2106. *Riccardo Zandonai: Atti del Convegno di Studi sulla Figura e l'Opera. . . .* Ed. Renato Chiesa. Milan: Unicopli, 1984. 376p. ISBN 88-7861-8846. ML410 .Z277 C66.

Eighteen papers from a conference held in the composer's birthplace, Rovereto, 29–30 April 1983. Contributions deal with his life and with *Francesca da Rimini, Giulietta e Romeo,* and *I cavalieri di Ekebù.* There are useful studies of his vocal writings and instrumentation. Chronology, index of names and topics.

2107. Dryden, Konrad Claude. *Riccardo Zandonai: A Biography.* Frankfurt am Main: Lang, 1999. 530p. ISBN 3-361-34374-4. ML410 .Z277 D79.

A plain life story, with program notes on the stage works (genesis and reception). Footnoted but with only a token bibliography; a notably poor index, and a worklist giving titles only.

Alexander von Zemlinsky (1871–1942)

Eine florentinische Tragödie is in *ASO* 186 (1999).

2108. Bek, Mikuláš. "On the Dramaturgy of Zemlinsky's *Eine florentinische Tragödie.*" *COJ* 7-2 (July 1995): 165–174.

Genesis, showing changes from the Oscar Wilde play, description of the opera, and some critical responses to it.

2109. Clayton, Alfred Eberhard Stephan. "The Operas of Alexander Zemlinsky." Ph.D. diss., Cambridge U., 1984.

Bernd Zimmermann (1918–1970)

Die Soldaten is in *ASO* 156 (1993).

Johann Rudolf Zumsteg (1760–1802)

Die Geisterinsel is in *GO*, v.12.

XVIII. Countries

Listed in this chapter are works that provide information about operatic composition and operatic performance, arranged geographically. The intention is to describe the most significant works that are specifically or primarily concerned with opera in each country (beginning with one region, Latin America). Works of a more general nature, in which some operatic facts may be found, are cited when no specialized publications are available. In some cases such citations are brief, with pointers to more substantial descriptions in *IOM* or elsewhere.

The reader is reminded that the content of many general histories and other reference works already entered in earlier chapters includes attention to individual countries.

Names of countries are rendered in the native spelling first, transliterated if necessary into Roman script, with English and other names following if such forms appear in the important literature. Country names are in alphabetical order under their English names.

Material under each country is usually set forth in a standard sequence:

1. Editions
2. Bibliographies
3. Music in general
    a. Collections
    b. Histories
    c. Biographies
4. Opera
    a. Collections
    b. Histories (subdivided by period as appropriate)
    c. Biographies
    d. Cities, regions, and theaters

These subdivisions are used as needed and modified in some cases.

Latin America

A useful, if now rather dated, guide to writings about music in the region and in each country is *IOM* 2, which presents 493 annotated entries.

2110. *South America, Mexico, Central America, and the Caribbean.* Ed. Dale A. Olsen and Daniel E. Sheehy. New York: Garland Publishing, 1998. ISBN 0-8240-4947-0.

Coverage of all Latin American countries. Includes glossary, bibliography, discography, videography, and index.

2111. Druesedow, John. "Music . . . Bibliography." In *Latin America and the Caribbean: A Critical Guide to Research Sources,* ed. Paula H. Covington, 575–588 (New York: Greenwood, 1992; A400 .L3225).

An annotated list of 151 books and articles on music, with a guide to library collections, and an essay by Gérard Béhague on Latin American music scholarship.

2112. Günther, Robert. *Die Musikkulturen Lateinamerikas im 19. Jahrhundert.* Regensburg: Bosse, 1982. 464p. ISBN 3-7649-2208-7. ML199 .M987.

Essays by many scholars, on individual countries (Argentina, Bolivia, Brazil, Chile, Costa Rica, Jamaica, Mexico, Puerto Rico, and Uruguay) and certain cities (Santiago de Chile, Valparaíso) and some more general studies. English summaries for each chapter. Good footnotes, illustrations, musical examples. Much biographical information throughout, and 19th-century operatic life is well covered. Name index.

2113. "Caribbean Music History: A Selective Annotated Bibliography with Musical Supplement." *Inter-American Music Review* 4–1 (Fall 1981): 1–112.

Covers to 1975. Richly informative annotations make this list very useful, even if one does not have access to the sources described. Valuable data appear passim (e.g., list of opera premieres in Haiti).

2114. Stevenson, Robert Murrell. "The South American Lyric Stage (to 1800)." *Inter-American Music Bulletin* 87 (July–October 1973): 1–27. ML1 .I57.

A scholarly account, with 164 footnotes, packed with useful data. Much attention to early opera in Peru. Gives synopses of major works, details of productions, and lists of operas by major composers.

2115. Stevenson, Robert Murrell. "American Awareness of the Other Americas to 1900." In *Essays on Music* (#67), 181–205.

A valuable review of musical activity in Latin America and the extent to which it was noted in the U.S. The operatic settings of *Montezuma,* by Frederick Gleason and Roger Sessions are compared, and the operas of Antonio Carlos Gomes and other Latins are discussed.

Current periodicals that deal with Latin American music are the *Inter-American Music Review,* 1978–, and the *Latin American Music Review,* 1980–. The *Handbook of Latin American Studies,* 1936–, includes classified bibliographies and detailed contents of periodicals and composite works.

See also #2747.

Argentina

The essential histories of music are Rodolfo Arizaga, *Enciclopedia de la música argentina,* 1971 (*IOM* 0919), which includes an appendix list of Argentine operas, and Vicente Gesualdo, *Historia de la música en la Argentina,* 1961 (*IOM* 0920), which gives strong coverage of opera in Buenos Aires and presents a list of scores published in the country, 1830–1900. Operatic life has been centered in the Teatro Colón of Buenos Aires, which opened in 1857, was destroyed in 1888, and rebuilt for a performance of *Aida* on May 25, 1908.

2116. Caamaño, Roberto. *La historia del Teatro Colón, 1908–1968.* Buenos Aires: Cinetea, 1969. 3v. ML1717.8 .B9 C3.

Excellent color plates (artists, scenes, costumes, and stage designs) make up most of the content, but there is also useful text in the form of essays by various scholars. Coverage of the building itself, personnel, performances (all casts given), critics, etc. Composer and artist indexes. The same author has written several brief accounts of the theater (*IOM* 0942ff.). A collection of documents on the theater was assembled by Ernesto de la Guardia and Roberto Herrera, *El arte lírico en el Teatro Colón (1908–1933),* 1933 (*IOM* 0943).

2117. Kuss, Malena. "Nativistic Strains in Argentine Operas Premiered at the Teatro Colón (1908–1972)." Ph.D. diss., U. of California at Los Angeles, 1976. xii, 523p.

Considers the operas of 12 major composers and gives a history of opera in Argentina; also a discussion of opera in other Latin countries, p.373–386. Worklists, bibliography of about 350 titles, no index.

2118. Fiorda Kelly, Alfredo. *Cronología de las óperas, dramas líricos, oratorios, himnos, etc., cantados en Buenos Aires.* Buenos Aires: Riera, 1934. 83p. ML1717.8 .B9 F5.

Covers performances in all theaters, 1825–1933; arranged by date, with lists also by composer and title. Cast and performer information is included. Another useful treatise is Mariano Bosch, *Historia del teatro en Buenos Aires,* 1910 (*IOM* 0944).

2119. Gesualdo, Vicente. *Pablo Rosquellas y los orígenes de la ópera en Buenos Aires.* Buenos Aires: Artes en América, 1962. 55p. ML1717.8 B9 G4.

Rosquellas was a singer, composer, and violinist who lived in the city from 1823 to 1833 and organized the first opera performances there. The book gives casts and production information on the early stagings, with biographical sketches of the singers and critical reviews. Thoroughly footnoted but without bibliography or index.

2120. Valenti Ferro, Enzo. *Las voces: Teatro Colón, 1908–1982.* Buenos Aires: Arte Gaglianone, 1983. 499p. ISBN 9-5090-0436-7. ML1717.8 .B92 T44 V18.

A list of about 800 singers and their roles, by season, with brief biographies and critical comments about them. The operas are also listed by composer.

2121. Dillon, César A., and Juan A. Sala. *El teatro musical en Buenos Aires: La ópera, la opereta, la zarzuela, la comedia musical—Teatro Doria, Teatro Marconi.* Buenos Aires: Arte Gaglianone, 1997. xxii, 485p. ISBN 950-720-051-7. ML1717.8 .B92 D55.

A narrative account of both theaters and a chronology of performances with casts. The Doria was active from 1887 to 1903, the Marconi from 1903 to 1966 (when it became a variety house, then was demolished). Good indexing locates companies, singers, directors, and works given.

Australia

2122. *Oxford Companion to Australian Music.* Ed. Warren Bebbington. New York: Oxford U.P., 1997. xvi, 608p. ISBN 0-1955-3432-8. ML101 .A9 O94.

A useful gathering of biographical and topical articles. "Opera and Opera Companies" (p.430–435) is the main operatic entry. It says Opera Australia is the only full-time company; it was established in 1956 as sthe Australian Opera and is based at the Sydney Opera House. A monthly journal, *Opera Australasia,* is mentioned in the article but has not been seen. No index.

2123. Crisp, Deborah. *Bibliography of Australian Music: An Index to Monographs, Journal Articles, and Theses.* Armidale, N.S.W.: Australian Music Studies Project, 1982. xiv, 260p. ML120 .A86 C7.

Covers 1790–1981, with 2,218 entries and a subject index.

2124. Cargher, John. *Opera and Ballet in Australia.* Stanmore, N.S.W.: Cassell Australia, 1977. xiii, 352p. ISBN 0-7269-1360-X. ML1751 .A9 C37.

Primarily a photo book, with an earthy popular commentary. Historical summary and discussion of recent performances in Melbourne and Sydney. Name and title index.

2125. Love, Harold. *The Golden Age of Australian Opera: W. S. Lyster and His Companies, 1861–1880.* Sydney: Currency Press, 1981. 309p. ML1751 .A9 L68.

A detailed history of the period indicated, with biographical notes on singers. Chief impresario William Lyster is discussed, and many dates and casts are given. There is no actual chronology, but one appeared for 1861–1868 in *Australasian Drama Studies* 2 (October 1983): 113–124.

2126. Mackenzie, Barbara, and Findlay Mackenzie. *Singers of Australia from Melba to Sutherland.* Melbourne: Lansdowne, 1967. xvii, 309p. ML400 .M27.

Long, footnoted chapters on Nellie Melba and Joan Sutherland. Good coverage of Frances Alda (born in New Zealand), Peter Dawson, John Brownlee, and Marjorie Lawrence; shorter treatment of 60 others. Useful introductory essay on opera in Australia. Bibliography of about 200 books and articles, name index.

2127. *Opera and the Australian Composer.* Ed. Kay Dreyfus. Camberwell, Victoria: K. Dreyfus, 1973. iv, 102p. ISBN 0-9598595-0. ML1751 .A9 O6.

Reports on a symposium sponsored by the International Society for Contemporary Music. A chatty view of the "current scene" has little value. An essay by Elizabeth Wood, "1840–1965: Precedents and Problems for the Australian Opera Composers," includes a few facts. No index.

2128. Australian Music Centre. *Directory of Australian Composers Represented in the Collection of the Australian Music Centre.* 2nd ed. Ultimo, N.S.W.: The Centre, 1988. i, 38p. ISBN 0-900168-25-3. ML21 .A86 L46.

First edition, 1978. Lists the works of about 150 persons. The index identifies about 60 operas.

The spectacular Sydney Opera House opened in 1970 and has spawned a number of descriptive publications. This one seems to cover the main points:

2129. Hubble, Ava. *More than an Opera House.* Sydney: Sydney Opera House, 1978. 67p.

Not seen; described in *RILM* as an illustrated booklet on "planning, design, construction, decoration, management, financing, organization and uses" of the house; with dimensions, facilities, photographs, and notes on artists and others associated with the complex. Other writings on the opera house are listed in Stoddard (#127). Annual reports of Opera Australia have been issued since 1972, with details on all productions.

Austria (French: Autriche; German: Österreich)

The vast literature on opera in Austria, especially in Vienna, is represented here by only a few useful works. A larger selection, including materials of wider scope in which opera has its place, will be found in *IOM* 1576–1643. Two handbooks form convenient entry points:

Music in General

2130. Goertz, Harald. *Musikhandbuch für Österreich.* 3rd ed. Vienna: Doblinger, 1993. xii, 168p. ISBN 3-900-6952-53. ML21 .A9 G6.

First edition, 1983. A good collection of information on musical life: schools, archives and libraries, theaters, orchestras and other performing groups, church music, radio and television, record studios, associations, institutions, and publishers. Locations (street names) of monuments are given, and these are numerous in Austria: Vienna alone has 21 for Beethoven, and Graz has 4 for Schubert. Bibliography, index.

The other handbook of interest is an older one by Brody, in the series noted at #144*. Concert and opera reviews are found in several periodicals, of which this is the best known:

2131. *Österreichische Musiikzeitschrift,* 1–, January 1946–. Vienna: H. Bauer, 1946–. Monthly. ML5 .O1983.

Includes some scholarly articles as well as short feature material. All musical topics are covered, with emphasis on Austria. Calendars and reviews of performances in Austria and neighboring countries, reviews of books and recordings.

2132. Dace, Wallace. *National Theaters in Larger German and Austrian Cities*. New York: Richards Rosen, 1980. 468p. ISBN 0-8239-0527-6. PN2044 .G4 D3.

A book of photographs and floor plans, plus names of operas given with performance information and financial statistics. Covers Vienna, Linz, West Berlin, Nuremberg, Stuttgart, Düsseldorf, Frankfurt, Cologne, Munich, and Hamburg. Institutions for research and library collections in Austria and Germany are also surveyed. Bibliography of about 150 items, name and title index.

Calendars of operatic performances are given at the website <www.austriaculture. net>.

2133. *The New Grove Second Viennese School: Schoenberg, Webern, Berg*. Ed. Oliver Neighbour et al. New York: Norton, 1983. 201p. ISBN 0-393-01686-2. ML390 .N34.

Three articles from *NG*, updated, indexed, and with strong worklists.

Other material on aspects of opera in Austria appears in various local histories; a selection of these is described in *IOM* 1608–1620.

Cities and Regions

Vienna (German: Wien)

The principal theaters and their opening dates: Kaiserhof, 1625; Theater am Kärntnerthor, 1708; Theater bei der Hofburg (Burgtheater), 1748; Freihaustheater auf der Wieden, 1787; Theater an der Wien, 1801, renovated and reopened 1962; Theater in der Josefstadt, 1788, reopened 1822 (with Beethoven's *Consecration of the House*); Oper am Ring (Staatsoper; Hofoper), 1869–1945, reopened 1955; Wiener Volksoper, 1898, reopened 1945.

2134. Heartz, Daniel. *Haydn, Mozart, and the Viennese School, 1740–1780*. New York: Norton, 1995. xviii, 780p. ISBN 0-393-96533-3. ML246.8 .V6 H4.

Vienna's musical life; details on the Burgtheater and Kärntnerthor (the buildings, repertoire, administration); court composers. Gluck has one chapter, Haydn two, Mozart three. Discussion of operas by Wagenseil, Bonno, Traetta, Gassmann, Salieri, and Dittersdorf. Detailed analyses of Haydn's *Le pescatrici, L'incontro improvviso, L'infedeltà delusa*; accounts of the early Mozart operas. Bibliography of about 300 items, index.

2135. Butterweck, Georg. *Veranstaltungssäle in Wien*. Vienna: Institut für Stadtforschung, 1973. 128p. ML21 .B88.

Describes 576 halls, which are grouped by locality (*Bezirk*) in the city. Every venue with seating for at least 100 persons is included. Floor plans for about 50 principal auditoriums. Vienna's total seating capacity is calculated at 159,124.

2136. Pirchan, Emil, et al. *300 Jahre Wiener Operntheater: Werk und Werden*. Vienna: Fortuna, 1953. 312p. ML1723.8 .V62 O77.

Covers all stage presentations from the baroque onward. Biographies, bibliography of about 120 items, 233 plates and name index.

2137. Witeschnik, Alexander. *Wiener Opernkunst von den Anfängen bis zu Karajan.* Vienna: Kremayr & Scherian, 1959. 332p. ML1723.8 .V6 W55.

Surveys operatic history from the beginnings; illustrated with nine plates and black-and-white photos and drawings. Bibliography, index.

2138. Wallaschek, Richard. *Das K. K. Hofoperntheater. Die Theater Wiens, v.4.* Vienna: Gesellschaft für Vervielfältigende Kunst, 1899–1909. 4v. in 6. PN2216 .V5 T4.

The fourth volume of a general history of Viennese theater is about opera and musical life. It includes narrative accounts and performance chronologies for the Kärntnerthortheater, 1763–1870, and the Hofoperntheater, 1869–1894. Bibliography of about 130 titles, name and title index.

2139. Kaufman, Thomas G. "Italian Performances in Vienna, 1835–59." *DSJ* 4 (1980): 53–72.

Operas and casts of Italian performances at Kärntnerthor by a troupe brought in by impresario Bartolomeo Merelli. Their season (April–June) was annual, except for 1848–1850. Events are listed chronologically.

2140. Wellesz, Egon. "Die Opern und Oratorien in Wien von 1600–1708." *Studien zur Musikwissenschaft* 6 (1919): 5–138.

A rich narrative account, with a list of about 60 operas given and their dates. Chapters on instrumental music in the operas, on individual composers (Badia, Ziani, the Bononcinis), vocal forms, libretti, and aria structure. Musical examples and notes but no index.

2141. *Opera buffa in Mozart's Vienna.* Ed. Mary Hunter and James Webster. New York: Cambridge U.P., 1997. xii, 459p. ISBN 0-521-57239-8. ML1723.8 .V6 O64.

A valuable collection of essays by various scholars, dealing with the Viennese context, patrons, audiences, librettists, singers, and set designers of the 75 *opere buffe* staged in Vienna in 1783–1792 (of the 75, only the three by Mozart are still in the repertoire). Useful contributions include Marvin Carlson, "*Il re alla caccia* and *Le roi et le fermier*: Italian and French Treatments of Class and Gender"; Edmund J. Goehring, "The Sentimental Muse of *opera buffa*"; Michael F. Robinson, "The Alternative Endings of Mozart's *Don Giovanni*"; and John Platoff, "Operatic Ensembles and the Problem of the *Don Giovanni* Sextet." These are entered separately in this guide: Jessica Waldoff on the finale in Aristotelian terms (#1310), Sergio Durante on operatic theory (#411), and James Webster on analysis and unity (#417). Bibliography, expansive index.

2142. Rommel, Otto. *Die alt-wiener Volkskomödie.* Vienna: A. Schroll, 1952. 1,096p. PN2616 .V5 R6.

The definitive history of stage comedies, comic opera, and operetta in Vienna from the baroque into the mid–19th century. About 250 illustrations, bibliography of some 750 items. Name and title index.

2143. Bauer, Anton. *Oper und Operetten in Wien: Verzeichnis ihrer Erstauf-führungern in der Zeit von 1629 bis zur Gegenwart.* Graz: H. Böhlaus Nachf., 1955. xii, 156p. ML1723.8 .V6 B22.

> All 4,856 stage works premiered from 1629 are listed in title order. Indexed by date, composer, and librettist. A map shows locations of the theaters. Bibliography of about 100 items.

See also material on Gluck in Vienna (#896) and #2349.

Vienna: Das Wiener Opernhaus (Staatsoper)

The Hofoper became the Staatsoper in 1918. This is the famous Vienna Opera. It was destroyed in a bombing on 12 March 1945, rebuilt and reopened on 5 November 1955. Of the many histories, these are the most useful:

2144. Beetz, Wilhelm. *Das Wiener Opernhaus, 1869 bis 1945.* 2nd ed. Vienna: Panorama, 1955. 288p. ML1723.8 .V62 O73.

> First edition, 1949 (the only one seen). A statistical history, with many lists and tables: complete record of performances of 337 German operas and *Singspiele,* 42 Italian and French operas; ballets and other stage works, 1869–1919. Lists of directors and performers, including orchestral musicians, by nationality and by instrument or specialty. Table of titles of all works given, with premiere and later productions of each year, 1869–1944; chronology of notable performances, 1926–1944. The 80 plates show the interior and exterior. Access to all these data is slow, since there is no index.

2145. Haas, Robert. *Die Wiener Oper.* Vienna: Eligius, 1926. 70p. and plates. ML1723.8 .V62 S825.

> A strong, concise narrative history. Much information on design and construction of the 1869 building, including names of painters and sculptors, etc. The architects, August Siccard von Siccardsburg and Eduard van der Nüll, receive considerable attention. Details of doorways, statuary, salons, lunettes, and exteriors are shown in 59 plates. No index.

2146. Hadamowsky, Franz. *Die Wiener Hoftheater (Staatstheater), 1776–1966.* Vienna: G. Prachner, 1966–1975. 2v. PN2616 .W7 H2.

> A well-documented narrative account of the Vienna Opera and its predecessor, the Hoftheater. Includes a list of performances from 1811 to 1974, with staff—but not casts—identified. Name indexes.

Three popular histories of the Vienna Opera have been translated into English:

2147. Klein, Rudolf. *The Vienna State Opera.* Vienna: Lafite, 1969. 80p. ML1723.8 .V62 S83.

> Originally *Die Wiener Staatsoper* (1967). A well-illustrated volume, with a list of premieres 1869–1969 and a list of opera directors.

2148. Kralik, Heinrich. *The Vienna Opera.* Vienna: Brüder Rosenbaum, distributed in the U.S. by Heineman, 1963. 189p. ML1723.8 .V6 K7.

Originally *Die Wiener Oper* (1962). A narrative history with fine illustrations, including drawings and watercolors of the star singers. Name index.

2149. Prawy, Marcel. *The Vienna Opera.* New York: Praeger, 1969. 228p. ML1723.8 .V62 O775.

Originally *Die Wiener Oper* (Zurich: Molden, 1969). A lavishly illustrated history, with emphasis on 20th-century personalities (portraits of about 150 of them). Name index.

2150. Rode-Breymann, Susanne. *Die Wiener Staatsoper in den Zwischenkriegsjahren.* Tutzing: Schneider, 1994. 485p. ISBN 3-7952-0772-4. ML1723.8 .V62 R63.

An interesting review of culture and politics between the world wars. Discusses the directorships of Franz Schalk and Clemens Kraus; composers and stagings. List of works performed, by composer, with critical responses to them. Backnotes, bibliography of about 350 items, expansive index.

2151. Christian, Hans, and Harald Hoyer. *Wiener Staatsoper, 1945–1980: Eine Dokumentation.* 408p. No ISBN. ML1723 .V62 S815.

Lists the performances at the Staatsoper, as well as the Theater an der Wien, Volksoper, and Redoutensaal; arranged by opera instead of chronologically. Identifies all the singers for each role. Index.

Vienna: Theater an der Wien

2152. Bauer, Anton. *150 Jahre Theater an der Wien.* Zurich: Amalthea, 1952. 515p. ML1723.8 V62 O72.

The theater opened on 13 June 1801. From late 1945 to 1954 it housed the productions of the Wiener Oper while that building was being reconstructed. This is a scholarly narrative history, with a large foldout plan and other good illustrations. Performance chronology, 1801–1939 and 1945–1951, without casts. Name and topic index.

2153. Lang, Attila. *Das Theater an der Wien. Vom Singspiel zum Musical.* 2nd ed. Vienna: Jugend und Volk, 1977. 134p. ISBN 3-7141-6096-5. ML1723.8 .V6 T55 L2.

A footnoted review of light opera (Lortzing, Kálmán, Offenbach, and other standard composers, plus recent works like *Gigi* and *Pippin*), with a chronology of premieres and a chronology of all performances from 6 October 1945 to 11 March 1976. List of directors, 1801–1965. No bibliography; name index.

Vienna: Burgtheater

2154. Heartz, Daniel. "Nicholas Jadot and the Building of the Burgtheater." *MQ* 68–1 (January 1982): 1–31.

The theater opened on 14 May 1748, and opera flourished there throughout the 18th century. After 1801 and the opening of Theater an der Wien, the Burgtheater was used more for spoken drama (its present function) but was still the site of many important productions in the 19th century until the opening of the Hofoper (now the Wiener Staatsoper) in 1869. Jean Nicolas Jadot was the architect. The article gives pictures and floor plans, plus useful notes on early works performed.

2155. Michtner, Otto. *Das alte Burgtheater als Opernbühne, von die Einführung des deutschen Singspiels (1778) bis zum Tod Kaiser Leopolds II (1792)*. Vienna: Hermann Böhlaus Nachf., 1970. 566p. ISBN 3-205-03204-7. PN2610 .T5 v.3, pt.1.

A segment of *Theatergeschichte Österreichs*. This volume covers the *Singspiel* productions by season, 1778–1783; Italian opera, 1783–1790; and opera under Leopold II, 1790–1792; full chronologies are given. Lists of singers and operas, bibliography of about 500 entries, and indexes of places, titles, and persons.

2156. Link, Dorothea. *The National Court Theatre in Mozart's Vienna*. New York: Oxford U.P., 1998. ix, 549p. ISBN 0-19-816673-7. ML1723.8 .V6 L56.

A performance chronology for the Burgtheater, 1783–1792. Eyewitness accounts of the same period, by Count Karl Zinzendorf (p.191–398), are of interest. Much valuable data throughout: currency, account books of the theater, companies, subscribers. Useful bibliography of primary and secondary material, about 150 items; indexes of names and titles.

2157. Lewy, Patricia. "Burgtheater, Vienna, 1873–1891: The Singers and Their Repertory." Ph.D. diss., U. of California, Berkeley, 1991. 465p.

See also Brockpähler (#2349) and Cole in #288.

Graz

2158. List, Rudolf. *Oper und Operette in Graz*. 2nd ed. Ried im Innkreis: Oberösterreichischer Landesverlag, 1974. xvi, 312p. ML1723.8 .G72 L6.

First edition, 1966. A general narrative for 1736–1974, giving some of the casts; with 213 photos; no index.

Innsbruck

2159. Senn, Walter. *Musik und Theater am Hof zu Innsbruck: Geschichte der Hofkapelle von 15. Jahrhundert bis zu deren Auflösung im Jahre 1748*. Innsbruck: Österreichisches Verlaganstalt, 1954. xx, 447p. ML246.8 .I5 S4.

A detailed, well-documented history, including biographical sketches of composers and performers (covering many minor figures). Bibliography of about 150 items, indexes of persons and places.

Linz

2160. Wimmer, Heinrich. *Das Linzer Landestheater, 1803–1958*. Linz: Oberösterreichischer Landesverlag, 1958. 204p.

Not examined.

Salzburg

2161. Kaut, Josef. *Festspiele in Salzburg.* 2nd ed. Salzburg: Residenz, 1969. 584p. ML246.8 .S18 K3.

First edition, 1965. A scholarly narrative of 1,000 years in the city's musical life, including ballet. Description of the Festspielhaus and index of works performed there from 1920 to 1969; artists are named. Bibliography, index to musicians but no general index.

2162. Kaut, Josef. *Die Salzburger Festspiele, 1920–1981.* Salzburg: Residenz, 1982. 499p. ISBN 3-7017-0308-6. ML246.8 .S2 F379.

A beautifully illustrated narrative history, updating the previous entry; chronologies for each year to 1982.

2163. Steinberg, Michael P. *The Meaning of the Salzburg Festival: Austria as Theater and Ideology, 1890–1938.* Ithaca, N.Y.: Cornell U.P., 1989. xvi, 253p. ISBN 0-801423-627. ML246.8 .S2 F435.

A cultural history, discussing the persons involved in the festival, government motivations, and social forces. The institution is essentially conservative, returning to baroque ideals. The important role of Hugo von Hoffmansthal is well described. Bibliography of about 150 items, index.

2164. Fuhrich, Edda, and Gisela Prossnitz. *Die Salzburger Festspiele: Ihre Geschichte in Daten, Zeitzeugnissen und Bildern. V.1: 1920–1945.* Salzburg: Residenz, 1990. 327p. ISBN 3-7017-0630-1. ML38 .S267 .S45.

Only this volume was seen. It is a chronology with extensive comments and many photos, plus extracts from critical reviews of performances. Index of titles and names.

See also #319.

Belarus (White Russia; Belorussia of the former Soviet Union)

There is no literature in Western languages. Three works in Russian have useful information: *Muzykal'naia kultura Belorusskoi SSR* (Moscow: Muzyka, 1977; ML309 .W5 M9; includes a chapter on opera), and two books by Bronislav Sil'vestrovich Smol'skii: *Belorusskii muzykal'nyi teatr* (Minsk: Nauka i Techhnika, 1963; ML1737 .S64; a scholarly narrative history), and *Beloruskii Gosudarstvennyi Orden Lenina Bol'shoi Teatr Opery i Baleta* (Minsk: Gos. Izd- vo BSSR, 1963; ML1741.8 M55 B44; a narrative with chronology for 1852–1961).

Belgium (French: Belgique; German: Belgien)

The country and its literature are bilingual, with Dutch (Flemish) spoken in Flanders (Vlaanderen; principal city, Antwerp) and French spoken elsewhere.

Brody's guidebook (#144*) has general directory information but is more than 20 years old. The website <www.belgium.fgov.be> has current opera calendars.

2165. Renieu, Lionel. *Histoire des théâtres de Bruxelles depuis leur origine jusqu'à ce jour.* Paris: Duchartre & Van Buggenhoudt, 1928. 2v. PN2706 .B7 R4 or ML1726.8 .B7 R4.

First performances and historical accounts of the major theaters in Brussels, including all forms of stage works. Bibliography of about 300 titles, no index.

2166. Salès, Jules. *Théâtre Royal de la Monnaie, 1856–1970.* Nivelles: Havaux, 1971. 454, xi p. ML1726.8 .B7 T43.

The first Monnaie was built in 1700; the present structure dates from 1856, extensively renovated and reopened in 1986. Renamed the Opéra National in 1963, it is the major opera house of the country. This is a chronology of performances, with casts and a title index. Bibliography has only six items.

2167. Couvreur, Manuel. *Le Théâtre de la Monnaie au XVIIIe siècle.* Brussels: Université Libre, 1996. 355p.

Not examined.

2168. Pols, André. *Vijftig jaar Vlaamsche Opera.* Antwerp: Pierre Dirix, 1943. 63p. and picture section. ML1726.8 .A7 P6.

The Royal Flemish Opera (Vlaamsche Opera) opened in 1893; this is a chronology of works performed through 1942–1943, with a historical narrative. All operas in the house are sung in Flemish. *Kaufman* mentions a book (not seen by him; title not verified) that extends the chronology: *Koninklijke vlaamse oper Antwerpen gedenkklanken 1893–1963,* by Renaat Verbruggen (Antwerp, 1965).

2169. Sanders, L. *Onderzoek opera en publiek te Antwerpen.* Antwerp: Dienst Sociologie, 1974. 2v. ML1726.8 .A7 S25.

Essentially a statistical study of operagoing and financial-sociological considerations but does give some facts on several Belgian opera companies. Bibliography of about 100 entries is of some use despite its incomplete data. No index.

2170. Auda, Antoine. *La musique et les musiciens de l'ancien pays de Liège: Essai bio-bibliographique sur la musique liègeoise depuis ses origines jusqu'à la fin de la Principauté (1800).* Brussels: Saint-Georges, 1930. 291p. ML265.8 .L4 A82.

Not seen.

Bosnia-Herzegovina

The country declared its independence from Yugoslavia in 1992. There is no music literature in Western languages. Only one item in Serbo-Croatian has been seen:

2171. Narodno Pozorište Sarajevo. Opera. *Jubilarna godina Sarajevske Opere, 1946–1966.* Sarajevo: Sarjevska Opera Narodnog Pozorišta, 1967. 64p. ML1751.8 .S27 N4.

An illustrated history with chronologies of performances for the period.

Brazil (Portuguese and Spanish: Brasil)

A rather old introduction to opera in the country is found in *150 anos de música no Brasil, 1800–1950,* by Luis Heitor Corrêa de Azevedo (1956; *IOM* 0976); the same author has a chapter on opera in his *Música e músicos do Brasil* (1950; *IOM* 0986). Even older is the reliable history by Renato Almeida, *História da música brasileira* (1942; *IOM* 0975).

Writings on musical topics are listed in two bibliographies:

2172. Corrêa de Azevedo, Luiz H. *Bibliografia musical brasileira (1820–1950).* Rio de Janeiro: Instituto Nacional do Livro, 1952. 252p. ML120 .B7 C6.

An annotated bibliography of 1,639 entries. Coverage of books on Brazilian music and by Brazilian authors on any musical topic. Includes some articles in Brazilian periodicals. Broad subject arrangement. Illustrations, author index.

2173. Antônio, Irati. *Bibliografia de música brasileira, 1977–1984.* São Paulo: Universidade de São Paulo, 1988. viii, [ii], 275p. ML120 .B7 A58.

A bibliography of 2,239 entries. Coverage includes books, parts of books, dissertations, and periodical articles. Well indexed by subject, author, and periodical titles. According to *Duckles,* 4.293, projected volumes will fill in the earlier period. Opera is hardly visible: there are 10 references in the subject index.

2174. *Enciclopédia da música brasileira: Erudita, folclóroica, popular.* São Paulo: Art Editora, 1977.

Not seen. According to *Duckles,* 1.129, it includes a chronological list of Brazilian operas and a description of theaters in the country.

2175. Lange, Francisco Curt. "La ópera y las casas de ópera en Brasil colonial." *Boletín interamericano de música* 44 (November 1964): 3–11.

An illustrated, footnoted account of opera in Rio de Janeiro, Vila Rica, and Cuyaba, 1770–1795. List of works performed.

2176. Corrêa de Azevedo, Luiz Heitor. *Relaçao das óperas de autores brasileiros.* Rio de Janeiro: Ministério de Educação e Saude, 1938. 116p. ML1717 .B8 C6.

A chronological list of 97 operas by Brazilians, with historical and biographical information.

2177. Chaves Júnior, Edgard de Brito. *Memórias e glórias de um teatro: Sessenta anos de história do Teatro Municipal de Rio de Janeiro.* Rio de Janeiro: Companhia Editôra Americana, 1971. 683p. ML232.8 .R5 T43.

The Teatro Municipal, major opera house of Rio, opened in 1909. This book gives a daily chronology of works performed to 1970, with discussions of the various genres: opera, operetta, ballet, etc. Illustrated; no bibliography or index.

2178. Pena, Luiz Carlos Martins. *Folhetins, a seman lírica.* Rio de Janeiro: Instituto Nacional de Livro, 1965. 387p. ML1717.8 .R5 P5.

Consists of long reviews of the season 1846–1847 in Rio, originally published in the *Jornal do comércio.* Name and title index.

2179. Cerquera, Paulo de Oliveira Castro. *Um século de ópera em São Paulo.* São Paulo: Editória Guia Fiscal, 1954. 327p. ML1717 .C44.

A valuable discussion of each season, 1874–1951, in each theater, with all casts given; then a title list of all operas performed, with dates and casts. Photos of singers, index of names.

2180. Magaldi, Cristina. "Concert Life in Rio de Janeiro, 1837–1900." Ph.D. diss., U. of California at Los Angeles, 1994. xi, 486p.

Bulgaria

There is hardly anything written on art music in Western languages. *MGG* offers a usable introduction; *NG* has a superficial treatment. A German dissertation may be the most extended presentation:

2181. Pantschewa, Eugenie. "Die Entwicklung der Oper in Bulgarien von ihren Anfängen bis 1915 . . ." Ph.D. diss., U. of Vienna, 1950.

Two valuable contributions in German are found in *Oper heute* (#151) 2: "Opern bulgarischer Komponisten, 1900–1978" (a chronology of about 60 works), and Maria Kostakewa, "Entwicklungs Prozesse in der bulgarischen Oper," which is a general survey of recent writing.

Writings in Bulgarian offer a range of approaches. The *Entsiklopediia na bŭlgarskata muzikalna kultura* (1967; *IOM* 1680; *Duckles* 1.131) includes chronologies and composer worklists as well as topical articles. Rozaliia Aleksandrova Biks has a scholarly history of Bulgarian opera: *Bŭlgarski operen teatŭr* (1976; *IOM* 1690). Stories and backgrounds of 23 native works are found in Liubomir Sagaev, *Sŭvremennoto bŭlgarsko operno tvorchestvo* (1974; *IOM* 1692). A history of the national opera theater includes a chronology, 1909–1953/1954: Zlata Bozhkova, *Sofiiska Narodna Opera memoari* (1975; *IOM* 1691); this chronology is updated in *Narodno Opera Sofiia 1944–1969*, issued by the Opera (no date; *IOM* 1692).

Canada

The useful survey in the *Oxford Dictionary of Opera* (#47) says that "permanent companies had no lasting success until the middle of the 20th century." In 1950 the Canadian Opera Company was established in Toronto; it now performs regularly in many Canadian cities. Schedules for that company and for 11 others in Canada are found through the website: <www.coc.ca/index>. The print literature is sparse.

2182. Wehrle, Marlene. "Reference Sources on Canadian Music: A Supplement to Guy Marco, *Information on Music,* Volume II." *Fontes Artis Musicae* 41–1 (1994): 40–52.

IOM has 64 annotated entries; Wehrle adds 94. Opera is nearly a nonsubject in these lists.

2183. Morey, Carl. *Music in Canada: A Resource and Information Guide.* Music Research and Information Guides, 20. New York: Garland, 1997. xiii, 283p. ISBN 0-8153-1603-8. ML120 .C2 M67.

A useful handbook of 928 annotated entries in topical arrangement, with brief annotations. Opera is not one of the topics, but there are 21 entries for opera in the subject index (caution: the index citations are to page numbers, not item numbers). The titles are mostly brief notices and biographical pieces about singers, but two academic papers seem substantial:

2184. Cooper, Dorith Rachel. "Opera in Montréal and Toronto: A Study of Performance Traditions and Repertoire, 1783–1980," Ph.D. diss., U. of Toronto, 1983. xxx, 1,399p.

2185. Barrière, Mireille. "La société canadienne-française et le théâtre lyrique à Montréal entre 1840 et 1913." Ph.D. diss., U. Laval, 1990. xv, 583p.

2186. Cancelled entry.

2187. *Encyclopedia of Music in Canada.* 2nd ed. Ed. Helmut Kallmann et al. Toronto: U. of Toronto Press, 1992. xxxii, 1,524p. ISBN 0-8020-2881-0. ML106 .C3 E52.

First edition, 1981. Also in French: *Encyclopédie de la musique au Canada* (Montreal: Fides, 1993). More than 3,000 articles, covering all aspects of music, with emphasis on biographical material. The article "Opera Composition" lists about 50 Canadian operas. "Opera Performance" is a survey from 1783. There are also entries for Opéra de Montréal, Opéra de Québec, Opéra Français, Opera Guild of Montreal, Opera Hamilton, Opera West, and Opéra National de Québec.

2188. Baille, Joan Parkhill, and William Kilbourn. *Look at the Record: An Album of Toronto's Lyric Theatres, 1825–1984.* Oakville, Ont.; New York: Mosaic Press, 1985. 293p. ISBN 0-88962-236-1. ML1713 .B24.

A picture book, arranged by theater (50 are covered), giving plans, interior/exterior views, and reproductions of newspaper pages. Chronologies for the theaters (1825–1984) as well as opera lists by title and composer. Name and title index.

2189. Canadian Music Centre. *List of Canadian Operas Available from the Canadian Music Centre.* Toronto: The Centre, 1982. 20p.

Current news of national and international operatic life, with calendars and notices, is given in *Opera Canada,* 1960–, a quarterly issued by the Canadian Opera Association.

See also #141 and #144.

Chile

2190. Cánepa Guzmán, Mario. *La ópera en Chile, 1839–1930.* Santiago: Alonso Ovalle, 1976. 305p. ML1717 .C5 C3.

A straightforward general history with some footnotes. Good portraits of the singers. Bibliography of about 50 items, no index.

Opera is covered adequately in two general histories: Eugenio Pereira Salas, *Historia de la música en Chile, 1850–1900* (Santiago: Editorial del Pacífico, 1957; *IOM* 1051), and Samuel Claro Valdés, *Historia de la música en Chile* (Santiago: Orbe, 1973; *IOM* 1052). One book is entirely about light opera:

2191. Abascal Brunet, Manuel. *Apuntes para la historia del teatro en Chile: La zar-zuela grande.* Santiago: Imprenta Universitaria, 1941–1951. 2v. ML1717.A25.

A footnoted historical study of the period 1628–1882, with facts about singers and a chronology of performances. Bibliography of 20 entries, name indexes.

2192. Ribera, Salvador A., and Luis Alberto Aguila. *La ópera.* Santiago, 1895.

Not seen. Described by *Kaufman* as a general opera dictionary, useful for its chronology of performances at the Teatro Municipal in Santiago, 1873–1895, and rosters of singers for each season.

Further references are available in:

2193. Pereira Salas, Eugenio. *Bio-bibliografía musical de Chile desde los orígenes a 1886.* Santiago: Universidad de Chile, 1978. 136p. ML106 .C5 P4.

A biographical dictionary of 199 composers with worklists.

Colombia

2194. Perdomo Escobar, José Ignacio. *La ópera en Colombia.* Bogotá: Litografía Arco, 1979. 107p. ML1717 .C6 P43.

A fine account of native opera composers, singers and companies, theaters, and periodicals. A list of operas performed in the country, by composer, shows primarily the standard European works, but a number of Latin composers are included. Good color plates; partly annotated bibliography of about 50 items. No index. Operatic topics are also covered in the same author's *Historia de la música en Colombia* (3rd ed.; Bogotá: Editorial ABC, 1963; *IOM* 1083). Another useful general history is Andrés Pardo Tovar, *La cultura musical en Colombia* (Bogotá: Lerner, 1966; *IOM* 1082).

Croatia

The country declared its independence from Yugoslavia in 1991. The chapter on music in *Croatia: Land, People, Culture,* ed. Francis Eterovich (Toronto: U. of Toronto Press, 1964), identifies leading opera singers and Zagreb's operatic institutions. The only substantial study of opera seen is in Serbo-Croatian:

2195. Zagreb. Hrvatsko Narodno Kazalište. *Sto godina opere, 1870/71–1970/71.* Zagreb: Grafički Zavod Hrvatske, 1971. Not paged. ML1751.8 Z3.

Commemorates the first centennial of the national theater. Includes a historical text with illustrations and a chronology. Also portraits of artists, composer index.

2196. *Enciklopedija Hrvatskoga Narodnoga Kazališta u Zagreb, 1894–1969.* Zagreb: Grafički Zavod Hrvatske, 1969. 721p.

Not seen. It is described as an encyclopedia of the national theater, with entries for plays, operas, and performers.

Cuba

2197. Orovio, Helio. *Diccionario de la música cubana: Biográfico y técnico.* 2nd ed. Havana: Letras Cubanas, 1992. 516p. ISBN 9-5910-0048-X. ML106 .C8 O76.

Not seen.

2198. Tolón, Edwin Teurbe, and Jorge A. Gonzáles. *Óperas cubanas y sus autores.* Havana: Ucar, 1943. 472p. ML1714 .T6.

A scholarly study of 12 composers, with portraits. No bibliography or index. The same authors also wrote *Historia del teatro en La Habana* (Santa Clara, Cuba: U. Central de las Villas, 1961; *IOM* 1123).

2199. Gonzalez, Jorge Antonio. *Composición operística en Cuba.* Havana: Letras Cubanas, 1986. 591p. No ISBN. ML1714 .G63.

A general undocumented narrative, with program notes on the operas. Very poor illustrations and musical examples. No bibliography or index.

Czech Republic

The country of Czechoslovakia was divided in 1993 into two new nations: Czech Republic (capital: Prague, or Praha), which includes the old Bohemia and Moravia, and Slovakia (capital: Bratislava). Most of the literature on music was written under the earlier designation, so the qualifier "Czech" may refer to both Czech and Slovakian music.

2200. Tyrrell, John. *Czech Opera.* New York: Cambridge U.P., 1988. xvi, 325p. ISBN 0-521-23531-6. ML1724 .T95.

A valuable, documented history of opera written to Czech texts, beginning in 1892. Works of Smetana and Janáček are given much attention. Musical and literary factors are considered, with useful consideration of meter and inflection in the Czech language and approaches to vocal aspects. Bibliography of about 150 items, index.

2201. Eckstein, Pavel. *A Brief Outline of Czechoslovak Opera.* Prague: Theatre Institute, 1964. 115p. ML1724 .E3.

Historical survey; list of operas with name of librettist, premiere data, and photos. No index.

2202. Eckstein, Pavel. *The Czechoslovak Contemporary Opera: Pictures and Information.* Prague: Panton, 1967. 50p. ML1724.5 .E26.

Text in English and German. Photos and brief descriptions of 50 operas premiered between 1921 and 1966.

2203. Teuber, Oscar. *Geschichte des Prager Theaters.* Prague: Hasse, 1883–1888. 3v. in 2. PN2859 .C9 T4.

A narrative of all theaters, with many casts, but no actual chronology. Index.

2204. "Tschechische und slowakische Opern seit 1946." *Musikbühne* 1975: 141–151.

A list of 125 operas in date order, with librettists and premiere information. Titles are in the original languages, with German translations. In the same issue of the journal there is a list of about 125 operettas written since 1946. The list of premieres is carried through 1979 in v.4 of *Oper heute* (#151).

2205. Buchner, Alexander. *Opera v Praze = Opera in Prague*. Prague: Panton, 1985. 236p. No ISBN. ML1724.8 .P72 B8.

> A popular history in Czech, Russian, and English. Fine pictures; list of about 200 Czech operas with premiere data. Title and name index.

Even in Eastern languages there seems to be just one history of early opera: Igor' Fedorovich Belza, *Cheshskaiia opernaia klassika* (Moscow: Iskusstvo, 1951). Several detailed accounts of the national theater are available in Czech:

2206. Němeček, Jan. *Opera Národního Divadla v období Karla Kovařovice, 1900–1920*. Prague: Divadelní Ústav, 1968. 2v. ML1724.8. P9 N43.

> Kovařovic was director of the national theater from 1900 to 1920. His biography is given here, with a survey of Bohemian opera of his time. The repertoire of the theater is presented in tabular form and through seasonal chronologies. Well documented with 745 footnotes but without bibliography. Indexed.

2207. Pala, František. *Opera Národního Divadla v období otokara ostrčila*. Prague: Ústav, 1962–1970. 4v. ML1724.8 .P9 N18.

> A narrative of each season in the national theater of Prague from 1918/1919 through 1928/1929, with considerable attention to notable personalities. Well documented but not indexed.

Some of the earlier times are covered in the next entries:

2208. Kamper, Otakar. *Hudební Praha v XVIII. věku*. Prague: Melantrich, 1936. 254p. ML247 .K15.

> A narrative of Prague musical life in the 18th century, with a chronology of operas and oratorios performed.

2209. Volek, Tomislav. *Repertoir Nosticovského Divadla v Praze z let 1794, 1796–8*. Prague: Ústav pro Dejiny Hudby pri Universite Karlove 1961. 191p. ML1724.8 .P9 V9.

> Mostly a narrative account of four early years of the opera in Prague, with tables of works performed and personnel lists. No index.

See also #2349.

2210. Bartos, Josef. *Prozatímní Divadlo a Jeho Opera*. Prague: Sbor pro Zrízení Druhého Národního Divadla 1938. 397p. ML1724.8 .P72 N32.

> Not seen. Described by *Kaufman* as an account of the provisional Czech theater of 1861–1883, predecessor of the national opera that opened in 1883. There is no formal chronology, but many dates and casts are given. Indexed.

2211. Bondi, Gustav. *Funfundzwanzig Jahre Eigenregie: Geschichte des Brünner Stadttheaters 1882–1907*. Brno: Author, 1907. 256p. PN2616 .B87 B7.

> A season-by-season narrative of opera in Brno (Brünn), with a foldout chart giving staff and singers. Name index, composer and librettist index.

Information on opera in other Czech cities is found in the local histories cited in *IOM* 1772a ff. A publisher's catalogue is a useful tool: *Catalogue of Selected Music-*

Dramatical Works (Prague: Dilia, 1971); it lists about 450 operas and ballets, with librettist, instrumentation, cast, and voice types. A useful yearbook, *Musical Events in Czech Republic and in Slovak Republic* (Prague: Hudební Informacní Stredisko Ceského Hudební Fondu Praha, 1993–) carries news of concerts, opera performances, competitions, festivals, and musicians.

Denmark (Danish: Danmark; French: Danemark; German: Dänemark)

The national theater, Danske Nationalteatr (formerly Der Kongelige Teatr and Hofteatr), was established in 1748. Its history is traced in several volumes:

2212. Roepstorff, Thorkild. *Operahuset i København. Bygningens historie skrevet i 50 året for landsrettens indflytning.* Copenhagen: Nyt Nordisk Forlag, 1970. 139p. ISBN 87-17-01261-9. ML1743.8 .C62 R6.

   A well-documented history of the opera house, with 72 illustrations, emphasizing architectural features. No repertoire or artists' list. Name and subject index.

2213. Leicht, Georg, and Marianne Hallar. *Det Kongelige Teaters repertoire, 1889–1975.* Copenhagen: Bibliotekscentralens Forlag, 1977. 437p. ISBN 87-552-0416-3. PN2746 .C62 K693.

   A useful chronology of opera, drama, and ballet performances for 1889–1975, with names of directors, conductors, and stage designers (but not of actors or singers); many photos of productions. Includes visiting companies. Lists of titles of works in original languages and Danish; indexes of authors, composers, choreographers, designers, and conductors. No general index. Bibliography of about 70 entries.

2214. Schepelern, Gerhard. *Italierne pas Hofteatret.* Copenhagen: Rhodos, 1976. 2v. ML1743 .S34

   Summary in German. A study of Italian touring opera companies that performed in Copenhagen during 1841–1854. The second volume has more general information: chronological list of Danish operas performed in Copenhagen, 1789–1899, and another list of works by non-Danes, 1703–1899. Bibliography of about 300 titles, indexes of names and titles. Additional works are in:

2215. Aumont, Arthur, and Edgar Collin. *Det Danske Nationaltheater, 1748–1889.* Copenhagen: J. Jørgensen, 1896–1897. 2v. PN2746 .C8 K82.

   For the period covered, gives lists of plays and operas performed. No casts or details.

2216. Kragh-Jacobsen, Svend. "Le théâtre musical depuis 1931." In *La vie musicale au Danemark,* ed. Sven Lunn, 97–128 (Copenhagen: Bianco Lunos, 1962; ML311 .L87).

   A useful essay from a volume prepared for an exposition of Danish music. The author gives a narrative account of operas performed since 1931, identifying prominent persons.

Outside of Copenhagen, there has been an active operatic history in Aarhus.

2217. Albeck, Gustav, and Gerhard Schepelern. *Opera i Aarhus: En historisk frem-stilling udgivet i anledning af den Jyske Opera's 25 års jubilaeum.* Aarhus: Universitetsforlaget, 1972. 313p. ML1743.8 .A2 A45.

A history and chronology of performances (with casts and staff lists) for 1947–1972. Works are listed by composer, with performances statistics. Singers, premieres, essays on the chorus and the new Jyske Opera house. Bibliography of about 250 titles, name index.

2218. *Musical Denmark,* 1–, 1952–. Copenhagen: Danske Selskab, 1952–. Irregular.

Popular articles about Danish musical events and Danish music performed in other countries. Selective lists of newly published music and books on music; discographies.

A similar title, *Musical Denmark Yearbook* (1994–) is in the Library of Congress catalogue (ML27 .D3 D36); it has not been seen.

2219. McLoskey, Lansing D. *Twentieth-Century Danish Music: An Annotated Bibliography and Research Directory.* Music Reference Collection, 65. Westport, Conn.: Greenwood, 1998. xxi, 149p. ISBN 0-313-30293-6. ML120 .D3 M35.

A topical bibliography, with entries for history of opera, opera companies, and works. Composers are listed both chronologically and alphabetically in two appendixes.

The website <www.kgl-teater.dk/dkt/> gives current opera calendars.

Finland (Finnish: Suomen)

No scholarly writing about opera in Finland exists in a common language. There are some brief surveys in English.

2220. "Finland." *Musikrevy* 30 (1975): 99–180. ML5 .M9635.

A special English-language issue of a Swedish journal, all about Finnish music, in popular style. Covers operatic life and gives short biographies of 16 composers and some opera singers.

2221. Hillila, Ruth-Esther, and Barbara Blanchard Hong. *Historical Dictionary of Music and Musicians in Finland.* Westport, Conn.: Greenwood, 1997. x, 473p. ISBN 0-313-27728-1. ML101 .F5 H55.

Consists of about 900 entries, most of them biographies of composers and performers, with worklists and bibliographies. Opera is not an entry topic or index entry. Chronology of Finnish music history, bibliography of about 60 items, index.

2222. De Gorog, Lisa, and Ralph Paul de Gorog. *From Sibelius to Sallinen: Finnish Nationalism and the Music of Finland.* New York: Greenwood, 1989. ix, 252p. ISBN 0-313-267405. ML269.5 .D4.

A popular survey, with a chapter on "Stage and Vocal Music in Finland," 173–193. Bibliography, index.

2223. Jellinek, George. "The Summers and Winters of Finnish Opera." *OQ* 11-3 (1995): 39–44.

A useful glimpse of recent operas and performances in Helsinki and Savonlinna. The key figures have been Martti Talvela, who developed the Savonlinna festival, and composers Aulis Sallinen and Joonas Kokkonen.

France (German: Frankreich; Italian: Francia)

Editions

2224. *French Opera in the 17th and 18th Centuries*. Ed. Barry Brook. Stuyvesant, N.Y.: Pendragon, 1983–. 75v. M1500 .M49 S89. (Cited in this guide as *FO*.)

Each volume has a full score (facsimile) and significant background information about the work: biography, worklist, librettist, genesis, performance history, reception, variant editions, plots, bibliographies. Individual volumes are entered in this guide under the names of composers.

2225. *Chefs d'oeuvre classiques de l'opéra français. Publiés sous la direction de T. Michaelis* . . . Paris, 1880. Reprint, New York: Broude, 1971. 40v. (Cited in this guide as *Chefs*.)

Editions (piano-vocal scores) of operas by 14 composers, including 11 by Lully and 7 by Rameau. Also includes the music of *Le ballet-comique de la reine*, by Balthazar de Beaujoyeulx (1581), a notable precursor of 17th-century opera. The works in this set are cited separately under the names of their composers elsewhere in this guide.

Bibliographies

This is a useful list of French operas:

2226. Crozet, Felix. *Revue de la musique dramatique en France* . . . Grenoble: Prudhomme, 1866. 477p. Supplement, 1872. 39p. ML1727.4 .C7.

Premiere data and plot synopses for about 1,000 works, with notes; chronology of 386 operas presented 1671–1842. No bibliography, no index.

Music in General: 17th and 18th Centuries

2227. *The New Grove French Baroque Masters: Lully, Charpentier, Lalande, Couperin, Rameau*. Ed. James R. Anthony et al. New York: Norton, 1986. ix, 318p. ISBN 0-393-02286-2. ML390 .N46.

Derived from entries in *NG*, with added material to incorporate recent research and a new index of names, titles, and topics. Bibliographies are in *New Grove* style, with incomplete data.

2228. Benoit, Marcelle. *Dictionnaire de la musique en France aux XVIIe et XVIIIe siècles*. Paris: Fayard, 1992. xvi, 811p. ISBN 2-2130-2824-9. ML 101 .F8 D543.

About 2,500 articles by specialists on individuals, works, instruments, and genres. Bibliography, by subject, of 1,751 items, with 241 entries for "Musique vocale profane," and indexes (really classified lists of articles in the volume) of names, terms, and topics.

2229. Benoit, Marcelle. *Musiques de cour: Chapelle, chambre, écurie. Recueil de documents, 1661–1733.* La vie musicale en France sous le rois Bourbons, 20. Paris: Picard, 1971. xxii, 553p. ML270 .B45.

Proclamations, lists of players, accounts, and *lettres patents,* in chronological order. Occupational index.

2230. Benoit, Marcelle. *Versailles et les musiciens du roi, 1661–1773: Étude institutionelle et sociale.* La vie musicale en France sous les rois Bourbons, 19. Paris: Picard, 1971. 474p. ML170.8 .V47 B45.

Institutions, family life of the musician, structure and economics of the music profession. Lists of performers by instrument. Illustrations include 29 coats of arms of musical families. Documented; bibliography of manuscript sources plus 392 books and articles. Index of names and topics.

2231. Anthony, James R. *French Baroque Music from Beaujoyeulx to Rameau.* 3rd ed. Portland, Ore.: Amadeus, 1997. 590p. ISBN 1-57467-021-2. ML270.2 .A6.

First edition, 1973; second edition, 1978. French translation of the 1978 ed. (with updating and corrections): *La musique en France à l'époque baroque, de Beaujoyeulx à Rameau,* trans. Béatrice Vierne (Paris: Flammarion, 1981), 536p. ISBN 2-08064-322-3. ML270.2 .A614.

Covers approximately 1581–1733, dealing with societal background, instruments, instrumental and vocal music, connections with Italian music, individual musicians, concerts, and documents. Bibliography of about 400 items. Index.

2232. Isherwood, Robert M. *Music in the Service of the King: France in the Seventeenth Century.* Ithaca, N.Y.: Cornell U.P., 1973. xiv, 422p. ISBN 0-8014-0734-6. ML270.2 .I8.

Music "in the context of French political and social history," covering court life, ceremonies and pageants, etc.; opera and ballet. Bibliography, index of titles.

2233. Lagrave, Henri. *Le théâtre et le public à Paris de 1715 à 1750.* Paris: Klincksieck, 1972. 717p. ISBN 2-252-01434-2. PC13 .B6 ser.C, v.37 or PN2636 .P3 L26.

An expansive table of contents facilitates access to this imposing work. It covers the halls, the public, seasons, programs, finances, and critical reception; music of the fairs, the Comédie Française, the Opéra, and Opéra-Comique; also taste of the times and administrative matters. With 32 plates, including plans; bibliography of about 400 items, name and title index.

2234. Parfaict, François. *Dictionnaire des théâtres de Paris . . . contenant toutes les pièces qui ont été représentés jusqu'à présent sur les différens théâtres françois. Par les frères Parfaict.* Paris: Lambert, 1756; Paris: Rozet, 1767. 7v. in 2. ML102 .O6 P2.

Lists of works performed from 1552 in all Paris theaters, with names of casts and much detail. The Nouveau Théâtre Italien is especially well covered.

2235. Rice, Paul F. *The Performing Arts at Fontainebleau from Louis XIV to Louis XVI.* Studies in Music, 102. Ann Arbor, Mich.: UMI Research, 1989. xiii, 299p. ISBN 0-8357-1869-7. PN2636 .F66 R53.

A chronology of performances, including plays, ballets, and operas, from 1661 to 1792. History and description of the building and its halls; the royal family and the theater.

2236. Burney, Charles. *Music, Men and Manners in France and Italy, 1770.* Ed. H. Edmund Poole. London: Folio Society, 1969. xxix, 245p. ML195 .B961.

Fascinating, valuable account of musicians, concerts, and libraries, as well as nonmusical events, in June–December 1770. Burney was collecting material for his 1776 music history, one of the first in English. His other research travels are described at #61.

2237. Striffling, Louis. *Esquisse d'une histoire de goût musicale en France au XVIIIe siècle.* Paris: Delagrave, 1912. 286p. Reprint, New York: American Musicological Society, 1978. ML270.3 .S7.

Critical responses to music by journalists, theorists, diarists, philosophers, and poets. Discussion of methodology and sources for a study of opera and other genres of the period.

2238. Didier, Béatrice. *La musique des lumières: Diderot, l'encyclopédie, Rousseau.* Paris: Presses Universitaires de France, 1985. 479p. ML79 .O5.

Recounts scientific and philosophical approaches to music, including opera, from the 1740s to the Revolution. Attention to the human voice, the opera disputes, librettists, the nature of opera. Extensively footnoted but without a bibliography.

Opera: 17th and 18th Centuries

The predecessor and companion form to French opera was the *ballet de cour,* which is well covered in these two works:

2239. McGowan, Margaret M. *L'art du ballet de cour en France, 1581–1643.* Paris: Centre National de la Recherche Scientifique, 1963. 351p. ML3460 .M146.

A narrative history, footnoted, with 24 plates. Description and location of all source materials; references to contemporary criticism. Bibliography of about 300 items, name and title index.

2240. Christout, Marie-Françoise. *Le ballet de cour de Louis XIV, 1643–1672.* Paris: Picard, 1967. 276p. ML270 .A1 V5 v.12.

A scholarly history with 24 plates; much attention to costume, music, and scenography. Chronology of ballets, with bibliographic references. Bibliography of primary and secondary materials, about 200 entries. Name and title index.

Early ballet and opera are covered in this landmark study:

2241. La Valière, Louis César de La Baume Le Blanc, duc de. *Ballets, opera, et autres ouvrages lyriques, par ordre chronologique depuis leur origine; avec une table alphabetique des ouvrages et des auteurs*. Paris: C. J. B. Bauche, 1760. viii, 300p. Reprint, London: H. Baron, 1967. ML102 .O6 L16.

Works are listed in sequence from 1548 to 1673, with information on performance (including names of casts in some cases) and publishing data. Also a chronological list of composers and their works. Name and title index.

During the late 17th and 18th centuries, leading to the establishment of Théâtre National de l'Opéra-Comique in 1801 (see #2312ff.), light opera-like entertainments were presented at the Paris fairs (*les foires*); they came to be called *opéras-comiques*. Those productions are well covered in:

2242. Parfaict, François. *Memoires pour servir a l'histoire des spectacles de la foire, par un acteur forain*. Paris: Briasson, 1743. 2v. Facsimile ed., New York: AMS, 1978. ISBN 0-404-60179-0. PN2633 .P3.

An account ascribed to one of the actors but thought to be by both Claude and François Parfaict, dealing with the fairs of S. Germaine and S. Laurent from 1697 to 1742. Extracts from official documents concerning the *foire*. Much production information, including comments on the actors and the music. An alphabetical list of works with premiere dates is in v.2.

2243. Le Sage, Alain René. *Le Théâtre de la Foire* . . . Paris: P. Gandouin, 1737. 9v. in 10. PQ1211 .L62.

History and repertoire for 1724–1731.

2244. Isherwood, Robert. *Farce and Fantasy: Popular Entertainment in Eighteenth-Century Paris*. New York: Oxford U.P., 1986. ix, 324p. ISBN 0-19-503648-4. DC729 .I84.

Discusses music at the various fairs, singing on the Pont-Neuf, and beginning of the genre known as *opéra-comique*. Bibliography and index.

2245. Barnes, Clifford Rasmussen. "The Théâtre de la Foire (Paris, 1697–1792): Its Music and Its Composers." Ph.D. diss., U. of Southern California, 1965. iv, 531p.

In 1697 there was a formalization of fair performances under the name Théâtre de la Foire and in 1715 under the name Opéra-Comique. Barnes considers the evolution of the genre from vaudevilles to Grétry, Italian influences (the fairs had taken over the repertoire of a troupe known as the Comédie-Italien, which was expelled in 1697), songs, and instruments.

2246. Brown, Bruce Alan. "Éditions anciennes et modernes d'opéras-comiques: Problèmes et méthodologies." In *Grétry* (#927), 355–365.

Of the composers of *opéra comique,* only Gluck and Grétry have critical editions. None is planned for Galuppi or Paisiello. Considers status and difficulties of publication of *vaudevilles*. Ascribes lack of modern productions of the *opéra-comique* repertoire to lack of suitable editions.

2247. Charlton, David. "*Opéra-comique* and the Computer." In *Grétry* (#927), 367–378.

Describes the database established in 1989 at U. of East Anglia, in Norwich, England. It offers a day-by-day repertoire, 1755–1815, with extensive information about each work. The database will correct errors in standard sources, such as *NG*.

2248. *L'opéra-comique en France au XVIIIe siècle*. Ed. P. Vendrix. Liège: Mardaga, 1992. 377p. ISBN 2-8700-9482-5. ML1727 .O63.

A well-documented account of the origins of the genre, early librettists and composers, stagings of 1762–1789, and the audiences. Useful comments on *opéra-comique* as literature and as music, in German lands (especially Vienna), in Scandinavia, the Low Countries, Britain, Italy, and Russia. Bibliography of about 400 items, primary and secondary sources, name and title indexes.

2249. *Dictionnaire de l'opéra-comique français, sous la direction de Francis Claudon*. Bern: Peter Lang, 1995. 533p. ISBN 3-906753-42-5. ML1727 .D53.

A history of the genre, not of the company, presenting "une approche esthétique"; comparisons with *Singspiel* and *opera buffa*. Pages 83–526 are on individual composers and their works: historical backgrounds, plots, and program notes. Footnoted but without bibliography or index.

2250. Couvreur, Manuel. "La folie à l'Opéra-Comique: Des grelots de Momus aux larmes de Nina." In *Grétry* (#927), 201–219.

Folie was a frequent theme in the *ballet de cour* and *comédie italien*. The 18th-century view of madness was that it resulted from excess passion. Opinion moved from negative to positive about it—by 1745 Diderot found nobility in madness. It ceased to be comical after midcentury, becoming instead attached to love. This evolution is reflected in the *opéra-comique*. With 60 footnotes to the relevant literature.

2251. *L'opéra au XVIIIe siècle: Actes du colloque organisé à Aix-en-Provence par le Centre Aixois d'Études et des Recherches sur le XVIIIe Siècle, 29 avril et 1er mai, 1977*. Aix-en-Provence: Publications Université de Provence, 1982. 578p. ML1704 .O63.

Consists of 29 papers, mostly on aspects of opera in the second half of the century. Three of the papers are entered separately in this guide: #901, #2292, and #2294. Three others are summarized in Foster (#1535).

2252. Demuth, Norman. *French Opera: Its Development to the Revolution*. Sussex, England: Artemis, 1963. xii, 337p. Reprint, New York: Da Capo, 1982. ISBN (Da Capo) 0-306-77576-X. ML1727 .D44.

A popular treatment with useful lists: documents held by the Académie Royale de Musique, 1669–1802; all theaters occupied by the Académie, 1671–1794, etc. With 19 plates, bibliography, and index.

2253. Prunières, Henry. *L'opéra italien en France avant Lulli*. Paris: Champion, 1913. 512p. ML1727.2 .P9. Reprint, Geneva: Minkoff, 1974, and Paris: Champion, 1975.

A scholarly account of Italian opera at the French court and its influence. Letters and documents, performance chronology. Bibliography (10 pages), index.

2254. Cucuel, Georges. *Les créatures de l'opéra-comique français*. Paris: Alcan, 1914. 243p. ML1727.3 .C9.

A history of the genre, not the company. Deals with origins, fairs, influence of opera buffa, early masters of the form (Gluck, La Ruette, and Duni), and, with much detail, the works of Monsigny, Philidor, and Grétry. With a section on the impact of the Revolution. Footnotes, brief bibliography, no index.

2255. Fajon, Robert. *L'opéra à Paris: Du roi soleil à Louis bien-aimé*. Geneva: Slatkine, 1984. 440p. ISBN 2-05100-5389. ML1727.8 .P2 F16.

An exhaustive, scholarly examination of the period 1643–1774. In narrative form, with some analysis of works; background and reception of individual operas; table of performances by type. Poor, hand-scrawled musical examples detract from usefulness. Bibliography of about 75 items.

See also #1143.

2256. Cancelled entry.

A debate about the relative merits of French and Italian opera occupied many minds and filled many pages in the mid-18th century; the debate is referred to as the Quarrel of the Buffoons, or *La querelle des bouffons*. A leading philosopher was one of the instigators:

2257. Rousseau, Jean-Jacques. *Lettre sur la musique française*. Paris, 1753. 92p. English trans. in *Strunk*.

Despite his nationality, Rousseau sided with the Italian mode, *opera buffa*, rather than with the French classical style. He himself composed a successful light (Italian-type) opera, *Le devin du village* (1752; see item #1596); it had considerable influence in the development of French *opéra-comique*.

2258. *La querelle des bouffons: Textes des pamphlets*. Ed. Denise Launay. Geneva: Minkoff, 1973. 3v. ML1727.33 .A1 Q5.

A huge (2,381 pages) collection of primary materials, such as Rousseau's letter, issued 1752–1754. Useful discussion of the dispute, chronology of the writings and of opera performances, attributions for anonymous pamphlets, running commentary, and index.

See also #89 and #378. Other documents relating to the quarrel are in Fubini (#98).

2259. Lowinsky, Edward E. "Taste, Style and Ideology in Eighteenth-Century Music." In *Aspects of the Eighteenth Century,* ed. Earl Wasserman, 163–206 (Baltimore: Johns Hopkins U.P., 1965. CB411. W3).

A learned examination of the French-Italian opera dispute, with special attention to the role of Rousseau and his *Le devin du village,* comparing it with *La serva padrona* by Pergolesi (1733), which was an inspiration for Rousseau.

The Italian incursions actually had begun a century earlier:

2260. Zaslaw, Neal. "The First Opera in Paris: A Study in the Politics of Art." In *Jean-Baptiste Lully* (#1130), 7–23.

Il giuditio della ragione, by Marco Marazzoli, was performed at the Palais Royal on 28 February 1645, introducing the Italian style (all sung) and leading to French imitators. This is a valuable account of the event and its political-cultural ramifications.

2261. Charlton, David. "The *romance* and Its Cognates: Narrative, Irony and *vraisemblance* in Early *opéra-comique*." In *Die opéra-comique* (#93), 43–92.

Investigates "the origins and dramaturgy of song forms (mainly strophic, but certainly not always so) in *opéra-comique*." When such songs occur, there is a detachment from the action, and the actor performs "in quotation marks." Charlton, elaborating on earlier work by Daniel Heartz, gives a history of the *romance* in opera. A "plurality in strophic forms" emerged after 1762.

2262. Cook, Elisabeth. *Duet and Ensemble in the Early "opéra-comique."* New York: Garland, 1995. xx, 317p. ISBN 0-8153-1893-6. ML1950 .C66.

A valuable study of ensemble composition in all the French and Italian genres prior to 1750. Attention to ensembles in French serious opera after 1750, with analysis of Philidor's *Ernelinde*. Deals with dramatic and literary aspects and with theoretical writings that considered ensemble composition. Rousseau receives particular notice. Notes, bibliography of about 150 items, expansive index.

2263. Jacobshagen, Arnold. "Formstrukturen und Funktionen der Chor-Introduktion in der *opéra-comique* des späten 18. und frühen 19. Jahrhunderts." In *Die opéra-comique* (#93), 151–167.

Observes that *opéra-comique* in this period usually opened, after the overture, with a choral number, followed by a solo. Discovers various patterns of the solo-duet-ensemble-chorus that were built around this practice and analyzes operas by Sacchini, Dalayrac, Cherubini, Berton, and others showing how it was done. In the 19th century this set assumed the form of a rondo.

Instrumental accompaniment to operas has been studied by several scholars:

2264. Sadler, G. "The Role of the Keyboard Continuo in French Opera, 1673–1776." *Early Music* 8 (1980): 148–157.

Observes that figures (figured bass) are abundant in the solo vocal numbers but absent from the instrumental and dance numbers. Concludes that harpsichord accompaniment was used only for the voice parts, primarily in recitative. The harpsichord was abandoned at the Opéra by 1776.

See also Milliot (#2294) on the orchestra and Cyr (#2295) on the continuo.

Scenic effects were of great importance. They are well illustrated in:

2265. Cohen, H. Robert et al. *Les gravures musicales dans "L'Illustration,"* 1843–1899. Quebec: Université Laval, 1982. 3v. ISBN 2-7637-6833-4. ML270.4 .G7.

Engravings of set designs, costumes, portraits, and performances.

2266. Lesure, François. *L'opéra classique français, 17e et 18e siècles*. Iconographie musicale, 1. Geneva: Minkoff, 1972. vi, 121p. ISBN 2-8266-0000-1. ML89 .L285.

A collection of 93 plates, showing stage design and machinery, with valuable introduction and commentary. Bibliography, no index.

2267. Coeyman, Barbara. "Opera and Ballet in Seventeenth-Century French Theaters: Case Studies of the Salle des Machines and the Palais Royal Theater." In *Opera in Context* (#288), 37–72.

The Salle des Machines, in the Tuileries Palace, opened 1662; it had a capacity of 6,000–8,000 persons. Coeyman explores structural features of French theaters and how they served performances, presenting a political and cultural context. While Italy had permanent opera houses in the 17th century, French buildings were unstable and temporary. By the start of the 18th century, French theaters were more like the Italian.

Music in General: 19th and 20th Centuries

2268. *The New Grove Twentieth Century French Masters: Fauré, Debussy, Satie, Ravel, Poulenc, Messiaen, Boulez*. Ed. Jean-Michel Nectoux et al. New York: Norton, 1986. 291p. ISBN 0-333-40239-1. ML390 .N48.

Articles from *NG*; each is entered in this guide under the composer.

2269. Bloom, Peter. *Music in Paris in the Eighteen-thirties = La musique à Paris dans les années mil huit cent trente*. Papers from the International Conference on Music in Paris in the Eighteen Thirties, Smith College, Northampton, Mass., April 1982. La vie musicale en France au XIXe siècle, 4. Stuyvesant, N.Y.: Pendragon, 1987. xiv, 641p. ISBN 0-918728-71-1. ML1727.8 .P2 S78.

Consists of 23 essays by various specialists. On opera: "Verdi et la culture parisienne des années 1830," by Marcello Conati; "Music at the Théâtre-Italien," by Philip Gossett; "The Boulevard Theaters and Continuity in French Opera of the 19th Century," by Karin Pendle; "The Influence of French Grand Opera on Wagner," by John Warrack; and "La musique dans le mélodrame des théâtres parisiens," by Nicole Wild. The books ends with the only "postface" so far discovered and an index.

Opera: 19th and 20th Centuries

2270. Bruyas, Florian. *Histoire de l'operette en France, 1855–1965*. Lyon: Vitte, 1974. 693p. ML1727 .B78.

A narrative account, with interesting descriptions of Parisian musical life in the years 1850, 1871, 1900, and 1945. Bibliography of about 30 items, name and title index.

2271. Fulcher, Jane F. *The Nation's Image: French Grand Opera As Politics and Politicized Art*. New York: Cambridge U.P., 1987. x, 280p. ISBN 0-521-32774-1. ML1727 .F84.

The politics of opera, mostly in the period 1830–1870: radicalization, repression, politicized attacks on composers and librettists. Theater as a "subtly used tool of the state." Essentially a cultural history, with attention to audience responses. Thoroughly documented, with strong bibliography of about 400 items and an expansive index.

2272. Gerhard, Anselm. *The Urbanization of Opera: Music Theater in Paris in the Nineteenth Century.* Trans. Mary Whittall. Chicago: U. of Chicago Press, 1988. xxi, 503p. ISBN 0-2262-8857-9. ML1728.8 P2 G38.

Originally *Die Verstädterung der Oper: Paris und das Musiktheater des 19. Jahrhunderts* (Stuttgart: J. B. Metzler, 1992; 491p.; ISBN 30-476-00850-9). "Urbanization" is Gerhard's term for the changes in opera that occurred in Paris in the early 19th century. Opera was freed from the court and became dependent on public acceptance for its success. Thus "new forms and conventions that have nothing to do with the historical predecessors of grand opera" emerged. Such conventions included the tragic ending, the indecisive hero, and large choral scenes with the chorus in the role of a destructive mob. Aesthetics of "the marvelous" continued to dominate at the Opéra until 1826. With chapters on Rossini, Scribe, Meyerbeer, Victor Hugo as librettist, and Verdi. Valuable bibliography of about 600 books, articles, and primary sources; name and title index.

2273. Barbier, Patrick. *Opera in Paris, 1800–1850: A Lively History.* Trans. Robert Luoma. Portland, Ore.: Amadeus, 1995. vii, 243p. ISBN 0-931340-83-7. ML1727.8 .P2 B313.

Originally *La vie quotidienne à l'Opéra au temps de Rossini et de Balzac* (Paris: Hachette, 1987). A social history in popular "you are there" style. Considers the impact of the emperor's taste, management at the Opéra and Opéra-Comique, audiences, artistic life, and role of the press. Rossini's debut at the Opéra is interestingly presented. Backnotes, bibliography of about 150 items, name index.

2274. Spies, André Michael. *Opera, State and Society in the Third Republic, 1875–1914.* Studies in Modern European History, 23. New York: Peter Lang, 1998. vii, 264p. ISBN 0-8204-3696-8. ML1727.8 .P2 S78.

An analysis of 138 French libretti premiered at the Opéra and the Opéra-Comique from 1875 to 1914. Spies, like Gerhard (#2272), ascribes great social content to these texts, seeing them as bearers of ideology. He asserts that the "nineteenth-century idea that opera can only be amusing or beautiful" is in decline. The problem he sees is how to distinguish social comment from mere topical reference and local color. The social messages emanating from the two opera houses (via the libretti) were similar until ca. 1879, then they diverged: the Opéra remained proaristocratic, while the Comique became more democratic. Libretti were modified accordingly by the administrators of the opera houses, who selected them in the first place because of their social messages. Much useful background information included on the audiences, theatrical customs (e.g., only men were allowed in the first 10 rows of seats at the Opéra), and the librettists. Bibliography, index.

2275. Wild, Nicole. *Dictionnaire des théâtres parisiens au XIXe siècle: Les théâtres et la musique.* Domaine musicologique, 4. Paris: Amateurs de Livres, 1989. 509p. PN2636 .P3 W54.

History, repertoire, and principal staff for opera houses and other theaters. Useful bibliography (p.457–480) covers primary and secondary materials. Name index.

2276. Pendle, Karin. "Boulevard Theaters." In *Music in Paris* (#2269), 509–535.

No premieres of importance took place at the Opéra between 1819 and 1828, but the boulevard theaters were flourishing. *Comédie-vaudeville,* melodrama, *Cirque-Olympique,* and *spectacles d'optique* (dioramas with lighting effects) are described by Pendle, who notes that elements of these performances were incorporated into French grand opera.

2277. Bäcker, Ursula. *Frankreichs Musik zwischen Romantik und Moderne.* Regensburg: G. Bosse, 1965. 324p. ML270.4 .E32.

Extracts a view of French music in the period 1848 to 1914 from writings in the French press; with extensive commentary. Emphasis on the place of Wagner. Bibliography of about 1,000 items, name index.

2278. *Le théâtre lyrique français, 1945–1985.* Ed. Pierre Ancelin. Paris: H. Champion, 1987. 481p. ISBN 2-8520-3041-1. ML1727.5 .T5.

An account of opera and musical theater, with a chronology of French operas and foreign operas performed. List of composers most played on French radio (Offenbach the winner) and of operas most performed in all French theaters (*Carmen* first). French singers and composers; recent architecture; opera in cities outside Paris. Bibliography, index.

2279. Cohen, H. Robert, and Marie-Odile Gigou. *One Hundred Years of Operatic Staging in France (ca. 1830–1930): A Descriptive Catalogue of Staging Manuals, Annotated Libretti and Annotated Scores in the Bibliothèque de l'Association de la Regie Théâtrale (Paris).* Musical Life in Nineteenth-Century France, 2. Stuyvesant, N.Y.: Pendragon, 1986. lviii, 334p. ISBN 0-918728-69-4. ML128 .O4 C63.

Title also in French. An inventory of about 700 manuals, alphabetical by title. Their content is fully described and is accessible through indexes by composer, librettist, other names, and theaters (by country and city).

See also #2300.

2280. Nectoux, Jean-Michel. "Trois orchestres." In *Music in Paris* (#2269), 471–505.

History of the orchestras of the Opéra, Théâtre-Italien, and the Conservatoire. Conditions of employment for the players and conductors; identification of all of them.

The operatic scene is well described in writings about individuals; see, for example, #462 (Scribe), #728 (David), and #1178 (Méhul). See also *Die "Opéra-comique" und ihr Einfluss* (#93).

Cities and Regions

The next sections identify works about specific opera companies. Certain difficulties are presented by this literature. One is that the words *opéra* and *opéra-comique* are used in a generic sense and also as names of formal institutions. Usually, capital letters identify the latter, which is convenient in French titles where the generics would normally appear in lowercase; but in English and German titles, capitalization applies to both the generic and specific uses of the words. Another troublesome point is the fact that the formal names of major institutions have changed frequently over their lives and that names overlap different entities at times. Finally, we have the ubiquitous abbreviation of formal names. All in all, a bibliography of works on French opera may be a nest of ambiguities. The same ambiguities are carried into histories, and the articles in works like *NGDO* are often a tangle of shifting terminology.

Paris: Théâtre National de l'Opéra

This is the institution usually referred to as the Paris Opera, or L'Opéra. It has been primarily housed in the structure known as Opéra Bastille since 1990 but remains identified with the glorious building it occupied from 1875, the Palais Garnier (now used for nonoperatic performances). As an entity it was created in 1669. Some writers about L'Opéra include attention to the 1645 performances of Italian opera at the Palais Royal (see #2260 and #2267). The titles that follow are arranged according to the periods they cover.

2281. Pitou, Spire. *The Paris Opéra: An Encyclopedia of Operas, Ballets, Composers, and Performers.* Westport, Conn.: Greenwood, 1983–1990. 3v. in 4. ISBN 0-313-21420-4. ML1727.8 .P2 P5.

   A major compilation of articles, in alphabetical order, on works performed (with synopses of plots), artists, entities, and topics. Appendixes list male and female singers and dancers, 1671–1982, and the repertoire in chronological sequence, 1671–1715. Index of names, works, and subjects.

2282. Gregoir, Edouard G. J. *Des gloires de l'Opéra et la musique à Paris.* Brussels: Schott, 1878–1881. 3v. ML1727.8 .P2 G7.

   A documentary chronology of performances through 1880. Includes *ballets de cour* and the *concerts spirituel,* with much detail provided. No index.

2283. Gourret, Jean. *Les hommes qui on fait l'Opéra, 1669–1984.* Paris: Albatros, 1984. 298 p. No ISBN. ML1727.8 .P2 G63.

   A valuable gathering of documents, beginning with the privilege given to Perrin in 1669 and concluding with the 1978 *Decret,* which established the "Théâtre National de l'Opéra de Paris," an umbrella agency that supervises the various theaters and companies. Also biographies of all 54 directors who served from 1669 to 1983, as well as annual budgets and accounts, amplified with helpful commentary. Notes, bibliography of sources, name/topic index.

2284. Gourret, Jean. *Dictionnaire des cantatrices de l'Opéra de Paris.* 2nd ed. Paris: Albatros, 1987. 319p. plus 40 plates. No ISBN. ML1727.8 .P2 G636.

First edition, 1981. Accounts of some 1,100 female singers who performed for the company from 1671 to 1987, listed in chronological order by date of first appearance. Biographical data, roles; information varies according to availability (none at all in some cases). Name index.

2285. Gourret, Jean. *Dictionnaire des chanteurs de l'Opéra de Paris.* Paris: Albatros, 1982. 331p. plus 32 plates. No ISBN. ML1717.8 .P2 G7.

A chronological list (by date of debut) of entries for about 1,600 male singers who have performed for the Opéra, 1671–1980. For many persons there is biographical information and comments on the voice, as well as identification of principal roles. Name index.

The Opéra has had 13 homes. Its longest occupancies were in the Palais Royal (1673–1763), Salle Le Peletier (1821–1873), and the Palais Garnier (1875–1990). All the houses except the new Bastille Opéra are described in:

2286. Gourret, Jean. *Histoire des salles de l'Opéra de Paris.* Paris: Tredaniel, 1985. 255p. ISBN 2-857-07180-9. ML1727.8 .P2 G66.

Includes numerous plans and drawings of facades, with illuminating commentary. Footnotes, bibliography (primary and secondary sources), index of names.

2287. Durey de Noinville, Jacques-Bernard, and Louis-Antoine Travenol. *Histoire du Théâtre de l'Académie Royale de Musique en France, depuis son etablissment jusqu'à présent.* 2nd ed. Paris: Duchesne, 1757. 384p. Reprint, Geneva: Minkoff, 1972. ISBN 2-8266-0327-2. ML1727.8 .A2.

First edition, 1753. Covers 1645–1747, with a supplement of performances "par les musiciens italiens," 1752–1754. In addition to texts and documents, gives biographies and both alphabetical and chronological lists of operas staged, with casts for many.

2288. Blaze, François-Henri Joseph Castil. *L'Académie Imperiale de Musique: Histoire littéraire, musicale, choréographique, pittoresque, morale, critique, facétieuse, politique, galante de ce théâtre de 1645 à 1855.* Paris: Castil-Blaze, 1855. 2v. ML1727.8 .P2 B61.

A narrative history, with little documentation but with useful features. Staff lists include directors and administrators as well as singers and dancers. List of 647 performances in date order. Volume 2, p.416, offers a valuable table of dimensions for the 25 largest theaters in Europe (the largest were La Scala in Milan, San Carlo in Naples, and Carlo Felice in Genoa, with the Paris hall—Le Peletier—fourth). Blaze gives some interesting comments on the history by Durey de Noinville (#2287). No index.

2289. Prod'homme, Jacques-Gabriel. *L'Opéra (1669–1925).* Paris: Delagrave, 1925. 188p. Reprint, Geneva: Minkoff, 1972. ISBN 2-8266-0411-2. ML1727.8 .P2 P8.

A general history, enhanced by useful lists: houses occupied, directors, performers, performances (chronological, 1671–1925), and dancers. Palais Garnier is described in great detail. Bibliography of about 400 items, no index.

2290. Desarbres, Nérée. *Deux siècles à l'Opéra (1669–1868): Chronique anecdotique, artistique, excentrique, pittoresque et galante.* Paris: E. Dentu, 1868. 297p. ML1727.8 .P2 N382.

Principally a collection of brief biographies of performers and administrators, with a chronology of 684 events, 1671–1868. An appendix identifies 37 busts in the opera house (Le Peletier). No index.

2291. Lajarte, Théodore Dufaure de. *Bibliothèque musicale du Théâtre de l'Opéra.* Paris: Libraire des Bibliophiles, 1878. 2v. Reprint, Hildesheim: Olms, 1969. ML136 .P2 O6.

A descriptive catalogue of 241 operas, 110 ballets, and 243 other works performed at the Opéra, in date order, 1671–1876. For each opera, mentions what music (scores, parts) survives; gives cast and other premiere information; identifies the most celebrated arias and numbers. Includes biographical sketches and indexes by composer and title.

2292. Fajon, Robert. "Les incertitudes du succès: Étude du répertoire de l'Académie Royale de Musique des origines à 1750." In *L'opéra au XVIIIe siècle* (#2251), 287–344.

A study of changing public taste as reflected in the repertoire of the Opéra from 1671 to 1750. Since revivals resulted from demand, they are good indicators of preferences. Tables show those revivals (and premieres) by decade and revivals in chronological order.

2293. Ducrot, Ariane. "Les représentations de l'Académie Royale de Musique à Paris au temps de Louis XIV (1671–1715)." *Recherches* 10 (1970): 19–55.

An intensive, scholarly review of a brief period, describing the typical opera season (days and hours of performances, etc.). Table of premieres at the court and in Paris, as well as chronology of all works.

2294. Milliot, Sylvette. "Vie de l'orchestre de l'Opéra de Paris au XVIIIe siècle à travers les documents du temps." In *L'opéra au XVIIIe siècle* (#2251), 263–285.

Describes the changing instrumentation of the orchestra between Lully and Rameau. Explains how musicians were selected and paid and what their duties were.

2295. Cyr, Mary. "Basses and *basse continue* in the Orchestra of the Paris Opéra 1700–1764." *Early Music* 10 (1983): 155–170.

Takes issue with the assumption that the double bass was a typical element in the continuo accompaniment, suggesting that it was reserved for special effects like tempest scenes.

2296. Rosow, Lois. "French Opera in Transition: *Silvie* (1765) by Trial and Berton." In *Critica musica: Essays in Honor of Paul Brainard,* ed. John Knowles, 333–364 (Amsterdam: Gordon & Breach, 1996; ML60 .B72 C7).

The author "aims to illustrate the atmosphere at the Paris Opéra in the mid–1760s, by concentrating on a single successful, historically important new opera, the *pastorale-héroique Silvie,* by Jean-Claude Trial (1732–71) and

Pierre-Montan Berton." A long genesis account of the opera, plot, and production details. *Silvie* was one of the first operas to be staged with the chorus in movement, as opposed to the traditional static pose. During the two years that *Silvie* was produced, there were also changes in the seating of the orchestra and place of the conductor; and dancers appeared for the first time without masks. *Silvie* was successful, although not in the reform style that was popular at the time, but simply because it was well composed and staged.

2297. Campardon, Émile. *L'Académie Royale de Musique au XVIII siècle: Documents inédits decouverts aux Archives Nationales.* Paris: Berger-Levrault, 1884. 2v. Reprints, Geneva: Minkoff, 1970; New York: Da Capo, 1971. ISBN (Da Capo) 0-306-70090-5. ML1727.8 .P2 C2.

Covers the 1700s. Unpublished archival documents relating to the theater and persons associated with it. About 200 biographical notices, with letters, baptismal certificates, and the like. List of roles taken by each performer. In the appendix, individuals are grouped by occupation or title. Index.

2298. Rushton, Julian Gordon. "Music and Drama at the Académie Royale de Musique, Paris, 1774–1789." Ph.D. diss., U. of Oxford, 1969.

Gives particular attention to the Gluck-Piccinni rivalry.

2299. Pendle, Karin, and Stephen Wilkins. "Paradise Found: The Salle le Peletier and French Grand Opera." In *Opera in Context* (#288), 171–207.

A vivid description, with illustrations, of the fourth-largest theater in Europe and three of its productions: *La muette de Portici* (1828), *La juive* (1835), and *Le prophète* (1849). Remarkable effects were created, including "an electric arc instrument used to represent the sun" in *Le prophète*. With 93 notes.

2300. Cohen, H. Robert. *The Original Staging Manuals for Ten Parisian Operatic Premieres, 1824–1843 = Dix livrets de mise en scène lyrique datant des créations parisiennes, 1824–1843.* Musical Life in 19th-Century France, 6. New York: Pendragon, 1998. xxii, 218p. ISBN 0-945193-61-0. ML1727.8 .P2 D58.

Cohen, H. Robert. *The Original Staging Manuals for Twelve Parisian Operatic Premieres = Douze livrets de mise en scène lyrique datant des créations parisiennes.* Musical Life in 19th-Century France, 3. New York: Pendragon, 1991. xxxiv, 282p. ISBN 0-918728-70-3. ML1727.8 .P2 O7.

These two books by Cohen offer facsimile reprints of the staging books used at the Paris Opéra. These *livrets,* in the Bibliothèque Historique de la Ville de Paris, are a collection of some 1,700 items pertaining to about 600 operas produced between 1830 and 1930. They are important for descriptions of stage arrangements and actions, with diagrams and a few sketches and pictures. Much detail on costumes.

See also #2279.

2301. Wild, Nicole. *Décors et costumes du XIXe siècle. Tome 1: Opéra de Paris.* Paris: Bibliothèque Nationale, 1987. 307p. ISBN 2-7177-1753-6. PN2067 .W54.

Considers about 500 operas performed in French theaters, identifying and illustrating costumes and scenic features. Names persons responsible in specific productions and gives biographies of many. About 100 black-and-white illustrations and 20 color plates; poor name index.

See also #784.

The next group of titles refers to the Opéra after 1875, housed in the Palais Garnier.

2302. Paris Opéra. *Petite encyclopédie illustrée de l'Opéra de Paris*. Paris: Théâtre National de l'Opéra, 1974. 160p. ML1727.8 .P2 P284.

Covers, in dictionary arrangement: architectural history and details, with dimensions; the library and museum; the wardrobe; artworks in the building; the ballet; lighting and electrical installations; the great staircase; finances, stage machinery; the orchestra; and administration. Excellent illustrations but no index or bibliography.

2303. Dupêchez, Charles. *Histoire de l'Opéra de Paris: Un siècle au Palais Garnier, 1875–1980*. Paris: Librairie Académique Perrin, 1984. 445p. ISBN 2-262-00338-6. ML1727.8 .P2 D8.

A footnoted narrative history of the period, with good photographs. Thorough chronology of performances includes ballets and solo recitals, giving names of principals. Bibliography, index of names and titles.

2304. Moatti, Jacques. *L'Opéra de Paris: Palais Garnier*. Photographs by Jacques Moatti; text by Martine Kahane and Thierry Beauvert. Paris: A. Biro, 1987. Ca. 200p. ISBN 2-8766-6004-8. ML1727.8 .P2 M7. Translated as *The Paris Opera: Palais Garnier* (New York: Vendome, 1988; ISBN 0-88565-092-6).

An unpaged book of splendid photographs, folio size, most of them in color. Includes the best pictures seen of the grand staircase. No index or documentation.

2305. Wolff, Stéphane. *L'Opéra au Palais Garnier, 1875–1961*. Paris: L'Entr'acte, 1962. 565p. ML1727.8 .P2 W8.

Lists all operas performed, in order by title, with premiere casts; total number of presentations of each work in the Opéra and in other Paris theaters; principal interpreters of major roles with dates of their appearances. Similar information for ballets and dramatic works. Artist section of some 3,000 names, with dates of debuts and major appearances. Chronology of performances from 1875 to June 1962. Without index.

2306. Duault, Alain. *L'Opéra de Paris*. Paris: Sand, 1989. 245p. ISBN 2-7107-0449-8. ML1727.8 .P2 D38.

An informal institutional history, of interest for its account of the German occupation and for productions of the 1980s.

2307. Join-Diéterle, Catherine. *Les décors de scène de l'Opéra de Paris à l'époque romantique*. Paris: Picard, 1988. 295p. ISBN 2-7084-03630X. ND2887 .F8 J65.

A useful gathering of 153 illustrations with extensive commentary, exhibiting the scenography of the first half of the 19th century. List of works staged, 1807 to 1850; biographies of scenographers; 489 backnotes; bibliography of about 150 items; name index.

2308. Kahane, Martine. *Les artistes et l'Opéra de Paris; dessins de costumes, 1920–1950*. Paris: Herscher/Bibliothèque-Musée de l'Opéra, 1987. ISBN 2-7335-0148-8. ML1727.8 .P2 B5.

Not seen.

2309. Rosow, Lois. "From Destouches to Berton: Editorial Responsibility at the Paris Opéra." *JAMS* 40 (1987): 285–309.

A perspective on the 18th century, when "music editing was an important activity at the Paris Opéra," because each revival entailed revisions of the score as tastes changed and operatic styles evolved. Rosow analyzes editing practice and its administrative place in the Opéra.

2310. Urfalino, Philippe. *Quatre voix pour un opéra: Une histoire de l'Opéra Bastille* . . . Paris: Métailié, 1990. 310p. ML1727.8 .P2 Q3.

A documented story of the new structure, with a chronology from 1981, description of the inauguration on 13 July 1989, the architectural competition (757 applied; Carlos Ott was chosen), and the new role of the Palais Garnier (for ballet). Myung-Whum Chung was appointed music director on 26 May 1989. Backnotes, bibliography of about 150 items, no index.

2311. Charlet, Gérard. *L'Opéra Bastille*. Paris: Éditions du Moniteur, 1990. Unpaged. ISBN 2-281-19039-0. ML1727.8 .P2 C47.

A picture book, with 71 excellent photographs and commentary. No index.

See also Liebermann (#313).

Paris: Théâtre National de l'Opéra-Comique

Established in 1715, this is the second great opera company of Paris. The initial organization grew out of the Théâtre de la Foire (see #2242ff.). In 1801 it was reorganized, incorporating two other companies. Like the Opéra, it has had many homes; its present theater is the Salle Favart, rebuilt after a fire in 1887 and reopened in 1898 on Place Boieldieu. Although the early repertoire favored varieties of opera buffa, it became a venue for serious as well as comic genres. Among its important premieres were *Carmen* (1875) and *Lakmé* (1883). The government closed the entity in 1972, then reopened it in 1976; it is no longer a principal venue of professional performance but is being used as an opera studio.

2312. Bartlet, M. Elizabeth. "Archival Sources for the Opéra-Comique and Its *registres* at the Bibliothèque de l'Opéra." *19thCM* 7 (1983): 119–129.

Describes documents including regulations that controlled the theaters, finances, internal management, rehearsal schedules, contracts, payment receipts, and letters. Prompters' manuscript libretti are of special value. Published inventories of the theater's own library are noted. The *registres* recorded daily rehearsals and the singers involved.

2313. Cucuel, Georges. "Sources et documents pour servir a l'histoire de l'Opéra-Comique en France." *L'année musicale* 3 (1913): 247–282.

Descriptions of manuscripts and unpublished documents on *les foires* and other precursors of the Opéra-Comique. Also print sources: memoirs, theoretical texts, official publications.

2314. Desboulmiers, Jean Auguste Julien. *Histoire du Théâtre de l'Opéra-Comique* . . . Paris: Lacombe, 1769. 2v. ML1727.8 .P2 D44.

An inventory with commentary of works performed 1712–1761, with a list of performers and their roles.

2315. Cancelled entry.

2316. Pougin, Arthur. *L'Opéra-Comique pendant la Révolution de 1788 à 1801.* Paris: A. Savine 1891. 337p. Reprint, Geneva: Minkoff, 1973. ISBN 2-8266-0656-7. ML1727.3 .P85.

A year-by-year record of performances, business transactions, and official documents. Material is drawn from the *registres* of the Comédie Italien, predecessor of the Opéra-Comique. The approach is scholarly but without notes or index.

2317. Soubies, Albert, and Charles Malherbe. *Histoire de l'Opéra-Comique. La seconde Salle Favart, 1840–1887.* Paris: Flammarion, 1892–1893. 709 columns. Reprint, Geneva: Minkoff, 1974. ISBN 2-8266-0629-8. ML1727.8 .P2 S6.

Detailed and scholarly study of the company and the building it occupied until the fire of 1887. Repertoire, personnel, finances, documents, and list of works performed.

2318. Soubies, Albert. *Soixante-neuf ans à l'Opéra-Comique en deux pages.* Paris: Fischbacher, 1894. x, 30p. plus 2 folded leaves of plates.

A tabular presentation of the repertoire, with premiere dates and number of performances for each work, by season, 1825–1894.

2319. Wolff, Stéphane. *Un demi-siècle d'Opéra-Comique (1900–1950); les oeuvres, les interprètes.* Paris: André Bonne, 1953. 339p. ML1717.8 .P22 O79.

A list of 401 works by 206 composers, arranged by title. Names of performers, total number of performances, and data on premieres and on selected later presentations. Names of about 2,500 artists, with facts on their debuts and other roles they sang or danced. List of ballet masters, directors, electricians, etc.

2320. Charlton, David. "Orchestra and Chorus at the Comédie-Italien (Opéra-Comique), 1775–1799." In *Slavonic and Western Music: Essays for Gerald Abraham,* ed. Malcolm Hamrick, 87–108 (Ann Arbor, Mich.: UMI Research, 1985; ML55 .A18).

A study of two sources: the *registres* of the Comédie-Italien, 1717–1832, and *Les spectacles de Paris,* which were annual guides to music and theaters. These were the *registres* that served as the main source for Pougin (#2316) and were organized by Brenner (#2323). Among the topics are the way a musician gained membership in the orchestra, the performance forces, conducting practice, and the increased use of the chorus after 1762. In the orchestra, clarinets, horns, and trumpets made their appearance in the 1770s, trombones in the 1790s.

2321. Krakovitch, Odile. "L'Opéra-Comique et la censure." In *Die "Opéra-comique"* (#93), 211–234.

Different theaters had varying degrees of censorial attention in the early 19th century. The Opéra-Comique was treated indulgently in matters of morals but more strictly in matters of politics and religion. Censorship followed the principle that theater is a mode of public education. Censors' reports of 1807–1867 are examined to exhibit their norms and concerns.

Paris: Théâtre Italien

The *querelle de bouffons* did not settle the matter of style in Paris, and both Italian and French forms continued to be performed. But the Opéra remained essentially French, so other venues became associated with the Italian manner. The first Théâtre Italien, traceable to the 17th-century Comédie Italien, became—after many adventures—part of the Opéra-Comique formed in 1801. A second company of the same name opened in 1801, with Napoleon's support, occupying the Salle Olympique. The company came to rival the Opéra and Opéra-Comique; Rossini was its director from 1824 to 1826 (although his own works premiered at the Opéra). Important premieres included Bellini's *I puritani* (1835) and Donizetti's *Don Pasquale* (1843).

2322. Gossett, Philip. "Music at the Théâtre-Italien." In *Music in Paris* (#2269), 327–364.

This theater was the point of entry into Paris for Italian composers. The works of Bellini, Donizetti, and Mercadante were staged there, with alterations in most cases. Italians dominated in Paris but were influenced to rethink their standard procedures.

2323. Brenner, Clarence Dietz. *The Théâtre-Italien: Its Repertory, 1716–1793.* Berkeley: U. of California Press, 1961. vii, 531p. PB13 .C3.

A presentation of material found in the *registres* (see #2320).

2324. *Le nouveau Théâtre Italien, ou recueil général des comédies . . .* 2nd ed. Paris: Briasson, 1753. 10v. PQ1231 .I5 N6.

An account of the period 1716–1752, describing in rich detail 648 works performed.

2325. Origny, Antoine Jean-Baptiste Abraham d'. *Annales du théâtre italien depuis son origine jusqu'à ce jour.* Paris: Veuve Duchesne, 1788. 3v. PN2636 .P3185.

An elaborate chronology of performances to 1788, including *comédies,* ballets, and parodies; with accounts of the theater and anecdotes about the actors.

2326. Desboulmiers, Jean Auguste Julien. *Histoire anecdotique et raisonée du Théâtre Italien, depuis son rétablissement en France, jusqu'à l'année 1769.* Paris: Lacombe, 1769. 7v. PN2633 .D4.

Not seen.

2327. Parfaict, François, and Claude Parfaict. *Histoire de l'ancien theatre italien depuis son origine en France jusqu'à sa suppression en l'année 1697*. Paris: Rozet, 1767. xiv, 455, iii p. Facsimile reprint, New York: AMS Press, 1978. PN2632 .P3.

Les Comédiens Italiens began performing on 19 May 1577 in Paris. A second troupe arrived in 1584, a third in 1588. Presented here are plots and descriptions of many plays, names of casts, and extracts from relevant privileges and documents. Despite the book's title, the period covered in the volume seen is 1645–1674.

2328. Soubies, Albert. *Le Théâtre-Italien de 1801 à 1913*. Paris: Fischbacher, 1913. iv, 186, iv p. ML1717.8 .P3 T3.

Features a vast foldout chart: "Tableau des pièces représentées," which shows performances of each work by season. Also letters, documents, good pictures, and a narrative of each season. Without notes, index, or bibliography.

Paris: Théâtre Lyrique

This company was established in 1851 as an outgrowth of a Théâtre National that began in 1847, taking its present name in 1852. It was the site of several major premieres, including Gounod's *Faust* (1859), Berlioz's *Les troyens à Carthage* (1863), and Gounod's *Roméo et Juliette* (1867).

2329. Walsh, T. J. *Second Empire Opera: The Théâtre Lyrique, Paris 1851–1870*. New York: Riverrun; London: Calder, 1981. x, 348p. ISBN 0-7145-3659-8. ML1727 .W227.

A thorough history, with much information on finances and audiences. Lacks attention to concurrent activity in the Opéra and other Parisian houses, thus offering an isolated view of "second empire opera." Poorly printed illustrations, backnotes, bibliography of about 100 entries, partly expansive index of names and titles.

2330. Lasalle, Albert de. *Mémorial du Théâtre-Lyrique* . . . Paris: Lecuir, 1877. 107p. ML1727.8 .P2 L33.

Covers 1847–1870. Chronology of performances with casts and comments; various statistical tables. Index of names and titles.

2331. Soubies, Albert. *Histoire du Théâtre-Lyrique, 1851–1879*. Paris: Fischbacher, 1899. ML1727.8 .P2 L35.

The repertoire of the period, in a foldout chart, tabular format.

Paris: Other Theaters

2332. Malliot, Antoine Louis. *La musique au théâtre*. Paris: Amyot, 1863. viii, 432p. ML1727 .M15

The history and repertoire of L'Opéra, L'Opéra-Comique, the Lyrique, L'Odéon, Théâtre des Nouveautés, La Renaissance, and (in most detail) Les Bouffes-Parisiens. The last named, which opened on 5 July 1855, presented almost all of Offenbach's operas and became known as the Théâtre Offenbach. Without documentation, index, or bibliography.

2333. Deierkauf-Holsboer, Sophie-Wilma. *Le Théâtre du Marais*. Paris: Nizet, 1954–1958. 2v. PN2636 .P3 T47.

The theater opened in 1634, was renamed Théâtre des Étrangers in 1792, and then Théâtre des Amis des Arts in 1793. This book covers the 17th century, in a footnoted narrative of persons and events. Documents and details on the building. Bibliography, index in each volume.

Other French cities are now taken up in alphabetical order.

Lyon

2334. Vallas, Leon. *Un siècle de musique et de théâtre à Lyon, 1688–1789*. Lyon: P. Masson, 1932. viii, 561p. Reprint, Geneva: Minkoff, 1971. ISBN 2-8266-0428-7. ML270.8 .L95 V3.

A documented narrative, with some illustrations and musical examples. Biographies of about 300 persons; list of about 100 libretti published in the city, 1688–1789. Bibliography of nine pages, name index.

2335. Sallés, Antoine. *L'opéra italien et allemand à Lyon au 19. siècle (1805–1882)*. Paris: E. Fromont, 1906. 122p. ML1727.8 .L9515.

Consists of journal articles previously published in *La revue musicale de Lyon*.

2336. Vuillermoz, Gustave Marie Joseph. *Cent ans d'opéra à Lyon: Le centenaire du Grand Théâtre de Lyon, 1831–1931*. Lyon: L. Bascou, 1932. 118p.

Not seen. *Kaufman* says it names the companies of each season and gives dates and casts for local premieres.

Marseille

2337. Harris, Claude. *Opéra à Marseille, 1685–1987*. Marseille: P. Tacussel, 1987. 269p. ISBN 2-9039-6328-2. ML1728.8 .M32 O6.

An informal history, without documentation but with a strong bibliography of about 100 items. Useful list of directors through the period and a chronology of performances 1787–1919, 1924–1986. No index.

2338. Segond, André. *L'opéra de Marseille, 1787–1987*. Marseille: J. Laffitte, 1987. 173p. ISBN 2-8627-6140-0. ML1727.8 .M32 O65.

A pictorial account, strong on architecture and plans, with drawings and photos of the interior of the new Théâtre d'Opéra (1924). Without notes or bibliography; with name and title index.

2339. Combarnous, Victor. *Notes et souvenirs: L'histoire du Grand-Théâtre de Marseille, 31 octobre 1787–13 novembre 1919*. Marseille: Imprimerie Méridionale, [1928?]. 370p.

Not seen. Described in *Kaufman* as a narrative history with dates and casts of most local premieres.

Nantes

2340. La Laurencie, Lionel de. *La vie musicale en province au 18e siècle. L'Académie de Musique et le Concert de Nantes à l'Hotel de la Bourse (1727–67)*. Paris:

Société Française d'Imprimerie et de la Librairie, 1906. xxvi, 213p. Reprint, Geneva: Minkoff, 1972. ISBN 2-8266-0350-7. ML270.8 .N19.

Describes all musical activities, including opera; with accounts of the repertoire, socioeconomic matters, music schools, instruments, and individual musicians.

Rouen

2341. Geispitz, Henri. *Histoire du Théâtre-des-Arts de Rouen, 1882–1913*. Rouen: Lestrignant, 1913.

Neither this book nor a second volume covering 1913–1940 (Rouen: Lecerf, 1951) was examined. Described in *Kaufman* as a seasonal account of companies and repertoire, with casts and dates for most productions.

Savoie (English: Savoy)

2342. Dufour, Auguste, and François Rabut. *Les musiciens, la musique et les instruments de musique en Savoie du XIIe au XIXe siècle*. Chambery: Albert Bottero, 1878. 232p. Reprint, Geneva: Minkoff, 1972. ISBN 2-8266-0326-4. ML270.7 .S29 D8.

A chronological review of all musical activity, with relevant documents presented. Index of names and topics.

Germany (German: Deutschland; French: Allemande; Italian: Germania)

Much of the literature reflects the division of the country after World War II into Bundesrepublik Deutschland (BRD), or West Germany, and Deutsche Demokratische Republik (DDR), or East Germany. Postwar literature on opera in Berlin was also divided, according to the control of the city by the BRD (the West Berlin zone) and DDR (the East Berlin zone). Die Deutsche Oper was in West Berlin, while Die Staatsoper and Die Komische Oper were in East Berlin. These geographical aspects were annulled with the reunification of Germany in 1990 under the official name Bundesrepublik Deutschland.

Editions

2343. *German Opera 1770–1800*. Ed. Thomas Bauman. New York: Garland, 1985–1986. 22v. ISBN and LC numbers vary with individual volumes. (Cited in this guide as *GO*.)

Consists of facsimiles of scores and libretti for 20 operas. Each is entered separately under its composer in this guide.

Music in General

The most comprehensive history of German music is the book-length article in *MGG*. In English there is a useful source:

2344. *Of German Music: A Symposium*. Ed. Hans-Hubert Schönzeler. New York: Barnes & Noble, 1976. 321p. ISBN 0-06-496113-3. ML275.1 .O4.

Essays by various authors, which taken together form a coherent history from the baroque into the mid-20th century. Worklists, name and subject index.

A number of histories of German music by period and by locality are entered in *IOM* 2116–2153.

Opera

2345. Flaherty, Gloria. *Opera in the Development of German Critical Thought.* Princeton, N.J.: Princeton U.P., 1976. xi, 382p. ISBN 0-691-06370-2. ML1729 .F6.

About critical writing related to opera in the 17th–19th centuries. Covers philosophical disputes, reforms, the assertion of German cultural identity, and the European romantic context. Backnotes, bibliography of about 400 items, expansive index.

2346. Schmitt, Anke. *Der Exotismus in der deutschen Oper zwischen Mozart und Spohr.* Hamburger Beiträge zur Musikwissenschaft, 36. Hamburg: K. D. Wagner, 1988. 608p. ISBN 3-8897-9035-6. ML1704 .S35.

By "exotic" was meant the Middle East and the Far East, including India. Interest in those lands was fired by travelers' accounts and led to impressions of the regions by painters and writers. All musical forms had their exotic elements, which are well described here. Among the themes employed in opera were Mohammed, the Crusades, Mongols, the French in Egypt, Turks, and Spanish Moors. Schmitt is specific in describing how those effects were gained through musical devices and plots. Special attention to the exotic operas of E. T. A. Hoffmann, Weber, and Spohr. Bibliography of about 450 items, name index.

2347. *Deutsches Bühnen Jahrbuch: Theatergeschichtliches Jahr- und Adressbuch,* 1–, 1890–. Hamburg: Genossenschaft Deutscher Bühnen-Angehörigen, 1890–. Annual. PN2640 .D45.

Publisher and title vary. Annual fact book about theatrical life, covering German, Austrian, and Swiss cities. Daily chronologies, organizations, theaters by city with seating capacities, opera companies with staff lists, events, and persons. Name index.

2348. Schletterer, Hans Michel. *Das deutsche Singspiel von seinen ersten Anfängen bis auf die neueste Zeit.* Hildesheim: Olms, 1975. x, 340p. ISBN 3-487-05577-5. ML1729.3 .S34.

Analyzes the works of Opitz, Reblun, Betuleium, Ruff, von Braunschweig, and other leading figures, in a historical context. Footnotes, list of sources, no index.

Opera: 17th and 18th Centuries

2349. Brockpähler, Renate. *Handbuch zur Geschichte der Barockoper in Deutschland.* Emsdetten: Lechte, 1964. 394p. ML1729.3 .B78.

A documentation of operatic life in 48 German cities, plus Vienna and Prague. Includes bibliographies, historical summaries, names of persons and institutions, and opera performances in date order. Name index.

2350. Wade, Mara R. *The German Baroque Pastoral "Singspiel."* New York: P. Lang, 1990. 353p. ISBN 3-261-04186-2. ML1729.2 .W3.

A narrative history, focused on three works as examples: *Seelewig* (1644), *Psyche* (1652), and *Amelinde* (1657). The term *Singspiel* is discussed, and the genre is said to have a "literary quality equal to, and in many instances superior to spoken drama." Music is not taken up. Chapter endnotes, bibliography of about 250 items, no index.

2351. Bauman, Thomas. *North German Opera in the Age of Goethe.* New York: Cambridge U.P., 1985. xi, 444p. ISBN 0-521-260272. ML1729 .B38.

Political and social background for opera in 1766–1799, covering the cities of Leipzig, Berlin, Hamburg, Weimar, Gotha, Dresden, Breslau, and Königsberg. Libretti, personalities, reception accounts. Most of the operas of the period have vanished from the stage, having been too insular for wide audiences. Viennese and Italian operas replaced them. Catalogue of the operas, musical examples, indexes.

2352. Allen, Sheila Marie. "German Baroque Opera (1678–1740) with a Practical Edition of Selected Soprano Arias." Ph.D. diss., Eastman School of Music, 1974. 187p.

2353. *Das deutsche Singspiel im 18. Jahrhundert: Quellen und Zeugnisse zu Ästhetik und Rezeption.* Ed. Renate Schusky. Bonn: Bouvier, 1980. 145p. ISBN 3-4160-1530-4. ML1704 .D48.

A useful gathering of 18 articles, prefaces, and extracts from books of the time. Commentary, but without footnotes on the individual items. Bibliography of about 75 titles, no index.

Opera: 19th Century

2354. Goslich, Siegfried. *Die deutsche romantische Oper.* Tutzing: Schneider, 1975. 460p. ISBN 3-7952-0161-6. ML1729.5 .G67.

A thorough, scholarly narrative of the second half of the 19th century. Works of Marschner, Lortzing, Spohr, Nicolai, and Weber are emphasized. Musical examples, illustrations, bibliography of about 400 items, name index.

Opera: 20th Century

2355. "Musikbühnen-Uraufführungen in der DDR seit 1945." *Musikbühne* 1977: 157–177.

A list of about 250 operas and operettas, in date order, by composers of the DDR, with librettists and premiere data.

2356. Neef, Sigrid, and Hermann Neef. *Deutsche Oper im 20. Jahrhundert: DDR, 1949–1989.* Berlin: P. Lang, 1992. 595p. ISBN 2-8603-2011-4. MT95 .N36.

Discusses the works of 32 composers, generally not known outside of the DDR: plots and program notes. Index of names and titles.

2357. Tschulik, Norbert. *Musiktheater in Deutschland: Die Oper im 20. Jahrhundert.* Vienna: Österreichischer Bundesverlag, 1987. 347p. ISBN 3-2150-6278-X. ML1729.5 .T75.

Discusses works of Pfitzner, Orff, Hindemith, Egk, and Henze. Backnotes, bibliography of about 125 items, name index.

See also Cook (#1055).

Cities and Regions

Berlin

The principal theaters are:

Die Deutsche Staatsoper, also known as Die Lindenoper. Originally (1742) Die Königlichen Hofoper unter den Linden, renamed Die Staatsoper, in 1919. Destroyed in 1941 or 1943 (sources differ), rebuilt and again destroyed in 1945, reopened in 1955.

Die Nationaltheater, opened in 1786. Mozart's operas performed there from 1788. The company moved in 1800 with the name Nationaltheater, occupying the Schauspielhaus to 1817 (burned) and Neues Schauspielhaus, 1821.

Kroll Oper, 1844. In 1895 became part of the Schauspieltheater, renamed Neues Königlichen Operettentheater, in 1900; destroyed in 1943 and not rebuilt. Kroll was also the familiar name given to the Staatsoper am Platz der Republik, under the direction of Otto Klemperer, 1927–1931 (closed).

Die Komische Oper, 1905–1911; at the Metropol Theater from 1947, under the direction of Walter Felsenstein; new building, 1966, director Götz Friedrich.

Die Deutsche Oper Berlin, so named from 1961 with the restoration of the theater. Opened in 1912 as Deutsches Opernhaus, under the direction of Hartmann; renamed Städtische Oper in 1925. Reorganized in 1933 under the Nazis, as Deutsches Opernhaus (Goebbels director); renamed Städtische Oper in Teater des Westens in 1945.

2358. Henzl, Christoph. *Quellentexte zur Berliner Musikgeschichte im 18. Jahrhundert.* Wilhelmshaven: Noetzel, 1999. 235p. ISBN 3-7959-0761-6. ML275.8 .B515 Q3.

A valuable gathering of 80 documents with library locations and commentaries. All of musical life is covered, with many resources on opera. The documents include letters, parts of books, newspaper notices, and official papers. Secondary literature about the materials is cited. Backnotes, name index.

2359. Freydank, Ruth. *Theater in Berlin von den Anfängen bis 1945.* Berlin: Argon, 1988. 494p. ISBN 3-87024-125-X. PN2656 .B4 F74.

A documented, narrative history of all the theaters, including those devoted to opera. One or two illustrations on every page, mostly black and white. Interesting chapters on the Nazi period and on the destruction of buildings during the war. Bibliography of some 750 items, name index.

Berlin: Staatsoper

2360. Kapp, Julius. *Geschichte der Staatsoper Berlin.* Berlin: Hesse, 1937. 264p. Revised reprint, 1942. ML1729.8 .B53 S93.

Examines early opera in the city; gives a list of works performed 1786–1942; tables of operas with number of performances for each; staff lists. Without footnotes or bibliography but with 600 illustrations and name index. A companion picture book by Kapp, *200 Jahre der Staatsoper im Bild* (Berlin: Hesse, 1942), has 247 pages of illustrations.

2361. Fetting, Hugo. *Die Geschichte der Deutschen Staatsoper.* Berlin: Henschelverlag, 1955. 283p. ML1729.8 .B53 S914.

A footnoted history from 1741 to 1954. Includes names of operas performed and about 200 photographs of scenes, artists, and the building itself, which was rebuilt in 1955 according to the original plans. No index.

2362. Schäffer, Carl, and Carl Hartmann. *Die Königlichen Theater in Berlin: Statistlischer Rückblick.* Berlin: Comtoir, 1886. 304p. ML1729.8 .B52 K68.

A fact book covering 1786–1855, including a list of about 2,500 works performed, with dates and total number of performances. Also seasonal chronologies, lists of all performers and their seasons, and accounts of the buildings that had housed the opera.

2363. Rösler, Walter, et al. *Das "Zauberschloss" unter den Linden: Die Berliner Staatsoper, Geschichte von den Anfängen bis heute.* Berlin: Edition q, 1997. 251p. ISBN 3-8612-4334-2. ML275.8 .B47 R647.

A popular narrative history, covering 1742–1997. Well illustrated, with many color plates. Bibliography of about 50 entries, no index.

See also Yorke-Long (#87).

Berlin: Neues Schauspielhaus

2364. Bomberger, E. Douglas. "The Neues Schauspielhaus in Berlin and the Premiere of Carl Maria von Weber's *Der Freischütz*." In *Opera in Context* (#288), 147–169.

The theater opened in 1821 with the Weber premiere. Elaborate detail is given on that production, including rehearsal schedules and special effects. The Wolf's Glen scene used the most advanced machines available, among them various color flames and sound machines. Floor plans and interior views of the theater, which had a capacity of 1,200 if standing room is counted. With 63 footnotes to the contemporary sources.

Berlin: Komische Oper

2365. Jacobsohn, Fritz. *Hans Gregors Komische Oper, 1905–1911.* Berlin: Osterheld, [1911?]. 115p. ML1729.8 .B5 J19.

An undocumented narrative history, with illustrations of scenes and a list of singers with their roles. No index.

2366. *Jahrbuch der Komischen Oper Berlin*, 1–12, 1960/1961–1971/1972. Berlin: Henschelverlag, 1960–1971.

See #151 for continuations. In *Oper heute* 2 there is a useful descriptive article on the Komische Oper; in v.3 there is a chronology of productions, 1947–1979.

2367. *Die Komische Oper*. Ed. Hans-Jochen Genzel. Berlin: Nicolai, 1997. 239p. ISBN 3-8758-4656-7. ML1729.8 .B53 K655.

> Consists of 44 popular-style essays by various authors, including Walter Felsenstein. Chronology, 1946–1997, with casts; tour appearances of the company, 1949–1997; fine illustrations. Name and title index.

See also #299 and #300.

Berlin: Deutsche Oper Berlin

2368. *Die Deutsche Oper Berlin*. Ed. Gisela Huwe. Berlin: Quadriga-Verlag Severin, 1984. 341p. ISBN 3-88679-111-4. ML1729.8 .B53 D525.

> Popular essays by various writers, with fine illustrations and a useful chronology of the theater, 1961–1984, with names of principals. No bibliography; name index.

2369. *Dreissig Jahre Deutsche Oper Berlin, 1961–1991*. Berlin: Hessling, 1962. 519p.

> Not examined. It is a sequel to another work by the same publisher, not available for examination: Werner Bollert, *50 Jahre Deutsche Oper Berlin, 7 November 1912–7 November 1962* (1962).

The other German cities are now taken up in alphabetical order.

Bayreuth

The city's famous venue is the Richard-Wagner Festspielhaus, opened in 1876, closed in 1944, and reopened under Wieland Wagner in 1951. The current director is Wolfgang Wagner, grandson of Richard Wagner.

2370. Karbaum, Michael. *Studien zur Geschichte der Bayreuther Festspiele (1876–1976)*. Regensburg: Bosse, 1976. 106p. ISBN 3-7649-2060-2. ML410 .W15 K18.

> A thorough, footnoted history of the festival, with pertinent documents reprinted. Bibliography of about 50 items, no index.

2371. Skelton, Geoffrey. *Wagner at Bayreuth*. 2nd ed. London and New York: White Lion, 1976. 251p. Reprint, New York: Da Capo, 1983. ISBN 0-306-76157-2. ML410 .W2 S55.

> A popular history, without notes. Useful list of productions, singers, and their roles, 1876–1975. Bibliography of about 50 entries, expansive index of names and titles.

2372. Spotts, Frederic. *Bayreuth: A History of the Wagner Festival*. New Haven, Conn.: Yale U.P., 1994. x, 334p. ISBN 0-300-05777-6. ML410 .W2 S6.

> The standard English history. Deals with Wagner's vision and plans and how they were fulfilled; the Wagner family—Cosima, Siegfried, Wolfgang, Winifred, and (the hero) Wieland—and their political adventures; singers, directors, conductors, "kings, kaisers, Hitler and Goebbels, and American soldiers in 1945." Great detail on the productions and reception. Emergence of

"Bayreuth style," which emphasizes text (slow tempo) and clarity in singing. Bibliography, index.

2373. Mayer, Hans. *Richard Wagner in Bayreuth, 1876–1976*. Stuttgart: Belser, 1976. 248p. ISBN 3-7630-9018-5. ML410 .W2 M46.

An English translation by Jack Zipes, with the same title, is available (New York: Rizzoli, 1976). It is a large photo book, with ample commentary in historical sequence. Some comments on previous writings, but no notes. Name index.

See also Baker in #288.

Cologne (Köln)

The Theater in Glockengasse operated from 1872 to 1944. In 1957 the new Theater in Offenbachplatz opened.

2374. Hiller, Carl H. *Vom Quaternmarkt zum Offenbachplatz, 400 Jahre Musiktheater in Köln*. Cologne: Bachem, 1986. 185p. ISBN 3-7616-0853-5. ML1729.8 .C7 H54.

An illustrated, narrative history, without documentation. Of interest for coverage of recent times: "Phönix aus der Asche, 1945–1975," and "Zu neuen Ufern, 1975–1986." A list of Cologne's premieres is included, with a token bibliography and name index.

2375. Mies, Paul, and Klaus Wolfgang Niemöller. "Bibliographie zur Musikgeschichte der Stadt Köln." In *Beiträge zur Musikgeschichte der Stadt Köln zum 70. Geburtstag von Paul Mies*, ed. Karl Gustav Fellerer, 55–80 (Cologne: Arno Volk-Verlag, 1959; ML279.8 .C73 F4).

A list of about 750 articles, books, and dissertations; not annotated.

Darmstadt

The Grosses Haus opened in 1819, burned in 1871, new building opened in 1879, destroyed in 1944. A new Grosses Haus opened in 1972.

2376. Kaiser, Hermann. *Barocktheater in Darmstadt: Geschichte des Theaters einer deutschen Residenz am 17. und 18. Jahrhunderts*. Darmstadt: E. Roether, 1951. 181p. PN2656 .D24 K3.

A documented, narrative history of theatrical performances, including opera. With a title list of works staged, by theater. Name index.

2377. Kaiser, Hermann. *300 Jahre Darmstädter Theater in Berichte von Augenzeugen*. Darmstadt: Roether, 1972. 191p. ISBN 3-7929-0006-6. PN1582 .G4 K17.

Interesting accounts by 173 persons who witnessed or participated in theatrical performances in the city. Among those reporting are Weber, Spohr, Wagner, Felix Weingartner, and Jenny Lind. Backnotes, name index, title index.

2378. Kaiser, Hermann. *Modernes Theater in Darmstadt, 1910–1933*. Darmstadt: E. Roether, 1955. 211p. PN2656 .D3 K3.

Not seen.

Dresden

There has been opera in the city since 1638. The first opera house opened in 1667. The Königlich Sächsisches Hoftheater (known as the Semper, for the architect Gottfried Semper) opened in 1841, burned in 1869. A second Semper, 1878, was renamed the Staatsoper; it was destroyed in 1945. The new Semper opened on 13 February 1985.

2379. Schnoor, Hans. *Dresden: Vierhundert Jahre deutsche Musikkultur.* Dresden: Dresdener Verlagsgesellschaft, 1948. 294p. ML1729.8 .D72 M88.

A narrative history of all kinds of music, with a chronology of performances from 1548 to 1948 and many details. Poor-quality photos, no footnotes. Useful annotated bibliography of about 500 entries. Name index.

2380. Schnoor, Hans. *Die Stunde des Rosenkavaliers.* Munich: Süddeutscher Verlag, 1968. 226p. ML1729.8 .D72 S84.

A general narrative of opera in Dresden, covering much the same ground as the preceding item but with excellent illustrations. The chronology is repeated. Emphasis in the text is on early 20th-century activity (*Der Rosenkavalier* premiered in Dresden in 1911). No bibliography; name index.

2381. *Oper in Dresden: Festschrift zur Wiedereroffnung.* Ed. Horst Seeger and Mathias Rank. Berlin: Henschelverlag, 1985. 117p. No ISBN. ML1729. O63. ML1729 .O63.

Consists of 15 essays by various authors, presenting historical perspectives. One is a chronology, 1627–1984. Fine illustrations, including a number that show war damage. No notes or index.

2382. *Semperoper: Gottfried Sempers Opernhaus zu Dresden.* Ed. Hella Bartnig. Meissen: Lerchl, 1995. 193p. ISBN 3-9803-3643-3. ML1729.8 .D72 S46.

A narrative history of opera in Dresden and of the Semper. Exterior and interior details of the theater are shown in 147 superb color illustrations. A useful chapter on the reconstruction, which began in 1967; cornerstone laid in 1977, opened in 1985. Chronology 1627 to present. Bibliography of about 50 items, no index.

See also Yorke-Long (#87).

Frankfurt am Main

The Opernhaus was built in 1880, mostly destroyed in 1943, and rebuilt in 1964.

2383. Valentin, Caroline. *Geschichte der Musik in Frankfurt am Main vom Anfange des XIV. bis zum Anfange des XVIII Jahrhunderts.* Frankfurt: Völcker, 1906. xii, 280p. Reprint, Walluf bei Wiesbaden: M. Sändig, 1972. ISBN 3-500-24710-5. ML279.8 .F8 V1.

A scholarly narrative of all musical activity. Good illustrations in the original printing are poorly reproduced in the reprint. Name and topic index.

2384. Mohr, Albert Richard. *Das Frankfurter Opernhaus 1880–1980* . . . Frankfurt: Kramer, 1980. 372p. ISBN 3-7829-0232-7. ML1729.8 .F8 M8.

A narrative history of productions and conductors, with interesting details on the postwar reconstruction of the building. Chapters for each Intendant. Fine illustrations but no footnotes or bibliography. Name index.

2385. Mohr, Albert Richard. *Die Frankfurter Oper 1924–44*. Frankfurt: Kramer, 1971. 752p.

A review of the seasons with chronology and press notices; name index.

2386. Eggert, Mara, and Hans-Klaus Jungheinrich. *Durchbruche: Die Oper Frankfurt: 10 Jahre Musiktheater mit Michael Gielen*. Weinheim: Quadriga, 215p. ISBN 3-8867-9151-3. ML1729.8 .F72 F73.

Not seen.

Halle

2387. Serauky, Walter. *Musikgeschichte der Stadt Halle*. Halle: Buchhandlung des Waisenhauses, 1935–1943. 3v. Reprint, Hildesheim: Olms, 1971. No ISBN. ML279.8 .H14 S4.

Detailed, well-illustrated, and documented history of music in the city from the Middle Ages. Name and place index.

Hamburg

The first public opera house in Germany, the Opern-Theatrum, opened on 2 January 1678; it was known as the Gänsemarkt (Goosemarket); closed in 1738, demolished in 1763. Das Cömodienhaus (Ackermannisches Komödienhuas) opened in 1764, renamed Deutsches Nationaltheater in 1797; renamed Hamburgisches Stadttheater in 1810. A Neues Stadttheater opened in 1827 (Theater am Dammtor); renamed Hamburgisches Staatstheater in 1933, then Hamburgische Staatsoper in 1934, destroyed in 1943; a new house opened in 1955, under the direction of Günther Rennert; Rolf Liebermann was director from 1959 to 1973, succeeded by Götz Friedrich.

2388. Sittard, Josef. *Geschichte des Musik- und Concertwesens in Hamburg vom 14. Jahrhundert bis auf die Gegenwart*. Leipzig: Reher, 1890. xi, 392p. Reprint, Hildesheim: Olms, 1971. ISBN 3-487-0401-0. ML283 .H19 S5.

Not seen.

2389. Wolff, Hellmuth C. *Die Barockoper in Hamburg: 1678–1738*. Wolfenbüttel: Möseler, 1957. 2v. ML1729.8 .H19 W6.

V.1 has a detailed account of the Gänsemarkt building: rooms, artworks, stage machinery. Operas performed there (by Keiser, Mattheson, Telemann, Graupner, etc.) are described and their stylistic features discussed. Also a chapter on ballet. With 38 plates, bibliography of about 300 items, and index of titles and names. V.2 consists entirely of musical examples.

2390. *300 Jahre Oper in Hamburg: 1678–1978*. Hamburg: Christians, 1977. 191p. ISBN 3-7672-0528-9. ML1729.8 .H192 H32.

A collection of essays by various authors, including a study of the period 1740–1840 (connecting with the preceding entry) by Kurt Stephenson; a summary of the preceding entry by its author, with some updating; the postwar era to 1977, by Erich Lüth; a history of the 1898–1943 period by Hans Worbs; and a list of key dates over the 300-year period by Joachim E. Wenzel.

2391. Busch, Max W., and Peter Dannenberg, eds. *Die Hamburgische Staatsoper*. Zurich: M&T Verlag, 1988–1990. 3v. ISBN 3-7265-6013-0. ML1729.8 .H2 H353.

V.1, 1678–1945; v.2, 1945–1988; v.3, *Sonderausgabe*. V.1 has 11 essays by various authors, dealing with the period 1678–1738; the Stadttheater of 1827–1897; conductors Mahler and Klemperer; Lotte Lehmann; wartime destruction; and ballet 1827–1944. There are 17 essays in v.2 by various authors, including material on the directors Rennert, Heinz Titjen, and Rolf Liebermann; singers, conductors, ballet, and designers. Also a chronology. Neither volume has notes, bibliography, or index.

2392. Meyer, Reinhart. *Die Hamburger Oper*. Munich: Kraus, 1980–1984. 4v. ISBN 3-601-00136-5. ML48 .H36.

V.1–3 consist of facsimiles of libretti for performances of 1678–1730. V.4 is a commentary. It presents a useful assortment of facts in topical chapters, then a list of operas performed with casts and references to writings, notes on the scenes, etc. Index of librettists and literature about them, name index, bibliography covering the contemporary building.

2393. Schröder, Dorothea. *Zeitgeschichte auf der Opernbühne: Barockes Musiktheater in Hamburg im Dienst von Politik und Diplomatie (1690–1745)*. Göttingen: Vandernhoeck und Ruprecht, 1998. vi, 366p. ISBN 3-525-27900-0. ML1729.8 .H19 S34.

The musical setting in the light of the political situation: censorship, financing, the opera, the audience, festivals and entertainments. Also accounts of performances and reception of individual operas. Bibliography of primary and secondary materials, about 150 items; chronology; name index.

2394. Braun, Werner. *Vom Remter zum Gänsemarkt: Aus der Frühgeschichte der alten Hamburger Oper, 1677–1697*. Saarbrücker Studien zur Musikwissenschaft, n.s., 1. Saarbrücken: Saarbrücker Druckerei und Verlag, 1987. 207p. ISBN 3-9250-3617-2. ML1729.8 .H19 B7.

Considers the sources and problems to be dealt with in the writing of a definitive history of German opera in Hamburg. Among the topics are libretti, chronology, performance conditions, stage technique, sacred opera, and opera in other cities. Analysis of *Orontes* (1677) and operas by Johann Sigismund Kusser (Cousser), who was music director from 1694 to 1696. Bibliography of about 300 items, index.

2395. *Studien zur Barockoper.* Ed. Constanin Floros et al. Hamburger Jahrbuch für Musikwissenschaft, 3. Hamburg: Verlag der Musikalienhandlung, 1978. 306p. ML1703 .S8.

> Consists of 11 essays by various authors, covering the research about opera in the city, the singers in the Gänsemarkt, Italian opera of 1600–1640, and stage design. Also consideration of individual works by Telemann, Alessandro Scarlatti, and Gasparini. Full contents in *Baron,* 1264.

Hannover (English: Hanover)

Opera was presented in the ducal palace from 1689 until the structure was demolished in 1854. The Grosse Schlosstheater opened in 1689, closed in 1714. A new house opened in 1818, named in 1837 the Hofoper. Another building, Königliche Hoftheater, became Städtliches Opernhaus in 1921, was destroyed in 1943, and rebuilt and opened in 1950. In 1970 it became the Niedersächische Staatstheater.

2396. Hammer, Sabine. *Oper in Hannover: 300 Jahre Wandel im Musiktheater einer Stadt.* Hannover: Schlütersche Verlaganstalt, 1990. 208p. ISBN 3-87706-298-9. ML1729.8 H24 H22.

> Popular essays with excellent illustrations, many in color. A city view of 1690 shows the Königlichen Hoftheater, and there is a chronology of operas given there 1815–1835. Name and title index.

2397. Sievers, Heinrich. *Hannoversche Musikgeschichte: Dokumente, Kriterien und Meinungen.* Tutzing: Schneider, 1979–1984. 2v. ISBN 3-3952-0282-5; 3-7952-0396-1. ML275.8 .H3 S48.

> V.1 considers the theaters, the contributions of Agostino Steffani as opera director, the brief directorship of Handel, the role of Gottfried Leibniz, and musical theater. There is also a historical narrative of all aspects of music, including theater. V.2 gives descriptive inventories of documents, with running historical commentary. Chapter endnotes, no indexes.

Kassel

2398. *Theater in Kassel: Aus der Geschichte des Staatstheaters Kassel von den Anfängen bis zur Gegenwart.* Kassel: Bärenreiter, 1959. 247p. PN2656 .K36 S77.

> Destroyed in 1943, the old Staatstheater (opened in 1764) was not rebuilt, but a new building, the Opernhaus, opened in 1959. This book gathers studies by various authors dealing with all historical periods; plays, operas, and operettas are discussed. A list of the most performed operas since 1814 is included. Bibliography of about 100 entries, name and subject index.

Leipzig

The first opera house opened in 1693. The Schauspielhaus opened in 1766, was rebuilt 1817, and named Stadttheater. The Neues Stadttheater of 1867 was destroyed in 1943 and rebuilt as Opernhaus in 1960.

2399. *Musikgeschichte Leipzigs in drei Bänden.* Leipzig: Kistner & Siegel, 1926–1941. 3v. ML280.8 .L3 M9.

A well-documented, detailed history ending with 1800. Topical chapters cover forms and approaches, including opera, but most of the work deals with instrumental works, in particular those of J. S. Bach. Name and topic indexes.

2400. Mueller, Georg Hermann. *Das Stadt-Theater in Leipzig, 1862–1887.* Leipzig, 1887.

Not seen. Described by *Kaufman* as a seasonal narrative with names of singers and dates of local premieres; no chronology.

Mannheim

The Nationaltheater opened in 1779, was destroyed in World War II, and replaced by a new building in 1957. Earlier opera in the city took place in the palace theater, 1742–1795.

2401. Meyer, Herbert. *Das Nationaltheater Mannheim, 1929–1979.* Mannheim: Bibliographisches Institut, 1979. 368p. ISBN 3-4110-1563-2. PN2656 .M42 N27.

A narrative history, organized into chapters for each director. Chronology with casts, 1929–1979. Bibliography of about 100 items, name index.

Munich (München)

Opera was heard in the city from 1653, at a granary in Salvatorplatz. The Residenztheater (Cuvilliéstheater) opened in 1753, was destroyed in 1944, and was rebuilt in 1958. The Hoftheater opened in 1818, was renamed Hof.- und Nationaltheater, destroyed in 1943, reopened in 1963, and now houses the Bavarian State Opera (Bayerische Staatsoper). Rudolf Hartmann and Günther Rennert have been directors.

2402. Zenger, Max. *Geschichte der Münchener Oper.* Munich: Verlag für Praktische Kunstwissenschaft, 1923. 547p. ML1729.8 .M96 Z47.

A general narrative of operatic life from 1653, with some illustrations. Name and topic index.

2403. Bolongaro-Crevenna, Hubertus. *"L'arpa festante": Die Münchener Oper, 1653–1825.* Munich: G. D. W. Callwey, 1963. 272p. ML1729.8 .M96 B6.

A documented (218 footnotes) study of the period, with a chronology of performances, giving casts and comments. Bibliography of about 90 titles, place and name index. The book's title recalls the first opera given in Munich, in August 1653.

2404. Wagner, Hans. *200 Jahre Münchener Theaterchronik, 1750–1950.* Munich: Robert Lerche, 1958. 263p. *Nachträge* (Supplement for 1957–1960), 1965. PN2656 .M7 W3.

A daily record of events in 12 theaters. Index of composers with all their works listed; portraits; performer index. Separate indexes for the supplement.

2405. Brunner, Herbert. *Altes Residenztheater in München.* Munich: Bayerische Verwaltung der Staatlichen Schlösser, Gärten und Seen, 1972. 47p. ML1729.8 .M962 R52.

A narrative and chronology of events, with much detail on the plan, decor, and artwork of the structure. François Cuvilliés was the architect of the outstanding building.

2406. Lachner, Johann, and Hildegard Steinmetz. *Das Alte Residenztheater zu München, "Cuvilliés Theater."* Starnberg: J. Keller, 1960. 113p. and 66 plates. NA6840 .G31 M9 S82.

The text is an undocumented historical summary. The book's value is in the fine plates, which show exterior and interior details, statues, and ornamentation.

2407. Böhmer, Karl. *Wolfgang Amadeus Mozarts "Idomeneo" und die Tradition der Karnavalsopern in München.* Mainzer Studien zur Musikwissenschaft, 39. Tutzing: H. Schneider, 1999. x, 443p. ISBN 3-7952-0997-8. ML410 .M93 B676.

A scholarly account of opera in Munich 1745–1777 and of the carnivals of 1767–1777. Discusses libretti and music (recitative, aria, form analysis, *Singspiel*, ballet). *Idomeneo* is analyzed (p.197–334): text, all musical elements, ballet, chorus, instrumentation. Bibliography of about 350 items, no index.

2408. *Nationaltheater: Die Bayerische Staatsoper.* Ed. Hans Zehetmair and Jürgen Schläder. Munich: Bruckman, 1992. 367p. ML1729.8 .M96 N37.

Seventeen essays by various scholars. Topics include Mozart in Munich, Rossini and other Italians, Wagner, the Munich Festspiele, ballet, political context, audiences, and the directorship of Wolfgang Sawallisch. List of premieres 1653–1992. Photos of plans, scenes, persons, and the building. Bibliography of about 200 items, index of names and titles.

See also #308, #309, and #321.

Nuremberg (Nürnberg)

2409. Sandberger, Adolf. "Zur Geschichte der Oper in Nürnberg in der zweiten Halfte des 17. und zu Anfang des 18. Jahrhunderts." *AfM* 1 (1918–1919): 84–107.

A technical discussion, with musical examples, of various works given, among them *Galathea* by Maximilian Zeidler and *Arminius* and *Theseus* by Johann Löhner.

Passau

2410. Schäffer, Gottfried. *Das Fürstbischöfliche und Königliche Theater zu Passau (1783–1883).* Passau: Vereins für Ostbairische Heimatforschung, 1973. xvii, 193p. No ISBN. ML1729.8 .P3 F8.

Foldout plans are included in this general history, plus 18th-century staff lists and performance chronologies with casts. Name index.

Stuttgart

The Komödienhaus opened in 1674, was renamed Hoftheater in 1815, and burned in 1902. Grosses und Kleines Haus opened in 1912, sustained little damage in World War II, and was renovated for reopening in 1984 as Grosses Haus, home of the Stuttgarter Staatsoper.

2411. Gonnenwein, Wolfgang, ed. *Die Oper in Stuttgart: 75 Jahre Littmann-Bau.* Stuttgart: Deutsche Verlags-Anstalt, 1987. 368p. ISBN 3-4210-6379-6. ML1729.8 .S82 S86.

Not seen.

See also Yorke-Long (#87).

Weimar

The city's Hoftheater had a number of distinguished directors and conductors, among them Goethe, Liszt, Hummel, von Bülow, and Richard Strauss. Its golden age is recounted in:

2412. Huschke, Wolfram. *Musik im klassischen und nach-klassischen Weimar, 1756–1861.* Weimar: Böhlaus, 1982. 240p. ML284.8 .W34 H96.

A narrative history, with valuable reference features: chronology of all performances 1848–1858, general musical chronology 1756–1861, table of Mozart performances (280 of them) 1791–1817, etc. Bibliography of about 200 entries, name index, 36 plates. The book is updated by:

2413. Bartels, Adolf. *Chronik des Weimarischen Hoftheaters 1817–1907.* Weimar: Hof- Buchdruckerei, 1908. xxxvi, 375p. PN2656 .W4 B3.

A chronology with dates and casts of local premieres. Indexes of composers, authors, and titles.

Hungary (Hungarian: Magyarország; French: Hongrie; German: Ungarn)

2414. Kertész, Iván. *A Magyar Állami Operaház.* Budapest: Magyar Állami Operaház, 1975. 64p. ML1725.8 .B82 O63.

A narrative account with color photographs of the opera house, dating from 1884; it was formerly known as the Magyar Királyi Operaház (Royal Opera). Without index, chronologies, or other reference features. Text is in five languages.

2415. *A Budapesti Operaház 100 éve.* Budapest: Zeneműkiadó, 1984. 592p.

Not seen, but a summary English translation appeared in *New Hungarian Quarterly* 25 (1984): 194–206; 26 (1985): 194–200. It is a narrative of opera in Budapest before the construction of the new house (the first opera was staged in 1784), with emphasis on the earlier Nemzeti Szinház; then a chronicle of new productions in the new building (no casts), with a list of the regular singers and their seasons; good illustrations. This was the celebration book for the 100th anniversary of the Operaház. Previous celebratory volumes are still of use for certain features. *A Magyar Királyi Operaház* (Budapest: Globus, 1935) has lists of all operas given, and *A Magyar Királyi Operház 1884–1909* (Budapest: Markovits és Gerai, 1909) details the construction of the building and gives a chronology. The next item is the best assemblage of facts:

2416. *A hetvenötéves Magyar Állami Operaház, 1884–1959*. Budapest: Magyar Állami Operaház, 1959. 251p. ML1725.8 .B82 M34.

Includes a composer list of operas and oratorios given both in the present house and in the Nemzeti Szinház. Premiere dates and number of performances of each work (*Faust* was most popular, with 776 performances); also lists of ballets. Portraits of singers and pictures of the theater, staff lists for the 1958–1959 season. No index.

2417. Horányi, Mátyás. *The Magnificence of Eszterháza*. Budapest: Akadémiai Kiadó, 1962; Chester Springs, Penn.: Dufour, 1963. 260p. ML1725.8 .F4 H58.

Originally in Hungarian, 1959. A description of the castle and theater; narrative of music and drama in the 18th century; the opera repertoire (date list of 113 works); list of singers and their years of activity. With 206 footnotes and 82 pictures. Name index. Other material on Eszterháza is at #1022ff.

About 25 recent Hungarian operas are listed in *Oper heute* 1 (#151).

Ireland

The Republic of Ireland, or Eire, comprises the 26 southern counties of the island; it has been independent of Great Britain since 1949. Dublin is the only city with an important operatic history. Its chronicler has been T. J. Walsh.

2418. Walsh, T. J. *Opera in Dublin, 1705–1797: The Social Scene*. Dublin: Figgis, 1973. xv, 386p. ML1731.8 .D82 W3.

A scholarly history of music in the city. The first opera was given in 1705, the first Italian opera in 1761. Casts, notices and reviews, list of premieres of "more important operas," tabulations of performances of French and Italian works given 1761–1789, and information on the first theater building. Bibliography of manuscripts, microfilms, newspaper sources, books, and articles. Name and topic index.

2419. Walsh, T. J. *Opera in Dublin, 1798–1820: Frederick Jones and the Crow Street Theatre*. New York: Oxford U.P., 1993. xiv, 294p. ISBN 0-19-816397-5. ML1731.8 .D82 W242.

Continues the preceding chronicle.

2420. Walsh, T. J. *Opera in Old Dublin, 1819–1838*. Wexford, Ireland: Wexford Festival, 1952. 103p. ML1731.8 .D8 W22.

Emphasizes Italian opera seasons; much information on individual singers. Also a review of the theaters in Dublin. This period was also dealt with in an older work:

2421. Levey, Richard N. *Annals of the Theatre Royal, Dublin, from Its Opening in 1821 to Its Destruction by Fire.* Dublin: Joseph Dollard, 1880.

Not seen. *Kaufman* notes that it is mostly about Italian opera, giving a daily account of visiting companies with dates and casts.

Italy (Italian: Italia; French: Italie; German: Italien)

Editions

2422. *Italian Opera, 1640–1770.* Ed. with introductions by Howard Mayer Brown. New York: Garland, 1977–1983. 60v. ISBN and LC numbers vary. (Cited in this guide as *IO–1640.*)

All volumes are entered under their composers. The set consists of facsimiles of scores with commentaries, except that v.51–60 contain libretti only. A second series, v.61–97, added further scores and, in v.92–97, libretti.

2423. *Italian Opera, 1810–1840.* Ed. with introductions by Philip Gossett. New York: Garland, 1985–1991. 25v. ISBN and LC numbers vary. (Cited in this guide as *IO–1810.*)

Originally to be in 58 volumes, the set emerged in 25v. but with the planned volume numbering retained. Consists of facsimiles, in some cases composite facsimiles from different sources. The works chosen represent a little-known repertoire from the period. They are entered here under their composers.

Bibliographies

2424. Vogel, Emil. *Bibliografia della musica italiana vocale profana pubblicata dal 1500 al 1700.* Rev. ed. Ed. François Lesure and Claudio Sartori. Pomezia: Staderini-Minkoff, 1977. 3v. ML120 .I8 B58.

Originally *Bibliothek der gedruckten weltlichen Vocalmusik Italiens aus den Jahren 1500–1700* (Berlin: A. Haack, 1892; 2v.). The new edition has an added title page: *Il nuovo Vogel. IOM 0439* has a detailed account of the first edition and supplements. *Duckles 5.605* describes the new one. This a basic source of data on vocal music, including operas, arranged by composer; bibliographic information is given, with library locations. Indexes for composers not cited on the titles pages, poets, singers and others mentioned, and first lines. A review of the work, by Howard Mayer Brown (*JAMS* 36 [1983]:142–150) puts the entire effort into perspective.

2425. Caselli, Aldo. *Catalogo delle opere liriche pubblicate in Italia.* Historiae musicae cultores, Biblioteca, 27. Florence: Olschki, 1969. xi, 891p. ML128 .O4 C39.

A list of some 9,000 works produced in Italy, 1600–1800, arranged by composer, identifying the premiere city. General index, city index, title index, libretto index.

Music in General

2426. Levarie, Siegmund. *Musical Italy Revisited: Monuments and Memorabilia: A Supplement to Guidebooks.* New York: Macmillan, 1963. xii, 212p. Reprint, Westport, Conn.: Greenwood, 1973. ISBN 0-8371-6916-4. ML290 .L33

A graceful, learned introduction to Italian musical culture in the form of a guide to each city. Considers history and landmarks of 34 cities. Sixteen plates, bibliography, index.

Elaine Brody's guidebook (#144*) is also useful for landmarks.

2427. *Annuario musicale italiano,* 1–, 1990–. Rome: CIDM, 1990–. Annual. No ISBN or ISSN given. ML21 .I88 A5.

Directory information for associations, performing groups, festivals, soloists, publishers, journals, music business, competitions, music education, government agencies. All opera houses and companies are listed, by city—a useful source of their correct names, in Italian. The 1995 issue is in two volumes, the first in 738 pages, with the second (93p.) being a name index. Another yearbook focuses on opera: *Annuario EDI / CIDIM dell'opera lirica in Italia* (Turin: EDT, 1987–).

Opera: Histories

2428. Bianconi, Lorenzo, and Giorgio Pestelli, ed. *Storia dell'opera italiana.* Turin: EDT, 1987–1988. 6v. ISBN varies. ML1733.S75.

The standard history of opera in the country, each volume consisting of essays by various specialists. Well documented and indexed (combined indexes in v.3 and v.6), with useful city indexes included. Composer indexes and valuable title index with all the composers who set each text. An English translation of v.4, part 2, as *Opera Production and Its Resources,* was done by Lydia G. Cochrane (Chicago: U. of Chicago Press, 1998).

2429. Austin, William W., ed. *New Looks at Italian Opera: Essays in Honor of Donald J. Grout.* Ithaca, N.Y.: Cornell U.P., 1968. ix, 290p. Reprint, Westport, Conn.: Greenwood, 1976. ISBN 0-8371-8761-3. ML1733.1 .A92.

Consists of eight essays, of which the most useful are Claude Palisca, "The Alterati of Florence, Pioneers in the Theory of Dramatic Music" (describing a group that had priority over the Camerata in approach to the music drama); Nino Pirrotta, "Early Opera and Aria" (#654); and William Carl Holmes, "Giacinto Andrea Cicognini's and Antonio Cesti's *Orontea,* 1649" (#682). Indexed by name and title.

2430. Kimbell, David R. B. *Italian Opera.* New York: Cambridge U.P., 1991. xviii, 684p. ISBN 0-521-23533-2. ML1733 .K55.

A popular-style overview of opera history, primarily covering to the end of the 19th century. Social and political background is well outlined, and representative operas are discussed. Monteverdi, Cesti, Metastasio, and Bellini get particular attention. Bibliography of some 400 items, expansive index.

2431. Bonaventura, Arnaldo. *Saggio storico sul teatro musicale italiano.* Livorno: Raffaello Giusti, 1913. xii, 414p. ML1733 .B77.

A well-documented narrative, covering the antecedents of opera, then the 16th and 17th centuries by city, and general trends to 1910. Bibliography and index of names and titles.

Opera: Libretto Studies

For catalogues of libretti see #212ff.

2432. Freeman, Robert S. *Opera without Drama: Currents of Change in Italian Opera, 1675 to 1725.* Studies in Musicology, 35. Ann Arbor, Mich.: UMI Research, 1981. xii, 347p. ISBN 0-8357-1152-8. ML1733 .F73.

Examines changes in the opera libretti before and during the reform period of Zeno and Metastasio. Contemporary writing about opera is carefully evaluated, along with the texts themselves; Zeno gets special attention. Full documentation and bibliography.

2433. Hoffmann, Andreas. *Tugendhafte Helden—Lasterhafte Tyrannen: Italienische Oper am Ende des siebzehnten Jahrhunderts.* Bonn: Orpheus, 1996. 406p. ISBN 3-922626-83-1. ML1733.2 .H644.

The title (Virtuous heroes, wicked tyrants) hardly suggests the wide scope of this important volume. It deals with Venetian libretti on war themes, offering the best sourcebook on the topic. Material considered and documented includes instruments, arias, tonality, rhythm, recitative, and theaters. A list of about 250 singers with their roles and venues includes writings about them. About 1,600 arias are listed, with their sources. Other lists cover impresarios, *ingegnieri,* stage designers, costumers, ballets, and works performed by city. Footnotes, extensive musical examples, chronology for 1682–1745, bibliography of about 150 items, index.

2434. Sartori, Claudio. *I libretti italiani a stampa dalle origini al 1800: Catalogo analitico.* Cuneo: Bertola & Locatelli, 1990–1994. 6v. in 7. No ISBN. ML136 .S270.

Preface in Italian and English. A valuable inventory of 25,437 libretti, with full bibliographic descriptions and library locations. Indexes by place, author, composer, impresario, scene designer, architect, choreographer, costumer, machinists, instrumentalists, singers and roles—insofar as these facts appear in the libretti. Using the city index, one has a chronological performance history in each town, mostly in Italy, but also in other countries.

2435. Goldin, Daniela. "Aspetti della librettistica italiana fra 1770 e 1830." *Analecta musicologica* 21 (1982): 128–191.

Examines trends and techniques of the period, through study of individual authors (Metastasio, Calzabigi, Goldoni, Bertati) and genres. Both *buffa* and *seria* texts are analyzed.

Opera: Theaters

2436. Bustico, Guido. *Bibliografia delle storie e cronistorie dei teatri italiani: Il teatro musicale italiano.* Milan: Bollettino Bibliografico Musicale, 1929. 83p. Z2354 .D8 B9.

A list of books and articles, with some annotations, on theater in the country and by city.

2437. Giovine, Alfredo. *Bibliografia di teatri musicali italiani: Storia e cronologie.* Bari: Laterza, 1982. 67p. ML120 .I8 G51.

About 800 entries, for books, parts of books, and periodical articles; arranged by city. No annotations.

Opera: Precursors and 17th Century

2438. Solerti, Angelo. *Gli albori del melodramma.* Milan: R. Sandron, 1904. 3v. ML1702 .S68.

A scholarly study of ballets, masques, and other precursors of opera up to the early 17th century. Documents and complete texts of many works. No index.

2439. Solerti, Angelo. *Le origini del melodramma: Testimonianze dei contemporanei* ... Turin: Bocca, 1903. vi, 262p. Reprint, Hildesheim: Olms, 1969. ML1702 .S682.

Discusses 54 operas from *Dafne* of 1600 to *La Licasta* of 1644, with full bibliographic detail on publications; reception and analysis. Bibliography of about 100 items, no index.

2440. Donington, Robert. *The Rise of Opera.* Boston: Faber & Faber, 1981. 399p. ISBN 0-571-11674-4. ML1700 .D683 R5.

A major history, covering through the 17th century: well documented and carefully presented. A particularly useful section is on calendars and dating problems. Valuable bibliography of about 450 entries; fine expansive index of names, titles, and subjects.

2441. Palisca, Claude, ed. *The Florentine Camerata: Documentary Studies and Translations.* New Haven, Conn.: Yale U.P., 1989. 234p. ISBN 0-300-03916-6. MT5 .F63.

The emergence of opera in Florence is linked to the activities of an academy known as the Camerata, which met in the home of Count Giovanni Bardi. This is a valuable collection of Italian texts and English translations of eight documents that cast light on the group and their views. The writers are Carlo Valgulio, Vincenzo Galilei (four items), Giovanni Bardi, and Giovanni Batista Strozzi. Palisca has added footnotes to explicate the material and an expansive index. He had an earlier article: "The *Camerata fiorentina:* A Reappraisal," *Studi musicali* 1 (1972): 203–236; reprint, *GL,* v.11.

2442. Pirrotta, Nino, and Elena Povoledo. *Music and Theater from Poliziano to Monteverdi.* New York: Cambridge U.P. , 1981. xi, 382p. ISBN 0-521-23529-7. ML1733 .P5713.

Originally *Li due Orfei, da Poliziano a Monteverdi* (Turin: ERI, 1969). Consists of essays on pre-opera genres (strambotti, intermedie, pastoral, etc.), early arias and recitative, with useful notes and musical examples. No bibliography or index.

2443. Pirrotta, Nino. *Music and Culture in Italy from the Middle Ages to the Baroque: A Collection of Essays.* Cambridge, Mass.: Harvard U.P., 1984. xv, 485p. ISBN 0-674-59108-9. ML290.1 .P57.

A valuable gathering of scholarly essays originally published between 1954 and 1975, of which nine are on the 17th century. Topics include the orchestra, the Camerata, Monteverdi, the libretti of Francesco Melosio. Names of the essays are in *Baron,* 24. Pirrotta finds no central theory that animated the opera pioneers; Caccini was interested in refined singing, and Cavalieri in elegant staging, while Peri and Rinuccini were concerned with dramatic expression.

2444. Sternfeld, Frederick W. *The Birth of Opera.* New York: Oxford U.P., 1993. x, 266p. ISBN 0-19-8161-30-1. ML1733.2 .S73.

An important overview of the new art, considering precursors, definitions, and topics such as the lament, finale, and aria. Sternfeld expanded on the aria study in "*Con che soavità*" (#2461). He died before finalizing and documenting this text. Bibliography of about 600 items, expansive index.

2445. Tomlinson, Gary. "Pastoral and Musical Magic in the Birth of Opera." In *Opera and the Enlightenment* (#91), 7–20.

Relates 16th-century pastoral drama to the early operas through "undercurrents of Neo-Platonism and its persistent magic." The nonverisimilitude of the singing actors was a mimesis of an invisible reality (Platonic idea). This applied both to pastorals (which were partly sung; but all their music is lost) and opera. Early opera was "a product of the same vision of reality, broader than ours, that gave rise to pastoral drama. It was a late outgrowth of the esotericism that burgeoned in Renaissance thought in the wake of the 15th-century revival of Neo-Platonism and related forms of ancient mysticism." Later in the 17th century, operatic magic was "rationalized, concealed behind a willing suspension of skepticism."

2446. Goldschmidt, Hugo. *Studien zur Geschichte der italienishcen Oper im 17. Jahrhundert.* Leipzig: Breitkopf und Härtel, 1901–1904. 2v. Reprints, Hildesheim: Olms, 1967; Wiesbaden: Breitkopf und Härtel, 1967. ML1733.2 .G62.

A scholarly study of baroque opera, stressing Monteverdi, opera in Rome, the orchestra, and comic opera. The entire score of *L'incoronazione di Poppea* is among the musical examples. Poetic and musical structure in typical works is analyzed, along with characterization. Bibliography, index.

2447. Torchi, Luigi. "L'accompagnamento degl'instrumenti nei melodrammi italiani della prima metà del seicento." *RMI* 1 (1894): 7–38.

A study of the opera orchestra, following Agazzari (see #343) in distinguishing between foundation and ornamental instruments. Although sources are few and ambiguous, they suggest that players exhibited great skill in improvising while keeping a balanced sound in the ensemble. Still, Torchi wonders whether the result could typically have been other than a "*charivari.*" Finally he decides that it could have worked, without the need for further written parts of some kind (as suggested by Goldschmidt).

2448. Arteaga, Stefano. *Le rivoluzioni del teatro musicale italiano dalla sua origine fino al presente.* Bologna: C. Trenti, 1783–1788. 3v. ML17333 .A7.

A history and theory of opera. The author finds that opera, in comparison with spoken drama, is better able to move the emotions. Arteaga puts emphasis on elegance, deploring excessive spectacle, crude plot elements, and demonstrative singers. Gluck represents his ideals for simplicity and realism, but he gives little credit to Calzabigi.

2449. Bianconi, Lorenzo. "Production, Consumption and Political Function of Seventeenth- Century Opera." *Early Music History* 4 (1984): 209–296.

Concerns the political and economic context of early Italian opera. Works of Mazzocchi and Cavalli are discussed from that aspect. A useful appendix presents many relevant documents.

2450. Brumana, Biancamaria. "Il Tasso e l'opera nel seicento." In *Tasso, la musica, i musicisti,* ed. Maria Antonella Balsano and Thomas Walker, 137–164 (Florence: Olschki, 1988). ML5 .Q13.

A discussion of Tasso's influence on early opera, with a list of some 200 works based on his poems.

Opera: 18th Century

2451. Strohm, Reinhard. *Die italienische Oper im 18. Jahrhundert.* Wilhelmshaven: Heinrichshofen, 1979. 398p. ISBN 3-7959-0110-3. ML1703 .S87.

A scholarly treatment of 24 operas, *commedie per musica,* intermezzi, and *opere buffe,* citing editions and secondary literature. The composers are discussed and the works analyzed. Bibliography of 261 items, name and topic index.

2452. Strohm, Reinhard. *"Dramma per musica": Italian "opera seria" of the 18th Century.* New Haven, Conn.: Yale U.P., 1998. x, 326p. ISBN 0-380006-454-3. ML1733.3 .S87.

Consists of previously published essays, given here in English. Strohm's basic theme is that Italian opera was "theatre in the first place and music in the second"; thus, he focuses on the libretti. These tended to be serious, since the Arcadian reform had rejected comedy. There is notably strong material on Hasse and Handel. Bibliography of about 250 items, index.

2453. Burt, Nathaniel. "Opera in Arcadia." *MQ* 41 (1955): 145–170.

The Accademia degli Arcadi, established in Rome, 1670, gave its name to the Arcadian movement or reform. Operas written according to Arcadian precepts began with Pollarolo's *La forza del virtù* (1693), which was the "point of origin for the development of Metastasian *opera seria*." That work is analyzed, as is *La Dori* (1663) by Appolonio Appoloni. Changes from 17th- to 18th-century opera are discussed in terms of form, tone, and structure, defining a move away from "bawdiness and emotional wallowing" toward a "well balanced edifice, a play reasonable in its architecture"—that is, Arcadian—"a moral atmosphere so rarefied as to be almost unbreathable."

2454. Zanetti, Roberto. *Storia della musica italiana da Sant'Ambrogio a noi.* Busto Arsizio: Bramante, 1978. 3v. ML290.3 .Z36.

A thorough scholarly history, with great value for its view of the 18th century. Considers all genres of opera and all the major composers and librettists. Places opera in the context of other stage presentations. Bibliography, index.

2455. Algarotti, Francesco. *Saggio sopra l'opera in musica.* 2nd ed. Livorno: Coltellini, 1763. 157p. ML3858 .A37.

First edition, 1755. Translated as *An Essay on the Opera Written in Italian by Count Algarotti . . .* (Glasgow: R. Urie, 1768). There is a partial translation in *Strunk.* Algarotti's essay was greatly influential in shaping ideas about good and bad in opera. Mythological subjects were good, historical subjects bad. Most of what Algarotti saw was in need of change: overtures were irrelevant, secco recitative boring, arias lacked dramatic truth, stage behavior was foolish, dances were extraneous. He called for reform, along more austere French lines.

2456. Lühning, Helga. "Die *cavatina* in der italienischen Oper um 1800." *Analecta musicologica* 21 (1982): 333–368.

In the 18th century the open form and usual brevity of the *cavatina* contrasted with the formal and lengthy *aria seria.* In the 19th century *cavatina* was simply the name given to the opening aria of a lead singer—it had the same form and length as any other. The transition is demonstrated through 17 extended examples and a sure technical analysis.

2457. Dent, Edward. "Ensembles and Finales in 18th-Century Italian Opera." *SIMG* 11 (1909–1910): 543–569; 12 (1910–1911): 112–138.

A major study of the ensembles and finales in earlier Neapolitan operas, especially those by Alessandro Scarlatti. His ensembles are found to be like arias, in the sense of conveying a single emotion instead of a complex interaction among the characters. The evolving freedom in treatment of comic ensembles is discussed.

2458. Heartz, Daniel. "The Creation of the *buffo finale* in Italian Opera." *PRMA* 104 (1977–1978): 67–78.

Traces the *buffo finale* to Galuppi's *L'Arcadia in Brenta* (1749) and *Il mondo della luna* (1750). The texts were by Goldoni, who put a similar *finale* into Mozart's *La finta giardiniera.*

2459. *The New Grove Italian Baroque Masters: Monteverdi, Frescobaldi, Cavalli, Corelli, Alessandro Scarlatti.* Ed. Denis Arnold. London: Macmillan, 1984. 376p. ISBN 0-333-38235-8. ML390 .N492.

Authoritative essays, revised from articles in *NG,* with updated bibliographies. Expansive index.

2460. Strohm, Reinhard. "Italienische Opernarien des frühen Settecento (1720–1730)." *Analecta musicologica* 16, part 1: 1–268; part 2: 1–342.

Two full volumes of the journal are devoted to this valuable monograph, which considers the economic and social context of opera in Italy and the demands of audiences. It was audience preference for certain kinds of aria that led composers to standardize the form. Strohm uses 18 arias to exemplify his views, drawing on such composers as Alessandro Scarlatti, Vinci, Gasparini, Pollarolo, Porpora, Leo, Vivaldi, and Hasse. He examines their scoring, declamation, musical structure, and the da capo form that emerged as typical of the period.

2461. *"Con che soavità": Studies in Italian Opera, Song, and Dance, 1580–1740.* Ed. Iain Fenlon and Tim Carter. New York: Oxford U.P., 1995. viii, 336p. ISBN 0-19-816370-3. ML1633 .C66.

A valuable collection of 13 essays, including these on opera which are cited separately: Eric Cross on Vivaldi's *Tamerlano* (#1961), Winton Dean on *Alcina* (#979), William Porter on laments (#1229), Michael Talbot on Albinoni's *Pimpinone* (#456), and Reinhard Strohm on Neapolitans in Venice (#2532). Indexed. The book's title is drawn from a Monteverdi madrigal.

2462. "Crosscurrents and the Mainstream of Italian Serious Opera, 1730–1790." *Studies in Music* (U. of Western Ontario) 7–1 (1982).

A journal issue devoted to six papers from a symposium held at the U. of Western Ontario in February 1982. Included are Nino Pirrotta, "Metastasio and the Demands of His Literary Environment," Don Neville, "Moral Philosophy in the Metastasian Drama," Michael F. Robinson, "The Ancient and the Modern: A Comparison of Metastasio and Calzabigi," and one entered separately: Stephen Willis on Cherubini (#698). An essay by Daniel Heartz, "Mozart's Tragic Muse," was reprinted in his *Mozart's Operas* (#1276).

2463. Corte, Andrea della. *L'opera comica italiana nel '700.* Bari: Laterza, 1923. 2v. ML1733.3 .C68.

Considers the antecedents of comic opera, such as comic parts in serious opera, and the fully developed comic works of all the important composers in the 18th century. Footnoted but without musical examples or bibliography. Name and title index.

2464. Verti, Roberto. "Indizi su repertorio, geografia e milieu delle farse per musica." In *I vicini di Mozart* (#90), v.2, 597–624.

Addresses the problem of defining the *farsa* and discusses the diffusion of the form from Venice to other cities. Table of performances in various cities, 1783–1794. *Farsa* in the 19th century is taken up by Morelli (#2477).

2465. Troy, Charles E. *The Comic Intermezzo: A Study in the History of Eighteenth-Century Italian Opera.* Studies in Musicology, 9. Ann Arbor, Mich.: UMI Research, 1979. xvi, 242p. ISBN 0-8357-0992-2. ML1733.3 .T6.

Comic elements were introduced into serious opera via the intermezzo, a humorous sketch performed between the acts. Its origin is ably traced in this useful study, along with its principal composers, singers, and troupes. The libretti are taken up, as well as elements of the comic style. There is discussion of musical elements: recitative, aria, duet, and accompaniment. Backnotes, bibliography of primary and secondary materials (about 300 items), index of names and titles.

See also Talbot (#456).

Opera: 19th Century

2466. Nicolaisen, Jay. *Italian Opera in Transition, 1871–1893*. Ann Arbor, Mich.: UMI Research, 1980. 315p. ISBN 0-8357-1121-X. ML1733 .N5.

Based on the author's dissertation, U. of California, Berkeley, 1977. A thorough, interesting examination of a period that is receiving much current attention. Concentrates on the development of the dramatic potential in compositions that followed the period of Rossini. Combines historical and analytic modes; well documented with footnotes, musical examples, list of scores consulted, and list of writings consulted (about 120 items). There is a list of all reviews for each opera and a list of operas most performed at La Scala, 1870–1890 (leaders were *Aida, L'ebrea (La juive), Gli ugonotti,* and *Faust*). An appendix gives a table of revisions Puccini made for *Edgar*. Texts are quoted in Italian only, without translations. Expansive name, title, and topic index. Treatments of individual composers are entered separately in this guide.

2467. Weaver, William. *The Golden Century of Italian Opera, from Rossini to Puccini*. New York: Thames & Hudson, 1980. 256p. ISBN 0-5000-1240-7. ML1733 .W41.

A popular survey, without notes or bibliography. Good pictures, index.

2468. Rosselli, John. *The Opera Industry in Italy from Cimarosa to Verdi: The Role of the Impresario*. New York: Cambridge U.P., 1984. 214p. ISBN 0-521-25732-8. ML1733 .R78.

An economic history of opera in Italy, dealing with commercial matters (receipts, fees), governance, agents, journalists, and the individual impresarios. Rosselli made a thorough examination of archives in theaters and towns, as well as the correspondence of singers and other players of the time. With eight tables and a graph on opera production, ca. 1750–1900. The power of the impresario was at its peak from 1780 to 1830. Backnotes, no bibliography, expansive index of names and topics. The same ground is covered in a popular (undocumented) style in the author's *Music and Musicians in Nineteenth-Century Italy* (Portland, Ore.: Amadeus, 1991; ML290.4 .R677).

2469. Balthazar, Scott L. "Aspects of Form in the *ottocento* Libretto." *COJ* 7 (1995): 23–35.

During the first half of the 19th century "eventual replacement of circular and static elements of design with more linear ones, and the fusion of separate temporal states into a continuum" took place in opera stories. The article shows how 18th-century plot devices were rejected in this period and how new ideas—tragic endings, intense personal conflicts, the love triangle—appeared.

2470. Cancelled entry.

2471. Balthazar, Scott L. "The *primo ottocento* Duet and the Transformation of the Rossinian Code." *JM* 7–4 (Fall 1989): 471–497.

Rossini's procedures were maintained in the early 19th century. Later, Bellini, Donizetti, and Verdi changed the musical and dramatic design. Duets of 1815–1830 are analyzed.

See also #511.

2472. Budden, Julian. "Wagnerian Tendencies in Italian Opera." In *Music and Theatre* (#68), 299–332.

Lohengrin was the first Wagner work to be performed in Italy (Bologna, 1871, in Italian); the premiere was a success, but at La Scala in 1873 there was rioting. *Tristan* was acclaimed in Bologna, 1888; that event, and the publication in 1894 of an Italian translation of *Oper und Drama,* brought Wagner great renown; among younger composers he was the "major prophet of the age." Puccini and Catalani were enthralled by him. However, Wagnerian theory never took root in Italy, and the *Ring* was not admired. Clear influences on Puccini are described: his orchestra tells of "things that are not in the text," and motives foreshadow events to come.

2473. Celletti, Rodolfo. "Il vocalismo italiano da Rossini a Donizetti." *Analecta musicologica* 5 (1968): 267–294; 7 (1969): 214–247.

The first part of this study, on Rossini, was also published separately (#1579). It concerns the sunset of *bel canto,* marked by the changing roles given to tenor, soprano, baritone, and contralto and their voice ranges. Rossini's practice of writing out voice parts entirely replaced the earlier freedom of singers to improvise and ornament.

2474. Gossett, Philip. "The Chorus in *Risorgimento* Opera." *COJ* 2 (1990): 41–64.

Considers the chorus as a political statement—representing "a people," usually dominated by a foreign power. Examples are Rossini's *La donna del lago* and *Guillaume Tell* and Verdi's *La battaglia di Legnano.*

2475. Powers, Harold S. "One Halfstep at a Time: Tonal Transposition and 'Split Association' in Italian Opera." *COJ* 7 (1995): 135–164.

Departures from original tonality were often made via half-step transpositions to suit performers. Powers agrees with Allan Atlas (#1484), who thought that Puccini, at least, did those things in the context of an alternative tonal structure. Powers also deals with the views of Roger Parker and James Hepokowski on the transposition issue. His conclusion is that in nearly all cases of transposition there were musical justifications: they "allow the passage in question to participate in the web of tonalities in a different manner, but not one that is random or without tonally expressive implications."

2476. Maehder, Jürgen. "The Origins of Italian *Literaturoper*: *Guglielmo Ratcliff, La figlia di Iorio, Parisina,* and *Francesca da Rimini.*" In *Reading Opera* (#218), 92–128.

A *Literaturoper* is "an opera based on a text that existed as a play before it was set to music," the play and the libretto being by different persons. Discusses Mascagni's *Guglielmo Ratcliff,* drawn from a text by Heinrich Heine; Franchetti's *La figlio d'Iorio,* from a play by D'Annunzio; and Mascagni's *Parisina,* also from D'Annunzio. The librettists all made some effort to retain the poetic or textual nature of the original text. But after World War I there was no more *Literaturoper*. The emphasis shifted to the ready-made libretto.

2477. Morelli, Giovanni. "Ascendenze farsesche nella drammaturgia seria italiana del grande ottocento." In *I vicini di Mozart* (#90), v.2, 641–688.

Discusses the term *farsa* and the nature of its texts. Notes similarity to serious drama, in plots that had reversal of fortunes, and use of contemporary themes and events—precursors of *verismo*. Also cites differences between comic and serious stories. The analysis is about textual features, not music, but Morelli does comment at the end on the gradual increase of singing and the decline of spoken lines.

2478. Senici, Emanuele. "Virgins of the Rocks: Alpine Landscape and Female Purity in Early Nineteenth-Century Italian Opera." Ph.D. diss., Cornell U., 1998. 306p.

2479. Smart, Mary Ann. "*Dalla tomba uscita*: Representations of Madness in Nineteenth-Century Italian Opera." Ph.D. diss., Cornell U., 1994. 352p.

2480. *The New Grove Masters of Italian Opera: Rossini, Donizetti, Bellini, Verdi, Puccini.* Ed. Philip Gossett et al. New York: Norton, 1983. 353p. ISBN 0-393-01685-4. ML390 .N473.

Articles from *NG,* with updated worklists and an index to the volume.

Opera: 20th Century

2481. Rossi, Nick. *Opera in Italy Today: A Guide.* Portland, Ore.: Amadeus, 1995. 432p. ISBN 0-9313-4077-2. ML1733 .R8.

A tour of opera houses, including regional theaters, and festivals. Bibliography and index.

2482. Fearn, Raymond. *Italian Opera since 1945.* Amsterdam: Harwood Academic Publishers, 1997. xviii, 258p. ISBN 90-5755-002-4. ML1733 .P43.

A useful examination of works by Dallapiccola, Goffredo Petrassi, Berio, Nono, Giacomo Manzoni, Maderna, Rota, Bussotti, Camillo Togni, Aldo Clementi, Lorenzo Ferrero, Azio Corghi, and Luca Lombardi. Technical analysis, genesis, letters and writings of the composers, reception, overview of opera in society. Chronology of principal operas, bibliography of about 50 items, discography, expansive index.

2483. Stenzl, Jürg. *Von Giacomo Puccini zu Luigi Nono: Italienische Musik 1922–1952: Faschismus, Resistenz, Republik*. Buren (Netherlands): Frits Knuf, 1990. 237p. ISBN 90-6027-639-6. ML290.5 .S84.

A narrative review of the period, well documented; stresses the political roles of the composers. Useful bibliographic essay, index of names and titles.

Cities and Regions

Arezzo

2484. Grandini, Alfredo. *Cronache musicali del Teatro Petrarca di Arezzo: Il primo cinquantennio (1833–1882)*. Florence: Olschki, 1995. xi, 377p. ISBN 88-222-43552. ML1733.8 .A752 P4.

A well-documented history and a chronology with casts, plus fine color plates of the theater and scenes from operas presented. Bibliography of about 100 items, name index.

Bari

2485. Giovine, Alfredo. *L'opera in musica in teatri di Bari: Statistiche delle rappresentazioni dal 1830 al 1969*. Bari: Civiltà Musicale Publiese, 1969. 116p. ML1733.8 .B3 G76.

A list of 215 operas, ballets, and operettas given in 20 theaters, for a total of 4,080 events during 1830–1969. Seasonal tabulations of performances. Discussion of the opera houses and names of musicians. No index.

2486. Giovine, Alfredo. *Il Teatro Petruzzelli di Bari: Stagioni liriche dal 1963 al 1982*. Bari: Fratelli Laterza, 1983. 188p. No ISBN. ML1733.8 .B37 T42.

A chronology, with commentary, of the 158 operas (3,070 performances) given in the major theater of the city. The Petruzzelli opened in 1903, burned in 1991; it was the fourth largest of Italy's theaters. Indexes of titles, composers, and participants. Giovine has similar books on two other Bari theaters: Teatro Margherita di Bari (1967) and Teatro Piccinni (1970).

Bergamo

2487. Comuzio, Ermanno. *Il Teatro Donizetti*. Bergamo: Lucchetti, 1990. 2v. ISBN 8-8858-3965-8. ML1733.8 .B4.

The Teatro Riccardi opened in 1791 and was renamed for the city's favorite son in 1897. This is a documented history, with a chronology of performances to 1989.

Bologna

2488. Trezzini, Lamberto, Sergio Paganelli, and Roberto Verti. *Due secoli di vita musicale: Storia del Teatro Comunale di Bologna*. 2nd ed. Bologna: Nuova Alfa, 1987. 3v. ISBN 88-7779-90024. ML1733.8 .B442 .T43.

First edition, 1966. V.1, a narrative history, with photos of the building; v.2, chronology, 1763–1966; v.3, chronology, 1966–1986. The chronologies include cast information, publications, and references. Footnoted, with indexes of persons and titles.

2489. Bignami, Luigi. *Cronologia di tutti gli spettacoli rappresentati nel Gran Teatro Comunale di Bologna*. Bologna: Agenzia Commerciale, 1880. 248p. ML1733.8 .B7 B4.

A chronology of operas and ballets given in the Teatro Comunale from 1763 to 1880, with reprints of advertising and names of casts. Indexes of titles, companies, composers, artists (including orchestral players), and staff. No general index.

2490. Giacomelli, Renzo. *Il Teatro Comunale di Bologna: Storia aneddotica e cronache di due secoli, 1763–1963*. Bologna: Tamari, 1965. 216p. ML1733.8 B7 G5.

Letters, documents, and anecdotes, including some chronologies and cast information. List of ballets in title order, 1763–1879; lists of dramatic performances and operas. Composer list but no index.

2491. Ricci, Corrado. *I teatri di Bologna nei secoli XVII e XVIII: Storia aneddotica*. Bologna: Monti, 1888. xxi, 736p. PN2686 .B6 R5.

A footnoted, narrative history of each theater, with chronologies 1600–1799. Index of titles, theaters, names, and topics.

2492. Hill, Laura Callegari. *La librettistica bolognese nei secoli XVII e XVIII: Catalogo ed indici*. Rome: Torre d'Orfeo, 1989. xliii, 350p. ISBN 88-85147-21-6. ML1733 .C24 L4.

A list in date order of libretti published for some 1,327 operas, oratorios, dramatic cantatas, and serenades; with useful commentaries. Indexed by title, genre, place of performance, composers, librettist, singers, choreographers, dancers, and dedicatees.

An older work describes the earliest performances of opera, which began in 1600: Alessandro Machiavelli, *Serie cronologica de' drammi recitati su de' pubblici teatri di Bologna dall'anno 1600 sino al corrente 1727* (Bologna: Soci Filopatri, 1737; 94p.; ML1733.8 .B7). Splendid color photos of the Comunale with scenes from 20th-century productions are in *Il teatro per la città* (Bologna: Teatro Comunale, 1998; 183p.; ML1733.8 .B442 T437). An extensive renovation of the theater was completed in 1981.

Catania

2493. Danzuso, Domenico, and Giovanni Idonea. *Musica, musicisti e teatri a Catania*. Palermo: Publisicula, 1985. 513p. ML290.8 .C27 D25.

Not seen. Described in *Kaufman* as a "magnificent" volume, with chapters on native sons Bellini and Pacini and the many opera houses in the city. Most important is the old Teatro Comunale, later the Teatro Massimo Bellini. Stories of the singers, chronologies of all the houses with casts, color plates.

Cremona

2494. Santoro, Elia. *Il teatro di Cremona*. Cremona: Pizzorini, 1969–1972. 4v. ML1733.8 .C72 N44.

A documented history with seasonal chronologies, giving casts; photos of persons and advertising posters. Bibliography, comprehensive index of names and titles.

Florence (Firenze)

2495. Nagler, Alois Maria. *Theatre Festivals of the Medici, 1539–1637.* Trans. George Hickenlooper. New Haven, Conn.: Yale U.P., 1964. xx, 190p. and 136 full-page illustrations. Reprint, New York: Da Capo, 1976. ISBN 0-3067-0779-9. PN2679 .N18.

The festivals, mostly for weddings, were spoken plays with musical intermezzi until 1608; then they became pure opera. Nagler gives elaborate descriptions of all aspects of 16 presentations, keyed to the illustrations. Details of the Uffizi Theater (1586). Name index.

2496. Weaver, Robert Lamar, and Norma Wright Weaver. *A Chronology of Music in the Florentine Theater, 1590–1750.* Detroit Studies in Music Bibliography, 38. Detroit: Information Coordinators, 1978. 421p. ISBN 0-911772-83-9. ML1733.8 .F6 W4.

A documented history with chronological lists of stage works performed; casts are given, along with library locations of scores and libretti. Bibliography, name and title index. Continued by the next entry:

2497. Weaver, Robert Lamar, and Norma Wright Weaver. *A Chronology of Music in the Florentine Theater, 1751–1800: Operas, Prologues, Farces, Intermezzos, Concerts, and Plays with Incidental Music.* Detroit Studies in Music Bibliography, 70. Warren, Mich.: Harmonie Park, 1993. xxxvii, 996p. ISBN 0-8999-0064-X. ML113 .D44, no. 70.

Extends the preceding entry.

2498. De Angelis, Marcello. *La musica del Granduca: Vita musicale e correnti critiche a Firenze, 1800–1855.* Florence: Vallecchi, 1978. 225p. No ISBN. ML290.8 .F6 D27.

A description of musical life, drawn from contemporary periodicals.

2499. Morini, Ugo. *La R. Accademia degli Immobili ed il suo teatro "La Pergola," 1649–1925.* Pisa: F. Simoncini, 1926. vi, 298p. ML1733.8 .F6 I7.

The Immobili produced opera as early as 1649 and built the great theater La Pergola in 1656—it still stands. This is a narrative history, without tables or lists, but it does cite works performed in each season. Chronologies for the years 1913–1925 are given. No index.

2500. Pinzauti, Leonardo. *Il Maggio Musicale fiorentino dalla prima alla trentesima edizione.* Florence: Vallecchi, 1967. 501p. ML38 .F63 P66.

A narrative history and chronology of the music festival, giving casts, 1928–1967. With 109 plates, most in color. Name index.

2501. Holmes, William C. *Opera Observed: Views of a Florentine Impresario in the Early Eighteenth Century.* Chicago: U. of Chicago Press, 1993. ix, 256p. ISBN 0-226-34970-5. ML1733.8 .F6 H6.

Presents the personal papers of Luca degli Albizzi (1638–1704) and his son Luca Casimiro Albizzi (1664–1745), located in the Palazzo Guicciardini, Florence, and related materials in the Accademia degli Immobili. Casimiro was involved in productions at La Pergola from 1718 to 1738; most of the observations are his. Interesting letters are included, to composers (e.g., Vivaldi) and singers; as well as details on productions, including stage design. Bibliography, index.

Genoa (Genova)

2502. *Teatro Comunale dell'Opera.* Genoa: Teatro Comunale, 1973. Not paged. ML1733.8 .G3 B8.

A popular history of opera in the city, featuring many fine photographs. Lists of singers and their roles, with performance dates, 1900–1930. No index.

2503. Schmuckher, Aidano. *Storia del Teatro Carlo Felice.* Genoa: Compagnia dei Librai, 1987. v, 163p. ML1733.8 .B32 S3.

A straight narrative; well documented, from the opening of the theater (third largest in Europe) in 1828; of interest primarily for the account of reconstruction after the damage of World War II. (The new Carlo Felice was inaugurated in 1991.) Essays on the directors of the orchestra; black-and-white photographs. Bibliography of more than 1,000 entries, name and title index.

2504. Frassoni, Edilio. *Due secoli di lirica a Genova.* Genoa: Cassa di Risparmio, 1980. 2v. ML1733 .F72 D83.

Not seen.

2505. Vallebona, G. B. *Il Teatro Carlo Felice: Cronistoria di un secolo, 1828–1928.* Genoa: Cooperativa Fascista Poligrafici, 1928. 363p. ML1733.8 .G3 V2.

A very detailed account of the building from its opening, including drawings, dimensions, and photographs. An informative chronology gives names of artists and comments on reception. The total number of performances was 15,776. List of dramatic companies, by date, with their artists. Title index of 339 operas and 350 ballets, with number of times each was staged and the dates.

2506. Brocca, Ambrogio. *Il Teatro Carlo Felice: Cronistoria dal 7 aprile 1828 al 27 febbraio 1898.* Genoa: A. Montorfano, 1898. 248p. ML1733.8 .G3 B8.

Largely superseded by the preceding entry but has some additional facts in the historical notes on performers and productions. Annual list of works, with casts. Title list of operas, with number of performances; same for ballets. Name index.

2507. Giazotto, Remo. *La musica a Genova nella vita pubblica e privata dal XIII al XVIII secolo.* Genoa: Società Industrie Grafiche e Lavorazioni Affini, 1951. 371p. ML290.8 .G33 G4.

A narrative of music history, drawing on all archival documents and illustrating them. Index of names and libraries.

Lucca

2508. Biagi Ravenni, Gabriela. *Diva panthera: Musica e musicisti al servizio dello stato lucchese*. Lucca: Accademia Lucchese di Scienze, Lettere, ed Arti, 1993. 215p. ML290.8 .L93 B5.

> Not seen. Described in *Duckles* 4.319 as a music history with bibliography and indexes. The Teatro Pantera gave its name to the title of the book.

2509. Paoli Catelani, Bice. *Il teatro comunale del "Giglio" di Lucca*. Pescia: Artidoro Benedetti, 1941. 111p. ML1733.8 .L8 P4.

> A history of opera in the city and a description of the theater. Chronology for 1819–1936 with names of principal singers; list of operas according to number of performances (*Il barbiere di Siviglia* was first, *Traviata* second).

2510. Diquinzio, Mary Elizabeth. "Opera in the Duchy of Lucca, 1817–1847." Ph.D. diss., Catholic U., 1997. 210p.

Mantua (Mantova)

2511. Amadei, Giuseppe. *I centocinquant'anni del Sociale nella storia dei teatri di Mantova*. Mantua: C.I.T.E.M., 1973. viii, 662p. ML1733.8 .M22 T42.

> The Sociale, which opened in 1822, was one of the two important houses of Mantua, the other being the Andreani (1862). Chronologies for both theaters and of others in the city are given by genre, with a historical narrative, composer list of works performed, and 79 illustrations. Bibliography of about 75 items, name index.

2512. Fenlon, Iain. *Music and Patronage in Sixteenth-Century Mantua*. New York: Cambridge U.P., 1980. 2v. ISBN 0-521-22905-7. ML290.8 .M2 F4.

> A documented history of the period, centered on the Gonzaga family and its control of cultural life. The second volume is a collection of music by Mantuan composers, including Monteverdi. Bibliography and name index.

2513. Fenlon, Iain. "Music and Spectacle at the Gonzaga Court, c. 1580–1600." *PRMA* 103 (1976–1977): 90–105.

> A chronology of theatrical presentations, with comments that bring out the influences of Ferrara and Florence on the theater of Mantua.

2514. Parisi, Susan Helen. "Ducal Patronage of Music in Mantua 1587–1627: An Archival Study." Ph.D. diss., U. of Illinois, 1989. xxii, 782p.

Messina

2515. Uccello, Leobaldo. *Lo spettacolo nei secoli a Messina*. Palermo: Publisicula, 1986. 564p.

> Not seen. *Kaufman* describes it as "stunning" if not always reliable; it gives chronologies for all houses.

2516. Scaglione, Nitto. *La vita artistica del Teatro Vittorio Emanuele.* Messina: La Sicilia, 1921.

Not seen. *Kaufman* describes it as an "excellent chronology" with dates and casts, 1852–1908.

Milan (Milano)

2517. Manzella, Domenico, and Emilio Pozzi. *I teatri di Milano.* Milan: Mursia, 1971. 306p. PN2686 .M5 M3.

Histories of all the theaters, including cabarets; well illustrated. No chronologies. Bibliography, index of theaters and of names.

2518. Daulmi, Davide. *Le origini dell'opera a Milano (1598–1649).* Amsterdam: Brepols, 1998. xvii, 626p.

Not seen. A review in *NRMI* says that it "brings the times to life." It describes the historical and cultural conditions that permitted the rise of opera in the city: palaces, festivals, carnivals, the influence of Marguerite of Austria. Sources, illustrations, chronology.

2519. Cambiasi, Pompeo. *Rappresentazioni date nei reali teatri di Milano, 1778–1872.* 2nd ed. Milan: Ricordi, 1872. 120p. PN2686 .M6 C2.

Chronologies for La Scala and the Teatro della Canobbiana, with lists of all participants (conductors, impresarios, orchestra players).

Milan: Teatro alla Scala

Il Teatro alla Scala (La Scala) opened in 1778, the largest theater in Europe. It was nearly destroyed by bombs in 1943 and was rebuilt in 1946. Of the great many books available, these offer a good combination of history and iconography:

2520. Tintori, Giampiero. *Cronologia: Opere, balletti, concerti, 1778–1977.* Gorie: Grafica Gutenberg, 1979. xiii, 475p. ML1733.8 .M5 T45.

The most complete chronology, covering all events in the Teatro and the associated Piccola Scala. Names of all performers are given. Footnoted and indexed. Introduction in Italian and English, but the text is in Italian only.

2521. Gatti, Carlo. *Il Teatro alla Scala nella storia e nell'arte (1778–1963).* Milan: Ricordi, 1964. 2v. ML1733.8 .M5 G3.

A narrative history, without footnotes. Also a chronology of all performances, arranged by genre, and lists of directors. With 22 color plates and 76 pages of photographs. Indexes of titles, names, and genres.

2522. Arruga, Lorenzo. *La Scala.* New York: Praeger, 1975. 314p. ISBN 0-275-53680-7. ML1733.8 .M6 A772.

The best popular history in English, including 476 photographs. Index of names and works. No chronology or bibliography.

Milan: Other Theaters

2523. Gutierrez, Beniamino. *Il Teatro Carcano (1803–1914).* 2nd ed. Milan: Sonzogno, 1916. viii, 197, xvi p.

Not seen. The theater was a poor rival to La Scala but did have premieres of *La sonnambula* and *Anna Bolena*.

2524. Paglicci Brozzi, Antonio. *Il Regio Ducal Teatro di Milano nel secolo XVIII.* Milan: Ricordi, 1894. 129p. ML1733.8 .M5 P3.

A history of the theater, with detailed chronology.

2525. Viale Ferrero, Mercedes. "Torino e Milano nel tardo settecento: Repertori a confronto." In *I vicini di Mozart* (#90), v.1, 99–138.

Considers operas performed at La Scala and the Teatro Canobbiana in Milan, and at the Teatro Regio and Teatro Carignano in Turin, for the period 1778–1815. There was little overlapping of repertoire between the two cities. Of 282 comic operas given in one or the other city, only 95 were staged in both. And there was little concordance in *opera seria* either. Economic and political reasons are proffered, along with full chronologies for the four theaters.

Modena

2526. Tardini, Vincenzo. *I teatri di Modena.* Modena: Gorghieri, Pellequi, 1899–1902. 3v. Supplement (1903) bound in v.3. ML1733.8 .M6 T2.

The first two volumes are concerned with spoken dramas, the third is about opera. Chronology from 1594 (Orazio Vecchi's madrigal-comedy, *L'Amfiparnaso)* to 1903, with casts. Name and title index. Earlier years are tabulated in Alessandro Gandini, *Cronistoria dei teatri di Modena dal 1539 al 1871* (Modena: Tipografia Sociale, 1873; 3v.).

2527. Gherpelli, Giuseppe. *L'opera nei teatri di Modena.* Modena: Artioli, 1988. 298p. ML1733.8 .M6 G43.

An illustrated narrative of the stage, with a chronology of each theater. Bibliography, index of names and titles.

Naples (Napoli; German: Neapel)

2528. Degrada, Francesco. "L'opera napoletana." In Barblan (#76), part 1, v.1, 237–332.

The best recent study of opera in Naples and the operatic style associated with its composers. Covers terminology, theaters, management, conservatories, social aspects, composers, and technical elements of the works.

2529. Downes, Edward O. D. "The Neapolitan Tradition in Opera." In *Report of the Eighth Congress of the International Musicological Society, New York, 1961,* ed. Jan La Rue, 277–284 (Kassel: Bärenreiter, 1961).

The designation "Neapolitan school" was long applied to operas by composers of Naples (among them Porpora, Vinci, Leo, Pergolesi, Traetta, Piccinni, Sacchini, Paisiello, Alessandro Scarlatti, and Cimarosa) in the 18th century. Downes questioned the validity of this concept, and other scholars have followed. It is not clear whether Neapolitan composers had a style distinguishable from that of other regions.

2530. Wolff, Hellmuth Christian. "The Fairy Tale of the Neapolitan Opera." In *Studies in Eighteenth-Century Music* (#73), 401–406.

Supports Downes (previous entry) and other skeptics about the existence of a distinct style, holding that the term "Neapolitan opera" "can best be employed for certain Neapolitan dialect comedies, but will certainly not serve for the characterization of the whole Italian opera from about 1700 to 1750." Indeed the so-called innovations attributed to the Neapolitans actually began in Venice. A possible designation for Italian opera of the period is "Metastasian opera." Wolff reviews the earlier literature on the subject. Daniel Heartz is one who favors retaining the term "Neapolitan opera" and gives reasons in "Opera and the Periodization of Eighteenth-Century Music," in *Report of the Tenth Congress of the International Musicological Society, Ljublana, 1967,* 160–168 (Kassel: Bärenreiter, 1970). Reprint, *GL,* v.11.

See also #2532.

2531. Robinson, Michael F. *Naples and Neapolitan Opera.* Oxford: Clarendon, 1972. ix, 281p. Reprint, New York: Da Capo, 1984. ISBN (Oxford) 0-19-816124-7. ML12733.8 .N3 R6.

A valuable examination of texts and scores, with extended musical examples, for the period from 1650 to 1800. Covers serious and comic opera, including overtures and other orchestral pieces. Extensive footnotes, bibliography, index.

2532. Strohm, Reinhard. "The Neapolitans in Venice." In *"Con che soavità"* (#2461), 249–274.

Notes that little has been published since the 1970s on the "Neapolitan school," because "the whole principle of style periodization in music has gone out of fashion." Still it is worth asking "what happened to Italian opera—especially *opera seria*—in the 18th century, and whether a qualified case for Neapolitan leadership can be made after all. I believe it can." He suggests that an approach through "operatic practice and business" rather than musical style may clarify how the composers of Naples took over the Venetian stage.

See also #2529, #2530.

2533. Tintori, Giampiero. *L'opera napoletana.* Milan: Ricordi, 1958. 301p. ML1733.8 .N3 T5.

A history, most useful for its list of about 2,000 operas, arranged by composer, with librettists and premiere data. Index to persons and theaters.

2534. *Napoli e il teatro musicale in Europa tra sette e ottocento: Studi in onore di Friedrich Lippmann.* Ed. Bianca Maria Antolini and Wolfgang Witzenmann. Quaderni della Rivista musicale italiana di musicologia, 28. Florence: Olschki, 1993. 448p. ISBN 88-222-4026-X. ML1733 .N26 or ML5 Q13, no. 28.

A useful collection of 20 essays; these are entered separately: G. Salvetti on Pietro Guglielmi (#936), Marita McClymonds on Haydn's *Armida* (#1038), and Fabrizio della Seta on *La traviata* (#1935).

2535. *La musica a Napoli durante il seicento. Atti del Convegno Internazionale di Studi.* Ed. Domenico Antonio D'Alessandro and Agostino Ziino. Rome: Torre d'Orfeo, 1987. xii, 730p. ML503.2 .M87.

Papers from a conference held in Naples, 11–14 April 1985, dealing with instrumental and sacred music as well as opera. The most useful is Pier Luigi Ciapparelli, "I luoghi del teatro a Napoli nel seicento: Le sale private," which describes the palaces, salons, and other nonpublic venues for opera, with extensive primary documentation.

2536. Hardie, Graham. "Neapolitan Comic Opera, 1707–1750: Some Addenda and Corrigenda for the *New Grove.*" *JAMS* 36 (1983): 124–127.

Provides bibliographic data for operas omitted in the *NG* worklists and offers added commentaries for certain pieces that are cited in those lists.

2537. Stalnaker, William Park. "The Beginnings of Opera in Naples." Ph.D. diss., Princeton U., 1968.

2538. Viviani, Vittorio. *Storia del teatro napoletano.* Naples: Guida, 1969. 971p. PN2686 .N2 V8.

A history of the theater from ancient times. Includes chapters on 17th-century dialect comedy and on Andrea Perrucci, librettist for many comic intermezzi.

Naples: Theaters

2539. Croce, Benedetto. *I teatri di Napoli, dal rinascimento alla fine del secolo decimottavo.* 2nd ed. Bari: Laterza, 1916. 336p. PN2686 .N2 C92.

First edition, *I teatri di Napoli, secolo XV-XVIII* (Naples: Pierro, 1891; xi, 786p). In the preface to the revised edition, Croce describes the book as an abridged, corrected reprint with some additions. It is a footnoted narrative beginning with the first public theaters at the end of the 16th century. Lists of musical works performed in some seasons. Name index.

2540. Florimo, Francesco. *La scuola musicale di Napoli e I suoi conservatorii.* Naples: Morano, 1880–1882. 4v. in 3. Reprint, Bologna: Forni, 1969. ML290.8 .N2 F6.

V.1–3, biographies and documents; v.4, chronology of all premiere performances in the city, 1651–1881. *Kaufman* notes that there are numerous errors in the list. Name index in v.3.

2541. Schletterer, Hans Michael. "Die Opernhäuser Neapels." *Monatshefte für Musikgeschichte* 14 (1882): 175–181; 184+; 15 (1883): 12–19.

Describes all the venues for opera, beginning with the mid–16th-century Commedia Vecchia, Teatro della Pace, and Teatro San Bartolommeo (opened in 1583). The principal old houses were Teatro dei Fiorentini (1652), Teatro Nuovo (1724), and Teatro San Carlo (1737; see following entries). Important productions and singers are named, and good information is given on establishments and closings.

Naples: Teatro San Carlo

Teatro di San Carlo opened in 1737, burned in 1816, and was rebuilt in six months. Damaged but not destroyed in World War II, it is the oldest structure still in use for opera.

2542. Ajello, Raffaelo, et al. *Il Teatro di San Carlo*. Naples: Guida, 1987. 2v. ISBN 88-7042-7315. ML1733.8 .N32 S27.

> V.1 consists of essays by various writers, forming a documented, illustrated, narrative history. V.2 is a chronology, 1737–1986/1987, with index of singers and titles.

2543. Jellinek, George. "The San Carlo Celebrates." OQ 6-2 (1988–1989): 69–76.

> An informal look at people and events associated with the theater: the Neapolitans Piccinni, Paisiello, Cimarosa, and Zingarelli; then Rossini's 10 operas for Naples; many of Donizetti's (including *Maria Stuarda* and *Lucia*). Caruso is almost missing: he sang there in 1901, was not well received, and never returned.

2544. *Cento anni di vita del Teatro di San Carlo, 1848–1948*. Naples: Ente Autonomo del Teatro di San Carlo, [1948]. 219p. ML1733.8 .N32 S23.

> Essays by various authors, presenting useful details on the present building (1817), documents of musical life, a list of impresarios from 1848–1948, and a chronology for that period (no casts). With 95 good illustrations, five in color. No index. This work is continued by *Cronache del Teatro di San Carlo, 1948–1968* (1968), which gives full casts in the chronology.

2545. Mancini, Franco, et al. *Il Teatro di San Carlo, 1737–1987*. Naples: Electa, 1987. 3v. ISBN 88-4352-4143. ML290.8 .N2 M3.

> A detailed history, dealing with events, the buildings, dance, scenery, and costumes. Chronology of performances; list of scenic designers and their productions, 1948–1987; list of administrators, 1737–1987. Bibliography in v.1; no indexes.

2546. Columbro, Marta. *La raccolta di libretti d'opera del Teatro San Carlo di Napoli*. Ancilla musicae, 3. Lucca: Libreria Musicale Italiana, 1992. xiii, 107p. ISBN 88-7096-0625. ML136 .N21 .T43.

> A title list of 262 entries, with full bibliographic descriptions, characters and persons associated with each work, and premiere data. Indexes of names and places and a chronological array. All the libretti are in Italian.

2547. Filippis, Felice de, and R. Arnese. *Cronache del Teatro di S. Carlo (1737–1960)*. Naples: Edizioni Politica Popolare, 1961–1963. 2v. ML1733.8 .N2 F45.

> A vaguely conceived chronicle: not a chronology but a list of works in approximate order. Casts are sometimes given. *Kaufman* warns against numerous errors. But the work is useful for a librettist index and a singer index.

Naples: Teatro Nuovo

2548. Filippis, Felice de, and M. Mangini. *Il Teatro Nuovo di Napoli*. Naples: Berisio, 1967. 193p. ML1733.8 .N3 F48.

A narrative history, with a list of *opere buffe* that premiered in the house, 1724–1880.

Padua (Padova)

2549. Pallerotti, A. *Spettacoli melodrammatici e coreografici rappresentati in Padova nei teatri Obizzi, Nuovo, e del Prato della Valle, dal 1751 al 1892*. Padua: Prosperini, 1892. 72p. ML1733.8 .P2 P15.

A list of about 750 productions, by date, with names of artists. No index.

2550. Brunelli Bonetti, Bruno. *I teatri di Padova dalle origini alla fine del secolo XIX*. Padua: A. Draghi, 1921. viii, 546p. PN2686 .P2 B7.

A scholarly narrative that describes the theaters and many of the works performed, including both operas and spoken dramas. No chronologies or lists. Indexes of names and titles.

Palermo

2551. Leone, Guido. *L'opera a Palermo dal 1653 al 1987*. Palermo: Publisicola, 1988. 2v. No ISBN. ML1733.8 .P25 M4.

A narrative history of operatic life, then a chronology for each theater. Title index.

2552. Tiby, Ottavio. *Il Real Teatro Carolino nell'ottocento musicale palermitano*. Florence: Olschki, 1957. 457p. ML1733.8 .P25 T5.

A valuable study of musical life in the city, including orchestral concerts and opera. The Teatro Carolino opened in 1809 as an enlarged reconstruction of a building that had housed opera since 1726. Its name was changed to Teatro Bellini in 1860. The later Teatro Massimo, opened in 1897, became the principal opera house. Chronologies for the seasons 1808/1809–1896/1897; title list; and lists of composers, impresarios, directors, and singers. No general index.

2553. Ciotti, Ignazio. *La vita artistica del Teatro Massimo di Palermo (1897–1937)*. Palermo: Fratelli Vena, 1938.

Not seen. *Kaufman* describes it as an "excellent chronology of the house, with indexes of artists and operas."

2554. Maniscalco Basile, Luigi. *Storia del Teatro Massimo di Palermo*. Florence: Olschki, 1984. 374p. ISBN 8-8222-3299-2. PN2686 .P18 T25.

The theatrical scene in Palermo in 1860 is described, then the building project for the Teatro Massimo is related, with much detail on the construction and specifications. The theater opened on 16 May 1897 with *Falstaff*. Its history is told to 1974, when it closed, with good photographs. Indexes give excellent access: titles, composers, soloists, librettists, scene designers, costumers, choreographers, and conductors.

2555. *Il Teatro Massimo: Cento e più anni fa. Fonti storico-documentarie.* Ed. Eliana Calandra. Palermo: Archivio Storico Comunale, 1997. 163p. No ISBN. PN2686 .P282 T437.

A celebratory volume marking the reopening of the theater on 12 May 1997. It had closed in 1974. Official documents relating to the planning and financing of the reconstruction, and to the competition to select the architect (G. B. F. Basile). Blueprints, drawings of fixtures, color illustrations. No index.

Parma

The city has a distinguished operatic past, boasting one of the oldest extant theaters, the Farnese (opened in 1628), and later associations with Verdi—it is the home of the Istituto di Studi Verdiani—and then Toscanini. The present center for opera is the Teatro Regio, which opened in 1829; it was named Teatro Ducale until 1849.

2556. Ferrari, Paolo-Emilio. *Spettacoli drammatico-musicali e coreografici in Parma dall'anno 1628 all'anno 1883.* Parma: Aderni, 1884. 383p. Reprint, Bologna: Forni, 1969. ML1733.8 .P28 F375.

Tabular chronologies by theater, with casts of singers and other participants. Commentaries and notes; detailed index to all persons, titles, and topics.

2557. Alcari, Cesare. *Il Teatro Regio di Parma nella sua storia dal 1883 al 1929.* Parma: Fresching, 1929. 179p. ML1733.8 .P28 A6.

A narrative history of the theater from its opening. Personalities are much discussed, followed by a chronology of concerts and operas. Directors are named but not the singers. The title index of works does show the singers who performed leading roles. No general index. The chronology is continued in the next entry.

2558. Corradi-Cervi, Maurizio. *Cronologia del Teatro Regio di Parma, 1928–1948.* Parma: Luigi Battei, 1955. 119p. ML1733.8 .P282 T43.

Carries forward the chronology of the preceding item, in similar format.

See also Yorke-Long (#87).

Pavia

2559. De Silvestri, Lodovico. *Civico Teatro Fraschini di Pavia: Cenni storici, notizie, documenti.* Pavia: Artigianelli, 1938. 202p.

Not seen. *Kaufman* notes that it has seasonal chronologies, without dates or casts.

Piacenza

2560. Forlani, Maria Giovanna. *Teatro Municipale di Piacenza (1804–1984).* Piacenza: Cassa di Risparmio di Piacenza, 1985. 479p. No ISBN. ML1733 .F675.

A thorough, documented account of the building, its administration, orchestra, singers, chorus, composers, and public. A chronology 1804–1984/1985 gives casts and relevant documents. Bibliography, name index, general index.

Pisa

2561. Dell'Ira, Gino. *I teatri di Pisa (1773–1986)*. Pisa: Giardini, 1987. 400p. and about 100 unnumbered pages of pictures. No ISBN. ML1733.8 .P58 D4.

> Good histories of the Teatro Ravviati (later the Teatro Rossi) and the Politeama Nuovo (later the Teatro Verdi), with chronologies and casts. Covers all works given in the city. Each theater has a separate index. Bibliography, general index.

Prato

2562. Fioravanti, Roberto. *La musica a Prato dal duecento al novecento*. Prato: Azienda Autonoma Turismo, 1973. 387p. No ISBN. ML290.8 .P7 F52.

> A scholarly history, with inventory of sources and illustration of major documents. Considers all musical life from the 13th century, with a complete list of works performed at the Teatro Metastasio, 1830–1964, with casts. Bibliography and index of names.

Ravenna

2563. Ravaldini, Gaetano. *Spettacoli nei teatri e in altri luoghi di Ravenna, 1555–1977*. Realtà Regionale. Fonte e studi, 3. Bologna: University Press, 1978. 398p. No ISBN. PN2686 .R3 R28.

> Chronologies for each theater, with casts; these include operas among other stage works. Good documentation; 59 illustrations; useful indexes of titles, conductors, singers, ensembles, companies, and instrumentalists.

Reggio Emilia

2564. Fabbri, Paolo, and Roberto Verti. *Due secoli di teatro per musica a Reggio Emilia: Repertorio cronologico delle opere e dei balli, 1645–1857*. Reggio Emilia: Teatro Edizioni del Municipale Valli, 1987. 479p. No ISBN. ML1733 .R4 F3.

> A history of the Teatro Comunale, with chronology and casts and performance details. Title index and name index arranged by occupation.

2565. Seragnoli, Daniele. *L'industria del teatro: Carlo Ritorni e lo spettacolo a Reggio Emilia nell'ottocento*. Proscenio, 4. Bologna: Società Editrice Il Mulino, 1987. 400p. ISBN 88-1501-55631. ML1733.7 .R4 S6.

> A footnoted history of theatrical life, centered on the initiatives of the *podestà* Count Carlo Ritorni, a writer and supporter of the opera. Documents are reproduced; no index.

2566. Degani, Giannino, and Mara Grotti. *Teatro Municipale di Reggio Emilia: Opere in musica, 1857–1976*. Reggio Emilia: Teatro Municipale, 1976. 4v.

> Not seen. *Kaufman* says it has a chronology with casts and dates, with an index of artists.

> Another work, not seen, should be useful for its illustrations: *Teatro a Reggio Emilia*, ed. Sergio Romagnoli and Elvira Garbera (Florence: Sansoni, 1980; 2v.); it has 162p. of plates.

Rome (Roma)

Operatic life in Rome displays an unsteady past. There were performances as early as 1606, and the first comic opera (Virgilio Mazzocchi's *Chi soffre speri*) was given in the Palazzo Barberini in 1637, but there was sporadic papal opposition to opera (Pope Innocent had the Teatro Tordinona, built in 1671, demolished in 1697), and the city never reached the distinction of other centers in Italy. The Teatro Argentina opened in 1732. In the same year the Tordinona was rebuilt; it was renovated in 1764, burned in 1781, rebuilt in 1795 as Teatro Apollo, and demolished in 1889. Other theaters: Teatro Drammatico Nazionale, 1886–1929; Politeama Romana, 1862–1883; Teatro Manzoni, 1876–; Politeama Adriano, later Teatro Adriano, 1898–. The principal venue at present is the Teatro dell'Opera, which opened as Teatro Costanzi in 1880, was renovated and renamed Teatro Reale dell'Opera in 1928, then given its present name. One pope was an opera patron, Clement IX: he was in fact a librettist of 12 operas, under the name Giulio Rospigliosi (see #446).

2567. Hammond, Frederick. *Music and Spectacle in Baroque Rome: Barberini Patronage under Urban VIII.* New Haven, Conn.: Yale U.P., 1995. xxiv, 369p. ISBN 0-300-05528-5. ML1733.8 .R6 H35.

A thorough treatment of patronage by the Barberini family in the 17th century: their palaces, paintings, and music sponsored for church, chamber, and stage. It all began with Maffeo Barberini (1568–1644), who became Pope Urban VIII in 1623. Details of opera production, theaters, orchestra placements; chronology of spectacles 1628–1644, with 73 period illustrations. Backnotes, excellent bibliography of about 450 items, expansive index.

2568. Ademollo, Alessandro. *I teatri di Roma nel secolo XVII: Memorie sincrone, inedite o non conosciute.* . . . Rome: Pasqualocci, 1888. xxviii, 283p. Reprint, Bologna: Forni, 1969. PN2686 .R6 A4.

A documented history of the 17th-century stage, based on archives, diaries, letters, and official announcements. A modern study of the next century, not seen: Giorgio Petrocchi, *Il teatro a Roma nel settecento* (Rome: Istituto della Enciclopedia Italiana, 1989; 2v.).

2569. Cametti, Alberto. *Il Teatro Tordinona poi di Apollo.* Tivoli: Arti Grafiche Aldo Chicca, 1938. 2v. PN2686 .R77 A64.

A scholarly history of the theater from 1671, recounting the numerous destructions and rebuildings, to its demise in 1889. Background on theatrical life of the time, patrons, composers, and artists. V.2 is a chronology for 1671–1697 and 1733–1888. Indexes of titles, dances, composers, poets, and performers.

2570. Radiciotti, Giuseppe. *Teatro e musica in Roma nel secondo quarto del secolo XIX (1825–50).* Rome: R. Accademia dei Lincei, 1905. 166 p. ML290.8 .R79 R2.

Not seen. *Kaufman* says it includes seasonal chronologies for the Teatro Apollo, Teatro Valle, and Teatro Argentina. Rosters of artists are given.

2571. Rinaldi, Mario. *Due secoli di musica al Teatro Argentina*. Florence: Olschki, 1978. 3v. ML1833.8 .R76 R57.

A documented narrative history, with a chronology 1732–1976. Valuable bibliography of more that 500 primary and secondary sources, name and title index.

2572. Frajese, Vittorio. *Dal Costanzi all'Opera*. Rome: Capitolum, 1928. 4v.

Not seen. *Kaufman* refers to it as a "model set," including complete chronologies with casts for Teatro Costanzi and (its later names) Teatro Reale dell'Opera, Teatro dell'Opera.

2573. Leoni, Edilio. *Un medico e un teatro: Mezzo secolo all'Opera di Roma*. Milan: Electa, 1987. 272p. ISBN 88-4352-1721. ML1733.8 .R62 T42.

A history covering 1880–1928; not seen. A continuation, also not available: Jole Tognelli, *Cinquant'anni del Teatro dell'Opera Roma, 1928–1978* (Rome: Bestetti, 1979; 293p.).

Turin (Torino)

2574. Bouquet, Marie-Thérèse, and Alberto Basso. *Storia del Teatro Regio di Torino*. Turin: Cassa di Risparmio di Torino, 1976. 2v. PN2686 .T82 R437.

The lively operatic history of Turin was concentrated on the great Teatro Regio from its opening in 1740 until its destruction by fire in 1936. It was finally rebuilt and reopened in 1973. This is a scholarly history, with thousands of footnotes and a presentation of all relevant documents. Outstanding color plates, chronologies with casts. Much detail is offered, such as the salaries paid to singers for performances. Each volume has a name and title index. Alberto Basso continued the story with *Il nuovo Teatro Regio di Torino* (Turin: Cassa di Risparmio di Torino, 1991; xiii, 541p.).

See also #2525.

Venice (Venezia; German: Venedig)

It was in Venice that opera became a public rather than a private spectacle. The first public opera house in the world, San Cassiano, opened in 1637, followed quickly by many others (there is a convenient list in *Oxford Dictionary of Opera* (#47). In 1792 the famous theater La Fenice opened, thought by many to be the most beautiful of all opera houses. It burned down on 29 January 1996 and is still (as of 1999) under reconstruction.

2575. Muraro, Maria Teresa, ed. *Venezia e il melodramma nel seicento*. Florence: Olschki, 1976. 400p. No ISBN. ML17333.8 .V8 V45.

A valuable collection of 19 articles, originally conference papers. They include Marie-Françoise Christout, "L'influence vénitienne exercée par les artistes italiens sur les premiers spectacles à machines montés à la Cour de France durant la Régence (1645–1650)"; Mercedes Viale Ferrero, "Repliche a Torino di alcuni melodrammi venziani e loro caratteristiche"; Pierluigi Petrobelli, "La partitura del *Massimo Pupieno* di Carlo Pallavicino (Venezia 1684)"; Hellmuth Christian Wolff, "Manierismus in den venezianischen Opernlibretti des 17. Jahrhunderts"; Ferruccio Marotti, "Lo spazio scenico del melodramma, esaminato sulla base della trattatistica teatrale italiana"; and these entered separately: Bruno Brizi on Busenello (#236), Ellen Rosand on Cavalli's arias (#672), William C. Holmes on *Orontea* (#683), Lionello Cammarota on Monteverdi's orchestration (#1249), and Giovanni Morelli and Thomas R. Walker on San Cassiano (#2584).

2576. Muraro, Maria Teresa, ed. *Venezia e il melodramma nel settecento.* Florence: Olschki, 1978, 1981. 2v. ISBN v.2 88-2223-057-3. ML1733.8 .V4 V46.

V.1 consists of 23 papers, including Mercedes Viale Ferrero, "Giovanni Battisti Crosato e la sua attività di scenografo al Teatro Regio di Torino"; Marian Hanna Winter, "Venice: Proving Ground and Arbiter for Italian Choreographers"; Francesco Degrada, "Origini e sviluppi dell'opera comica napoletana"; Nicola Mangini, "Sulla diffusione dell'opera comica nei teatri veneziani"; Nicola Mangini, "Sui rapporti del Vivaldi col Teatro di Sant'Angelo"; Hellmuth Christian Wolff, "Johann Adolf Hasse und Venedig"; Klaus Hortschansky, "Die Rezeption der Wiener Dramen Metastasios in Italien"; and Carolyn Gianturco, "*Il trespolo tutore* di Stradella e di Pasquini." Entered separately: Daniel Heartz on Hasse, Galuppi, and Metastasio (#1007) and Claudio Gallico on Rinaldo di Capua (#1567).

V.2 has 15 papers, including Stefan Kunze, "Elementi veneziani nella librettistica di Lorenzo Da Ponte"; and these entered separately: Daniela Goldin on *opera buffa* (#243), Daniel Heartz on *L'Arcadia in Brenta* (#250), Michael F. Robinson on Goldoni (#252), Sven H. Hansell on Bertoni (#572), Hellmuth Christian Wolff on *La sposa fedele* (#937), Daniela Goldin on the text of *Il barbiere di Siviglia* (#1376) and Gianfranco Folena on *La serva padrona* (#1396).

2577. Rosand, Ellen. *Opera in Seventeenth-Century Venice: The Creation of a Genre.* Berkeley: U. of California Press, 1991. 684p. ISBN 0-520-06808-4. ML1733.8 .V4 R67.

The indispensable study of the period, based on primary sources that are presented in appendixes. Examines the Venetian environment in which opera took on the identity it still holds, departing from austere Florentine beginnings. Commercialization of opera is traced, as well as the impact of the public. Many works are discussed, with 91 long musical examples, but actual musical analysis is light. Copious notes, strong bibliography, indexing by title and topic.

2578. Worsthorne, Simon Towneley. *Venetian Opera in the Seventeenth Century.* Oxford: Clarendon, 1954. vii, 194p. ML1733.8 .V4 W77.

A scholarly account, with a good review of earlier research. Discusses the place of opera in the thought of the times, the theaters of Venice, and musical life in general. Casts for operas before 1700 but no actual chronology. Stage scenes are shown in 23 plates. Bibliography of about 150 entries, index.

2579. Bryant, David. "La farsa musicale: Coordinate per la storia di un genere non-genere." In *I vicini di Mozart* (#90), v.2, 431–456.

Developing from various precursors, the *farsa* emerged in Venice in the 1790s; seven were staged in the carnival season of 1794. By 1800 there had been 28 premieres, but then the genre lost favor. Bryant discusses works of Paisiello, Paër, Portogallo, Cimarosa, Mayr, Piccinni, and other leading practitioners. Chronological table.

2580. Salvioli, Giovanni. *I teatri musicali di Venezia nel secolo XVII (1637–1700): Memorie storiche e bibliografiche raccolte ed ordinate da Livo Niso Galvani* [pseudonym]. Milan: Ricordi, 1879. 193p. Reprint, Bologna: Forni, 1969. ML1733.8 .V4 S3.

Useful chronologies for 16 theaters, with casts and names of all others associated with the events, and commentaries. Composer, title, name, and librettist indexes.

2581. Wiel, Taddeo. *I teatri musicali veneziani del settecento: Catalogo delle opere in musica rappresentate nel secolo XVIII in Venezia (1701–1800).* 2nd ed. Rev. Reinhard Strohm. Leipzig: Peters, 1979. lxxx, 635p. ML1733.8 .V4 W6.

First edition, 1897. The revision has a new introduction and an updated bibliography but does not change the text of the original. It is a chronology of all theaters, recording 1,274 performances. For each, the composer, librettist, singers and their roles, and miscellaneous information is given, but exact dates are lacking—reference is to seasons. Indexes to titles, librettists, musicians, singers, choreographers, and dancers.

2582. Glixon, Beth L. "Recitative in Seventeenth-Century Venetian Opera: Its Dramatic Function and Musical Language." Ph.D. diss., Rutgers U., 1985. 462p.

2583. Brown, Jennifer Williams. "*Con nuove arie aggiunte*—Aria Borrowing in the Venetian Opera Repertory, 1672–1685." Ph.D. diss., Cornell U., 1992. 611p.

2584. Morelli, Giovanni, and Thomas R. Walker. "Tre controversie intorno al San Cassiano." In *Muraro* (#2576), 97–120.

Describes documents about San Cassiano and about Francesco Cavalli in the Archivio di Stato di Venezia and the Monastero di S. Maria dell'Orazion a Malamocco. The materials concern economic activity of the theater and administrative procedures. Cavalli was one of the founders of an academy for performing at the theater (1638). The sources cast light on audience, reception, and competition among productions for the years 1635–1650.

Venice: Il Teatro La Fenice

2585. *Gran Teatro La Fenice.* Text by Giandomenico Romanelli et al. Photography by Graziano Arici. Padua: Evergreen, 1999. 337p. ISBN 3-8228-7062-5. ML1733.8 .V4 G7313.

A splendid photo book, mostly color, with English-language text. Originally published in Italian, 1996. Pictures of the building in great detail and of playbills and scenes. Dance and opera are well covered. Commentaries are of interest as well. No chronologies. The project aims to restore the building "looking as it did before it fell into flames." Many photos show the fire (29 January 1996) in progress and the condition of the structure after the conflagration.

2586. Nani Mocenigo, Mario. *Il teatro La Fenice: Notizie storiche e artistiche.* Venice: Industrie Poligrafiche Venete, 1926. 71, xxxiii p. ML1733.8 .V4 N18.

Diverse essays on the theater itself (opened in 1791) and on early performances. Chronology of operas and ballets 1792–1925, with names of artists; commentaries on the works, with details of critical reception.

2587. Hannemann, Beate. *Im Zeichen der Sonne: Geschichte und Repertoire des Opernhauses "La Fenice" von seiner Gründig bis zum Wiener Kongress (1787–1814).* Dialoghi/Dialogues, 2. Frankfurt: Peter Lang, 1996. 332p. ISBN 3-631-30261-4. ML1733.8 .V4 H36.

Based on the author's dissertation, U. of Hannover. A useful exploration of the political background in which the theater was planned, its financing, architecture and decoration, choice of its name, and critical response to the new structure. An account of the impresarios, repertoire, librettists, premieres, and the variable stability of the enterprise during the period. Extensively footnoted, bibliography of about 400 primary and secondary sources, name index.

2588. Girardi, Michele. *Il Teatro La Fenice: Cronologia degli spettacoli, 1938–1991.* Venice: Albrizzi, 1992. xxiii, 650p. ISBN 88-3175-5099. ML1733.8 .V4 G57.

A detailed chronology, with casts, for 4,089 performances. Bibliography, index of persons and titles. An earlier volume by Girardi, covering 1792–1936, was not available for examination.

Venice: Teatro Grimani

2589. Saunders, Harris. "Repertoire of a Venetian Opera House, 1678–1714: The Teatro Grimani di San Giovanni Grisostomo." Ph.D. diss., Harvard U., 1985. 568p.

Vicenza

2590. Schivao, Remo. *A Guide to the Olympic Theatre.* 2nd English ed. Trans. Patricia Anne Hill. Vicenza: Accademia Olimpica, 1981. 160p.

Not seen. Originally *Guida al Teatro Olimpico. Kaufman* describes it as a stunning coffee-table book, with historical text but no chronologies. Index of titles and singers.

Lithuania (Lietuvos Respublika; Lietuva)

The country declared its independence from the Soviet Union in 1991. All the scholarly writing on opera is in Lithuanian, except a master's thesis by Vytas Nakas, "Jurgis Karnavičius: *Gražina,* the First Lithuanian Opera" (Indiana U., 1974); the abstract in *RILM* indicates coverage of Lithuanian opera in general. Three items in Lithuanian:

2591. Mažeika, Vytautas. *Opera: Lietuvių tarybinio operos teatro raida, 1940–1965.* Vilnius: Mintis, 1967. 207p. ML1751 .L58 M4.

A popular narrative of opera history in the period noted, with a chronology of premieres. Staff list but no other reference features. No index.

2592. *Muzika ir teatras: Almanachas.* Vilnius: Valstybinė Grožines Literatūros Leidykla, 1962–. Annual. ML21 .M96.

A yearly review of opera and dramatic events in the country. Feature articles on individual works and on composers. No actual chronicles. Contents pages seen were in English and Russian as well as Lithuanian.

2593. Yla, Stasys. *Lietuvių nacionalinė opera.* Vilnius: Valstybinė Politinės ir Mokslinės Literatūros Leidykla, 1960. 103p. ML1738 .L5 Y4.

Essays by various authors about Lithuanian national opera. Most of them are about individual composers or works. No reference features, no index.

Mexico (México)

2594. Stevenson, Robert Murrell. *Music in Mexico: A Historical Survey.* New York: Crowell, 1952. 300p. ML210 .S8.

A scholarly, comprehensive study covering all periods and genres. The operatic 19th century is thoroughly discussed in a 50-page chapter with 92 footnotes. Musical examples, 11-page bibliography, index of names, titles, and topics.

2595. Olavarria y Ferrari, Enrique de. *Reseña histórica del teatro en México . . .* 3rd ed. México City: Porrua, 1961. 6v. PN2311 .O43.

Opera is treated along with other stage presentations in this imposing work; coverage is 1538–1961. A chronology of performances, 1911–1961, is in v.5, and there is an index of names, organizations, theaters, places, and publications in the last volume.

2596. Pulido Granata, Francisco Ramon. *La tradicion operatística en la Ciudad de México, siglo 19.* Mexico City: Cuadernos de Cultura Popular, 1970.

Not seen. There was also a continuation for 1900–1911 (1981). *Kaufman* describes these works as narratives for each season in the capital, with dates and casts for many performances but without actual chronologies.

2597. Díaz Du-Pond, Carlos. *Cinquenta años de opera en México: Testimonio operístico.* Mexico City: UNAM, 1978. 326, 64p. ML1715 .D5.

A popular history of the period 1924–1973, with dates and casts of many performances. No index. The review in *Inter-American Music Review* 5–1 (Fall 1982) makes favorable comments but observes that the book should be "re-edited with careful insertion or confirmation of dates, places, and names. Footnotes should be added, identifying person and places casually mentioned. Above all an index is needed."

2598. *50 años de opera en el Palacio de Bellas Artes, 1934–1984.* Mexico City: Instituto Nacional de Bellas Artes, 1986. 252p.

Not seen. *Kaufman* describes it as a coffee-table book of illustrations, with descriptions of each season and chronologies.

Monaco

2599. Walsh, T. J. *Monte Carlo Opera, 1879–1909*. Dublin: Gill & Macmillan, 1975. xix, 321p. ISBN 0-7171-0725-6. ML1751 .M66 W3.

The basic study: a scholarly narrative, well documented and illustrated. Includes a chronology of operas performed, with casts; performances by the company abroad; number of performances of each opera; and seasonal reports. Bibliography, name and title index. The next item is an update.

2600. Walsh, T. J. *Monte Carlo Opera, 1910–1951*. Kilkenny, Ireland: Boethius Press, 1986. 443p. ML1751 .M66 W341.

Continues the preceding. Under director Raoul Gunsbourg, the opera became "one of the world's finest." Premieres given include *Don Quichotte* (1910), *Pénélope* (1913), and *La rondine* (1917). The book is in narrative form, with capsule singer biographies and a chronology with casts. Name index. Some updating is provided in:

2601. Favre, Georges. *Histoire musicale de la Principauté de Monaco du XVIe au XXe siècle*. Paris: Picard; Monaco: Archives du Palais Princier, 1974. 154p. No ISBN. ML325 .M6 F3.

A heavily footnoted narrative history, quoting original sources. The chapter on opera, p.80–113, deals mostly with the accomplishments of Raoul Gunsbourg. Bibliography of 28 items, name index.

2602. Scott, Michael. "Raoul Gunsbourg and the Monte Carlo Opera." *OQ* 3-4 (Winter 1985–1986): 70–78.

An account of Gunsbourg's 59 years as director, 1893–1951. Many world premieres were given, as well as revivals of operas by Lully, Rameau, Monteverdi, Cimarosa, and Paisiello. The important international singers took part.

Netherlands (Dutch: Nederland, or Holland; French: Hollande, or Pays-Bas; German: Niederlande. Holland is acceptable in English.)

2603. *Algemene muziek encyclopedie*. Ed. Jozef Robijns and Miep Zijlestra. Haarlem: De Haan, 1979–1984. 10v. ML100 .A41.

An expansion of the *Algemene muziekencylopdie*, ed. A. Corbet and Wouter Paap (Antwerp: Zuid-Nederlandse Uitg., 1957–1963; 6v. and supplement 1972). It is universal, but coverage of national topics is strongest. Articles are in Dutch only, although contributors come from many countries. Reference features include chronological tables, worklists for composers, bibliographies, and discographies, but there is no general index.

2604. Monnikendam, Marius. *Nederlands componisten van heden en verleden*. Amsterdam: A. J. G. Strengholt, 1968. 280p. ML390 .M658 N4.

A strong introduction to past and present musical life, including a chapter on opera. Name index.

2605. Bottenheim, S. A. M. *De opera in Nederland*. 2nd ed. Amsterdam: P. N. van Kampen & Zoon, 1983. 281p. ML1735 .B68.

First edition, 1946. The only general history of opera in Holland. It is a plain narrative, with some illustrations. No chronologies, bibliography, or index.

New Zealand

2606. Brusey, Phyllis Wilkins. *Ring Down the Curtain.* Wellington: C. Rex Monigatti, 1973. xii, 192p. and 48p. of plates. ML1751 .N5 N56.

A well-illustrated popular history of operatic life in the country. Includes a list of productions of the New Zealand Opera Company from 1954 to 1971. No bibliography or index.

2607. Hurst, Maurice Gordon. *Music and the Stage in New Zealand, 1840–1943.* Auckland: C. Begg, 1944. 112p. ML1751 .N5 H6.

A narrative account of companies and performances; no chronologies.

Norway

2608. Grinde, Nils. *A History of Norwegian Music.* Trans. William H. Halverson and Leland B. Sateren. Lincoln: U. of Nebraska Press, 1991. xxiii, 418p. ISBN 0-8032-2135-5. ML312 .G7513.

Originally *Norsk musikhistorie,* 3rd ed. (Oslo, 1971). Grinde updated his work for this, the first English translation. It is a readable narrative in popular idiom, with excellent photos and portraits and long musical examples. Biographies and worklists for major composers. Bibliography, index.

2609. Blanc, Tharald. *Christiania Theater's historie, 1827–77.* Oslo: J. W. Cappelen, 1899. xii, 318p. PN2766 .C5 B5.

A narrative account of opera and opera companies in the capital city (named Christiania until 1924), with details on some performances.

2610. Anker, Oyvind. *Christiania Theater's repertoire 1827–99.* Oslo: Gyldendal, 1956. 182p. PN2766 .O7 K91.

A title list of all works performed, with their dates (no casts) from the 1827 opening of the theater to its final day, 15 June 1899. Introduction in Norwegian and English, text in Norwegian only. Author and composer indexes.

Peru (Spanish: Perú)

2611. Stevenson, Robert Murrell. *The Music of Peru: Aboriginal and Viceroyal Epochs.* Washington, D.C.: Pan American Union, 1960. xii, 331p. ML236 .S8.

The basic history, thoroughly documented, offering much detail on all musical topics. Early opera is amply discussed. Bibliography, musical examples, index. The same author has a major study of opera:

2612. Stevenson, Robert Murrell. *Foundations of New World Opera, with a Transcription of the Earliest Extant American Opera, 1701.* Lima: Ediciones CULTURA, 1973. 300p. ML1717 .S83.

A valuable study of early Peruvian opera, including a transcription and analysis of Tomás de Torrejón y Velasco's opera *La púrpura de la rosa,* the first Western Hemisphere opera for which music has survived.

2613. Claro, Samuel. "Música dramática en el Cuzco durante el siglo XVIII y catá-
logo de manuscritos de música del seminario de San Antonio Abad (Cuzco,
Perú)." *Yearbook for Inter-American Musical Research* 5 (1969): 1–48.

A scholarly, documented, 23-page examination of colonial-era musical theater
in Cuzco, followed by a 16-page classified catalogue of music manuscripts in
the Cuzco seminary. Musical examples.

2614. Prieto, Juan Sixto. "El Perú en la música escénica." *Fénix, revista de la Biblioteca Nacional* 9 (1953): 278–351. Z761 .F35.

A chronology (without casts) of operas, ballets, and other musical dramatic
works with Peruvian subject matter, 1658–1927. Bibliographic data and performance history; mostly concerns European composers and production.
Footnotes, many illustrations, bibliography of about 90 sources. Title, composer, and librettist indexes.

Poland (Polish: Polska; German: Polen)

Almost all the scholarly literature is in Polish. Since those writings are cited in Smialek
(#2615) they are mostly passed over in this guide. A few titles are entered here if they
present lists or other reference features that are accessible to those who do not read
the language.

2615. Smialek, William. *Polish Music: A Research and Information Guide.* Music
Research and Information Guides, 12. New York: Garland, 1989. xii, 260p.
ISBN 0-8240-4614-5. ML120 .P6 S6.

A valuable handbook of writings on all aspects of Polish music and musical
life, consisting of 989 annotated entries and an index of names and topics.
There are 36 references to opera in the index, most of them in Polish.

2616. Jarociński, Stefan. *Polish Music.* Warsaw: PWN, 1965. viii, 327p. ML306
.J28.

Essays on various aspects of musical culture, among them a collection of opera
statistics, 1949–1962, and a historical chronology through 1963. Excellent
bibliography of about 200 items, name index.

2617. Glowacki, John M. "The History of Polish Opera." Ph.D. diss., Boston U.,
1952. 215p.

Discusses early opera in the country and works by Polish composers and lists
all Polish operas with their premiere dates.

2618. Abraham, Gerald. "The Early Development of Opera in Poland." In *Essays on
Opera* (#72), 148–165.

A useful summary, beginning with the earliest performance of opera in the
country (1633) and the first Polish opera (1778). Titles are in Polish, and there
are 40 reference footnotes.

2619. Neuer, Adam. *Polish Opera and Ballet of the Twentieth Century: Operas, Ballets, Pantomimes, Miscellaneous Works.* Krakow: Polskie Wydawnictwo
Muzyczne, 1986. 132p. ISBN 83-2240-3003. ML1736.5 .P6413.

Not seen. Smialek (#2615) describes it as a title list of 262 works for stage, radio, or television. Information given includes synopsis, duration, instrumentation, and recordings. Indexes of composers and librettists and a chronology.

2620. Michalowski, Kornel. *Opery polskie: Katalog.* Krakow: Polskie Wydawn. Muzyczne, 1954. 277p. ML128 .O4 M5.

A list of about 250 Polish operas arranged by title, giving names of composers, librettists, and premiere data. Chronology for 1778–1953. Also a list of operas by non-Poles with Polish themes or settings. Bibliography of about 300 entries, composer index.

Two articles by Józef Kański in *Musikbühne 76* give some views of recent work: "Die neue polnischer Oper" and "Opern polnischer Komponisten seit 1951."

Individual Cities

Gdansk (Gdańsk)

2621. *Państwowa Opera i Filharmonia Baltycka w Gdańsku* . . . Gdansk: Morskie, 1971. 162p. ML1740.8 .D3 P3.

Miscellaneous essays on concert, opera, and ballet activity. Gives list of operas performed 1950–1970 with casts and illustrations. Names of artists in the company are listed. No bibliography, no index.

Krakow (Kraków; Cracow)

2622. Reiss, Józef. *Almanach muzyczny krakowa, 1780–1914.* Krakow: Nakładem Tow. Miłośników Historii i Zabytków Krakowa, 1939. 2v. ML21 .R42.

Not seen. Described by Smialek (#2615) as a chronicle of operas and concerts, with a list of concerts 1780–1914. Index of names.

Poznan (Poznań:)

2623. Waldorff, Jerzy. *Opera Poznańska, 1919–1969.* Poznan: Wydawn. Poznańskie, 1970. 219p. DK4750 .A2 B5 no.30.

A history of opera in the city, including biographies of leading figures. Chronology of 412 performances; 111 photographs. No index.

Warsaw (Warszawa)

The capital is the main opera center. The Teatr Wielki (Grand Theater) was built in 1833, destroyed in 1939, and rebuilt and reopened in 1965.

2624. Kański, Józef. *Teatr Wielki w Warszawie.* Warsaw: Wydawnictwa Artystyczne i Filmowe, 1965. Not paged. ML1740.8 .W4 T44.

A picture book prepared for the reopening of the theater. Preface is in five languages, and captions are in French and Polish, but the main text is in Polish only. List of the 230 operas and ballets performed in the Teatr Wielki and in the earlier Warsaw theater from 1778 to 1965, with directors and choreographers named (not the singers); also a list of administrators since 1821. No index.

2625. *Dwadzieścia pięc' lat opery Warszawskiej w Polsce Ludowej, 1945–1970.* Warsaw: Teatr Wielki, 1970. 339p. ML1740.8 W4 T446.

Mostly a book of photographs showing scenes, posters, portraits, and many views of the new Grand Theater. Also a chronology 1945–1970, naming directors but not singers. No index.

2626. Filler, Witold. *Rendez-vous z warszawską operetką.* Warsaw: Państwowy Instytut Wydawniczy, 1961. 355p. ML1740.8 .W4 S5.

A popular history of light operas by Poles and others that have been given in Warsaw. List of works by composer, with dates, 1859–1939 (titles in Polish and original language). Bibliography of 54 items, name and title index.

Portugal

2627. Stevenson, Robert Murrell. "Portuguese Music: A Historical Résumé." *Journal of the American Portuguese Cultural Society* 4 (Summer–Fall 1970): 1–13. DP501 .A5.

Not many libraries have this journal, but the article is worth searching out as the most dependable brief review. It begins in the early sixth century. Opera in the 18th century has considerable attention, and modern works are discussed.

2628. De Brito, Manuel Carlos. *Opera in Portugal in the Eighteenth Century.* New York: Cambridge U.P., 1989. xv, 254p. ISBN 0-521-35312-2. ML1748 .B75.

Originally the author's dissertation, U. of London, 1985. Praised by *Baron* as the best English-language summary of baroque opera in the country, "full of scholarly data." Discusses the period 1708–1797, covering Italian influences, the tenure of Domenico Scarlatti in Lisbon 1719–1729, public and court theaters, important singers, "musical inclinations of the royalty and aristocracy," and the puppet operas of the dramatist António José da Silva. Chronology for the period, without casts. Appendix of documents, backnotes, bibliography of about 200 items, and index of names and topics. De Brito's essay in *Teatro y música* (#2667) presents useful citations to recent articles dealing with opera in Portugal.

2629. Marques, José Joaquim. *Cronologia da ópera em Portugal* . . . Lisbon: Artística, 1947. 159p. ML1748 .M3.

Although most of this volume concerns a form of cantata called *vilhancico,* it does include a chronology of operatic and other dramatic performances 1640–1793. No bibliography or index.

Six monographs by one of the most important Portuguese scholars are found in Mário de Sampayo Ribeiro, *Achegas para a história da música em Portugal, 1932–61* (Lisbon: Pereira Rosa, 1932–1961; 6v. in 3). Francisco Marques de Sousa Viterbo, *Subsídios para a história da música em Portugal* (Coimbra: Imprensa da Universidade, 1932), presents historical data in the form of a biographical dictionary. Another biographical work, *Os músicos portuguezes: Biographia-bibliographia,* by Joaquím Antonio da Fonseca E. Vasconcellos (Pôrto: Imprensa Portugueza, 1870; 2v.), is useful for worklists and historical context; it includes a chronology of performances of operas by Marcos Portugal (1762–1830). A chronology for Lisbon's principal theater, 1793–1863, is in *O Real Theatro de S.Carlos de Lisboa desde a sua fundação em 1793 até á actualidade,* by Francisco da Fonseca Benevides (Lisbon: Castro Irmão, 1883). Some updating is given in the same author's *O Real Theatro de S. Carlos de Lisboa: Memorias, 1883–1902* (Lisbon: R. de Souza & Salles, 1902). See also #1080.

Romania (The spelling Rumania is also used.)

2630. Cosma, Viorel. *România muzicală*. Bucharest: Editura Muzicală, 1980. 131p. ML258 .C7.

Includes essays on opera companies and other musical institutions. Bibliography, no index.

An earlier review of the musical situation: Petre Nitulescu, *Muzica românească de azi* (Bucharest: Sindicatul Ariştilor Instrumentişti din România, 1939), has considerable detail on the operatic institutions. Petre Brâncusi, *Muzica în România socialistă* (Bucharest: Editura Muzicală, 1973), is a popular introduction to opera and other musical activities, stressing socialist values. A scholarly history of opera, emphasizing the 19th and 20th centuries:

2631. Massoff, Ioan. *Teatrul romînesc; privire istorică*. Bucharest: Editura Pentru Literatură, 1961–. PN2841 .M3.

Only one volume has been seen, in what was planned as a multivolume history. It gives details on opera houses, companies, and individuals. There is just one chronology, for one theater, 1852–1860. Bibliography of about 600 entries, no index. The next item is a good supplement:

2632. Cosma, Octavian L. *Opera romînească: Privire istorică asupra creatiei lirico-dramatice*. Bucharest: Editura Muzicală, 1962. 332p. ML1751 .R8 C68.

Considers opera and ballet after World War I: well illustrated and footnoted. List of opera composers and their works (about 300 operas). Chronology of performing groups in Bucharest, 1772–1921. Bibliography of about 200 titles, index of persons and titles. The same author's *Hronicul muzicii romanesti* (Bucharest: Editura Muzicală, 1983), not seen, is described by *Kaufman* as the best of the Cosma books: a history of the companies that have performed in Romania, with biographies of Romanian singers.

2633. Burada, Teodor. *Istoria teatrului în Moldova*. Bucharest: Minerva, 1975. xxiii, 809p. No ISBN. PN2845 .M6 B9.

A history of stage performances in the province of Moldova (Moldavia), 1846–1896. Narrative style, with casts, comments, and press notices. The story ends with the opening of the Teatru Naţional on 1 December 1896. Bibliography, title index, name index.

Russia (Russian: Rossiia; French: Russie; German: Russland)

From 1917 to 1991 the country was named the Union of Soviet Socialist Republics (Soiuz Sovetskikh Sotsialisticheskikh Respublik, or SSSR) and referred to in the West as the USSR or Soviet Union. Belarus, Lithuania, and Ukraine—former republics of the Soviet Union—are now independent nations and have their own entries in this guide. Since most of the scholarly literature on music was written during the Soviet period, the researcher will encounter the old names of the country and the 15 republics that composed it. All those designations are given in *IOM* 3, 299–354, where the principal Russian music literature is identified. In the present guide, the emphasis is on material in Western languages. Russian works included are those that have notable illustrations, chronologies, or title lists—the kind of reference features that should be accessible to persons who can read the alphabet, if not the language.

Russian words are transliterated according to a modification of the Library of Congress system, in which the supradiacritics are omitted. This procedure is becoming more common in the age of online catalogues. The reader will bear in mind that there are many other transliteration systems for Cyrillic and that the system used in a given publication will affect the indexing and other alphabetical approaches to the material.

A further complication in the life of the researcher in the U.S. is that library collections have demonstrated extremely vague acquisition practice for books and journals published in Russia. Neither the Library of Congress nor any other great library consulted in the preparation of this volume gave evidence of a coherent collection policy for Russian musical materials, so it may well be that important items are missing in this inventory and that certain titles cited have been superseded by later editions or new works.

Of the English-language musical reference works, only *NGDO* can be recommended for its coverage of opera in Russia. The article "Russia" (v.4, 98–104) by Richard Taruskin is an excellent overview. Taruskin also made valuable contributions with entries for individual cities.

Music in General

Gerald Abraham has written widely on Russian music. Many of his essays appear in three collections:

2634. Abraham, Gerald. *Slavonic and Romantic Music: Essays and Studies*. New York: St. Martin's, 1968. 360p. ML300 .A16 S6.

Consists of 14 studies about Russian and Eastern European composers, plus 15 essays on non-Slavonic topics. "Tchaikovsky's Operas" is a particularly useful contribution. Name index.

2635. Abraham, Gerald. *Studies in Russian Music*. London: Reeves, 1935. vi, 355p. Reprint, Freeport, N.Y.: Books for Libraries Press, 1968. ML300 .A16 S8.

Essays on individual works by Glinka, Musorgsky, Balakirev, and, in particular, Rimsky-Korsakov (*The Maid of Pskov, May Night, Snow Maiden, Sadko, Tsar's Bride, The Invisible City of Kitezh*, and *The Golden Cockerel*). Name index.

2636. Abraham, Gerald. *On Russian Music*. London: Reeves, 1939. 279p. Reprint, Freeport, N.Y.: Books for Libraries Press, 1970. ISBN 0-8369-1909-9. ML300 .A16 S82.

Essays on various composers, emphasizing their operas. The studies of *Mlada* and *Tsar Sultan* by Rimsky-Korsakov are especially interesting. Name index.

The preferred general history in English is:

2637. Leonard, Richard Anthony. *A History of Russian Music.* New York: Macmillan, 1957. Reprint, Westport, Conn.: Greenwood, 1977. ISBN 0-8371-9658-2. ML300 .L45.

A useful survey of main trends, drawn from secondary sources in Western languages. Good summary of operatic development. Bibliography of about 100 titles, expansive index of names and titles.

2638. Mooser, Robert Aloys. *Annales de la musique et des musiciens en Russie au XVIIIe siècle.* Geneva: Mont-Blanc, 1948–1951. 3v. ML300 .M84.

Based on primary documents, which are quoted extensively, this is the preferred Western-language account of the 18th century. Incudes much biographical detail. Appendixes of letters, programs, and other contemporary materials. The impressive bibliography has about 800 titles, unfortunately rendered in French translation only. Name and title indexes.

In Russian the significant studies of the 18th century are by Iurii Keldysh (*IOM* 3193) and Nikolai Findeizen (*IOM 3194).* For the 19th century the most esteemed Russian writers are Boris V. Asaf'ev (*IOM* 3197) and Vladimir V. Stasov *(IOM* 3198; Stasov must be read cautiously [see #2644]); some of this work is available in translations (noted in the *IOM* entries). There is a useful account in English of 20th-century trends:

2639. Schwarz, Boris. *Music and Musical Life in Soviet Russia, 1917–1970.* 2nd ed. Bloomington: Indiana U.P., 1983. xiii, 722p. ISBN 02-5333-9561. ML300.5 .S41.

First edition, 1972. A musical and political history, since the two spheres were united under the Soviets. A valuable study, perhaps most important for "the final two chapters of this book, newly written for the enlarged edition, [which] focus on Soviet consent and dissent" and bring out the adjustments in scores and attitudes by such masters as Shostakovich and Prokofiev. Schwarz observes that "next to the Italians, the Russians are probably the world's most opera-loving and most opera-conscious people." Backnotes, bibliography of about 200 items, expansive index of names and topics.

2640. *Russian and Soviet Music: Essays for Boris Schwarz.* Ed. Malcolm Hamrick Brown. Ann Arbor, Mich.: UMI Research, 1984. viii, 327p. ISBN 0-8357-1545-0. ML55 .S398.

Consists of 18 essays by various authors, plus a bibliography of writings by Schwarz, and an index. These are entered separately in this guide: Richard Taruskin on 19th-century opera (#2649), Laurel E. Fay on Shostakovich's *Nose* (#1670), and Royal S. Brown on *Lady Macbeth* (#1669).

2641. Moldon, David. *A Bibliography of Russian Composers.* London: White Lion, 1976. xviii, 364p. ISBN 0-7285-0010-7. ML120 .R8 M6.

A useful bibliography with some annotations of about 3,000 books, parts of books, articles, and unpublished materials in English. Sixty journals were searched. About 370 entries deal with the period 1883–1973; then there is a list of writings about 113 composers. Index of authors, editors, compilers, translators, and illustrators; subject index.

2642. *The New Grove Russian Masters 1: Glinka, Borodin, Balakirev, Musorgsky, Tchaikovsky.* Ed. David Brown et al. New York: Norton, 1986. 260p. ISBN 0-393-30102-8. ML390 .N475.

Articles from *NG*, with some updating and an index to the volume.

2643. *The New Grove Russian Masters 2: Rimsky-Korsakov, Skryabin, Rakhmaninov, Prokofiev, Shostakovich.* Ed. Gerald Abraham et al. New York: Norton, 1986. 240p. ISBN 0-393-02283-8. ML390 .N4751.

Continues the preceding entry.

Opera in General

2644. Newmarch, Rosa. *The Russian Opera.* London: Herbert Jenkins, 1914. xv, 403p. Reprint, Westport, Conn.: Greenwood, 1972. ISBN 0-8371-4298-9. ML1741 .N49.

Newmarch was one of the first scholars of the West to study the music of Eastern Europe. She lived in Russia and studied under Stasov, which was a mixed blessing; her book is, according to Richard Taruskin, "a mirror of the prejudices . . . of Vladimir Stasov, surely one of the most partisan and biased 'historians' that ever lived." With that in mind, one can make some use of this book for personal details and unusual information, notably about Rimsky-Korsakov. Index.

2645. Neef, Sigrid. *Handbuch der russischer und sowjetischen Oper.* Berlin: Henschelverlag, 1985. 760p. No ISBN. MT95 .N38.

A valuable work, with chapters on opera in each of the Soviet republics and then consideration of about 200 operas by 64 composers. For each opera the Russian and German titles are given, with genesis, synopsis, premiere information, reception, publications, and bibliography. For leading composers there is also musical analysis. Index of titles (in German only) and names.

2646. Maximovitch, Michel. *L'opéra russe, 1731–1935.* Lausanne: L'Age d'Homme, 1987. 432p. No ISBN. ML1737 .M33.

A popular narrative history, with synopses and program notes for selected works. Also information on theaters. All opera titles are in French only, in the text and in the index.

2647. Morrison, Simon Alexander. "Russian Opera and Symbolist Poets." Ph.D. diss., Princeton U., 1997. 277p.

2648. Taruskin, Richard. *Opera and Drama in Russia as Preached and Practiced in the 1860's.* Ann Arbor, Mich.: UMI Research, 1981. xvii, 560p. Reprint, Rochester: U. of Rochester Press, 1993. ISBN (UMI) 0-8357-1245-1. ML1737 .T37.

An important, exhaustive analysis of the period, emphasizing Glinka, Serov, and Cui. Works are identified in both Russian and English. Footnotes, 90 pages of extended musical examples in score, index of names and topics. The 1993 reprint has a new preface that connects its material to the author's collection of essays on Musorgsky (#1346).

2649. Taruskin, Richard. "'The Present in the Past': Russian Opera and Russian Historiography, ca. 1870." In *Russian and Soviet Music* (#2640), 77–146.

An intriguing view of a time when high art was taken seriously, as an obligation of thoughtful men. Historical study was also a serious matter, and opera was seen as a didactic occasion for historical subjects. To show how composers approached historical themes, Taruskin compares the first and second versions of *Boris* and Rimsky-Korsakov's *Maid of Pskov* with Tchaikovsky's *Oprichnik* (both about Ivan the Terrible). As background for this exercise, there is a discussion of the anti-Ivan history of Nikolai Karamzin and the more favorable views of Sergei Solovyov. Rimsky went along with the latter, while Tchaikovsky was more neutral. *Boris* was informed by Karamzin and also Nikolai Kostomarov: through the historians Musorgsky found an authentic basis for the opera's second version. So the three eminent composers were "directly involved with the works and issues raised by the three most eminent historians of their time." With long musical examples, technical analysis, and 142 footnotes.

2650. Karlinsky, Simon. "Russian Comic Opera in the Age of Catherine the Great." *19thCM* 7 (1984): 318–325.

Comic opera came to Russia with a French touring company in the period 1764–1768. Some Russian efforts in the genre, by Alexander Ablesimov, Mikhail Matinski, and Nikolai Lvov, are described.

2651. Mooser, Robert. *Opéras, intermezzos, ballets, cantates, oratorios joués en Russie durant le XVIIIe siècle.* 2nd ed. Geneva: R. Kister, 1955. xiv, 169p. ML128 .V7 M8.

First edition, 1945. A title list of operas and stage works with music that were performed in Russia during the 18th century. Theater and date are given for each performance, along with sources of data. Also a list of musical dramatic works by Russians that were performed outside the country. Index by composer.

2652. Buckler, Julie A. "Divas in the Drawing Room: Opera as Literature in Pre-Revolutionary Russia." Ph.D. diss., Harvard U., 1996. 455p.

2653. Hofmann, Rostislav. *Un siècle d'opéra russe (de Glinka a Stravinsky).* Paris: Corrêa, 1946. 254p. ML1741 .H7.

A useful summary, organized by composer: chapters on Glinka, Rimsky-Korsakov, Dargomyzhskii, Musorgsky, Borodin, and Tchaikovsky. Genesis, program notes, and reception for their major operas. No index.

There is a useful list of about 350 operas by Soviet composers, with names of librettists and premiere dates, in "Sowjetische Opern seit 1945," *Musikbühne* 1974: 174–197. Unfortunately the titles are given only in German translation. Three Russian works are of interest:

2654. *Teatral'naia entsiklopediia.* Moscow: Sovetskaia Entsiklopediia, 1967. 5v. PN2035 .T4.

Covers all stage genres in all countries, with emphasis on the Soviet Union. Each republic has a long article on opera, with details on theaters, chronologies and casts, and bibliographies. No index.

2655. *Ruskii sovetskii teatr.* Leningrad: Iskusstvo, 1975. 2v. PN2724 .R874.

Contents pages are in several languages, but the text is in Russian only. There are descriptive and historical essays on all the theaters of Leningrad (St. Petersburg) and Moscow. All performances and casts are given for 1917–1926. Index of theaters, name index.

2656. Bernandt, Grigorii Borisovich. *Slovar' oper.* Moscow: Sovetskii Kompozitor, 1962. 554p. ML102 .O6 B45.

Includes program notes and premiere details on major operas of 1736–1959, a chronology of premieres by city, and indexes to composers, librettists, conductors, ballet masters, stage managers, and other personnel. Arrangement is by title.

Individual Cities

Moscow (Moskva)

Moscow developed as a major opera center only in the later 19th century, although it had an opera house as early as 1742. The famous Bol'shoi Teatr opened in 1825, burned in 1853, and was rebuilt in 1856. It has been the subject of many books in Russian, of which these two histories are the most informative:

2657. *Bol'shoi Teatr SSSR: Opera, balet.* Moscow: Gosudarstvennoe Muzykal'noe Izdatel'stvo, 1958. 238p. PN2726 .M62 G52.

An oversized book of color pictures of the building and of scenes from opera and ballet, with a historical narrative and a bibliography of more than 1,000 entries. No index.

2658. Bocharnikova, Ella. *Bol'shoi Teatr: Kratkii istoricheskii ocherk.* Moscow: Moskovskii Rabochii, 1987. 187p. and 48p. of plates. No ISBN. ML1741.8 .M72 G715.

An illustrated gathering of historical essays on the theater. No index.

An annual publication presents accounts of all events, with pictures and personnel lists: *Bol'shoi Teatr SSSR, 1969/70–*. ML1741.8 .M7 C5. A useful book in English is available:

2659. Pokrovsky, Boris Alexandrovich, and Yuri Nikolayevich Grigorovich. *The Bolshoi: Opera and Ballet at the Greatest Theater in Russia.* New York: Morrow, 1979. 238p. ISBN 0-6880-3492-6. ML1741.8 .M7 P762.

A large photo book, with historical summary. Includes a repertoire list that shows only 42 different operas presented since 1842. Only eight composers were foreigners, and Wagner was never produced. Index of titles. Premieres at the theater 1917–1980 were listed in *Oper heute* 4.

St. Petersburg (Leningrad)

The first opera was seen in 1736. Principal houses were the Mariinskii Teatr (1860, replacing an earlier structure, renamed the Kirov—see full name in #2660—in 1935, renamed Marinskii Teatr in 1991) and the Mikhailovskii (1833, rebuilt in 1859, renamed the Malyi Opernyi Teatr after the Revolution). A theater for comic opera opened in 1927. The *NGDO* article on the city is informative with regard to the history of these theaters. For details there are several useful works in Russian:

2660. *Leningradskii Gosudarstvennyi Ordena Lenina Akademischskii Teatr Opery i Baleta Imeni S. M. Kirova, 1917–1967.* Leningrad: Muzyka, 1967. 328p. ML1741.8 .L4 G74.

A well-illustrated history of the theater, now known simply as the Kirov Teatr. A chronological list of works staged 1917–1967 includes names of directors and ballet masters but not singers. No index.

2661. *Leningradskii Teatr Muzykal'noi Komedii.* Leningrad: Muzyka, 1972. 182p. ML1741.8 .L4 L4.

A popular, illustrated history of the theater known for its comic opera productions. Includes a chronology, with casts, 1929–1971. No index.

Slovakia

See note at Czech Republic.

2662. Hoza, Štefan. *Opera na Slovensku.* Martin: Vydavatel'stvo Osveta, 1952–1954. 2v. ML1724 .H7.

A very well illustrated account of opera in Slovakia, with special attention to Bratislava. Details on the seasons of 1920–1931. Footnoted but without bibliography. Name and title indexes.

2663. Vajda, Igor. *Slovenska Opera.* Bratislava: Opus, 1988. ML1724.7 .S6 V34.

Not seen. Library of Congress record indicates it has illustrations and a six-page bibliography. A coffee-table book of illustrations, *Slovenskeho Narodneho Divadlo* (Bratislava: Slovenske Vyd. Krasnej Literatury, 1960; 522p.) was not seen; *Kaufman* says it has a chronology 1920–1960, without casts. Several bibliographies by Juraj Potúček are of use for references to operatic matters; they are identified in *Duckles* 4.340–4.342.

Spain (Spanish: España)

Music in General

2664. Subirá, José. *Historia de la música española y hispano-americana.* Barcelona: Salvat Editores, 1953. 1,003p. ML315 .S897.

The standard history: a comprehensive account covering to 1950. All musical forms are discussed, and biographical information is given. Copiously illustrated. Index.

2665. Chase, Gilbert. *The Music of Spain.* 2nd ed. New York: Dover, 1959. 383p. ISBN 0-486-20549-5. ML315 .C4.

First edition, 1941. The preferred English-language history: a survey from the Middle Ages to the mid–20th century; all forms are considered. Musical examples, illustrations, 25-page bibliography, and index.

Opera

2666. Subirá, José. *Historia de la música teatral en España.* Barcelona: Labor, 1945. 214p. ML1747 .S83.

Historical survey from medieval liturgical drama through opera and zarzuela of the 19th century. Musical examples and photos, no bibliography or index.

2667. *Teatro y música en España (siglo XVIII): Actas del Simposio Internacional Salamanca 1994.* Ed. Rainer Kleinertz. Kassel: Reichenberger, 1996. viii, 234p. ISBN 0-930700-72-7. ML315.3 .S554.

Consists of 11 papers from the conference; one is about Portugal, the others are about stage music of Spain. Of special interest: Reinhard Strohm, "Francesco Corselli's Operas for Madrid" (#717); and Rainer Kleinertz, "La zarzuela del siglo XVIII entre ópera y comedia."

2668. Subirá, José. *La tonadilla escénica.* Madrid: Tipografía de Archivos, 1928–1930. 3v. ML1747 .S8.

The definitive history and analytical study of the 18th- and early-19th-century opera-in-miniature, the scenic *tonadilla.* Includes extensive appendixes of supplementary materials: documents, chronologies, casts, lists of works, performers, musical transcriptions, libretti, and composer biographies. No index or bibliography.

2669. Cotarelo y Mori, Emilio. *Historia de la zarzuela, o sea el drama lírico en España desde su origen a fines del siglo XIX.* Madrid: Tipografía de Archivos, 1934. 618p. ML1747 .C6 H5.

A comprehensive study, tracing the zarzuela from its origins in the 17th century to 1857. Focus is on performance history rather than on musical aspects. Illustrations but no musical examples, bibliography, or index.

2670. Bussey, William M. *French and Italian Influences on the Zarzuela, 1700–1770.* Ann Arbor, Mich.: UMI Research, 1982. 297p. ISBN 0-8357-1285-0. ML1950 .B87.

A scholarly account of the era, with musical examples and analyses, production histories, and description of primary and secondary sources. A useful glossary of terms, bibliography of some 500 items, index of names, titles, and topics.

2671. Fernández-Cid, Antonio. *Cien años de teatro musical en España, 1875–1975.* Madrid: Real Musical, 1975. 610p. ISBN 84-387-0021-7. ML1747 .F47.

A useful, illustrated survey of opera, zarzuela, and other stage music for the century. List of librettists and biographical section for composers. No bibliography; with index.

2672. Boyd, Malcolm, and Juan José Carreras. *Music in Spain during the Eighteenth Century.* New York: Cambridge U.P., 1998. vii, 269p. ISBN 0-521-48139-2. ML315.3 .M87.

Consists of 18 essays by various authors. The only one on opera is a useful summary by Xoán M. Carreira, "Opera and Ballet in Public Theatres of the Iberian Peninsula"; it has 14 footnotes to the relevant literature. The volume has a name and topic index.

Cities and Regions

Barcelona

The Gran Teatro del Liceo opened in 1847, burned in 1861, and was rebuilt and reopened in 1862.

2673. Subirá, José. *La ópera en los teatros de Barcelona: Estudio histórico cronológico desde el siglo XVII al XX.* 2nd ed. Barcelona: Librería Milla, 1960. 2v. in 1. ML1747.8 .B18 S8.

First edition, 1946. A detailed history of opera performances in the city to 1936. Without index or bibliography.

2674. Virella Cassanes, Francisco. *La ópera en Barcelona: Estudio histórico-crítico.* Barcelona: Redondo y Xumetra, 1888. vii, 380p. ML1747.8 .B18 V2.

A history with a chronology from 1788 to 1888. Appendix gives a list of singers and a list of works performed. No bibliography or index.

2675. Alier Aixalà, Roger. *L'ópera a Barcelona: Origines, desenvolupamente i consolidacio de l'ópera com a espectacle.* Barcelona: Societat Catalana de Musicologia, 1990. 651p. No ISBN. ML1747 .A45.

Originally the author's dissertation, U. of Barcelona, 1979. A thorough study covering to 1800. Narrative style, with chronologies of seasons 1708–1801. Economic data, information on singers. Bibliography, no index.

2676. Alier Aixalà, Roger. *El Gran Teatro Liceo.* Madrid: Daimon, 1986. 119p. ISBN 9-6860-2487-5. ML1747.8 .B18 A3.

A footnoted history of the theater, with architectural details but with few illustrations. The repertoire of the 1870s is described, and there is a list of 369 operas performed 1847–1986. No index.

2677. Sabat, Antonio. *Gran Teatro del Liceo.* Barcelona: Escudo de Oro, 1979. 96p.

Not seen. *Kaufman* describes it as a narrative history with pictures. *Kaufman* also mentions José Artís, *Primer centenario de la Sociedad del Gran Teatro del Liceo, 1847–1947* (Barcelona, 1950).

Cadiz

2678. Carreira, Xoán M. "Origenes de la ópera en Cadiz: Un informe de 1768 sobre el Coliseo de Óperas." *Revista de musicologia* 10 (1987): 581–599.

A collection of documents on the theater, without introduction or commentary.

Madrid

The Teatro Real opened in 1850, was bombed in the Spanish Civil War, was rebuilt as a concert hall, and underwent restoration in the 1990s. It had a distinguished history in the 19th century. The first opera "broadcast" took place there in 1896, the transmission being by telephone. This interesting fact is one of many provided in:

2679. Gómez de la Serna, Gaspar. *Gracias y desgracias del Teatro Real.* 2nd ed. Madrid: Ministerio de Educación y Ciencia, 1975. viii, 78p. ISBN 8-4369-0455-9. ML1747.8 M32 T44.

Begins with a useful review of theaters in Madrid in 1850, when the Real opened. Gives a general account (no chronologies) of each season, 1868–1924/1925. The theater closed in 1925 and was not reopened until 1966. Illustrations; no notes, bibliography, or index.

2680. Subirá, José. *Historia y anecdotario del Teatro Real.* Madrid: Plus-Ultra, 1949. 820p. ML1747.8 .M32 T48.

A survey of the theater's history, with chronologies and a list of works performed. Index.

2681. Buck, Donald C. "Aesthetics, Politics, and Opera in the Vernacular: Madrid, 1737." OQ 10-3 (1994): 71–91.

Examines the city's theaters—the Cruz and the Principe—and their administration. Spanish companies presented zarzuelas and by 1737 were also giving native operas. Buck compares their "performance aesthetic" with that of Italian companies. One difference was that castrati took part in Italian performances, while in Spanish productions women took female and male roles.

Málaga

Kaufman cites D. B. Fernandez Serrano, *Annales del Teatro Cervantes de Málaga* (1903), as a narrative history 1870–1903, with good coverage of performances and playbills for each season; and Enrique del Pino, *Historia del teatro en Málaga durante el siglo XIX, 1792–1914* (2v., 1985).

Oviedo

Kaufman cites Luis Peon Arrones, *Historia de la ópera en Oviedo* (3v.; 1981–1987), as a history to 1948, with details on each season from then to 1985: dates, casts, reviews, and pictures.

Valencia

2682. Zabala, Arturo. *El teatro en la Valencia de finales del siglo XVIII.* Valencia: Institución Alfonso el Magnanimo, 1982. 461p. ISBN 8-4000-5084-3. PN2785 .V18 Z16.

A documented narrative history of all theatrical genres, including the *tonadilla,* dealing much with administration, the public, and the critics. Seasonal chronologies, 1790–1801. No index.

2683. Zabala, Arturo. *La ópera en la vida teatral Valenciana del siglo XVIII.* Valencia: Diputación Provincial de Valencia, 1960. 330p. ML1747.8 .V18 Z16.

A strong history of 18th-century performances, in narrative style, with chronologies 1727–1797 (no casts). No bibliography, but 525 footnotes identify the relevant writings. Index of names, topics, and titles.

IOM 2905–2918 and 2955–2968 give many other perspectives on Spanish opera in the cities and regions.

Sweden (Swedish: Sverige; German: Schweden)

Major opera productions have taken place in Stockholm since the mid–18th century. The first permanent theater was built in the suburb of Drottningholm in 1754; it burned in 1762, was rebuilt in 1766, and is still in use. Its story is told in:

2684. Beijer, Agne. *Drottningholms slottsteater på Lovisa Ulrikas och Gustaf III's tid.* Stockholm: LiberFörlag, 1981. 359p. ISBN 91-38-72351-4. PN2776 .D72.

A history of the baroque court theater from its rebuilding in 1766 to 1809. Details on the structure, scenery, and repertoire. Bibliography, indexes of works and persons.

2685. Prieberg, Fred K. *Musik und Musikpolitik in Schweden.* Herrenberg: Döring, 1976. 112, [12] p. ML313.5 .P74.

Describes the Institutet för Rikskonserter and other state institutions for the dissemination of musical performances, covering the 1960s and early 1970s. Name index.

2686. Institutet för Rikskonserter. *Music for Sweden. The Institute for National Concerts (INC).* Stockholm: INC, 1972. 50p. ML27 .S85 I6.

The INC was formed in 1968 to support Swedish composers. The book narrates its work and presents a general picture of Swedish musical life, together with maps and lists of orchestras, opera houses, and music schools. No index.

2687. Roth, Lena. *Musical Life in Sweden.* Stockholm: Swedish Institute, 1987. 167p. ISBN 0-15200-2012. ML313.5 .M8.

This useful overview of musical activity includes a section (p.61–87) on musical theater. It gives brief notes about opera composers and the performances at the Royal Opera and other theaters. Index.

2688. Ralf, Klas. *Kungliga Teatern repertoar 1773–1973: Opera, operett, sångspel, balett.* Stockholm: Operan, 1974. 219p. ML1745.8 .S82 K88.

A valuable account of the Royal Opera Company (Kungliga Teatern; established 1773), with chronologies and casts. The company has had numerous venues, culminating in the opening of today's principal theater, the Kungliga Teatern, in 1898. Tours of the company, as well as visiting companies in Stockholm. Composers and their works, with performance statistics (the most popular opera, by far, has been *Carmen;* the only native opera on the list is Blomdahl's *Aniara,* number 66). Titles are in Swedish and the original language, and there is a two-page summary of the contents in English. Ballet is in a separate section. Name index and title index of about 1,400 names. The next item provides some later data.

2689. Sällström, Åke. *Opera på Stockholmsoperan.* Stockholm: Norstedt, 1977. 197p. ISBN 91-773051-1. ML1745.8 .S82 K86.

A popular, illustrated history of the Royal Opera Company. Includes a list of artists, with portraits and works they have sung, and a title list of all operas performed through 1977 (names in original languages or in Swedish) with dates. Name index.

A guide to a large body of publications about Swedish music:

2690. Davidsson, Åke. *Bibliografi over svensk musiklitteratur 1800–1945 = Bibliography of Swedish Music Literature 1800–1945.* 2nd ed. Stockholm: Almqvist & Wiksell, 1980. 267p. ISBN 91-85092-10-X. ML120 .S8 D33.

First edition, 1948. A classified list of 6,756 titles by and about Swedish music; no annotations. Author and title index.

2691. *Fran Sveagaldrar till Reliken: Svenska musikdramatiska verk 1890–1975.* Stockholm: Swedish Music Information Center, 1977. 58p. ISBN 91-85470-04-X.

About 150 operas listed by title. Cast requirements, instrumentations, durations, and publishers. Composer index.

Short articles on artists, events, and recordings appear in the journal *Musikrevy: Nordisk tidskrift för musik och grammofon,* 1–, 1946–; ML5 .M9635. A special issue (1967) in English dealt with "Swedish Music Past and Present." The website <www.kungligaoperan.se/> gives current opera calendars and notices.

Switzerland (French: Suisse; German: Der Schweiz; Italian: Svizzera)

2692. Gaillard, Paul-André. "Les compositeurs suisses et l'opéra." *Schweizerische Musikzeitung* 114 (July–August 1974): 219–225; 114 (September–October 1974): 280–286. ML5 .S34.

Consists of interviews with opera composers and comments on their works. Gaillard states that there is no specifically Swiss style of opera. Footnotes lead to important earlier literature, and there is a bibliography of 15 items. An older view appeared in the same journal:

2693. Refardt, Edgar. "Schweizer Oper und Opernkomponister." *Schweizerische Musikzeitung* 85 (1945): 385–389.

An inventory of names and titles, with some commentary, covering activity from the 18th century to the 20th.

Cities and Regions

Basel

2694. Merian, Wilhelm. *Basels Musikleben im XIX. Jahrhundert.* Basel: Helbing und Lichtenhahn, 1920. xi, 238p. ML320.8 .B31 M5.

Opera is included among other musical events in this general, undocumented history. Bibliography of 15 items, index of composers and their works, name index. A century of the principal opera house is covered in Fritz Weiss, *Basler Stadttheater 1834–1934* (Basel: Benno Schwabe, 1934); not seen.

Geneva (Genève)

The Grand Théâtre, so named in 1910, was opened in 1879.

2695. Tappolet, Claude. *La vie musicale à Genève au dix-neuvième siècle (1814–1918)*. Geneva: Alex Jullien, 1972. 215p. ML320.8 .G3 T3.

A scholarly account of musical activity for the period: festivals, societies, composers, the Grand Théâtre, Victoria Hall, and the Orchestre de la Suisse Romande. Documents, letters, 24 plates illustrating programs and theaters. Name and institution index.

2696. Candolle, Roger de. *Histoire du théâtre de Genève*. Geneva: Braillard, 1978. 303p. ML1749.8 G42 G72 C2.

An illustrated narrative of stage music. Includes seasonal chronologies for the Grand Casino 1952/1953–1961/1962, and the Grand Théâtre 1962/1963–1978/1979. List of premieres and of pieces most performed. Extensive index of names.

Vaud

Vaud is the southwestern canton that includes Lausanne, Geneva, and Montreux. There is a good history of its music:

2697. Burdet, Jacques. *La musique dans le pays de Vaud sous le régime Bernois (1536–1798)*. 692p. ML320 .B8 M8.

Theatrical music is covered with all other forms. Full documentation; musical examples and illustrations, bibliography of 11 pages, index of names and instruments.

Zurich (Zürich)

The famous auditorium of the city is the Tonhalle, used for concerts. The Stadttheater (new Opernhaus Zürich, opened in 1984) is the venue for opera.

2698. *150 Jahre Theater in Zürich*. Zurich: Orell Fussli, 1984. 193p. ISBN 3-2800-1521-9. PN2806 .Z92 O6413.

Not seen. *Kaufman* describes it as a volume issued to observe the opening of the new theater. It gives a history of opera in the city as well as of the new house. Color illustrations; little on the musical aspects.

Ukraine (Ukraïna)

The country declared its independence in 1991. Earlier music literature identifies it as the Ukrainskaia Sovetskaia Sotsialisticheskaia Respublika, or Ukrainskaia SSR. Nearly all the writing about music and opera is in Russian or Ukrainian; a selection of that material is in *IOM* 3406–3436. The titles given here have features of use to those who do not read Russian.

2699. Stefanovych, Mykhaïlo Pavlovych. *Kyïvs'kyi Derzhavnï Ordena Lenina Akademichnyï Teatr Opery ta Baletu URSR imeni T. H. Shevchenka.* 2nd ed. Kiev: Zhovten', 1966. 274p. ML1741.8 .K5 S8.

First edition, 1960. Musical life in Kiev during the 19th century; opera in Ukraine from 1867 to 1917; and the Akademichnyï Teatr (Shevchenko State Academic Theater of Opera and Ballet) from 1917 to 1967. Chronology 1917–1967, along with names of staff (not singers). Illustrations, no index.

2700. Stanischevs'kyi, Iurii Oleksandrovych. *Opernyi teatr Radians'koi Ukraïny: Istoriia i suchasnist'.* Kiev: Muzychna Ukraïna, 1988. 246, [40] p. of plates. ISBN 58-8510-0209. ML1741 .S86.

A plain history of opera in Kiev, with bibliographic references but with no chronologies, index, or other reference features.

United Kingdom

The United Kingdom (U.K.) comprises England, Scotland, Wales, and Northern Ireland. Great Britain—usually termed "Britain"—the larger of the two principal islands, includes England, Scotland, and Wales.

Music in General

2701. *The Lost Chord: Essays on Victorian Music.* Ed. Nicholas Temperley. Bloomington: Indiana U.P., 1989. 180p. ISBN 0-25333-3518-33. ML285.4 .L68.

A scholarly study of the period, with theatrical music covered in a chapter on English romantic opera and a chapter on Verdi in the U.K. Index, no bibliography.

2702. *The New Grove Twentieth Century English Masters.* Ed. Diana McVeagh et al. New York: Norton, 1986. 307p. ISBN 0-393-02285-4. ML286.5 .N48.

Articles from *NG,* with updated worklists and an index. Composers covered are Elgar, Delius, Vaughan Williams, Holst, Walton, Tippett, and Britten.

The *British Music Yearbook* (1975–) gives directory information and occasional lists. *London Musical Events* (1946–) is a monthly calendar.

Opera

2703. White, Eric Walter. *A History of English Opera.* 2nd ed. London: Faber & Faber, 1983. 472p. plus 32p. of plates. ISBN 0-571-10788-5. ML1731 .W59.

First edition, as *The Rise of English Opera* (New York: Philosophical Library; London: Lehmann, 1951). Development of opera in Britain up to the 1970s; treats composers, librettists, management, and organizations. List of about 750 works with premiere dates; list of operas produced in English translation. The author notes the "increase and sharpening of focus in the last 30 years or so," as over 150 new operas were produced 1945–1975. Bibliography; name, title, and theater index.

2704. White, Eric Walter. *A Register of First Performances of English Operas and Semi-Operas from the 16th Century to 1980*. London: Society for Theatre Research, 1983. v, 130p. ISBN 0-8543-0036-8. ML1731 .W59.

A list in date order—from ca. 1517—of premieres of English operas and "semi-operas" (masques, operettas, and the like). Entries name the composer, librettist, and premiere location. Some annotations, title index.

2705. Dent, Edward Joseph. *Foundations of English Opera: A Study of Musical Drama in England during the Seventeenth Century*. Cambridge: Cambridge U.P., 1928. xv, lx, 241p. Reprint, New York: Da Capo, 1965. ML1731.2 .D4.

Examines precursors, continental influences, chamber opera, and other developments up to and including Purcell. Footnotes and musical examples, no bibliography, index of names, titles, and topics. Dent's evidence and conclusions are critically assessed in:

2706. Buttrey, John. "The Evolution of English Opera between 1656 and 1695: A Re-Investigation." Ph.D. diss., U. of Cambridge, 1967. 2v.

Author's abstract in *RILM* indicates a wide range of corrections to Dent (previous entry). Says that opera in England did not begin until 1674. Discusses all operas to 1695, with particular attention to *Dido and Aeneas*.

2707. Fiske, Roger. *English Theatre Music in the Eighteenth Century*. 2nd ed. London: Oxford U.P., 1996. xiv, 684p. ISBN 0-19-316409-4. ML1731.8 .F38.

First edition, 1973. A scholarly study of all stage genres: masque, pantomime, ballad opera, etc. Includes biographies of about 50 singers, musical examples, and a bibliography of about 250 entries. An important index gives the names of all works from 1695 to 1800 that have survived in full score or vocal score; also a name index, with works under composers.

2708. Gänzl, Kurt. *British Musical Theatre*. London: Oxford U.P., 1986. 2v. ISBN 0-19-520509-X. ML1731.8 .L7 G36.

Plots, reviews, casts, and musical excerpts from several genres of stage works. Criteria for inclusion are vague, but operetta, comic opera, and musicals are present. The period covered is 1865–1984. Index.

On the 19th century see also Biddlecombe (#473).

2709. Adams, Nicky, ed. *Who's Who in British Opera*. Aldershot: Scolar Press; Brookfield, Vt.: Ashgate, 1993. xvii, 339p. ISBN 0-85967-894-6. ML102 .O6 A3.

Covers 493 living persons: singers, conductors, designers, directors, critics. An appendix groups them by occupation.

2710. Northouse, Cameron. *Twentieth-Century Opera in England and the United States*. Boston: G. K. Hall, 1976. viii, 400p. ISBN 0-8161-7896-8. ML128 .O4 N87.

Comprises several useful lists: (1) first performances of 20th-century English and American operas, 1900–1974, arranged by year, with city, date, and librettist—a total of 1,612 works; (2) an additional 941 operas for which complete performance information is lacking; (3) operas based on literary works. Indexed by composer, librettist, title, literary title, and literary author.

Cities and Regions

London

2711. *The London Stage, 1660–1800: A Calendar of Plays, Entertainments and After-pieces* . . . Carbondale: Southern Illinois U.P., 1960–1979. 11v. PN2592 .L6.

An important list of all stage productions, by date, with their casts. Financial data and critical reviews are given. Music and dance components of each work are identified. The final volume is a vast index of more than a half million references, citing all titles and persons. A companion work by the same publisher:

2712. Highfill, Philip H., Jr. et al. *A Biographical Dictionary of Actors, Actresses, Musicians, Dancers, Managers, and Other Stage Personnel in London, 1660–1880.* Carbondale: Southern Illinois U.P., 1973–1993. 16v. ISBN 0-8093-0518-6. PN2597 .H5.

Gives information on about 16,00 persons, half of them musicians. Also maps, theater plans, and much miscellaneous data.

2713. Price, Curtis Alexander. *Music in the Restoration Theatre.* Studies in Musicology, 4. Ann Arbor, Mich.: UMI Research, 1979. xxi, 302p. ISBN 0-8357-0998-1. ML1731 .P74.

Not about opera but about songs and music that were performed within spoken plays. The tangled management picture of London theaters is well described. Backnotes, indexes of songs and stage works.

2714. Petty, Frederick C. *Italian Opera in London, 1760–1800.* Ann Arbor, Mich.: UMI Research, 1980. xi, 426p. ISBN 0-8357-1073.4. ML1731.8 .L7 P512.

Based on the author's dissertation (Yale U., 1971). A scholarly account of operas, performers, productions, institutions, audiences, critical reactions, and miscellaneous facts. Includes chronology of the 1760–1800 seasons in the King's Theatre and a table of performances of the operas of each composer. The most popular opera was Piccinni's *La buona figliuola* (112 times), followed by three of Paisiello's. Only two works of importance in the period remain in the repertoire: *Alceste* and *Il matrimonio segreto.* Excellent bibliography of about 500 entries, name index, and index to operas and arias.

2715. Smith, William Charles. *The Italian Opera and Contemporary Ballet in London, 1789–1820.* London: Society for Theatre Research, 1955. xviii, 191p. ML1731.8 .L7 S5.

A discussion of each season, concentrating on the King's Theatre and the Haymarket Theatre. Casts of all performances given. Index of titles, singers, ballet artists, composers, and instrumentalists.

2716. Knapp, J. Merrill. "Eighteenth-Century Opera in London before Handel, 1705–1710." In *British Theatre and the Other Arts, 1660–1800,* ed. Shirley

Strum Kenny, 67–104 (Washington, D.C.: Associated University Presses, 1984; PN2592 .B74).

Describes the London opera scene and lists the works staged 1705–1710.

For the period 1830–1859 there is a book of reviews by the critic of the *Athenaeum*: Henry F. Chorley, *Thirty Years' Musical Recollections* (New York: Knopf, 1926; originally published 1862). Chorley was a good observer of Italian opera, but he did not appreciate Wagner. Interesting opinions are gathered in Percy Alfred Scholes, *The Mirror of Music, 1844–1944: A Century of Musical Life in Britain in the Pages of the "Musical Times"* (London: Novello, 1947). See also Lumley (#314), Klein (#429), and Schmidgall on Shaw (#433) for other critical views of the London opera.

London: Theaters

The history of London theaters is a complex one, involving numerous rebuildings and name changes. This summary may be useful.

Drury Lane: Four buildings have occupied the site, dating from 1663, 1674, 1794, and 1812 (the present structure). Important in the 19th century, the theater is no longer used regularly for opera.

Her Majesty's Theatre: This is the theater in the Haymarket, opened in 1705 as the Queen's Theatre, renamed the King's Theater in 1714—the name changed after that to accord with the gender of the sovereign—burned in 1789, rebuilt in 1791, burned in 1867, demolished in 1891, and rebuilt in 1897. It was the exclusive home of Italian opera but is no longer used for opera.

The Royal Opera House, Covent Garden, has had three buildings: 1732 (burned in 1808), 1809 (burned in 1856), and 1858. Closed for renovation; reopened in December 1999.

Sadler's Wells: The first house opened in 1765 and was the site of occasional opera until it fell into disuse in the late 19th century. Renovated in 1931, moved to the Coliseum Theatre in 1968, renamed English National Opera in 1974.

London: Royal Opera

2717. Rosenthal, Harold D. *Two Centuries of Opera at Covent Garden*. London: Putnam, 1958; Chester Springs, Penn.: Dufour, 1964. xiv, 849p. ML1731.8 .L72 C67.

A well-illustrated popular account, with casts of all performances 1847–1956/1957. The arrangement is by title, not in chronological order. Information is not always reliable. Index of names, operas, and topics.

2718. Donaldson, Frances Londsale. *The Royal Opera House in the Twentieth Century*. London: Weidenfeld & Nicholson, 1988. xvii, 238p. ISBN 0-2977-9178-8. ML1731.8 .L72 C624.

A narrative of the periods 1888–1985/1986, covering opera and ballet. Deals with administrative and economic matters, the company's tours abroad, and the emergence—under Georg Solti in 1958–1971—of "an international opera house." Backnotes, expansive index of names and theaters.

See also Haltrecht (#325).

London: Drury Lane

2719. Girdham, Jane Catherine. *English Opera in Late Eighteenth-Century London: Stephen Storace at Drury Lane*. New York: Oxford U.P., 1997. xiv, 272p. ISBN 0-19-816254-5. ML1731.8 .L72 G57.

The theater scene, biography of Storace, music at Drury Lane, music publishing. All scenes and numbers of the Storace operas are listed, along with a list of all works performed. Bibliography of about 250 items, expansive index.

London: King's (Queen's) Theatre

2720. Price, Curtis, et al. *The King's Theatre, Haymarket, 1778–1791*. New York: Oxford U.P., 1995. xxv, 698p. ISBN 0-19-816166-2. ML1731.8 .L72 P76.

A narrative history from 1704; considers the operatic scene, administration and daily operation of the theater, performance practice, rowdy audiences, temperamental singers, various directors, ballet, destruction of the building and its reconstruction in 1789–1791. Seasonal analysis of works performed.

2721. Stahura, Mark W. "Handel's Haymarket Theatre." In *Opera in Context* (#288), 95–116.

The theater was Handel's venue, 1710–1739; 30 of his 44 operas were written for it. Plans, dimensions, and illustrations of the building are given, but "little is known about the working mechanisms of the stage." A case study of *Rinaldo* presents available information about the scenic and mechanical effects. It is noted that music was always played while the machinery operated, possibly to absorb the noise.

2722. Nalbach, Daniel. *The King's Theatre, 1704–1867: London's First Italian Opera House*. London: Society for Theatre Research, 1972. xii, 164p. ISBN 0-8543-0003-1. ML1731.8 .L8 K52.

Architecture of the first structure, its managers (1710–1789), artists, and audiences. The new building of 1791–1867, with its managers. Scenery of the entire period. After the second Haymarket theater burned (1867) it was rebuilt (1897) but was no longer a leading opera house. Nalbach notes that this building is not the same one as the Theatre Royal, Haymarket, and not the Pantheon Theatre (King's Theatre, Pantheon). Index of names and topics.

London: Sadler's Wells

For Sadler's Wells there are two popular accounts: Dennis Arundell, *The Story of Sadler's Wells* (2nd ed., London: Hamish Hamilton, 1977), and Richard Jarman, *A History of Sadler's Wells Opera* (London: English National Opera, 1974).

London: The Royal Academy of Music

2723. Gibson, Elizabeth. *The Royal Academy of Music (1719–1728): The Institution and Its Directors*. Outstanding Dissertations in Music from British Universities. New York: Garland, 1989. 465p. ISBN 0-8240-2342-0. ML1731.8 . L72 R73.

A footnoted seasonal narrative, with documents, of the venue founded to present Italian opera. No bibliography or index.

Information on 910 London theaters is given in Diana Howard, *London Theatres and Music Halls* (London: The Library Association, 1970).

See also Radice (#1522).

Glyndebourne

Notable operatic performances have been given since 1934 on John Christie's estate in Sussex. Fritz Busch was director until his death in 1951. The original building was demolished in August 1992, and a new one opened on 28 May 1994.

2724. Hughes, Patrick Cairns (Spike). *Glyndebourne.* 2nd ed. London, North Pomfret, Vt.: David & Charles, 1981. 388p. ISBN 0-7153-7891-0. ML1731.8 .G63 H89.

First edition, 1965, is updated in the revision by extending the chronology of that volume to 1979. Casts, artists and their roles, and recordings are identified. There is also a popular account of the history of the festival, well illustrated. Index of names and titles.

2725. Binney, Marcus. *Glyndebourne: Building a Vision.* London: Thames & Hudson, 1994. 160p. ISBN 0-5002-7754-0. ML38 .G63 G64.

Primarily a book of color photos, with commentary, backnotes, a summary chronology of events from 1933, and index of names and titles.

2726. Joliffe, John. *Glyndebourne: An Operatic Miracle.* London: John Murray, 1999. xii, 284p. ISBN 0-7195-5578-7. ML38 .G63 G64.

A popular narrative, of interest for details on the construction of the new house. List of works performed, by composer; expansive index of names.

See also Blunt (#297) and Higgins (#306).

Liverpool

2727. Broadbent, R. J. *Annals of the Liverpool Stage.* Liverpool: Edward Howell, 1908. 393p. PN2596 .L5 B8.

A footnoted narrative going back to the medieval mystery plays, arranged by theater. Opera, variety shows, and spoken drama are covered. No chronology. Name index.

Oxford

2728. White, Eric Walter. "A Note on Opera at Oxford." In *Essays on Opera* (#72), 168–176.

The Oxford University Opera Club was responsible for a number of important stagings. The first British performances of Monteverdi's *Orfeo* (1925) and *Poppea* (1927) led to the revival of interest in the composer. *Incognita* by Egon Wellesz was premiered there in 1951. A list of 41 club productions 1925/1926–1970/1971 is given; they represent all styles and periods.

Scotland

The Scottish Opera was founded in 1961. Its early time is described in Conrad Wilson, *Scottish Opera: The First Ten Years* (Glasgow: Collins, 1972). A longer period is covered by Cordelia Oliver, *It Is a Curious Story: The Tale of Scottish Opera, 1962–1987* (Edinburgh: Mainstream, 1987).

Wales

2729. Fawkes, Richard. *Welsh National Opera*. London: Julia Macrae, 1986. x, 368p. ISBN 0-86203-184-2. ML1731.7 .W3 F4.

An informal narrative, covering 1943–1985, with a chronology 1946–1985. No bibliography. General index, and indexes of conductors and singers with their roles.

United States

Editions

2730. *Nineteenth-Century American Musical Theater*. Ed. Deane L. Root. New York: Garland, 1994. 16v. ISBN 0-8153-1365-9. LC numbers vary. (Cited in this guide as *19CAMT.*)

A series of original printed or manuscript sources for stage works, published for the first time. Genres included are ballad opera, pantomime, plays with incidental music, parlor entertainments, temperance shows, ethnic theater, minstrelsy, and operettas. Individual volumes are entered separately.

Bibliographies

2731. Horn, David. *The Literature of American Music in Books and Folk Music Collections: A Fully Annotated Bibliography*. Metuchen, N.J.: Scarecrow, 1977. 570p. ISBN 0-8108-0996-6. ML120 .U5 H7. *Supplement 1*, by David Horn and Richard Jackson, 1988. 586p. ISBN 0-8108-1997-X. ML120 .U5 H7 Suppl.

These two volumes present the core monographic literature about American music and music in the U.S. There are 3,862 entries, most of them extensively annotated. Author, title, and subject indexes.

2732. Marco, Guy A. *Literature of American Music III, 1983–1992*. Lanham, Md.: Scarecrow, 1996. xviii, 449p. ISBN 0-8108-3132-5. ML120 .U5 M135. Cited in this guide as *LOAM-3*.

A continuation of the Horn volumes, presenting 1,302 annotated entries. Together the three books offer an inventory of all significant writings in monographic form. With a title index, subject index (using Library of Congress headings), and joint-author index. The author index is in a separate volume:

2733. Marco, Guy A. *Checklist of Writings on American Music, 1640–1992*. Lanham, Md.: Scarecrow, 1996. v, 236p. ISBN 0-8108-3133-3. ML120 .U5 .M127.

A cumulative author index to all three volumes of *Literature of American Music,* covering some 5,100 titles.

2734. Heintze, James R. *American Music before 1865 in Print and on Records*. 2nd ed. I.S.A.M. Monographs, 30. Brooklyn: Institute for Studies in American Music, 1990. xiii, 248p. ISBN 0-9146-7833-7. ML120 .H6 H4.

First edition, 1976. Consists of 1,300 entries in alphabetical order, giving all editions and recordings of early compositions. Indexed by composer, compiler, title, and record label.

2735. Heintze, James R. *Early American Music: A Research and Information Guide*. Music Reference and Information Guides, 13. New York: Garland, 1990. xii, 511p. ISBN 0-8240-4119-4. ML120 .U5 H46.

A selective, annotated bibliography of 1,959 books, articles, and dissertations that deal with American music and musicians up to about 1820. Overlap with #2731–#2733 is limited to monographs. Author, title, and subject indexes.

2736. Krummel, Donald W., et al. *Resources of American Music History: A Directory of Source Materials from Colonial Times to World War Two*. Urbana: U. of Illinois Press, 1981. vi, 463p. ISBN 0-252-00828-6. ML120 .U5 R47.

A valuable review of library collections by state, with attention to materials for historical research. Index of names, topics, and types of materials.

2737. Krummel, Donald W. *Bibliographical Handbook of American Music*. Urbana: U. of Illinois Press, 1987. 269p. ISBN 0-252-01450-2.ML120 .U5 K78.

A thorough, annotated list of 760 reference works that concern American music. Includes bibliographies, trade lists, library catalogues, discographies, and guides to the literature. All genres of music are covered. Important critical commentaries. Index by author, title, and subject.

Other bibliographical materials are identified in *IOM*, 0817ff.

Music in General

Directories

2738. *Handel's National Directory for the Performing Arts*. 5th ed. New York: Bowker, 1992. 2v. ISBN 0-8352-3250-6. ML18 .H1.

Fourth edition, 1988. A list of about 7,000 organizations and facilities for music, dance, and theater, grouped by state. V.2 presents information on schools.

See also #141, #142, and #144.

Encyclopedias

2739. *The New Grove Dictionary of American Music*. Ed. H. Wiley Hitchcock and Stanley Sadie. New York: Grove's Dictionaries of Music, 1986. 4v. ISBN 0-943818-36-2. ML101 .U6 N48.

NG emphasized "European musical and cultural traditions" to the neglect of American topics; this work (often referred to as "Amerigrove") is a valuable supplement to it that fills the gap. All aspects of musical life are usefully dealt with in signed articles by authorities. Weaknesses of *NG* are unfortunately preserved: weak bibliographies and lack of an index. The whole field of sound recording is passed over in silence. Fuller descriptions in *Duckles* 1.120 and *LOAM-3,* S2–65.

Biographies

2740. *The New Grove Twentieth Century American Masters: Ives, Thomson, Sessions, Cowell, Gershwin, Copland, Carter, Barber, Cage.* Ed. William Austin et al. New York: Norton, 1988. xiv, 312p. ISBN 0-393-30353-5. ML390 .N469.

   Articles from *NG*, updated and with an index to the volume.

Other biographical coverage of American musicians is found in many works; see *IOM* 0778–0789a.

Histories

2741. Chase, Gilbert. *America's Music, from the Pilgrims to the Present.* 3rd ed. New York: McGraw-Hill, 1987. xxiv, 712p. ISBN 0-252-00454-X. ML200 .C5.

   First edition, 1955. A major history, dealing with all genres in chronological format. Chapter endnotes, musical examples, bibliography of about 1,200 items (including books, articles, and dissertations). Expansive index of persons, titles, and subjects.

2742. Hitchcock, H. Wiley. *Music in the United States: A Historical Introduction.* 3rd ed. Englewood Cliffs, N.J.: Prentice-Hall, 1988. xviii, 365p. ISBN 0-13-608407-9. ML200 .H58.

   First edition, 1969. A valuable work that combines readability with scholarship. All genres are treated, but the emphasis is on what Hitchcock calls the "cultivated" idiom rather than the "vernacular" (folk and pop). Strong bibliographic essays conclude each chapter. Expansive index.

2743. Kingman, Daniel. *American Music: A Panorama.* 2nd ed. New York: Schirmer, 1990. xix, 684p. ISBN 0-02-873370-3. ML200 .K55.

   First edition, 1979. A fine, balanced account of all genres, with considerable attention to pop forms. Chapter endnotes and bibliographic references, expansive index.

2744. Howard, John Tasker. *Our American Music: A Comprehensive History from 1620 to the Present.* 4th ed. New York: Crowell, 1965. xii, 944p. ML200 .H82.

   First edition, 1931. Title varies. A classic history with a full range of topics; biographies and worklists included. Valuable bibliographies: one is a list of histories in date order, another is of 21 regional and state histories. Indexed.

2745. Sablosky, Irving. *What They Heard: Music in America, 1852–1881, from the Pages of "Dwight's Journal of Music."* Baton Rouge: Louisiana State U.P., 1986. xiv, 317p. ISBN 0-8071-1258-5.

The leading music periodical of the mid-19th century was *Dwight's*: it covered all sorts of events, including opera performances around the country. Sablosky's illuminating commentary puts it all into perspective. Biographical register of artists, expansive index.

See also #434. Other general and specialized histories are described in *IOM* 0707–0745a.

Opera

Bibliography

2746. Borroff, Edith. *American Operas: A Checklist.* Ed. J. Bunker Clark. Detroit Studies in Music Bibliography, 69. Warren, Mich.: Harmonie Park, 1992. xxiv, 334p. ISBN 0-8999-00631.

A useful list of about 4,000 operas by 2,000 composers. Arranged by composer, then chronologically. Information given: librettist, number of acts, casting, timing, premiere data (city and date; no theaters named). No title index.

2747. Johnson, H. Earle. *Operas on American Subjects.* New York: Coleman-Ross, 1964. 125p. ML128 .O6 J6.

A useful inventory of operas having any subject matter related to North or South America, whatever the composer's nationality. Gives synopses and critical notices. Also has an interesting list of American and British literary works that have been adapted as opera libretti. Subject and title indexes.

Histories

2748. Dizikes, John. *Opera in America: A Cultural History.* New Haven, Conn.: Yale U.P., 1993. xi, 611p. ISBN 0-300-05496-3. ML1711 .D6.

A scholarly narrative of operatic activity in the U.S., covering from 1735. Treats all cities, conductors, singers, audiences, and buildings. Backnotes and expansive index, no bibliography.

2749. Lahee, Henry Charles. *Grand Opera in America.* Boston: L. C. Page, 1902. 348p. Reprint, New York: AMS, 1973. ML1711 .L18.

A useful historical survey, considering artists and performances. Stresses the influences of England, Italy, and Germany. Indexed.

2750. Mates, Julian. *The American Musical Stage before 1800.* New Brunswick, N.J.: Rutgers U.P., 1962. ix, 331p. ML1711 .M4.

A scholarly history of theaters, orchestras, audiences, companies, artists, works, and criticism, with 67 pages of notes and 14 pages of bibliography. Mates uncovered a musical stage heritage in the 18th century that other writers had ignored. It was not *The Black Crook* (1866) but *The Archers* (1796) that should be recognized as "the first extant musical performed in America and written by Americans." Name and topic index.

2751. Mattfeld, Julius. *A Handbook of American Operatic Premieres, 1731–1962.* Detroit Studies in Music Bibliography, 5. Detroit: Information Service, 1963. 142p. ML128 .O4 M3.

A title list of about 2,000 operas (with some operettas and musicals) by Americans, including those premiered outside the U.S. Information given: language, number of acts, date and locale of premiere. Composer index.

2752. Sonneck, Oscar G. T. *Early Opera in America*. New York: Schirmer, 1915. viii, 230p. Reprint, New York: B. Blom, 1963. ML1711 .S73.

An essential, learned account of the 18th-century situation, based on newspapers and other primary documents. Much detail on productions and performers, with good bibliographical references. Emphasis on the East Coast and the South and on French opera companies. Indexed.

2753. Virga, Patricia H. *The American Opera to 1790*. Ann Arbor, Mich.: UMI Research, 1982. xix, 393p. ISBN 0-8357-1374-1. ML1711 .V816.

Discusses the first music-stage works written in America, the ballad and comic operas. Special attention to *The Disappointment* (1767). Includes musical analyses and comments on productions. Informative backnotes, bibliography of about 400 items, expansive index of names, titles, and topics.

2754. Porter, Susan L. *With an Air Debonair: Musical Theatre in America, 1785–1815*. Washington, D.C.: Smithsonian Institution Press, 1992. xiv, 631p. ISBN 1-56098-063-X. ML1711 .P67.

A scholarly treatment of genres and styles of performance, theaters, and companies in a strong historical context. Types of theater covered include ballad opera, pastiche, comic opera, ballet, and melodrama. A wide range of primary sources used, such as playbills, pictures, and theater chronicles. Appendix of about 1,100 musicals performed 1785–1815; another appendix of shows given in New York, Philadelphia, Boston, Charleston, and Baltimore, 1801–1815. Endnotes, bibliography of 300 sources, and index.

2755. Nelson, Molly Sue. "Operas Composed in America in the Nineteenth Century." Ph.D. diss., U. of North Carolina, 1976.

2756. Ottenberg, June C. *Opera Odyssey: Toward a History of Opera in 19th-Century America*. Contributions to the Study of Music and Dance, 32. Westport, Conn.: Greenwood, 1994. xi, 203p. ISBN 0-313-27841-5. ML1711 .O88.

A breezy style and celebrity emphasis obstruct the author's purpose, which is to show that the success of opera in America can be attributed to Veblenesque desires of the rich to exhibit their wealth. This oversimplification is not well supported by the facts presented, and the author's credibility is affected by her naive responses to such works as Fry's *Leonora* and Bristow's *Rip van Winkle*. Chapter endnotes, bibliography, index.

See also #2786.

2757. *Opera and the Golden West: The Past, Present, and Future of Opera in the U.S.A.* Ed. John L. Di Gaetani and Josef P. Sirefman. Rutherford, N.J.: Fairleigh Dickinson U.P., 1994. 311p. ISBN 0-8386-3519-9. ML1711 .O64.

Consists of 24 brief, footnoted papers from a conference held at Hofstra U. Topics deal with singers, impresarios, companies, performances and reception of European operas (and a few native works) more or less west of Chicago. Puccini's *Fanciulla del West* is the topic of several papers. Among the many intriguing accounts is Nadine Sine's reception study for *Salome,* with quotations from horrified critics. Index of names and places.

2758. Davis, Ronald L. *A History of Opera in the American West.* Englewood Cliffs, N.J.: Prentice-Hall, 1965. 178p. ML1711 .D4.

The title conceals the actual coverage, which includes Chicago and New Orleans as well as states from Texas to California. A documented story of stage activity in all major cities and the important smaller centers like Central City and Santa Fe. Well illustrated; name and title index but no bibliography.

2759. Preston, Katherine K. *Opera on the Road: Traveling Opera Troupes in the U.S. 1825–60.* Urbana: U. of Illinois Press, 1993. xvii, 479p. ISBN 0-252-01974-1. ML1711.4 .P73.

An account of various Italian companies, Max Maretzek's troupe, along with Pyne & Harrison, and other English companies. Itineraries, illustrations, backnotes, bibliography of about 600 entries, and expansive index of names, titles, and places.

2760. Drummond, Andrew H. *American Opera Librettos.* Metuchen, N.J.: Scarecrow, 1972. 277p. ISBN 0-8108-0553-7. ML1711 .D8.

Examines 40 libretti of works that were performed at the New York City Opera, 1948–1971. Includes a good bibliography of about 300 items and an NYCO chronology. Name and title index.

2761. Kornick, Rebecca Hodell. *Recent American Opera: A Production Guide.* New York: Columbia U.P., 1991. xvii, 352p. ISBN 0-231-06920-0. MT955 .K82.

A useful list of 213 works—including some operettas and musicals—mostly written since 1972. Information given: synopsis, roles and their vocal ranges, instrumental and choral requirements, and other production matters. Critical reviews are quoted. Indexes of titles, publishers, durations. No overlap with Eaton (#284).

Theaters and Companies

2762. Zietz, Karyl Lynn. *Opera Companies and Houses of the United States: A Comprehensive, Illustrated Reference.* Jefferson, N.C.: McFarland, 1995. xv, 335p. ISBN 0-89950-955-X. ML13 .Z54.

A valuable handbook of information on 92 opera companies in 41 states, giving their history, repertoire, premieres, staff, and publications. Opera houses are illustrated. Bibliography of about 150 items, index of names, titles, and institutions.

2763. Zietz, Karyl Lynn. *The National Trust Guide to Great Opera Houses in America.* New York: Wiley, 1996. xi, 228p. ISBN 0-4711-4421-5. NA6830 .Z54.

A summary of opera house construction, 1766–1865, by region and a review of restoration activity. Houses no longer extant are listed. Construction details and dimensions, black-and-white photos. Bibliography, index.

2764. Bishop, Cardell. *San Carlo Opera Company of America*. Santa Monica, Calif.: Author, 1980–1981. 2v.

> Not seen. Described by *Kaufman* as "crammed with dates and casts, especially for performances in New York, Los Angeles, and San Francisco." The company performed across the U.S. and Canada, with such artists as Tito Schipa and Titta Ruffo.

Singers

2765. Davis, Peter G. *The American Opera Singer: The Lives and Adventures of America's Great Singers in Opera and Concert from 1825 to the Present*. New York: Doubleday, 1997. 626p. ISBN 0-385-47495-4. ML400 .D33.

> Facts about the stars, told in a popular style. The vapid jargon of journalistic criticism is pervasive: Aprile Millo "lacked inner conviction," and Jennie Tourel's voice had an "intriguing tang and pungency." Backnotes, bibliography of about 150 titles, index.

Cities and Regions

The only works cited are those devoted to opera, but some information on opera will be found in the more generalized city and regional histories identified in *IOM* v.2. Treatises on the stage history of particular cities are often useful for operatic studies; citations are given in *IOM* and in *GRB*.

Boston

Boston had an unsteady operatic history until the foundation in 1958 of the Opera Company of Boston, under Sarah Caldwell.

2766. Eaton, Quaintance. *The Boston Opera Company*. New York: Appleton-Century-Crofts, 1965. xiv, 338p. ML1711.8 .B7 E14.

> A popular, undocumented story, with 55 illustrations. Gives complete casts for all performances, material on the singers, and a chapter on the Boston critics. Expansive index of names and titles.

2767. Bishop, Cardell. *Boston National Opera Company and Boston Theatre Opera Company*. Santa Monica, Calif.: Author, 1981. vii, 41 leaves. ML1711.8 .B7.

> A history of the companies, 1914–1918, with chronologies and casts. Index.

Chautauqua

2768. Cowden, Robert H. *The Chautauqua Opera Association, 1929–1958: An Interpretative History*. [University, Miss.]: National Opera Association, 1974. iv, 85p. ML1711.8 .C45.

> The Chautauqua Institute was founded in 1874; its music program was initiated in 1878. This useful survey includes a list of 72 operas (titles only) presented from 1929 to 1958 with the dates on which they were given. The research literature on Chautauqua is covered by 173 backnotes.

Chicago

Performances were heard in the city as early as 1850, and an opera house was constructed in 1865 (Crosby's, which burned in the great fire of 1871). The superb Auditorium, designed by Louis Sullivan and Dankmar Adler, was the home of visiting companies, 1889–1920, then of the new Chicago Grand Opera Company. In 1929 opera moved to the new Civic Opera House, but the depression of the 1930s put an end to the local company. In 1954 the Lyric Theater, later the Lyric Opera, began its highly successful seasons. This intricate tale is without a scholarly literature.

2769. Hackett, Karlton. *The Beginning of Grand Opera in Chicago (1850–1859)*. Chicago: Laurentian, 1913. 60p.

Not seen.

2770. Moore, Edward C. *Forty Years of Opera in Chicago*. New York: Liveright, 1930. 430p. ML1711.8 .C5 M7.

A popular history of opera in the Auditorium, 1889–1929. Without documentation or index but has yearly staff lists and many illustrations.

2771. Davis, Ronald. *Opera in Chicago: A Social and Cultural History, 1850–1965*. New York: Appleton-Century, 1966. 393p. ML1711.8 .C5 D4.

Although the author states that "the bulk of the material presented here is drawn from contemporary Chicago newspapers," he does not provide exact references, and there is no bibliography. The result is a popular account, emphasizing personal lives of the singers. A useful feature is the listing of casts for performances, 1910–1965. Index.

2772. Cropsey, Eugene M. "Mr. Crosby's Temple of Art: The Inaugural Season, Chicago, 1865." OQ 12-1 (Autumn 1995): 99–126.

An interesting, documented study of the house, with illustrations of the sumptuous interior and a chronology with casts, 1865–1871; 76 backnotes.

2773. Cassidy, Claudia. *Lyric Opera of Chicago: Twenty Years, A Pictorial Souvenir*. Chicago: R. R. Donnelly for the Lyric Opera, 1979. 80p. ML1711.8 .C4 L95.

An attractive coffee-table book with some commentary and cast lists, 1954–1979.

Cincinnati

2774. Thierstein, Eldred A. *Cincinnati Opera, from Zoo to Music Hall*. Hillsdale, Mich.: Deerstone Books, 1995. 316p. ISBN 0-964-6068-0-1. ML1711.8 .C56 T5.

The city zoo had a band shell from 1877, which was enlarged in 1920 and became the home of the Cincinnati Summer Opera. This is a footnoted narrative, with annals of performances and casts, 1920–1995. List of administrators, title and name indexes.

2775. Wolz, Larry Robert. "Opera in Cincinnati . . . 1801–1920." Ph.D. diss., U. of Cincinnati, 1983.

Denver

2776. Jennings, Harlan. "Grand Opera Comes to Denver, 1864–1881." OQ 13-3 (Spring 1997): 57–84.

Traveling companies performed on occasion from 1864. In 1881 the Tabor Opera House opened with Emma Abbott and her troupe. In 1890 the Broadway Theatre opened and eclipsed the Tabor, although celebrities continued to appear there (e.g., the Mapleson troupe with Adelina Patti, Minnie Hauk, and Lillian Nordica). Nellie Melba sang in 1899, and the Metropolitan appeared in 1900. The Tabor was torn down in 1964. This interesting article has 82 notes to the relevant literature.

Kansas City

2777. Jennings, Harlan. "The Early Days of Grand Opera in Kansas City, Missouri, 1860–1879." OQ 15-4 (Autumn 1999): 677–696.

In 1860 soprano Anna Bishop sang in the outpost town of 6,000; the first professional opera performance was given in 1869 by the Brignoli Opera Company. The Coates Opera House opened in 1870. During 1860–1879 there were 14 performances of 10 different operas. Some pictures and information on more recent times are in Russell Patterson, *A View from the Pit: 30 Years of Opera Theater in Mid-America* (Kansas City, Mo.: Lowell, 1987; xx, 94p; ISBN 0-9328-4525-8; ML1711.8 .K36 P37). It is a celebratory volume for the 30th anniversary of the Lyric Opera of Kansas City.

Los Angeles

2778. Wilson, Neil E. "A History of Opera Activities in Los Angeles, 1887–1965." Ph.D. diss., Indiana U., 1967. 329p.

2779. Bishop, Cardell. *The Los Angeles Grand Opera Association, 1924–1934: A Short Career in a Big City.* Santa Monica, Calif.: Author, 1979. vii, 54p. ML1711.8 .L6 B57.

A survey history, with complete chronology and casts.

2780. Sanders, J. "Los Angeles Grand Opera Association: The Formative Years." *Southern California Quarterly* 55 (1973): 261–302.

Recounts the establishment of the company in 1924 by Gaetano Merola, who had earlier created the San Francisco Opera. Claudia Muzio and Beniamino Gigli were among the luminaries who appeared in 1924. Casts of all performances, 1924–1926; 145 footnotes.

New Orleans

2781. Belsom Jack. *Opera in New Orleans.* New Orleans: New Orleans Opera Association, 1993. 20p. ML1711.8 .N25 B45.

Not seen.

2782. Kmen, Harry A. *Music in New Orleans: The Formative Years, 1791–1841.* Baton Rouge: Louisiana State U.P., 1967. 314p. ML200.8 .N48 K6.

A scholarly survey of musical activity, including opera. French and Italian companies appeared; some dates and casts are given. Indexed.

2783. Baroncelli, Joseph Gabriel de. *Le théâtre français à la Nlle Orleans 1791–1906.* New Orleans: G. Muller, 1906.

Not seen. *Kaufman* says it is a narrative account with company rosters and casts for some performances.

New York City

Ballad operas and similar works were heard in New York in the early 18th century; the first Italian company arrived in 1825. Various houses and companies competed for audiences through the 19th century, among them the Astor Place Opera, under Maretzek, 1847–1852 (see #316), and the Academy of Music, under Mapleson, 1854–1925 (see #315). The Metropolitan Opera opened on 22 October 1883, with *Faust.* The Met moved to its new quarters in Lincoln Center in 1966. The city's other company is the New York City Opera, founded in 1944.

New York City: Histories—19th Century

2784. Odell, George Clinton Densmore. *Annals of the New York Stage.* New York: Columbia U.P., 1927–1949. 15v. PN2277 .N5 O4.

A vast chronology for the period 1699–1894, covering spoken plays, opera, and operetta. Casts are given, with portraits and critics' comments. Informal style but rich in detail. Each volume has an expansive index of names, titles, and topics.

2785. Rogers, Delmer D. "Public Music Performances in New York City from 1800 to 1850." *Anuario interamericano de investigación musical* 6 (1970): 5–50.

Describes sacred and secular music concerts, opera performances, variety shows, and dance programs. Casts given, with commentaries and bibliographic references. Summary in Spanish.

2786. Ahlquist, Karen. *Democracy at the Opera: Music, Theater, and Culture in New York City, 1815–1860.* Urbana: U. of Illinois Press, 1997. xvii, 248p. ISBN 0-252-02272-6. ML1711.8 .N3 A4.

Asserts that opera was a tool of the elite for class domination. The theory does not account for the fact that the elite already had political and economic power. Many errors and dubious assumptions were ascribed to the book by its reviewer in *OQ.*

See also #2756.

2787. Krehbiel, Henry Edward. *Chapters of Opera: Being Historical and Critical Observations and Records Concerning the Lyric Drama in New York from Its Earliest Days Down to the Present Time.* 3rd ed. New York: Holt, 1911. xvii, 460p. ML1711.8 .N3 K73.

Surveys the years before 1825 and operatic events of the 19th century. Krehbiel was a critic for the *New York Tribune,* a witness to much of what happened. A chronology for the seasons 1908–1911 is included. See continuation at #2791.

2788. Lawrence, Vera Brodsky. *Strong on Music: The New York Music Scene in the Days of George Templeton Strong. Volume One: Resonances, 1836–1849.* New York: Oxford U.P., 1987. lvi, 608p. Reprint, Chicago: U. of Chicago Press, 1995. ISBN (Oxford) 0-19-503199-2. ML200.8 .N5 L4.

A valuable account of the city's musical culture, based on Strong's diary. A lawyer and music lover, Strong made articulate observations on concerts, singers, composers, and all aspects of the art milieu. Extensive commentaries by Lawrence and an expansive index that leads to critical writings and such miscellaneous facts as the addresses of music stores. Bibliography of about 400 primary and secondary sources. See next entry.

2789. Lawrence, Vera Brodsky. *Strong on Music: The New York Music Scene in the Days of George Templeton Strong. Volume Two: Reverberations, 1850–1856* Chicago: U. of Chicago Press, 1995. xxii, 863p. ISBN 0-226-47010-5. ML200.8 .N3 C42. *Volume Three: Repercussions, 1857–1862.* Chicago: U. of Chicago Press, 1999. xvii, 630p. ISBN 0-226-47015-6. ML200.8 .N3 C43.

Continuations of the preceding entry.

New York City: Histories—20th Century

The writings of music critics give good perspectives on concert and opera life. Collections of New York criticisms already cited: Aldrich (#425), Henderson (#427), and Porter (#432). Others:

2790. Downes, Olin. *Olin Downes on Music: A Selection from His Writings during the Half-Century 1906 to 1955.* Ed. Irene Downes. New York: Simon & Schuster, 1957. 473p. ML60 .C73.

Downes wrote for the *New York Times* and earlier for the *Boston Post*. The book offers about 150 reviews, with a name and title index.

2791. Krehbiel, Henry Edward. *More Chapters of Opera: Being Historical and Critical Observations and Records Concerning the Lyric Drama in New York from 1908 to 1918.* New York: Holt, 1919. xvi, 474p. ML1711.8 .N3 K74.

Continues #2787; has tables of performances and singers.

New York City: The Metropolitan Opera ("The Met")

2792. Mayer, Martin. *The Met: One Hundred Years of Grand Opera.* New York: Simon & Schuster for the Metropolitan Opera Guild, 1983. 368p. ISBN 0-671-47087-6. ML1711.8 .N3 M46.

The official history of the Met's first century: a fluid narrative, with backnotes, 212 pleasing illustrations, and a name-title index.

2793. *Annals of the Metropolitan Opera: The Complete Chronicle of Performances and Artists; Chronology 1883–1985.* Ed. Gerald Fitzgerald. New York: Metropolitan Opera Guild; Boston: G. K. Hall, 1989. 2v. ISBN 0-8161-8903-X. ML1711.8 .N3 M38.

V.1: chronology, with casts. V.2: lists of performers, composers and librettists, production personnel, locations, broadcasts, staff, chorus and ballet masters, and premieres. Name index cites sections of the book only, not exact pages. Supersedes the pioneering *Metropolitan Opera Annuals* of William H. Seltsam (*IOM 0694*).

2794. Jackson, Paul. *Saturday Afternoons at the Old Met: The Metropolitan Opera Broadcasts, 1931–1950.* Portland, Ore.: Amadeus, 1992. xvi, 569p. ISBN 0-931-340-48–9. ML1711.8 .N3 M434.

A valuable presentation of the Met's radio history, with casts, photos, stories about the artists, and perceptive critiques. More than 200 broadcasts have been preserved in whole or in part; the Met has complete recordings only from 1950. Notes, bibliography, expansive index of names and titles. See next entry.

2795. Jackson, Paul. *Sign-Off for the Old Met: The Metropolitan Opera Broadcasts, 1950–1966.* Portland, Ore.: Amadeus, 1997. xv, 644p. ISBN 1-57467-030-1. ML1711.8 .N3 M4343.

Extends the preceding entry, in the same format; covers about 200 broadcasts.

2796. Eaton, Quaintance. *Opera Caravan: Adventures of the Metropolitan on Tour, 1883–1956.* New York: Farrar, Straus, & Cudahy, 1957. xv, 400p. Reprint, New York: Da Capo, 1978. ML1711.8 .N3 M425.

A chronology of all tours, by city, with casts and interesting photos. Breezy text with invented conversations. Name, title, and city index.

2797. Jacobson, Robert. *Magnificence: Onstage at the Met: Twenty Great Operas.* New York: Simon & Schuster, 1985. 255p. ISBN 0-671-5572-38. ML1711.8 .N3 M435.

An elaborate photo book, with commentary, presenting views from 20 operas. Name index.

2798. Seligman, Paul. *Debuts and Farewells: A Two-Decade Photographic Chronicle of the Metropolitan Opera.* New York: Knopf, 1972. 180p. ISBN 0-394-47983-1. ML1711.8 .N3 M597.

A picture book of singers, onstage and off, and of the buildings.

2799. Tuggle, Robert. *The Golden Age of Opera.* With the photographs of Herman Mishkin. New York: Holt, Rinehart & Winston, 1983. 246p. ISBN 0-03-057778-0. ML400 .T855.

Consists of 200 photos from 1906 to 1932, most showing singers in costume, with some casual biographies. Expansive index of names and titles.

2800. Fellers, Frederick. *Metropolitan Opera on Record.* Westport, Conn.: Greenwood, 1984. xix, 101p. ISBN 0-313-23952-5. ML156.4 .O46 F4.

Full detail on 477 recordings, including cast and release labels. Indexes of artists, operas, and arias.

See also the memoirs of impresarios Bing (#295, #296) and Gatti-Casazza (#305).

New York City: Other Opera Companies

2801. Cone, John. *The First Rival of the Met.* New York: Columbia U.P., 1983. 257p. ISBN 0-231-05748-2. ML1711.8 .N32 A22.

A scholarly account of Colonel Mapleson's opera troupe, which performed in the New York Academy of Music from 1878. The seasons 1883–1886 are the only ones covered. Backnotes, bibliography of about 50 items, expansive index of names and topics.

2802. Sokol, Martin. *The New York City Opera: An American Adventure.* New York: Macmillan, 1981. xiv, 562p. ISBN 0-02-612280-4. ML1711.8 .N3 N58 S6.

A general history with little documentation. Useful seasonal chronology, with all casts. Good photos, tables of broadcasts, television appearances, films, and recordings. Index of names, titles, and topics.

See also Drummond (#2760).

2803. Cone, John. *Oscar Hammerstein's Manhattan Opera Company.* Norman: U. of Oklahoma Press, 1966. 399p. ML1711.8 .N3 M153.

An illustrated account of the company, which operated 1906–1910. Chronology with casts, bibliography of about 200 items, index of names, titles, and topics.

Philadelphia

Philadelphia is the home of the oldest opera house in continuous use in the U.S., the Academy of Music (1857); it is now the home of the Philadelphia Orchestra. Resident opera companies have not shown comparable longevity.

2804. Albrecht, Otto. "Opera in Philadelphia, 1800–1830." *JAMS* 32-3 (Fall 1979): 499–515.

A narrative of the period, with a list of operas performed and references to other literature on Philadelphia opera.

2805. Armstrong, William. *A Record of the Opera in Philadelphia.* Philadelphia: Porter & Coates, 1884. 274p. Reprint, New York: AMS, 1976. ISBN 0-404-12853-X. ML1711.8 .P5 A7.

A useful history, with a list of operas produced by all major companies, 1827–1883. Detail on the Academy building and some interesting comparative information on world opera houses. (Capacities are given, with internal dimensions and colors of the interiors. Prague is white, Moscow amber, Philadelphia—like most of the great houses—crimson.) Lists of Academy directors, 1852–1883. No bibliography. Name and title index.

San Francisco

The first opera performance in San Francisco took place in 1851; within a few years 11 theaters were presenting many visiting companies. *Carmen* was sung—by Enrico Caruso, Olive Fremstad, and Marcel Journet—on the day of the 1906 earthquake.

The San Francisco Opera was founded in 1923; since 1932 its home has been the War Memorial Opera House.

2806. Bloomfield, Arthur J. *The San Francisco Opera, 1922–78.* Rev. ed. Sausalito, Calif.: Comstock Editions, 1978. 552p. ISBN 0-89174-032-5. ML1711.8 .S2 B65.

First edition, 1961. The book is a popular, journalistic account by a local music critic. Casts for each season are given, and the repertoire is arrayed by composer. Name and topic index.

2807. Hixon, Don. *Verdi in San Francisco 1851–1869: A Preliminary Bibliography.* Irvine, Calif.: Author, 1980. vi, 89p. ML410 .V4 H591.

A list of operas performed, with dates, theaters, casts, and citations to reviews.

2808. Gagey, Edmond McAdoo. *The San Francisco Stage: A History.* New York: Columbia U.P., 1950. 264p. PBN2277. S4 G22.

A theatrical history, giving attention to various short-lived opera companies: Maguire's, Shiel's, Gray's, and Wade's. Each had occupancy of an opera house, and their seasons are discussed, without chronologies. Bibliography, index.

Santa Fe

2809. Scott, Eleanor. *The First Twenty Years of the Santa Fe Opera.* Santa Fe, N. Mex.: Sunstone Press, 1976. 166p. ML1711.8 .S25 S27.

A seasonal narrative with performer index; no chronology.

Seattle

2810. Salem, Mahmoud M. *Organizational Survival in the Performing Arts: The Making of the Seattle Opera.* New York: Praeger, 1976. 210p. ISBN 0-275-05670-8. ML1711.8 .S4 S47.

Primarily a story of financial problems and successes; some references to the opera performances here and there. Expansive index of names, titles, and topics.

St. Louis

2811. Carson, William G. *St. Louis Goes to the Opera, 1837–1941.* St. Louis: Missouri Historical Society, 1946. 44p. ML1711.8 .S15 C3.

Not seen. *Kaufman* says it is a history, with no chronologies.

2812. Jennings, Harlan. "Grand Opera in St. Louis in 1886: A Champion Season?" *OQ* 10-3 (1994): 131–143.

Mapleson's company had its eighth and last season in the city. Herman Grau's troupe was also there in 1886, with a week of German opera, featuring artists from the Met. The American Opera Company, directed by Theodore Thomas, was also performing. There were controversies and uproars over all three groups.

Washington, D.C.

2813. Squares, Roy. "The Washington Opera, Inc., 1956–1977." Master's thesis, American U., 1977. 112p.

Not seen. The author's abstract in *RILM* states that it offers names of works given at the Kennedy Center, 1971–1977; Wolf Trap Farm Park, 1971–1978; and by the Opera Society of Washington, 1956–1977.

Uruguay

2814. Ayesterán, Lauro. *La música en el Uruguay.* Montevideo: Difusión Radio Elétrica, 1953. 817p. ML237 .A9.

The standard music history, covering all genres to 1860. Opera chronologies, illustrations, musical examples, name index.

Venezuela

2815. Calzavara, Alberto. *Historia de la música en Venezuela: Periodo hispánico, con referéncias al teatro y la danza.* Caracas: Fundación Pampero, 1987. xiii, 342p. ISBN 9-8026-5838-3. ML238 .C33.

Primarily a narrative of choral and instrumental performance since the 16th century, with emphasis on Caracas, and a section on each Venezuelan province. Except for a few pages on the *tonadilla escénica* there is hardly anything about stage works. Bibliography, index.

2816. Calcaño, José Antonio. *400 años de música caraqueña.* Caracas: Círculo Musical, 1967. 98p. ML238.8 .C3 C34.

A lavishly illustrated volume that gives a good overview of musical life in Caracas from 1567.

2817. Mikulan, Marta. *Centenario del Teatro Municipal de Caracas.* Caracas: Fundación Teresa Carreño, 1980.

Not seen. *Kaufman* describes it as a lavishly illustrated volume, with chronology and casts (except for 1885–1901) of the theater's 100 years.

2818. Salas, Carlos. *Historia del teatro en Caracas.* Caracas: Imprenta Municipal, 1967. 391p. PN2552 .C2 S2.

An informal narrative, with emphasis on performers (many pictures of them). Chronology 1951–1961. No index.

2819. Salas, Carlos, and Eduardo Feo Calcaño. *Sesquicentenario de la ópera en Caracas.* Caracas: Vargas, 1960. 185p. ML1717.8 .C37 S3.

A narrative by season, 1808–1858, with singers named. List of visiting companies by year, as well as newspaper notices. Photos and reproductions of programs. No index.

Yugoslavia (Jugoslavia)

Since the creation of independent nations in 1991 and 1992, the former Socialist Federated Republic of Yugoslavia has been reduced to what had been the republics of Serbia and Montenegro. Material on the new Croatia and Bosnia-Herzegovina is entered separately in this guide. Most of the literature is in local languages (see *IOM* 3609a–3676).

2820. *Yugoslav Music.* Sarajevo: Zvuk, 1967. 154p. ML260 .Y83.

Title and text in English, French, and German. A useful collection of essays by topic and locality; musical and operatic life of each major city is discussed.

2821. Andreis, Josip, and Slavko Zlatič. *Yugoslav Music.* Trans. Karla Kunc. Belgrade: Edition Jugoslavija, 1959. 158p. ML260 .A5.

The history and current musical scene in each republic, with accounts of opera in the important cities.

2822. Cvetkovič, Sava V. *Repertoar Narodnog Pozorišta u Beogradu, 1868–1965.* Belgrade: Muzej Pozorišne Umetnosti, 1966. 172p. PN2856 .B4 C9.

Seasonal lists of plays, operas, operettas, and ballets. Names of directors but not the singers. There were 1,926 total performances. Bibliography, name and title index.

Index of Opera Titles

Citations are to entry numbers. This is a list of opera titles specifically named in citations or in annotations. It includes the names of operas in major compilations, such as *FO* and *IO-1640*, since all the works in those compilations have separate citations. Although the list may be useful as an inventory of principal operas, it is important to note that many important works are not found in it, because they are not named in citations or annotations. For example, there are only two Gilbert and Sullivan operas. An asterisk following an entry number indicates that there is material about the opera in the text that follows that entry. Alphabetizing is word by word—*Al gran sole* before *Albert Herring*—and initial articles and diacritics in all languages are ignored.

Index of Subjects

Citations are to entry numbers. An asterisk following an entry number indicates that there is material about the subject in the text after that entry. The distinction between the headings "Opera" and "Operas" may not be immediately apparent. "Opera" and its subdivisions are for materials about opera as a genre, and "Operas" and its subdivisions are for materials about individual operas.

In general, the headings in the subject index are also used as subheadings under the names of composers, but the composer entries are modified in accordance with the publications about each person. Entries for cities are listed under their countries.

Alphabetizing is word by word: Martin y Soler, Vicente, before Martini, Jean-Paul Egide. Compound names and hyphenated words are treated as one word. Initial articles and diacritics in all languages are ignored in alphabetizing.

Index of Authors and Main Entries

Citations are to entry numbers. An asterisk following an entry number indicates that there is material about the person or title in the text that follows that entry. This list includes the names of sole authors and of those whose names appear first among several (joint) authors on a title page. (Names of other joint authors, whose names are not first on the title page, are included in the Index of Secondary Authors.) Composite works of various kinds, which are cited by title rather than by an author or editor, are the "main entries" that also appear. Those main entries are the only title entries given in the index.

Collaborative works for which an author has the primary entry (name being first on the title page) appear ahead of works for which that person is sole author.

Alphabetizing is word by word:

Berg, Alban
The Berg Companion
Berg, Karl Georg Maria
Berger, Christian

As those items indicate, initial articles in all languages are ignored in alphabetizing. In compound surnames, any apostrophes and spaces are also ignored in alphabetizing; that is, the names are treated as single words:

Dalayrac, Nicolas
D'Albert, Eugen
Dallapiccola, Luigi
Damrosch, Walter
D'Annunzio, Gabriele
Da Ponte, Lorenzo

Diacritical marks in all languages are also ignored in alphabetizing. Numerals file ahead of words:

50 años de opera en el Palacio de Bellas Artes, 1934–1984, 2598
150 Jahre Theater in Zürich, 2698
300 Jahre Oper in Hamburg: 1678–1978, 2390

Blunt, Wilfrid. *John Christie of Glyndebourne,* 297
Blyth, Alan. *Opera on CD: The Essential Guide to the Best CD Recordings of 100 Operas,* 437; *Opera on Record,* 437
Bobeth, Marek. *Borodin und seine Oper "Fürst Igor": Geschichte, Analyse, Konsequenzen,* 610
Bocharnikova, Ella. *Bol'shoi Teatr: Kratkii istoricheskii ocherk,* 2658
Bögel, Hartweg. *Studien zur Instrumentation in den Opern Giacomo Puccinis,* 1456
Bogosavljević, Srdan. "Hofmannsthal's 'Mythological' Opera *Arabella,*" 1708
Böhmer, Karl. *Wolfgang Amadeus Mozarts "Idomeneo" und die Tradition der Karnavalsopern in München,* 2407
Bohuslav Martinů: Anno 1981, 1156
Bokina, John. *Opera and Politics: From Monteverdi to Henze,* 82
Boldrey, Richard. *Guide to Operatic Duets,* 27; *Guide to Operatic Roles & Arias,* 28
Bollert, Werner. *50 Jahre Deutsche Oper Berlin, 7 November 1912–7 November 1962,* 2369; *Die Buffo-Opern Baldassare Galuppis,* 850
Bolongaro-Crevenna, Hubertus. *"'L'arpa festante': Die Münchener Oper, 1653–1825,* 2403
Bol'shoi Teatr SSSR, 1969/70, 2658*
Bol'shoi Teatr SSSR: Opera, balet, 2657
Bomberger, E. Douglas. "The Neues Schauspielhaus in Berlin and the Premiere of Carl Maria von Weber's *Der Freischütz,*" 2364
Bonaventura, Arnaldo. *Saggio storico sul teatro musicale italiano,* 2431
Bondi, Gustav. *Funfundzwanzig Jahre Eigenregie: Geschichte des Brünner Stadttheaters 1882–1907,* 2211
Bonnert, Olivier H. "Autour des persans dans l'opéra au XVIIIe siècle," 933
Bontinck-Küffel, Irmgard. *Opern auf Schallplatten, 1900–1962,* 438
Borchmeyer, Dieter. *Richard Wagner: Theory and Theatre,* 1985; *Das Theater Richard Wagners,* 1985; "Wagner Literature: New Light on the Case of Wagner," 1967
Borroff, Edith. *American Operas: A Checklist,* 2746; *An Introduction to Elisabeth-Claude Jacquet de La Guerre,* 1098
Bortolotto, Mario. "Sul sestetto nell' opera *Lucia di Lammermoor,*" 798
Borwick, Susan. "The Music for the Stage Collaborations of Weill and Brecht," 234; "Weill's and Brecht's Theories on Music in Drama," 233
Bosch, Mariano. *Historia del teatro en Buenos Aires,* 2118
Bossarelli, Anna Mondolfi. "Ancora intorno al codice napoletano della *Incoronazione di Poppea,*" 1210
Boston, Margie Viola. "An Essay on the Life and Works of Léo Delibes," 745
Bottenheim, S. A. M. *De opera in Nederland,* 2605
Boubel, Karen A. "The Conflict of Good and Evil: A Musical and Dramatic Study of Britten's *Billy Budd,*" 630
Bouissou, Sylvie. "*Les Boréades* de J.-Ph. Rameau: Un passé retrouvé," 1545; "Jean-Philippe Rameau: *Les Boréades,*" 1545
Boulay, Jean-Michel. "Monotonality and Chromatic Dualism in Richard Strauss's *Salome,*" 1745
Bouquet, Marie-Thérese, and Alberto Basso. *Storia del Teatro Regio di Torino,* 2574
Bourgeois, Thomas-Louis, 611*
Bourne, Joyce. *Who's Who in Opera: A Guide to Opera Characters,* 29
Bowles, Garrett H. *Ernest Krenek: A Bio-Bibliography,* 1097
Boyd, Malcolm, and Juan José Carreras. *Music in Spain during the Eighteenth Century,* 2672
Bozhkova, Zlata. *Sofiiska Narodna Opera memoari,* 2181
Bradley, Carol June. *Music Collections in American Libraries: A Chronology,* 124
Bradley, Ian. *The Complete Annotated Gilbert and Sullivan,* 1763
Brainard, Paul. "Aria and Ritornello: New Aspects of the Comparison Handel/Bach," 968
Brâncusi, Petre. *Muzica în România socialistă,* 2630*
Braun, Edward. *Meyerhold: A Revolution in Theatre,* 317

Corse, Sandra. *Opera and the Uses of Language: Mozart, Verdi, and Britten,* 385; "The Voice of Authority in Wagner's *Ring*," 2051; *Wagner and the New Consciousness: Language and Love in the "Ring,"* 2047

Corte, Andrea della. "Aspetti del 'comico' nella vocalità teatrale di Monteverdi," 1210; *L'opera comica italiana nel '700,* 2463; *Paisiello,* 1372; "Saggio di bibliografia delle critiche al *Ballo in maschera,*" 1869; "Saggio di bibliografia delle critiche al *Rigoletto,*" 1920; "Saggio di bibliografia delle critiche alla *Forza del destino,*" 1889

Cosma, Viorel. *Hronicul muzicii romanesti,* 2632; *Opera romînească: Privire istorică asupra creatiei lirico-dramatice,* 2632; *România muzicală,* 2630

Cotarelo y Mori, Emilio. *Historia de la zarzuela, o sea el drama lírico en España desde su origen a fines del siglo XIX,* 2669

Couch, John Philip. *The Opera Lover's Guide to Europe,* 143

Couvreur, Manuel. "La folie à l'Opéra-Comique: Des grelots de Momus aux larmes de Nina," 2250; *Jean-Baptiste Lully: Musique et dramaturgie en service du prince,* 1131; *Le Théâtre de la Monnaie au XVIIIe siècle,* 2167

Covell, Roger David. "Monteverdi's *L'incoronazione di Poppea*: The Musical and Dramatic Structure," 1237

Cowart, Georgia. *Origins of Modern Musical Criticism: French and Italian Music, 1600–1750,* 421

Cowden, Robert H. "Acting and Directing in the Lyric Theater: An Annotated Checklist," 280; *The Chautauqua Opera Association, 1929–1958: An Interpretative History,* 2768; *Classical Singers of the Opera and Recital Stages: A Bibliography of Biographical Materials,* 160; *Concert and Opera Conductors: A Bibliography of Biographical Materials,* 161; *Opera Companies of the World: Selected Profiles,* 138

Craft, Robert. *Stravinsky: Glimpses of a Life,* 1750

Craggs, Stewart R. *Arthur Bliss: A Bio-Bibliography,* 590; *Richard Rodney Bennett: A Bio-Bibliography,* 525; *William Walton: A Catalogue,* 2079; *William Walton: A Source Book,* 2079

Crain, Gordon F. "The Operas of Bernardo Pasquini," 1380

Cramer, Thomas. "*Lohengrin,* Edition und Untersuchung," 2023

Crawford, John C. "*Die glückliche Hand*: Schoenberg's *Gesamtkunstwerk,*" 1632

Crest, Renzo. *Linguaggio musicale di Luciano Chailly,* 688

Crisp, Deborah. *Bibliography of Australian Music: An Index to Monographs, Journal Articles, and Theses,* 2123

Croatia: Land, People, Culture, 2195*

Croccolo, Enrico. *Donizetti a Lucca: Storia delle opere di Donizetti rappresentate a Lucca dal 1827 al 1858,* 776

Croce, Benedetto. *I teatri di Napoli, dal rinascimento alla fine del secolo decimottavo,* 2539; *I teatri di Napoli, secolo XV-XVIII,* 2539

Croissant, Charles. *Opera Performances in Video Format: A Checklist of Commercially Released Recordings,* 444

Croll, G. "Agostino Steffani (1654–1728): Studien zur Biographie, Bibliographie der Opern und Turnierspiele," 1683

Cronache del Teatro di San Carlo, 1948–1968, 2544

Cronin, Charles P. D., and Betje Black Klier. "Théodore Pavie's *Les babouches du Brahmane* and the Story of Delibes's *Lakmé,*" 749

Cronin, Charles P. D. "The Comic Operas of Gaetano Donizetti and the End of the *opera buffa* Tradition," 778

Cropsey, Eugene M. "Mr. Crosby's Temple of Art: The Inaugural Season, Chicago, 1865," 2772

Cross, Eric. *The Late Operas of Antonio Vivaldi, 1727–1738,* 1954; "The Relationship between Text and Music in the Operas of Vivaldi," 1951; "Vivaldi and the Pasticcio: Text and Music in *Tamerlano,*" 1961

Cross Index Title Guide to Opera and Operetta, 50

"Crosscurrents and the Mainstream of Italian Serious Opera, 1730–1790," 2462

Crowell's Handbook of Gilbert & Sullivan, 1766

Crowell's Handbook of World Opera, 45

Eisenschmidt, Joachim. *Die szenische Darstellung der Opern Händels auf der Londoner Bühne seiner Zeit*, 967

Ellis, W. A. *Richard Wagner's Prose Works*, 1981

Emerson, Caryl, and Robert William Oldani. *Modest Musorgsky and Boris Godunov: Myths, Realities, Reconsiderations*, 1351

Emerson, Caryl. "Back to the Future: Shostakovich's Revision of Leskov's *Lady Macbeth of Mtensk District*," 1668; "Musorgsky's Libretti on Historical Themes: From the Two Borises to *Khovanshchina*," 1348

Emery, Ted. *Goldoni as Librettist: Theatrical Reform and the "drammi giocosi per musica*," 247

Emmanuel, Maurice. "*Pelléas et Mélisande" de Debussy: Ètude et analyse*, 737

Emslie, Barry. "Woman as Image and Narrative in Wagner's *Parsifal*: A Case Study," 2032

En travesti: Women, Gender Subversion, Opera, 389.

Enciclopédia da música brasileira: Erudita, folclóroica, popular, 2174

Enciklopedija Hrvatskoga Narodnoga Kazališta u Zagreb, 1894–1969, 2196

Encyclopedia of Music in Canada, 2187

Encyclopedia of Recorded Sound in the United States, 434.

Encyclopédie de la musique au Canada, 2187

Engel, Hans. "Die *finali* der Mozartschen Opern," 1292; "Über Richard Wagners Oper *Das Liebesverbot*," 2020

Engelbert, Barbara. "Wystan Hugh Auden, 1907–1973: Seine Opern-aesthetische Anschaung in seine Tätigkeit als Librettist," 230

Engelbert Humperdinck zum 70. Todestag, 1064

Engelhardt, Markus. *Die Chore in den frühen Opern Giuseppe Verdis*, 1862

Engländer, Richard. "Die erste italienische Oper in Dresden, Bontempis *Il Paride in musica* (1662)," 607

English National Opera Guides [series], 150

Enix, Margery. "A Reassessment of *Elektra* by Strauss," 1724

Entsiklopediia na bŭlgarskata muzikalna kultura, 2181*

Eősze, László. *Zoltán Kodály: His Life and Work*, 1093

Ermanno Wolf Ferrari, 2105

"Ernani" ieri e oggi: Atti del Convegno Internazionale di Studi, Modena, Teatro San Carlo, 9–10 dicembre 1984, 1876

Ertelt, Thomas F. *Alban Bergs "Lulu": Quellenstudium und Beiträge zur Analyse*, 538

Erwin, Charlotte Elizabeth. "Richard Strauss's *Ariadne auf Naxos*: An Analysis of Musical Style Based on a Study of Revisions," 1714

Esotismo e colore locale nell'opera di Puccini, 1439

Essays on Music for Charles Warren Fox, 67.

Essays on Opera and English Music: In Honour of Sir Jack Westrup, 72

Essays Presented to Egon Wellesz, 70

Evans, John. "Benjamin Britten's *Death in Venice*: Perspectives on an Opera," 632; "*Death in Venice*: The Apollonian/Dionysian Conflict," 631

Evans, Peter. *The Music of Benjamin Britten*, 622

Everett, Andrew. "Meyerbeer in London," 1190

Everist, Mark. "Lindoro in Lyon: Rossini's *Le barbier de Séville*," 1582; "Meyerbeer's *Il crociato in Egitto*: Mélodrame, Opera, Orientalism," 1196

Evidon, Richard. "Film," 445*

Ewans, Michael. *Janáček's Tragic Operas*, 1075

Ewen, David. *The Book of European Light Opera* , 200; *The New Encyclopedia of the Opera*, 32

Fabbri, Paolo, and Roberto Verti. *Due secoli di teatro per musica a Reggio Emilia: Repertorio cronologico delle opere e dei balli, 1645–1857*, 2564

Fabbri, Paolo. *Il secolo cantante: Per una storia del libretto d'opera nel seicento*, 215; *Monteverdi*, 1217

Failoni, Judith Weaver. "Tradition and Innovation in Jacques Ibert's Opera, *Persée et Andromède*," 1065

Saffle, Michael. *Franz Liszt: A Guide to Research*, 1116

Sagaev, Liubomir. *Săvremennoto bŭlgarsko operno tvorchestvo*, 2181

Saint-Evremond, Charles. *Sur les opéras*, 1129

Sala, Emilio. "Alla ricerca della *Pie voleuse*" [sources for *La gazza ladra*], 1570; "Réécrit-ures italiennes de l'opéra comique française," 93; "Women Crazed by Love: An Aspect of Romantic Opera," 394

Salas, Carlos, and Eduardo Feo Calcaño. *Sesquicentenario de la ópera en Caracas*, 2818

Salas, Carlos. *Historia del teatro en Caracas*, 2818

Salem, Mahmoud M. *Organizational Survival in the Performing Arts: The Making of the Seattle Opera*, 2810

Salès, Jules. *Théâtre Royal de la Monnaie, 1856–1970*, 2166

Sallés, Antoine. *L'opéra italien et allemand à Lyon au 19. siècle (1805–1882)*, 2335

Sällström, Åke. *Opera på Stockholmsoperan*, 2689

Salvetti, Guido. "Alcuni criteri nella rielaborazione ed orchestrazione dell'*Incoronazione*," 1243; "Un maestro napoletano di fronte alla riforma: L'*Alceste* di Pietro Alessandro Guglielmi," 936

Salvioli, Giovanni. *I teatri musicali di Venezia nel secolo XVII (1637–1700): Memorie storiche e bibliografiche raccolte ed ordinate da Livo Niso Galvani* [pseudonym], 2580

Samuel, Rhian. "Birtwistle's Gawain: An Essay and a Diary," 577

Sandberger, Adolf. "Zur Geschichte der Oper in Nürnberg in der zweiten Halfte des 17. und zu Anfang des 18. Jahrhunderts," 2409

Sanders, Ernest. "*Oberon* and *Zar und Zimmerman*," 1119

Sanders, J. "Los Angeles Grand Opera Association: The Formative Years," 2780

Sanders, L. *Onderzoek opera en publiek te Antwerpen*, 2169

Sansone, Matteo. "Verga and Mascagni: The Critics' Response to *Cavalleria rusticana*," 1160; "The *verismo* of Ruggero Leoncavallo: A Source Study of *Paglicacci*," 1109

Santi, Piero. "Intorno al *Grand macabre*," 1113; "Il mondo della *Dèbora*," 1419; "Tempo e spazzio ossia colore locale in *Bohème, Tosca, e Madama Butterfly*," 1465

Santore, Jonathan Conrad. "Dramatic Action, Motive Deployment, and Formal Structure in Hindemith's *Sancta Susanna* and *Native Soil*," 1056

Santoro, Elia. *Il teatro di Cremona*, 2494

Saracino, Egidio. *Tutti i libretti di Donizetti*, 759

Sartori, Claudio. "*Il Dafni* di Alessandro Scarlatti," 1617; *I libretti italiani a stampa dalle origini al 1800: Catalogo analitico*, 2434

Saunders, Harris. "Repertoire of a Venetian Opera House, 1678–1714: The Teatro Grimani di San Giovanni Grisostomo," 2589

Savage, Roger, Barry Millington, and John Cox. "Production," 281

Savage, Roger. "Calling Up Genius: Purcell, Roger North, and Charlotte Butler," 1514; "Producing *Dido and Aeneas*: An Investigation into Sixteen Problems," 1524; "The Shakespeare-Purcell Fairy Queen: A Defense and Recommendation," 1528; "Staging of Opera," 77; "The Theatre Music," 1516

Sawkins, Lionel. "Rameau's Last Years: Some Implications of Rediscovered Material at Bordeaux," 1556; "*Trembleurs* and Cold People: How Should They Shiver?" 1514

Saya, Virginia Cotta. "The Current Climate for American Musical Eclecticism as Reflected in the Operas of Dominick Argento," 461

Scaglione, Nitto. *La vita artistica del Teatro Vittorio Emanuele*, 2516

Scarpatta, Umberto. "Un opera pietroburghese: il *Castro e Polluce*," 1610

Schäffer, Carl, and Carl Hartmann. *Die Königlichen Theater in Berlin: Statistlischer Rückblick*, 2362

Schäffer, Gottfried. *Das Fürstbischöfliche und Königliche Theater zu Passau (1783–1883)*, 2410

Schebera, Jürgen. *Kurt Weill, 1900–1950: Eine Biographie in Texten, Bildern, und Dokumentation*, 2104; *Kurt Weill: An Illustrated Life*, 2104

Schepelern, Gerhard. *Italierne pas Hofteatret*, 2214

Scheppach, Margaret A. *Dramatic Parallels in Michael Tippett's Operas: Analytical Essays on the Musico-Dramatic Techniques*, 1785

Scherliess, Volker. "*Il barbiere di Siviglia*: Paisiello and Rossini," 1375

Index of Secondary Authors

Citations are to entry numbers. An asterisk following an entry number indicates that there is material relevant to the person in the text that follows that entry. The names listed here are those of persons whose names appear in citations but who are not the primary authors of the works cited. Primary authors are in the Index of Authors and Main Entries. Included here are joint authors, editors, compilers, translators, and illustrators.

Alphabetizing practice is the same as that in the Index of Authors and Main Entries.